"Building on an extensive and careful study of every passage in the Pauline corpus pertaining to union with Christ, Constantine Campbell demonstrates the theme's important role in Paul's theology—a role he describes as being that of the 'webbing' that holds the theology together. His book is a helpful reminder of how essential this idea is for our understanding of Paul."

—Morna D. Hooker, Lady Margaret's Professor of Divinity
Emerita, University of Cambridge

"With the increased prominence of attention to union with Christ in Paul in recent decades, Campbell's contribution is most welcome. Impressive for its comprehensive scope, its careful attention to exegetical detail yet with the overall theological picture also in view, and its balanced and fair conclusions, this book is bound to benefit anyone interested in this important topic."

—Richard B. Gaffin Jr., Professor of Biblical and Systematic Theology, Emeritus, Westminster Theological Seminary, Philadelphia

"Union with Christ, a vital and debated theme in Paul's theology, has not received the attention it deserves. Constantine Campbell seeks to redress this situation with a thorough exegetical analysis of all the relevant Pauline texts. His study both makes its own contribution and provides a great foundation for continuing discussion."

—Douglas J. Moo, Wessner Chair of Biblical Studies, Wheaton College; Chair, Committee on Bible Translation

"Campbell provides a lucid and lively study of union with Christ. Few authors are able to combine exegetical skill with theological acumen on such a complex topic as Campbell does here. It is a brilliant study about what a constellation of images of union, participation, identification, and incorporation into Christ actually means. Campbell's *tour de force* will be the authoritative book on the subject for decades to come."

—Michael Bird, Lecturer in Theology and New Testament, Crossway College in Brisbane, Australia

"The unifying theme of 'union with Christ' in Paul is often interpreted vaguely or in surprisingly different ways, with little attention to the apostle's specific language. Dr. Campbell carefully examines all the expressions related to 'in Christ,' sensibly explains their meaning within each context, and insightfully integrates the results into Paul's overarching teaching and practice. This book is an invaluable tool."

—Peter T. O'Brien, senior research fellow at Moore Theological College

PAUL AND UNION WITH CHRIST

AN EXEGETICAL AND THEOLOGICAL STUDY

CONSTANTINE R. CAMPBELL

ZONDERVAN

Paul and Union with Christ
Copyright © 2012 by Constantine R. Campbell

Requests for information should be addressed to:

Zondervan, 3900 Sparks Dr. SE, Grand Rapids, Michigan 49546

Library of Congress Cataloging-in-Publication Data

Campbell, Constantine R.
      Paul and union with Christ : an exegetical and theological study / Constantine R.
Campbell.
         p. cm.
     Includes bibliographical references (pp.445-63) and indexes.
     ISBN 978-0-310-32905-3 (softcover)
     1. Bible. N.T. Epistles of Paul—Criticism, interpretation, etc. 2. Mystical union. I. Title.
BS2655.M85C36 2012
     227'.06—dc23   2012009068

Cover design: John Hamilton Design
Cover photography: Erich Lessing / Art Resource, NY
Interior design: Matthew Van Zomeren

Printed in the United States of America

17 18 19 20 /DCI/ 23 22 21 20 19 18 17 16 15 14 13 12 11 10 9 8 7 6 5

For Jasmine, Xanthe and Lukas

Contents

EXEGETICAL STUDY

THEOLOGICAL STUDY

CHAPTER 8
Union with Christ and the Work of Christ 327

CHAPTER 9
Union with Christ and the Trinity 353

ACKNOWLEDGEMENTS

I am indebted to two outstanding New Testament scholars, Dr Peter O'Brien and Dr Francis Watson. Dr O'Brien first implanted the idea that I might conduct research on the Pauline theme of union with Christ. He pointed out that the theme is both extremely important and in need of serious treatment. That—combined with the fact that I had been lecturing on Paul's epistle to the Ephesians and was already intrigued by the concept—immediately settled the matter as to what my next major research task should engage. Dr O'Brien also studied the manuscript carefully, which offered great reassurance to me since his attention to detail and exegetical prowess is world-renowned.

My interactions with Dr Francis Watson during the course of my research became highly influential on the shape of this study. We have met together annually at the SBL conventions in the United States over the last five years, and each meeting provided fresh stimulus, challenge, and direction as I conducted my work. One of his suggestions—that I ought to conduct a thorough examination of Paul's relevant prepositional phrases—accounts for roughly half this book. I have richly benefitted from Dr Watson's penetrating insight into Pauline theology and scholarship, for which he is highly acclaimed.

I am grateful for the community of Moore College in various ways. Frequent discussions with students and faculty about union with Christ have helped to sharpen my thinking, and the very nature of our theological community has provided the ideal context in which to pursue this study. I am grateful to our Principal, Dr John Woodhouse, and our Governing Board for providing a semester-long study leave in 2009, in which about a third of this book was written. Thanks are also due to Peter Baker, who served as my research assistant in the summer of 2009–2010. He provided wonderful assistance in tracking down 160 journal articles that I needed.

I wish to thank my friends at Zondervan Academic, with whom it is a pleasure to work, and I am grateful for their vision for this project. In particular, I offer thanks to my editors, Katya Covrett and Verlyn Verbrugge, for their friendship and encouragement as well as their exceptional editorial skill.

Finally, I am ever grateful for my family—a constant source of love, nourishment, and entertainment. Without my wife, Bronwyn, I am fairly certain that I simply would not function. Our children, Jasmine, Xanthe, and Lukas, are precious blessings in every way. I dedicate this book to them.

Soli Deo Gloria

Christmas Eve, 2011

ABBREVIATIONS

AB   Anchor Bible

AJT   *Asia Journal of Theology*

AnBib   Analecta biblica

AThR   *Anglican Theological Review*

BBR   *Bulletin for Biblical Research*

BDAG   Walter Bauer, Frederick W. Danker, William F. Arndt, and Wilbur Gingrich, *A Greek–English Lexicon of the New Testament and other Early Christian Literature*. 3rd ed. Chicago: University of Chicago Press, 2000.

BDF   F. Blass, A. Debrunner, and Robert A. Funk, *A Greek Grammar of the New Testament and other Early Christian Literature*. Chicago: University of Chicago Press, 1961.

BNTC   Black's New Testament Commentary

BSac   *Bibliotheca sacra*

CBC   Cambridge Bible Commentary

CBQ   *Catholic Biblical Quarterly*

CGTC   Cambridge Greek Testament Commentary

CTM   *Concordia Theological Monthly*

CurTM   *Currents in Theology and Mission*

CV   *Communio Viatorum*

EHPR   Études d'histoire et de philosophie religieuses

ESV   English Standard Version

EvQ   *Evangelical Quarterly*

ExpTim   *Expository Times*

HCSB   Holman Christian Standard Bible

HNTC   Harper's New Testament Commentaries

HTR   *Harvard Theological Review*

ICC   International Critical Commentary

IJST   *International Journal of Systematic Theology*

Int   *Interpretation*

JBL   *Journal of Biblical Literature*

JETS   *Journal of the Evangelical Theological Society*

JSNT   *Journal for the Study of the New Testament*
JSNTSup   Journal for the Study of the New Testament Supplement Series
JTS   *Journal of Theological Studies*
LXX   Septuagint
NASB   New American Standard Bible
Neot   *Neotestamentica*
NCB   New Century Bible
NEB   New English Bible
NIBC   New International Biblical Commentary
NICNT   New International Commentary on the New Testament
NIGTC   New International Greek Testament Commentary
NIV   New International Version
NovT   *Novum Testamentum*
NRSV   New Revised Standard Version
NSBT   New Studies in Biblical Theology
NTS   *New Testament Studies*
PNTC   Pillar New Testament Commentary
RTR   *Reformed Theological Review*
SBET   *Scottish Bulletin of Evangelical Theology*
SBG   Studies in Biblical Greek
SJT   *Scottish Journal of Theology*
TBT   *The Bible Today*
TDNT   G. Kittel and G. Friedrich, eds., *Theological Dictionary of the New Testament*. 10 vols. Trans. Geoffrey W. Bromiley. Grand Rapids: Eerdmans, 1964–76.
THNTC   Two Horizons New Testament Commentary
TNTC   Tyndale New Testament Commentary
TJ   *Trinity Journal*
ThTo   *Theology Today*
VE   *Vox Evangelica*
WBC   Word Biblical Commentary
WTJ   *Westminster Theological Journal*
WUNT   Wissenschaftliche Untersuchungen zum Neuen Testament
WW   *Word and World*
ZNW   *Zeitschrift für die neutestamentliche Wissenschaft und die Kunde*

Part 1

Introductory
Matters

CHAPTER 1

INTRODUCTION AND METHODOLOGY

1.1 PAUL AND UNION WITH CHRIST

The theme of union with Christ in the writings of the apostle Paul is at once dazzling and perplexing. Its prevalence on every page of his writings demonstrates his proclivity for the concept, and yet nowhere does he directly explain what he means by it. This creates a problem for any student of Paul's theology, since union with Christ is both important yet obtuse.

These two realities have amply been demonstrated in the New Testament scholarship of the twentieth and twenty-first centuries. The volume of scholarly activity conducted in search for Paul's meaning speaks to the obtuseness of union with Christ. The degree of controversy surrounding the theme speaks to its importance. Consequently, two of the central concerns addressed in this book include what union with Christ actually is and what role it performs in Paul's theology.

The path to addressing these concerns is not straightforward. As explained below, we cannot presume to speak of Paul's theology before engaging his writings through detailed exegesis. And yet, it is difficult to know what to look for in exegesis if we have not already determined what Paul considers to be relevant to the theme of union with Christ. While building on previous advances of scholarship, I take nothing for granted in this book. Instead, it represents a fresh investigation of the Pauline material, examining the exegetical minutiae and moving through to the wide spheres of Paul's thought. The work is therefore self-consciously exegetical-theological, allowing exegesis to shape theology and vice versa.

1.2 AN EXEGETICAL-THEOLOGICAL APPROACH

Within the literature concerning the theme of union with Christ, there appear two opposite tendencies among various methodological approaches. Some contributors write of union with Christ as a broad theological concept that is used within a theological matrix of ideas and themes within the Pauline canon. It is discussed in relation to justification, trinitarianism, ethics, and so forth. This is a valid and important direction to be pursued, since union with Christ *is* connected to many such themes within Paul's writings; it is a theologised concept. One weakness of such an approach, however, is that the theme almost immediately turns abstract, sometimes without careful analysis of the key texts that give rise to the conception of union with Christ—that is, without an exegetically derived description of what union with Christ is. While it is important to understand how this theme relates to other themes and to Paul's theology as a whole, the conclusions of some investigations must be received with caution, since the detailed groundwork has yet to be established.

By contrast, some contributors investigate union with Christ on a purely terminological basis, focusing on a Pauline 'formula'—usually ἐν Χριστῷ—and exploring the various uses of the formula in the contexts in which it is found.[1] Again, this is an important and valuable endeavour since it is the kind of exploration that produces the groundwork sometimes missing from the aforementioned approach. A weakness here, however, is that the discussion can become severely limited, as though a phrase such as ἐν Χριστῷ tells the whole story of the theme of union with Christ.[2] Even from a purely exegetical approach, it is apparent that the ideas expressed by ἐν Χριστῷ are related to other phrases too, such as σὺν Χριστῷ, εἰς

---

1. Neugebauer's monograph, for instance, is restricted to the phrases ἐν Χριστῷ and ἐν κυρίῳ; Fritz Neugebauer, *In Christus: Eine Untersuchung zum paulinischen Glaubensverständnis* (Göttingen: Vandenhoeck & Ruprecht, 1961).

2. Admittedly, some such studies are not interested in 'union with Christ' per se; they are only interested in a feature of Paul's language as it pertains to his body of writings.

Χριστόν, and διὰ Χριστοῦ.[3] In other words, 'pure exegesis' leads away from a narrow investigation of ἐν Χριστῷ alone and requires the inclusion of other elements of Paul's language.

But is there such a thing as 'pure exegesis' in the first place? Paul was a theologian and, while not 'systematic' in modern terms, he presented his thinking through the interaction of themes that are broader than the use of so-called formulas. Consequently, a proper approach to Paul must be theological as well as exegetical. Indeed, for a theological writer such as Paul, the two approaches become inextricably entwined. In this book, therefore, exegesis and theology will be conducted hand in hand, while the structure of the book (to be explained below) will move from an exegetical pole to a theological one. We will begin with attention to the details of Paul's language, investigating the relevant phrases in context, then widening the scope to consider metaphorical devices. From there, the interest becomes dominantly theological as the results of the exegetical analyses are interpreted with respect to Paul's broader thought. This study, then, is exegetical-theological, belonging to the discipline of New Testament theology. It will be apparent that this differs from traditional systematic theology in that it begins with textual minutiae and develops through to the conceptual big picture; it does not start with the whole, but progresses from one pole to the other.

1.3 DETERMINING THE EXEGETICAL DATA

In order to begin at the 'exegetical pole' of the topic, we must address the essential task of determining which data this will include. Such an endeavour is at once both simple and complex. On the one hand, it involves surface-level analysis. We are concerned to ask which texts within the Pauline canon are relevant to the wider task at hand. This is simply a question of what's in and what's not; what are the parameters of the discussion from a textual point of view? Along such lines, the task here is to delineate which texts are of interest.

On the other hand, the manner in which the relevant texts are

---

3. This is Bouttier's advance beyond Neugebauer's contribution; his net is cast wider than the phrase ἐν Χριστῷ; Michel Bouttier, *En Christ: Étude d'exégèse et de théologie Pauliniennes* (EHPR 54; Paris: Presses Universitaires de France, 1962).

ascertained is far from simple. The most perplexing question concerns the issue of how we know which texts are about union with Christ and which are not. Clearly, the use of some notable phrases will automatically signal a text's relevance. But how far does the concept permeate when such phrases are not extant? Which other phrases may be regarded as related to the topic? Which ideas and metaphors are connected to the concept of union?

The issue is more complicated than merely chasing down the phrase 'in Christ' and describing how it is used and what it means. That Paul may discuss the concepts raised by the phrase 'in Christ' without actually using the phrase in certain instances is a reasonable presupposition. Observation of the workings of human language demonstrates that we may speak of concepts and ideas through variegated expressions. Rarely, if ever, is the communication of a concept limited to one phrase or peculiar locution. Sophisticated language users may summon synonymous, parallel, symmetrical, analogous, metaphorical, and otherwise related means by which to speak of their chosen themes.[4]

As such, our endeavour to demarcate the texts of relevance to the theme of union with Christ is more complicated than it first appears. To find the theme, we must first know what the theme is. What is union with Christ? How are we to define this topic? What are the essential ingredients that establish the concept of interest? The problem here, of course, is that we cannot know what the theme is until we examine the relevant texts. And yet we have already established that we may not know what the relevant texts are until we are able to recognise the theme within them. The task at hand, therefore, is inevitably circular. We must examine texts that deal with union with Christ in order to know what union with Christ is, and yet we cannot know which texts deal with union with Christ until we know what union with Christ is.

This kind of circularity is not unique. Several areas of research are beset

---

4. Indeed, it is possible to discuss a concept at length *without* the explicit use of the most obvious phrases or terminology. While many examples of this phenomenon could be offered, one from popular culture seems apt. The film *The Godfather* is a fictional account of the inner workings of the Mafia. The basic subject of the film is never in question and is implied by a plethora of subtle and unsubtle indicators. And yet the term that most obviously describes the subject matter of the film is entirely absent. The term *Mafia* is not once mentioned in the film. In spite of such an omission, the subject matter is securely grounded beyond doubt. The concept indicated by this key word may also be indicated by a combination of other features, even in its absence.

with similar problems of definition and method. In the study of verbal semantics within linguistics, for example, the issue of semantic circularity is at once a foundational and highly obtuse problem of methodology.[5] In order to secure data, texts are examined with semantic presuppositions already in place. As the data are assessed, evidence is gathered to support the semantic conclusions that were assumed at the outset. Thus, the evidence is corrupted from the beginning because it is assembled in order to prove propositions that are already accepted. If a different set of propositions was presupposed, the data would lead to a different result, which would be in keeping with those presuppositions. And so it goes.

The methodological circularity identified here is unavoidable, and yet the point at which one 'enters the circle' will affect the shape of the discussion that ensues. In order to minimize the distorting effects of circularity, the starting point at which we enter must be determined as objectively as possible. We must search for an objectively derived tangent into the circularity—a 'way in' that will lead to commendable results rather than weak conclusions skewed by unwitting circularity.

The most obvious tangent into the methodological circularity is the phrase ἐν Χριστῷ. Scholars unanimously regard this phrase to be central to the theme of union with Christ, so beginning here is uncontroversial. It will be necessary to observe all the uses of this phrase to gather our preliminary data. The two most important questions that we will seek to address are as follows. First, what appear to be the unifying features of the usage of 'in Christ' language? Second, how may we move out beyond this phrase to detect other phrases or indicators of the theme of union with Christ? These two questions will shape how we move from the phrase ἐν Χριστῷ into the broader discussion.

1.4 Prepositions, Formulas, Idioms

The prepositional phrase ἐν Χριστῷ is often described as a *formula*. What that means differs, but it usually connotes the conviction that the phrase refers to the same thing each time it is used. The idea is that the 'formula'

---

5. On this problem for the Koine Greek verbal system, see my *Verbal Aspect, the Indicative Mood, and Narrative: Soundings in the Greek of the New Testament* (SBG 13; New York: Peter Lang), 29–30.

compresses a theological conviction into a convenient locution, and its usage conveys the fully orbed concept it represents. Scholars have firmly rejected this assumption, however, particularly those of the second half of the twentieth century. No proposal as to what is meant by the 'formula' has ever found wide acceptance, which is why Markus Barth, for instance, concludes that the phrase is flexible.[6]

In fact, ἐν Χριστῷ has a range of usage determined by the elasticity of the preposition ἐν, and close exegesis of the phrase in context demonstrates this, as we will see in chapter 3. Consequently, it is best to abandon the term *formula* when referring to the phrase ἐν Χριστῷ; it is misleading at best. Strictly speaking, ἐν Χριστῷ is a prepositional phrase, and there is no reason not to label it such. Paul's fondness of the phrase, however, suggests that it might also be described as an *idiom*. Its frequency indicates that it is not an accidental combination of preposition and proper name, and yet it does not convey a fixed meaning every time it occurs. *Idiom* usefully captures these nuances. Thus, ἐν Χριστῷ is a frequent Pauline idiomatic expression with flexible usage.

We have already noted that the theme of union with Christ is not limited by the idiom ἐν Χριστῷ; there are other related phrases, perhaps also idioms, that contribute to the theme. What has yet to be ascertained is how these phrases are distinct and what such distinctions tell us about their functions. The key element that distinguishes these phrases is their prepositions. What meanings are evoked by the ἐν of ἐν Χριστῷ? And how do they differ from the εἰς of εἰς Χριστόν? What is meant by the σύν of σὺν Χριστῷ? The syntax and semantics of Greek prepositions are complex, and it will not be possible to offer a full treatment.[7] Nevertheless, given the

---

6. 'The impossibility of elaborating a final definition of the meaning of "in Christ" may well have a simple cause: namely that Paul used the formula *in more than one sense*'; Markus Barth, *Ephesians: Introduction, Translation, and Commentary on Chapters 1–3* (AB; Garden City, NY: Doubleday, 1974), 69 [italics are original].

7. As Heinfetter, writing in 1850, laments: 'Is there a Scholar that will venture to deny, that many of the differences between men, qualified to judge, not only in respect of their learning, but also of their Truth and Sincerity, exist, in the Ambiguous Senses now attributed to the Greek Preposition? by [*sic*] which, not only the same Sense is supposed to be conveyed by various Prepositions, but even the same Preposition, is considered to convey, not only different, but even opposing Senses; a state of things, in which the wonder is not, that differences of opinion exist, but rather, that any Material Point of Union can be found'; Herman Heinfetter, *An Examination into the Significations and Senses of the Greek Prepositions* (London: Cradock, 1850), 5.

importance of prepositions to the theme of union with Christ, it is necessary to explore the function and meaning of the relevant prepositions, at least in a limited way.

On this lexical issue, the role of BDAG is both essential and troublesome. Despite its flaws,[8] BDAG currently remains the standard lexicon for our literature and is drawn into the discussion at several points. While the lexicon is explored for the range of usage of each preposition, its conclusions about how each prepositional occurrence *functions* are not accepted prima facie. The editors of BDAG have listed particular occurrences of prepositions under certain functions by observation of context and through exegesis. We will reproduce those steps here and are therefore not dependent on the lexicon's analyses. As such, this study relies on BDAG insofar as it describes the scope of possible functions for each preposition. Beyond that, BDAG is a useful companion with which we are free to disagree, as we can do with any commentator.

Subsequent chapters will investigate each preposition in turn and the functions of the idiomatic phrases to which they belong. Finally, some synthesis of how each preposition contributes to the theme of union with Christ will be attempted.

1.5 THE PAULINE CANON

In keeping with the current climate in New Testament scholarship, most recent studies of Pauline theology are based on a truncated canon, putting the Pastoral Epistles, and often Ephesians and Colossians, to one side. While these so-called 'deutero-Pauline' letters are sometimes addressed in appendices, they are not integrated into the fabric of Paul's reconstructed thought. The approach taken in this book, however, is to work with the entire Pauline corpus, in keeping with the arguments advanced by Brevard Childs.[9] The goal of his 'canonical hermeneutic' is 'to reflect on the

---

8. For his devastating critiques of BDAG, see John A. L. Lee, *A History of New Testament Lexicography* (SBG 8; New York: Peter Lang, 2003); idem, 'The Present State of Lexicography of Ancient Greek', in *Biblical Greek Language and Lexicography: Essays in Honor of Frederick W. Danker* (ed. Bernard A. Taylor et al.; Grand Rapids: Eerdmans, 2004), 66–74.

9. Informing Childs' approach is his understanding of the nature of canon: 'The essence of canon was not, however, its formal privileging of texts. Rather, the act of canonization derived from its substance, the christological content of Scripture. The canon served as a rule designating the arena within which the truth of the gospel was heard. It functioned also as a

theology expressed in various forms within the Pauline corpus'.[10] While he acknowledges that there may at times be a distinction between the theology of the 'historical Paul' and that of the Pauline corpus, Childs resists 'any permanent separating of a reconstructed "historical Paul" from the witness of the "canonical Paul"'.[11] The failure of scholarly approaches to Paul lies in 'the assumption that one could recover Paul's theology apart from its ecclesial reception'.[12]

This means that the Pauline authorship, or otherwise, of various elements of the canon is not taken into account here. Childs does not assume direct Pauline authorship of all the letters bearing his name, but rather acknowledges 'their status within a traditional apostolic collection'.[13] The author(s) of each letter that bears his name will be addressed as Paul, regardless of which part of the canon is in view. Some readers may prefer to understand the author as 'Paul (so-called)', depending on the letter in question, but no such distinction will permeate this study.

As Childs suggests, the study of Pauline theology is not ultimately for the purpose of reconstructing a purified 'theology of Paul', but rather to operate within the larger context of the Bible, in order 'to understand the full range of the message of the Pauline corpus whose witness continues to instruct, admonish, and sustain the apostolic faith of the church'.[14] Finally, then, acceptance of the entire Pauline canon is necessary here because this book is not for academia alone. It is also for the church.

1.6 THE SHAPE OF THE STUDY

The book consists of three parts. Part 1 raises introductory matters in this chapter, and the following chapter provides a selective survey of major academic developments through the twentieth century to the present time.

---

negative criterion to mark off those claims of truth that fell outside the circle of faith'; Brevard S. Childs, *The Church's Guide for Reading Paul: The Canonical Shaping of the Pauline Corpus* (Grand Rapids: Eerdmans, 2008), 16.

10. Ibid., 77.

11. Ibid.

12. Ibid. After all, 'the historical Paul of the first century has been transmitted by Christian tradents who have received and shaped their testimony into the form of a canonical Paul' (ibid., 256).

13. Ibid., 79.

14. Ibid., 112.

Part 2 comprises roughly half the book, addressing the exegesis of relevant texts. Chapters 3, 4, 5, and 6 each deal with a prepositional phrase and their respective alterations: ἐν Χριστῷ, σὺν Χριστῷ, εἰς Χριστόν, and διὰ Χριστοῦ. Chapter 7 explores Paul's use of metaphor for expressing union with Christ. Part 3 draws on the results of the exegetical studies conducted in Part 2 and seeks to integrate them into the broad spheres of Paul's thought. Chapters 8, 9, 10, and 11 address the work of Christ, Paul's trinitarian thought, Christian living, and justification, respectively. Chapter 12 draws together the fruit of the entire study in order to articulate a comprehensive description of union with Christ. This chapter also includes a discussion about the conceptual antecedents of Paul's thought. Chapter 13 explores the implications of the book's conclusions and marks out future directions for research. The two implications explored are, first, the role of union with Christ in Paul's theological framework vis-à-vis other themes and concerns, and, second, the theological structure of his thought.

1.7 THE MAJOR CONCLUSIONS OF THE STUDY

The major conclusions and implications of this study are established in chapters 12 and 13, but it is worth outlining them from the outset. First, the term 'union with Christ' is deemed insufficient to convey all that Paul includes in the theme. Indeed, other terms such as 'participation' and 'mysticism' are likewise insufficient. To do justice to the full spectrum of Paul's thought and language, the terms *union, participation, identification, incorporation* are adopted, in place of previous terminology. These four umbrella terms successfully capture the full range of prepositional phraseology, metaphorical conceptualisations, and theological interactions that Paul draws on to communicate what it means to be united to Christ. Some of the characteristics of the metatheme of *union, participation, identification, incorporation* include locality, instrumentality, trinitarianism, eschatology, and spiritual reality.

Second, certain conceptual antecedents that give rise to Paul's metatheme of *union, participation, identification, incorporation* can be found in Jewish theology and the Old Testament, but most profoundly in the words of Jesus, beginning with his words *to Paul* on the Damascus road. While such antecedents inform Paul's thinking, his conception remains boldly original in its language, scope, and pervasiveness.

Third, the metatheme of *union, participation, identification, incorporation* is regarded to be of utmost importance to Paul, yet does not occupy the 'centre' of his theological framework. It is, rather, the essential ingredient that binds all other elements together.

CHAPTER 2

THE STATE OF
THE UNION

2.1 INTRODUCTION

The Pauline theme of union with Christ has risen to prominence in the
current world of New Testament scholarship. This, of course, did not
happen overnight, but is the fruit of labours over more than a century.
While union with Christ has been discussed and explored at various times
in the history of the Christian church, the volume and intensity of such
discussions and exploration became significantly heightened through the
twentieth century. Among the issues that preoccupied scholarly inquiry
is the conceptual background of Pauline mysticism and what union with
Christ actually means to Paul. As the theme rose to prominence through
the twentieth century, it became increasingly important to understand
how it relates to other themes in Pauline thought, since it was perceived
by some to displace other traditionally significant themes.

It is important to understand the trajectory of thought regarding union
with Christ and what factors led to the current state of play. Accordingly, this
chapter consists of a survey of major contributions of the scholars who have
significantly shaped the current discussion through the twentieth century to
the present day.[1] Clearly, such a survey will be limited in its depth of coverage, but the aim is to portray accurately the main lines of thought of each
scholar, highlighting their distinctives and offering some elucidation of the

---

1. It is not possible to survey every significant contributor here, but those included define
the parameters of the field in a way that sets the scene for the ensuing discussion.

connections between them. Following this survey I will include a brief synthesis of the key lines of thought across the body of contribution. This will be useful for bringing into focus the salient issues, as well as those about which there is common assent and those about which there is still disagreement.

2.2 ADOLF DEISSMANN (1892)

James D. G. Dunn acknowledges that it was Adolf Deissmann who brought the idiom 'in Christ' to centre stage in twentieth-century New Testament scholarship.[2] Deissmann described union with Christ as *Christ mysticism*, which he regarded as a response to Paul's 'mystical experience' at Damascus — 'a mystical initiation arising from a divine initiative'.[3] For Deissmann, this Christ mysticism was not in the first instance about doctrine or Paul's theological formulation; rather, it had to do with fellowship with Christ — what he described as 'Christ-intimacy'.[4] 'Paul lives "in" Christ, "in" the living and present spiritual Christ, who is about him on all sides, who fills him, who speaks to him, and speaks in and through him.'[5] Describing how this fellowship with Christ is manifested, Deissmann suggested that because Christ is Spirit he can live in Paul, while Paul lives in him. He offers an analogy with air: 'Just as the air of life, which we breathe, is "in" us and fills us, and yet we at the same time live in this air and breathe it, so it is also with the Christ-intimacy of the Apostle Paul: Christ in him, he in Christ.'[6]

Deissmann regarded Christ mysticism as taking its place within mysticism in general. Hellenistic influence was surely at work in Paul's conception, which likewise spoke of 'inspired people who were filled with their God and given power by their God'.[7] Having said this, however, Deissmann employed the German word *Mystik* in its wider sense, by which he would describe any religious tendency that connects to God 'through inner experience without the mediation of reasoning'.[8] Conse-

---

2. James D. G. Dunn, *The Theology of Paul the Apostle* (Grand Rapids: Eerdmans, 1998), 391.

3. Adolf Deissmann, *Paul: A Study in Social and Religious History* (2nd ed.; trans. William E. Wilson; London: Hodder & Stoughton, 1926), 130–31.

4. Ibid., 135–36; see also Adolf Deissmann, *Die Neutestamentliche Formel "In Christo Jesu"* (Marburg: N. G. Elwert'sche Verlagsbuchhandlung, 1892), 81–82.

5. Deissmann, *Paul*, 135–36; also Deissmann, *In Christo Jesu*, 97–98, 118–24.

6. Deissmann, *Paul*, 140.

7. Ibid., 147.

8. Ibid., 149.

quently, he did not wish to employ the term *Mystik* in any technical sense; rather, Paul's conception could be described as mysticism simply because it involved contact with the deity, which, according to Deissmann, is the 'constitutive element in mysticism'.[9]

Within mysticism, Deissmann distinguished between two types. The first, which he labelled 'ego-centric mysticism', affirmed union with the divine, oneness with God, loss of human personality, transformation into the deity, aesthetic intoxication, and denial of personality.[10] This type of mysticism did not respect the boundaries between humanity and deity, but rather sought to merge one into the other. The second type of mysticism, clearly preferred by Deissmann and labelled 'Theo-centric mysticism', affirmed communion rather than union with God, the sanctification of personality, conformation of the human toward the divine, ethical enthusiasm, and personality.[11] Not surprisingly, Deissmann regarded Paul's mysticism as of the second type, in which Paul 'was not deified nor was he transformed into spirit by this communion, nor did he become Christ'.[12]

Regarding Paul's language of mysticism, Deissmann claimed that the apostle used the genitive 'of Jesus Christ' in a unique manner. He argued that in several instances of Paul's usage of this phrase, the normal classes of subjective and objective genitive were insufficient to describe accurately what Paul meant. Deissmann believed that Paul used a special type of genitive, 'which might be called the "genitive of fellowship" or the "mystical genitive," because it indicates mystical fellowship with Christ'.[13] He goes so far as to say that the phrase 'of Jesus Christ' is basically identical with 'in Christ'.[14] This claim led Deissmann to argue that the phrases 'justification out of faith' or 'through faith' should be understood as 'justification "in" faith', that is 'justification "in Christ"', 'justification "in the name of Jesus Christ"', 'justification "in the blood of Christ"'.[15]

Deissmann concluded by arguing that while Paul's Christ mysticism is distinctly Pauline in origin and meaning,[16] it is not inconsistent with the

9. Ibid.
10. Ibid., 150–51.
11. Ibid.
12. Ibid., 152–53.
13. Ibid., 162–63.
14. Ibid., 163.
15. Ibid., 169–70.
16. Deissmann, *In Christo Jesu*, 72–73.

teaching of Christ. Rather, Christ mysticism appropriates the benefits of Christ to those who share in fellowship with him:

> The Christ-centred Christianity of Paul is therefore neither a breach with the Gospel of Jesus nor a sophistication of the Gospel of Jesus. It secures for the many the Gospel experience of God which had been the possession of the One, and it does so by anchoring these many souls in the Soul of the One.[17]

2.3 WILHELM BOUSSET (1913)

Alongside Deissmann's contribution, the early twentieth-century discussion about Christ mysticism was indebted to Wilhelm Bousset. He described the Christ piety of Paul as 'the intense feeling of personal belonging and of spiritual relationship with the exalted Lord'.[18] The 'in Christ' formula is for Paul a summary of the fact that Christ has become 'the supra-terrestrial power which supports and fills with its presence his whole life'.[19]

Bousset regarded it as obvious that Paul connected his Christ mysticism to the sacrament of baptism. 'For him baptism serves as an act of initiation in which the mystic is merged with the deity, or is clothed with the deity.... Thus in baptism the Christians have become one with the Son, and hence themselves have become sons.'[20]

Bousett drew a strong connection between the 'in Christ' formula and the 'in the Spirit' expression and regarded the two expressions as immediately parallel and analogous.[21] The Christian is in Christ as he is in the Spirit, and the 'two formulas coincide so completely that they can be interchanged at will'.[22] Bousset claimed that in Paul's thought all the benefits and expressions of the Christian life can be traced back to the Spirit or to Christ.[23]

Of all the twentieth-century contributions concerning union with Christ, arguably it is Bousset's work that deals most thoroughly with the

---

17. Deissmann, *Paul*, 258.
18. Wilhelm Bousset, *Kyrios Christos: A History of Belief in Christ from the Beginnings of Christianity to Irenaeus* (trans. John E. Steely; Nashville: Abingdon, 1970), 153.
19. Ibid., 154.
20. Ibid., 158.
21. Ibid., 160.
22. Ibid.
23. Ibid.

issue of Pauline mysticism and Hellenistic mysticism. While he maintained some parallel between them, he began by stating that 'at first glance … it is not altogether easy to find such parallels at all'.[24] The goal of Greek mysticism was deification; it did not concern life in or with the deity but sought to be the deity. The Greek mystery system was 'individualistic, eudaemonistic, egoistic; the individual mystic achieves for himself the blessed state of deification. The divine is completely absorbed into the human. These perils are avoided in Paul.'[25] In contrast, Bousset noted, Paul's 'in Christ' conception meant a new world; it meant that the individual was swept up into 'one great surpassing, world-embracing will which is expressed in the totality of a comprehensive fellowship'.[26]

Having said as much, however, Bousett nevertheless draws some connection between Paul and Greek religion. The Greek notion of the religious superman is in part stirring in Paul; thus 'there remains a certain affinity between the Pauline Christ mysticism and that mystery piety portrayed above'.[27]

2.4 ALBERT SCHWEITZER (1930)

If Deissmann brought the formula 'in Christ' to centre stage in twentieth-century New Testament scholarship, it was Albert Schweitzer who dominated the discussion. Schweitzer began by defining mysticism in a similar manner to Deissmann — it has to do with the connection between the human and divine. 'We are always in the presence of mysticism when we find a human being looking upon the division between earthly and super-earthly, temporal and eternal, as transcended, and feeling himself, while still externally amid the earthly and temporal, to belong to the super-earthly and eternal.'[28]

While Schweitzer, like Deissmann, located Paul's mysticism within the wider mystical tradition, he regarded it as standing high above the religious conceptions of primitive mysticism. He argued that Paul never

---

24. Ibid., 164.
25. Ibid., 166.
26. Ibid., 168–69.
27. Ibid., 170.
28. Albert Schweitzer, *The Mysticism of Paul the Apostle* (trans. William Montgomery; Baltimore: John Hopkins Univ. Press, 1998), 1.

speaks of being one with God or of a mystical union with God himself; rather, his relation to God is mediated 'by means of the mystical union with Christ'.[29] While Paul describes believers as sons of God, this does not envisage an immediate mystical relation to God. In part, it is this mediated mystical relationship that makes Paul unique among mystical traditions.

A key distinctive in Schweitzer's approach to Pauline mysticism was the central significance of eschatology. He argued that 'God-mysticism' was a thing of the future: 'Before that, they are those who have the assurance of having been called to this sonship and are therefore, by anticipation, denominated Children of God.'[30] Thus, God mysticism is recognised by Paul, but it cannot be concurrent with Christ mysticism; they are 'chronologically successive, Christ-mysticism holding the field until God-mysticism becomes possible'.[31] In other words, Christ mysticism is the experience or state of believers in this present age until Christ returns. It is mediatory and penultimate in its meaning and scope.

Schweitzer acknowledged that a peculiarity of Pauline mysticism is its 'extraordinarily realistic character', in which the believer has 'a real co-experiencing' of Christ's dying and rising again.[32] A further un-Hellenistic characteristic of the apostle's mysticism is that the concept of deification is foreign to it.[33] The believer has fellowship with Christ and shares the experience of Christ's dying and rising again, but Paul goes no further than that. Schweitzer's claim was that this feature of Paul's thought set his mysticism apart from Hellenistic versions:

> Through this alone it is clear that Hellenistic and the Pauline mysticism belong to two different worlds. Since the Hellenistic mysticism is founded on the idea of deification and the Pauline on the idea of fellowship with the divine being, it is impossible to find in the Hellenistic literature parallels for the characteristic phrases 'with Christ' and 'in Christ' which dominate the Pauline mysticism.[34]

---

29. Ibid., 3.
30. Ibid., 12.
31. Ibid., 12–13.
32. Ibid., 13.
33. Ibid., 15.
34. Ibid., 16.

Schweitzer outlined several other differences between Paul's mysticism and that of Hellenism. Among these are Paul's connection of predestination to mysticism,[35] the historico-cosmic dimension of Paul's mysticism as compared to mythical Hellenism,[36] Paul's collective mysticism versus Hellenism's individualistic mystery religions,[37] and the focus of Paul's mysticism on the end of the world, whereas Hellenistic mysticism is oriented toward the remote beginnings of the world.[38] All in all, Schweitzer drew compelling evidence of the absolute uniqueness of Pauline mysticism when compared against Hellenistic mysticism.[39]

Having demonstrated that Pauline mysticism did not originate in Hellenistic thought, Schweitzer also concluded that it did not come from mainstream Judaism either. He claimed that the Jewish conception of the deity as transcendental in character and the antithesis between present and future, this world and the other world, 'are opposed to mysticism'.[40] Schweitzer does, however, regard late Jewish eschatology as holding promise.[41]

As for the place of mysticism in Paul's thought, Schweitzer viewed it as his solution to an eschatological problem. He viewed Paul's conception of redemption as eschatological, which meant that Paul was forced to account for how believers living in this world might appropriate now the benefits of redemption, which properly lie in the future.[42]

> In consequence of his eschatological view of redemption Paul is obliged to maintain that the powers of death and resurrection which were made manifest in Jesus, now, from the moment of His dying and rising again onwards, are at work upon the corporeity of those who are elect to the Messianic Kingdom and render them capable of assuming the resurrection mode of existence before the general resurrection of the dead takes place.[43]

---

35. Ibid.
36. Ibid., 23.
37. Ibid.
38. Ibid., 23–24.
39. He expressed it poignantly: 'Since all his conceptions and thoughts are rooted in eschatology, those who labour to explain him on the basis of Hellenism, are like a man who should bring water from a long distance in leaky watering-cans in order to water a garden lying beside a stream' (ibid., 140).
40. Ibid., 36.
41. Ibid., 37.
42. Ibid., 75.
43. Ibid., 101.

As such, Schweitzer regarded mysticism as the means by which Paul was able to reconcile the otherwise contradicting elements of his eschatology. Redemption is future, and yet believers are able to experience Christ's death and resurrection in their present existence because they share with Christ.

While Christ mysticism solves Paul's eschatological 'problem', it raised a new problem for Schweitzer: 'But how is such mysticism possible?'[44] He asked how it is conceivable that the elect, who are earthly, natural people, should have fellowship with Christ, who is now in a supernatural state.[45] The answer to this question that Schweitzer settled on is that 'these Elect are in reality no longer natural men, but, like Christ Himself, are already supernatural beings, only that in them this is not yet manifest'.[46] Consequently, Schweitzer was able to say that Paul's mysticism is nothing else than 'the doctrine of the making manifest, in consequence of the death and resurrection of Jesus, of the pre-existent Church (the Community of God)'.[47] In this sense, he could claim that the expression 'being-in-Christ' is 'merely a shorthand reference for being partakers in the Mystical Body of Christ'.[48]

According to Schweitzer, the concept of this Mystical Body of Christ was the heart of Paul's mysticism. While the phrase 'in Christ' is dominant in its number of references, the original conception is the 'sharing by the Elect in the same corporeity with Christ'.[49] Futhermore, Schweitzer regarded the Mystical Body of Christ as an actual reality in Paul's mind; it was not metaphorical or symbolic in nature.[50]

Having satisfied himself on the issue of origin, role, and meaning of Pauline mysticism, Schweitzer went on to explore its connection to other themes in Paul's thought. These include the Spirit, the Law, the sacraments, righteousness, forgiveness of sins, and ethics.

2.5 RUDOLF BULTMANN (1948 – 1953)

Contrary to Schweitzer's best effort to eliminate any connection between Pauline mysticism and Hellenism, Bultmann embarked upon that path at

---

44. Ibid., 109.
45. Ibid.
46. Ibid., 110.
47. Ibid., 116.
48. Ibid., 122.
49. Ibid., 125.
50. Ibid., 127.

full bore: '*Paul describes Christ's death in analogy with the death of a divinity of the mystery religions.*'[51] He described the significance of the sacraments as parallel to participation in the fate of the mystery-divinity, which grants the initiate participation into the dying and reviving of the divinity, and he claimed that Paul interprets the death of Christ through the categories of the gnostic myth.[52] This gnostic myth involves the presupposition that gnostic men constitute a unity with the Redeemer, such that what happens to the Redeemer happens to his whole 'body'.[53]

Bultmann argued that the 'in Christ' terminology did not refer to mystic union, but was primarily an ecclesiological formula.[54] 'It means the state of having been articulated into the "body of Christ" by baptism, although baptism need not be directly implied in every instance'.[55] Bultmann did, however, allow meaning for the phrase beyond baptism into the body, but only by extension. It can also express 'the state of being determined by Christ', by which he meant that this was Paul's way of referring to people as 'Christian', before that adjective had come into frequent use.[56]

Bultmann took this line of argumentation so far as to say the exact reverse of Schweitzer: *in Christ* 'denotes not, to be sure, an individual mysticism relationship to Christ'[57]. In fact, 'it makes no difference whether Paul speaks of the believer's being in Christ or of Christ's being in the believer.... Either one means nothing else than that conditioning of concrete life which Paul also calls the "law of Christ"'.[58]

It is difficult to imagine a more extreme reaction to Schweitzer than that witnessed in Bultmann's analysis of 'in Christ'. He affirmed the gnostic roots of the conception, whereas Schweitzer strenuously denied them. He regarded 'in Christ' language to refer simply to membership in the church, without any mystical connection to Christ. Schweitzer regarded mystical union with Christ as central to Paul's thought.

---

51. Rudolf Bultmann, *Theology of the New Testament* (trans. Kendrick Grobel; London: SCM, 1952), 298, §33 [italics are original].
52. Ibid.
53. Ibid.
54. Ibid., 311, §34.
55. Ibid.
56. Ibid.
57. Ibid., 328, §36.
58. Ibid.

2.6 JOHN MURRAY (1955)

Taking a theological approach to union with Christ as opposed to an historico-exegetical approach, John Murray claimed that 'nothing is more central or basic than union and communion with Christ'.[59] Murray argued that union with Christ is the 'central truth of the whole doctrine of salvation' and 'underlies every step of the application of redemption'.[60]

Murray took care to explore what type of union pertains between a believer and Christ:

> This brings us to note, in the second place, that union with Christ is *Spiritual* because it is a spiritual relationship that is in view. It is not the kind of union that we have in the Godhead — three persons in one God. It is not the kind of union we have in the person of Christ—two natures in one person. It is not the kind of union we have in man—body and soul constituting a human being. It is not simply the union of feeling, affection, understanding, mind, heart, will, and purpose. Here we have union which we are unable to define specifically. But it is union of an intensely spiritual character consonant with the nature and work of the Holy Spirit so that in a real way surpassing our power of analysis Christ dwells in his people and his people dwell in him.[61]

Rejecting the tendency of some toward deification, Murray stated clearly that union with Christ 'does not mean that we are incorporated into the Godhead. That is one of the distortions to which this great truth has been subjected.'[62] Nevertheless, believers' union with Christ is the highest kind of unity that exists for creatures, and 'it is attested by nothing more than this that it is compared to the union that exists between the Father and the Son in the unity of the Godhead.'[63] More than that, union with Christ achieves for believers union with the Father, Son, and Spirit.[64]

Along such lines, Murray regarded Christ mysticism as the highest order of mysticism. Rather than being vague, unintelligible, or rapturous,

---

59. John Murray, *Redemption—Accomplished and Applied* (Grand Rapids: Eerdmans, 1955), 201.
60. Ibid.
61. Ibid., 206 [italics are original].
62. Ibid., 208.
63. Ibid., 208–9.
64. Ibid., 212.

it is 'the mysticism of communion with the one true and living God, and
... only because it is communion with the three distinct persons of the
Godhead in the strict particularity which belongs to each person in that
grand economy of saving relationship to us'.[65]

2.7 ALFRED WIKENHAUSER (1960)

The Catholic theologian Alfred Wikenhauser began by acknowledging
that there is no agreement concerning mysticism, and this is in part due to
Protestant antipathy toward the issue.[66] Wikenhauser defined mysticism
as *'that form of spirituality which strives after (or experiences) an immediate
contact (or union) of the soul with God'*,[67] and acknowledged the diversity of
its forms. All mysticism may be described as either 'the entry of man into
Divinity' or 'the entry of Divinity into man'. Either may exist without the
other, or both may exist together.[68] Wikenhauser did not regard Pauline
mysticism as an example of Hellenistic mysticism. Some of the key differences between the two include the fact that Paul had a monotheistic
concept of God, while Hellenistic mysticism was pantheistic. Paul's theology contains a clearly defined eschatology, of which there is no such thing
in Hellenism. Paul's mysticism involves being united with a person rather
than being united with infinity.[69]

On Paul's use of language to refer to mysticism, Wikenhauser observed
that some instances of 'in Christ' speak of 'Christ as the vehicle of God's
work',[70] and sometimes it refers to the union between the Christian and
Christ. Wikenhauser acknowledged that the references that speak of God's
action in Christ have no mystical meaning. He also observed the difficulty
of determining whether or not a specific passage has a mystical meaning.[71]

In an interesting twist, however, Wikenhauser suggested that the use of
'in Christ' language, when 'by Christ' would do, is significant. 'Evidently
[Paul] wished to bring out the point that to some extent Christ was the

---

65. Ibid.
66. Alfred Wikenhauser, *Pauline Mysticism: Christ in the Mystical Teaching of St. Paul*
(trans. Joseph Cunningham; Freiburg: Herder and Herder, 1960), 13–14.
67. Ibid., 14 [italics are original].
68. Ibid., 19.
69. Ibid., 166–67.
70. Ibid., 24.
71. Ibid.

abode of God's gracious presence, the place where God willed and worked the salvation of men.'[72] In this way, passages that do not relate to mysticism in terms of the human-Christ relationship nevertheless indicate a union of sorts—between the Father and the Son.

Contrary to the types of assertions made by Bultmann, Wikenhauser regarded the believer's relationship to Christ as not merely ethical; 'it is ontological.... The man who "puts on Christ" gains a share in Christ's being.'[73]

Wikenhauser engaged Deissmann's belief in the so-called 'mystical genitive'. While he acknowledged the sharp critique of this new category by E. von Dobschütz, Wikenhauser nevertheless allowed for the possibility of mystical nuance in the genitival phrase. 'We could not say *a priori* that this use of the genitive must necessarily convey a mystical meaning. But in the light which other texts shed on his doctrine of union with Christ, it is clear that this genitive is often used in a mystical sense.'[74]

As for Wikenhauser's relation to the work of Schweitzer, there is some agreement and some disagreement. Schweitzer's focus on the eschatological subsistence of 'in Christ' was echoed by Wikenhauser when he said that being *with* Christ is the final goal of the Christian, whereas '"being in Christ" comes to an end when it attains its purpose and we are "with Christ"'.[75] However, whereas Schweitzer conceived of a 'quasi-physical' union with Christ, Wikenhauser declared that Paul was not thinking of a physical location in Christ; 'there is no question here of any idea of spatial presence.'[76]

Wikenhauser denied any pantheistic sense of absorption into God, which was common in Hellenistic mysticism.[77] A Christian's personality is not lost through absorption into Christ; 'the only union which he knows preserves the individuality of the person, and also the relationship of master and servant with Christ.'[78]

Somewhat uniquely, Wikenhauser denied that mysticism arises from

---

72. Ibid., 25.
73. Ibid., 32.
74. Ibid., 39–40 [italics are original].
75. Ibid., 62–63, cf. 200.
76. Ibid., 64.
77. Ibid., 96.
78. Ibid., 102.

faith in Christ and that Protestant arguments along such lines were quite unacceptable.[79] He argued that Paul envisaged an objective relationship with Christ, and this was 'established by a sacramental act, namely by Baptism'.[80] The mystical union is not even achieved through a combination of faith and baptism for Wikenhauser: 'We may say without qualification that Baptism, and not faith, establishes the mysticism relationship with Christ.'[81] While union with Christ is not established by faith, Wikenhauser is clear that without faith, there is no union with Christ. Faith, then, is a precondition of union, which 'presupposes faith in the resurrection of Christ.... Only one who has attained this faith can enter upon a mystical relationship with Christ.'[82]

2.8 FRITZ NEUGEBAUER (1961)

After publishing an article on the topic in 1958,[83] Fritz Neugebauer's 1961 monograph constituted one of the twentieth-century's major exegetical studies of the Pauline 'in Christ' and 'in the Lord' phrases. Rather than being interested in the theological theme of union with Christ or Pauline mysticism, Neugebauer's research was limited to the meaning and significance of these phrases.

First, Neugebauer examined the individual elements contained in the phrases 'in Christ (Jesus)' and 'in the Lord', with an extensive discussion of Paul's use of the preposition ἐν,[84] followed by his use of Ἰησοῦς, Χριστός, and κύριος.[85] He then proceeded to a major discussion of the meaning of the formula ἐν Χριστῷ (Ἰησοῦ) through the subsections of salvation in Christ,[86] the church in Christ,[87] and the apostle in Christ.[88]

Through this discussion, Neugebauer develops a salvation-historical approach to the topic, in which 'in Christ' depicts the objective reality of

---

79. Ibid., 110.
80. Ibid.
81. Ibid., 123.
82. Ibid., 129.
83. Fritz Neugebauer, 'Das paulinische "in Christo,"' *NTS* 4 (1957–58): 124–38.
84. Neugebauer, *In Christus*, 34–44.
85. Ibid., 44–64.
86. 'Das Heil in Christo'; see ibid., 72–92.
87. 'Die Ekklesia in Christo'; see ibid., 92–112.
88. 'Der Apostel in Christo'; see ibid., 113–30.

Christian existence and the work of God in the death and resurrection of Christ. Salvation 'in Christ' is an eschatological event that is determined by the love and will of God.[89] The fact of eschatological salvation in Christ establishes the church as a new creation.[90] And what is true of the church in Christ is true also for Paul the apostle.[91]

Neugebauer argued that Paul used ἐν Χριστῷ for indicative statements, while he employed ἐν κυρίῳ for imperatival material. Thus, ἐν Χριστῷ indicates that eschatological salvation has happened, is happening, and will happen. It harks back to the events of the cross and resurrection and looks forward to the final consummation. Ἐν κυρίῳ, however, occurs in contexts in which believers are encouraged to persevere on the basis of what has been received ἐν Χριστῷ. Neugebauer therefore defined ἐν Χριστῷ as a 'definition of circumstances' and ἐν κυρίῳ as 'determined by the circumstances that Jesus Christ is Lord of human history, and as such calls for (certain) actions'.[92]

While Neugebauer's study is enlightening with respect to these two Pauline phrases, he did not include other expressions that are, arguably, related or synonymous. Moreover, the various metaphorical concepts through which Paul expresses corporate relationship with Christ are ignored. As an exegetical investigation concerned with these formulae only, Neugebauer does not explore the theological notions of Pauline mysticism or union with Christ, having enunciated the reality of being 'in Christ' purely through the lens of salvation history.

2.9 MICHEL BOUTTIER (1962)

Soon after Neugebauer's monograph followed a second major exegetical study, published in 1962 by Michel Bouttier. Bouttier desired to arrive at a unified translation of ἐν Χριστῷ in order to preserve the integrity of

---

89. 'Doch nicht nur Gnade und Friede finden ihre Determination in Christo Jesus, sondern auch die Liebe und der Wille Gottes'; ibid., 90.

90. 'Der Mensch auf dieser Erde ist in Christo jetzt schon neue Schöpfung, weil die Ekklesia neue Schöpfung ist. Eschatologisches Heil ist geschehen'; ibid., 112.

91. 'Weil die Christusformel der gemeinsam bestimmende Umstand für Apostel wie Ekklesia ist, darum bedeutet die Verwendung von "in Christo" zur Charackterisierung des apostlischen Wirkens für die Ekklesia das Einheitsmoment, das beide gleicherweise konstituiert'; ibid., 127.

92. Neugebauer, 'Das paulinische "In Christo"', 132, 135.

Pauline usage.[93] Beginning with the presupposition that a unified translation was possible, Bouttier offered a limited categorization of the uses of ἐν Χριστῷ. He saw Paul's usage comprehensively accounted for by instrumental, inclusive and communal, and eschatological categories.[94] The instrumental, or historical, category of usage referred to Paul's references to crucifixion and resurrection of Christ. The inclusive and communal category referred to the elevation of Christ to the Father's right hand and his presence in the church. The eschatological category referred to the establishment of the kingdom of God.[95]

The two most substantial sections of Bouttier's monograph deal with exegetical analysis and theological synthesis in turn. The first offers a significant advance upon Neugebauer's work by considering several other phrases alongside ἐν Χριστῷ and ἐν κυρίῳ.[96] These include διὰ Χριστοῦ,[97] εἰς Χριστόν,[98] σὺν Χριστῷ,[99] ἐν πνεύματι,[100] the so-called 'mystical genitive',[101] and the concept of 'we in Christ—Christ in us'.[102]

Bouttier concludes that ἐν Χριστῷ is the most comprehensive of these phrases, while the others each perform a specialized function. The use of ἐν Χριστῷ is grounded in the past events of Christ's narrative while also expressing both the present characteristics of Christian life and the consummation in the eschaton. The phrase διὰ Χριστοῦ is more objective than ἐν Χριστῷ, establishing Christ as Saviour and Lord and leading to the relationship described as ἐν Χριστῷ. The phrase σὺν Χριστῷ functions to relate believers to the death and resurrection of Christ as well as to the future union with him beyond death. The use of ἐν κυρίῳ tends to depict the present activities of life in Christ, thus associated with the ethical imperative. The phrase εἰς Χριστόν indicates transference into the realm of Christ.

---

93. 'Tenons donc fermement à l'unité de in Christo et maintenons indéfectiblement la même traduction, partout, envers et contre tout' (Bouttier, *En Christ*, 30).

94. Ibid., 133.

95. Ibid.

96. 'Sur les Frontières de "in Christo"'; see ibid., 31–86.

97. Ibid., 31–35.

98. Ibid., 35–38.

99. Ibid., 38–53.

100. Ibid., 61–69.

101. Ibid., 69–79.

102. Ibid., 80–85.

The second significant section attempts to set the exegetical results of the first into Paul's theological thought.[103] Bouttier analyses the work of Christ in relation to the past and his future coming, and he speaks of a mystical element in relation to the present.[104] In his later work of 1966, Bouttier concluded:

> In Christ we share in him who is the same yesterday, today, and for ever. Jesus' death and resurrection fulfilled the promise of the old covenant as well as the mysterious expectation of the Gentiles, and answered the sighs of creation; henceforth everything is embodied in him; in him there meet there various threads of revelation; God's plan is summed up and at the same time goes on anew.[105]

2.10 KARL BARTH (1932 – 1968)

While Barth expounded his fully developed thinking about union with Christ in *Church Dogmatics* IV/3.2, Neder notes that this stands in relation to a twofold form of *participation in Christ* that had been developed from as early as II/2.[106] There is an objective form of participation in Christ, which is the ground for a subjective form. The objective form refers to Barth's conviction that human nature does not exist apart from its being in Christ. In one sense, all of humanity, by definition, is 'in Christ'. The subjective form is the *telos* of the objective form, which is realised in obedience.[107] Once Barth reached IV/3.2 he adopted the term *union with Christ* as a synonym for the subjective form of participation earlier developed.

Barth regarded the Christian to be united with Christ in the whole of his existence and experience.[108] As such, union with Christ is not induced through psychological experience.[109] While it is personal rather than impersonal, union with Christ does not eliminate the 'distinction between

---

103. 'Dimensions de "in Christo"'; see ibid., 87–133.

104. Ibid., 93, 98, 132.

105. Michel Bouttier, *Christianity According to Paul* (trans. F. Clarke; London: SCM, 1966), 118–19.

106. Adam Neder, *Participation in Christ: An Entry into Karl Barth's* Church Dogmatics (Columbia Series in Reformed Theology; Louisville: Westminster John Knox, 2009), 78.

107. Ibid., 17–18.

108. Ibid., 78.

109. Karl Barth, *Church Dogmatics* IV/3.2: *The Doctrine of Reconciliation* (ed. G. W. Bromiley and T. F. Torrance; trans. G. W. Bromiley; Edinburgh: T&T Clark, 1962), 536.

the Creator and creature or the antithesis between the Holy One and sinners'.[110] It does not bring about a loss of 'specific character, role and function in relation to the other'.[111] While such a distinction remains, union with Christ is nevertheless a 'true, total and indissoluble union'—a 'single totality', which is a 'genuine and solid unity'.[112] Barth regarded the fellowship between Christians and Christ to be a perfect fellowship, 'inasmuch as what takes place in it is no less than their union with Christ'.[113]

For Barth, the phenomenon of being in Christ stems from the trinitarian nature of God: 'This historical being in Christ is decisively determined, of course, by the fact that first and supremely God was "in Christ" reconciling the world to Himself.'[114] In other words, being in Christ is not just a relationship between people and Christ; it is first a relationship between the Father and the Son. Indeed, believers who are in Christ 'acquire and have a direct share in what God first and supremely is in Him, what was done by God for the world and therefore for them in Him, and what is assigned and given to them by God in Him'.[115] Even so, Barth is emphatic in his rejection of deification throughout *Church Dogmatics*, and especially in IV/2.

In a manner similar to Schweitzer, Barth regarded the word 'in' in the phrase 'in Christ' to have a 'local signification'.[116] While believers and Christ do not lose their identity and particularity in their union, 'the "in" must indeed indicate on both sides that the spatial distance between Christ and the Christian disappears, that Christ is spatially present where Christians are, and that Christians are spatially present where Christ is, and not merely alongside but in exactly the same spot.'[117] Against Schweitzer (who is not named), however, Barth rejected the use of the term *mysticism*, 'unless we state precisely what we have in view' by it.[118] Since there is no compelling reason to use the term, he recommended avoiding it.[119]

---

110. Ibid.
111. Ibid., 540.
112. Ibid.
113. Ibid.
114. Ibid., 546.
115. Ibid.
116. Ibid., 547.
117. Ibid.
118. Ibid., 539.
119. Ibid., 540.

Contrary to the views of Wikenhauser, Barth did not allow a disjunction between becoming a Christian and the relationship of union with Christ. Rather, 'a man becomes and is a Christian as he unites himself with Christ and Christ with him.'[120] This fellowship of union with Christ was regarded by Barth to be the starting point for everything else that 'is to be thought and said concerning what makes the Christian a Christian'.[121]

2.11 ROBERT C. TANNEHILL (1967)

Tannehill critiqued previous theological discussion for its lack of attention to the motif of dying and rising with Christ. He argued that through dying and rising with Christ, the believer *partakes* in the events of Christ's death and resurrection rather than simply benefiting from them. 'Furthermore, these events continue to give their stamp to the life of the believer, for he continues to participate in Christ's death and resurrection in his daily life, especially through suffering.'[122] As such, Paul's use of the motif falls into two groups: in reference to 'dying with Christ as a decisive, past event' and in reference to 'dying with Christ as a present experience'.[123]

Tannehill's monograph consists of three parts. In part 1, he explores the motif of dying with Christ as the basis of the new life. The key element here is that dying and rising with Christ relates to two dominions and their rulers, indicating transference from one to the other.[124] Consequently, the motif is inextricably bound to Paul's eschatological vision: 'When Paul speaks of dying and rising with Christ, he is referring to Christ's death and resurrection as eschatological events.'[125] By the believer's participation in Christ's death and resurrection, he or she is grounded in new life through dying to the old age and rising to the new.

In part 2, Tannehill deals with dying with Christ as the structure of the new life, referring to the present aspect of Christian action and suffering. Since Paul uses the motif to interpret *present* experience *and* to refer

---

120. Ibid., 548–49.
121. Ibid., 549.
122. Robert C. Tannehill, *Dying and Rising with Christ: A Study in Pauline Theology* (1967; repr. Eugene, OR: Wipf & Stock, 2006), 1.
123. Ibid., 6.
124. Ibid., 7.
125. Ibid., 39.

to a *past* event, it is clear that 'existence in the new dominion takes on a structure which corresponds to the founding events of death and resurrection, and there is a sense in which we can say that the Christian *continually* dies with Christ.'[126] Dying with Christ in present experience and suffering leads to life on the basis of the pattern of Christ. 'By God's power Jesus' death led to his resurrection. So also God brings life from death in the existence of the believer.'[127]

In part 3, Tannehill explores the notion of rising with Christ at his coming. Paul indicates that 'dying with Christ is the necessary condition for rising with Christ'.[128] Moreover, it is rising with Christ that gives significance to dying with him. 'Dying with Christ is without meaning unless God is now exercising his power for life in the midst of this dying and unless God manifests this power for life fully through the resurrection of the dead.'[129]

While Tannehill's work is narrowly defined — focusing on the motif of dying and rising with Christ rather than the full theme of union with Christ — his contribution has become significant for the following discussions of the latter. Alongside the well-established significance of 'in Christ' language, the motif of dying and rising with Christ envisions an eschatological participation in the events of Christ that informs the current and future experience of the believer.

2.12 W. D. DAVIES (1970)

Schweitzer's analysis, which drew a sharp dichotomy between Jewish and Hellenistic concepts, came under sharpest critique through the work of W. D. Davies. He pointed out that since Schweitzer's work, our understanding of mystical elements in first-century Judaism has been transformed.[130] The Dead Sea Scrolls in particular confirmed that pre-Christian Judaism did 'exhibit incipient tendencies towards later Gnosticism: they have made it luminously clear that much that has often been labelled Hellenistic may well have been Palestinian and Semitic'.[131]

---

126. Ibid., 80 [italics are original].
127. Ibid., 89.
128. Ibid., 131.
129. Ibid.
130. W. D. Davies, *Paul and Rabbinic Judaism* (3rd ed.; London: SPCK, 1970), ix–x.
131. Ibid., ix–x. He does, however, regard the attempt to trace the influence of mystery religions on Paul's teaching as a failure (ibid., 91).

In a second and related point of critique, Davies regarded Schweitzer's purely eschatological analysis of Paul's thought to be corrupted. Schweitzer drew a sharp distinction between apocalyptic and Pharisaism, which, as a result of studies and discoveries since Schweitzer, must be rejected. Davies acknowledged that such discoveries have demonstrated that 'apocalyptic and Pharisaism—differing as they did in emphases—were not alien to each other but often, if not always, enjoyed a congenial coexistence'.[132]

> What has happened since Schweitzer is that the simple picture of a normative Pharisaic Judaism standing over against apocalyptic and Hellenism has vanished. Its fast colours have become blurred and mixed. Judaism has emerged as more varied, changing, and complicated than Schweitzer could have appreciated. In particular, the Dead Sea Scrolls have triumphantly confirmed the suspicions of those who had already suspected Schweitzer's neat dichotomies.[133]

Davies observed that Schweitzer's eschatological emphasis, which led him to locate the believer's quasi-physical solidarity with Christ as the centre of Paul's thought, was supported by appeal to apocalyptic sources.[134] The apocalyptic Judaism that Schweitzer appealed to, however, was an 'emasculated' Judaism, 'not the varied Judaism of Pharisaism, Qumran, and other currents'.[135] Instead, Davies suggested that the way for Pauline studies to move beyond Schweitzer was to evaluate Paul not only in light of apocalyptic, but 'in the whole complex of Judaism'.[136]

Davies argued that mysticism was not alien to Judaism and indeed could be found within Pharisaism.[137] Nevertheless, when Paul claimed that being 'in Christ' was fundamental to being the people of God rather than being 'in Israel', he contradicted his rabbinic contemporaries at the core of their message.[138]

While Davies affirmed the conclusions of recent scholarship that regarded 'in Christ' to be a social concept, he also affirmed its personal

---

132. Ibid., xi.
133. Ibid., xii.
134. Ibid.
135. Ibid., xiv–xv.
136. Ibid., xv.
137. Ibid., 15.
138. Ibid., 85.

particularity; 'there can be no question that to be "in Christ" signified for Paul the most intensely personal relation to Christ.'[139]

The real difficulty with the concept that has been problematic for all the scholars engaged with Christ mysticism is to understand the exact nature of this personal union. Davies affirmed previous conclusions by saying that being in Christ 'involves an identity of experience with Christ. The union of the individual with Christ is such that the experiences of Christ are re-enacted in the experience of the individual Christian.'[140] The effect of union with Christ is that the past events of Christ's life are shared, which is why 'Paul could speak of Christ being formed in a person and carrying on his life in that person'.[141]

2.13 E. P. SANDERS (1977)

Sanders left an indelible mark on modern New Testament studies with his comparison of the patterns of religion of Paul and Palestinian Judaism. As part of this comparison, Sanders revitalized the concept of participation with Christ, describing Paul's pattern of religion as 'participationist eschatology'.[142]

Sanders was strongly indebted to Schweitzer but differed at various important points. For instance, Sanders adopted the term 'participation' to replace Schweitzer's 'mysticism', making 'participation' the current favourite term in modern New Testament studies for union with Christ.[143] Furthermore, Sanders identified a problematic element in Schweitzer's theory as a whole, namely, that 'Schweitzer did not see the *internal connection* between the righteousness by faith terminology and the terminology about life in the Spirit, being in Christ and the like'.[144] Schweitzer had driven too much of a wedge between juristic and participationist categories for Sanders' liking, who claimed that 'righteousness by faith and participation in Christ ultimately amount to the same thing'.[145]

---

139. Ibid., 86–87.

140. Ibid., 88.

141. Ibid.

142. E. P. Sanders, *Paul and Palestinian Judaism: A Comparison of Patterns of Religion* (Minneapolis: Fortress, 1977), 549.

143. Ibid., 440.

144. Ibid.

145. Ibid., 506.

Salvation and participation categories coincide completely in Paul, according to Sanders, who regarded the primary significance of Christ's death as facilitating a change of lordship; 'by *sharing* in Christ's death, one dies to the *power* of sin or to the old aeon, with the result that one *belongs to God*.... The transfer takes place by *participation* in Christ's death.'[146] Sanders summarizes Paul's conception of salvation as follows:

> God has appointed Christ as Lord and saviour of the world. All who believe in him have the Spirit as the guarantee of future full salvation and are at present considered to participate in Christ's body, to be one Spirit with him. As such, they are to act in accordance with the Spirit, which is also to serve Christ as the Lord to whom they belong.[147]

While seeking to keep righteousness and participation categories together, Sanders nevertheless gives priority to the latter: 'The real bite of his theology lies in the participatory categories, *even though he himself did not distinguish them this way*.'[148] And yet, Sanders acknowledges the difficulty in articulating the reality of participation with Christ: 'But what does this mean? How are we to understand it?... I must confess that I do not have a new category of perception to propose here. This does not mean, however, that Paul did not have one.'[149]

Nevertheless, Sanders regards participatory union as 'real': 'The participatory union is not a figure of speech for something else; it is, as many scholars have insisted, real.'[150] He also argues that to belong to Christ is not different from being 'in' him. This is because the Spirit of Christ claims believers for Christ; in any case, 'we see the close connection between belonging, indwelling and being indwelt'.[151] Putting it all together, then, Sanders describes the essence of Paul's theology in the following manner:

> The basic insight was that the believer becomes one with Christ Jesus and that this effects a transfer of lordship and the beginning of a transformation which will be completed with the coming of the Lord. The

---

146. Ibid., 467–68 [italics are original].
147. Ibid., 463.
148. Ibid., 502 [italics are original].
149. Ibid., 522–23.
150. Ibid., 455.
151. Ibid., 462.

sequence of thought, and thus the pattern of Paul's religious thought, is this: God has sent Christ to be the saviour of all, both Jew and Gentile ... one participates in salvation by becoming one person with Christ, dying with him to sin and sharing the promise of his resurrection.... It seems reasonable to call this way of thinking 'participationist eschatology'.[152]

2.14 RICHARD B. GAFFIN (1978)

Gaffin argued that union with Christ is primarily 'experiential' in nature. 'It is a union which is constitutive as well as descriptive of the actual existence of the individual believer.'[153] While he regarded 'in Christ' language to refer in several instances to 'solidarity with Christ in the past, definitive, historical experiences' of Christ,[154] nevertheless, the 'existential "in Christ"' is not eclipsed in Paul's writings by either the 'predestinarian "in Christ"', nor the 'redemptive-historical "in Christ"'.[155] For Gaffin, this existential union with Christ is entered into through baptism. 'Baptism signifies and seals a *transition* in the experience of the recipient, a transition from being (existentially) apart from Christ to being (existentially) joined to him.'[156]

In a similar manner to Murray's analysis, Gaffin was primarily concerned with the theological relationships between union with Christ and other Pauline themes. He regarded the existential union with Christ to be basic to Paul's soteriology.[157] Nevertheless, this existential union should not be abstracted out from the other two types of union that Gaffin identified—predestinarian union and past historical union. These are the basis for and give rise to the other. This 'organic bond' is essential, and a failure to appreciate it as such represents 'a subtle danger to which the interpretation of Paul is constantly exposed'.[158]

While Gaffin expounded Paul's stress on the organic bond between Christ's past historical experience and the present existence of the believer,

152. Ibid., 549.
153. Richard B. Gaffin, *The Centrality of the Resurrection: A Study in Paul's Soteriology* (Grand Rapids: Baker, 1978), 50.
154. Ibid.
155. Ibid.
156. Ibid.
157. Ibid., 51.
158. Ibid.

he also recognized that Paul does not obscure 'the definitive and completed character of the former'.[159] And yet, the 'solidaric tie' between the two things—Christ's historical experience and the realization of redemption in the life history of the believer—is so strong that the latter can only be understood and expressed in terms of the former. 'The redemptive-historical perspective is both dominant and determinative.'[160]

Part of Gaffin's concern was to demonstrate how union with Christ relates to the so-called *ordo salutis* of theological soteriology. He argued that the crucifixion, death, burial, and resurrection 'are not distinct or separate occurrences in the experience of the individual believer'.[161] Rather, union with Christ applies each of these elements of sharing in Christ's experience as a coherent totality. 'Each is not a separate stage in an *ordo salutis* but an aspect of the single, indivisible event of being joined to Christ experientially.'[162] By the same token, justification, adoption, sanctification, and glorification are not viewed by Paul as distinct acts, 'but as different facets or aspects of the *one act* of incorporation with the resurrected Christ'.[163]

The outworking of this for justification is that 'the justification of the ungodly is not arbitrary but according to truth';[164] that is, 'imputed righteousness' is not a 'legal fiction', but is a corollary of being united to the resurrected and righteous Christ. Gaffin articulated this by nuancing the traditional formulation: 'Not justification by faith but union with the resurrected Christ by faith (of which union, to be sure, the justifying aspect stands out perhaps most prominently) is the central motif of Paul's applied soteriology.'[165]

2.15 JAMES D. G. DUNN (1998)

After briefly surveying some of the major contributions to the field through the twentieth century, Dunn outlined three broad categories for the use of 'in Christ' and related language. The first category is an objective usage,

---

159. Ibid., 59.
160. Ibid.
161. Ibid., 52.
162. Ibid.
163. Ibid., 130–31.
164. Ibid., 132.
165. Ibid.

which refers to the redemptive act that has occurred 'in Christ'.[166] The second category is a subjective usage, in which Paul speaks of believers as being 'in Christ'.[167] The third category deals with Paul's own activity, or the actions and attitudes that his readers are to adopt.[168]

Dunn affirmed Deissmann and Bousset's belief that 'in Christ' language refers to an experience of the risen Christ, not just a belief about Christ.[169] This, together with the locative sense of 'in', at least in several instances, 'makes it hard to avoid talk of something like a mystical sense of the divine presence of Christ within and without, establishing and sustaining the individual in relation to God'.[170]

Dunn reiterated the conclusions of others by acknowledging the eschatological implications of union with Christ as well as its social and participatory ramifications.[171] By its very nature, 'it is a shared experience which involves creation as well. The "with Christ" cannot be fully enacted except as a "with others" and "with creation."'[172]

While he was contented to adopt the term 'mysticism', Dunn acknowledged its inadequacy to indicate the profundity of the 'sense of participation with others in a great and cosmic movement of God centred on Christ and effected through his Spirit'.[173]

2.16 MICHAEL S. HORTON (2007)

In relation to the works surveyed so far, Horton took a somewhat unique approach to the matter of union with Christ by examining its place within a tightly defined covenantal theology. He pointed out that E. P. Sanders correctly identified the contrast between covenant nomism and participationist eschatology, yet 'failed to see the complementary—indeed, inextricable—relationship between the themes of covenant and participation' because of Sanders' restrictive view of the meaning of the noun

---

166. Dunn, *Paul the Apostle*, 397.
167. Ibid., 398.
168. Ibid.
169. Ibid., 400.
170. Ibid., 401.
171. Ibid., 403–4.
172. Ibid., 404.
173. Ibid.

covenant.[174] Horton did not allow any 'facile oppositions between law and love, the courtroom and the family room, a verdict of righteousness *extra nos* and an organic, living, and growing relationship in which the justified grow up into Christ'.[175]

According to Horton, union with Christ brings together all the disparate elements of salvation: 'past, present, and future, as well as the objective and subjective, historical and existential, corporate and individual, forensic and transformative'.[176] Horton regarded Reformation thought to be consistent with this analysis; the Reformers recognized 'the integral connection of justification and sanctification, the imputation of righteousness, and the impartation of Christ's holy love in the lives of those united to him through faith'.[177] For Calvin, Horton elucidated, mystical union enables believers to share with Christ in the gifts he has received. As for the Reformation doctrine of imputed righteousness, the implication is clear: 'While our righteousness is indeed external to us—an alien righteousness that belongs properly to Christ rather than to us—Christ himself does not remain alien, but joins himself to us and us to him.'[178]

In contrast to Gaffin, the all-embracing nature of union with Christ does not, for Horton, obliterate the concept of an *ordo salutis*. Rather, an *ordo salutis* is descriptive of the incorporation of believers through mystical union. While identity 'in Christ' is realized in the history of redemption (*historia salutis*), individual believers are included in this history of redemption through mystical union—it is this aspect that Horton labels the *ordo salutis*.[179]

Horton reaffirmed the mutuality of justification and union with Christ: one does not displace the other; rather, union 'emphasizes that everything that God gives to believers—not only justification but also sanctification and glorification—subsist properly "in him," not "in us"'.[180] This mutuality of justification and union with Christ is emblematic of the

---

174. Michael S. Horton, *Covenant and Salvation: Union with Christ* (Louisville: Westminster John Knox, 2007), 130.

175. Ibid. [italics are original].

176. Ibid., 131.

177. Ibid., 141.

178. Ibid., 145.

179. Ibid., 151.

180. Ibid.

relationship between union and the 'covenant of grace'. In fact, according to Horton, these 'are not simply related themes, but are different ways of talking about one and the same reality'.[181]

2.17 MICHAEL J. GORMAN (2009)

In his 2001 publication Gorman expounded Paul's spirituality through the concept of *cruciformity*, which is grounded in participation in the death of Christ: '*Paul conceives of identification with and participation in the death of Jesus as the believer's fundamental experience of Christ.*'[182] The notion of cruciformity was then further developed in his 2009 work, which he acknowledged to be the logical continuation of the first book.[183] Drawing on Paul's robust trinitarianism, Gorman argued that 'to be in Christ is to be in God. At the very least, this means that for Paul cruciformity—conformity to the crucified Christ—is really theoformity, or theosis.'[184] He therefore claims that 'Paul's famous phrase "in Christ" is his shorthand for "in God/in Christ/in the Spirit".'[185] Thus, Paul's christocentricity is an implicit trinitarianism.

Gorman defined theosis in such a way that avoids the inference that believers become 'little gods'; rather, 'theosis means that humans become *like* God'.[186] He describes it as the 'transformative participation in the kenotic, cruciform character of God through Spirit-enabled conformity to the incarnate, crucified, and resurrected/glorified Christ'.[187] While not entirely comfortable with the notion of a centre to Paul's theology, Gorman nevertheless regarded theosis to occupy that position.[188]

The concept of theosis is worked through the themes of Christ's kenosis, justification, holiness, and the end of violence. Christ's act of kenosis and crucifixion is viewed as the definitive theophany.[189] Justification

---

181. Ibid., 181.

182. Michael J. Gorman, *Cruciformity: Paul's Narrative Spirituality of the Cross* (Grand Rapids: Eerdmans, 2001), 32 [italics are original].

183. Michael J. Gorman, *Inhabiting the Cruciform God: Kenosis, Justification, and Theosis in Paul's Narrative Soteriology* (Grand Rapids: Eerdmans, 2009), 1.

184. Ibid., 4.

185. Ibid.

186. Ibid., 4–5.

187. Ibid., 7.

188. Ibid., 171.

189. Ibid., 35.

stems from participation in Christ's resurrection, which is effected by co-crucifixion with him.[190] Holiness is regarded as a participation in the very life of God.[191] There is freedom from the practice of violence through confidence in the eschatological judgment of God.[192]

2.18 SYNTHESIS

This chapter has surveyed significant academic contributions concerning union with Christ through the twentieth century to the present day. We must now begin to piece together the various strands of thought that run throughout. Our survey revealed a range of issues, reflecting the prominence they achieved through the last century. We will attempt to delineate these issues here and briefly canvass the main positions that scholars have adopted regarding them. The purpose of this synthesis is to sharpen our ability to interact with the history of scholarship in following chapters by identifying the pivotal issues that will require analysis and shape the subsequent discussion.

2.18.1 CONCEPTUAL ANTECEDENTS

A principal theme of the twentieth-century discussion, particularly through the first half of the century, is the relationship that Pauline mysticism exhibits to other types of mystical formulations. Scholars were interested in detecting parallels between Paul and, in particular, Hellenistic mystery religions. This raised two keys issues. First, to what extent were these supposed parallels actually analogous? Second, was Hellenistic mysticism the correct religious background against which to compare Paul?

The three scholars who most deliberately drew parallels between Pauline mysticism and Hellenistic mysticism were Deissmann, Bousset, and Bultmann. While the term 'mysticism' itself was employed by these, and other, scholars in its broadest sense — as referring to any kind of direct relationship between a human being and the divine — nevertheless, Hellenistic mysticism provided some clues for interpreting Paul's conception.

Deissmann and Bousset present the most rigorous elucidations of Paul

---

190. Ibid., 40.
191. Ibid., 122.
192. Ibid., 158.

in light of Hellenism, and yet both conclude that Paul is unique among mystics. While there are some basic elements of parallel between Paul and Hellenism in the broadest sense of mysticism, most of the analogies are negative in that Pauline mysticism is *not* like Hellenistic mysticism. At almost every point of possible parallel, Paul's presentation is stridently distinct; he does not share the ethos or trajectory of Hellenism, and at several important junctures he takes an opposite path.

Interestingly, Bultmann draws an unreserved connection between Pauline mysticism and Hellenistic mystery religions. This apparently analogous relationship is multifaceted and virtually unqualified in Bultmann's view.

The most significant challenge to any kind of Hellenistic analogous relationship to Pauline mysticism came from Schweitzer. While he was content to employ the term *mysticism* in its broadest sense, he forcefully argued for any such ancient parallels to be found in late Jewish eschatology rather than Hellenistic mystery religions. While, of course, the parallels between Paul and Jewish eschatology require appropriate nuance, nevertheless there are deep and overarching points of connection.

Schweitzer altered the course of discussion for the remainder of the twentieth century and, with the exception of Bultmann, none of the following major contributors seriously engaged the possibility of Hellenistic parallels to Paul, except by way of negative analogy—Hellenism served to assist in the grappling of what Pauline mysticism was by contrasting it to what it was not. In fact, the whole question of conceptual parallels between Pauline mysticism and other ancient sources became a good deal less significant for the discussion in the latter half of the twentieth century. Instead, the theological importance of union with Christ and its relationship to other strands of Pauline theology rose to prominence.

2.18.2 DEFINING PAULINE MYSTICISM

Perhaps the most central question through the whole discussion concerns the matter of what Pauline mysticism, or union with Christ, actually *is*. This is also the most important question that scholarship has grappled with in respect to the topic, and yet is most elusive, generating the most complex range of possibilities. Consequently, it is difficult to summarize the key positions that were established through the twentieth century while doing justice to the nuance and perplexity of the issue.

To begin with, Markus Barth provides a candid snapshot of the range of interpretations that have been proffered:

> This key term of Paul's theology ['in Christ'] is a puzzle that has been treated in any number of monographs and excurses. Mythical (Schlier in his commentary), mystical (Schweitzer), existential, sacramental (Bouttier), local (Deissmann), historical and eschatological (Lohmeyer, Neugebauer, Bouttier), juridicial (Parisius), and ecclesiastical (Grossouw) interpretations compete for recognition or are grouped together in various selections.[193]

Rather than delineate every position represented throughout the twentieth century, we will focus on the most significant and widely held analyses regarding what Pauline mysticism, or union with Christ, actually is. Part of the difficulty of this task lies in the fact that the majority of scholars have recognized that Paul's 'in Christ' language serves more than one purpose and enjoys a wide range of use. Nevertheless, it seems that several contributors were content to identify one central element or motif that most characterised this Pauline theme.

While the 'in Christ' language is capable of multifarious functions, there is apparently, according to many scholars, a key meaning that gives rise to the rest. In aligning various scholars to the main positions, it is important to acknowledge that each of the other positions are in some measure represented in their own analyses; it is simply a matter of which elements are regarded as central and which as contingent. In other words, the main positions that will now be outlined are not mutually exclusive and may be identified at least in part by the majority of contributors.

The first 'definition' of Pauline mysticism or union with Christ is the 'local' conception. This is the description championed by Deissmann. According to this definition, union with Christ encapsulates a spatial-spiritual relationship, whereby Paul is 'in' Christ, and Christ is 'in' Paul. Just as we need air 'inside' us, so we live 'in' air.

The second definition is the 'relational' conception, of which Bousset and Murray are key exponents. For Bousset, Pauline mysticism envisages the intense feeling of personal and spiritual relationship. For Murray,

---

193. M. Barth, *Ephesians 1–3*, 69.

union with Christ refers to intensely spiritual relationship consonant with the nature and work of the Holy Spirit.

The third understanding of union with Christ is the 'eschatological' formulation. This is, of course, Schweitzer's great contribution. According to this view, the primary designation of union with Christ is to connect the believer to the risen Christ, and through him, the anticipation of the new age.

The fourth model of union with Christ is that of trinitarian fellowship. The leading exponent of this model is Karl Barth. According to Barth, being in Christ is determined first and foremost by the fact that God is in Christ. The nature of our fellowship with Christ stems from the mutual indwelling of Father and Son within the Godhead.

The final conception of union with Christ included here is the existential model. With Gaffin as the major exponent of this description, union with Christ is perceived as solidarity with Christ. It is constitutive and descriptive of the actual experience of the believer, since solidarity means that what Christ experienced becomes part of the 'experience' of the believer.

To reiterate, these 'definitions' of union with Christ are not the only ones that have been conceived, but they appear to be the most significant within the twentieth-century discussion. Again, these are not mutually exclusive; there are elements of most of these to be found in most analyses in one form or another. Nevertheless, insofar as a central concept may be deemed definitive, these represent the five primary options.

2.18.3 ROLE WITHIN PAUL'S THEOLOGY

The significance of union with Christ within Paul's theological framework is a matter of note. All contributors regard the theme to be vital to Paul's thought and of great significance. None of the major contributors investigated here argues for the insignificance of union, nor do they assume a low position for it.

There is some room for evaluation, however, as to whether union with Christ is to be regarded as displacing some other feature of Pauline theology at its centre. Certainly from the late twentieth century on there has been, in some quarters, a tendency to view the greater acknowledgment of the importance of union with Christ as somehow displacing justification as Paul's theological centre. To what extent union with Christ is to be regarded as the centre of Paul's theology—if indeed, there is such a centre—is a matter for further exploration.

Schweitzer did indeed regard righteousness as a 'subsidiary crater' within the main crater of being in Christ.[194] For most scholars (including Schweitzer), however, the recognition of union's central significance does not mean that it should be pitted against justification somehow, nor is it intended to marginalise justification. The two things are inextricably linked, and one does not occur without the other in Paul's thought. While union with Christ is regarded by most as occupying the centre of Paul's doctrine of salvation, it serves as the ground for justification; it does not displace it or create an 'alternative' to it.

The key difference between justification and union with Christ in terms of their respective roles within Paul's thought world may be elucidated through the notion of extent. Justification is a relatively discrete concept that has a concrete field of reference. While it is related to other themes, it occupies its own 'space', as it were. Union with Christ, however, is all-pervading. It relates to everything with which Paul is concerned and is the grounding for important themes such as justification and resurrection.

In relation to the *ordo salutis*, Gaffin argues that union with Christ does away with any sense of temporal ordering between the elements of salvation. Teachings such as justification, sanctification, and glorification all occur for the believer as one inclusive act through becoming united to Christ. Horton, by contrast, seeks to retain the validity of an *ordo salutis*, but sees it as conditioned by union with Christ.

2.18.4 SACRAMENTALISM

The only other reasonably significant issue of dispute is that of the connection between union with Christ and sacramentalism—baptism in particular. While most scholars recognize some relationship between baptism—whether spiritually defined or the concrete act—and union with Christ, Wikenhauser in particular raises this relationship to some degree of prominence. He argues that union with Christ is established by the sacramental act of baptism and not by faith, though faith is prerequisite.

---

194. Schweitzer, *Mysticism*, 225.

While there has been some disagreement among scholars regarding the issues surveyed above, the remaining issues reflect points at which there is widespread, if not unanimous, agreement.

2.18.5 PERSONHOOD AND DEIFICATION

For each of the major contributors, Pauline mysticism or union with Christ does not compromise the integrity of an individual's personhood. This is stated time and time again, and Paul's view of this is often contrasted against Hellenistic forms of mysticism, in which personhood is lost, or at least significantly diluted. Rather, a believer's union with Christ allows for profound identification and sharing with Christ, while not blurring either Christ's identity or that of believers.

Related to personhood is the issue of deification. In Hellenism, mystical union with a god meant that the person becomes divine. Not so for Paul's mysticism, and the major scholars presented here agree on the matter (notwithstanding Gorman's use of the term *theosis*). While there is a trinitarian element involved, insofar as the Father is 'in' the Son just as believers are 'in' Christ, so that they share in something of the nature of the fellowship within the persons of the Trinity, nevertheless there is no divinisation of the believer as a result.

Certainly, deification has been evident as a strand of Christian theology at various points within the history of the church — especially in Orthodoxy and Lutheranism — but of the scholars who have made the most significant contributions concerning Pauline mysticism through the twentieth century, the issue is not in doubt. Paul has no place for divinisation, even though the fellowship that believers share with Christ is profoundly trinitarian in character.

2.18.6 BODY OF CHRIST

Another issue about which there is a good level of agreement is that concerning the body of Christ and its relationship to union. It is well established that Pauline mysticism is not individualistic, as in Hellenism, but corporate in nature. As such, the church is formed as each individual is incorporated into Christ; by being 'in him' believers are joined together as his body. This metaphor itself relates to union with Christ, since the head is organically and essentially connected to his body.

In this chapter, we have surveyed significant academic contributions that are concerned with Pauline mysticism or union with Christ from the turn of the twentieth century to the present day. The two towering figures in the discussion are Deissmann and Schweitzer—the first for raising Pauline mysticism to central stage in New Testament scholarship, and the second for changing the course of exploration and putting an indelible stamp on virtually everything to follow. We have seen that among the key issues of investigation are conceptual parallels for Paul's mysticism, what Pauline mysticism actually means, and the place of union with Christ in Paul's theological framework. While there is some level of agreement on these important topics, they remain unsettled in various ways, and the latter two in particular would benefit from further investigation. It is to this task that the remainder of this volume is dedicated.

PART 2

EXEGETICAL
STUDY

CHAPTER 3

Ἐν Χριστῷ

3.1 INTRODUCTION

Several studies have focused on the phrase ἐν Χριστῷ, which is generally regarded to be language of central concern for the theme of union with Christ. This is, then, a natural place with which to begin our analysis of Paul's language. Furthermore, it has been commonplace to treat ἐν Χριστῷ as a technical formula in Paul's usage. While this understanding of the phrase requires scrutiny, it means that it will be prudent to examine the precise phrase in its own right before exploring the several variations of the phrase that Paul is capable of employing.

There are seventy-three occurrences of the precise phrase ἐν Χριστῷ in the Pauline corpus, all of which are cited below. It is immediately possible to observe certain patterns that emerge, and these seventy-three instances of ἐν Χριστῷ are therefore grouped together in subgroups, each of which demonstrates a relatedness of the phrase to particular Pauline themes (some references will naturally suit more than one subgroup, so are repeated as appropriate). The subgroupings that are employed have not been artificially predetermined, nor do they follow any particular agenda. These are simply groupings that broadly describe features that certain texts share in common, and they are arranged in no particular order.[1]

---

1. Such groupings may, however, seem premature at this stage. One reason for this impression is that the methodological 'circle' has not yet had opportunity to develop—we are primarily gathering our data so that reflection on that data might ensue. The subgroups listed below merely represent a preliminary effort to group the material as it is adduced—from the ground up, as it were.

A second concern here will be to attempt to ascertain the manner in which the ἐν in the phrase ἐν Χριστῷ is operating. This will necessarily involve some cautious speculation, since it will not always be clear which of the various possibilities is in view. Context is our only reliable guide, but even so we may encounter genuine ambiguity. Furthermore, there is no compelling reason to assume that all uses of ἐν in the phrase ἐν Χριστῷ are identical. In fact, the results of previous studies suggest that there are grounds for distinguishing between the various uses of ἐν Χριστῷ.[2] To begin, therefore, we contemplate the meaning and function of the preposition ἐν.

3.2 ʾΕν

The semantic analysis of prepositions is a complex enterprise. As Bortone describes, 'prepositions are described as semantically poor, but very dense … a way of saying that their meaning is ill-defined but their nuances are manifold: not only is the basic sense (if any) unclear, but the semantic ground covered can be vast and cannot easily be predicted.'[3]

From a diachronic viewpoint, Bortone's 'localist hypothesis' states that the concrete spatial meanings of prepositions are the earliest ones, and that 'spatial meanings evolve into non-spatial ones but not vice-versa'.[4] Growing out of such spatial meanings, there are 'plenty of other "abstract" meanings that can be brought within the scope of localism'.[5] Indeed, a preposition 'may have different, even incompatible meanings synchronically, or may develop them diachronically'.[6] This raises the question of how we are to clarify the various meanings of a preposition; 'Are they truly separate meanings, or variations on a basic single one?'[7]

Without question, the preposition ἐν is the most significant and, at

---

2. For example, Markus Barth: 'The impossibility of elaborating a final definition of the meaning of "in Christ" may well have a simple cause: namely that Paul used the formula in more than one sense' (*Ephesians 1–3*, 69). See also Friedrich Büchsel, '"In Christus" bei Paulus', *ZNW* 42 (1949): 141–58; Neugebauer, 'Das paulinische "in Christo"'; Bouttier, *En Christ*.

3. Pietro Bortone, *Greek Prepositions: From Antiquity to the Present* (Oxford: Oxford Univ. Press, 2010), 41–42.

4. Ibid., xii.

5. Ibid., 70.

6. Ibid., 42.

7. Ibid.

the same time, the most perplexing of the relevant prepositions,[8] as is acknowledged by BDAG: 'The uses of this prep. are so many and various, and oft. so easily confused, that a strictly systematic treatment is impossible. It must suffice to list the main categories, which will help establish the usage in individual cases.'[9] The main uses of this preposition are listed by BDAG as following:[10]

1. marker of a position defined as being in a location, *in, among*
2. marker of a state or condition, *in*
3. marker of extension toward a goal that is understood to be within an area or condition, *into*
4. marker of close association within a limit, *in*
5. marker introducing means or instrument, *with*
6. marker of agency: *with the help of*
7. marker of circumstance or condition under which something takes place [*in view of*]
8. marker denoting the object to which something happens or in which something shows itself, or by which something is recognized, *to, by, in connection with*
9. marker of cause or reason, *because of, on account of*
10. marker of a period of time, *in, while, when*
11. marker denoting kind and manner [*according to*]
12. marker of specification or substance ... *consisting of*

Each heading within the BDAG entry for ἐν contains several more nuances and subcategories that add to the perplexity of analysing this preposition. Immediately obvious, however, is that this preposition has a wide range of usage and is enormously flexible. Indeed, it is so much a 'maid-of-all-work' that Moulton suggests that this accounts for its ultimate disappearance in the language, being 'too indeterminate'.[11] It has functions that are spatial (1), broadly instrumental (including agency; 5,

---

8. It is also by far the most commonly used preposition in the New Testament; see Daniel B. Wallace, *Greek Grammar beyond the Basics: An Exegetical Syntax of the New Testament* (Grand Rapids: Zondervan, 1996), 357, 372; BDF, 117, § 218.

9. BDAG, 326.

10. Ibid., 326–29.

11. James Hope Moulton, *A Grammar of New Testament Greek*; vol. 1, *Prolegomena* (3rd ed.; Edinburgh: T&T Clark, 1908), 103.

6, 9), temporal (10), personal (4), and others. It appears that BDAG regard the fourth category, 'marker of close association within a limit, *in*', as most closely associated with the Pauline use of ἐν Χριστῷ.[12] It will become clear, however, that the meaning of ἐν in this Pauline idiom cannot be limited to one function.

Robertson suggests that 'the only way to know the resultant meaning of ἐν is to note carefully the context. It is so simple in idea that it appears in every variety of connection.'[13] Harris concurs: 'Sometimes all the exegete can do is to reduce the number of possible meanings of *en* by examining the context.'[14] As a rule of thumb, the most basic use of the preposition, which is spatial, is an appropriate starting point, as Oepke points out: 'The spatial sense is always the starting-point, but we have to ask how far there is an intermingling of other senses, esp. the instrumental.'[15] Oepke regards the use of ἐν with πνεῦμα as local: 'The thought of the Spirit in man is local.... The converse that man is in the Spirit ... is also based on a spatial sense'.[16] With reference to its use with Christ, however, the matter becomes more complicated. The usage cannot 'be wholly explained in terms of a mystically local conception'.[17] Speaking of Romans 5:12–21, Oepke regards the spatial

---

12. BDAG, 327–28: 'c. esp. in Paul. or Joh. usage, to designate a close personal relation in which the referent of the ἐν-term is viewed as the controlling influence: *under the control of, under the influence of, in close association with* (cp. ἐν τῷ Δαυιδ εἰμί 2 Km 19:44): of Christ εἶναι, μένειν ἐν τῷ πατρί (ἐν τῷ θεῷ) J 10:38; 14:10f ... and of Christians 1J 3:24; 4:13, 15f; *be* or *abide in Christ* J 14:20; 15:4f; μένειν ἐν τῷ υἱῷ καὶ ἐν τῷ πατρί 1J 2:24. ἔργα ἐν θεῷ εἰργασμένα *done in communion with God* J 3:21 (but s. 1e above).—In Paul the relation of the individual to Christ is very oft. expressed by such phrases as ἐν Χριστῷ, ἐν κυρίῳ etc., also vice versa ... ἐν ἐμοὶ Χριστός Gal 2:20, but here in the sense of a above.... Paul has the most varied expressions for this new life-principle: life in Christ Ro 6:11, 23; love in Christ 8:39; grace, which is given in Christ 1 Cor 1:4; freedom in Chr. Gal 2:4; blessing in Chr. 3:14; unity in Chr. vs. 28. στήκειν ἐν κυρίῳ *stand firm in the Lord* Phil 4:1; εὑρεθῆναι ἐν Χ. *be found in Christ* 3:9; εἶναι ἐν Χ. 1 Cor 1:30; οἱ ἐν Χ. Ro 8:1.—1 Pt 5:14; κοιμᾶσθαι ἐν Χ., ἀποθνῄσκειν ἐν κυρίῳ 1 Cor 15:18.—Rv 14:13; ζῳοποιεῖσθαι 1 Cor 15:22.'

13. A. T. Robertson, *A Grammar of the Greek New Testament in the Light of Historical Research* (4th ed.; Nashville: Broadman, 1934), 589.

14. Murray J. Harris, 'Appendix: Prepositions and Theology in the Greek New Testament', in *New International Dictionary of New Testament Theology* (ed. Colin Brown; Carlisle: Paternoster, 1976), 3:1191. Indeed, 'any sensible exegete will hesitate to dogmatize'; H. A. A. Kennedy, 'Two Exegetical Notes on St. Paul', *ExpTim* 28 (1916–17): 322.

15. Albrecht Oepke, 'ἐν', *Theological Dictionary of the New Testament* (ed. Gerhard Kittel; trans. Geoffrey W. Bromiley; Grand Rapids: Eerdmans, 1964), 2:538.

16. Ibid., 2:540.

17. Ibid., 2:541–42.

concept as 'the clue to the true significance of the formula ἐν Χριστῷ Ἰησοῦ and its parallels'. And yet, 'here, too, there is both a local and an instrumental element'.[18]

Porter acknowledges that some have interpreted ἐν Χριστῷ as 'a physical locative metaphor for some sort of corporate mystical union between the believer and Christ'.[19] He offers an alternative option, however, in which the phrase is regarded as 'a spherical use, according to which it is said that one is in the sphere of Christ's control'.[20] Lending some support to this is Moule's verdict, that to 'interpret it in a quasi-material way, as though Christ were the "atmosphere" or "locality" in which believers are placed, seems to do less than justice to its deeply *personal* significance'.[21] A spherical reading would not equate Christ to 'atmosphere' or 'locality', but rather the sphere over which Christ reigns, which is a more personal notion, even while it is somewhat spatial. According to Harris, the basic figurative sense of 'en corresponds to its original local signification. It is used to denote the sphere within which some action occurs or the element or reality in which something is contained or consists.'[22]

Turner argues that ἐν Χριστῷ 'is neither the instrumental *en* ... nor is it simply the local meaning of "in"'. In fact, it 'is not to be taken in a local sense, which is crude and meaningless, but neither is it a metaphor'.[23] Rejecting such notions that have been commonly suggested by others, Turner regards this language as referring to '"Christification," a sharing of the *physis* or nature of Christ—an adumbration of what in later theology was known as the *theosis* or deification of human nature'.[24] He warns against treating *en* as having a merely instrumental meaning ('by' or 'with'), 'for the predominant meaning is still "in," "within," "in the sphere of," at this period'.[25] It is not clear if Turner's approach easily accords with

---

18. Ibid., 2:542.
19. Stanley E. Porter, *Idioms of the Greek New Testament* (2nd ed.; Biblical Languages: Greek 2; Sheffield: Sheffield Academic, 1994), 159.
20. Ibid.
21. C. F. D. Moule, *An Idiom Book of New Testament Greek* (2nd ed.; Cambridge: Cambridge Univ. Press, 1959), 80.
22. Harris, 'Prepositions and Theology', 3:1191.
23. Nigel Turner, *Grammatical Insights into the New Testament* (Edinburgh: T&T Clark, 1965), 119.
24. Ibid.
25. Ibid., 120–21.

Porter and Moule. There may be some common ground, however, in that when a verb is followed by ἐν, 'a new situation is in mind, and ... it is the mystical conception of Christification once again'.[26] If this 'new situation' may be correlated with the 'sphere' of Christ's rule, then Turner's conception is not necessarily incompatible with Porter and Moule's.

Harris argues that in the Pauline formula of ἐν Χριστῷ, 'the *en* has no uniform function',[27] but rather seems to express the following range of ideas or relationships: incorporative union, sphere of reference, agency or instrumentality, cause, mode, location, and authoritative basis.[28] This moves us away from regarding ἐν as purely spherical within the formulaic uses. While 'sphere of reference' appears to be a commonly acknowledged notion, Harris does not regard it as the sole nuance to be appreciated. He does not rule out incorporation, agency, and so forth. Again, context remains determinative.

To add to these variables, an observation of Dutton concerning the use of ἐν within Ancient Greek may have some bearing on the discussion of ἐν Χριστῷ. Dutton recognises a use that appears to resemble the Latin word *penes*, conveying the sense 'it is in one's power' or 'depends upon some one or some thing'.[29] Some examples of this usage are as follows: ἐν σοὶ γὰρ ἐσμέν, 'we are in your hand' (Sophocles, *Oed. tyr.* 314); ἐν ὕμμι γὰρ ὡς θεῷ κείμεθα τλάμονες, 'on you, as on a god, we depend in our misery' (Sophocles, *Oed. col.* 247); ἐν σοὶ πᾶσ' ἔγωγε σῴζομαι, 'my welfare is entirely in your hands' (Sophocles, *Aj.* 519); ἐν σοὶ τὸ πλεῖν ἡμας, 'it depends on you whether we sail' (Sophocles, *Phil.* 963); ἐν σοὶ δ' ἐσμεν καὶ μή, 'whether we live or not is in your power' (Euripides, *Alc.* 278); καὶ τἄμ' ἐν ὑμιν ἐστιν ἢ καλῶς ἔχειν, 'I am in your hands, whether I am to succeed' (Euripides, *Iph. taur.* 1057).[30]

It is difficult to ascertain whether or not such phenomena have any bearing on Pauline usage, but at the very least these examples demonstrate that ἐν is capable of expressing the sense of being under the power

---

26. Ibid., 121.

27. Harris, 'Prepositions and Theology', 3:1192.

28. Ibid. 1192. See also Murray J. Harris, *Prepositions and Theology in the Greek New Testament* (Grand Rapids: Zondervan, 2012), 123–25.

29. Emily Helen Dutton, *Studies in Greek Prepositional Phrases: διά, από, ἐκ, εἰς, ἐν* (Chicago: Univ. of Chicago Press, 1916), 201.

30. See ibid, for more examples.

of another. Luraghi adds that, in older Greek, ἐν used with reference to a person (such as ἐν Χριστῷ) 'must be understood as based on a metonymy: "to be in somebody's power/will"'.[31]

It is unfortunate that the preposition ἐν remains so elusive. Due to its enormous range and elastic flexibility, it is difficult to conclude with much certainty what exactly it conveys in the formula ἐν Χριστῷ. Additionally, the fact that this phrase is central to the entire theme of union with Christ further compounds the difficulty of arriving at concrete conclusions about the wider concept at large. Indeed, it may not be an overstatement to suggest that the pervading ambiguity of the theme of union with Christ is due in no small measure to the ambiguity of this little word, ἐν.

What, then, may we conclude about this preposition? There is agreement that the word is flexible and that pinning it down to one function, even within the formula ἐν Χριστῷ, invites difficulty. There is agreement that the role of context in understanding the various functions of ἐν is of utmost importance. It is also reasonable to regard the spatial sense of the preposition to be primary, and this should be our first consideration when analysing each instance. Even when moving to figurative uses of ἐν, it is generally agreed that a spatial understanding of figurative senses is to be preferred where possible, and that the notion of 'sphere' appears to be one of the key uses of ἐν within the Pauline idiom. It also seems prudent to accept that the phrase ἐν Χριστῷ denotes a personal relatedness. Even with its more spatial connotations—such as the sphere of Christ's rule—these should be regarded as pertaining to the person of Christ rather than viewing him as an abstract quantity of some sort. At this juncture, it is appropriate to examine the evidence in detail, and so we turn to analyse each occurrence of the formula ἐν Χριστῷ and group them according to various subthemes.

3.3 THINGS ACHIEVED FOR/GIVEN TO PEOPLE IN CHRIST

Several instances of ἐν Χριστῷ in the letters bearing Paul's name occur with reference to things that have been achieved for believers. They are the

---

31. Silvia Luraghi, *On the Meaning of Prepositions and Cases: The Expression of Semantic Roles in Ancient Greek* (Amsterdam: John Benjamins, 2003), 87. Luraghi notes (93) that the instrumental meaning of ἐν owes to a later evolution, and 'one can speak of real Instrument expressions only starting with the New Testament'.

beneficiaries of work that has been accomplished on their behalf, or recipients of gifts given to them *in Christ*. Of the seventy-three occurrences of ἐν Χριστῷ, twenty are accommodated by this subgroup.

Rom 3:24 δικαιούμενοι δωρεὰν τῇ αὐτοῦ χάριτι διὰ τῆς ἀπολυτρώσεως τῆς ἐν **Χριστῷ** Ἰησοῦ

*They are justified freely by His grace through the redemption that is **in Christ Jesus**.*

There is a connection here of ἐν Χριστῷ to justification, but the more immediate connection is to redemption. The redemption that is in Christ Jesus refers to the redeeming activity of Christ, which has accomplished the emancipation of those who were in bondage to sin. For example, *locative* (the redemption that is found in the sphere of Christ), *instrumental* (the redemption that is achieved [by God] through Christ), *agency* (the redemption achieved by Christ), *causal* (the redemption that exists because of Christ) are all plausible options in the context.

The wording διὰ τῆς ἀπολυτρώσεως τῆς ἐν Χριστῷ Ἰησοῦ resembles an appositional construction, in which *in Christ Jesus* qualifies *redemption*. Thus, the sense of the sentence is as following: *they are justified by grace through redemption, and that redemption is of Christ*. While more than one of the categories put forth by BDAG for the use of ἐν might apply here, the most likely is that of association, since the expression is appositional. It is not *any* kind of redemption that justifies believers—it is the redemption associated with Christ. This conclusion accords well with Cranfield's suggestion that the thought here 'is of the accomplishment of the redeeming action in the past, not of the availability of redemption in the present through union with Christ'.[32]

Rom 6:23 τὰ γὰρ ὀψώνια τῆς ἁμαρτίας θάνατος, τὸ δὲ χάρισμα τοῦ θεοῦ ζωὴ αἰώνιος ἐν **Χριστῷ** Ἰησοῦ τῷ κυρίῳ ἡμῶν

*For the wages of sin is death, but the gift of God is eternal life **in Christ Jesus** our Lord.*

---

32. C. E. B. Cranfield, *The Epistle to the Romans* (ICC; London: T&T Clark, 1975), 1:208. Dunn concludes similarly regarding the accomplishment of redemption in the past, though finds it 'difficult to exclude the thought of a redemption which is "in Christ" for those who are "in Christ Jesus"'; James D. G. Dunn, *Romans 1–8* (WBC; Dallas: Word, 1988), 170.

Here eternal life is a gift given by God and found in Christ Jesus. It is clear that God is the logical subject—he is the giver of the gift that is eternal life. There are a few different possibilities for understanding this *eternal life in Christ Jesus*: *locative* (eternal life found in the sphere of Christ); *instrumental* (eternal life wrought [by God] through Christ); *agency* (eternal life achieved by Christ); *causal* (eternal life that is given [by God] because of Christ). A further complication arises when we consider what exactly the gift of God is. Is it *eternal life*, which is then qualified somehow by *Christ Jesus our Lord*? Or is the gift *eternal life in Christ Jesus our Lord*, in which *Christ Jesus our Lord* is regarded as part of the gift (the gift of God is eternal-life-in-Christ-Jesus-our-Lord)?

To attempt to answer these questions, we note the parallelism within the verse: *wages* is juxtaposed with *gift*; *sin* is juxtaposed with *God*; *death* is juxtaposed with *eternal life*. While *death* may be juxtaposed with *eternal-life-in-Christ-Jesus-our-Lord*, it seems rather more likely that it is simply juxtaposed with *eternal life*, thus making *in Christ Jesus our Lord* a qualification of sorts regarding this eternal life. Consequently, this probably rules out the locative option, since it does not refer to *eternal life found in the sphere of Christ*. Since God is the actor (it is the gift of God), agency is also ruled out because God is the agent.[33] Cause is possible, in that the gift of God is given because of Christ, but it tends to undermine the agency of God somewhat, making his gift dependent on Christ. Thus it seems most prudent to regard the instrumental understanding as best in this case. God is the agent—the giver of eternal life—and this is achieved through the work of Christ. With this understanding, God's agency is not compromised and the gift remains a straightforward contrast to death. Christ is the one through whom God has worked to give eternal life.

Against this conclusion stands Dunn's reading of this verse, in which participation in the life of Jesus is in view: 'eternal life is simply a sharing in the unending risen life of Christ'.[34] While we cannot disagree with the theological sentiment here, such participation is not likely in view in this

---

33. It is important to distinguish between the terms *agency* and *instrumentality*. Throughout this work, *agency* will denote the originator of an action rather than the instrument through which/whom it occurs. *Instrumentality* will denote the one through whom actions are accomplished. See §6.2.

34. Dunn, *Romans 1–8*, 356.

verse. Participation in the death and life of Christ is featured in the first part of the chapter (6:1 – 11), but that is not in view in the final section (6:15 – 23). This section deals with the fruit of slavery to sin versus the fruit of slavery to God, and concludes that the fruit of slavery to God is sanctification, of which eternal life is the end (6:22). Thus in this section, eternal life is regarded as the fruit of slavery to God, not of participation in the life of Christ (though the two are not mutually exclusive, of course); this makes unlikely that participation is the meaning of ἐν Χριστῷ Ἰησοῦ in 6:23. Rather, Christ is the instrument through which God liberates believers from sin, which enables their slavery to God, the fruit of which is eternal life.

> 1 Cor 1:2 τῇ ἐκκλησίᾳ τοῦ θεοῦ τῇ οὔσῃ ἐν Κορίνθῳ, ἡγιασμένοις ἐν Χριστῷ Ἰησοῦ, κλητοῖς ἁγίοις, σὺν πᾶσιν τοῖς ἐπικαλουμένοις τὸ ὄνομα τοῦ κυρίου ἡμῶν Ἰησοῦ Χριστοῦ ἐν παντὶ τόπῳ, αὐτῶν καὶ ἡμῶν

> *To God's church at Corinth, to those who are sanctified **in Christ** Jesus and called as saints, with all those in every place who call on the name of Jesus Christ our Lord—both their Lord and ours.*

In this instance ἐν Χριστῷ is connected to sanctification. Paul refers to people who have been sanctified *in Christ*—it is a work accomplished for them and in them. The function of ἐν in this case might be *locative* (sanctified in the sphere of Christ), *instrumental* (sanctified through Christ), *agency* (sanctified by Christ), or *causal* (sanctified because of Christ). The locative option seems least likely here, since there does seem to be causation at work—*in Christ Jesus* appears to offer some kind of explanation as to how it is that the Corinthians are sanctified—whether that be agency, instrumental, or causal. This is confirmed by what follows in the verse, which may be taken as epexegetical of the first part of the verse: the Corinthians are described as *sanctified* (ἡγιασμένοις), and they were called to be *saints* (ἁγίοις) with all who call on the name of the Lord Christ. The cognates ἡγιασμένοις and ἁγίοις suggest that the same thing is under discussion in both parts of the verse: they are sanctified, which has taken place by their being called to be saints. And being called to be saints is shared with all who call on the name of the Lord, which suggests that calling on his name is key to their sanctification. As such, their calling to be saints, which occurs in connection with calling on the name of the Lord, suggests that the way in which they are sanctified is in view. Consequently, agency, instrumental, or causal uses of ἐν provide the best fit.

On first glance, agency seems most likely. While Wallace claims that the dative expression of agency is 'an *extremely rare* category in the NT, as well as in ancient Greek in general',[35] he notes four keys to identification, all of which are met by this passage. First, the dative must be personal, which Christ clearly is. Second, the person specified by the dative noun must be portrayed as exercising volition—something that can easily be assumed for this passage. Third, the example should include a perfect passive verb, which is supplied here by ἡγιασμένοις. Fourth, the agent of a passive verb can become the subject of an active verb, which Christ could be for an active form of *sanctify*. Thus, while rare, this verse seems to meet the criteria for a dative of agency.

However, there is one fatal strike against this usage, which involves an implicit reference to God as the ultimate agent. The key here relates to the *calling* language. The believers in Corinth are sanctified in Christ Jesus, and they have been *called* to be saints—the connection of these two ideas has already been shown to be epexegetical in nature. Yet we see in 1:1 that Paul was also called (to be an apostle), and this occurred 'by the will of God'. It follows, therefore, that the calling of believers was also issued by God. The call of God initiates their transformation into saints, even though the mechanism for such is their calling upon the name of the Lord Jesus Christ. Consequently, it appears that God is agent of this work, and Christ is the (personal) instrument; sanctification occurs through and by him to fulfill the call of God.[36]

1 Cor 1:4 εὐχαριστῶ τῷ θεῷ μου πάντοτε περὶ ὑμῶν ἐπὶ τῇ χάριτι τοῦ θεοῦ τῇ δοθείσῃ ὑμῖν **ἐν Χριστῷ** Ἰησοῦ

*I always thank my God for you because of God's grace given to you **in Christ Jesus**.*

---

35. Wallace, *Greek Grammar*, 163 [italics are original].
36. So Fee: 'Thus the phrase ἐν Χριστῷ Ἰησοῦ is probably not locative here, but a kind of instrumental: "By what God has accomplished through Christ they have been sanctified";' Gordon D. Fee, *The First Epistle to the Corinthians* (NICNT; Grand Rapids: Eerdmans, 1987), 32.

This example demonstrates the use of ἐν Χριστῷ with reference to the gift of grace. God's grace has been given *in Christ* to believers. As with the example above, this ἐν is probably best understood as instrumental. This is due, again, to the implicit agency of God. Paul thanks *God* for the Corinthians for (ἐπὶ) the grace of *God* that has been given to them. By thanking God for this and by describing the gift as having its source in God (τῇ χάριτι τοῦ θεοῦ), Paul apparently views this work as originating with the Father. And yet this grace was given to the Corinthians *in Christ Jesus*. Given the agency of God that is inherent in the verse, the instrumental use provides the best fit for this occurrence of the Pauline formula.[37]

2 Cor 3:14 ἀλλὰ ἐπωρώθη τὰ νοήματα αὐτῶν. ἄχρι γὰρ τῆς σήμερον ἡμέρας τὸ αὐτὸ κάλυμμα ἐπὶ τῇ ἀναγνώσει τῆς παλαιᾶς διαθήκης μένει, μὴ ἀνακαλυπτόμενον ὅτι **ἐν Χριστῷ** καταργεῖται

*But their minds were closed. For to this day, at the reading of the old covenant, the same veil remains; it is not lifted, because it is set aside only **in Christ**.*

In this example ἐν Χριστῷ is used to indicate that the veil may only be set aside through Christ. The ability to see truly, unhindered by the veil, is something accomplished *in Christ* for the believers' benefit. The use of ἐν here could be locative (it is set aside in the realm of Christ), instrumental (it is set aside through Christ), or agency (it is set aside by Christ). The locative option seems least likely since it is the action of setting aside that is in view rather than the state of affairs that the setting aside might produce—which would then be manifested within the realm of Christ. The instrumental option is more likely, but it is hindered by the lack of any hint of the ultimate agency of another (i.e., God). Through the whole pericope (3:12–18), there is no explicit or implicit reference to God the Father (unless one regards the multiple references to 'the Lord' in vv. 16–18 as referring to God rather than Christ, though this seems

---

37. While Thiselton affirms the agency of God in this verse, he adopts an eschatological understanding of ἐν Χριστῷ here, stating that to be in Christ is 'to experience the eschatological tension whereby God has already showered his grace upon them'; Anthony C. Thiselton, *The First Epistle to the Corinthians* (NIGTC; Grand Rapids: Eerdmans, 2000), 90. This conclusion, however, appears to be based on a theological assertion that is read into ἐν Χριστῷ rather than identifying its particular function on exegetical grounds.

unlikely). While the instrumental use is not dependent on an explicit reference to the ultimate agent, the lack thereof suggests that a different option might be preferable.[38]

As such, agency may well provide the best understanding in this instance, even though it does not qualify according to Wallace's criteria. Of Wallace's four keys to identification, this passage meets three of the four, but fails to exhibit a perfect passive verb.[39] This, however, might be construed as the weakest of the four criteria. Wallace relies on BDF and Smyth for support on this matter and, while BDF suggests that there is only one occurrence of a dative of agent in the New Testament (a suggestion that Wallace regards as too strict),[40] Smyth only claims that the usage is found with passive verbs *'usually* in the perfect and pluperfect'.[41] Consequently, it does not seem too far-fetched to regard this instance of ἐν Χριστῷ as expressing agency: Christ is the ultimate subject of the action and the one who sets aside the Mosaic veil.

> 2 Cor 5:19 ὡς ὅτι θεὸς ἦν **ἐν Χριστῷ** κόσμον καταλλάσσων ἑαυτῷ, μὴ λογιζόμενος αὐτοῖς τὰ παραπτώματα αὐτῶν καὶ θέμενος ἐν ἡμῖν τὸν λόγον τῆς καταλλαγῆς
>
> *That is, **in Christ**, God was reconciling the world to Himself, not counting their trespasses against them, and He has committed the message of reconciliation to us.*

As well as the clear Trinitarian inference here, this example demonstrates the connection of ἐν Χριστῷ to reconciliation. The world is reconciled to God through his work, and this is accomplished *in Christ*. The meaning of ἐν Χριστῷ in this example is more than a little perplexing. The first question to resolve is whether or not ἦν ... καταλλάσσων is to be regarded as a periphrastic construction. If it is *not* periphrastic,

---

38. Contra Bultmann, who seems to adopt an instrumental reading: 'bis heute is die Decke liegengeblieben, nicht abgenommen, weil sie (nur) in (und durch) Christus beseitigt wird'; Rudolf Bultmann, *Der zweite Brief an die Korinther* (Göttingen: Vandenhoeck & Ruprecht, 1976), 90.

39. Wallace, *Greek Grammar*, 164.

40. BDF, 102, §191; Wallace, *Greek Grammar*, 164.

41. Herbert Weir Smyth, *Greek Grammar* (rev. by Gordon M. Messing; Cambridge, MA: Harvard Univ. Press, 1920), 343, §1488 [emphasis added].

then θεὸς ἦν becomes immediately qualified by ἐν Χριστῷ, such that it reads *God was in Christ*. If that is the correct reading, this would be a use of ἐν that marks close association; God and Christ relate and operate within a tight solidarity, of the kind found in John 14:10–11.

It is more likely, however, to regard ἦν ... καταλλάσσων as a periphrasis, with ἐν Χριστῷ κόσμον nested within it in order to modify the participle.[42] Porter enunciates the criteria for Greek verbal periphrases in strict fashion:

> The Participle not only must be grammatically in suitable agreement with the auxiliary but must be adjacent to it, either before or after.... Except for connectives, εἰμί and the Participle may be separated only by adjuncts or complements of the Participle as predicate, otherwise the Participle is considered not to form a periphrastic construction. Insertion of elements modifying or specifying the auxiliary (e.g. the subject) between the auxiliary and Participle is seen as a formal means of establishing the independence of the auxiliary, whereby a complement or adjunct of the Participle is fully compatible with its verbal use and draws no special attention.[43]

Though Porter sets narrow criteria for verbal periphrasis, he nevertheless regards the verse in question as a legitimate example of it.[44] Accordingly, therefore, the use of ἐν probably does not here mark a relationship of close association or solidarity. The most likely contender, then, is the instrumental use: God was reconciling the world to himself through the person of Christ.[45]

Gal 2:4 διὰ δὲ τοὺς παρεισάκτους ψευδαδέλφους, οἵτινες παρεισῆλθον κατασκοπῆσαι τὴν ἐλευθερίαν ἡμῶν ἣν ἔχομεν **ἐν Χριστῷ** Ἰησοῦ, ἵνα ἡμᾶς καταδουλώσουσιν

*[This issue arose] because of false brothers smuggled in, who came in secretly to spy on the freedom that we have **in Christ** Jesus, in order to enslave us.*

---

42. Stanley E. Porter, *Verbal Aspect in the Greek of the New Testament with Reference to Tense and Mood* (SBG 1; New York: Peter Lang, 1989), 462.

43. Ibid., 453.

44. Ibid., 462.

45. So also Ralph P. Martin, *2 Corinthians* (WBC; Waco: Word, 1986), 153–54. Martin helpfully rebuffs Harris's reading, which does not acknowledge the periphrasis (cf. Harris, 'Prepositions and Theology', 3:1193).

The reference here to 'our freedom that we have in Christ Jesus' refers to the freedom given to believers through Christ's redeeming activity. Nevertheless, it is not necessarily the redeeming activity of Christ that is in view here; rather, Paul reflects on a state of existence (ἔχομεν) that has arisen out of such activity. Freedom belongs to him and all believers, *in Christ Jesus*. Since it is unlikely that the activity of achieving freedom is in view, the instrumental and agency uses of ἐν are best discounted — these most naturally suit the depiction of action, either through an instrument or by an agent.

One possibility would be to regard this example as expressing cause: Paul speaks of the freedom that they have because of Christ Jesus. This understanding does no violence to the text, though there is another possibility that does it more justice. The verse appears to set up a contrast between the freedom in Christ that Paul and his fellow believers enjoy and the slavery that the false-brothers would bring upon them (καταδουλώσουσιν). For Paul, slavery is not just a regrettable state of affairs; it is an entirely different dominion, from which believers have been rescued and set free (Gal 4:24–25; 5:1). Thus, the freedom 'which we have in Christ Jesus' represents the experience of those who have been transferred into a new and superior dominion — that of Christ. Consequently, this use of ἐν Χριστῷ is best understood as locative, referring to the freedom that is found within the personal realm and dominion of Christ.[46]

Gal 3:14 ἵνα εἰς τὰ ἔθνη ἡ εὐλογία τοῦ Ἀβραὰμ γένηται ἐν Χριστῷ Ἰησοῦ, ἵνα τὴν ἐπαγγελίαν τοῦ πνεύματος λάβωμεν διὰ τῆς πίστεως

---

46. Longenecker regards this example as indicating *both* instrumentality and locality, such that freedom 'results from both what Christ effects in our lives (instrumentality) and our being brought into personal union with Christ (locality)'; Richard N. Longenecker, *Galatians* (WBC; Dallas: Word, 1990), 52. This, however, seems unlikely for two reasons. First, there is no linguistic support to undergird the suggestion that ἐν Χριστῷ should bear *two* functions at once. In fact, every discussion of the lexical nature of the preposition ἐν regards context as the determinative factor in establishing its (*one*) function in any given situation. This is not to say, of course, that from a *theological* perspective the instrumentality of Christ may be included alongside a locative sense, together with several other facets of union with Christ. Rather, the point is that from a linguistic and exegetical perspective, we are required to ascertain the particular function of the preposition in its specific context. Second, instrumentality — while possible — is not favoured here because of the lack of explicit reference to an agent, not to mention the point above that the *activity* of achieving freedom is not in view in this instance.

*The purpose was that the blessing of Abraham would come to the Gentiles **by Christ** Jesus, so that we could receive the promised Spirit through faith.*

Here we see that the blessing of Abraham was intended to extend to the Gentiles, and this blessing comes *by Christ*. The two most likely contenders for this use of ἐν Χριστῷ are those of agency and instrumentality.[47] At first glance, it would appear that agency may be appropriate, since there is little hint of an ultimate agent other than Christ. Certainly the pericope 3:10–14 nowhere mentions the work of God as the ultimate source of Christ's activity, which might imply that Christ is the actual agent here. There is, however, implicit agency that stems back to 3:8, where we are told that 'God would justify the Gentiles by faith' and that he 'preached the gospel beforehand to Abraham, saying, "In you shall all the nations be blessed."' This verse clearly informs our reading of 3:14. God promised that the Gentiles would be blessed (ἐνευλογηθήσονται; 3:8), and it is that promise that is fulfilled in 3:14: 'in Christ Jesus the blessing (εὐλογία) of Abraham' has come to the Gentiles. So we see that the work of Christ in bringing this blessing upon the Gentiles is an outworking of the promise of God. It is therefore most likely that this use of ἐν Χριστῷ is instrumental: the blessing of Abraham upon the Gentiles is ultimately the work of God's initiative, which has been wrought through the work of Christ.

Eph 1:3 εὐλογητὸς ὁ θεὸς καὶ πατὴρ τοῦ κυρίου ἡμῶν Ἰησοῦ Χριστοῦ, ὁ εὐλογήσας ἡμᾶς ἐν πάσῃ εὐλογίᾳ πνευματικῇ ἐν τοῖς ἐπουρανίοις **ἐν Χριστῷ**

*Praise the God and Father of our Lord Jesus Christ, who has blessed us **in Christ** with every spiritual blessing in the heavens.*

Once again, ἐν Χριστῷ is here used with reference to the gift of God; in this case the bestowal of every spiritual blessing is in view, and it occurs *in Christ*. There are grounds for regarding this use of ἐν Χριστῷ as loca-

---

47. The English translation provided suggests a third option, in which the Gentiles are described as being in Christ ('Gentiles in Christ Jesus'), but this is not supported by the Greek word order, which literally translated reads 'to the Gentiles the blessing of Abraham would come in Christ Jesus'.

tive: the preceding phrase ἐν τοῖς ἐπουρανίοις is most likely locative and ἐν Χριστῷ could be read in apposition to it. It might then be paraphrased as *every spiritual blessing in the heavens—that is, in the realm of Christ.*[48] Indeed, there is support found elsewhere for this reading: Ephesians 2:6 reads καὶ συνήγειρεν καὶ συνεκάθισεν ἐν τοῖς ἐπουρανίοις ἐν Χριστῷ Ἰησοῦ, *[He] raised us up with him and seated us with him in the heavenly places in Christ Jesus* (ESV). This could be understood as *seated us with him in the heavenly realms—that is, in the realm of Christ*. Additionally, 2 Timothy 4:18 describes the kingdom of Christ using the same adjective: ῥύσεταί με ὁ κύριος ἀπὸ παντὸς ἔργου πονηροῦ καὶ σώσει εἰς τὴν βασιλείαν αὐτοῦ τὴν ἐπουράνιον, *The Lord will rescue me from every evil deed and bring me safely into his heavenly kingdom* (ESV). This verse demonstrates that it is possible to refer to the realm of Christ as 'heavenly', which adds weight to the locative reading of Ephesians 1:3.

Nevertheless, further investigation of the adjective ἐπουρανίοις suggests that it is probably best not to view ἐν Χριστῷ as appositional to ἐν τοῖς ἐπουρανίοις. Ephesians 3:10 and 6:12 speak of the rulers and authorities, powers of darkness, and spiritual forces of evil *in the heavens* (ἐν τοῖς ἐπουρανίοις). These are surely not included within the realm of Christ, which stands in opposition to such forces. While it may be argued that ἐν Χριστῷ is in apposition to ἐν τοῖς ἐπουρανίοις for precisely that reason—to specify the heavenly realm *of Christ*, rather than that of his enemies—it is more likely that ἐν τοῖς ἐπουρανίοις is a technical term that refers to all spiritual reality, in which the realm of Christ stands in opposition to the realm of the powers of darkness. It is thus unlikely that the realm of Christ would be described as the heavens, even if that is qualified as the Christ-heavens.

As for the example of 2 Timothy 4:18, which clearly associates ἐπουράνιος with the realm of Christ, this is expressed quite differently. Christ's kingdom has been explicitly specified (τὴν βασιλείαν αὐτοῦ), which is then modified by the adjective (τὴν ἐπουράνιον). This is not a substantival use of the adjective, which ἐν τοῖς ἐπουρανίοις clearly is—it means *heavenly*, while the latter means *the heavens*. The difference between the two is substantial enough to disregard 2 Timothy 4:18 as

---

48. While ἐπουρανίοις is an adjective, it does not qualify ἐν Χριστῷ, since the two phrases do not agree in number. It is, rather, an adjective functioning as a substantive.

evidence supporting the substantive use of ἐπουρανίος as referring to the realm of Christ.

If, then, ἐν τοῖς ἐπουρανίοις ἐν Χριστῷ is not to be regarded as an appositional use of ἐν Χριστῷ, how should it be understood? The most straightforward rendering would be to regard ἐν Χριστῷ as instrumental.[49] There is clear reference to the agency of God (*Blessed be the God and Father of our Lord Jesus Christ, who has blessed us*), and it is therefore likely that the verse should be read as *Blessed be the God and Father of our Lord Jesus Christ, who has blessed us through Christ with every spiritual blessing in the heavens.*

> Eph 2:6 καὶ συνήγειρεν καὶ συνεκάθισεν ἐν τοῖς ἐπουρανίοις ἐν Χριστῷ Ἰησοῦ
>
> *He also raised us up with Him and seated us with Him in the heavens, in Christ Jesus.* (pers. trans.)

This occurrence relates to God's work in raising believers and seating them with Christ in the heavens. Believers are passive recipients of the work of God *in Christ*. Again, this usage of ἐν Χριστῷ is not straightforward. It is argued above that the identical phrase in 1:3 (ἐν τοῖς ἐπουρανίοις ἐν Χριστῷ) is not appositional; if that is correct, this instance is also unlikely to be so. It is also argued above that the phrase in 1:3 is instrumental, but that diagnosis presents some problems here. If ἐν Χριστῷ is instrumental here, it would mean that God raised believers with Christ and seated them with Christ, all *through* Christ. It seems a little odd to understand this verse as teaching that through Christ God raised us up with Christ. Putting aside for the moment the apparent tautology, it appears somewhat oxymoronic that God *raised* Christ and yet this is performed *through* Christ.

While ἐν Χριστῷ may not be appositional and therefore not locative with respect to the realm of Christ, it may be locative in a concrete manner: believers are seated in the heavens *with Christ*. An objection here is

---

49. O'Brien correctly regards ἐν Χριστῷ as modifying the verb *blessed*, signifying that God's gifts come through Christ; Peter T. O'Brien, *The Letter to the Ephesians* (PNTC; Grand Rapids: Eerdmans, 1999), 97. While he employs the term *agency* to describe this, he clarifies in a footnote that he understands agency as synonymous with instrumentality (97, n. 49).

that this reading would be tautologous since the verse already contains 'raised with Him' and 'seated with Him'. The verse would then read *He also raised us up with Him and seated us with Him in the heavens, with Christ Jesus.* However, this apparent tautology is produced by translation. The fact is that συνήγειρεν καὶ συνεκάθισεν needs not be translated as *raised us up with Him and seated us with Him.* To begin with, 'Him' is not found in the Greek but is only implied by the συν- prefix and the context. These verbs could be translated *co-raised us and co-seated us,* which would then avoid tautology when put beside *with Christ.*[50] The verse would then read *He also co-raised us and co-seated us in the heavens with Christ Jesus.*

One strength of this reading is that it better matches the preceding verse: καὶ ὄντας ἡμᾶς νεκροὺς τοῖς παραπτώμασιν συνεζωοποίησεν τῷ Χριστῷ, *even when we were dead in trespasses (he) made us alive together with Christ* (ESV). We notice here that another συν-prefix is used, though this time translated *made us alive together,* which parallels *co-raised* and *co-seated.* The phrase τῷ Χριστῷ is translated *with Christ* (or the whole phrase συνεζωοποίησεν τῷ Χριστῷ can simply mean *made alive with Christ*). Nevertheless, it seems coincidental that this συν-prefixed word is matched with τῷ Χριστῷ, while the two συν-prefixed words in 2:6 are matched with ἐν Χριστῷ. Certainly it could be argued that the difference between the two phrases indicates that they are not to be understood as synonymous, but that argument would be inconclusive.

The reality of language phenomena is that synonymity frequently occurs in normal usage, without any intended distinction between synonyms. Such may occur for stylistic, idiolectic, or indiscernible concerns. The case for synonymity between τῷ Χριστῷ and ἐν Χριστῷ may be argued by recognizing the inherent parallels between vv. 5 and 6. The συν-prefixed words are obvious parallels, but so is the underlying theme that God has performed these actions for believers in conjunction with Christ. In other words, the two verses continue the same idea — though interrupted by χάριτί ἐστε σεσῳσμένοι, *by grace you are saved.* As such, this parallelism provides decent grounds on which to claim that τῷ Χριστῷ and ἐν Χριστῷ are to be understood as synonymous. In conclusion, then,

---

50. This point appears to have been missed by Lincoln, who regards the συν-prefixed verbs next to the phrase 'in Christ Jesus' as 'characteristic of Ephesians' redundancy of style for the sake of emphasis'; Andrew T. Lincoln, *Ephesians* (WBC; Dallas: Word, 1990), 105.

the use of ἐν Χριστῷ in 2:6 is best understood as concrete and locative: believers are *with Christ*.

Eph 2:7 ἵνα ἐνδείξηται ἐν τοῖς αἰῶσιν τοῖς ἐπερχομένοις τὸ ὑπερβάλλον πλοῦτος τῆς χάριτος αὐτοῦ ἐν χρηστότητι ἐφ᾽ ἡμᾶς ἐν Χριστῷ Ἰησοῦ

*So that in the coming ages He might display the immeasurable riches of His grace through His kindness to us **in Christ Jesus**.*

This occurrence relates to the kindness and grace extended by God *in Christ* to believers. The use of ἐν Χριστῷ does not appear to be locative or instrumental. The former category is ruled out because there is no hint here of locality—be it metaphorical or otherwise. The latter category tends to be found in association with a distinct action (of God), whereas here the formula is used in connection with the noun χρηστότητι. While it might be argued that ἐν Χριστῷ is indeed modifying a verbal idea—namely, ἐνδείξηται—this seems to be too much of a stretch; it most naturally modifies χρηστότητι.

If such is the case, in what sense is this kindness *in Christ*? In context ἐν Χριστῷ could be construed as revelatory somehow of the kindness of God. Certainly, revelation is already in view, as the use of ἐνδείξηται underlines; the verse is about God displaying the immeasurable riches of his grace. As such, this use of ἐν Χριστῷ may be understood by the category that BDAG describes as: 'marker denoting the object to which someth. happens or in which someth. shows itself, or by which someth. is recognized, *to, by, in connection with*'. Ours would relate to the third of these—the recognition of something. This would mean that ἐν Χριστῷ leads to the recognition or revelation of God's kindness. As Best concludes, Christ is 'the place where, or means whereby, God's grace is exhibited'.[51] Indeed, it could also be argued that ἐν χρηστότητι ἐφ᾽ ἡμᾶς conveys the same function, in that God's kindness is revelatory of his immeasurable grace. An expanded paraphrase captures the sense of this: *so that in the coming ages He might display the immeasurable riches of His grace, which is evident in his kindness to us, which is evident in Christ Jesus.*

---

51. Ernest Best, *Ephesians* (ICC; London: T&T Clark, 1998), 225.

Eph 2:10 αὐτοῦ γάρ ἐσμεν ποίημα, κτισθέντες **ἐν Χριστῷ** Ἰησοῦ
ἐπὶ ἔργοις ἀγαθοῖς οἷς προητοίμασεν ὁ θεὸς, ἵνα ἐν αὐτοῖς
περιπατήσωμεν

*For we are His creation, created **in Christ** Jesus for good works,*
which God prepared ahead of time so that we should walk in them.

God's work of creating people is described as ἐν Χριστῷ. This appears
to be a straightforward case of instrumentality. The agency of God is
explicitly stated: *we are His creation* (the context making clear that the
antecedent of *His* is God the Father), and yet we have been created in
Christ Jesus. The simplest way to put these two things together is to recognize that the 'creation' spoken of belongs to God and has its ultimate
source in him, but is brought about by the work of Christ. As Lincoln
states, "'in Christ Jesus" here is shorthand for "through God's activity in
Christ."'[52] The relationship between agent and personal instrument is also
evident in the second half of the verse, in which believers are created in
Christ Jesus *for good works*, and these good works have been prepared by
God. In other words, God has prepared the works that believers will do,
and Christ has prepared believers to do them.

Eph 2:13 νυνὶ δὲ **ἐν Χριστῷ** Ἰησοῦ ὑμεῖς οἵ ποτε ὄντες μακρὰν
ἐγενήθητε ἐγγὺς ἐν τῷ αἵματι τοῦ Χριστοῦ

*But now **in Christ** Jesus, you who were far away have been brought*
near by the blood of the Messiah.

The work of God in bringing near those who were far off is conveyed
in connection to ἐν Χριστῷ. At first glance, an instrumental reading of
ἐν Χριστῷ appears to provide the best fit: God has brought Gentiles near
through the work of Christ. The problem with that reading, however, is
that it creates an apparent tautology within the verse, which would read:
But now by Christ Jesus, you who were far away have been brought near by
the blood of the Messiah. In other words, this reading construes two instrumental phrases, both modifying the same action. As Best asserts, however,
'two instrumental phrases both introduced by ἐν would be clumsy and, if

---

52. Lincoln, *Ephesians*, 114.

instrumental, 'in Christ Jesus' ought to have been more closely linked to ἐγενήθητε ἐγγὺς'.[53]

The context suggests that a locative meaning might be appropriate: *in the realm of Christ*. In this section, Paul sets up a stark contrast between the former condition in which Gentiles found themselves and their new situation in Christ. They were 'in the flesh', 'uncircumcised', 'separated from Christ', 'alienated' from Israel, 'without God' (2:11–12). The dramatic contrast to this former state is introduced by νυνὶ δὲ, *but now*, and Gentiles have been 'brought near', reconciled to Israel and to God, and have been given access to the Father by the Spirit (2:13–18). These descriptions constitute two strikingly different eras of the Gentile experience. Consequently, a locative understanding of ἐν Χριστῷ, in which the realm or sphere of Christ is in view, provides an appropriate contribution to the rhetorical aims of the section. In the new realm of Christ, Gentiles have been brought near by the blood of Christ.

Eph 4:32 γίνεσθε [δὲ] εἰς ἀλλήλους χρηστοί, εὔσπλαγχνοι, χαριζόμενοι ἑαυτοῖς, καθὼς καὶ ὁ θεὸς **ἐν Χριστῷ** ἐχαρίσατο ὑμῖν

*And be kind and compassionate to one another, forgiving one another, just as God also forgave you **in Christ**.*

The forgiveness of God is, in Christ, extended toward believers. An instrumental reading of ἐν Χριστῷ appears to provide a good fit here — God forgave through Christ. But, once again, this may not offer the best solution. The difficulty of an instrumental understanding is that it implies that the forgiveness of God is somehow mechanistic. While it might be the case that the work of Christ deals with sin such that God is able to offer forgiveness, this is not quite the same as saying that God forgives *through* Christ. While this may not be argued from the context, it seems more likely from a theological point of view to regard this phrase as expressing *cause* in some sense. It is because of Christ that God forgives.

This offers a subtle but important distinction compared to instrumentality. While God's redemptive and reconciliatory work is carried out through Christ (instrumental), his forgiveness is based on that work; God forgives on account of Christ. This reading also makes better sense of

---

53. Best, *Ephesians*, 247.

the exhortation to believers that they should forgive each other 'just as' God forgave them. If ἐν Χριστῷ were instrumental, that would imply that believers are also to forgive each other *through* Christ—a perplexing notion.[54] If, however, God's forgiveness is offered *on account of* Christ, this provides an appropriate model for believers to follow: they too are to forgive on account of Christ.

Phil 4:7 καὶ ἡ εἰρήνη τοῦ θεοῦ ἡ ὑπερέχουσα πάντα νοῦν φρουρήσει τὰς καρδίας ὑμῶν καὶ τὰ νοήματα ὑμῶν **ἐν Χριστῷ Ἰησοῦ**

*And the peace of God, which surpasses every thought, will guard your hearts and your minds **in Christ Jesus.***

Here ἐν Χριστῷ is connected to the work of God in guarding believers' hearts. As for the meaning of the phrase in this context, there are three plausible options. First, a locative reading would suggest that the peace of God is something that characterizes life within the realm of Christ. The main weakness of this approach, however, is that the context suggests that the realm of Christ is not in view here. The preceding verse—*Don't worry about anything, but in everything, through prayer and petition with thanksgiving, let your requests be made known to God*—addresses anxiety and indicates that the right response to the vagaries of life is to trust God in prayer. Verse 7 then appears to offer a result of that trust in God—the peace of God will guard your hearts and minds. Since the relationship between these two verses is apparently causal (v. 6 brings about v. 7), it seems unlikely that v. 7 is addressing a universal condition of those who exist within the realm of Christ.

Second, an instrumental reading suggests that God is the agent of this 'guarding of hearts and minds', and Christ is the personal instrument through which God achieves this blessing. But the main difficulty of this approach is that it is not strictly the case that God is the agent of this activity. The explicit statement of the verse is that the *peace of God* is the ultimate agent with respect to the guarding of hearts and minds.

---

54. Best acknowledges the difficulty; 'it may also carry a comparative sense (forgive in the way God forgives ...) though the 'in Christ' would appear to invalidate the comparison'; Best, ibid., 464.

While it may be queried as to whether an impersonal force such as this may legitimately be described as an *agent*, the point is that the agent is *not* simply God himself. Without God as agent and with an impersonal agent that is perhaps better not labelled as such, an instrumental reading of ἐν Χριστῷ appears unlikely.

Third, the use of ἐν Χριστῷ might indicate *cause*. The grounds on which the peace of God may guard hearts and minds is the person and work of Christ. While it is correctly argued that the cause of this guarding is presented in the preceding verse (see above) — it is brought about through prayer and trust in God — ἐν Χριστῷ may provide grounds for that too. That is, prayer to God is made effective through the mediation of Christ; therefore, the extension of the peace of God to those who pray is ultimately grounded in Christ. Indeed, it follows that the whole thrust of 4:6 – 7, which may be summarized as *anxiety – prayer – peace*, has Christ as its raison d'être.[55] Consequently, it is probably best to regard this occurrence of ἐν Χριστῷ as indicating cause or grounds.

> Phil 4:19 ὁ δὲ θεός μου πληρώσει πᾶσαν χρείαν ὑμῶν κατὰ τὸ πλοῦτος αὐτοῦ ἐν δόξῃ **ἐν Χριστῷ** Ἰησοῦ
>
> *And my God will supply all your needs according to His riches in glory **in Christ Jesus.***

Here God's work of provision is associated with ἐν Χριστῷ. Again, it is possible to regard this occurrence as locative, indicating the realm of Christ in which God's provision is manifested according to his riches. In the immediate context Paul is addressing the financial partnership that he enjoys with the Philippian church. He praises them for their generosity (4:15 – 16, 18), then states that their own needs will be met by God. It is possible, then, that Paul is implicitly evoking the reality of God's provision for those who dwell within the realm of Christ. While possible, however, this reading is weakened by an apparent lack of 'realm contrast'; the realm of Christ is not juxtaposed against the realm of the flesh, the world, or

---

55. So Fee: 'It is their relationship to God through Christ, in whom they trust and in whom they rejoice, that is the key to all of these imperatives and this affirming indicative.... Everything that makes for life in the present and the future has to do with their being "in Christ Jesus"'; Gordon D. Fee, *Paul's Letter to the Philippians* (NICNT; Grand Rapids: Eerdmans, 1995), 411.

the devil. While Paul's previous discussion in 4:10–18 addresses certain realities of life within the real world, these are not particularly negative in his portrayal and are not, therefore, set against the realm of Christ in this context. While it is probably not necessary to observe such 'realm contrast' in order to arrive at a locative reading of ἐν Χριστῷ, its absence does weaken its plausibility.

An instrumental reading of ἐν Χριστῷ is also possible, in which the verse depicts the provision of God executed through Christ. The only weakness here—and it is not a particularly great weakness—is the word order. It can be precarious making exegetical decisions based on word order—and there is much that we still do not understand about its importance for conveying meaning—and yet in this case it may give weight to another alternative. While it is not necessary for the instrument to be mentioned in immediate proximity to the agent, as we have observed in several examples above, the placement of ἐν Χριστῷ following κατὰ τὸ πλοῦτος αὐτοῦ ἐν δόξῃ makes the instrumental reading a little awkward.

If anything, the most natural way to read the sentence is to see ἐν Χριστῷ connected to ἐν δόξῃ, or possibly τὸ πλοῦτος αὐτοῦ ἐν δόξῃ, so that it qualifies it somehow. Consequently, the best category for understanding this use of ἐν Χριστῷ is probably that of close association. Under such a reading, the idea would be that God's riches in glory are closely associated with Christ. To speak of the riches of God is to implicate Christ Jesus; they are inextricably entwined, as Bruce summarizes: 'Paul cannot even think of the divine riches now without linking them with Christ Jesus.'[56]

1 Tim 1:14 ὑπερεπλεόνασεν δὲ ἡ χάρις τοῦ κυρίου ἡμῶν μετὰ πίστεως καὶ ἀγάπης τῆς **ἐν Χριστῷ** Ἰησοῦ

*And the grace of our Lord overflowed, along with the faith and love that are **in Christ** Jesus.*

Here we see ἐν Χριστῷ employed in connection with the gift of grace, faith, and love. One possibility for understanding the function here of ἐν Χριστῷ might be the category listed in BDAG as a 'marker denoting the object to which someth. happens or in which someth. shows itself, or by

56. F. F. Bruce, *Philippians* (NIBC; Peabody: Hendrickson, 1989), 155.

which someth. is recognized, *to, by, in connection with*'. In this case the idea would be that faith and love are directed toward Christ ('the object to which someth. happens'). The problem with that understanding is that the context seems to portray things that are given to Paul rather than things that are directed toward Christ. In other words, if ἐν Χριστῷ is the object to which something happens, the faith and love mentioned in this verse become directed toward him rather than being the gift of God to Paul, which is what the context appears to demand.

One clue to note is the existence of τῆς preceding ἐν Χριστῷ Ἰησοῦ. Being a genitive feminine article, this agrees with πίστεως and ἀγάπης, which implies that the phrase τῆς ἐν Χριστῷ Ἰησοῦ is appositional to πίστεως καὶ ἀγάπης. As such, ἐν Χριστῷ is to be regarded as conveying something more about the faith and love rather than indicating the way in which faith and love are delivered or on what basis they exist. Of the categories listed in BDAG, the most appropriate for this use is that indicating state or condition. Thus ἐν Χριστῷ refers to the state or condition of πίστεως and ἀγάπης; faith and love are conditioned by Christ. This conclusion is compatible with Marshall's suggestion that the form of expression 'may well be determined by the need to contrast the Christian way of salvation and genuine Christian existence ... with competing claims to spirituality'.[57] In other words, the faith and love in view is conditioned by Christ in juxtaposition to false versions thereof.

> 2 Tim 1:1 Παῦλος ἀπόστολος Χριστοῦ Ἰησοῦ διὰ θελήματος θεοῦ κατ᾽ ἐπαγγελίαν ζωῆς τῆς **ἐν Χριστῷ** Ἰησοῦ
>
> *Paul, an apostle of Christ Jesus by God's will, for the promise of life **in Christ** Jesus.*

The promise of life, which is in accord with God's will, is given ἐν Χριστῷ. This use appears to be similar to that of the previous example: there is a substantive followed by τῆς ἐν Χριστῷ Ἰησοῦ, again employing the genitive feminine article before ἐν Χριστῷ, which suggests that ἐν Χριστῷ is in apposition to ἐπαγγελίαν ζωῆς. There is also no explicit verbal action specified, which tends to rule out an instrumental use of ἐν Χριστῷ. It is therefore probably best to regard this use as the same as that

---

57. I. Howard Marshall, *The Pastoral Epistles* (ICC; London: T&T Clark, 1999), 396.

above, indicating state or condition. The promise of life is conditioned by Christ Jesus.

2 Tim 1:9 τοῦ σώσαντος ἡμᾶς καὶ καλέσαντος κλήσει ἁγίᾳ, οὐ κατὰ τὰ ἔργα ἡμῶν ἀλλὰ κατὰ ἰδίαν πρόθεσιν καὶ χάριν, τὴν δοθεῖσαν ἡμῖν **ἐν Χριστῷ** Ἰησοῦ πρὸ χρόνων αἰωνίων

*He has saved us and called us with a holy calling, not according to our works, but according to His own purpose and grace, which was given to us **in Christ** Jesus before time began.*

God's purpose and grace are given to believers ἐν Χριστῷ. There are three compelling reasons to regard this use of ἐν Χριστῷ as instrumental.[58] First, it is directly connected to a verbal idea (τὴν δοθεῖσαν ἡμῖν), which appears to be a prerequisite for the instrumental function. Second, the agency of God is clearly present. He is explicitly referred to at the end of the previous verse (*share in suffering for the gospel, relying on the power of God*) and is therefore the subject of *saved us and called us*, and he is the antecedent of the pronoun in the phrase *His own purpose and grace*. Third, the apparent instrumentality of Christ continues into the next verse: *This has now been made evident through the appearing of our Savior Christ Jesus, who has abolished death and has brought life and immortality to light through the gospel.*

2 Tim 2:10 διὰ τοῦτο πάντα ὑπομένω διὰ τοὺς ἐκλεκτούς, ἵνα καὶ αὐτοὶ σωτηρίας τύχωσιν τῆς **ἐν Χριστῷ** Ἰησοῦ μετὰ δόξης αἰωνίου

*This is why I endure all things for the elect: so that they also may obtain salvation, which is **in Christ** Jesus, with eternal glory.*

God's gift of salvation is here associated with the phrase ἐν Χριστῷ. It might be argued that salvation is not just associated with Christ but is also achieved by Christ; therefore this use of ἐν Χριστῷ should be understood as instrumental. One problem for this reading, however, is that ἐν Χριστῷ clearly modifies the noun σωτηρίας rather than any verbal action. As with two instances above (1 Tim 1:14; 2 Tim 1:1), ἐν Χριστῷ follows a genitive

---

58. Or, as Marshall expresses it, 'He is the "channel" through which God effects his purpose' (ibid., 706).

feminine article, which puts it in apposition to a substantive—σωτηρίας in this case. A second problem for this reading is that the agency of God is not explicitly evoked; thus, an instrumental reading is unlikely. But since this use of ἐν Χριστῷ is so similar to the uses in the aforementioned verses, it is probably best to regard it as indicating a state or condition. Salvation is conditioned by Christ, such that ἐν Χριστῷ marks out 'the specifically Christian character of the salvation to be obtained'.[59]

3.3.1 SUMMARY

In each occurrence of ἐν Χριστῷ above, the term is used in connection to acts of God that are performed for, or upon, believers, or in connection to gifts given to, or for the benefit of, believers. While the more specific functions of ἐν Χριστῷ within this subcategory of God's acts and gifts toward believers may only be put tentatively, we have observed some interesting results. Of twenty uses of ἐν Χριστῷ, eight are arguably instrumental (Rom 6:23; 1 Cor 1:2, 4; 2 Cor 5:19; Gal 3:14; Eph 1:3; 2:10; 2 Tim 1:9), three are locative (Gal 2:4; Eph 2:6, 13), three indicate state or condition (1 Tim 1:14; 2 Tim 1:1; 2:10), two indicate association (Rom 3:24; Phil 4:19), two are causal (Eph 4:32; Phil 4:7), one indicates agency (2 Cor 3:14), and one is a marker of recognition (Eph 2:7). While these results demonstrate a variety of uses of ἐν Χριστῷ, there is a clear tendency toward the instrumental function.

Clearly, then, the phrase ἐν Χριστῷ performs a characteristic role in the description of God's acts and gifts of kindness toward his people. In some sense, it would seem, God's acts towards believers are performed through Christ or are in some way conditioned or associated with Christ. It may not be too much to claim at this early stage that such usages of ἐν Χριστῷ primarily have to do with the role of Christ in mediating the work of God toward believers.

3.4 BELIEVERS' ACTIONS IN CHRIST

This next subcategory deals with actions that believers (particularly Paul) perform and are described in connection to ἐν Χριστῷ. The phrase seems

---

59. Donald Guthrie, *The Pastoral Epistles* (TNTC; 2nd ed.; Leicester, UK: Inter-Varsity Press, 1990), 156.

to denote the manner or mode in which these actions are performed. Some of the descriptions of these actions appear to employ ἐν Χριστῷ in order to indicate that such actions are performed under the banner of Christ— they are done in his name. Other descriptions of these actions seem to employ ἐν Χριστῷ in order to indicate the manner in which they are performed: if an action is performed ἐν Χριστῷ, it will be defined by certain characteristics that are consonant with Christ himself. Furthermore, some instances employ ἐν Χριστῷ in order to express cause, revealing the reason or motivation for certain activities. Out of the seventy-three total uses, there are seven uses of ἐν Χριστῷ that may be gathered in this subgroup.

Rom 9:1 ἀλήθειαν λέγω **ἐν Χριστῷ**, οὐ ψεύδομαι, συμμαρτυρούσης μοι τῆς συνειδήσεώς μου ἐν πνεύματι ἁγίῳ

*I speak the truth **in Christ**—I am not lying; my conscience is testifying to me with the Holy Spirit.*

Paul's activity of speaking the truth is described as being in Christ. It appears that an instrumental reading of ἐν Χριστῷ would not be appropriate, since it would be odd to regard Paul as the ultimate agent while Christ accomplished the task as his instrument.

An important element for consideration is the fact that a parallel phrase is used at the end of the verse: ἐν πνεύματι ἁγίῳ. Paul is not lying, and his conscience testifies to him in—or with—the Holy Spirit. Before attempting to ascertain what this phrase means, we would do well to ask whether or not the two phrases— ἐν Χριστῷ and ἐν πνεύματι ἁγίῳ—should be read the same way just because they occur together in the same sentence. While there does not seem to be any compelling reason why they must be read the same way, it may be preferable to do so if one category does justice to the use of both phrases. Indeed, both phrases are used in connection to the utterance of testimony—Paul speaks the truth in Christ; his conscience confirms it in the Holy Spirit—which suggests that they could profitably be understood the same way.

The ἐν Χριστῷ phrase could be understood as locative so that Paul is saying that, as someone who is in the realm of Christ, he speaks the truth. This view, however, suffers two weaknesses. First, the locative understanding does not directly qualify the action that Paul performs, but rather communicates something about Paul's identity (he is in the realm of Christ), which then in turn affects his action. While this may be possible, the phrase is better read as qualifying Paul's action directly. It is saying something about his speaking.

Probably the best understanding of ἐν Χριστῷ is to regard it as a marker of close association. One of the subcategories of the marker of close association, as listed by BDAG, is as follows: 'esp in Paul. or Joh. usage, to designate a close personal relation in which the referent of the ἐν-term is viewed as the controlling influence: *under the control of, under the influence of, in close association with*'.[60] Indeed, BDAG include this verse under that subcategory. Furthermore, BDAG comment: 'The use of ἐν πνεύματι as a formulaic expression is sim.'[61] Not only is our verse listed under this category, but so is the expression ἐν πνεύματι. As such, this category may be applied to both ἐν Χριστῷ and ἐν πνεύματι ἁγίῳ and do justice to both phrases. Consequently, the verse is understood as following: *I speak the truth under the control of Christ—I am not lying; my conscience is testifying to me under the control of the Holy Spirit.* Dunn expresses a view similar to this when he regards Paul as 'one who is conscious of his dependence on the living Christ and on his authorization and approval'.[62]

Rom 15:17 ἔχω οὖν [τὴν] καύχησιν **ἐν Χριστῷ** Ἰησοῦ τὰ πρὸς τὸν θεόν

*Therefore I have reason to boast **in Christ** Jesus regarding what pertains to God.*

Paul's action of boasting is conducted in Christ. The category explored under the previous entry—the marker of close association—may be appropriate here but seems unlikely. In what sense would Paul boast *under the control* or *under the influence* of Christ? That would imply that Christ somehow compels Paul to boast, which is doubtful. It is not doubtful, however, that Paul might be caused to boast *about* Christ. Yet, while Paul would have no difficulty boasting about Christ, that does not appear to be the concern here since Paul's boast concerns τὰ πρὸς τὸν θεόν.

60. BDAG, 327.
61. Ibid., 328.
62. James D. G. Dunn, *Romans 9–16* (WBC; Dallas: Word, 1988), 523.

Arguably the most natural way to read ἐν Χριστῷ here is to view it as modifying the verbal idea ἔχω … καύχησιν. If such is the case, ἐν Χριστῷ conveys an adverbial function, which may be accommodated by the category in BDAG—'marker denoting kind and manner, esp. functioning as an auxiliary in periphrasis for adverbs'.[63] If this category applies here, the sense of ἔχω … καύχησιν ἐν Χριστῷ Ἰησοῦ would be that Paul has a boast characterized by Christ; that is, he boasts *Christ-ly*. The strength of this reading is that ἐν Χριστῷ Ἰησοῦ makes Paul's boasting acceptable; he is not boasting in a self-righteous manner. Rather, his Christ-ly boasting is appropriate precisely because it pertains to Christ.

What exactly this means becomes evident in the following verse: οὐ γὰρ τολμήσω τι λαλεῖν ὧν οὐ κατειργάσατο Χριστὸς δι᾽ ἐμοῦ εἰς ὑπακοὴν ἐθνῶν, λόγῳ καὶ ἔργῳ *For I would not dare say anything except what Christ has accomplished through me to make the Gentiles obedient by word and deed.* Whatever Paul claims for his ministry, according to 15:18, is ultimately grounded in the work of Christ.[64] Thus in this sense 15:18 interprets 15:17: everything Paul says (including his boasting) is *Christ-ly*.

1 Cor 4:17 διὰ τοῦτο ἔπεμψα ὑμῖν Τιμόθεον, ὅς ἐστίν μου τέκνον ἀγαπητὸν καὶ πιστὸν ἐν κυρίῳ, ὃς ὑμᾶς ἀναμνήσει τὰς ὁδούς μου τὰς **ἐν Χριστῷ** [Ἰησοῦ], καθὼς πανταχοῦ ἐν πάσῃ ἐκκλησίᾳ διδάσκω

*This is why I have sent Timothy to you. He is my dearly beloved and faithful son in the Lord. He will remind you about my ways **in Christ** Jesus, just as I teach everywhere in every church.*

As Paul speaks here about his 'ways in Christ Jesus', he is describing the activities (and perhaps attitudes) that define his general conduct. His activities, customs, and basic practices are in Christ. Thus, it may be best to regard this use of ἐν Χριστῷ in the same way as the previous entry—denoting kind or manner, in an adverbial capacity. While the phrase τὰς ὁδούς μου contains no verb, it nevertheless implies verbal activities, so that an adverbial function for ἐν Χριστῷ is not inappropriate.

It is worth noting, however, that τὰς ὁδούς μου probably does not refer

---

63. BDAG, 330.
64. Cranfield, *Romans*, 2:757–58.

only to Paul's conduct, since the following clause states that he teaches these everywhere in every church.[65] In other words, Paul's 'ways in Christ Jesus' probably refers to his life *and* doctrine, and his exhortation in 4:16 to imitate him therefore implies that the Corinthians ought to follow his teaching as well as its embodiment in his own life. In this sense, the use of ἐν Χριστῷ to denote kind or manner pertains to Paul's entire life and teaching.

2 Cor 2:17 οὐ γάρ ἐσμεν ὡς οἱ πολλοὶ καπηλεύοντες τὸν λόγον τοῦ θεοῦ, ἀλλ᾽ ὡς ἐξ εἰλικρινείας, ἀλλ᾽ ὡς ἐκ θεοῦ κατέναντι θεοῦ ἐν Χριστῷ λαλοῦμεν

*For we are not like the many who market God's message for profit. On the contrary, we speak with sincerity **in Christ**, as from God and before God.*

Here Paul describes his speaking as ἐν Χριστῷ. The immediate context suggests that the phrase is used to define the character of his speaking; unlike those who pedal God's message as a trade, Paul speaks with sincerity. If this is the function of ἐν Χριστῷ here, this occurrence provides another example of the adverbial usage, denoting kind or manner.

While this reading is possible, however, it may not provide the strongest account of Paul's intent. For one thing, it would make Paul's statement slightly tautologous: he has already mentioned that he and his fellow workers speak with sincerity; to say that they also speak *Christ-ly* would overlap with this. While this would not represent a complete tautology, it is nevertheless a little awkward. Furthermore, Paul's critique of those who would make a trade of proclaiming the word of God is not directly aimed at the *manner* in which they speak, but the motivation, or cause, of their speaking, which is for profit.

If, therefore, Paul's critique against the peddlers has to do with their motivation or cause of speaking, it follows that the way in which he contrasts his own speaking is along similar lines. In other words, the most likely reading of ἐν Χριστῷ in this context is as a marker of cause. Paul

---

65. Fee correctly dismisses the claims of those who 'would limit Paul's "ways" to his doctrinal instruction only, on the basis of the last clause', pointing out that for Paul '"doctrine" includes ethics, or it is no doctrine at all'; Fee, *1 Corinthians*, 189, n. 37.

speaks on account of Christ rather than for profit. This is Martin's conclusion, who states: 'Paul's message is "from God" (ἐκ θεοῦ) and proclaimed "in God's presence" (κατέναντι θεοῦ) and ἐν Χριστῷ, "in Christ," i.e., as Christ's servant ought to do, pointing on to 4:5.'[66] Martin's reference to 4:5 is instructive, since there Paul states his obligation to proclaim Christ rather than himself *because of Jesus* (διὰ Ἰησοῦν).

2 Cor 12:19 πάλαι δοκεῖτε ὅτι ὑμῖν ἀπολογούμεθα. κατέναντι θεοῦ **ἐν Χριστῷ** λαλοῦμεν· τὰ δὲ πάντα, ἀγαπητοί, ὑπὲρ τῆς ὑμῶν οἰκοδομῆς

You have thought all along that we were defending ourselves to you.
*No, in the sight of God we are speaking **in Christ**, and everything,*
dear friends, is for building you up.

As with the entry above, ἐν Χριστῷ is employed here in relation to Paul's speaking. And, again, as with the entry above, the best reading of ἐν Χριστῷ is cause. Paul argues that he has not been motivated by the desire to defend himself (*You have thought all along that we were defending ourselves to you*), and so it follows that when he describes his speaking as ἐν Χριστῷ, he is providing the correct motive with which he speaks: Christ is the cause and the reason for his speech, not self-defense.

Phil 3:3 ἡμεῖς γάρ ἐσμεν ἡ περιτομή, οἱ πνεύματι θεοῦ λατρεύοντες καὶ καυχώμενοι **ἐν Χριστῷ** Ἰησοῦ καὶ οὐκ ἐν σαρκὶ πεποιθότες

For we are the circumcision, the ones who serve by the Spirit of God,
*boast **in Christ** Jesus, and do not put confidence in the flesh.*

Once again Paul uses the phrase ἐν Χριστῷ in relation to boasting. I argued above that in Romans 15:17 the phrase is a marker of kind or manner and is thus adverbial in function. In that instance, however, the situation is slightly different. The content of Paul's boast is stated as *what pertains to God* (τὰ πρὸς τὸν θεόν), and so the probable function of ἐν Χριστῷ is adverbial — Paul speaks *Christ-ly*. In Philippians 3:3, however, no content or cause for the boasting is provided, unless that cause is

---

66. Martin, *2 Corinthians*, 50.

Christ. Thus, in this context, it is less likely that ἐν Χριστῷ is functioning adverbially, qualifying the nature of Paul's boasting. Rather, ἐν Χριστῷ is most likely the cause of his boasting; he boasts on account of Christ.

In fact, BDAG lists a subcategory within the category of 'marker of cause or reason' as follows: 'w. verbs that express feeling or emotion, to denote that toward which the feeling is directed; so: εὐδοκεῖν (εὐδοκία), εὐφραίνεσθαι, καυχᾶσθαι, χαίρειν et al.'[67] Note that the activity of boasting (καυχᾶσθαι) is explicitly accomodated within this subcategory. This reading also serves as a juxtaposition to the latter part of the verse — *and do not put confidence in the flesh* — in that instead of trusting in the flesh, Paul boasts (and therefore expresses confidence) on account of Christ.[68]

Phlm 20 ναὶ ἀδελφέ, ἐγώ σου ὀναίμην ἐν κυρίῳ· ἀνάπαυσόν μου τὰ σπλάγχνα **ἐν Χριστῷ**

*Yes, brother, may I have joy from you in the Lord; refresh my heart **in Christ**.*

While this is a command rather than a straightforward action, it envisages the activity of refreshing Paul's heart in connection to ἐν Χριστῷ. This use of ἐν Χριστῷ could be construed as depicting cause, in the sense that Paul is saying to Philemon that because of Christ, he should refresh Paul's heart. It might also denote instrumentality, so that Philemon would refresh Paul's heart *through* Christ. More likely than either of these, however, is the use of ἐν Χριστῷ that marks close association. As with Romans 9:1 above, the subcategory within 'marker of close association' that is described as *under the control of, under the influence of, in close association with* may provide the best fit here. Philemon is to refresh Paul's heart under the influence of Christ.

This may overlap somewhat with cause (Christ is the cause of this action), but also implies that Christ is somehow involved in the activity of refreshing: it is performed under his influence and in association with him. Rather than Christ being an instrument of this activity, as though subject to the agency of Philemon, he is influential over (as well as involved in) this task.

---

67. BDAG, 329.
68. So Fee, *Philippians*, 301.

3.4.1 SUMMARY

While it is clear that the phrase ἐν Χριστῷ may be used in descriptions of God's action toward people, it is also evident from the passages above that it may also be used in descriptions of people's action. Of the seven uses of ἐν Χριστῷ within this subcategory, three arguably depict cause (2 Cor 2:17; 12:19; Phil 3:3), two express kind and manner (Rom 15:17; 1 Cor 4:17), and two convey close association (Rom 9:1; Phlm 20). Thus we see that ἐν Χριστῷ is employed in association with the behaviour of believers, providing the grounding for their activity as well as the mode in which it is executed.

3.5 CHARACTERISTICS OF THOSE *IN CHRIST*

Alongside descriptions of God's activity toward believers and believers' activity, as delimited by the two subgroups above, the following instances employ the phrase ἐν Χριστῷ in connection to descriptions of believers themselves. Rather than focusing on their *actions* (as does the previous subcategory), this subcategory focuses on the observable characteristics of believers — the things that express their character and attitudes, such as wisdom, confidence, maturity, and so forth. This subcategory marks a distinction between the characteristics of believers and the status or spiritual state of believers (e.g., *alive in Christ*). While these things are no doubt related, the present subcategory will treat the former while a separate subcategory below will deal with the latter. Of the seventy-three total uses of ἐν Χριστῷ, eleven are accommodated by this subcategory.

Rom 16:10 ἀσπάσασθε Ἀπελλῆν τὸν δόκιμον **ἐν Χριστῷ**. ἀσπάσασθε τοὺς ἐκ τῶν Ἀριστοβούλου.

Greet Apelles, who is approved **in Christ**. *Greet those who belong to the household of Aristobulus.*

In this instance, ἐν Χριστῷ is connected to the description of Apelles, who is described as approved. While his being approved implies an action performed by another (the one/s who approve/s him), it is ultimately a statement concerning Apelles's character: he is worthy of approval. This occurrence of ἐν Χριστῷ might be understood as a marker of close association in that Apelles is worthy of approval as one who is under the influence, or control, of Christ. In this sense, his approval is subject to Christ's influence.

Another approach is to regard ἐν Χριστῷ as a 'marker of circumstance or condition under which someth. takes place'.[69] Under this reading, Apelles would be regarded as worthy of approval under the condition of Christ or — perhaps better — with reference to Christ. He is approved under the conditions that pertain to Christ and with reference to him. To put it another way, Apelles's approval in Christ does not necessarily mean that he would be approved by Caesar; it is with reference to *Christ* that Apelles is approved, or worthy of approval.[70]

1 Cor 4:10 ἡμεῖς μωροὶ διὰ Χριστόν, ὑμεῖς δὲ φρόνιμοι **ἐν Χριστῷ**· ἡμεῖς ἀσθενεῖς, ὑμεῖς δὲ ἰσχυροί· ὑμεῖς ἔνδοξοι, ἡμεῖς δὲ ἄτιμοι

*We are fools for Christ, but you are wise **in Christ**! We are weak, but you are strong! You are distinguished, but we are dishonored!*

Quite clearly mocking his readers, Paul describes them as 'wise in Christ'. The first point of interest is the apparent parallel between διὰ Χριστόν and ἐν Χριστῷ: Paul and his fellow-workers are fools διὰ Χριστόν, and the Corinthians are wise ἐν Χριστῷ. A pertinent question here is whether these should be read as parallel — using different prepositions to mean the same thing — or as deliberately distinct for the very reason that different prepositions are used. On the one hand, the latter approach seems most sensible; why use different prepositions if the same meaning is intended? But on the other hand, the inverted parallelism between Paul and company being *fools* and the Corinthians being *wise* pushes the matter toward the former approach.

But perhaps therein lies the clue. Just as *fools* and *wise* are inverted, perhaps διὰ Χριστόν and ἐν Χριστῷ are also to be understood as inverted.

---

69. BDAG, 329.

70. Some commentators suggest that Paul might mean that Apelles had proved himself in some kind of trial, particularly since δόκιμιον often denotes the proven character resulting from a difficulty. Moo and Cranfield also acknowledge, however, that it just as likely indicates respect. See Douglas J. Moo, *The Epistle to the Romans* (NICNT; Grand Rapids: Eerdmans, 1996), 924; Cranfield, *Romans*, 2:791.

That is to say, that the fools are made so on account of Christ; proclaiming Christ has actually caused them to 'become a spectacle to the world' (4:9), and that, in fact, is an expression of suffering for Christ. Whereas, if the Corinthians are described as wise in Christ and perhaps puffed up in their knowledge about Christ, that is to their shame. They have not been made fools for Christ but have become puffed up in their 'understanding' of Christ.

Having suggested that διὰ Χριστόν and ἐν Χριστῷ are deliberately distinct, we are left to consider exactly what the latter term refers to here. If the above reading is correct, then it follows that ἐν Χριστῷ most probably refers to the substance of their wisdom or the content of their knoweldge. BDAG lists a category of the usage of ἐν that we have not yet employed, which captures this exact sense—'marker of specification or substance'—and provides the example πλούσιος ἐν ἐλέει, *rich in mercy* (Eph 2:4).[71] *Rich in mercy* appears to be a similar type of expression as *wise in Christ*. In both expressions, the ἐν-phrase designates the content of the leading adjective. The Corinthians are wise in Christ, but because they have not also become fools for Christ, their wisdom is not true knowledge of Christ.

1 Cor 15:31 καθ' ἡμέραν ἀποθνῄσκω, νὴ τὴν ὑμετέραν καύχησιν, [ἀδελφοί], ἣν ἔχω **ἐν Χριστῷ** Ἰησοῦ τῷ κυρίῳ ἡμῶν

*I affirm by the pride in you that I have **in Christ** Jesus our Lord: I die every day!*

Paul's pride in the Corinthians is connected to ἐν Χριστῷ. This use is similar to that found in Romans 15:17 (above), which is described as denoting kind and manner. In both instances, ἐν Χριστῷ is found in an ἔχω ... ἐν Χριστῷ Ἰησοῦ expression, which is used in relation to καύχησιν.[72] It is likely, then, that this use is the same as that in Romans 15:17; it denotes kind and manner, so that Paul has pride (or has a boast) in a *Christ-ly* way.

---

71. BDAG, 330.

72. Thiselton (*1 Corinthians*, 1251) seems to suggest that 'in Christ Jesus our Lord' modifies the Corinthians, so that Paul has 'pride in what they are in Christ Jesus our Lord, and thus it is by them and their status in God's grace and shared Christ-union with Paul that he chooses "to affirm"'. This reading, however, seems to miss the fact that the phrase modifies Paul's *boast* in the Corinthians, not the Corinthians themselves.

Phil 1:26 ἵνα τὸ καύχημα ὑμῶν περισσεύῃ **ἐν Χριστῷ** Ἰησοῦ ἐν ἐμοὶ διὰ τῆς ἐμῆς παρουσίας πάλιν πρὸς ὑμᾶς

*So that, because of me, your confidence may grow **in Christ** Jesus when I come to you again.*

Just as καύχησιν has twice been used in relation to ἐν Χριστῷ, so here καύχημα—a cognate of καύχησιν—is employed with the phrase. A preliminary question here is whether ἐν Χριστῷ should be regarded as modifying the verb (περισσεύῃ) or the noun (καύχημα). If it modifies the verb, the sense will be *your confidence may grow-in-Christ*, which would indicate that the *growing* happens in Christ. If ἐν Χριστῷ modifies the noun, the sense will be *your confidence in Christ may grow*, which would indicate that it is specifically their confidence in Christ that may grow. While either is possible, the verse more naturally reads as being about the Philippians' confidence (or boast) in Christ; thus we should take ἐν Χριστῷ as modifying the noun rather than the verb. The most likely reading of ἐν Χριστῷ here is as a marker of specification or substance: Christ is the one in whom their confidence is growing.[73]

Phil 2:1 εἴ τις οὖν παράκλησις **ἐν Χριστῷ**, εἴ τι παραμύθιον ἀγάπης, εἴ τις κοινωνία πνεύματος, εἴ τις σπλάγχνα καὶ οἰκτιρμοί

*If then there is any encouragement **in Christ**, if any consolation of love, if any fellowship with the Spirit, if any affection and mercy.*

This instance of ἐν Χριστῷ appears to be parallel with the two genitive nouns ἀγάπης and πνεύματος. That is, *encouragement* is said to be *in Christ* in the same manner in which *consolation* is *of love* and *fellowship* is *with the Spirit*. Taking this third phrase first, κοινωνία πνεύματος need not indicate that *Spirit* is the object of *fellowship*, as it is translated here (*fellowship with the Spirit*); the phrase could just as easily be rendered as *fellowship of the Spirit*, which would indicate fellowship that is issued from the Spirit, or at least fellowship that is characterised by the Spirit.

---

73. Fee (*Philippians*, 154–55) notes that καύχημα here refers to putting one's trust or confidence in something or someone, and secondarily to 'glorying' in that something or someone. He also notes the awkard syntax, in which 'in Christ' immediately follows 'overflow', but he maintains that Christ is the grounds for such boasting (ibid.,155, n. 21).

One of these latter two senses is preferable to the translation provided above because of the way in which they may be seen to parallel the preceding phrase, *consolation of love*. This second phrase, παραμύθιον ἀγάπης, is likewise best understood as indicating either consolation that is *issued* from love or consolation that is *characterised* by love. Of these two options, the former seems most likely, such that consolation is seen to arise from love; love is the cause or ground for said consolation.

If the second and third phrases—*consolation of love* and *fellowship of the Spirit*—are best understood as expressing qualities that arise from love and from the Spirit respectively, it follows that *encouragement in Christ* might also be read this way.[74] In other words, encouragement issues, or arises, from Christ. Such a reading of ἐν Χριστῷ is accommodated by the BDAG category 'marker of cause or reason': the encouragement that Paul envisions is possible *because of* Christ, or *on account of* Christ.[75]

Phil 2:5 τοῦτο φρονεῖτε ἐν ὑμῖν ὃ καὶ ἐν **Χριστῷ** Ἰησοῦ

*Make your own attitude that **of Christ** Jesus.*

The translation offered here is not particularly helpful for understanding the nuances of the Greek wording. Most literally, this verse may be rendered as *think this among yourselves, which is also in Christ Jesus*. We note two instances of parallelism in the verse: τοῦτο is the antecedent of ὅ; and ἐν ὑμῖν is parallel to ἐν Χριστῷ Ἰησοῦ. It would seem, therefore, that the key to understanding this use of ἐν Χριστῷ lies in its relationship to ἐν ὑμῖν.

The first question is whether the apparent parallelism between ἐν ὑμῖν and ἐν Χριστῷ means that the ἐν should be understood the same way in both phrases. For example, ἐν ὑμῖν might mean *among you*, so that the phrase reads *think this among you*, while ἐν Χριστῷ could mean *from Christ*, so that that phrase reads *which is also from Christ*. Read this way, the verse means that the way of thinking that is to be found among the Philippians *comes from Christ*. While it is possible that the two uses of ἐν

---

74. O'Brien, however, notes the difficulty of basing conclusions on the nature of the interrelationship between these phrases, 'since no certainty exists about the precise nature of that interrelationship'; Peter T. O'Brien, *The Epistle to the Philippians* (NIGTC; Grand Rapids: Eerdmans, 1991), 170–71. He nevertheless suggests that a parallel relationship between the phrases is more likely than other options (ibid., 171, n. 34).

75. BDAG, 329.

are here to be understood with different senses (i.e., *among* versus *from*), the most likely reading takes them the same way. The main reason for seeing this parallelism (beside the two counts of parallelism already noted) is the word καὶ. Following the relative pronoun, this conjunction should be read as *also*. As such, it is difficult to see how the two uses of ἐν could be taken differently here, since *also* implies that the parallelism between ἐν ὑμῖν and ἐν Χριστῷ indicates a parallel *sense* as well as form.

If, then, ἐν has the same function in both phrases, we may understand the meaning of ἐν Χριστῷ from ἐν ὑμῖν, since the latter phrase is more limited in its potential scope. In fact, ἐν ὑμῖν really must mean *among you*, so that Paul is instructing the Philippians to adopt a corporate way of thinking. This rendering of ἐν is best understood as locative—it is a marker of position—and BDAG provides a subcategory within this use of ἐν that may be particularly apt: 'to describe certain processes, inward'.[76] It is probably best to understand ἐν Χριστῷ the same way: Christ thinks this way 'within' himself.[77] While the gloss *among* does not work with reference to Christ since it does not suit singular nouns, this is a problem pertaining to English, not to Greek, where ἐν suits both singular and plural nouns. Accordingly, the Philippians are instructed to think a certain way among themselves—a way in which Christ also thinks.

> Col 1:28 ὃν ἡμεῖς καταγγέλλομεν νουθετοῦντες πάντα
> ἄνθρωπον καὶ διδάσκοντες πάντα ἄνθρωπον ἐν πάσῃ σοφίᾳ, ἵνα
> παραστήσωμεν πάντα ἄνθρωπον τέλειον **ἐν Χριστῷ**
>
> *We proclaim Him, warning and teaching everyone with all wisdom,
> so that we may present everyone mature **in Christ**.*

Perhaps the most obvious way to read this instance of ἐν Χριστῷ is to view ἐν as a marker of close association, 'to designate a close personal relation in which the referent of the ἐν-term is viewed as the controlling influence: *under the control of, under the influence of, in close association with*'.[78] Under this reading, *mature in Christ* simply refers to a state of

---

76. Ibid., 327.

77. So O'Brien: ἐν Χριστῷ Ἰησοῦ is understood as referring to the person of Jesus in whom this attitude of humility is found. No verb needs to be supplied in v. 5b, while the καί ('also') is given its full force, which is to bring out the parallel between ἐν ὑμῖν and ἐν Χριστῷ; O'Brien, *Philippians*, 205.

78. BDAG, 327–28.

maturity that is determined by Christ and is under his influence. This would certainly suit the context, in which maturity is understood as the goal of Paul's warning and teaching.

There is, however, another way to understand this use of ἐν Χριστῷ. Under BDAG's locative category for ἐν, a subcategory is provided in which ἐν is rendered as *before, in the presence of,* and can be understood in a forensic sense: '*in someone's court* or *forum*'.[79] Read this way, ἐν Χριστῷ means *before Christ* or *in the presence of Christ*, so that Paul's desire is to present everyone mature before Christ. While at first glance this understanding of ἐν Χριστῷ may seem less obvious than the option presented above, there is good reason for adopting it here. The key to this reading is found with the phrase ἵνα παραστήσωμεν. The verbal lexeme παρίστημι can be used as a legal term, meaning *to bring before a judge*.[80] Thus the use of this lexeme in connection with the forensic potential of ἐν is suggestive of a legal situation, in which Christ is portrayed as judge.

Further confirmation of this reading is found in Colossians 1:22, which reads: νυνὶ δὲ ἀποκατήλλαξεν ἐν τῷ σώματι τῆς σαρκὸς αὐτοῦ διὰ τοῦ θανάτου παραστῆσαι ὑμᾶς ἁγίους καὶ ἀμώμους καὶ ἀνεγκλήτους κατενώπιον αὐτοῦ: *But now He has reconciled you by His physical body through His death, to present you holy, faultless, and blameless before Him.* We here see the same verbal lexeme (παραστῆσαι), and in this context it is clear that the *presenting* has forensic overtones since people are presented *before Him* (κατενώπιον αὐτοῦ).[81] Insofar as v. 22 uses παρίστημι in connection with κατενώπιον αὐτοῦ, it is possible to conclude that in v. 28 παρίστημι in connection with ἐν Χριστῷ conveys a similar notion.[82] Since

---

79. Ibid., 327.

80. Ibid., 778.

81. Most commentators assume that God is the subject of ἀποκατήλλαξεν and παραστῆσαι (and the antecedent of κατενώπιον αὐτοῦ) in v.22, but this is problematic. Clearly Christ is the subject of ἐν τῷ σώματι τῆς σαρκὸς αὐτοῦ διὰ τοῦ θανάτου. To regard God as subject of the initial verb and the final clause of the verse but Christ as the subject of the two intervening prepositional phrases (without any *explicit* change of subject indicated) is awkward to say the least. It is more likely that Christ is the subject throughout the verse, such that *he* reconciled believers by *his* physical body through *his* death, so that *he* might present them holy and blameless before *himself.*

82. The connection between the two verses is noted by several commentators. See Peter T. O'Brien, *Colossians, Philemon* (WBC; Nashville: Nelson, 1982), 89; N. T. Wright, *Colossians and Philemon* (TNTC; Leicester, UK: Inter-Varsity Press, 1986), 92; Marianne Meye Thompson, *Colossians and Philemon* (THNTC; Grand Rapids: Eerdmans, 2005), 46.

we have already established the possibility of ἐν Χριστῷ here meaning *before Christ*, the apparent parallel with v. 22 provides confirmation. Thus, the most appropriate manner in which to understand ἵνα παραστήσωμεν πάντα ἄνθρωπον τέλειον ἐν Χριστῷ is as follows: *so that we may present everyone mature before Christ*.

2 Tim 1:13 ὑποτύπωσιν ἔχε ὑγιαινόντων λόγων ὧν παρ' ἐμοῦ ἤκουσας ἐν πίστει καὶ ἀγάπῃ τῇ ἐν **Χριστῷ** Ἰησοῦ

*Hold on to the pattern of sound teaching that you have heard from me, in the faith and love that are **in Christ** Jesus.*

While it is a little ambiguous as to whether the faith and love mentioned here are best regarded objectively or subjectively, it seems most likely that a subjective reading is correct: Paul is referring to the faith and love that is to characterise Timothy in his words and deeds. These characteristics are connected to the phrase ἐν Χριστῷ.

This instance of ἐν Χριστῷ offers several possible readings. First, the phrase could provide the object of *faith* and *love*: it is faith in Christ and love for Christ that are in view. A problem here, however, is that ἐν πίστει καὶ ἀγάπῃ appears to be adverbial in function, qualifying *Hold on to the pattern of sound teaching*; Timothy is to hold on to this pattern *in faith and love*. It is therefore a statement about the manner in which Timothy is to fulfill this command rather than about the object of his faith and love. This problem is not unsurmountable, however; the NIV translates ἐν πίστει καὶ ἀγάπῃ as *with faith and love in Christ Jesus*, which retains the adverbial function of the phrase while also ascribing Christ as the object of the faith and love. Then again, it seems awkward to regard ἀγάπῃ τῇ ἐν Χριστῷ Ἰησοῦ as describing love *of* Christ or love *for* Christ.

Second, it is possible to understand ἐν Χριστῷ as conveying close personal association, which is a reading with which we are now quite familiar. This would render Timothy's faith and love as under the influence or in connection with Christ. While this certainly is possible, it may not be the preferred option since it tends to make faith and love somewhat static; in the present context they more naturally appear dynamic.

Third, ἐν Χριστῷ may indicate kind or manner. This would then understand ἐν Χριστῷ as a periphrasis for an adverb and would be read as *Christ-ly faith* and *Christ-ly love*. While this option is possible, it seems unlikely: as indicated above, it is probable that the phrase ἐν πίστει καὶ ἀγάπῃ is itself adverbial (or at least an adverbial periphrasis). As such, there would be a double adverbial situation if ἐν Χριστῷ were also regarded as adverbial. This seems overly awkward.

Fourth, ἐν Χριστῷ may be the *ground* or *reason* of Timothy's faith and love, which would be a use parallel to that observed in Philippians 2:1 above. The strength of this reading is that this allows *faith* and *love* to retain their dynamism: Timothy is to hold on to the pattern of sound teaching in *faith that arises from Christ Jesus* and in *love that arises from Christ Jesus*. It is because of Christ that Timothy has faith and love, and it is with such faith and love that he is to hold to the pattern of teaching.[83] While this is only one of four possibilities, it appears most likely in this particular context.

2 Tim 2:1 σὺ οὖν, τέκνον μου, ἐνδυναμοῦ ἐν τῇ χάριτι τῇ ἐν Χριστῷ Ἰησοῦ

*You, therefore, my son, be strong in the grace that is **in Christ** Jesus.*

There are only two possible options for understanding what ἐν Χριστῷ means in this context. Ἐν Χριστῷ may denote close association: it is the grace that is so obviously associated with Christ that is in view. The weakness of this option, however, is that this particular use of the phrase is not personal. As defined by BDAG, the use of ἐν that serves as a marker of close association normally designates a close *personal* relation with the referent. In other words, this 'close association' use pertains to a *person* ἐν Χριστῷ; here we see *grace* that is ἐν Χριστῷ, which is obviously impersonal.[84]

The second possible option is to understand ἐν Χριστῷ as locative, once again indicating the realm of Christ. By this reading, Timothy is urged to be strong in the grace that exists within the realm of Christ. This option is to be preferred since grace is an abstract notion and therefore pairs well with the abstract concept of the realm of Christ. Grace pertains to, and

---

83. Mounce concludes similarly: 'this faith and love are not inherent qualities but rather supernatural gifts given to those who are "in Christ Jesus"'; William D. Mounce, *Pastoral Epistles* (WBC; Nashville: Nelson, 2000), 489.

84. While grace could be described as *relational*, this does not qualify it as *personal* in a grammatical sense—that is, its referent is not a person.

in no small measure characterises, the realm of Christ. Being within this realm, Timothy is to be characterised by the grace with which the realm of Christ is itself characterised.

2 Tim 3:12 καὶ πάντες δὲ οἱ θέλοντες εὐσεβῶς ζῆν ἐν Χριστῷ Ἰησοῦ διωχθήσονται

*In fact, all those who want to live a godly life **in Christ** Jesus will be persecuted.*

Here we see godly living described in association with ἐν Χριστῷ. There are several different ways in which one can understand how the phrase is functioning here. First, ἐν Χριστῷ may be indicating *cause* or *reason*, such that the verse speaks of living a godly life *because of Christ Jesus*. While this is possible, it does not seem altogether likely since the context proffers no reason to account for the cause of godly living.

Second, ἐν Χριστῷ may indicate agency, such that godly living is described as occuring through the work of Christ. Again, this is possible, and it is probably a better fit for Paul's ethical framework, but it also suffers from having no real role in the context.

Third, ἐν Χριστῷ might here be locative, indicating the realm of Christ. In this way, godly living is viewed as pertaining to the sphere and realm of Christ's rule. This is most likely the best reading, since the wider context contains a series of stark contrasts between false teachers and Paul's own ministry. With such striking contrasts throughout the chapter and the immediate context, a reading that takes ἐν Χριστῷ as referring to the realm of Christ provides a meaningful fit.[85]

Phlm 8 διὸ πολλὴν ἐν Χριστῷ παρρησίαν ἔχων ἐπιτάσσειν σοι τὸ ἀνῆκον

*For this reason, although I have great boldness **in Christ** to command you to do what is right.*

Paul describes his boldness as being ἐν Χριστῷ. This occurrence of the phrase is probably best understood as indicating *ground* or *cause*. Paul's

---

85. So Guthrie, who describes this as 'the mystical sphere in which Christian life is to be lived'; Guthrie, *Pastoral Epistles*, 173.

point is that because of Christ, he has boldness to command Philemon to do the right thing. The reason that this option is likely best is that Paul goes on *not* to command Philemon to do the right thing, but instead *appeals* to him in the following two verses: *I appeal, instead, on the basis of love. I, Paul, as an elderly man and now also as a prisoner of Christ Jesus, appeal to you for my child, whom I fathered while in chains—Onesimus.* Instead of boldly commanding Philemon, Paul appeals to him on the basis of love.

He then goes on to explain this love: as an elderly man he appeals for his *child*, whom he *fathered*—the love is of a parent for a child. The ground of his appeal is his loving spiritual fatherhood of Onesimus. If such is the basis of his appeal in vv. 9 and 10, this is contrasted with the basis of his (unissued) command in v. 8—his boldness that is grounded in Christ. Because of the contrast between v. 8 and vv. 9 and 10, it is best to understand ἐν Χριστῷ as providing ground or cause.[86]

3.5.1 SUMMARY

The above instances of ἐν Χριστῷ demonstrate that the phrase is commonly used in connection with descriptions of the characteristics of believers. Parallel to the subcategory of believers' actions performed ἐν Χριστῷ, this subcategory groups together uses of ἐν Χριστῷ that describe the believers themselves. Of the eleven uses of ἐν Χριστῷ in this subcategory, four are locative (Phil 2:5; Col 1:28; 2 Tim 2:1; 3:12), three depict cause or reason (Phil 2:1; 2 Tim 1:13; Phlm 8), two express specification or substance (1 Cor 4:10; Phil 1:26), one conveys circumstance or condition (Rom 16:10), and one indicates kind or manner (1 Cor 15:31).

3.6 FAITH *IN CHRIST*

This subgroup recognizes those instances of ἐν Χριστῷ that indicate the object of faith and hope—believers have faith *in Christ*. Because of the nature of this subcategory, there is much less scope for the range of

---

86. Interestingly, Wright appears to connect ἐν Χριστῷ to Paul's apostolic authority: 'he indicates that he is not denying the fact that as an apostle he has certain rights'; Wright, *Colossians and Philemon*, 180; so also John Woodhouse, *Colossians and Philemon: So Walk in Him* (Fearn, Scotland: Christian Focus, 2011), 287. It is not clear whether Wright and Woodhouse regard the phrase itself as functioning as a reminder of his apostleship, or that Paul's boldness in issuing a command flows from his apostolicity irrespective of ἐν Χριστῷ.

nuances that we have witnessed in previous subcategories. By definition, each reference here employs the phrase ἐν Χριστῷ as the object of faith or belief. Of the seventy-three total uses of the phrase, six instances of ἐν Χριστῷ belong here.

1 Cor 15:19 εἰ ἐν τῇ ζωῇ ταύτῃ **ἐν Χριστῷ** ἠλπικότες ἐσμὲν μόνον, ἐλεεινότεροι πάντων ἀνθρώπων ἐσμέν

*If we have put our hope **in Christ** for this life only, we should be pitied more than anyone.*

————

Gal 3:26 πάντες γὰρ υἱοὶ θεοῦ ἐστε διὰ τῆς πίστεως **ἐν Χριστῷ** Ἰησοῦ

*For you are all sons of God through faith **in Christ** Jesus.*

————

Eph 1:1 Παῦλος ἀπόστολος Χριστοῦ Ἰησοῦ διὰ θελήματος θεοῦ τοῖς ἁγίοις τοῖς οὖσιν [ἐν Ἐφέσῳ] καὶ πιστοῖς **ἐν Χριστῷ** Ἰησοῦ

*Paul, an apostle of Christ Jesus by God's will: To the saints and believers **in Christ** Jesus at Ephesus* (pers. trans.)

This last example could fit the previous subcategory in that the phrase καὶ πιστοῖς ἐν Χριστῷ Ἰησοῦ might be translated 'and faithful in Christ Jesus' (NIV, HCSB, ESV). If understood this way, the phrase would be descriptive of the believers whom Paul is addressing: they are faithful in Christ. If, however, the phrase is understood as it is translated above — 'believers in Christ Jesus' — it belongs here since ἐν Χριστῷ indicates the object of belief. Indeed, O'Brien, Lincoln, and Best all take πιστοῖς (πιστός) as 'believers' rather than 'faithful ones', since this is in keeping with Paul's substantival use of the word, which is found in contrast to 'unbelievers' in 2 Corinthians 6:15 (cf. 1 Tim 4:10, 12; 5:16; Titus 1:6).[87]

———

87. When used as an adjective rather than substantive, πιστός means 'faithful'. See O'Brien, *Ephesians*, 87; Lincoln, *Ephesians*, 6; Best, *Ephesians*, 101.

Col 1:4 ἀκούσαντες τὴν πίστιν ὑμῶν **ἐν Χριστῷ** Ἰησοῦ καὶ τὴν ἀγάπην ἢν ἔχετε εἰς πάντας τοὺς ἁγίους

*For we have heard of your faith **in Christ** Jesus and of the love you have for all the saints.*

―――――

1 Tim 3:13 οἱ γὰρ καλῶς διακονήσαντες βαθμὸν ἑαυτοῖς καλὸν περιποιοῦνται καὶ πολλὴν παρρησίαν ἐν πίστει τῇ **ἐν Χριστῷ** Ἰησοῦ

*For those who have served well as deacons acquire a good standing for themselves, and great boldness in the faith that is **in Christ** Jesus.*

―――――

2 Tim 3:15 καὶ ὅτι ἀπὸ βρέφους [τὰ] ἱερὰ γράμματα οἶδας, τὰ δυνάμενά σε σοφίσαι εἰς σωτηρίαν διὰ πίστεως τῆς **ἐν Χριστῷ** Ἰησοῦ

*And you know that from childhood you have known the sacred Scriptures, which are able to give you wisdom for salvation through faith **in Christ** Jesus.*

3.6.1 SUMMARY

These occurrences of ἐν Χριστῷ each indicate the object of believers' faith and hope—it is *in Christ* (1 Cor 15:19; Gal 3:26; Eph 1:1; Col 1:4; 1 Tim 3:13; 2 Tim 3:15). It would appear, then, that this usage of the phrase differs in nature to the three subcategories above. The first three subcategories gather together instances in which ἐν Χριστῷ is capable of a wide range of nuances. In this subcategory, however, ἐν Χριστῷ is the object of faith—believers have faith *in Christ*. In the first three subcategories, ἐν Χριστῷ is basically descriptive in function, adding shape and depth to concepts that might have functioned adequately even if the phrase were absent. In this subcategory, the phrase is integral to the concept at hand; it would be difficult to speak of faith in Christ without mentioning Christ!

3.7 JUSTIFICATION *IN CHRIST*

There are only two instances of ἐν Χριστῷ that are directly connected to the Pauline theme of justification.

Rom 3:24 δικαιούμενοι δωρεὰν τῇ αὐτοῦ χάριτι διὰ τῆς ἀπολυτρώσεως τῆς ἐν Χριστῷ Ἰησοῦ

*They are justified freely by His grace through the redemption that is **in Christ** Jesus.*

This first example has already been listed in a subcategory above, but it should also be included here. As argued above, this use of ἐν Χριστῷ is most likely that of association, since the expression is appositional. It is not any kind of redemption that justifies believers—it is the redemption associated with Christ. Here we see that justification occurs through redemption and that redemption is ἐν Χριστῷ.

According to this reading, *in-Christ-redemption* is the instrument of grace to bring about justification. In other words, grace is the agent for justification, and grace effects justification through its instrument, *in-Christ-redemption*. Thus, this example demonstrates a clear connection of ἐν Χριστῷ to the language of justification: justification occurs through *in-Christ-redemption*, which is the instrument of grace.

Gal 2:17 εἰ δὲ ζητοῦντες δικαιωθῆναι ἐν Χριστῷ εὑρέθημεν καὶ αὐτοὶ ἁμαρτωλοί, ἆρα Χριστὸς ἁμαρτίας διάκονος; μὴ γένοιτο

*But if we ourselves are also found to be 'sinners' while seeking to be justified **by Christ**, is Christ then a promoter of sin? Absolutely not!*

This occurrence of ἐν Χριστῷ demonstrates a direct connection to justification. There are two plausible options for understanding the force of ἐν Χριστῷ here. The first is to view ἐν Χριστῷ as indicating sphere or realm. This, then, would create the sense that people seek to be justified within the sphere of Christ. This is certainly a viable option, but it is probably not the most likely. The reason for this is provided by Paul's next two phrases: *if we ourselves are also found to be 'sinners'... is Christ then a promoter of sin?* By raising the question of whether Christ is a promoter of sin, Paul implies Christ has *acted* in the event of justifying sinners. If the apostle had simply been speaking of justification within the realm of Christ, the notion of Christ's activity would have been somewhat muted. In actual fact, the best sense is made of the question of whether Christ promotes sin by regarding him as actively involved in the event of justification. Consequently, the preferred reading of ἐν Χριστῷ here is to ascribe the notion of agency. Christ brings about justification.

3.7.1 SUMMARY

While, therefore, there are only two instances of direct connection between the phrase ἐν Χριστῷ and the language of justification, it is arguably the case that ἐν Χριστῷ conveys the instrumentality of Christ in the first (Rom 3:24) and the agency of Christ in the second (Gal 2:17) with respect to justification. The relationship between the two major themes of union with Christ and justification must be explored further, to be sure, both through the other phrases that give rise to the former theme and through theological reflection and integration into Paul's theological framework. It is noteworthy, nevertheless, that we have found only two instances of this lexical connection.

3.8 NEW STATUS IN CHRIST

This subcategory groups together instances of ἐν Χριστῷ that are in connection with descriptions of new states in which believers are found. These states represent major changes to status for those implicated. They have moved from death to life, from old creation to new, from strangers to family. By the nature of this subcategory, then, most entries here will exemplify uses of ἐν Χριστῷ that express the locative notion of being within the realm or sphere of Christ. Of the seventy-three total occurrences of ἐν Χριστῷ, nine may be included here.

> Rom 6:11 οὕτως καὶ ὑμεῖς λογίζεσθε ἑαυτοὺς [εἶναι] νεκροὺς μὲν τῇ ἁμαρτίᾳ ζῶντας δὲ τῷ θεῷ **ἐν Χριστῷ Ἰησοῦ**
>
> *So, you too consider yourselves dead to sin, but alive to God **in Christ Jesus**.*

Believers have moved from death to life, from being spiritually dead before God to being spiritually alive to him, and this new life is described as being ἐν Χριστῷ. The notion of being within, or under, the realm of Christ is implied through the contrasts between death and life, and sin and God. Furthermore, being dead to sin has already been established within the context as something of a realm transfer; vv. 9 and 10 indicate that death no longer rules over Christ, because he died to sin — Christ died to sin but is alive to God. Verse 11 simply implies that because such is the case for Christ, so it is for Paul's readers — they are dead to sin, but alive to God. As Murray states, 'the complementation of "dead unto sin" and "alive unto God," as parallel to Christ's death to sin and life to God, implies that the life to God is of abiding continuance just as being dead to sin is.'[88] Since this reality is predicated upon Christ's death to sin and his being alive to God — and this demarcates two different realms — so, for believers, being dead to sin and alive to God delineates two realms. The second realm is described as ἐν Χριστῷ.

Rom 8:1 οὐδὲν ἄρα νῦν κατάκριμα τοῖς **ἐν Χριστῷ** Ἰησοῦ

*Therefore, no condemnation now exists for those **in Christ** Jesus.*

The fact that believers now will face no condemnation represents a major shift in status — they have moved from being under God's wrath to being in a state of acquittal. This status exists under the auspice of the realm of Christ, which Dunn calls 'the epoch of Christ in distinction to that of Adam'.[89]

Rom 12:5 οὕτως οἱ πολλοὶ ἓν σῶμά ἐσμεν **ἐν Χριστῷ**, τὸ δὲ καθ᾽ εἷς ἀλλήλων μέλη

*In the same way we who are many are one body **in Christ** and individually members of one another.*

The status of being incorporated into the one body is probably not here related to realm transfer, since there is no contrast of realms in view. Contrasts between death and life, old and new creations, strangers and family give rise to the concept of realm transfer in their respective con-

---

88. John Murray, *The Epistle to the Romans* (NICNT; Grand Rapids: Eerdmans, 1959), 1:226.

89. Dunn, *Romans 1–8*, 415.

texts, but such is not evident here. It may be best, then, to regard this use of ἐν Χριστῷ as a marker of state or condition, so that it depicts the state in which the body is constituted: *in Christ*. The phrase may, Dunn suggests, provide 'a countermodel of social identity no longer reducible to merely ethnic or cultural categories'.[90]

1 Cor 15:18 ἄρα καὶ οἱ κοιμηθέντες ἐν **Χριστῷ** ἀπώλοντο

*Therefore, those who have fallen asleep **in Christ** have also perished.*

While falling asleep ἐν Χριστῷ may refer to a manner or kind of action, modifying the way in which death takes place, a better way to understand this use of ἐν Χριστῷ is to view it as describing the realm or sphere of Christ. The focus is not on *how* these people died, but rather on their current situation: they are asleep in Christ. The idea is that believers have died as people who are under Christ's realm, and being part of the sphere of Christ means that such people may be described as having fallen asleep—death is but temporary, since resurrection awaits all within his realm.[91]

2 Cor 5:17 ὥστε εἴ τις ἐν **Χριστῷ**, καινὴ κτίσις· τὰ ἀρχαῖα παρῆλθεν, ἰδοὺ γέγονεν καινά

*Therefore, if anyone is **in Christ**, he is a new creation; old things have passed away, and look, new things have come.*

Here we witness a direct correlation between being ἐν Χριστῷ and a new creation.[92] Anyone who is to be described as *in Christ* must therefore have attained the status of a new creation. Again, the most likely sense of ἐν Χριστῷ here is the portrayal of the realm of Christ, under which the status of new creation belongs. This is underscored by the realm contrast inherent to the verse (new creation; old things gone; new things come).

---

90. Dunn, *Romans 9–16*, 733.

91. See Thiselton for the 'logical "grammar" of sleep', which contains the expectation of the awakening of resurrection; Thiselton, *1 Corinthians*, 1220–21.

92. Martin reads ἐν Χριστῷ as modifying καινὴ κτίσις, not τις, thus producing the sense of a 'new eschatological situation which has emerged from Christ's advent'; Martin, *2 Corinthians*, 152. This reading, however, goes against the most natural way to take the Greek, in which ἐν Χριστῷ modifies that which it directly follows (cf. Hughes, Barnett, Kruse).

Gal 3:26 πάντες γὰρ υἱοὶ θεοῦ ἐστε διὰ τῆς πίστεως **ἐν Χριστῷ**
Ἰησοῦ

*For you are all sons of God through faith **in Christ** Jesus.*

This example has already been listed under the subcategory above that
deals with *faith in Christ*, and hence ἐν Χριστῷ is properly understood as
the object of faith.[93] This verse is listed again here because it also expresses
the existence of a new of status — that of being *sons of God.* This new status in Christ, however, is not described as a result of being under the realm
of Christ, but is rather seen as occurring through faith in Christ Jesus.

Gal 3:28 οὐκ ἔνι Ἰουδαῖος οὐδὲ Ἕλλην, οὐκ ἔνι δοῦλος οὐδὲ
ἐλεύθερος, οὐκ ἔνι ἄρσεν καὶ θῆλυ· πάντες γὰρ ὑμεῖς εἷς ἐστε **ἐν**
Χριστῷ Ἰησοῦ

There is no Jew or Greek, slave or free, male or female; for you are all
*one **in Christ** Jesus.*

A new status is clearly in view here, since the categories of Jew and
Greek, slave and free, male and female are rendered irrelevant with respect
to unity in Christ. The new status, described as ἐν Χριστῷ, is having been
made *one.* This oneness pertains to all who are included within the sphere
of Christ, which is implicitly contrasted with these other 'spheres' of Jew
and Greek and so on that promote division. Regarding this use of ἐν
Χριστῷ, Longenecker correctly regards the 'in' as local and personal, and
the 'Christ Jesus' as universal and corporate — both parts of the expression
therefore supporting the 'sphere' or 'realm' reading here.[94]

Eph 3:6 εἶναι τὰ ἔθνη συγκληρονόμα καὶ σύσσωμα καὶ συμμέτοχα
τῆς ἐπαγγελίας **ἐν Χριστῷ Ἰησοῦ** διὰ τοῦ εὐαγγελίου

The Gentiles are coheirs, members of the same body, and partners of
*the promise **in Christ** Jesus through the gospel.*

---

93. Bruce thinks that ἐν Χριστῷ Ἰησοῦ is not governed by πίστεως, thus rejecting the reading 'faith in Christ Jesus'. He argues that such a meaning is usually expressed by Paul with
the objective genitive, but this ought not exclude the reading here since similar expressions
found in Col 1:4; 1 Tim 3:13; and 2 Tim 3:15 seem also to express 'faith in Christ'. See F. F.
Bruce, *The Epistle to the Galatians* (NIGTC; Exeter, UK: Paternoster, 1982), 184.

94. Longenecker, *Galatians,* 158.

Here the changed status of Gentiles is in view: they are now coheirs with Israel, they are part of the same body, they share in the same promise. While ἐν Χριστῷ here could modify 'the same promise', it more likely modifies the Gentiles' status of co-inclusion: coheirs, members, and partners.[95] The phrase διὰ τοῦ εὐαγγελίου strengthens this reading as it suggests that the broader picture is in view, not simply the last-mentioned item in the list. Since this status of co-inclusion is the topic modified by ἐν Χριστῷ, it is best to regard this as a local use of the phrase depicting inclusion within the realm of Christ, which is the location of such status. As O'Brien notes, 'Christ Jesus is the *sphere* in which this incorporation of Gentiles occurs'.[96]

1 Thess 4:16 ὅτι αὐτὸς ὁ κύριος ἐν κελεύσματι, ἐν φωνῇ ἀρχαγγέλου καὶ ἐν σάλπιγγι θεοῦ, καταβήσεται ἀπ᾽ οὐρανοῦ καὶ οἱ νεκροὶ **ἐν Χριστῷ** ἀναστήσονται πρῶτον

*For the Lord Himself will descend from heaven with a shout, with the archangel's voice, and with the trumpet of God, and the dead **in Christ** will rise first.*

Being dead in Christ refers to a status that describes all who die as believers in Christ. The use of ἐν Χριστῷ here does not describe the manner in which such deaths took place,[97] but rather indicates the sphere under which the dead are situated: 'even death does not break the union; we are still *in* him'.[98]

3.8.1 SUMMARY

Through these occurrences of ἐν Χριστῷ, we observe its connection to various new statuses that are descriptive of believers. Because they are *in*

---

95. O'Brien, *Ephesians*, 236.

96. Ibid. [italics are original].

97. On this possibility, see Konstan and Ramelli, who claim that 'if Paul had wished to say "the dead in Christ will rise" or "those will rise who have died in Christ," he would have to have written οἱ ἐν Χριστῷ νεκροὶ ἀναστήσονται, or else οἱ νεκροὶ οἱ ἐν Χριστῷ ἀναστήσονται, which would have been unequivocal. As the sentence stands, however, οἱ νεκροὶ ἐν Χριστῷ ἀναστήσονται, it would seem far more natural to take it to mean "the dead will rise in Christ"'; David Konstan and Ilaria Ramelli, 'The Syntax of ἐν Χριστῷ in 1 Thessalonians 4:16', *JBL* 126 (2007): 590–91.

98. Leon Morris, *The Epistles of Paul to the Thessalonians* (TNTC; rev. ed.; Leicester, UK: Inter-Varsity Press, 1984), 93.

Christ, believers are a new creation; they are sons of God rather than his enemies; they are together now as one body rather than as opposing races. Of the nine uses of ἐν Χριστῷ in this subcategory, seven are locative, depicting the notion of realm transference (Rom 6:11; 8:1; 1 Cor 15:18; 2 Cor 5:17; Gal 3:28; Eph 3:6; 1 Thess 4:16), one expresses state or condition (Rom 12:5), and one indicates Christ as the object of faith (Gal 3:26).

3.9 *IN CHRIST* AS A PERIPHRASIS FOR BELIEVERS

There are several instances in which ἐν Χριστῷ seems to be employed as a label to indicate that people are Christian. In this way, ἐν Χριστῷ might be regarded as roughly equivalent to the modern label 'Christian'; Paul does not use the latter term, but its function is carried by the former term. This subcategory may appear similar to the use of ἐν Χριστῷ that indicates the realm or sphere of Christ. After all, anyone who is a 'Christian' is by definition under the realm of Christ.

A distinction, however, between the two may be discerned through the communicative purpose of each instance. Sometimes Paul is concerned with the notion of realm and the significance of realm transfer or the implications that proceed from incorporation under the realm of Christ. In other instances, it appears that Paul simply wants to indicate that someone is a believer in Christ, without any necessary focus on the notion of realm. It is to these cases that we now turn. By the nature of this subcategory, most instances of ἐν Χριστῷ will be seen to be expressing close association or personal relation. There are several occurrences of ἐν Χριστῷ that are accommodated by this category; of seventy-three total uses, fourteen are included here.

> Rom 16:3 ἀσπάσασθε Πρίσκαν καὶ Ἀκύλαν τοὺς συνεργούς μου ἐν Χριστῷ Ἰησοῦ
>
> *Give my greetings to Prisca and Aquila, my coworkers **in Christ** Jesus.*

To describe Prisca and Aquila as his coworkers in Christ Jesus, Paul means to mark them out as *Christian* coworkers, or coworkers in the cause of Christ. The use of ἐν Χριστῷ here is best understood as indicating close personal association: as 'Christians', Prisca and Aquila are people who are identified closely with Christ. As Cranfield concludes, 'ἐν Χριστῷ Ἰησοῦ clearly serves to indicate that it is in relation to Christ and in the work of the gospel of Christ rather than in any other sphere or matter that they are Paul's fellow-workers'.[99]

Rom 16:7 ἀσπάσασθε Ἀνδρόνικον καὶ Ἰουνιᾶν τοὺς συγγενεῖς μου καὶ συναιχμαλώτους μου, οἵτινές εἰσιν ἐπίσημοι ἐν τοῖς ἀποστόλοις, οἳ καὶ πρὸ ἐμοῦ γέγοναν ἐν **Χριστῷ**

*Greet Andronicus and Junia, my fellow countrymen and fellow prisoners. They are noteworthy in the eyes of the apostles, and they were also **in Christ** before me.*

Clearly Paul's use of ἐν Χριστῷ is intended to mean that Andronicus and Junia were believers in Christ before he was.[100] While this instance could be understood as indicating the realm of Christ—such that Andronicus and Junia are described as having come under the realm of Christ before Paul—Paul's interest here does not appear to be in the notion of realm. It is better simply to regard this statement as communicating the fact that Andronicus and Junia came to Christ—became Christians—at a time prior to Paul.[101]

Rom 16:9 ἀσπάσασθε Οὐρβανὸν τὸν συνεργὸν ἡμῶν ἐν **Χριστῷ** καὶ Στάχυν τὸν ἀγαπητόν μου

*Greet Urbanus, our coworker **in Christ**, and my dear friend Stachys.*

This example is parallel to Romans 16:3, above.

1 Cor 3:1 κἀγώ, ἀδελφοί, οὐκ ἠδυνήθην λαλῆσαι ὑμῖν ὡς πνευματικοῖς ἀλλ᾽ ὡς σαρκίνοις, ὡς νηπίοις ἐν **Χριστῷ**

*Brothers, I was not able to speak to you as spiritual people but as people of the flesh, as babies **in Christ**.*

---

99. Cranfield, *Romans*, 2:785. Cranfield also suggests, however, that 'the deeper meaning of the formula "in Christ" is also present to his mind', but this claim is difficult to demonstrate in the context.

100. Joseph A. Fitzmyer, *Romans* (AB; New York: Doubleday, 1993), 740.

101. Cranfield, *Romans*, 2:790.

Here Paul uses the phrase ἐν Χριστῷ with an almost mocking tone as he castigates the Corinthians for their lack of maturity. Apparently a locative sense—expressing the realm or sphere of Christ—is not the focus here; to describe the Corinthians as babies within the realm of Christ would not be consistent with the way in which the notion has been employed elsewhere. However, a use of ἐν Χριστῷ that simply labels the Corinthians as 'Christians' makes some sense: they are baby Christians; as believers they are not yet mature.[102]

1 Cor 4:15 ἐὰν γὰρ μυρίους παιδαγωγοὺς ἔχητε ἐν Χριστῷ ἀλλ' οὐ πολλοὺς πατέρας· ἐν γὰρ Χριστῷ Ἰησοῦ διὰ τοῦ εὐαγγελίου ἐγὼ ὑμᾶς ἐγέννησα

For you can have 10,000 instructors in Christ, but you can't have many fathers. Now I have fathered you in Christ Jesus through the gospel.

The first use of ἐν Χριστῷ appears to depict the idea of *Christian instructors*; ἐν Χριστῷ delimits the scope of potential instructors to those who are believers. Thiselton accepts the possibility of this reading, along with the option *with reference to your life as Christians*, thus taking ἐν Χριστῷ as modifying the Corinthians rather than their instructors.[103] The former reading is to be preferred, however, on the basis that the second reference to the phrase in the verse (ἐν . . . Χριστῷ Ἰησοῦ) makes best sense as referring to Paul's fathering action rather than to the Corinthians, thus forming a parallel to the aforementioned instructors in Christ. Nevertheless, both of Thiselton's options take ἐν Χριστῷ as periphrastic for *Christian*; whether it modifies the Corinthians or their instructors is largely beside the point for our purpose here.

Regarding the second use of ἐν Χριστῷ, Paul's 'begetting' (ἐγέννησα) of the Corinthians refers to his leading them to Christ; thus it does not adhere to the category of periphrasis for *Christian*—since the phrase modifies an action rather than a person—and will be dealt with below at §3.11.1.2.

---

102. Thiselton asks whether ἐν Χριστῷ is to be 'understood to mean *in union with Christ*, or **in Christian terms**', the latter term roughly approximating our 'periphrasis for believer'. Thiselton shys away from the 'full theological sense of *being-in-Christ*' here, preferring **in Christian terms**; Thiselton, *1 Corinthians*, 289 (see also n. 344) [emphases are original].
103. Ibid., 370.

1 Cor 16:24 ἡ ἀγάπη μου μετὰ πάντων ὑμῶν **ἐν Χριστῷ** Ἰησοῦ

*My love be with all of you **in Christ Jesus**.*

This use of ἐν Χριστῷ could conceivably express cause or ground, in that Christ Jesus is the ground on which Paul's love will be with the Corinthians. It is rather more likely, however, that ἐν Χριστῷ is descriptive of *you*—the Corinthians. This reading is strengthened by Thiselton's suggestion that the subtext of this verse is that Paul loves them *all*, not any particular faction or party within the Corinthian church.[104] In this way, ἐν Χριστῷ is understood as modifying *all*, such that Paul has all Corinthians Christians in view.

2 Cor 12:2 οἶδα ἄνθρωπον **ἐν Χριστῷ** πρὸ ἐτῶν δεκατεσσάρων, εἴτε ἐν σώματι οὐκ οἶδα, εἴτε ἐκτὸς τοῦ σώματος οὐκ οἶδα, ὁ θεὸς οἶδεν, ἀρπαγέντα τὸν τοιοῦτον ἕως τρίτου οὐρανοῦ

*I know a man **in Christ** who was caught up into the third heaven 14 years ago. Whether he was in the body or out of the body, I don't know, God knows.*

This description of a man ἐν Χριστῷ clearly depicts this man as a believer[105] and does not appear to have any more significance in the context than this.[106] Martin, however, regards the phrase as indicating that 'it was in Christ's power that the following visions and revelations took place'.[107] This reading takes ἐν Χριστῷ as an indicator of mode, such that the man presumably was 'caught up into the third heaven' while in a special mode of being in Christ. In other words, being in this special mode enabled his experience. There is scant evidence in the context, however, to read ἐν Χριστῷ in such a way, since there is no obvious indication in the Greek text that the phrase is meant to modify an action or capacity. Futhermore, Martin appears to view the prepositional phrase as modifying ἀρπαγέντα, which is a long way removed from ἐν Χριστῷ in Greek.

---

104. Ibid., 1353.

105. Murray J. Harris, *The Second Epistle to the Corinthians* (NIGTC; Grand Rapids: Eerdmans, 2005), 834.

106. So Colin G. Kruse, *The Second Epistle of Paul to the Corinthians* (TNTC; Leicester, UK: Inter-Varsity Press, 1987), 201.

107. Martin, *2 Corinthians*, 399.

Gal 1:22 ἤμην δὲ ἀγνοούμενος τῷ προσώπῳ ταῖς ἐκκλησίαις τῆς Ἰουδαίας ταῖς ἐν Χριστῷ

*I remained personally unknown to the Judean churches **in Christ**.*

In this example we see actual churches described as ἐν Χριστῷ. The most obvious way to understand the phrase here is as a label defining the sort of gatherings in mind: they are Christian gatherings in Judaea.[108]

Phil 1:1 Παῦλος καὶ Τιμόθεος δοῦλοι Χριστοῦ Ἰησοῦ πᾶσιν τοῖς ἁγίοις ἐν Χριστῷ Ἰησοῦ τοῖς οὖσιν ἐν Φιλίπποις σὺν ἐπισκόποις καὶ διακόνοις

*Paul and Timothy, slaves of Christ Jesus: To all the saints **in Christ** Jesus who are in Philippi, including the overseers and deacons.*

While perhaps being slightly tautologous, the phrase ἐν Χριστῷ here identifies the saints in Philippi as Christian. Fee reads the phrase as indicating 'those who belong to Christ Jesus, as those whose lives are forever identified with Christ'.[109]

Phil 1:13 ὥστε τοὺς δεσμούς μου φανεροὺς ἐν Χριστῷ γενέσθαι ἐν ὅλῳ τῷ πραιτωρίῳ καὶ τοῖς λοιποῖς πᾶσιν

*So that it has become known throughout the whole imperial guard, and to everyone else, that my imprisonment is **in the cause of Christ**.*

In this unusual example, the phrase ἐν Χριστῷ is employed with reference to Paul's imprisonment. *How* it is related to his chains, however, is somewhat ambiguous. O'Brien correctly points out that the Greek word order prevents the reading, 'so that my chains in Christ have become manifest', since φανεροὺς separates the two phrases τοὺς δεσμούς μου and ἐν Χριστῷ.[110] Thus ἐν Χριστῷ modifies the infinitival phrase that brackets it—φανεροὺς γενέσθαι—which means that somehow Paul's

---

108. Thus Bruce notes the NEB's rendering: 'Christ's congregations in Judaea'; Bruce, *Galatians*, 104.

109. Fee, *Philippians*, 65.

110. O'Brien, *Philippians*, 92.

chains have been revealed 'in Christ'. O'Brien renders this with 'my bonds have become manifest-in-Christ'.[111] It remains unclear, however, exactly *how* Paul's chains are 'manifest-in-Christ'. To read this as indicating that Christ has revealed Paul's chains is nonsensical, since his chains are not secret, nor are they spiritually discerned. Thus, it appears most likely that 'manifest-in-Christ' means that Paul's chains are revealed to be *for* Christ, or *because of* him. Indeed, O'Brien approvingly cites the NIV rendering, 'it has become clear . . . that I am in chains for Christ', which thus clarifies how he understands 'manifest-in-Christ'.[112]

While this example is not exactly parallel to the others in this sub-category, we nevertheless conclude that Paul's imprisonment pertains to Christ; he is in chains for the cause of Christ and, perhaps, because he shares in the sufferings of Christ. Thus it is not inappropriate to regard his chains as 'Christian' in the sense that this identifies the nature of his offence.

Phil 4:21 ἀσπάσασθε πάντα ἅγιον **ἐν Χριστῷ** Ἰησοῦ. ἀσπάζονται ὑμᾶς οἱ σὺν ἐμοὶ ἀδελφοί

*Greet every saint **in Christ** Jesus. Those brothers who are with me greet you.*

This example uses the phrase ἐν Χριστῷ in the same manner as Philippians 1:1, above, though with reference to each individual saint (πάντα ἅγιον) while 1:1 refers to the group (πᾶσιν τοῖς ἁγίοις).[113]

Col 1:2 τοῖς ἐν Κολοσσαῖς ἁγίοις καὶ πιστοῖς ἀδελφοῖς **ἐν Χριστῷ**, χάρις ὑμῖν καὶ εἰρήνη ἀπὸ θεοῦ πατρὸς ἡμῶν

*To God's holy people in Colossae, the faithful brothers and sisters **in Christ**: Grace and peace to you from God our Father.*

Here again we see the term *saints* connected to the phrase ἐν Χριστῷ, but not directly as it is in the two examples from Philippians, above.

---

111. Ibid.
112. Ibid.
113. O'Brien, *Philippians*, 553; Fee, *Philippians*, 458, however, takes ἐν Χριστῷ Ἰησοῦ here as modifying the imperative.

In this occurrence the term *faithful brothers* is directly connected to ἐν Χριστῷ. Once again, it is probably best to understand this as indicating that the believers in Colossae are *Christian brothers*.

Wright, however, argues that ἐν Χριστῷ here is to be understood in a locative sense, in balance with the locative ἐν Κολοσσαῖς. While this is certainly possible — and it should be noted that the 'periphrasis for *Christian*' usage cannot be divorced from the essential reality of location in the realm of Christ — Wright probably reads too much into the phrase at this point.

1 Thess 2:14 ὑμεῖς γὰρ μιμηταὶ ἐγενήθητε, ἀδελφοί, τῶν ἐκκλησιῶν τοῦ θεοῦ τῶν οὐσῶν ἐν τῇ Ἰουδαίᾳ **ἐν Χριστῷ Ἰησοῦ**, ὅτι τὰ αὐτὰ ἐπάθετε καὶ ὑμεῖς ὑπὸ τῶν ἰδίων συμφυλετῶν καθὼς καὶ αὐτοὶ ὑπὸ τῶν Ἰουδαίων

For you, brothers, became imitators of God's churches **in Christ** *Jesus that are in Judea, since you have also suffered the same things from people of your own country, just as they did from the Jews.*

This is similar to Galatians 1:22 in that we observe churches, or gatherings, described as ἐν Χριστῷ. While this example is best understood in the same way as Galatians 1:22 — as describing these gatherings as *Christian* — it is curious here that the gatherings are also defined as 'of God'. The use of ἐν Χριστῷ is not tautologous, however, since 'gatherings of God' could be understood to include synagogues and other Jewish gatherings, whereas Paul makes clear that he explicitly has *Christian* congregations in mind. Such a reading is made more plausible by the reference to Judea and the phrase 'just as they did from the Jews'; the demarcation between Jews and Christians is in view, which means that ἐν Χριστῷ Ἰησοῦ is most likely epexegetical of τοῦ θεοῦ.[114]

Phlm 23 ἀσπάζεταί σε Ἐπαφρᾶς ὁ συναιχμάλωτός μου **ἐν Χριστῷ Ἰησοῦ**

Epaphras, my fellow prisoner **in Christ** *Jesus, greets you.*

---

114. 'The Christian assemblies are distinguished as being "God's," and further as "in Christ Jesus"'; Leon Morris, *The First and Second Epistles to the Thessalonians* (NICNT; Grand Rapids: Eerdmans, 1991), 83.

Similar to the use of ἐν Χριστῷ in Philippians 1:13 in that it describes someone in imprisonment, this example of the phrase may again be understood as describing a believer as a *Christian* prisoner. Epaphras is in chains with Paul because he is a Christian.[115]

3.9.1 SUMMARY

With this subcategory we identify the use of ἐν Χριστῷ as an indicator that certain people and congregations belong to Christ. This subcategory constitutes one of the largest groupings of ἐν Χριστῷ usage, with fourteen occurrences. Of these uses of ἐν Χριστῷ, twelve convey close personal association (Rom 16:3, 7, 9; 1 Cor 3:1; 4:15 [first instance]; 16:24; 2 Cor 12:2; Gal 1:22; Phil 1:1; 4:21; Col 1:2; 1 Thess 2:14), and two indicate imprisonment for the cause of Christ (Phil 1:13; Phlm 23).

3.10 TRINITY *IN CHRIST*

This subcategory includes occurrences of ἐν Χριστῷ that are explicitly connected to references to God or the Spirit. Some of these instances have already appeared in other subcategories above for different reasons, yet are included here because they also make explicit connection to Paul's trinitarian thought.[116] Incidentally, there are citations above that arguably express an *implicit* trinitarianism but are not included here because of the criterion of *explicitness*. The instances below self-evidently meet this criterion.

Rom 8:2 ὁ γὰρ νόμος τοῦ πνεύματος τῆς ζωῆς ἐν **Χριστῷ** Ἰησοῦ ἠλευθέρωσέν σε ἀπὸ τοῦ νόμου τῆς ἁμαρτίας καὶ τοῦ θανάτου

*Because the Spirit's law of life **in Christ** Jesus has set you free from the law of sin and of death.*

This is a perplexing use of ἐν Χριστῷ because it is not clear what the phrase is modifying. There are several options. First, ἐν Χριστῷ could modify *life*, so that *life in Christ Jesus* is in view. Second, ἐν Χριστῷ could modify

---

115. While Wright is no doubt correct to describe Epaphras as engaged with Paul 'in the battle between Christ and the powers of the present age', this is probably too much to read into ἐν Χριστῷ here; Wright, *Colossians and Philemon*, 191.

116. In other words, this subcategory overlaps with others.

Spirit, so that the *Spirit in Christ* is meant. Third, ἐν Χριστῷ could modify *law*, so that the *law in Christ* is in view. Finally, ἐν Χριστῷ could modify *set you free*, so that *set you free in/by/through Christ* is intended.

Several commentators prefer this last option, including Cranfield, Moo, and Dunn. Each acknowledges, however, that ἐν Χριστῷ Ἰησοῦ could modify the phrase νόμος τοῦ πνεύματος τῆς ζωῆς, or one of its parts. The reasons put forth for taking ἐν Χριστῷ Ἰησοῦ with ἠλευθέρωσέν σε are not particularly strong, defaulting to the commentator's sense of what seems most likely.[117] Against this reading is the fact that had Paul intended ἐν Χριστῷ Ἰησοῦ to modify ἠλευθέρωσέν σε, he could have made this clear by placing the prepositional phrase after the verb rather than before it. As it stands, it is ambiguous, but the best reading is to allow the word order its natural influence so that ἐν Χριστῷ Ἰησοῦ modifies νόμος τοῦ πνεύματος τῆς ζωῆς (or some part of it), which it immediately follows.

Regardless of whether ἐν Χριστῷ Ἰησοῦ modifies νόμος τοῦ πνεύματος τῆς ζωῆς or some part of the phrase, it most likely refers to the realm or domain of Christ. Life in Christ Jesus, or the Spirit of life in Christ Jesus, or the law of the Spirit of life in Jesus Christ are each best understood as determined by their position within the realm of Christ. This is reinforced by the previous verse, which refers to the status of noncondemnation for those in the realm of Christ Jesus (see on Rom 8:1, above). Verse 2 then expands on the internal operations within the realm of Christ; the Spirit's law of life has set free those within the realm of Christ.

Of further consideration is the parallel statement at the end of the verse: *the law of sin and of death*. From this expression it may be observed that *sin* and *death* are not the content of the law; Paul is, after all, referring to the Torah.[118] What Paul means is that sin and death are the outworking of the law or the domain under which the law now exists (and these need not be mutually exclusive). The more likely of the two, however, is that Paul is referring to the domain of sin and death; this is due to the parallelism with the beginning of the verse in which *Spirit of life in Christ*

---

117. Cranfield, *Romans*, 1:374–75; Moo, *Romans*, 473, n. 21; Dunn, *Romans 1–8*, 418.

118. Dunn, *Romans 1–8*, 419; cf. Moo, *Romans*, 474–76, who takes both references to the law as a 'binding authority' or 'power'. In the following verse, however, the law is described as 'limited by the flesh', which strongly suggests that the Torah is in view. It can be described as 'the law of sin and of death' in v. 2 since that is what it produces in combination with the flesh.

Jesus should be understood as referring to dominion rather than result. By reading both parts of the parallelism against each other, we conclude that the *law of the Spirit of life in Christ Jesus* refers to a law that pertains to the domain of Christ,[119] while the *law of sin and of death* refers to a law that pertains to the domain of sin and death.

Also of interest is the way in which the *Spirit of life* correlates to this domain of Christ. Most likely the Spirit is viewed as part of the constitution of the sphere of Christ; the Spirit operates within Christ's realm. It may even be possible to posit the same kind of relationship between the Spirit and Christ that exists between sin and death. Elsewhere Paul regards sin as death's instrument and thus the servant of death. Perhaps the parallelism between the two laws in this verse can be pressed a little further so that the Spirit is seen as Christ's instrument and servant in a way that is parallel, mutatis mutandis, to the relationship between sin and death.

At this point we pause to reflect on Paul's trinitarian thinking, which constitutes the burden of this subcategory. One may question whether the Spirit operating within and under the realm of Christ is truly trinitarian, since it might imply inferiority. While such concerns deserve attention, they need not undermine the point at hand. Paul is no doubt conscious that Christ conducted himself under his Father's authority, as the Gospels report. And yet Christ's willing submission to the Father is not seen to undermine his status as the second person of the Trinity. By the same measure, the Spirit's operation under and within the realm and sphere of Christ need not undermine his status as the third person of the Trinity.

Rom 8:39 οὔτε ὕψωμα οὔτε βάθος οὔτε τις κτίσις ἑτέρα δυνήσεται ἡμᾶς χωρίσαι ἀπὸ τῆς ἀγάπης τοῦ θεοῦ τῆς **ἐν Χριστῷ** Ἰησοῦ τῷ κυρίῳ ἡμῶν

*Height or depth, or any other created thing will have the power to separate us from the love of God that is **in Christ** Jesus our Lord!*

The love of God is described here as ἐν Χριστῷ, which raises questions relating to the trinitarian expression of love as well as the way in which the phrase ἐν Χριστῷ modifies *the love of God*. From a trinitarian point of

---

119. This 'law' is best understood as a 'principle', 'authority', or 'power' of the Spirit; it is intended as an intential play on words in contrast to the law of Moses; Moo, *Romans*, 474–75.

view, we should note that the love is described as clearly directed toward believers: Paul says that nothing is able to separate us from it. Yet this love is described as being *in Christ Jesus*; it is not explicitly claimed that this love is *in believers*, from whom it cannot be separated—rather, it is in Christ. While this is a curious fact in its own right, we may also conclude that God's love being found ἐν Χριστῷ does not appear to lead to any kind of remoteness on the part of God. Nothing is able to separate believers from his love; such does not sound like love from afar—it is personal and imminent. Thus, the trinitarian nature of God's love means that it is both mediated through Christ and, yet, is personally imminent, such that any kind of separation from it is impossible.

As for the way in which ἐν Χριστῷ modifies *the love of God*, there are only two options among those we have observed thus far. First, there is the local use of the phrase, in which the realm or sphere of Christ is in view. Under this reading, the love of God is experienced as part of belonging to said realm. Just as the Spirit operates within and under this realm (see the previous example), so too, perhaps, does the love of God, as it is spread through the people belonging to the realm of Christ. A problem with this reading, however, is that it makes the love of God seem abstract. It is almost as though it is some kind of cosmic force that operates within the domain of Christ. This in itself may not be too problematic, but the verse does appear to portray love that is personally known.

Second, ἐν Χριστῷ could be employed instrumentally. This reading is not necessarily problematic in terms of Paul's mediatorial understanding of Christ. The main obstacle to an instrumental understanding, however, is that such is normally required to be adverbial in some sense. That is, an action will be performed through the means of an instrument. And presumably *the love of God* does not directly refer to an action. This obstacle is not unsurmountable, however, and the word *directly* in the previous sentence is significant. If Paul means to express more than meets the eye through the phrase *the love of God that is in Christ Jesus*, he may refer to love that is mediated through Christ, or perhaps expressed through Christ. The sense of the verse, then, would be that no one is able to separate believers from the love of God that is effected or manifested through Christ.

Given that the second reading requires an imported step, however, a third option may prove stronger. BDAG lists the following category under the entry for ἐν: 'marker denoting the object to which someth. happens or in which someth. shows itself, or by which someth. is recognized, *to, by, in connection with*'.[120] Through this use of ἐν, Paul's point may be that the love of God is *recognized* in Christ. This would be consistent with his description, earlier in the letter, of the way in which the love of God is demonstrated: *But God proves His own love for us in that while we were still sinners, Christ died for us* (Rom 5:8). God's love is demonstrated in Christ's act. If understood in this way, Romans 8:39 then may be rendered: *nor height, nor depth, nor any other created thing will have the power to separate us from the love of God that is seen in Christ Jesus our Lord!* This option is to be preferred over the previous two because it is simpler than the instrumental reading and it does not turn God's love into an abstraction; God's love is direct and personal and is recognized through Christ. As Murray concludes, 'only in Christ Jesus as our Lord can *we* know the embrace and bond of this love of God'.[121]

1 Cor 1:4 εὐχαριστῶ τῷ θεῷ μου πάντοτε περὶ ὑμῶν ἐπὶ τῇ χάριτι τοῦ θεοῦ τῇ δοθείσῃ ὑμῖν **ἐν Χριστῷ** Ἰησοῦ

*I always thank my God for you because of God's grace given to you **in Christ Jesus**.*

To reiterate the comments on this verse above (see §3.3), this example depicts the agency of God and the instrumentality of Christ in the giving of God's grace. The verse is listed again here for its obvious association with trinitarian thought.

1 Cor 1:30 ἐξ αὐτοῦ δὲ ὑμεῖς ἐστε **ἐν Χριστῷ** Ἰησοῦ, ὃς ἐγενήθη σοφία ἡμῖν ἀπὸ θεοῦ, δικαιοσύνη τε καὶ ἁγιασμὸς καὶ ἀπολύτρωσις

*But it is from Him that you are **in Christ** Jesus, who became God-given wisdom for us—our righteousness, sanctification, and redemption.*

Before exploring the trinitarian nature of this verse, we note the so far unusual use of the phrase ἐν Χριστῷ. This is one of the few examples in

120. BDAG, 329.
121. Murray, *Romans*, 1:335 [italics are original].

which we witness Paul claiming that believers are *in* Christ (ὑμεῖς ἐστε ἐν Χριστῷ Ἰησοῦ). There have certainly been many hints of the notion throughout, but it is rarely so directly stated. In other cases, ἐν Χριστῷ is employed somewhat indirectly; that is, believers might be described as fellow workers in Christ, or alive in Christ, and so forth. Here believers simply *are* in Christ.

On the one hand, this expression could be another instance of the use of ἐν Χριστῷ to describe people as *Christians*. This would provide a comfortable fit in the first part of the verse; the sense would be: *But from Him you are Christians*. On the other hand, the use of the phrase as a periphrasis for *Christian* does not provide the best fit for the remainder of the verse. Paul goes on to say that Christ *became God-given wisdom of us — our righteousness, sanctification, and redemption*. The most compelling way to understand this is to view it as indicating some kind of union with Christ: he became wisdom, righteousness, sanctification, and redemption *for us*. If the notion of union is in view here (as vague as that may seem at this stage), it would make better sense to read the first part of the verse as indicating something more than merely *Christian*. If Paul really does mean that believers are *in Christ*, it follows that some kind of union is meant by this. While we are yet to explore what it really means to be *in Christ*, it is safe to suppose that union is implicit therein. The two parts of the verse, then, coordinate neatly: *you are in Christ* (and therefore have union with him), and *he became wisdom, righteousness, sanctification, and redemption for us* (an outworking of this union).[122]

As for the trinitarian import of the verse, we observe that being in Christ comes from God (ἐξ αὐτοῦ). From v. 27, Paul catalogues acts of God in choosing his people, and v. 30 continues that line of thought by indicating that it is from God that the Corinthians are in Christ. The point of interest here is that ἐν Χριστῷ language is often used to describe the mediatorial work of Christ — on several occasions as the personal instrument of God's agency. Yet here it appears that the roles are reversed; rather than Christ working on God's behalf, or on the believers' behalf toward God, we see the Father working to bring people into union with Christ.

---

122. Roy E. Ciampa and Brian S. Rosner, *The First Letter to the Corinthians* (PNTC; Grand Rapids: Eerdmans, 2010), 108–9.

2 Cor 5:19 ὡς ὅτι θεὸς ἦν **ἐν Χριστῷ** κόσμον καταλλάσσων ἑαυτῷ, μὴ λογιζόμενος αὐτοῖς τὰ παραπτώματα αὐτῶν καὶ θέμενος ἐν ἡμῖν τὸν λόγον τῆς καταλλαγῆς

That is, **in Christ,** *God was reconciling the world to Himself, not counting their trespasses against them, and He has committed the message of reconciliation to us.*

The comments on this verse above (see §3.3) label the use of ἐν Χριστῷ as instrumental; God is the agent of reconciliation, through the instrumental work of Christ. The verse is cited again here because of its clear trinitarian connotation: the work of the Father and the Son are tightly coordinated.

Gal 3:14 ἵνα εἰς τὰ ἔθνη ἡ εὐλογία τοῦ Ἀβραὰμ γένηται **ἐν Χριστῷ** Ἰησοῦ, ἵνα τὴν ἐπαγγελίαν τοῦ πνεύματος λάβωμεν διὰ τῆς πίστεως

*The purpose was that the blessing of Abraham would come to the Gentiles by [**in**] Christ Jesus, so that we could receive the promised Spirit through faith.*

As indicated above (see §3.3), this use of ἐν Χριστῷ is best understood as instrumental. The verse is listed again here for its connection between ἐν Χριστῷ and the work of the Spirit. Paul says that the blessing of Abraham comes to the Gentiles *in Christ*, and this in turn leads to the reception of the promised Spirit.

Of the two ἵνα + subjunctive constructions in this verse, the second is of particular interest. While ἵνα + subjunctive ordinarily indicates *purpose*—the blessing of Abraham comes to the Gentiles in Christ, *in order that* we receive the promised Spirit—it can also indicate *result*—the blessing of Abraham comes to the Gentiles in Christ, *with the result that* we receive the promised Spirit.[123] There is, however, a third category for the use of ἵνα + subjunctive: *purpose-result*: 'Not only is ἵνα used for result in the NT, but also for purpose-result. That is, it indicates *both the intention and its sure accomplishment.*'[124] BDAG elaborates:

---

123. See Wallace, *Greek Grammar*, 473.
124. Ibid.

In many cases purpose and result cannot be clearly differentiated, and hence ἵνα is used for the result that follows according to the purpose of the subj. or of God. As in Semitic and Gr-Rom. thought, purpose and result are identical in declarations of the divine will.[125]

Given that this verse has divine purpose in view, it is reasonable to regard the use of ἵνα + subjunctive here as indicating *purpose-result*. As such, the reception of the Spirit is both the purpose and result of the Gentiles' reception of the blessing of Abraham. Since the blessing of Abraham comes to the Gentiles ἐν Χριστῷ, there is an obvious relationship between the work of Christ and the Spirit here.

Gal 3:26 πάντες γὰρ υἱοὶ θεοῦ ἐστε διὰ τῆς πίστεως ἐν Χριστῷ Ἰησοῦ

*For you are all sons of God through faith **in Christ** Jesus.*

This verse is listed here for the third time (see §§3.6, 3.8) — here because of its trinitarian nature. Faith ἐν Χριστῷ is the means through which people attain divine sonship. The Fatherhood of God is extended to human beings by nature of the relationship between the Father and Son; 'as he is God's Son inherently, so in him they become God's sons and daughters'.[126]

Eph 1:3 εὐλογητὸς ὁ θεὸς καὶ πατὴρ τοῦ κυρίου ἡμῶν Ἰησοῦ Χριστοῦ, ὁ εὐλογήσας ἡμᾶς ἐν πάσῃ εὐλογίᾳ πνευματικῇ ἐν τοῖς ἐπουρανίοις ἐν Χριστῷ

*Praise the God and Father of our Lord Jesus Christ, who has blessed us **in Christ** with every spiritual blessing in the heavens.*

As discussed above (see §3.3), this use of ἐν Χριστῷ is most likely instrumental. The trinitarian connotation here again envisages God as agent and Christ as instrument.

Eph 2:6 καὶ συνήγειρεν καὶ συνεκάθισεν ἐν τοῖς ἐπουρανίοις ἐν Χριστῷ Ἰησοῦ,

---

125. BDAG, 477.
126. Bruce, *Galatians*, 184.

*And God raised us up with Christ and seated us with him in the heavenly realms **in Christ Jesus**.*

This occurrence of ἐν Χριστῷ is best understood as locative in a concrete capacity (see the previous discussion of this verse in §3.3), describing the spiritual location of believers with Christ, seated in the heavens. From a trinitarian point of view, we notice again that it is the Father who acts on believers in conjunction with his acting on Christ.[127] As he raised Christ, and seated him in the heavens, so he did for believers. This 'direction' of divine activity counters the more usual pattern of the mediation of Christ between God and believers. Here God works on believers and Christ, while Christ's mediation is not the focus.

Eph 2:7 ἵνα ἐνδείξηται ἐν τοῖς αἰῶσιν τοῖς ἐπερχομένοις τὸ ὑπερβάλλον πλοῦτος τῆς χάριτος αὐτοῦ ἐν χρηστότητι ἐφ' ἡμᾶς **ἐν Χριστῷ** Ἰησοῦ

*So that in the coming ages He might display the immeasurable riches of His grace through His kindness to us **in Christ Jesus**.*

It is argued above (see §3.3) that this instance of ἐν Χριστῷ conveys the sense of God's grace and kindness being *evident* in Christ. The trinitarian implication of this relates to the intimate association between Father and Son: they are so closely identified that the kindness of one is revealed in the other. Christ is 'the place where, or means whereby, God's grace is exhibited'.[128] While it is the Father who acts to display (ἐνδείξηται) these characteristics, the Son's (passive?) involvement once again demonstrates the profoundly intimate coordination of their activity.

Eph 2:10 αὐτοῦ γάρ ἐσμεν ποίημα, κτισθέντες **ἐν Χριστῷ** Ἰησοῦ ἐπὶ ἔργοις ἀγαθοῖς οἷς προητοίμασεν ὁ θεός, ἵνα ἐν αὐτοῖς περιπατήσωμεν.

*For we are His creation, created **in Christ Jesus** for good works, which God prepared ahead of time so that we should walk in them.*

127. See the discussion in Lincoln, *Ephesians*, 106–9.
128. Best, *Ephesians*, 225.

Being another example of the instrumental function of ἐν Χριστῷ (see §3.3), this verse once again depicts the close nature of the operations of the persons within the Trinity. While believers may be described as *God's creation*, that work is conducted through Christ.[129]

Eph 3:21 αὐτῷ ἡ δόξα ἐν τῇ ἐκκλησίᾳ καὶ **ἐν Χριστῷ** Ἰησοῦ εἰς πάσας τὰς γενεὰς τοῦ αἰῶνος τῶν αἰώνων, ἀμήν.

*To Him be glory in the church and **in Christ** Jesus to all generations, forever and ever. Amen.*

This is an interesting use of the phrase ἐν Χριστῷ. Part of a doxology, Paul associates the glory of God with the church and with Christ. The nature of this association is intriguing because it is not immediately evident whether Paul envisages this glory as being *located* in the church and in Christ, or as being *brought about* by the church and by Christ, or as being *revealed* in the church and in Christ. All three options appear feasible.

First, the locative sense would understand ἐν Χριστῷ to be depicting the realm of Christ, which is a common enough phenomenon. This would presumably also require *the church* to be understood this way — as a realm or sphere. To regard the church in this way seems possible though somewhat unusual.

Second, the instrumental sense would depict the church and Christ as the means through which God's glory is attained. It would not be unusual to regard Christ as an instrument in the attainment of the glory of God. To say as much about the church seems less likely though not impossible.

Third, the revealing sense would understand ἐν Χριστῷ as the way in which the glory of God is made evident.[130] Such a reading can be applied to the church also; it is in the church and in Christ that the glory of God is seen.[131] The second part of the verse offers confirmation of this view.

---

129. Lincoln, *Ephesians*, 114–15.
130. This makes use of BDAG's category under the entry for ἐν: 'marker denoting the object to which someth. happens or in which someth. shows itself, or by which someth. is recognized, *to, by, in connection with*' (329).
131. Barth is startled by the sequence of the terms 'in the church' and 'in Christ Jesus' and asks: 'Why is the Messiah not mentioned before his people?' M. Barth, *Ephesians 1–3*, 375. This is only problematic, however, if our first reading — that the church is the location of

Paul prays that God's glory may be revealed in the church and in Christ *to all generations, forever and ever.* What is the meaning of the reference to *all generations?* Under the first two possible readings above, it is not clear how this fits in the verse as a whole. Under the third reading, however, it can be argued that *to all generations* refers to those to whom the glory of God will be evident. Paul desires God's glory to be revealed to all generations forevermore; they are the 'audience' for God's glory.

This option, then, provides a coherent reading of the verse that the other two options struggle to achieve. The wider context also helps to confirm this choice. A major burden of Paul's prayer, beginning at v. 14, is that his readers might know the love of Christ; the prayer is concerned with *revelation*. Given this wider concern, the third option is best: the glory of God is revealed in the church and in Christ to all generations.

Eph 4:32 γίνεσθε [δὲ] εἰς ἀλλήλους χρηστοί, εὔσπλαγχνοι, χαριζόμενοι ἑαυτοῖς, καθὼς καὶ ὁ θεὸς **ἐν Χριστῷ** ἐχαρίσατο ὑμῖν

*And be kind and compassionate to one another, forgiving one another, just as God also forgave you **in Christ**.*

As established above (see §3.3), this use of ἐν Χριστῷ indicates that God's forgiveness is offered on account of Christ. The trinitarian import of this verse involves the manner in which God's forgiveness relates to Christ: he is the ground of God's forgiveness. This relationship, however, need not indicate close personal association in this example. Without denying the existence of such close personal association between Father and Son, this particular reading of ἐν Χριστῷ does not convey it. It was observed above that God's forgiveness in Christ is parallel to the forgiveness that believers are to extend toward each other; as such, their forgiveness is also offered on account of Christ. That being the case, ἐν Χριστῷ expresses an abstract notion here and thus does not connote intimate personal relations.

God's glory—or second reading—that the church brings about God's glory—is adopted, in which case it would indeed be odd for the church to precede Christ. A strength of our third option is that it need not imply any credit to the church, since it is not its activity that brings about the glory of God, nor is the church its 'location'. Rather the very *existence* of the church declares God's glory, and this is wholly dependent on the work of Christ.

Phil 3:14 κατὰ σκοπὸν διώκω εἰς τὸ βραβεῖον τῆς ἄνω κλήσεως τοῦ θεοῦ ἐν Χριστῷ Ἰησοῦ

*I pursue as my goal the prize promised by God's heavenly call **in Christ** Jesus.*

This use of ἐν Χριστῷ is connected to the heavenly call of God. While ἐν Χριστῷ might be understood as modifying Paul's action *I pursue as my goal*, it is more likely modifying *God's heavenly call*. There are at least two plausible options for understanding the function of ἐν Χριστῷ here. First, the phrase may express an instrumental notion. Read this way, ἐν Χριστῷ would refer to the means by which the call of God is issued. The issuing of the call must be understood implicitly, since the actual wording denotes a nominal rather than verbal concept, but it may nevertheless be in view. Second, ἐν Χριστῷ may express *cause* or *reason*, such that the call of God is issued *on account of* Christ. In this way, the phrase would indicate that God's call is not necessarily mediated *through* Christ, but is issued because of his person and work.

These two interpretive options — an instrumental understanding of ἐν Χριστῷ and the expression of cause or reason — both seem possible, and there are no obvious factors to commend one over the other. While far from conclusive, the second option is preferred here. The preference arises from the nature of Paul's pursuance of his goal: it is in pursuit of a prize that is grounded in God's call. It follows, then, that since the concept of being *grounded* is already in view, it may be best to regard ἐν Χριστῷ as indicating *ground, cause*, or *reason*. Paul pursues the prize that is grounded in God's call, which is issued *on account* of Christ; so Martin acknowledges, 'Christ himself is the foundation of the divine summons to sinful men and women'.[132]

Similar to the example directly above, then, the trinitarian import of this verse involves the manner in which the call of God relates to Christ: he is the ground of that call. As above, this example need not convey close personal association.

Phil 4:7 καὶ ἡ εἰρήνη τοῦ θεοῦ ἡ ὑπερέχουσα πάντα νοῦν φρουρήσει τὰς καρδίας ὑμῶν καὶ τὰ νοήματα ὑμῶν **ἐν Χριστῷ** Ἰησοῦ

---

132. Ralph P. Martin, *The Epistle of Paul to the Philippians* (TNTC; rev. ed.; Leicester, UK: Inter-Varsity Press, 1987), 157.

And the peace of God, which surpasses every thought, will guard your hearts and your minds **in Christ Jesus.**

It is argued above (see §3.3) that ἐν Χριστῷ here expresses *cause* or *reason* such that Christ is regarded as the ground on which the peace of God will guard believers' hearts and minds. The trinitarian import of this verse, then, is much the same as the last two examples: it says little regarding the cooperation or intimate relationship between Father and Son. Moreover, in this instance, it is all the more so since *the peace of God* is an abstract concept.

Phil 4:19 ὁ δὲ θεός μου πληρώσει πᾶσαν χρείαν ὑμῶν κατὰ τὸ πλοῦτος αὐτοῦ ἐν δόξῃ **ἐν Χριστῷ Ἰησοῦ**

And my God will supply all your needs according to His riches in glory **in Christ Jesus.**

This use of ἐν Χριστῷ is most likely a marker of association: God's riches in glory are closely associated with Christ (see §3.3). The trinitarian relevance, therefore, is that God's riches are intimately identified with Christ. It is not possible to speculate further, solely on the basis of this verse, as to the nature of this association; we simply note the identification of God's riches with Christ.

1 Thess 5:18 ἐν παντὶ εὐχαριστεῖτε· τοῦτο γὰρ θέλημα θεοῦ **ἐν Χριστῷ Ἰησοῦ εἰς ὑμᾶς**

Give thanks in everything, for this is God's will for you **in Christ Jesus.**

In this example the phrase ἐν Χριστῷ is connected to the will of God. It is not immediately apparent how this use of the phrase should be understood, though three alternatives emerge. First, ἐν Χριστῷ might be locative, so that it connotes the realm or sphere of Christ. Read this way, the phrase would indicate that God's will permeates the realm of Christ's rule: whoever is incorporated into the realm of Christ is subject to God's will. A strength of this option is the correlation between *rule* and *will*: God's will is expressed in and through the rule of Christ, as it pertains to the realm of Christ. A weakness, however, is that it may imply that God's will is restricted to the realm of Christ, as though his will does not reach beyond it. Surely God's will *does* reach through all creation and over all people, regardless of whether they are currently located under the realm of Christ. Then again, the verse specifies the object of God's will: it is εἰς ὑμᾶς. Therefore, one can understand the restriction of God's will to the realm of Christ when applied to those within that realm.

A second option is to view ἐν Χριστῷ as indicating *close association*, such that the will of God is identified with Christ. Again, this alternative is possible, though a little vague. In what sense is the will of God associated with Christ? There are potentially many answers to that question, and that is exactly the point: it is vague. This does not rule out the possibility, but it does weaken its viability.

A third option is to view ἐν Χριστῷ as a 'marker denoting the object ... by which someth. is recognized, *to, by, in connection with*'.[133] Under this reading, God's will is made known in Christ; through his person and work, Christ reveals the will of God.[134] Again, this alternative is certainly possible, and Paul elsewhere speaks of the ways in which Christ reveals God's will. The question is whether this is the most appropriate reading. One difficulty is the sense in which Christ reveals God's will that believers give thanks in everything. To be sure, thanksgiving is an outworking of Christ's work, but in what sense is it revealed as *God's will* through Christ? This is not clear.

Given the strengths and weaknesses of the alternative readings of ἐν Χριστῷ here, it is difficult to decide the issue. Nevertheless, the first option is tentatively adopted here. In support of this reading—that the realm or sphere of Christ is in view—is the universality of the command (for believers, at least). They are to give thanks in *everything*, and the present imperative most likely issues a general command that is to characterize the behaviour of believers.[135] Such universality fits the idea that ἐν Χριστῷ indicates the realm of Christ. All believers are under his rule, the will of God for them pervades the realm of Christ, and believers are to give thanks in all things as part of their general conduct.

---

133. BDAG, 329.

134. So Morris, *Thessalonians*, NICNT, 175.

135. See Constantine R. Campbell, *Verbal Aspect and Non-Indicative Verbs: Further Soundings in the Greek of the New Testament* (SBG 15; New York: Peter Lang, 2008), 91–93.

We turn now to explore the trinitarian implications of this verse. If the tentative conclusion above is adopted, it means that God's will for believers is something that permeates the realm of Christ. Since this *realm of Christ* is a way of speaking of those who fall under the *rule* of Christ, it is interesting that God's will is expressed through Christ's rule. The trinitarian nature of Christ's rule involves the direct expression of the will of his Father.

3.10.1 SUMMARY

So we observe eighteen occasions in which ἐν Χριστῷ is explicitly connected to the work of the Father and the Spirit. While we will need to probe more deeply into these connections and what they mean, a few observations are possible at this stage. It is clear that the Father often works through the instrumentality of Christ. The deeds he performs, the promises he makes, and the attributes he shares with his people are mediated through Christ (1 Cor 1:4; 2 Cor 5:19; Gal 3:14; Eph 2:10). It has also been observed that there is coordination between the work of the Father, Son, and Spirit within the realm of Christ (Rom 8:2; Eph 2:6; 1 Thess 5:18). Certain attributes of the Father are revealed through Christ (Rom 8:39; Eph 2:7; 3:21). There is also the sense in which particular activities of the Father are offered on account of Christ (Eph 4:32; Phil 3:14; 4:7). In at least one case we see the notion of close association between Father and Son (Phil 4:19).

In terms of trinitarian formulation the emphasis is between the Father and Son with relatively little in connection to the Spirit, though of course he is not absent (Rom 8:2). The phrase ἐν Χριστῷ is employed, then, with various trinitarian overtones, some of which have now been explored. Further theological implications of union with Christ for trinitarian thought will be unfolded in due course.

3.11 VARIATIONS OF THE ἐν Χριστῷ IDIOM
3.11.1 IN ... CHRIST

The first step outside the precise phrase ἐν Χριστῷ is to examine occurrences of phrases that are almost identical. There are several instances in which ἐν Χριστῷ has been infiltrated by a word or two, and in many such

cases these will have the same functions as their 'pure' counterparts; ἐν ...
Χριστῷ will normally mean the same thing as ἐν Χριστῷ. Using the same
subcategories as above (as needed), it is to these instances we now turn.

3.11.1.1 Things achieved for/given to people in ... Christ

1 Cor 15:22 ὥσπερ γὰρ ἐν τῷ Ἀδὰμ πάντες ἀποθνήσκουσιν,
οὕτως καὶ ἐν τῷ **Χριστῷ** πάντες ζῳοποιηθήσονται

*For as in Adam all die, so also **in Christ** all will be made alive.*

It could be argued that ἐν τῷ Χριστῷ here has an instrumental meaning such that Paul means to say *so also through Christ all will be made alive.*
This reading is supported by the previous verse, which posits this exactly:
'For since death came through a man, the resurrection of the dead also
comes through a man'. The twice-occurring δι᾽ ἀνθρώπου expression in
v. 21 is probably best understood instrumentally.

On the other hand, the instrumentality of v. 21 might be used to argue
against such a reading in v. 22. If 'in Adam' and 'in Christ' are taken
instrumentally in v. 22, all this adds to v. 21 is illumination as to who the
two 'men' are; it is otherwise tautologous. This is not a defeating argument,
however, since there *is* new information given in v. 22 on an instrumental
reading. Nevertheless, it is more likely that v. 22 is not simply supplying the
names of the two 'men' of v. 21, but is also delimiting those to whom death
comes—those 'in Adam'—and those who will be made alive—those 'in
Christ'. Consequently, it may be better to regard 'in Adam' and 'in Christ'
as expressing the realms under which each group respectively belongs. The
representative nature of Adam and Christ is commonly understood in this
verse; 'Adam is, for Paul, both an individual and a corporate entity',[136] and
Christ likewise. Understood this way, a locative reading of ἐν τῷ Χριστῷ
is best since solidarity within the realm of Christ is in view.

2 Cor 2:14 τῷ δὲ θεῷ χάρις τῷ πάντοτε θριαμβεύοντι ἡμᾶς ἐν τῷ
Χριστῷ καὶ τὴν ὀσμὴν τῆς γνώσεως αὐτοῦ φανεροῦντι δι᾽ ἡμῶν
ἐν παντὶ τόπῳ·

---

136. Thiselton, *1 Corinthians*, 1125. Note, also, the notion of solidarity that Thiselton
explores in this regard (ibid., 1125–26).

> *But thanks be to God, who always puts us on display in Christ, and through us spreads the aroma of the knowledge of Him in every place.*

While the inference is slightly negative in the context, in that Paul's being put on display is not necessarily a happy fact for him, nevertheless, we see that ἐν τῷ Χριστῷ is used in connection with something done for, or to, Paul. In discerning the meaning of ἐν τῷ Χριστῷ, there are two likely contenders. First, Paul might mean ἐν τῷ Χριστῷ as a periphrasis for *Christian*, which was observed as a common use of ἐν Χριστῷ, above. Read this way the verse could be understood, *But thanks be to God, who always puts us Christians on display.* However, this might imply that *all* Christians are put on display — or, literally, in *triumphal procession* — which is not Paul's meaning since the context clearly refers to himself and his fellow workers.[137]

Second, ἐν τῷ Χριστῷ might be understood as providing *cause* or *reason*, such that Paul means, *But thanks be to God, who always puts us on display on account of Christ.* This is to be preferred as it provides a meaningful fit in the context. The triumphal procession refers to Paul's apostolic ministry, which is conducted on account of Christ's person and work, and so it follows that ἐν τῷ Χριστῷ is best understood as referring to that grounding in Christ.

Thus, of the two instances of ἐν ... Χριστῷ in this subcategory, one is locative (1 Cor 15:22) and one indicates cause or reason (2 Cor 2:14).

3.11.1.2 Believers' actions in ... Christ

1 Cor 4:15 ἐὰν γὰρ μυρίους παιδαγωγοὺς ἔχητε ἐν Χριστῷ ἀλλ' οὐ πολλοὺς πατέρας· ἐν γὰρ **Χριστῷ** Ἰησοῦ διὰ τοῦ εὐαγγελίου ἐγὼ ὑμᾶς ἐγέννησα

*For you can have 10,000 instructors in Christ, but you can't have many fathers. For I became your father in **Christ Jesus** through the gospel.*

---

137. Similarly, Hughes's mystical reading of ἐν τῷ Χριστῷ suffers the same problem; Philip Edgcumbe Hughes, *Paul's Second Epistle to the Corinthians* (NICNT; Grand Rapids: Eerdmans, 1962), 78. Cf. Kruse, *2 Corinthians*, 85–86.

The first instance of ἐν Χριστῷ in this verse is dealt with above (being a 'precise' example of the phrase) and is regarded as a periphrasis for *Christian*. The second occurrence—infiltrated by the postpositive conjunction γάρ—refers to Paul's 'begetting' (ἐγέννησα) of the Corinthians by leading them to Christ; thus, it does not adhere to the category of periphrasis for *Christian*, since it modifies an action rather than a person.

Nevertheless, there must be some relationship to the first instance of the phrase, since *instructors in Christ* is contrasted against *fathers (in Christ)* in the first part of the verse. This is then followed in the second part of the verse by begetting language (ἐγέννησα), which no doubt is to be regarded in light of the comment about fathers. Therefore, while ἐν γὰρ Χριστῷ Ἰησοῦ does not fit the category of periphrasis for *Christian* since it modifies a verb rather than a person, it should be understood as the closest verbal equivalent.

Accordingly, the most feasible category for understanding ἐν γὰρ Χριστῷ Ἰησοῦ is as a marker of close personal relationship, 'in which the referent of the ἐν-term is viewed as the controlling influence: *under the control of, under the influence of, in close association with*'.[138] This reading has the benefit of using the same BDAG category under which 'periphrasis for "Christian"' is found,[139] which thus demonstrates the desired relatedness to that use. Furthermore, the category accords well with the notion of Paul's 'begetting' believers; he can only do so under the control of Christ and by his power.

3.11.1.3 Faith in … Christ

Eph 1:12 εἰς τὸ εἶναι ἡμᾶς εἰς ἔπαινον δόξης αὐτοῦ τοὺς προηλπικότας **ἐν τῷ Χριστῷ**

*So that we who had already put our hope **in the Messiah** might bring praise to His glory.*

In this straightforward example, we observe that the phrase ἐν τῷ Χριστῷ indicates the *object* of hope: believers have put their hope in Christ.[140]

---

138. BDAG, 327–28.

139. Ibid., 328. The periphrasis alternative is restricted to nominal referents, while the wider category can include verbal referents.

140. Lincoln, *Ephesians*, 36–37.

3.11.1.4 New status in ... Christ

Gal 5:6 ἐν γὰρ **Χριστῷ** Ἰησοῦ οὔτε περιτομή τι ἰσχύει οὔτε ἀκροβυστία ἀλλὰ πίστις δι᾽ ἀγάπης ἐνεργουμένη

*For **in Christ** Jesus neither circumcision nor uncircumcision accomplishes anything; what matters is faith working through love.*

Here Paul is describing what really matters for believers — faith and love matter; circumcision and uncircumcision do not. This is connected to ἐν ... Χριστῷ. In the first instance, it appears that Christian behaviour is in view: circumcision *accomplishes* nothing; faith *works* through love. As such, it would follow that ἐν ... Χριστῷ takes on an adverbial character, modifying the activities in view.

Against this reading, however, is the wider context in which the new status of believers is in view. In 5:1 Paul states 'Christ has liberated us to be free', and this sets the topic for the remainder of the pericope (5:1 – 6). The status of freedom informs Paul's injunctions against circumcision in vv. 2 – 3. Verse 4 clarifies that status is still in view when he says, 'You who are trying to be justified by the law are alienated from Christ; you have fallen from grace!' In this context, v. 6 is best read in light of the status of freedom established in v. 1: 'In Christ Jesus neither circumcision nor uncircumcision accomplishes anything' is a statement about the irrelevancy of such things for those who have been liberated by Christ.

As with the examples above relating to new status (see §3.8), the most likely option for understanding this use of ἐν ... Χριστῷ is that it refers to the realm or sphere of Christ.[141] Within the realm of Christ — in which true freedom is found — circumcision and uncircumcision count for nothing; rather, it is faith working through love that matters to those who have been set free.

Eph 1:10 εἰς οἰκονομίαν τοῦ πληρώματος τῶν καιρῶν, ἀνακεφαλαιώσασθαι τὰ πάντα ἐν τῷ **Χριστῷ**, τὰ ἐπὶ τοῖς οὐρανοῖς καὶ τὰ ἐπὶ τῆς γῆς ἐν αὐτῷ

---

141. So Martyn: 'Paul and his comrades live in the realm established by the coming of Christ.' J. Louis Martyn, *Galatians* (AB; New York: Doubleday, 1997), 472.

*For the administration of the days of fulfillment—to bring every-
thing together **in the Messiah**, both things in heaven and things on
earth in Him.*

This example differs to others in this category in that it envisages a
new status of *everything*, not just that of believers. The new status is the
cosmic unity of all things in heaven and on earth. Here Paul refers to the
bringing together of everything *in ... Christ* and thus views Christ as a
central focal point in whom all things find unity.

While this example could be viewed as an instrumental use of ἐν τῷ
Χριστῷ, such that it means *to bring everything together by Christ*, this option
is not as compelling as a locative reading. One reason for this is that the
verse concludes with *in Him*, which seems to reiterate the point made in the
previous clause: everything together in Christ; things in heaven and earth
in him. This final phrase is more difficult to read as instrumental; it makes
best sense as expressing locality. For that reason, it is also best to regard the
ἐν τῷ Χριστῷ expression as conveying location rather than instrumentality.

Thus, a locative sense is seen here in that Christ is the centerpoint
toward whom all things are drawn—they are together *in him*. As O'Brien
writes, 'Christ is the one *in whom* God chooses to sum up the cosmos, the
one in whom he restores harmony to the universe. He is the focal point,
not simply the means, the instrument, or the functionary through whom
all this occurs.'[142]

Thus, both examples of ἐν ... Χριστῷ in this subcategory are regarded
as locative, expressing realm or sphere (Gal 5:6; Eph 1:10).

3.11.1.5 Trinity in ... Christ

Eph 1:20 ἣν ἐνήργησεν ἐν τῷ **Χριστῷ** ἐγείρας αὐτὸν ἐκ νεκρῶν
καὶ καθίσας ἐν δεξιᾷ αὐτοῦ ἐν τοῖς ἐπουρανίοις

*He demonstrated this power **in the Messiah** by raising Him from the
dead and seating Him at His right hand in the heavens.*

The phrase ἐν τῷ Χριστῷ appears to indicate the object toward which
God worked (ἐνήργησεν) his power,[143] being accommodated by the BDAG

---

142. O'Brien, *Ephesians*, 111–12.
143. This takes τὴν ἐνέργειαν (v. 19) as the antecedent of ἣν (v. 20), though it could also

category, 'marker denoting the object to which someth. happens or in which someth. shows itself, or by which someth. is recognized'.[144] Christ is certainly the object of *raising* and *seating*, so it seems reasonable to understand ἐν τῷ Χριστῷ in the same way.

The trinitarian import of this verse relates to how the power of the Father acts on the Son. While both persons of the Godhead share the divine nature, Paul sees no contradiction in viewing one as directly acting on another.

Eph 3:11 κατὰ πρόθεσιν τῶν αἰώνων ἣν ἐποίησεν **ἐν τῷ Χριστῷ** Ἰησοῦ τῷ κυρίῳ ἡμῶν

This is according to His eternal purpose accomplished **in the Messiah,** *Jesus our Lord.*

This use of ἐν τῷ Χριστῷ is most likely to be understood as instrumental, describing the manner in which God accomplished (ἐποίησεν) *His eternal purpose.*[145] Christ is the one in whom the Father has brought about his purpose. From a triniarian point of view, we once again witness the intimate cooperation of Father and Son, as the Son implements the will of the Father and as the Father's agency is brought to bear through the Son.

Of the two examples of ἐν ... Χριστῷ here, one indicates the object in which something shows itself (Eph 1:20), while one is instrumental (Eph 3:11).

3.11.1.6 Summary
All instances of ἐν ... Χριστῷ are accommodated within the same subcategories as the various uses of ἐν Χριστῷ. This is not surprising, and there does not seem to be any good reason for regarding these instances of ἐν ... Χριστῷ as functioning differently to ἐν Χριστῷ.

3.11.2 IN THE LORD
The next most sensible step out from ἐν Χριστῷ is to examine the instances of ἐν κυρίῳ. It is reasonable to assume that there is no serious distinction in

---

be τῆς ἰσχύος αὐτοῦ (or, less likely, τῆς δυνάμεως αὐτοῦ).

144. BDAG, 329.

145. Barth, *Ephesians 1–3*, 347. Barth uses the term 'agent' in the way I employ 'instrument'.

Paul's use of this phrase compared to ἐν Χριστῷ. In order to test the validity of this assumption, however, all the uses in Paul's letters of ἐν κυρίῳ are surveyed below. The phrases ἐν ... κυρίῳ are included in the same subcategory given there is likely no difference between these and ἐν κυρίῳ, as observed for ἐν Χριστῷ and ἐν ... Χριστῷ.

3.11.2.1 Things achieved for/given to people in the Lord

1 Cor 7:22 ὁ γὰρ **ἐν κυρίῳ** κληθεὶς δοῦλος ἀπελεύθερος κυρίου ἐστίν, ὁμοίως ὁ ἐλεύθερος κληθεὶς δοῦλός ἐστιν Χριστοῦ

*For he who is called **by the Lord** as a slave is the Lord's freedman. Likewise he who is called as a free man is Christ's slave.*

In this instance, it might be tempting to regard ἐν κυρίῳ as a periphrasis for *Christian*, since calling is in view. However, there is some cause not to do so and instead to regard it as instrumental in function here. The most compelling reason for this is the fact that the notion of being *Christian* already occurs twice in the verse, in parallel formation: *For he who is called by the Lord as a slave is the Lord's freedman. Likewise he who is called as a free man is Christ's slave.* Both slave and free belong to the Lord; they are *Christian* freedmen and slaves. If *he who is called by the Lord* is understood as *he who is called to be a Christian*, this would not only be redundant; it would unbalance the parallelism. Thus, it makes better sense to read the first phrase as *he who is called by the Lord*, rendering ἐν κυρίῳ as instrumental and viewing the parallelism of the Lord's freedman and the Lord's slave as the twin results of this instrumental action.[146]

An instrumental reading may raise an objection, namely, that there is no explicit agency in view. It is sound, however, to assume the agency of God. While such agency is not directly mentioned, which is unusual for clear cases of instrumentality, there is a hint of it in v. 24: *Brothers, each person should remain with God in whatever situation he was called.* By

---

146. Fee rejects an instrumental reading, which 'seems to miss the sense of the whole passage. The calling is to be "in Christ," which has to do with one's relationship with him'; Fee, *1 Corinthians*, 318, n. 53. Fee's verdict on the instrumental reading is subjective and his own interpretation is problematic. If Paul meant to say *he who is called to be in the Lord*, one would expect the verb *to be*, probably in the infinitive. Without the equative verb, Fee's reading is difficult and less appealing than a reading that does not require it.

describing a believer as *with God* (παρὰ θεῷ) when he is *called* (ἐκλήθη), Paul has established an oblique parallel with v. 22. In v. 22 the call of Christ results in people belonging to Christ; in v. 24 calling results in being with God. If belonging to Christ can be equated to being with God, then the call of v. 24 can be equated with the call of Christ in v. 22. This makes the parallel complete: just as the call of Christ results in belonging to Christ (v. 22), so the call of God results in being with God (v. 24). We have thereby established the agency of God in the act of calling, and it is effected through the instrumentality of Christ.[147]

1 Cor 11:11 πλὴν οὔτε γυνὴ χωρὶς ἀνδρὸς οὔτε ἀνὴρ χωρὶς γυναικὸς **ἐν κυρίῳ**

In the Lord, *however, woman is not independent of man, and man is not independent of woman.*

There are two likely contenders for understanding this instance of ἐν κυρίῳ. First, it may be locative in function, indicating the realm of Christ. The verse then expresses that under Christ's rule, woman is not independent of man and vice versa. Since Paul is addressing the issue of orderly conduct within Christian congregations, the relationship of women to men in the domain of Christ makes some sense. A potential weakness of this reading, however, is that from 11:8 Paul has widened his lens to refer to the relationship between men and women in creation: *For man did not come from woman, but woman came from man. And man was not created for woman, but woman for man* (11:8–9). Since Paul is discussing the creation order in the immediate context, it is less likely that ἐν κυρίῳ specifies a mutual dependence between men and women that is particular to the realm of Christ; such mutual dependence is a fact of creation, within Christ's realm and without.

Second, the phrase may indicate instrumentality, pointing to the work of the Lord in establishing the mutual dependence between man and woman. This reading suitably fits the creation motif of the immediate context. Indeed, the following verse reinforces the likelihood of this reading. Verse 12 relates to v. 11 in an epexegetical manner so that the

---

147. See also 1 Cor 7:17.

mutual dependence cited in v. 11 is explained in v. 12: *For just as woman came from man, so man comes through woman, and all things come from God.* While v. 12a–b unpacks the mutual dependence of v. 11, the final clause of v. 12 supports the instrumentality of ἐν κυρίῳ in v. 11. Just as *all things come from God* indicates that God is the ultimate agent (v. 12), so ἐν κυρίῳ indicates that the Lord is his instrument (v. 11).[148] For this reason, an instrumental reading of ἐν κυρίῳ is stronger than a locative reading.[149]

2 Cor 2:12 ἐλθὼν δὲ εἰς τὴν Τρῳάδα εἰς τὸ εὐαγγέλιον τοῦ Χριστοῦ καὶ θύρας μοι ἀνεῳγμένης **ἐν κυρίῳ**

When I came to Troas for the gospel of Christ, a door was opened to me **in the Lord** (pers. trans.).

There can be little doubt that in this instance ἐν κυρίῳ expresses the instrumentality of Christ.[150] The only other possibility would be to regard the phrase as expressing *cause* or *reason*, such that the verse is understood, *When I came to Troas for the gospel of Christ, a door was opened to me on account of the Lord.* This, however, is unlikely because it is unclear how or by whom the door was opened and why it would be opened on account of Christ.

Again, however, an objection may be raised here against instrumentality — that there is no explicit agent in view. But as with previous examples, it is safely assumed that the agency of God is understood[151] — indeed, a hint of this is evident in v. 14, which says *But thanks be to God, who always puts us on display in Christ.* This implies that God directs the apostle's path and

---

148. It is to be noted that ἐν κυρίῳ could refer to God rather than Christ, given the parallels between v. 11 and v. 12. On this reading, both verses would indicate agency; the Lord is agent in v. 11 and God in v. 12 — the same person in view in both verses. This is not essential, however, since the parallel does not necessitate agency in both verses, but more likely indicates instrumentality in v. 11 and agency in v.12. Moreover, standard Pauline usage pushes us to take κύριος as referring to Christ.

149. Ciampa and Rosner seem to prefer this option, citing that an instrumental reading would correspond perfectly to Jewish exegetical tradition about the Lord's role in the formation of every human being (*y. Berakot* 9:1; *Genesis Rabbah* 8:9; 22:2) and would strengthen the parallel between v. 11 and v. 12; Ciampa and Rosner, *1 Corinthians*, 535.

150. Note Martin's translation, *by the Lord*; Martin, *2 Corinthians*, 41. The NIV has: 'the Lord had opened a door for me'.

151. Victor Paul Furnish, *2 Corinthians* (AB; Garden City: Doubleday, 1984), 169.

controls his mission. As such, it follows that God's agency is at work when the Lord opens a door for Paul (2:12).

Eph 2:21 ἐν ᾧ πᾶσα οἰκοδομὴ συναρμολογουμένη αὔξει εἰς ναὸν ἅγιον **ἐν κυρίῳ**

*The whole building, being put together by Him, grows into a holy sanctuary **in the Lord.***

The most likely understanding of ἐν κυρίῳ here is that it expresses incorporation into the Lord. The immediate context provides plenty of evidence for this reading, beginning with the description of Christ as the cornerstone of the new building (2:20). The building metaphor on its own implies incorporation, since believers are built into this building of which Christ is the cornerstone; the formation of a 'building' together with the Lord inherently implies incorporation. Furthermore, this building is *being put together by Him* (2:21), which strengthens the implied incorporation already inherent to the building metaphor.

The following verse underscores the concept even further: [*in whom*] *you also are being built together for God's dwelling in the Spirit* (2:22). Not only is the building fitted together in him (2:21), it is also built together in him (2:22). The plethora of indications of incorporation in these few verses therefore make it the most compelling reading of ἐν κυρίῳ in 2:21. O'Brien captures the sense well, 'So to speak of the building being *joined together* refers not simply to the union of one stone with another, but also the union of the whole structure with (and in) the cornerstone.'[152]

Eph 6:10 τοῦ λοιποῦ, ἐνδυναμοῦσθε **ἐν κυρίῳ** καὶ ἐν τῷ κράτει τῆς ἰσχύος αὐτοῦ

*Finally, be strengthened **by the Lord** and by His vast strength.*

Despite first impressions, this is a difficult example to navigate. Not only is ἐν κυρίῳ inherently ambiguous—with the possible meanings *by the Lord* and *in the Lord*—but so is the verb accompanying it. The verb ἐνδυναμοῦσθε can be either middle or passive in voice, and each enables a different rendering of the meaning of the verse.

---

152. O'Brien, *Ephesians*, 219.

If ἐνδυναμοῦσθε is understood as passive in voice — translated as *be strengthened* — ἐν κυρίῳ is most naturally understood as instrumental, as rendered above: *be strengthened by the Lord*.[153] This is plausible, especially given the second half of the verse in which believers are to be strengthened not only by the Lord, but also by his vast strength. If, however, ἐνδυναμοῦσθε is understood as middle in voice — translated as *be strong* — then the phrase ἐν κυρίῳ has a few possible senses, the most likely of which is the expression of union. Under this reading, believers are closely associated or connected to the Lord and his vast strength and are commanded to be strong by virtue of that association; they are to be strong *in the Lord and in his vast strength*.

It is difficult to ascertain whether Paul intended ἐνδυναμοῦσθε to be middle or passive since other occurrences of the lexeme in Pauline usage attest to both possibilities (as well as active voice uses; see Rom 4:20; Phil 4:13; 1 Tim 1:12; 2 Tim 2:1; 4:17). Indeed, Paul can employ the verb to express the agency or instrumentality of the Lord (1 Tim 1:12) or solidarity with him (2 Tim 4:17). As such, similar notions within Paul's thinking do not shed enough light to be decisive. It will be more instructive, therefore, to rely on the internal logic of the passage in its immediate and wider context.

First, the following verse (6:11) contains a middle aorist imperative: *put on the full armor of God*. This lends some weight to the possibility of ἐνδυναμοῦσθε in 6:10 as being a middle imperative also, thus creating two adjacent and similar commands: *be strong in the Lord* and *put on the full armor of God*. Such parallelism would be neater than *be strengthened by the Lord* and *put on the full armor of God*, since the first command is to receive strengthening *passively*, while the second is to take up the armor of God *actively*.

Second, an instrumental reading of ἐν κυρίῳ in 6:10 contains a mild internal difficulty. There is tension between the command *be strengthened* and *by the Lord*, since the instrumentality (or agency) of the Lord is in view, and yet the command is directed to believers. This creates cognitive dissonance between the command itself and those commanded. In other words, believers are commanded to do this and yet it is the Lord who does

---

153. Note, however, that Lincoln takes ἐνδυναμοῦσθε as passive but does not read ἐν κυρίῳ as instrumental — it indicates relationship to Christ; Lincoln, *Ephesians*, 441–42.

it. But if the verse expresses union, such a disjunction is resolved since believers are instructed to be strong *in* the Lord—rather than strengthened *by* the Lord; the command is executed by those commanded rather than a third party.[154]

Third, the wider context suggests that an expression of union is more likely than an instrumental reading. Throughout Ephesians 6:10–17, the listed armour of God not only resonates with Roman military weaponry but also with descriptions of Yahweh (and/or his Messiah) in battle as found in Isaiah.[155] Thus, one of the implications of 6:10–17 is that believers are to put on the armour that the Lord himself wears in battle, which evokes a sense of union with him in the matter of spiritual warfare. Given that this union pervades the whole pericope, it is reasonable to conclude that ἐν κυρίῳ in 6:10 conveys union with the Lord.[156] The sense of the instruction, then, is that believers are to be strong by virtue of their union with Christ: they are to be strong *in the Lord* and in his vast strength. The ensuing passage teases out what that entails when it comes to spiritual warfare; through their union with Christ, believers share in his armour and have solidarity with him in battle.

Col 4:17 καὶ εἴπατε Ἀρχίππῳ· βλέπε τὴν διακονίαν ἣν παρέλαβες ἐν κυρίῳ, ἵνα αὐτὴν πληροῖς

*And tell Archippus, 'Pay attention to the ministry you have received **in the Lord**, so that you can accomplish it.'*

This instance of ἐν κυρίῳ could denote at least three different meanings. First, ἐν κυρίῳ could convey specification or substance (BDAG), in which *the Lord* is regarded as the substance of Archippus's ministry. This

---

154. Lincoln prefers the passive rather than middle voice reading because it reinforces 'the notion that the strength is to be drawn from an external source'; Lincoln, *Ephesians*, 441. However, a middle voice reading does not here imply that believers' own strength is to be drawn upon, since they are to be strong 'in the Lord'. Note that Barth takes a middle voice reading while affirming that 'a power which comes to man from outside is meant, rather than an increase in strength flowing from internal resources'; Markus Barth, *Ephesians: Introduction, Translation, and Commentary on Chapters 4–6* (AB; Garden City, NY: Doubleday, 1974), 760.

155. O'Brien, *Ephesians*, 463 ff.

156. So Lincoln, 'Believers' relationship to Christ gives them access to his power'; Lincoln, *Ephesians*, 442.

presumably would be a fitting description of his ministry, which no doubt centred on Christ. A weakness of this approach, however, is that ἐν κυρίῳ qualifies the verb *received* (παρέλαβες) rather than Archippus's ministry as such. Paul is not, then, specifying the substance of Archippus's ministry so much as describing the nature in which this ministry was received.

Second, ἐν κυρίῳ could convey cause or reason: *the ministry you have received because of the Lord*. Read this way, the phrase expresses the origin of Archippus's ministry — it exists because of the work (or person) of the Lord. Nevertheless, it seems a little strained to conceive of the ministry as being received *because of* the Lord. It is not clear why Archippus received his ministry because of the Lord, nor from whom he received it, since the reading implies the agency of a third party.

Third, then, is the reading that treats ἐν κυρίῳ as expressing agency: *the ministry you received from the Lord*. This option seems most likely as it provides the best fit for the verb *received*. If ἐν κυρίῳ does indeed qualify the verb rather than Archippus's ministry, as claimed above, then the agency of that action makes best sense.

Of the 6 uses of ἐν κυρίῳ in this subcategory, three are instrumental (1 Cor 7:22; 11:11; 2 Cor 2:12), one expresses incorporation (Eph 2:21), one indicates union (Eph 6:10), and one conveys agency (Col 4:17).

3.11.2.2 Believers' actions in the Lord

Rom 16:2 ἵνα αὐτὴν προσδέξησθε **ἐν κυρίῳ** ἀξίως τῶν ἁγίων καὶ παραστῆτε αὐτῇ ἐν ᾧ ἂν ὑμῶν χρῄζῃ πράγματι· καὶ γὰρ αὐτὴ προστάτις πολλῶν ἐγενήθη καὶ ἐμοῦ αὐτοῦ

*So you should welcome her **in the Lord** in a manner worthy of the saints and assist her in whatever matter she may require your help. For indeed she has been a benefactor of many — and of me also.*

This occurrence of ἐν κυρίῳ modifies the imperative *welcome* (προσδέξησθε) and is most likely either expressing cause or manner. If the former, the idea would be that *because of the Lord* the Romans are to welcome Phoebe. The Lord is the cause of their shared bond and fellowship and the Romans are to express this fellowship through their welcome of Phoebe among them. If the latter, the idea would be that the Romans are to welcome Phoebe in a manner that may best be described as *in the Lord*.

The latter reading—expressing kind or manner of action—is most likely here because of the immediate context. The phrase following ἐν κυρίῳ expresses manner through the adverbial phrase *in a manner worthy of the saints* (ἀξίως τῶν ἁγίων). It is possible that both phrases are correlated to the original imperative so that both express the manner in which the Romans are to welcome Phoebe; 'by it Paul simply means that the Roman Christians are to give Phoebe a "Christian" welcome. The additional qualification, "in a manner worthy of the saints," expands on this same point.'[157] Furthermore, the final phrase of the verse provides the cause for the imperative: *for indeed she has been a benefactor of many—and of me also.* As such, it is unlikely that ἐν κυρίῳ expresses cause since a different cause is offered only a few phrases later.

Rom 16:12 ἀσπάσασθε Τρύφαιναν καὶ Τρυφῶσαν τὰς κοπιώσας **ἐν κυρίῳ**. ἀσπάσασθε Περσίδα τὴν ἀγαπητήν, ἥτις πολλὰ ἐκοπίασεν **ἐν κυρίῳ**

*Greet Tryphaena and Tryphosa, who have worked hard **in the Lord.*** *Greet my dear friend Persis, who has worked very hard **in the Lord.***

Both these examples of ἐν κυρίῳ refer to work that is conducted *in the Lord.* The two most likely options for understanding what is meant are close association and cause. The former option would regard ἐν κυρίῳ as indicating work that has been conducted in close association in terms of controlling influence: these believers are *under the control of, under the influence of* the Lord (BDAG).

The latter option, however, might prove more likely. A causal reading understands ἐν κυρίῳ as expressing the reason for their work. They are working on account of, for, and with respect to Christ. In this way, Paul's intention is to indicate the kind of work in which these believers have been labouring; it is the Lord's work. This reading seems stronger than the former because Paul's praise is more likely related to the type of work that has occupied them than whether they have worked under the Lord's influence. Surely every believer is expected to work under the Lord's influence (whatever work that may be), so why would these

---

157. Moo, *Romans*, 915.

believers deserve special mention?[158] The mention is warranted because Paul refers to Christian ministry, which is entrusted to some. Hence, the Romans are to greet those who have laboured in Christian service.

Rom 16:22 ἀσπάζομαι ὑμᾶς ἐγὼ Τέρτιος ὁ γράψας τὴν ἐπιστολὴν ἐν κυρίῳ

*I Tertius, who wrote this letter **in the Lord**, greet you* (HCSB footnote trans.).

The difficulty of this occurrence of ἐν κυρίῳ is establishing whether the phrase modifies *who wrote this letter* (ὁ γράψας τὴν ἐπιστολὴν) or *I ... greet you* (ἀσπάζομαι ὑμᾶς), both of which are grammatically possible. The modification of *who wrote this letter* is the most straightforward in terms of word order, since ἐν κυρίῳ follows ὁ γράψας τὴν ἐπιστολὴν. If read this way, ἐν κυρίῳ describes either the activity of writing the epistle or the nature of the epistle itself.

The phrase could, however, be understood as modifying *I greet you*, if the participial clause ὁ γράψας τὴν ἐπιστολὴν functions as discontinuous syntax—that is, if it is 'bracketed' as a self-contained unit, while ἐν κυρίῳ then continues the principal clause ἀσπάζομαι ὑμᾶς ἐγὼ Τέρτιος. The ambiguity of the syntax is reflected in the translations. While the HCSB footnote translation (above) regards ἐν κυρίῳ as modifying ὁ γράψας τὴν ἐπιστολὴν, the NIV and ESV treat it as modifying ἀσπάζομαι: *I Tertius, who wrote this letter, greet you in the Lord* (ESV). Since either reading is possible and there are no other determining factors, it seems most prudent to adopt the most straightforward option and view ἐν κυρίῳ as modifying ὁ γράψας τὴν ἐπιστολὴν.[159]

The next difficulty relates to whether ἐν κυρίῳ modifies the participle ὁ γράψας, thereby contributing an adverbial nuance, or τὴν ἐπιστολὴν,

---

158. This stands against Moo's reading that takes ἐν κυρίῳ here in the same way that he understands it in 16:2; that is, 'christianly'; Moo, *Romans*, 925, 915. Again, surely all believers are to work 'christianly', so why are these workers singled out?

159. Most recent commentators follow Cranfield, who takes ἐν κυρίῳ with ἀσπάζομαι. While he acknowledges the attractiveness of the alternative, Cranfield concludes that 'the balance of probability would seem to lie with the more commonly held view that ἐν κυρίῳ should be taken with ἀσπάζομαι'; Cranfield, *Romans*, 2:806. Unfortunately, Cranfield does not specify what factors contribute to this balance of probability, while (somewhat ironically) he lists several factors in support of the alternative he rejects.

thereby contributing an adjectival element. If Tertius is describing the activity of writing this letter, it is not entirely clear how ἐν κυρίῳ modifies it. Some of the usual options are cancelled here by virtue of the fact that Tertius is not the apostolic author of Romans but merely the scribe. For instance, agency (*with the help of the Lord*), close association (*under the influence of the Lord*), and causal (*because of the Lord*) readings might apply to Paul as the author of the letter, but do not seem apposite for a scribe.

Nevertheless, it is appropriate to regard the letter itself as modified by ἐν κυρίῳ. In light of this, the most likely category recognized by BDAG would be that of *specification or substance*. The letter concerns the Lord, whose person and work form its substance. Consequently, Tertius sends his greetings to the Romans as the scribe who wrote this letter concerning Christ.

1 Cor 1:31 ἵνα καθὼς γέγραπται· ὁ καυχώμενος **ἐν κυρίῳ** καυχάσθω

*In order that, as it is written: The one who boasts must boast **in the Lord**.*

This instance of ἐν κυρίῳ clearly modifies the imperative καυχάσθω. The statement implies that boasting about oneself or one's own achievements is inappropriate, so if there is to be boasting at all, it must be boasting that glorifies and praises the Lord. Consequently, the most likely reading of ἐν κυρίῳ is that which denotes *specification* or *substance*: the boaster is to boast with reference to the Lord; he is the subject and content of such boasting.[160]

The only plausible alternative to this reading of ἐν κυρίῳ here is to regard it as indicating *kind* or *manner* such that boasting is to be conducted, that is, in a way that is pleasing to the Lord or consistent with his intentions and principles. The weakness of this alternative, however, is that it sanctions boasting itself as an activity; it would allow boasting — without specifying its content — so long as it is conducted in a manner worthy of the Lord. It is difficult to imagine what sort of boasting would be pleasing to the Lord if not in him, since human boasting is so often

---

160. See Ciampa and Rosner for the allusions here to Jer 9:24 and 1 Sam 2:10 LXX in support of this reading; Ciampa and Rosner, *1 Corinthians*, 110–11.

self-serving. Thus, the former reading that regards ἐν κυρίῳ as specifying the content of boasting is most appropriate.

1 Cor 9:1 οὐκ εἰμὶ ἐλεύθερος; οὐκ εἰμὶ ἀπόστολος; οὐχὶ Ἰησοῦν τὸν κύριον ἡμῶν ἑόρακα; οὐ τὸ ἔργον μου ὑμεῖς ἐστε **ἐν κυρίῳ;**

*Am I not free? Am I not an apostle? Have I not seen Jesus our Lord? Are you not my work **in the Lord**?*

This example is similar to Romans 16:12 (above) in which work conducted *in the Lord* refers to the labour of Christian ministry. The key difference here is that the 'work' is a noun rather than a verb and refers to *people*. It is probably best, however, to regard ἐν κυρίῳ as operating the same way as in Romans 16:12 in order to express the nature, cause, and purpose of Paul's work: it is Christian ministry to which he refers. The shift that has occurred here, however, in describing his work as *people* most likely indicates the *fruit* of his labour. The Corinthians are Paul's *work* insofar as their lives are the product of Paul's ministry among them.[161]

1 Cor 15:58 ὥστε, ἀδελφοί μου ἀγαπητοί, ἑδραῖοι γίνεσθε, ἀμετακίνητοι, περισσεύοντες ἐν τῷ ἔργῳ τοῦ κυρίου πάντοτε, εἰδότες ὅτι ὁ κόπος ὑμῶν οὐκ ἔστιν κενὸς **ἐν κυρίῳ**

*Therefore, my dear brothers, be steadfast, immovable, always excelling in the Lord's work, knowing that your labor **in the Lord** is not in vain.*

Again, this reference to *labor in the Lord* most likely describes Christian service. It is work conducted for the cause of Christ. This reading seems all the more likely in this passage for two reasons. First, this labour is referred to earlier in the verse as *the Lord's work* (ἐν τῷ ἔργῳ τοῦ κυρίου). This genitive expression is more explicit than the flexible dative ἐν κυρίῳ. While the latter could refer to labour that is conducted in a manner worthy of the Lord—and thus not necessarily denoting Christian service per se—the former does not allow such a broad possibility. The *work of the*

Lord or *the Lord's work* refers to Christian service conducted for the cause and purposes of the Lord.[162]

Second, Paul declares that such labour is not in vain. It is difficult, though perhaps not impossible, to imagine that Paul would claim such a thing about any kind of work. While it may be true that any work performed in honour of the Lord has integrity (cf. Col 3:23), Paul is here referring to the work itself rather than the manner in which the work is conducted. Not all work — even that conducted faithfully by Christians — can reasonably be described as *labor in the Lord*. Thus, this point, in conjunction with the first, suggests that *labor in the Lord* refers to Christian service; ἐν κυρίῳ specifies the nature of the work rather than the manner in which it is conducted.

1 Cor 16:19 ἀσπάζονται ὑμᾶς αἱ ἐκκλησίαι τῆς Ἀσίας. ἀσπάζεται ὑμᾶς **ἐν κυρίῳ** πολλὰ Ἀκύλας καὶ Πρίσκα σὺν τῇ κατ᾽ οἶκον αὐτῶν ἐκκλησίᾳ

*The churches of Asia greet you. Aquila and Priscilla greet you warmly **in the Lord**, along with the church that meets in their home.*

The notion of greeting someone *in the Lord* is similar to welcoming someone *in the Lord*, an example of which is provided above in Romans 16:2. In that instance, it is suggested that ἐν κυρίῳ expresses *kind* or *manner*, thus characterizing the activity of welcoming as Christian in nature. The same approach is likely here, so that Aquila and Priscilla's greeting is characterized as a *Christian* greeting. In other words, they greet the Corinthians as believers to believers, expressing their bond of common faith and fellowship.[163]

2 Cor 10:17 ὁ δὲ καυχώμενος **ἐν κυρίῳ** καυχάσθω

*So the one who boasts must boast **in the Lord**.*

---

162. Fee's comments are helpful, 'It is not absolutely certain what kind of activity Paul had in mind by the phrase "the work of the Lord." Minimally, it may refer more broadly to whatever one does *as a Christian* ... but along with the next word, "labor," Paul frequently uses it to refer to the actual ministry of the gospel. Probably in their case it covers the range but leans more toward the former. That is, there are those kinds of activities in which believers engage that are specifically Christian, or specifically in the interest of the gospel. This seems to be what Paul has in mind here'; Fee, *1 Corinthians*, 808.

163. Ciampa and Rosner, *1 Corinthians*, 861.

For this use see 1 Corinthians 1:31 above.

Eph 4:17 τοῦτο οὖν λέγω καὶ μαρτύρομαι **ἐν κυρίῳ**, μηκέτι ὑμᾶς περιπατεῖν, καθὼς καὶ τὰ ἔθνη περιπατεῖ ἐν ματαιότητι τοῦ νοὸς αὐτῶν

*Therefore, I say this and testify **in the Lord**: You should no longer walk as the Gentiles walk, in the futility of their thoughts.*

The two most likely possibilities for understanding this use of ἐν κυρίῳ are *causal* and *kind* or *manner*. If causal, the sense of the expression is that Paul speaks and testifies in this way because of the Lord; such is a plausible reading. If the phrase is understood as expressing kind or manner, however, Paul's meaning is that he speaks and testifies in a way that is characterized by the Lord. In other words, Paul uses ἐν κυρίῳ to underscore the truth, and perhaps also authority, of his testimony.

The second reading, in which ἐν κυρίῳ expresses kind or manner, is to be preferred here for one reason. The verb *testify* (μαρτύρομαι) introduces the notion of truth telling as a specific interest. Paul does not merely wish to say what he says; he says it as a word of testimony and of witness. As such, he is concerned to underscore the integrity and veracity of his statement. Consequently, understanding ἐν κυρίῳ to express the manner in which Paul testifies is apposite. Paul's testimony conforms to the Lord and is therefore genuine and authoritative.[164]

Eph 6:1 τὰ τέκνα, ὑπακούετε τοῖς γονεῦσιν ὑμῶν [**ἐν κυρίῳ**]· τοῦτο γάρ ἐστιν δίκαιον

*Children, obey your parents **in the Lord**, for this is right.* (NASB)

This instance of ἐν κυρίῳ could modify *your parents*, thus designating such parents as Christian, or the imperative *obey*, thus designating some kind of adverbial nuance. It is unlikely that Paul intends children only to obey Christian parents, so specifying the parents as Christian seems unnecessary.[165] The phrase ἐν κυρίῳ is, therefore, more likely modifying the imperative.[166]

---

164. O'Brien, *Ephesians*, 319.
165. Obedience of children to their parents was taken for granted in the ancient world (ibid., 441).
166. Best, *Ephesians*, 564.

The adverbial nature of ἐν κυρίῳ is probably not causal, since an explicit cause is given in the last clause of the verse: *for this is right.* The reason for children to obey their parents is simply that that is the right thing to do. While ἐν κυρίῳ could express kind or manner, such that children's obedience is *Christian* obedience, this also seems unlikely since obeying one's parents is *right*; it does not need to be Christian obedience to be so.

A possible solution is to regard ἐν κυρίῳ as locative, indicating the sphere of Christ. This would envisage the household code as characteristic of families that live under Christ's reign. Thus the adverbial sense of ἐν κυρίῳ contributes to the context of the imperative issued to children: they are members of families that live in the domain of Christ. This does not contradict the point made above, that obedience to parents is right whether Christian or not, but indicates that within the realm of Christ, families are to be characterized by what is right.

Phil 3:1 τὸ λοιπόν, ἀδελφοί μου, χαίρετε **ἐν κυρίῳ**. τὰ αὐτὰ γράφειν ὑμῖν ἐμοὶ μὲν οὐκ ὀκνηρόν, ὑμῖν δὲ ἀσφαλές

*Finally, my brothers, rejoice **in the Lord**. To write to you again about this is no trouble for me and is a protection for you.*

The most plausible reading of ἐν κυρίῳ here is that it expresses cause. Believers are to rejoice because of the Lord; presumably because of who he is and what he has done, the relationship that believers have with him that gives rise to such an instruction. Bruce acknowledges the echo here of an exhortation repeated in the Psalms (Pss 32:11; 33:1); 'The people of God rejoice in him because he is their "exceeding joy" (Ps 43:4).'[167]

Phil 4:1 ὥστε, ἀδελφοί μου ἀγαπητοὶ καὶ ἐπιπόθητοι, χαρὰ καὶ στέφανός μου, οὕτως στήκετε **ἐν κυρίῳ**, ἀγαπητοί

So then, my brothers, you are dearly loved and longed for—my joy and crown. In this manner stand firm in the Lord, dear friends.

This example of ἐν κυρίῳ could express cause, such that believers are instructed to stand firm *because of the Lord*; he is their reason and purpose for standing firm in their convictions. While possible, this reading is

---

167. Bruce, *Philippians*, 101.

weakened by the fact that the location or position of their standing is not specified if ἐν κυρίῳ expresses cause. Consequently, ἐν κυρίῳ most likely denotes the locative concept of the sphere of the Lord, thereby specifying the location and position in which believers are to stand firm.[168] The meaning, then, of the instruction *stand firm in the Lord* is that believers are to remain securely fixed within the domain of Christ.

Phil 4:2 Εὐοδίαν παρακαλῶ καὶ Συντύχην παρακαλῶ τὸ αὐτὸ φρονεῖν **ἐν κυρίῳ**

*I urge Euodia and I urge Syntyche to agree **in the Lord**.*

This example presents a few possibilities for understanding ἐν κυρίῳ. First, the phrase might express kind or manner, so that Euodia and Syntyche agree in a Christian way. While possible, however, this reading raises the question of how *Christian* agreement differs from simple agreement; surely the distinctive element of Christian agreement is the cause or means of such agreement. There are, therefore, more likely candidates for understanding ἐν κυρίῳ.

Second, then, it is possible that ἐν κυρίῳ specifies the cause of agreement: Euodia and Syntyche are to agree because of their common bond and fellowship in the Lord. It is their shared existence as believers that should drive them to reconciliation. While this reading is stronger than the first, it raises the question of why agreement necessarily follows from shared belief in the Lord. After all, Paul himself is content to disagree with others who share the same Lord.

Perhaps there is something inappropriate about the nature of the disagreement that calls for its discontinuation. If so, Paul's charge does not necessarily arise from their commonality in the Lord but from the requirement to adhere to a code of conduct. In other words, Euodia and Syntyche are to agree because it is right.[169] While such a reconstruction is admittedly speculative, it suggests that the best reading of ἐν κυρίῳ is to understand it as expressing the locative notion of the realm of Christ.

---

168. 'Here it can only be locative, indicating the sphere in which they are to stand fast'; Fee, *Philippians*, 388, n. 22.

169. O'Brien acknowledges this possibility as well as the reading that takes ἐν κυρίῳ as signifying a common bond in the Lord; O'Brien, *Philippians*, 478.

Since believers live within Christ's domain, they are expected to conform to behaviour that is appropriate to it. These two believers have inappropriately failed to reconcile, but because they are *in the Lord*—existing under his sphere of his rule—this will not do.

Phil 4:4 χαίρετε **ἐν κυρίῳ** πάντοτε· πάλιν ἐρῶ, χαίρετε

*Rejoice **in the Lord** always. I will say it again: Rejoice!*

For this use of ἐν κυρίῳ see Philippians 3:1 above.

Phil 4:10 ἐχάρην δὲ **ἐν κυρίῳ** μεγάλως ὅτι ἤδη ποτὲ ἀνεθάλετε τὸ ὑπὲρ ἐμοῦ φρονεῖν, ἐφ᾽ ᾧ καὶ ἐφρονεῖτε, ἠκαιρεῖσθε δέ

*I rejoiced **in the Lord** greatly that once again you renewed your care for me. You were, in fact, concerned about me but lacked the opportunity to show it.*

The two previous mentions of rejoicing ἐν κυρίῳ were treated as expressing cause, such that the Lord is the cause of believers' rejoicing. Although we may assume that conclusion to be correct and that there is consistency between those instances and this one, a causal reading is nevertheless not straightforward. The difficulty arises from the fact that the cause of Paul's rejoicing here is explicitly given in the following clause: *that now at last you have renewed your care for me.* This fact, however, need not rule out a causal understanding of ἐν κυρίῳ. It is possible that, given Paul's understanding of the sovereignty of God, he rejoices in the Lord who is at work behind the scenes as the Philippians renew their care for Paul. This would find a happy parallel in Paul's thanksgiving to God for the partnership of the Philippians (1:3–5); while it is their partnership that brings forth thanks, Paul directs the thanks to God in recognition of his sovereign hand. In the same way, then, Paul here recognizes the Lord's provision in the Philippians' care for him and thus is able to rejoice because of him.[170]

---

170. 'The arrival of the gift at the hands of Epaphroditus (4:18) is made the occasion of rejoicing *in the Lord* who has put this generosity in his people's hearts'; Martin, *Philippians*, 176.

Col 3:18 αἱ γυναῖκες, ὑποτάσσεσθε τοῖς ἀνδράσιν ὡς ἀνῆκεν **ἐν κυρίῳ**

*Wives, be submissive to your husbands, as is fitting **in the Lord.***

As with the instruction to children as part of the household code in Ephesians 6:1, this instance of ἐν κυρίῳ is best regarded as expressing what is proper within families that live in the realm of Christ. A wife's submission is fitting in the Lord because this accords to the pattern of family life in Christ's domain.[171]

Col 3:20 τὰ τέκνα, ὑπακούετε τοῖς γονεῦσιν κατὰ πάντα, τοῦτο γὰρ εὐάρεστόν ἐστιν **ἐν κυρίῳ**

*Children, obey your parents in everything, for this is pleasing **in the Lord.*** (pers. trans.)

Parallel to Ephesians 6:1 and following Colossians 3:18, this occurrence of ἐν κυρίῳ similarly expresses the locative notion of appropriate behaviour in the domain of the Lord. While some versions mistranslate τοῦτο γὰρ εὐάρεστόν ἐστιν ἐν κυρίῳ as *for this pleases the Lord* (NIV, RSV, ESV; cf. HCSB) — thus masking the locative sense of ἐν κυρίῳ — it is best rendered that children's obedience is *pleasing in the Lord*, because it is an appropriate expression of life in the sphere of Christ's rule. As O'Brien concludes, 'obedience to parents is fit and proper in that sphere in which the Christian now lives'.[172]

1 Thess 3:8 ὅτι νῦν ζῶμεν ἐὰν ὑμεῖς στήκετε **ἐν κυρίῳ**

*For now we live, if you stand firm **in the Lord.***

For this use of ἐν κυρίῳ see Philippians 4:1 above.

---

171. Marianne Meye Thompson summarizes, 'In the present passage, believers are urged to let their relationships be lived as "in the Lord" (3:18, 20), indicating that they fear the Lord (v. 22), that their actions are done for the Lord (v. 23), that they serve the Lord (v. 24), and that they ultimately have a Lord in heaven (4:1). The genius of Colossians is that all of life, from creation to redemption, is brought under the aegis of Christ's lordship; that includes the fundamental relationships of human life'; Thompson, *Colossians and Philemon*, 92.

172. O'Brien, *Colossians, Philemon*, 225.

1 Thess 4:1 λοιπὸν οὖν, ἀδελφοί, ἐρωτῶμεν ὑμᾶς καὶ
παρακαλοῦμεν **ἐν κυρίῳ** Ἰησοῦ, ἵνα καθὼς παρελάβετε παρ'
ἡμῶν τὸ πῶς δεῖ ὑμᾶς περιπατεῖν καὶ ἀρέσκειν θεῷ, καθὼς καὶ
περιπατεῖτε, ἵνα περισσεύητε μᾶλλον.

*Finally then, brothers, we ask and encourage you **in the Lord** Jesus,*
that as you have received from us how you must walk and please
God—as you are doing—do so even more.

This example of ἐν κυρίῳ Ἰησοῦ is clearly adverbial, modifying the verbs
ἐρωτῶμεν and παρακαλοῦμεν. As with Ephesians 4:17 above, the two most
compelling options for understanding the adverbial function of the phrase
are causal and kind or manner. If causal, Paul asks and encourages the
Thessalonians to please God *because of the Lord Jesus.* As in Ephesians 4:17,
this is a possible reading.

If, however, the phrase expresses kind or manner, Paul asks and encourages the Thessalonians in a manner consonant with the Lord Jesus. If so,
ἐν κυρίῳ Ἰησοῦ would add weight and authority to the petition. Indeed,
this reading is to be preferred over the former because of the parallel it
enables with the following verse: *For you know what commands we gave*
you through the Lord Jesus (4:2). Paul's commands are issued *through* the
Lord (διὰ τοῦ κυρίου Ἰησοῦ), thus cementing the inviolable connection
between Paul's instruction and the will of the Lord. If such is the case in
4:2, it increases the likelihood that 4:1 operates likewise: Paul is asking
and encouraging the Thessalonians in direct connection with the will of
the Lord.[173]

1 Thess 5:12 ἐρωτῶμεν δὲ ὑμᾶς, ἀδελφοί, εἰδέναι τοὺς κοπιῶντας
ἐν ὑμῖν καὶ προϊσταμένους ὑμῶν **ἐν κυρίῳ** καὶ νουθετοῦντας ὑμᾶς

Now we ask you, brothers, to give recognition to those who labor
*among you and lead you **in the Lord** and admonish you.*

Paul requests here that recognition be given to those who labour, lead,
and admonish ἐν κυρίῳ. While ἐν κυρίῳ follows *lead* (προϊσταμένους),

---

173. 'He speaks as one who has authority committed to him by the Lord.' Morris, *Thes-*
salonians (NICNT), 114.

it probably modifies *lead*, *labor* (τοὺς κοπιῶντας) as well as *admonish* (νουθετοῦντας). The three substantival participles form a TSKS construction (article-substantive-καί-substantive), as each are in the same case with an article preceding the first but not the second or third, while joined by καί.[174] While this does not qualify as a Granville Sharp construction since the participles are plural, there is no doubt that those who labour, those who lead, and those who admonish share the same referent. The participles προϊσταμένους and νουθετοῦντας then add further descriptions of the group first labeled τοὺς κοπιῶντας.[175] Consequently, ἐν κυρίῳ modifies all three.[176]

This then provides another example of labour described as *in the Lord*. As with previous instances (Rom 16:12; 1 Cor 9:1; 15:58), ἐν κυρίῳ most likely expresses *cause*: it is labour conducted because of the Lord. Paul has Christian service in mind, which is reinforced by the reference to leadership and admonishment. Thus, the Thessalonians are urged to offer recognition to those who work in Christian leadership among them.[177]

2 Thess 3:12 τοῖς δὲ τοιούτοις παραγγέλλομεν καὶ παρακαλοῦμεν **ἐν κυρίῳ** Ἰησοῦ Χριστῷ, ἵνα μετὰ ἡσυχίας ἐργαζόμενοι τὸν ἑαυτῶν ἄρτον ἐσθίωσιν

Now we command and exhort such people **by the Lord** *Jesus Christ that quietly working, they may eat their own food.*

The activities of commanding and exhorting are modified by ἐν κυρίῳ Ἰησοῦ Χριστῷ, which allows at least two plausible readings: causal and manner or kind. The similarity of this expression to that in 1 Thessalonians 4:1 is striking: *we ask and encourage you in the Lord Jesus*. Both instances modify the activities of asking or commanding, encouraging or exhorting, with ἐν κυρίῳ Ἰησοῦ. Indeed, both verses employ the verb παρακαλέω — translated here *exhort* and in 4:1 *encourage*. Given such

---

174. See Wallace, *Greek Grammar*, 270–86.

175. Morris, *Thessalonians* (NICNT), 165.

176. While ἐν κυρίῳ follows the *second* substantival participle of three, the force of the TSKS construction enables the prepositional phrase to qualify the whole chain regardless of its position.

177. Morris (ibid.) takes this to refer to the elders of the church: 'Who else would discharge this triple function?'

strong parallels, it is reasonable to conclude that ἐν κυρίῳ Ἰησοῦ here parallels 4:1. It expresses kind or manner, so that Paul's command and exhortation is consonant with the Lord Jesus; such instruction carries the weight and authority of the Lord.[178]

This subcategory of believers' actions contains twenty-one instances ἐν κυρίῳ, of which seven express cause (Rom 16:12; 1 Cor 9:1; 15:58; Phil 3:1; 4:4, 10; 1 Thess 5:12), six are locative (Eph 6:1; Phil 4:1, 2; Col 3:18, 20; 1 Thess 3:8), five indicate kind or manner (Rom 16:2; 1 Cor 16:19; Eph 4:17; 1 Thess 4:1; 2 Thess 3:12), and three refer to specification or substance (Rom 16:22; 1 Cor 1:31; 2 Cor 10:17).

3.11.2.3 Characteristics of those in the Lord

Rom 14:14 οἶδα καὶ πέπεισμαι **ἐν κυρίῳ** Ἰησοῦ ὅτι οὐδὲν κοινὸν δι' ἑαυτοῦ, εἰ μὴ τῷ λογιζομένῳ τι κοινὸν εἶναι, ἐκείνῳ κοινόν

*I know and am persuaded **by the Lord** Jesus that nothing is unclean in itself. Still, to someone who considers a thing to be unclean, to that one it is unclean.*

There are two major options for understanding the use of ἐν κυρίῳ Ἰησοῦ in this verse. First, a locative reading indicating the sphere of Christ would mean that because Paul is in Christ's domain, he therefore knows that nothing is unclean. The problem with this understanding is that it implies that those who do not know the same thing are therefore not under the same realm. In the context, we see that Paul wishes to accommodate the weaker brother who does not in every respect understand reality as he does. Nevertheless, Paul regards such a person as a weaker *brother*; though incorrect in minor issues, he is no less a brother in Christ and therefore in the realm of Christ. Thus, it makes little sense that Paul should designate the realm of Christ determinative for his understanding while others in said realm are of a different mind.

Second, and more likely, is the possibility that Paul uses ἐν κυρίῳ Ἰησοῦ to express *agency*. As translated above, Paul is persuaded by the Lord Jesus,

---

178. Gene L. Green, *The Letters to the Thessalonians* (PNTC; Grand Rapids: Eerdmans, 2002), 352.

who is therefore the agent of this outcome. While speculative, it may be that Paul has in mind Jesus' teaching recorded in Mark 7:18–19: 'And He said to them, "Are you also lacking in understanding? Don't you realize that nothing going into a man from the outside can defile him? For it doesn't go into his heart but into the stomach and is eliminated." (As a result, He made all foods clean.)'[179] If so, Jesus' agency in persuading Paul that nothing is unclean is not limited to his experience—it is available to all, even if some do not avail themselves of it.

Gal 5:10 ἐγὼ πέποιθα εἰς ὑμᾶς **ἐν κυρίῳ** ὅτι οὐδὲν ἄλλο φρονήσετε· ὁ δὲ ταράσσων ὑμᾶς βαστάσει τὸ κρίμα, ὅστις ἐὰν ᾖ

*I have confidence **in the Lord** you will not accept any other view. But whoever it is that is confusing you will pay the penalty.*

This occurrence of ἐν κυρίῳ modifies the verb πέποιθα (*I am persuaded; I have confidence*) and thus relates to why Paul believes the Galatians will not accept any other view. Paul has confidence that the Lord will act for the good of his people in Galatia. Consequently, ἐν κυρίῳ most likely expresses cause: because of the Lord, Paul believes the Galatians will come to their right minds.

It may be objected, however, that this does not do justice to the phrase εἰς ὑμᾶς, which apparently indicates confidence in the Galatians; but only if so translated. The preposition εἰς could effect the sense *I have confidence regarding you, that you will not accept any other view*, since it can express reference or respect (BDAG). In that case, Paul's confidence is not *in* them but is *in relation* to them.[180] His confidence is in the Lord, who will put the Galatians straight.

Eph 4:1 παρακαλῶ οὖν ὑμᾶς ἐγὼ ὁ δέσμιος **ἐν κυρίῳ** ἀξίως περιπατῆσαι τῆς κλήσεως ἧς ἐκλήθητε

*Therefore I, the prisoner **for the Lord**, urge you to walk worthy of the calling you have received.*

---

179. Cranfield acknowledges this possibility (as well as Matt. 15:10–11, 15–20); Cranfield, *Romans*, 2:712–13.

180. So Longenecker, *Galatians*, 231.

The strongest obvious option for understanding ἐν κυρίῳ in this example is to regard it as expressing cause or reason. Paul is a prisoner on account of the Lord, or, for the sake of the Lord.

Another possibility is that ἐν κυρίῳ indicates sphere or realm; 'since for Paul the whole sphere of Christian living was "in the Lord," his imprisonment was to be seen as no exception'.[181] It is not clear, however, what significance this would have for the remainder of the verse, in which Paul urges the Ephesians to walk worthy of their calling. To read ἐν κυρίῳ as indicating cause, however, relates well to this exhortation. Paul is imprisoned because of the Lord, which underscores his credibility as one who may issue such an encouragement.

Eph 5:8 ἦτε γάρ ποτε σκότος, νῦν δὲ φῶς **ἐν κυρίῳ**· ὡς τέκνα φωτὸς περιπατεῖτε

*For you were once darkness, but now you are light **in the Lord**. Walk as children of light.*

This instance of ἐν κυρίῳ could easily be understood as expressing cause or reason, indicating that believers are light because of the Lord's work. Alternatively, this might more accurately be described as agency: believers are light through the work of the Lord.

Notwithstanding these options, it may be better to understand ἐν κυρίῳ as locative, indicating the sphere of Christ. The pericope in which this verse is found draws strong contrast between competing domains: the immoral have no place in the kingdom of Christ and of God (5:5); unbelievers are described as 'the disobedient' (5:6), while believers are 'children of light' (5:8); at one time believers 'were darkness', but now they are 'light in the Lord' (5:8). This series of contrasts emphasizes the distinction between two realms—one of darkness and one of light. Thus, it is best to regard ἐν κυρίῳ with the thrust of the wider passage: it indicates the sphere of Christ, in which believers are located and may be described as 'light'.[182]

2 Thess 3:4 πεποίθαμεν δὲ **ἐν κυρίῳ** ἐφ' ὑμᾶς, ὅτι ἃ παραγγέλλομεν [καὶ] ποιεῖτε καὶ ποιήσετε

---

181. Lincoln, *Ephesians*, 234.
182. 'He is the one who has made the decisive difference, and it is through union with him that they have entered a new dominion and become *light*'; O'Brien, *Ephesians*, 367.

*We have confidence **in the Lord** about you, that you are doing and will do what we command.*

This example of ἐν κυρίῳ is similar to Galatians 5:10 above and expresses cause; the Lord is the ground of Paul's confidence.[183] In this instance it is clearer that Paul's confidence is not in his readers since the preposition ἐπί offers fewer possibilities than εἰς in this scenario. Thus, ἐφ᾽ ὑμᾶς can only express reference or respect: Paul's confidence is in the Lord with respect to the Thessalonians' progress.

Phlm 20 ναὶ ἀδελφέ, ἐγώ σου ὀναίμην **ἐν κυρίῳ**· ἀνάπαυσόν μου τὰ σπλάγχνα ἐν Χριστῷ

*Yes, brother, may I have joy from you **in the Lord**; refresh my heart in Christ.*

This verse has already received comment regarding ἐν Χριστῷ (see above). Since ἐν κυρίῳ and ἐν Χριστῷ are found in such proximity, and Paul is using both phrases in connection with his desire to receive something from Philemon, it is almost certain that the two phrases are employed in the same way.[184] For this reason, ἐν κυρίῳ is regarded as indicating close association, such that Philemon is required to act under the influence of the Lord. Just as he is to refresh Paul's heart under the influence of Christ (see above), so he is to act in such a way as to bring Paul joy (or benefit) under the influence of the the Lord.

This subcategory of characteristics of those ἐν κυρίῳ contains five different uses in six references. These uses are the expression of cause (Gal 5:10; Eph 4:1), agency (Rom 14:4), locative realm or sphere (Eph 5:8), reference or respect (2 Thess 3:4), and close association (Phlm 20).

3.11.2.4 Faith in the Lord

As with the parallel subcategory faith *in Christ*, these two instances of faith *in the Lord* indicate the object of faith.

---

183. Morris, *Thessalonians* (NICNT), 249.

184. So F. F. Bruce, *The Epistle to the Colossians, to Philemon, and to the Ephesians* (NICNT; Grand Rapids: Eerdmans, 1984), 221.

Eph 1:15 διὰ τοῦτο κἀγὼ ἀκούσας τὴν καθ' ὑμᾶς πίστιν **ἐν τῷ κυρίῳ** Ἰησοῦ καὶ τὴν ἀγάπην τὴν εἰς πάντας τοὺς ἁγίους

*This is why, since I heard about your faith **in the Lord** Jesus and your love for all the saints.*

———

Phil 2:19 ἐλπίζω δὲ **ἐν κυρίῳ** Ἰησοῦ Τιμόθεον ταχέως πέμψαι ὑμῖν, ἵνα κἀγὼ εὐψυχῶ γνοὺς τὰ περὶ ὑμῶν

*Now I hope **in the Lord** Jesus to send Timothy to you soon so that I also may be encouraged when I hear news about you.*

3.11.2.5 In the Lord as a periphrasis for believers

As established in §3.9 above on ἐν Χριστῷ, the function of ἐν κυρίῳ as a periphrasis for believers indicates close association or personal relation. It is due to the believer's close personal association with Christ that he or she may be described as ἐν κυρίῳ.

Rom 16:8 ἀσπάσασθε Ἀμπλιᾶτον τὸν ἀγαπητόν μου **ἐν κυρίῳ**

*Greet Ampliatus, my dear friend **in the Lord**.*

Ampliatus is not merely a dear friend to Paul; he is a dear *Christian* friend.

Rom 16:11 ἀσπάσασθε Ἡρῳδίωνα τὸν συγγενῆ μου. ἀσπάσασθε τοὺς ἐκ τῶν Ναρκίσσου τοὺς ὄντας **ἐν κυρίῳ**.

*Greet Herodion, my fellow countryman. Greet those who belong to the household of Narcissus who are **in the Lord**.*

This example seems to imply that not all in the household of Narcissus are believers. The construction τοὺς ὄντας ἐν κυρίῳ, *those being in the Lord*, need not necessarily indicate this, since it could simply describe the household of Narcissus—albeit in more cumbersome fashion than is Paul's custom. Still, his use of the preposition ἐκ suggests that he is thinking of people *from* the household of Narcissus rather than the whole household.

If so, this justifies the cumbersome phrase τοὺς ὄντας ἐν κυρίῳ since Paul actually intends to specify certain members of the household: those who are in Christ.[185] Consequently, ἐν κυρίῳ clearly indicates these people as *Christians* as opposed to other members of Narcissus' household.

> Rom 16:13 ἀσπάσασθε Ῥοῦφον τὸν ἐκλεκτὸν **ἐν κυρίῳ** καὶ τὴν μητέρα αὐτοῦ καὶ ἐμοῦ
>
> *Greet Rufus, chosen **in the Lord**; also his mother—and mine.*

It is unclear whether Rufus's being chosen ἐν κυρίῳ means that he was chosen *by* the Lord—an instrumental reading—or that this is a periphrasis for *Christian*. If the latter, the sense would be that his election is *Christian* election; that is, he has been chosen to be a Christian. Given the context, this is probably the best reading. Appearing within a list of greetings, there are several surrounding references to people who are also described as *Christians*: coworkers in Christ (16:3, 9); a convert to Christ (16:5); a friend in Christ (16:8); one approved in Christ (16:10). Thus, reading ἐν κυρίῳ as a periphrasis for *Christian* makes clear sense here.[186]

> 1 Cor 4:17 διὰ τοῦτο ἔπεμψα ὑμῖν Τιμόθεον, ὅς ἐστίν μου τέκνον ἀγαπητὸν καὶ πιστὸν **ἐν κυρίῳ**, ὃς ὑμᾶς ἀναμνήσει τὰς ὁδούς μου τὰς ἐν Χριστῷ Ἰησοῦ, καθὼς πανταχοῦ ἐν πάσῃ ἐκκλησίᾳ διδάσκω
>
> *This is why I have sent Timothy to you. He is my dearly loved and faithful son **in the Lord**. He will remind you about my ways in Christ Jesus, just as I teach everywhere in every church.*

By describing Timothy as his child ἐν κυρίῳ, Paul obviously refers to something other than the usual relationship of father and son. The metaphorical *child* depicts Timothy as *like* a son in certain respects. By modifying *child* with ἐν κυρίῳ, there is little doubt that Paul specifies the nature of this relationship: it is based on their shared belief in Christ and probably means that Paul led Timothy to new birth.[187] Timothy is Paul's *Christian* son.

---

185. Cranfield, *Romans*, 2:793.
186. Such is assumed by Cranfield; ibid., 2:794.
187. Thiselton, *1 Corinthians*, 374.

1 Cor 7:39 γυνὴ δέδεται ἐφ᾽ ὅσον χρόνον ζῇ ὁ ἀνὴρ αὐτῆς· ἐὰν δὲ κοιμηθῇ ὁ ἀνήρ, ἐλευθέρα ἐστὶν ᾧ θέλει γαμηθῆναι, μόνον **ἐν κυρίῳ**

*A wife is bound as long as her husband is living. But if her husband dies, she is free to be married to anyone she wants—only **in the Lord**.*

Paul here imposes one limiting qualification for whom a widow may marry. She may marry whom she wishes (ᾧ θέλει) as long as he is ἐν κυρίῳ. On the one hand, μόνον ἐν κυρίῳ could modify the verb *marry*, such that Paul would be describing the nature of their union as Christian. On the other hand, the phrase more likely modifies the potential marriage partner since μόνον provides a natural counterpoint for ᾧ θέλει such that they clearly go together. Thus, ἐν κυρίῳ specifies the nature of the widow's potential husband—he is to be a Christian.[188]

1 Cor 9:2 εἰ ἄλλοις οὐκ εἰμὶ ἀπόστολος, ἀλλά γε ὑμῖν εἰμι· ἡ γὰρ σφραγίς μου τῆς ἀποστολῆς ὑμεῖς ἐστε **ἐν κυρίῳ**

*If I am not an apostle to others, at least I am to you, for you are the seal of my apostleship **in the Lord**.*

This is a difficult example since it is not clear whether ἐν κυρίῳ modifies the Corinthians, such that they are a *Christian* seal of Paul's apostleship, or his apostleship itself, such that Paul is a *Christian* apostle. And the difficulty extends further since it is not clear what either option would denote; what does it mean for the Corinthians to be a Christian seal of Paul's apostleship, or for Paul to be a Christian apostle—as opposed to some other kind?

Perhaps a third possibility is more likely. The wider context sees Paul defending his apostleship and in turn his rights as an apostle (9:1–15). As part of the defense of his apostleship, he cites the Corinthians as the fruit of his labour: *Am I not free? Am I not an apostle? Have I not seen Jesus our Lord? Are you not my work in the Lord?* (9:1). Paul then acknowledges that while he may not be regarded an apostle by some, he is to the Corinthians: they are the seal of his apostleship (9:2). Surely, then, their witness to Paul's apostleship is due to his work in the Lord; they are the fruit of his

---

188. Fee, *1 Corinthians*, 356.

labour. And what does this imply? That because they are *Christian*, they constitute evidence of Paul's apostleship: their status as believers is the product of his apostolic work. In such light, ἐν κυρίῳ does not modify the Corinthians' seal or Paul's apostleship. Rather, Paul says that *because the Corinthians are in the Lord*, they confirm Paul's apostleship. Since they are Christians, they testify to his apostolic labours.[189]

Eph 6:21 ἵνα δὲ εἰδῆτε καὶ ὑμεῖς τὰ κατ' ἐμέ, τί πράσσω, πάντα γνωρίσει ὑμῖν Τύχικος ὁ ἀγαπητὸς ἀδελφὸς καὶ πιστὸς διάκονος **ἐν κυρίῳ**

Tychicus, our dearly loved brother and faithful servant in the Lord, will tell you all the news about me so that you be informed.

The most apparent function of ἐν κυρίῳ is to designate Tychicus a *Christian* brother and servant.[190]

Phil 1:14 καὶ τοὺς πλείονας τῶν ἀδελφῶν **ἐν κυρίῳ** πεποιθότας τοῖς δεσμοῖς μου περισσοτέρως τολμᾶν ἀφόβως τὸν λόγον λαλεῖν

Most of the brothers in the Lord have gained confidence from my imprisonment and dare even more to speak the message fearlessly.

This example likewise employs ἐν κυρίῳ to specify *Christian* brothers. While ἐν κυρίῳ could modify the following πεποιθότας rather than τῶν ἀδελφῶν, the word order favours the latter.[191]

Col 4:7 τὰ κατ' ἐμὲ πάντα γνωρίσει ὑμῖν Τύχικος ὁ ἀγαπητὸς ἀδελφὸς καὶ πιστὸς διάκονος καὶ σύνδουλος **ἐν κυρίῳ**

Tychicus, our dearly loved brother, faithful servant, and fellow slave in the Lord, will tell you all the news about me.

---

189. Leon Morris, *The First Epistle of Paul to the Corinthians* (TNTC; rev. ed.; Leicester, UK: Inter-Varsity Press, 1985), 130.

190. Charles Hodge, *A Commentary on the Epistle to the Ephesians* (New York, 1856; repr. Geneva Series Commentary; London: Banner of Truth, 1964), 396.

191. O'Brien correctly notes that τῶν ἀδελφῶν ἐν κυρίῳ does not occur elsewhere; however, we have seen ἐν κυρίῳ with the singular ἀδελφός in the previous entry: ὁ ἀγαπητὸς ἀδελφὸς καὶ πιστὸς διάκονος ἐν κυρίῳ (Eph 6:21). This fact also undermines the point that 'whenever the apostle speaks of "brethren" he usually means "Christians", so that to add "in the Lord" would seem superfluous'; O'Brien, *Philippians*, 94–95.

Tychicus is a *Christian* brother, a *Christian* servant, and a fellow *Christian* slave, as in the parallel Ephesians 6:21, above.

Phlm 16 οὐκέτι ὡς δοῦλον ἀλλ' ὑπὲρ δοῦλον, ἀδελφὸν ἀγαπητόν, μάλιστα ἐμοί, πόσῳ δὲ μᾶλλον σοὶ καὶ ἐν σαρκὶ καὶ **ἐν κυρίῳ**

*No longer as a slave, but more than a slave—as a dearly loved brother. He is especially so to me, but even more to you, both in the flesh and **in the Lord**.*

This is an interesting example in that Onesimus is described as a brother ἐν σαρκὶ, *in the flesh*, as well as ἐν κυρίῳ, *in the Lord*. The contrast between being a brother in the flesh and in the Lord offers the strongest evidence yet that one of the functions of ἐν κυρίῳ is to be periphrastic for *Christian*. That Onesimus may be described as a brother *both* in the flesh and in the Lord demonstrates that being a brother in the flesh is not negative. Contrary to the manner in which Paul often uses σάρξ to indicate a realm of the flesh in competition to the realm of the Lord, this occurrence does not. It probably, then, refers to the human bond of brotherhood—that is, a normal and common relationship.

Incidentally, this brotherhood need not refer to a blood relationship but can simply refer to a close affinity or association (BDAG). Likewise *flesh* can simply mean *human* and does not necessitate a blood brotherhood (BDAG). Consequently, this human brotherhood is coupled with brotherhood in the Lord, which strongly suggests that the latter refers to *Christian* brotherhood. Thus, Paul's point is that Onesimus is a dear Christian brother to him, but to Philemon he is a 'human' *and* Christian brother.[192]

All ten instances of ἐν κυρίῳ in this subcategory of usage as a periphrasis for believers indicate close association or personal relation (Rom 16:8, 11, 13; 1 Cor 4:17; 7:39; 9:2; Eph 6:21; Phil 1:14; Col 4:7; Phlm 16).

3.11.2.6 Summary

Perusal of the evidence appears to justify the validity of the original assumption, that ἐν κυρίῳ offers no clear distinction to ἐν Χριστῷ. Each

---

192. Murray J. Harris, *Colossians and Philemon* (Exegetical Guide to the Greek New Testament; Grand Rapids: Eerdmans, 1991), 267–68.

instance refers to Christ, not the Father or some other lord. Furthermore, the subcategories above parallel those of ἐν Χριστῷ, though not exhaustively.

3.11.3 IN HIM

Just as ἐν κυρίῳ is a natural step outside ἐν Χριστῷ, so ἐν αὐτῷ is the next step. Whenever the pronoun refers to Christ, it is assumed that ἐν αὐτῷ is another way to say ἐν Χριστῷ.

3.11.3.1 Things achieved for/given to people in Him

1 Cor 1:4–5 εὐχαριστῶ τῷ θεῷ μου πάντοτε περὶ ὑμῶν ἐπὶ τῇ χάριτι τοῦ θεοῦ τῇ δοθείσῃ ὑμῖν ἐν Χριστῷ Ἰησοῦ, ὅτι ἐν παντὶ ἐπλουτίσθητε **ἐν αὐτῷ**, ἐν παντὶ λόγῳ καὶ πάσῃ γνώσει

I always thank my God for you because of God's grace given to you in Christ Jesus, that **by Him** *you were enriched in everything—in all speech and all knowledge.*

Since ἐν Χριστῷ in 1:4 has been designated above (§3.3) as instrumental, such that the grace of God has been given through Christ, it is natural to regard ἐν αὐτῷ in 1:5 likewise. The correlation between these two instances does not rest merely on their proximity or on the fact that the latter instance is a pronoun whose antecedent is the former instance, but also on the fact that 1:5 has an epexegetical relationship to 1:4.[193] The grace of God in 1:4 is specified in 1:5 as pertaining to being made rich in everything. Given this epexegetical relationship, the case for an instrumental reading of ἐν αὐτῷ in 1:5 is strong.

2 Cor 1:19–20 ὁ τοῦ θεοῦ γὰρ υἱὸς Ἰησοῦς Χριστὸς ὁ ἐν ὑμῖν δι᾽ ἡμῶν κηρυχθείς, δι᾽ ἐμοῦ καὶ Σιλουανοῦ καὶ Τιμοθέου, οὐκ ἐγένετο ναὶ καὶ οὔ ἀλλὰ ναὶ **ἐν αὐτῷ** γέγονεν. ὅσαι γὰρ ἐπαγγελίαι θεοῦ, **ἐν αὐτῷ** τὸ ναί· διὸ καὶ δι᾽ αὐτοῦ τὸ ἀμὴν τῷ θεῷ πρὸς δόξαν δι᾽ ἡμῶν

---

193. The whole clause is of '"explicative" apposition' to the previous verse; Thiselton, *1 Corinthians*, 90.

*For the Son of God, Jesus Christ, who was preached among you by us—by me and Silvanus and Timothy—did not become "Yes and no"; on the contrary, a final "Yes" has come **in Him**. For every one of God's promises is "Yes" **in Him**. Therefore, the "Amen" is also spoken through Him by us for God's glory.*

These two instances of ἐν αὐτῷ are most likely instrumental. Paul says in 1:19 that *Yes* has come about in Christ, and he makes clear in 1:20 that this *Yes* refers to the fulfillment of God's promises. Since they are the promises of *God*, 1:20 provides a clear indication of God's agency. The promises are issued by God and fulfilled by Christ.[194] Thus, it appears that ἐν αὐτῷ in both verses indicates the manner in which God's promises have been fulfilled, namely, through the work of Christ; he is the personal instrument of God's agency.

Eph 1:4 καθὼς ἐξελέξατο ἡμᾶς **ἐν αὐτῷ** πρὸ καταβολῆς κόσμου εἶναι ἡμᾶς ἁγίους καὶ ἀμώμους κατενώπιον αὐτοῦ ἐν ἀγάπῃ

*For He chose us **in Him**, before the foundation of the world, to be holy and blameless in His sight.*

This instance of ἐν αὐτῷ qualifies God's choosing. Since the activity of God is in view and his agency is clear, it is reasonable to perceive an instrumental use of ἐν αὐτῷ. Furthermore, two facets of the immediate context support this view. First, the verse follows an occurrence of ἐν Χριστῷ, which has been designated instrumental (Eph 1:3, see §§3.3, 10); indeed, Χριστῷ is the antecedent of αὐτῷ. Second, *He predestined … through Jesus Christ* (1:5) parallels *He chose us in Him, before the foundation of the world* (1:4); both are concerned with the election of believers. In 1:5 Christ is explicitly designated the instrument through whom predestination occurs (διὰ Ἰησοῦ Χριστοῦ). Given this and the parallel between 1:5 and 1:4, it seems likely that ἐν αὐτῷ is also intended to be instrumental. Using different language, then, both verses speak of the predestination of believers through Christ.[195]

---

194. Paul Barnett, *The Message of 2 Corinthians: Power in Weakness* (Bible Speaks Today; Leicester, UK: Inter-Varsity Press, 1988), 39.

195. So Mitton, who uses the term 'agent' in the same way that we employ 'instrument':

178 · Exegetical Study

Eph 2:15 τὸν νόμον τῶν ἐντολῶν ἐν δόγμασιν καταργήσας, ἵνα τοὺς δύο κτίσῃ **ἐν αὐτῷ** εἰς ἕνα καινὸν ἄνθρωπον ποιῶν εἰρήνην

*He made of no effect the law consisting of commands and expressed in regulations, so that He might create **in Himself** one new man from the two, resulting in peace.*

The most likely reading of ἐν αὐτῷ here is that it expresses incorporation into Christ, such that Jew and Gentile become one new man united with him. Inherent to the verse itself is the notion of consolidation, as expressed in the phrase *one new man from the two.* Such consolidation supports the reading of incorporation for ἐν αὐτῷ.

Furthermore, the wider context underscores this conclusion. The pericope begins by addressing Gentiles, pointing out their former exclusion from God and his people: *At that time you were without the Messiah, excluded from the citizenship of Israel, and foreigners to the covenants of the promise, without hope and without God in the world* (2:12). This is sharply contrasted in the following verses, beginning with 2:13: *But now in Christ Jesus, you who were far away have been brought near by the blood of the Messiah.* Thus we see that Christ has overturned the exclusion of Gentiles; they have been brought near, and both groups have been made one (2:14–15).

Given this movement from exclusion and separation to unification and incorporation, it follows that ἐν αὐτῷ continues the same thrust: the two groups have been made one by incorporation with Christ; he has brought them together by joining them both to him.[196] Indeed, this is reinforced in the following verse: *He did this so that He might reconcile both to God in one body* (2:16). The mention of *in one body* specifies that incorporation is in view; Jew and Gentile are reconciled by incorporation into the one body of Christ.

Eph 4:21 εἴ γε αὐτὸν ἠκούσατε καὶ **ἐν αὐτῷ** ἐδιδάχθητε, καθώς ἐστιν ἀλήθεια ἐν τῷ Ἰησοῦ

*If indeed you have heard Him and have been taught **in Him**, just as truth is in Jesus.* (NASB)

Christ 'had been God's agent in planning the future salvation and commissioning of those who were now Christians'; C. Leslie Mitton, *Ephesians* (NCB; London: Oliphants, 1976), 50.
196. Best, *Ephesians*, 263.

There are at least two strong options for understanding ἐν αὐτῷ in this verse. First, the phrase may be treated as locative, indicating the domain of Christ. Under this reading, believers were taught the truth in the domain of Christ. It refers to true knowledge that steers away from the sinful behaviour depicted in 4:19–20 and is required under Christ's rule.

Second, ἐν αὐτῷ could express agency, specifying that believers are taught *by* Christ. A difficulty is the manner in which Christ teaches believers. Is it metaphorical? Or does Paul mean that Christ teaches through his Spirit and apostolic witness? It is not clear. However, αὐτὸν ἠκούσατε at the beginning of the verse adds support to this reading. The ESV and NIV—which render ἐν αὐτῷ *in Christ*—translate αὐτὸν ἠκούσατε *you have heard about him* (ESV) and *you heard of him* (NIV). These translations treat αὐτὸν ἠκούσατε as indicating the content of what believers heard: it was *about* Christ. If taken this way, the phrase supports the locative reading of ἐν αὐτῷ because Christ's teaching becomes indirect; believers heard *about* him and were taught by being in his domain.

If, however, αὐτὸν ἠκούσατε is rendered *you heard him*, it conveys that believers have heard Christ directly; they heard *him*, rather than *about* him.[197] This reading supports agency for ἐν αὐτῷ; *you heard him* (NASB) *and were taught by him* (HCSB). Being taught *by* Christ correlates to *hearing* Christ. Thus, while a locative reading of ἐν αὐτῷ is plausible, αὐτὸν ἠκούσατε makes agency more likely.

Col 1:16–17 ὅτι **ἐν αὐτῷ** ἐκτίσθη τὰ πάντα
ἐν τοῖς οὐρανοῖς καὶ ἐπὶ τῆς γῆς,
τὰ ὁρατὰ καὶ τὰ ἀόρατα,
εἴτε θρόνοι εἴτε κυριότητες
εἴτε ἀρχαὶ εἴτε ἐξουσίαι·
τὰ πάντα δι' αὐτοῦ καὶ εἰς αὐτὸν ἔκτισται.
καὶ αὐτός ἐστιν πρὸ πάντων
καὶ τὰ πάντα **ἐν αὐτῷ** συνέστηκεν

197. Commentators recognize that with the verb ἀκούω, 'the person whose words one hears stands in the genitive, the person about whom one hears stands in the accusative'; Lincoln, *Ephesians*, 280. This then produces the translation 'you heard about him', since the object is accusative (αὐτόν). Nevertheless, the commentators do not seem to consider the fact that if Christ spoke about himself, 'you heard him' would be an appropriate translation and would account for the accusative object, because he *is* one about whom he speaks. In any case, BDAG acknowledges exceptions to the rule (e.g., Rev 5:13).

*For everything was created **by Him**,*
in heaven and on earth,
the visible and the invisible,
whether thrones or dominions
or rulers or authorities—
all things have been created through Him and for Him.
He is before all things,
*and **by Him** all things hold together.*

In these verses, the double occurrence of ἐν αὐτῷ offers two possible readings. On the one hand, the phrase might indicate agency (or instrumentality), such that everything was created by Christ and is held together by Christ. This reading is possible and is reflected in the translation above, *by him* (for both occurrences).

On the other hand, ἐν αὐτῷ may be locative.[198] This reading would suggest that God, the implicit agent of creation (taking ἐκτίσθη as a 'divine passive'),[199] has created and sustains all things in the sphere of Christ.[200] There are at least two compelling facts that support such a reading. First, the thrust of the entire passage 1:15–23 is concerned with the supremacy of Christ and the reconciliation of things in him. All things hold together in him (ἐν αὐτῷ; 1:17), and all things are reconciled through him (δι' αὐτοῦ; 1:20). Given this reconciliation thread and the fact that Christ is the centrepoint of reconciliation, the locative ἐν αὐτῷ provides a strong fit.

Second, there is a curiously subtle parallel to be discerned between 1:16 and 1:19–20. Verse 16 contains ἐν αὐτῷ, δι' αὐτοῦ, and εἰς αὐτὸν, which are found again in 1:19–20. This parallel aligns with the two major concepts of the wider passage: 1:16 focuses on creation while 1:19–20 focuses on reconciliation. If these two themes are correlated by the parallel ἐν αὐτῷ, δι' αὐτοῦ, and εἰς αὐτὸν in 1:16 and 1:19–20, it follows that ἐν αὐτῷ in 1:16 is parallel to its meaning in 1:19. In 1:19, ἐν αὐτῷ is locative: *For God was pleased to have all His fullness dwell in Him*—this bespeaks

---

198. Moule takes both options—instrumental and local; C. F. D. Moule, *The Epistles to the Colossians and to Philemon* (CGTC; Cambridge: Cambridge Univ. Press, 1958), 65.

199. O'Brien, *Colossians, Philemon*, 45.

200. Bruce, *Colossians, Philemon, Ephesians*, 61–62; Harris, *Colossians and Philemon*, 45–45.

the indwelling of God in Christ.[201] Consequently, ἐν αὐτῷ in 1:16 (and 1:17) is most likely locative. All things were created (by God), and are sustained, in the sphere of Christ.

Col 2:10 καὶ ἐστὲ **ἐν αὐτῷ** πεπληρωμένοι, ὅς ἐστιν ἡ κεφαλὴ πάσης ἀρχῆς καὶ ἐξουσίας

*And you have been filled **by Him**, who is the head over every ruler and authority.*

This instance of ἐν αὐτῷ could express *substance* (BDAG), such that Paul is specifying that believers have been filled with Christ (or *by him*, as translated here). Notwithstanding the unusual usage, this reading is probably not the strongest possibility in the context.

It is better to regard ἐν αὐτῷ as expressing union with Christ.[202] Believers are 'filled' because of their union in him. The strength of this reading arises from the verses to either side of 2:10. First, 2:9 speaks of the fullness of God dwelling in Christ bodily. This does not mean that Christ's body is 'filled' with God, but that through his union with God, Christ shares in the fullness of his deity. Second, 2:11 speaks of being circumcised in the circumcision of Christ (ἐν ᾧ); 2:12 refers to being buried with Christ (συνταφέντες αὐτῷ) in baptism and being raised with him (ἐν ᾧ καὶ συνηγέρθητε); 2:13 speaks of being made alive with him (συνεζωοποίησεν ὑμᾶς σὺν αὐτῷ). These three verses thus contain several references to the realities that believers share with Christ through their union and participation with him. Given that its context so strongly commends union with Christ, ἐν αὐτῷ in 2:10 is likewise best understood this way.

2 Thess 1:12 ὅπως ἐνδοξασθῇ τὸ ὄνομα τοῦ κυρίου ἡμῶν Ἰησοῦ ἐν ὑμῖν, καὶ ὑμεῖς **ἐν αὐτῷ**, κατὰ τὴν χάριν τοῦ θεοῦ ἡμῶν καὶ κυρίου Ἰησοῦ Χριστοῦ

*So that the name of our Lord Jesus will be glorified by you, and you **by Him**, according to the grace of our God and the Lord Jesus Christ.*

---

201. 'He is the "place" … in whom God in all his fullness was pleased to take up residence'; O'Brien, *Colossians, Philemon*, 53.

202. Harris, *Colossians and Philemon*, 100; O'Brien, *Colossians, Philemon*, 113.

The most likely understanding of ἐν αὐτῷ in this instance is instrumental. The reciprocity in glorification reveals that a symmetrical activity is in view rather than a static local notion in which believers exist in the realm of Christ. It is possible that it indicates agency rather than instrumentality since there is no explicit reference to the agency of God; without agency, an instrumental reading is weakened. There is, however, a hint of implied agency at the end of the verse: *according to the grace of our God and the Lord Jesus Christ*. While it is unclear how the mutual glorification of Christ and believers is *according to* the grace of God, it is nevertheless consonant with, and perhaps arises from, God's grace. With the agency of God in the background, an instrumental reading of ἐν αὐτῷ is sound.

Of the ten instances of ἐν αὐτῷ in this subcategory, five are instrumental (1 Cor 1:5; 2 Cor 1:19, 20; Eph 1:4; 2 Thess 1:12), two are locative (Col 1:16, 17), one expresses incorporation (Eph 2:15), one indicates agency (Eph 4:21), and one conveys union (Col 2:10).

3.11.3.2 Believers' actions in Him

Col 2:6–7 ὡς οὖν παρελάβετε τὸν Χριστὸν Ἰησοῦν τὸν κύριον, **ἐν αὐτῷ** περιπατεῖτε, ἐρριζωμένοι καὶ ἐποικοδομούμενοι **ἐν αὐτῷ** καὶ βεβαιούμενοι τῇ πίστει καθὼς ἐδιδάχθητε, περισσεύοντες ἐν εὐχαριστίᾳ

*Therefore, as you have received Christ Jesus the Lord, walk **in Him**, rooted and built up **in Him** and established in the faith, just as you were taught, overflowing with gratitude.*

It is likely that these two instances of ἐν αὐτῷ are to be understood the same way since the participles ἐρριζωμένοι and ἐποικοδομούμενοι — modified by the second ἐν αὐτῷ (v. 7) — themselves modify the imperative ἐν αὐτῷ περιπατεῖτε (v. 6). They explicate how the imperative is to be obeyed.[203]

---

203. The participles could be middle or passive in voice. A passive reading would render believers the objects of the work of Christ (or God), which is certainly theologically plausible. However, the participles are most likely middle in voice as they modify an imperative. Since they provide more information as to how believers are to 'walk in him', the believers are the agents of *rooted* and *built up*.

A strong possibility for both occurrences of ἐν αὐτῷ is a locative reading. The participles ἐρριζωμένοι and ἐποικοδομούμενοι—*rooted* and *built up*—are suggestive of incorporation into Christ. To walk in him (ἐν αὐτῷ περιπατεῖτε) would then envisage conduct that is expected of those within the realm of Christ.

But there are at least three reasons to prefer an alternate reading of ἐν αὐτῷ here. These occurrences of the prepositional phrase are candidates for the subcategory recognized by BDAG: 'to designate a close personal relation in which the referent of the ἐν-term is viewed as the controlling influence: *under the control of, under the influence of, in close association with*'.[204] To 'walk in him' means to live in a way that is under the control of Christ. This is supported by the fact that τὸν κύριον stands in apposition to τὸν Χριστὸν Ἰησοῦν, a phrase that clearly emphasizes the lordship of Christ.

Furthermore, the language *you received* (παρελάβετε) *Christ Jesus the Lord* indicates the reception of *teaching* about Christ. This is clear from other uses of παραλαμβάνω in which the tradition and teaching about Christ and the gospel is in view (1 Cor 15:1, 3; Gal 1:9; Phil 4:9; 1 Thess 2:13; 4:1–2; 2 Thess 3:6).[205] This phrase is, therefore, consonant with the close association reading of ἐν αὐτῷ, since believers are to live in conformity with the *teaching* about Christ that they have received.

A third reason to accept the close association reading of ἐν αὐτῷ is the phrase βεβαιούμενοι τῇ πίστει (*established in the faith*; v. 7). While it does not employ the prepositional construction ἐν + *dative*, nevertheless the *article* + *dative* modifying another participle that is clearly connected to the previous two (ἐρριζωμένοι καὶ ἐποικοδομούμενοι καὶ βεβαιούμενοι) is highly suggestive that a similar syntactical force is to be expected.

This, then, raises the question of how τῇ πίστει is to be understood. It seems unlikely that *in (the) faith* is to be regarded as locative. While a 'realm of faith' is not inconceivable, it is nevertheless tenuous. Against a locative reading is the following phrase καθὼς ἐδιδάχθητε (*just as you were taught*), which again indicates that it is the reception of *teaching* that is in view. As such, τῇ πίστει is to be read as a controlling influence so that

---

204. BDAG, 327.

205. J. B. Lightfoot, *Saint Paul's Epistles to the Colossians and to Philemon* (1879; repr. Grand Rapids: Zondervan, 1968), 176.

being established in the faith means to be confirmed in the teaching (i.e., *the faith*) to which they are to be conformed. This understanding of τῇ πίστει is also suggested by the textual variants that read εν πιστει or εν τη πιστει in its place.[206]

Consequently, the imperative *walk in him* and the modifying participles *rooted and built up in him* are to be understood as instructing believers to live under the controlling influence of Christ, according to the teaching they have received about him.

3.11.3.3 Characteristics of those in Him

> 2 Cor 13:4 καὶ γὰρ ἐσταυρώθη ἐξ ἀσθενείας, ἀλλὰ ζῇ ἐκ δυνάμεως θεοῦ. καὶ γὰρ ἡμεῖς ἀσθενοῦμεν **ἐν αὐτῷ**, ἀλλὰ ζήσομεν σὺν αὐτῷ ἐκ δυνάμεως θεοῦ εἰς ὑμᾶς
>
> *In fact, He was crucified in weakness, but He lives by God's power. For we also are weak **in Him**, yet toward you we will live with Him by God's power.*

With this occurrence of ἐν αὐτῷ we observe a certain symmetry between the first half of the verse and the second: Christ was *crucified in weakness*, and Paul is *weak in him*; Christ lives by God's power, so Paul will live with him by God's power. The symmetry indicates that Paul models his ministry among the Thessalonians on the experience of Christ. Indeed, more than modeling the weakness of Christ and living by God's power, he shares in those things too. Consequently, ἐν αὐτῷ signifies union with Christ: his weakness is weakness in Christ, just as his living is with Christ; 'the believer is united with Christ not only in the weakness of His death and burial, but also in the glorious power of His resurrection'.[207]

> Eph 6:20 ὑπὲρ οὗ πρεσβεύω ἐν ἁλύσει, ἵνα **ἐν αὐτῷ** παρρησιάσωμαι ὡς δεῖ με λαλῆσαι
>
> *For this I am an ambassador in chains. Pray that I might be bold enough **in Him** to speak as I should.*

---

206. Nestle-Aland 27: εν π. A C I Ψ 2464 *pc* | εν τη π. ℵ D2 P 0278. 1739. 1881 M; Cl.
207. Hughes, *2 Corinthians*, 479.

This occurrence of ἐν αὐτῷ could express cause or agency.[208] If cause, Paul asks for prayer that he may speak boldly *because* of Christ; that is, on account of Christ. If agency, he asks for prayer that he would speak boldly *with the help* of Christ. He would not, then, be indicating *motive* for speaking boldly, but rather *how* he might speak boldly.

The latter option—that ἐν αὐτῷ expresses the agency of Christ—is preferred. Paul has already asked for prayer in the previous verse: *Pray also for me, that the message may be given to me when I open my mouth to make known with boldness the mystery of the gospel* (6:19). The parallels between 6:19 and 6:20 are obvious: Paul requests prayer that he might speak with boldness. In 6:19, however, he asks that *the message may be given to me*, which acknowledges his dependence on God's agency (or Christ's agency). It thus follows that ἐν αὐτῷ in 6:20 continues the same idea: he is dependent on the agency of Christ for boldness to speak as he should.

Of the two instances of ἐν αὐτῷ in this subcategory, 2 Cor 13:4 refers to union and Eph 6:20 indicates agency

3.11.3.4 Justification in Him

> 2 Cor 5:21 τὸν μὴ γνόντα ἁμαρτίαν ὑπὲρ ἡμῶν ἁμαρτίαν ἐποίησεν, ἵνα ἡμεῖς γενώμεθα δικαιοσύνη θεοῦ **ἐν αὐτῷ**
>
> *He made the One who did not know sin to be sin for us, so that we might become the righteousness of God **in Him**.*

There are three strong candidates for understanding this instance of ἐν αὐτῷ. First, the phrase could indicate the sphere or realm of Christ. The strongest argument in favour of this reading is that is how ἐν Χριστῷ is taken in 5:17 (see §3.8). The notion of realm transfer is in view in 5:17,

---

208. Heil translates ἐν αὐτῷ 'in it', referring to the gospel; 'within the dynamic realm in which the mystery which is the gospel is proclaimed, heard, and believed, Paul may "speak boldly"'; John Paul Heil, *Ephesians: Empowerment to Talk in Love for the Unity of All in Christ* (Atlanta: SBL, 2007), 294. It is certainly possible that 'the gospel' (v.19) is the antecedent of the pronoun—as apparently reflected in the NIV and ESV translations—in which case v.20 would fall outside the scope of this discussion. In favour of 'the gospel' as antecedent is that it is the nearest explicit candidate. Against it is the unusual use of ἐν αὐτῷ to depict the content of speech; αὐτό (accusative) would be the obvious choice if 'the gospel' were in view. Also against it is the idiomatic use of ἐν αὐτῷ elsewhere, which suggests that 'in the Lord' or 'in Christ' is meant.

which makes such a reading of ἐν Χριστῷ strong in that context. Against such a reading in 5:21, however, is the verb γενώμεθα: believers are not described as passing into the realm of God's righteousness but as *becoming the righteousness of God.*[209] This nuance, while subtle, pushes away from the notion of realm transfer.

Second, ἐν αὐτῷ could be instrumental. To properly appreciate the strength of this alternative, it is necessary to trace Paul's thought from 5:18. Paul states that *everything is from God* and that God has reconciled believers to himself *through Christ* (διὰ Χριστοῦ; 5:18). He then restates this point with different language: *that is, in Christ, God was reconciling the world to Himself* (5:19). The significance of these two verses is, first, the agency of God is explicitly in view: everything is from God and God reconciles believers through Christ (5:18) and in Christ (5:19). Second, there is a clear parallel between the expressions διὰ Χριστοῦ in 5:18 and ἐν Χριστῷ in 5:19, such that the latter phrase most likely expresses instrumentality. Consequently, verses 18–19 provide three explicit references to the agency of God and two explicit references to the instrumentality of Christ.

Once these factors are considered, they may influence our reading of 5:21. The verse begins with an explicit reference to God's agency: *He made the One who did not know sin to be sin for us.* And while the instrumentality of Christ in becoming sin for us is implicit, it is nevertheless plausible to read God as agent and Christ as instrument. The second half of the verse then indicates the purpose and result of this work: *so that we might become the righteousness of God in Him.* Given the frequent references to the instrumentality of Christ (both explicit and implicit)—and to the agency of God—throughout 5:18–21, an instrumental reading of ἐν αὐτῷ is a strong candidate.

Third, the phrase could indicate union with Christ: believers are made righteous by sharing in the righteousness of Christ. The strength of this reading comes from the apparent symmetry in the verse in which Christ becomes sin for us and believers become righteous in him. Since Christ— who knew no sin—was made 'sin', thus sharing in the plight of the sinful,

209. Martin equates ἐν αὐτῷ in v.21 with ἐν Χριστῷ in v.17, but apparently does not notice his own internal contradiction. On v.17 he argues that ἐν Χριστῷ does *not* refer to the believer but 'relates to the new eschatological situation which has emerged from Christ's advent'. On v.21 he clearly regards ἐν αὐτῷ as relating to believers; 'that we might become … in him'; Martin, *2 Corinthians*, 152, 158.

so sinners are made righteous by sharing in his right standing. Such symmetry speaks against the instrumental reading above; if believers become the righteousness of God *through* Christ (as instrument), it is not clear how this would parallel his being made sin for us. Rather, ἐν αὐτῷ as expressing union makes the symmetry intelligible. Christ was made 'sin', while believers become righteousness. Thus, while the wider context provides strong candidates in the sphere and instrument readings, the internal logic of the verse itself must finally be conclusive: ἐν αὐτῷ indicates union with Christ.

Phil 3:8–9 ἀλλὰ μενοῦνγε καὶ ἡγοῦμαι πάντα ζημίαν εἶναι διὰ τὸ ὑπερέχον τῆς γνώσεως Χριστοῦ Ἰησοῦ τοῦ κυρίου μου, δι' ὃν τὰ πάντα ἐζημιώθην, καὶ ἡγοῦμαι σκύβαλα, ἵνα Χριστὸν κερδήσω καὶ εὑρεθῶ **ἐν αὐτῷ**, μὴ ἔχων ἐμὴν δικαιοσύνην τὴν ἐκ νόμου ἀλλὰ τὴν διὰ πίστεως Χριστοῦ, τὴν ἐκ θεοῦ δικαιοσύνην ἐπὶ τῇ πίστει

*More than that, I also consider everything to be a loss in view of the surpassing value of knowing Christ Jesus my Lord. Because of Him I have suffered the loss of all things and consider them filth, so that I may gain Christ and be found **in Him**, not having a righteousness of my own from the law, but one that is through faith in Christ—the righteousness from God based on faith.*

There are two clear options for understanding this instance of ἐν αὐτῷ. The first is to regard it as locative, conveying the realm of Christ. The strength of this reading is that *being found* naturally suggests a *place* in which that occurs. The sense, then, is that while Paul has lost everything because of Christ, he is now located in Christ's domain.

The second option is to regard ἐν αὐτῷ as expressing union with Christ. Paul's point is to indicate that, while he has lost all things, he has gained Christ by becoming one with him. Indeed, this is stronger than the locative option because of the personal nature of gaining Christ; Paul does not refer merely to his 'location' within the sphere of Christ's rule, but regards his situation as one of personal connection such that he 'obtains' Christ somehow and is found in him.

This is reinforced by what follows: *not having a righteousness of my own from the law, but one that is through faith in Christ.* Regardless of whether πίστεως Χριστοῦ refers to faith in Christ or Christ's faithfulness, Paul's point is that he does not have a righteousness of his own but shares in the righteousness that comes from Christ. Paul's Christ-righteousness is an outworking of being found in him. Consequently, ἐν αὐτῷ is best regarded as expressing union with Christ: Paul has gained Christ, he is found in him, and he shares in his righteousness.[210]

Both instances of ἐν αὐτῷ in this subcategory refer to union (2 Cor 5:21; Phil 3:9).

3.11.3.5 Trinity in Him

2 Cor 1:20 ὅσαι γὰρ ἐπαγγελίαι θεοῦ, **ἐν αὐτῷ** τὸ ναί· διὸ καὶ δι' αὐτοῦ τὸ ἀμὴν τῷ θεῷ πρὸς δόξαν δι' ἡμῶν

For every one of God's promises is "Yes" **in Him**. *Therefore the "Amen" is spoken also through Him by us for God's glory.*

See above (§3.11.3.1) for the instrumental reading of ἐν αὐτῷ in this verse. It is included again under this subcategory because of its trinitarian nature. God's promises are fulfilled in Christ: God is the promissory agent who fulfills his will through the personal instrumentality of Christ.

2 Cor 5:21 τὸν μὴ γνόντα ἁμαρτίαν ὑπὲρ ἡμῶν ἁμαρτίαν ἐποίησεν, ἵνα ἡμεῖς γενώμεθα δικαιοσύνη θεοῦ **ἐν αὐτῷ**

He made the One who did not know sin to be sin for us, so that we might become the righteousness of God **in Him**.

See above (§3.11.3.4) for ἐν αὐτῷ expressing union in this verse. Its trinitarian nature is evident: believers' union with *Christ* establishes them as the righteousness of *God*. It appears that God's righteousness is so closely identified with Christ that union with him establishes believers *as* God's righteousness.

Eph 1:4 καθὼς ἐξελέξατο ἡμᾶς **ἐν αὐτῷ** πρὸ καταβολῆς κόσμου εἶναι ἡμᾶς ἁγίους καὶ ἀμώμους κατενώπιον αὐτοῦ ἐν ἀγάπῃ

---

210. O'Brien, *Philippians*, 392–93; and specifically on the relationship of righteousness to being in Christ, see pp. 415–17.

*For He chose us **in Him**, before the foundation of the world, to be holy and blameless in His sight.*

Again, see above (§3.11.3.1) for the instrumental reading of ἐν αὐτῷ here. This occurrence demonstrates the agency of God in partnership with the instrumentality of Christ.

Eph 1:9–10 γνωρίσας ἡμῖν τὸ μυστήριον τοῦ θελήματος αὐτοῦ, κατὰ τὴν εὐδοκίαν αὐτοῦ ἣν προέθετο **ἐν αὐτῷ** εἰς οἰκονομίαν τοῦ πληρώματος τῶν καιρῶν, ἀνακεφαλαιώσασθαι τὰ πάντα ἐν τῷ Χριστῷ, τὰ ἐπὶ τοῖς οὐρανοῖς καὶ τὰ ἐπὶ τῆς γῆς **ἐν αὐτῷ**

*He made known to us the mystery of His will, according to His good pleasure that He planned **in Him** for the administration of the days of fulfillment—to bring everything together in the Messiah, both things in heaven and things on earth **in Him**.*

The second instance of ἐν αὐτῷ reiterates ἐν τῷ Χριστῷ in 1:10, which is regarded as locative (see above, §3.11.1.4). Given these two locative references in 1:10, it would be natural to regard ἐν αὐτῷ in 1:9 as locative also. However, this case is not so simple since the two verses appear to use the phrases differently. In 1:10, location fits well with 'bringing everything together', but 1:9 refers to the planning activity of God (προέθετο ἐν αὐτῷ εἰς οἰκονομίαν).[211] To regard this as taking place in the realm of Christ is unintelligible. Rather, it refers to close association and shared purpose. As such, ἐν αὐτῷ in 1:9 is best understood as expressing union; it is unlikely that any other options make sense. The meaning, then, is that God has planned the revelation of his will in conjunction and in unity with Christ.

Col 1:19 ὅτι **ἐν αὐτῷ** εὐδόκησεν πᾶν τὸ πλήρωμα κατοικῆσαι

*For God was pleased to have all His fullness dwell **in Him**.*

As mentioned above in the discussion of Colossians 1:16–17, this use of ἐν αὐτῷ is locative in a spiritual manner; it depicts the indwelling of God in Christ.[212]

---

211. 'No doubt προέθετο does refer to God's eternal intent, but such a meaning has to be derived from contextual considerations rather than the form of the verb, as its use in Rom 1:13 indicates'; Lincoln, *Ephesians*, 31.

212. 'He is the "place" ... in whom God in all his fullness was pleased to take up residence'; O'Brien, *Colossians, Philemon*, 53.

Col 2:9 ὅτι **ἐν αὐτῷ** κατοικεῖ πᾶν τὸ πλήρωμα τῆς θεότητος σωματικῶς

*For **in Him** all the fullness of Deity dwells in bodily form.* (NASB)

In this verse ἐν αὐτῷ has significant trinitarian implications and expresses the union of God and Christ. While other instances included under this subcategory reflect Paul's trinitarian thinking in relation to other issues, this one is entirely concerned with the inner nature of the Godhead. The dwelling of God's nature in Christ denotes an association of profound connectedness and union. It 'speaks of the real, substantial, even tangible and visible presence of God' in Christ.[213]

Col 2:15 ἀπεκδυσάμενος τὰς ἀρχὰς καὶ τὰς ἐξουσίας ἐδειγμάτισεν ἐν παρρησίᾳ, θριαμβεύσας αὐτοὺς **ἐν αὐτῷ**

*He disarmed the rulers and authorities and disgraced them publicly; He triumphed over them **by Him**.*

This occurrence of ἐν αὐτῷ offers a fairly certain example of instrumentality. The agency of God is clearly in view (*He disarmed ... He triumphed...*), and the previous verse unambiguously assigns instrumentality to the cross of Christ: *He erased the certificate of debt... and has taken it out of the way by nailing it to the cross* (2:14). Given these factors, the instrumentality of ἐν αὐτῷ in 2:15 is overt. The trinitarian nature of this verse is also overt, with God acting as agent in the triumph achieved through Christ.

Of the seven occurrences of ἐν αὐτῷ in this trinitarian subcategory, three express union (2 Cor 5:21; Eph 1:9; Col 2:9), two are instrumental (Eph 1:4; Col 2:15), and two are locative (Eph 1:10; Col 1:19).

3.11.3.6 Summary

To conclude this section on ἐν αὐτῷ, we note that it is simply another way to express ἐν Χριστῷ. The two phrases are used in identical ways, found in matching contexts, and are apparently interchangable.

---

213. Woodhouse, *Colossians and Philemon*, 130.

3.11.4 IN WHOM

Following ἐν κυρίῳ and ἐν αὐτῷ, ἐν ᾧ is the next step outside ἐν Χριστῷ. Whenever the relative pronoun refers to Christ, it is assumed that ἐν ᾧ is another way to say ἐν Χριστῷ. Of note is that most translations render the relative pronoun with an English personal pronoun in most (if not all) instances. And in some cases, the phrase ἐν ᾧ is not directly rendered at all.

3.11.4.1 Things achieved for/given to people in whom

Eph 1:6 εἰς ἔπαινον δόξης τῆς χάριτος αὐτοῦ ἧς ἐχαρίτωσεν ἡμᾶς ἐν τῷ ἠγαπημένῳ.

*To the praise of His glorious grace that He favored us with **in the Beloved**.*

This example does not utilize the relative pronoun but is a miscellaneous reference with ἐν τῷ ἠγαπημένῳ referring to Christ.[214] It is included here because it directly preceeds v. 7, addressed next. The phrase ἐν τῷ ἠγαπημένῳ could express instrumentality, such that God dealt his favour to believers through the Beloved, or it could be locative, such that God's favour is poured out on those belonging to the realm of Christ.

If it could be argued that ἐν τῷ ἠγαπημένῳ modifies ἡμᾶς rather than ἐχαρίτωσεν, the locative reading would become most likely. The idea would be that God has shown favour to 'us who are in the realm of the Beloved'. In spite of word order, however, it is unlikely that ἐν τῷ ἠγαπημένῳ modifies ἡμᾶς. Modifying ἐχαρίτωσεν, therefore, ἐν τῷ ἠγαπημένῳ refers either to the instrument of this favour or to the realm in which God's favour is known. It is difficult to say which reading is correct, but since a locative reading is most likely for the phrase ἐν ᾧ in the next verse (see below) — in fact, τῷ ἠγαπημένῳ is the antecedent of the relative pronoun in v. 7 — this is cautiously adopted here too.[215]

Eph 1:7 ἐν ᾧ ἔχομεν τὴν ἀπολύτρωσιν διὰ τοῦ αἵματος αὐτοῦ, τὴν ἄφεσιν τῶν παραπτωμάτων, κατὰ τὸ πλοῦτος τῆς χάριτος αὐτοῦ

---

214. See Lincoln for discussion of this title for Christ; Lincoln, *Ephesians*, 26.

215. Lincoln takes the phrase as instrumental but does not argue for or defend that position; Lincoln, *Ephesians*, 26.

*We have redemption **in Him** through His blood, the forgiveness of our trespasses, according to the riches of His grace.*

This use of the phrase ἐν ᾧ could be regarded as *locative* (the redemption that is found in the sphere of Christ), *instrumental* (the redemption that is achieved [by God] through Christ), or *agency* (the redemption achieved by Christ). Of these options, an instrumental reading is unlikely given that role is assigned to Christ's blood (διὰ τοῦ αἵματος αὐτοῦ).[216]

Reading ἐν ᾧ as indicating agency is possible, especially if the phrase *according to the riches of His grace* refers to Christ rather than the Father. This would mean that according to the riches of Christ's grace, he has bestowed redemption on believers through his blood. While it is ambiguous, however, it is more likely that *according to the riches of His grace* refers to the Father rather than Christ, in keeping with similar statements in Ephesians (e.g., 2:7 – 8).[217] Consequently, agency is not the most robust reading of ἐν ᾧ here.

Thus, a locative reading is probably best.[218] Believers belong to the realm of Christ, to which redemption and forgiveness of trespasses pertain according to the riches of God's grace.

Eph 1:11 **ἐν ᾧ** καὶ ἐκληρώθημεν προορισθέντες κατὰ πρόθεσιν τοῦ τὰ πάντα ἐνεργοῦντος κατὰ τὴν βουλὴν τοῦ θελήματος αὐτοῦ

*We have also received an inheritance **in Him**, predestined according to the purpose of the One who works out everything in agreement with the decision of His will.*

While this use of ἐν ᾧ could possibly be instrumental in function, it is more likely locative. This is in keeping with the previous occurrence of ἐν ᾧ in v. 7 (see previous entry). Also in support of this conclusion is the cosmic nature of 1:10, in which Paul writes that everything is brought

---

216. William J. Larkin, *Ephesians: A Handbook on the Greek Text* (Baylor Handbook on the Greek New Testament; Waco, TX: Baylor Univ. Press, 2009), 9.

217. Best, *Ephesians*, 132.

218. So Rudolf Schnackenburg, *The Epistle to the Ephesians* (trans. Helen Heron; Edinburgh: T&T Clark, 1991), 56.

together in the Messiah, both things in heaven and things on earth. Verse 11 then narrows the focus to believers as a subset within the cosmos.[219]

This movement parallels 1:22–23, in which Paul writes that everything is put under Christ's feet, with a subsequent narrowing of focus to the church as Christ's body. In both 1:10–11 and 1:22–23, then, the body of believers are viewed as a subset within the cosmological whole. Therefore the cosmic sense of v. 10 supports a locative reading of v. 11 because the notion of dominion and realm is in view; it is within the realm of Christ that believers share in the inheritance. Furthermore, the phrase ἐν τῷ Χριστῷ in v. 10 is most likely locative also (see above, §3.11.1.4 and 3.11.3.5), which provides further confirmation of the locative reading of ἐν ᾧ in v. 11.

Eph 1:13 **ἐν ᾧ** καὶ ὑμεῖς ἀκούσαντες τὸν λόγον τῆς ἀληθείας, τὸ εὐαγγέλιον τῆς σωτηρίας ὑμῶν, **ἐν ᾧ** καὶ πιστεύσαντες ἐσφραγίσθητε τῷ πνεύματι τῆς ἐπαγγελίας τῷ ἁγίῳ

*When you heard the message of truth, the gospel of your salvation, and when you believed **in Him**, you were also sealed with the promised Holy Spirit.*

There are two instances of ἐν ᾧ in this verse. Regarding the former occurrence, a preliminary issue to address is the syntax of the verse, which is unusually complex with a series of subordinate clauses embedded within the principal clause.[220] Most likely the principal clause is ἐν ᾧ καὶ ὑμεῖς ... ἐσφραγίσθητε τῷ πνεύματι τῆς ἐπαγγελίας τῷ ἁγίῳ *In whom you also ... were sealed with the promised Holy Spirit*. The other clauses are bracketed by the two parts of the principal clause. This complexity most likely accounts for the HCSB's failure to translate the first ἐν ᾧ at all, but the ESV helpfully captures the clause structure: ***In him** you also, when you heard the word of truth, the gospel of your salvation, and believed **in him**, were sealed with the promised Holy Spirit.*

---

219. According to Best, ἐν ᾧ 'creates the bridge to the next stage of the eulogy in which attention returns from the cosmic to blessings granted more directly to believers'; Best, *Ephesians*, 144.

220. Indeed, this 'principal clause' is in fact also a subordinate (relative) clause, but the other clauses here are subordinate to *it*, hence creating a further level of subordination. The 'principal clause' is so named to clarify this point.

An understanding of the clausal structure clarifies that the first instance of ἐν ᾧ in the verse is the third in a string (vv. 7, 11 and 13), in which the phrase is connected with benefits received by believers (see above on 1:7, 11). In 1:7 believers have redemption *in him*; in 1:11 believers have received an inheritance *in him*; and here in 1:13 believers were sealed with the Holy Spirit *in him*. Given this pattern of parallel usage of ἐν ᾧ in vv. 7, 11, and 13, it is likely that the phrase functions the same way across all three verses — indeed this has already been established for 1:7 and 11 (above). Thus, the first occurrence of ἐν ᾧ in 1:13 is locative in function, indicating that believers have been sealed with the Spirit *in the realm of Christ*.

The second occurrence of ἐν ᾧ most likely resumes the first,[221] and this is for syntactical reasons. The phrase ἐν ᾧ καὶ ὑμεῖς ἀκούσαντες is a striking parallel to ἐν ᾧ καὶ πιστεύσαντες. Both phrases begin with ἐν ᾧ καί, which is then followed by an aorist participle. The parallel phrases are correlated by their depiction of human hearing and response in the realm of Christ; first hearing the word of truth, second believing. Thus both instances of ἐν ᾧ are locative in function depiciting the realm of Christ.[222]

Eph 2:21 – 22 ἐν ᾧ πᾶσα οἰκοδομὴ συναρμολογουμένη αὔξει
εἰς ναὸν ἅγιον ἐν κυρίῳ, ἐν ᾧ καὶ ὑμεῖς συνοικοδομεῖσθε εἰς
κατοικητήριον τοῦ θεοῦ ἐν πνεύματι

In whom *the whole building, being fitted together, is growing into a holy temple in the Lord,* **in whom** *you also are being built together into a dwelling of God in the Spirit.* (NASB)

It is argued above (§3.11.2.1) that the phrase ἐν κυρίῳ in 2:21 indicates incorporation into the Lord, in keeping with the sense of the building metaphor. While ἐν ᾧ in vv. 21 and 22 could be taken as instrumental, such that the building is fitted together *by him* (2:21) and believers are built together *by him* (2:22), this is not as likely as an incorporative sense. The entire thrust of the verse in context is the building together of believers in the Lord, and the two instances of ἐν ᾧ function according to this purpose alongside ἐν κυρίῳ.

---

221. Best, *Ephesians*, 148; O'Brien, *Ephesians*, 118.

222. This goes against both translations provided (HCSB, ESV), which take ἐν ᾧ as the object of πιστεύσαντες.

Col 1:14 ἐν ᾧ ἔχομεν τὴν ἀπολύτρωσιν, τὴν ἄφεσιν τῶν ἁμαρτιῶν

*We have redemption, the forgiveness of sins, **in Him**.*

The phrase ἐν ᾧ ἔχομεν τὴν ἀπολύτρωσιν is exactly paralleled in Ephesians 1:7. It is argued above that ἐν ᾧ there is locative, indicating the realm or sphere of Christ. While the parallel between the two verses is sufficient evidence for a locative reading here in Colossians 1:14, the context confirms this conclusion beyond doubt. The preceding verse reads *He has rescued us from the domain of darkness and transferred us into the kingdom of the Son He loves* (1:13). Realm transfer is clearly in view here, with believers transferred from the domain of darkness into Christ's kingdom. Furthermore, redemption, 'which connotes liberation from imprisonment and bondage',[223] also embodies overtones of realm transference. Consequently, a locative reading of ἐν ᾧ in 1:14 is highly likely; believers have redemption *in the realm of Christ*.

Col 2:3 ἐν ᾧ εἰσιν πάντες οἱ θησαυροὶ τῆς σοφίας καὶ γνώσεως ἀπόκρυφοι

*All the treasures of wisdom and knowledge are hidden **in Him**.*

While it is not immediately self-evident that this example refers to *things achieved for/given to people*, the context reveals this to be the case. In the preceding verse, Paul desires that believers would have *all the riches of assured understanding and have the knowledge of God's mystery — Christ* (2:2). He then states that all the treasures of wisdom and knowledge are hidden in Christ (2:3) — the implication being that the desired knowledge (2:2) may be found in Christ (2:3). Furthermore, a practical benefit of 2:3 for believers is that *no one will deceive you with persuasive arguments* (2:4). Thus, the verse is appropriately listed in this subcategory; the treasures of wisdom and knowledge are on offer to believers.

The language of such wisdom and knowledge being *hidden* (ἀπόκρυφοι) in Christ suggests a locative reading of ἐν ᾧ.[224] It is unclear, however, as

---

223. O'Brien, *Colossians, Philemon*, 28.

224. It is possible that the antecedent of ἐν ᾧ is μυστηρίου of 2:2, but 'it is more likely to be the nearer antecedent, Χριστοῦ'; Harris, *Colossians and Philemon*, 82.

to whether this locative sense ought to be understood in the customary way—as indicating location within the realm of Christ—or in a more personal capacity. Presumably Paul could envisage the treasures of wisdom and knowledge as 'hidden' in the domain of Christ, available to all who identify with his realm. Nevertheless the idea of hiddenness is not only suggestive of location, but also of personal seclusion.[225] Rather than referring to the realm of Christ, in all its pervasive broadness, this instance of ἐν ᾧ may point to the location of wisdom and knowledge *in Christ's person*. Indeed, this nuance might also be supported by the context, since in the preceding verse Paul wants believers to *have the knowledge of God's mystery—Christ*. Christ is the content of their knowledge; this too refers to the person of Christ rather than his domain. Consequently, the wisdom and knowledge Paul wishes for believers is to be found in the person of Christ.

Col 2:11 **ἐν ᾧ** καὶ περιετμήθητε περιτομῇ ἀχειροποιήτῳ ἐν τῇ ἀπεκδύσει τοῦ σώματος τῆς σαρκός, ἐν τῇ περιτομῇ τοῦ Χριστοῦ

*You were also circumcised **in Him** with a circumcision not done with hands, by putting off the body of flesh, in the circumcision of the Messiah.*

In this curious example that contains Paul's only *spiritual* use of the verb περιτέμνω (i.e., *a circumcision not done with hands*),[226] ἐν ᾧ could be understood as instrumental, such that the Colossians were circumcised *by Christ*. Apart from the awkwardness of the image of being circumcised by Christ, however, an instrumental reading is less likely than a local interpretation—believers have been transferred into the realm of Christ through spiritual 'circumcision'. Such circumcision occurs *by putting off the body of flesh*, which is the kind of language Paul uses with reference to realm transfer. Believers are no longer to live according to the flesh but according the Spirit.[227] If being circumcised in Christ is achieved by put-

---

225. These treasures of wisdom and knowledge are 'deposited' or 'stored up' in Christ; O'Brien, *Colossians, Philemon*, 95.

226. Other uses of the verb refer to the physical act of circumcision; 1 Cor 7:18; Gal 2:3; 5:2–3; 6:12–13; Col 2:11.

227. 'God himself had decisively effected the change from the old life to the new'; O'Brien, *Colossians, Philemon*, 116.

ting off the body of flesh, it stands to reason that circumcision in Christ refers to the transference of believers into the domain of Christ.[228] This reading is also supported by the last clause, *in the circumcision of the Messiah*, which can also be understood as referring to the realm of Christ.

Col 2:12 συνταφέντες αὐτῷ ἐν τῷ βαπτισμῷ, ἐν ᾧ καὶ συνηγέρθητε διὰ τῆς πίστεως τῆς ἐνεργείας τοῦ θεοῦ τοῦ ἐγείραντος αὐτὸν ἐκ νεκρῶν

*Having been buried with Him in baptism, you were also raised **with Him** through faith in the working of God, who raised Him from the dead.*

It is possible that ἐν ᾧ here has baptism as its antecedent rather than Christ, as the ESV renders it: *having been buried with him in baptism, **in which** you were also raised with him.* This seems unlikely, however, since nowhere else does Paul refer to being *raised* in baptism; that image (when spiritually applied) always refers to participation in Christ's death rather than his resurrection.[229] It also goes against the consistent usage of ἐν ᾧ in Colossians, which always refers to Christ (1:14; 2:3; and, most notably, the preceding verse, 2:11).[230]

Referring to Christ, then, ἐν ᾧ most likely indicates participation in the event of his resurrection. Participation language permeates the verse (on the σύν-compound words συνταφέντες and συνηγέρθητε, and their expression of participation with Christ, see ch. 5), which strongly suggests a participation reading for ἐν ᾧ. In this way, ἐν ᾧ καὶ συνηγέρθητε functions much the same way as the preceding phrase συνταφέντες αὐτῷ, with the dative pronoun working in conjunction with the σύν-compound word to create the periphrastic sense *you were raised with him.*

Of the eleven instances of ἐν ᾧ in this subcategory, eight are locative

---

228. Wright prefers to use the familial language here, but the notion of transference is nevertheless in view; 'the Colossians now belong first and foremost to the family of God, and not, therefore, to the human families (and their local "rulers") to which they formerly belonged'; Wright, *Colossians and Philemon*, 106.

229. Contra Harris, who claims that Rom 6:4, 8–11, 13 expresses resurrection with Christ in baptism, whereas those references confirm that baptism with Christ is only explicitly connected to participation with Christ in his death. While resurrection with Christ occurs in the context, it is not depicted with the image of baptism. Cf. Harris, *Colossians and Philemon*, 104.

230. So O'Brien, *Colossians, Philemon*, 118–19.

(Eph 1:6, 7, 11, 13 [x2]; Col 1:14; 2:3, 11), two indicate incorporation (Eph 2:21–22), and one expresses participation (Col 2:12).

3.11.4.2 Characteristics of those in whom

Eph 3:12 ἐν ᾧ ἔχομεν τὴν παρρησίαν καὶ προσαγωγὴν ἐν πεποιθήσει διὰ τῆς πίστεως αὐτοῦ

In Him *we have boldness and confident access through faith in Him.*

This example of ἐν ᾧ is most likely understood as a *marker of cause of reason*,[231] such that it is because of Christ that believers may have boldness and confidence in access to the Father.[232] This reading is supported by the previous verse, *This is according to His eternal purpose accomplished in the Messiah, Jesus our Lord* (3:11), which refers to Christ's achievement of the Father's purpose in bringing Jew and Gentile into the riches of Christ (3:6–10). While the Gentiles were once *excluded from the citizenship of Israel, and foreigners to the covenants of the promise, without hope and with-out God in the world* (2:12), now because of Christ's accomplishment, Jew and Gentile alike have confident access to God.

3.11.4.3 Summary

To conclude this section on ἐν ᾧ, we note that when the antecedent of the relative pronoun is Christ, the phrase is yet another way to express ἐν Χριστῷ. While ἐν ᾧ has a narrower range of usage, being far less common than ἐν Χριστῷ, the two phrases nevertheless share identical functions, are found in matching contexts, and are apparently interchangable.

3.12 Summary

This chapter has demonstrated that the idiom ἐν Χριστῷ is capable of a broad range of expressions, owing to the flexibility of the preposition ἐν and determined by context. Moreover, there is no discernable difference in function between ἐν Χριστῷ, ἐν κυρίῳ, ἐν αὐτῷ, and ἐν ᾧ (when Christ

---

231. BDAG, 329.

232. As Best summarizes, 'it is only through Christ … that they gain the right to speak without fear to God'; Best, *Ephesians*, 329.

is the antecedent of the personal and relative pronouns). These idioms can express instrumentality, close association, agency, recognition, cause, kind and manner, locality, specification or substance, circumstance or condition, the object of faith, incorporation, union, reference or respect, and participation. It is, therefore, impossible to define the meaning of these idioms by a single description as though they are formulaic. Virtually the full range of lexical possibilities of the preposition ἐν is extant for ἐν Χριστῷ and its variations.

These various uses of ἐν Χριστῷ and its variations are grouped into broader categories of usage, determined by the metafunction of the contexts to which they contribute. The phrases are found in reference to things achieved for/given to people, believers' actions, characteristics of believers, faith in Christ, justification, and new status. The phrases contribute to trinitarian contexts, and they frequently function as periphrases to denote that someone is a believer.

CHAPTER 4

Εἰς Χριστόν

4.1 INTRODUCTION

While it may seem less than clear as to where to proceed after ἐν Χριστῷ, ἐν κυρίῳ, and ἐν αὐτῷ, it is prudent to consider a preposition lexically similar to ἐν. The phrase εἰς Χριστόν provides such a candidate. Obviously εἰς is not identical to ἐν; nevertheless there is some lexical overlap between them, and εἰς is the preposition most similar to ἐν.

4.2 Εἰς

The relationship between ἐν and εἰς is widely acknowledged and may be seen through etymology as well as synchronic usage.[1] According to Robertson, εἰς developed as a later variation of ἐν and was originally *ἐνς. Once the ν in ἐνς disappeared, the form became εἰς through compensatory lengthening.[2] As for usage, Harris acknowledges that Hellenistic Greek is marked by 'a general tendency to confuse the categories of linear motion ("to") and punctiliar rest ("in")'.[3] As a result, there was mixed usage in both directions: εἰς denoting 'position', and ἐν implying 'movement'.

While this phenomenon is evident within Classical Greek usage, it is relatively infrequent when compared to the Koine period.[4] This is not to

---

1. 'eis had a comparatively late origin, having derived from en in some of the individual Greek dialects, presumably when the class of preverbs/adpositions was already well established as such'; Luraghi, *Prepositions and Cases*, 107.

2. Robertson, *Grammar*, 584–86, 591.

3. Harris, *Prepositions and Theology*, 84.

4. Ibid., 84–86. Contra Turner, who claims that 'in the Koine εἰς and ἐν are freely inter-

say that the interchange between the two prepositions is common within the Pauline canon. Within the New Testament, it is frequently observed only in Matthew and Luke-Acts, and the other New Testament authors 'do not ordinarily use *eis* for *en*'.[5] So Turner: 'The Pauline and Johannine epistles and Rev ... do not often confuse local ἐν and εἰς'.[6] Nevertheless, the etymological and synchronic relatedness between ἐν and εἰς is instructive, as long as the two dangers of which Harris warns are avoided. The first danger is to treat the two prepositions as synonymous in every case; the second is 'always to insist on a distinction between them'.[7]

The main uses of εἰς are listed by BDAG as following:[8]

1. extension involving a goal or place, *into, in, toward, to*
2. extension in time, *to, until, on*
3. marker of degree, *up to*
4. marker of goals involving affective/abstract/suitability aspects, *into, to*
5. marker of a specific point of reference, *for, to, with respect to, with reference to*
6. marker of a guarantee, *by*
7. distributive marker
8. the predicate nom. and the predicate acc. are somet. replaced by εἰς w. acc. under Semitic influence, which has strengthened Gk. tendencies in the same direction
9. marker of instrumentality, *by, with*
10. other uses of εἰς

As with ἐν, εἰς enjoys a wide range of functions, including spatial and temporal extension (1, 2), degree (3), goal (4), and reference (5). It is unclear,

---

changed ... εἰς often appearing for ἐν and more rarely ἐν for εἰς'; Turner, *Grammatical Insights*, 254. Turner's claims here seem to be overstated, though there is evidence of some interchange between the two prepositions in Koine papyri, as well as in the New Testament; see James Hope Moulton and George Milligan, *Vocabulary of the Greek Testament* (1929; repr. Peabody, MA: Hendrickson, 2004), 186, §1519.

5. Harris, 'Prepositions and Theology', 1185–86.

6. Turner, *Grammatical Insights*, 255.

7. Harris, 'Prepositions and Theology', 1186. See also Maximilian Zerwick, *Biblical Greek: Illustrated by Examples* (English ed. adapted from 4th Latin ed. by Joseph Smith; Scripta Pontificii Instituti Biblici 114; Rome: Pontificio Instituto Biblico, 1963), 33–37.

8. BDAG, 288–91.

however, which category (or categories) would be regarded by BDAG as appropriate to describe the Pauline expression εἰς Χριστόν and related phrases.

Moule discusses what might be called a 'pregnant' use of εἰς, 'apparently *combining* the ideas of motion and rest, the "linear" and the "punctiliar"—a line ending at a point, as it were'.[9] He identifies a metaphorical version of this pregnant use: εἰς τὸν καιρὸν αὐτῶν *at their proper time* (Luke 1:20); εἰς τὸ μέλλον, *in the future* (Luke 13:9); εἰς τὸ μεταξὺ σάββατον, *on the next sabbath* (Acts 13:42).[10] Moule suggests that some of these metaphorical pregnant uses of εἰς 'look uncommonly like synonyms for ἐν'.[11] While there may be some degree of synonymy between the two prepositions in the shared notion of 'rest'—a stative spatial concept—it would appear that the 'motion' that inheres the pregnant εἰς is not shared by ἐν. Thus, the so-called pregnant εἰς may be seen to overlap with ἐν while not being entirely synonymous. Porter concludes similarly, claiming that 'the historical and contextual evidence indicates that they overlap in meaning, while remaining distinct'.[12]

Oepke delineates a use of εἰς that denotes a 'friendly relationship' between man and man, as well as 'the love of the world and man for God'.[13] Faith that believes in or on Christ is expressed by the phrase πιστεύειν εἰς τὸν κύριον Ἰησοῦν. Oepke regards this kind of expression as original to the New Testament.[14] He claims, however, that εἰς Χριστόν 'never became a formula like ἐν Χριστῷ. There is hardly the slightest impulse in this direction in an expression like ἀπαρχὴ τῆς Ἀσίας εἰς Χριστόν (R. 16:5).'[15] Oepke also states that εἰς can replace the genitive or dative cases, offering the example of τὰ εἰς Χριστὸν παθήματα, which he translates 'the sufferings of Christ' (1 Peter 1:11).[16]

Dunn argues that in the phrase 'having been baptized into Christ', 'it is difficult to avoid the basic sense of *eis*, as movement into a location'.[17] This movement, Dunn suggests, refers to the motion with which believers become members of the body of Christ; 'to be baptized into Christ is com-

9. Moule, *Idiom Book*, 68.
10. Ibid., 68–69.
11. Ibid., 69.
12. Porter, *Idioms*, 151, 153.
13. Albrecht Oepke, 'εἰς', *TDNT*, 2:432.
14. Ibid.
15. Ibid., 433.
16. Ibid., 434.
17. Dunn, *Paul the Apostle*, 404.

plementary to or equivalent to assuming the persona of Christ'.[18] For other uses of εἰς Χριστόν, however, Dunn understands εἰς to convey the sense of 'towards, in reference to, for'.[19] He does not, however, overtly acknowledge a purely stative use of εἰς, which would be synonymous with ἐν.

Thus, for our purposes, it appears that the key issues concerning the use of εἰς relate to its synonymy or otherwise with ἐν, whether the preposition expresses movement toward a goal or is simply stative, and whether it may serve in place of a genitival or dative relation. We now turn to examine each occurrence of the phrase εἰς Χριστόν in its context, using the subcategories employed in the previous chapter.

4.3 THINGS ACHIEVED FOR/GIVEN TO PEOPLE *INTO CHRIST*

2 Cor 1:21 ὁ δὲ βεβαιῶν ἡμᾶς σὺν ὑμῖν **εἰς Χριστὸν** καὶ χρίσας ἡμᾶς θεός

*Now it is God who strengthens us, with you, **in Christ** and has anointed us.*

Two elements within the context bear upon the reading of this verse. The first is the partial parallelism of the following verse: *He has also sealed us and given us the Spirit as a down payment in our hearts* (1:22), which is more striking in the Greek phrasing. While 1:21 employs the substantival participial phrase ὁ δὲ βεβαιῶν ἡμᾶς, *[God] who strengthens us*, 1:22 has ὁ καὶ σφραγισάμενος ἡμᾶς, *[the one] who has also sealed us*. While 1:21 depicts some kind of confirmation *into Christ*, 1:22 conveys the giving *of the Spirit*. The question, therefore, is whether the parallels between the two verses should inform the way in which εἰς Χριστόν is to be understood. It is probably best, however, not to view confirmation *into Christ* as strictly parallel to the giving *of the Spirit*, since the activities of *confirming* and *giving* are distinct.

The second element within the context that bears on our reading of εἰς Χριστόν is the use of ἐν αὐτῷ and δι' αὐτοῦ in the previous verse: *For every one of God's promises is "Yes" **in Him**. Therefore the "Amen" is also*

18. Ibid., 405.
19. Ibid.

*spoken **through Him** by us for God's glory* (1:20). Thus we can observe an interesting string of three prepositional phrases through the two verses: ἐν αὐτῷ, δι᾽ αὐτοῦ, and εἰς Χριστόν.

I argued in the previous chapter that ἐν αὐτῷ in 1:20 is best understood as expressing instrumentality, such that Christ is the one through whom God has fulfilled his promises. And while we are yet to investigate the functions of the phrase δι᾽ αὐτοῦ, this too appears to reflect instrumentality, such that Paul's *Amen* is issued through Christ. Thus, the uses of ἐν αὐτῷ and δι᾽ αὐτοῦ in 1:20 are somewhat synonymous—the first phrase reflecting the *Yes* of God through Christ, which is answered by the second phrase, reflecting the *Amen* of Paul through Christ.

Consequently, we are led to wonder whether the third member of the string, εἰς Χριστόν, should also be regarded as instrumental. Certainly this seems possible, so that the sense of 1:21 would be that God confirms Paul, with the Corinthians, *through Christ*. Such a reading would be supported by the opinion of BDAG regarding the function of βεβαιόω here, which is that it conveys the idea of *strengthening*: '*the one who strengthens us in Christ*=makes us faithful disciples'.[20] The idea, then, would be that God performs this work of strengthening believers *through Christ*.

One wonders, however, whether 1:21 is actually concerned with *strengthening* disciples, as BDAG suggests. In this the parallel with 1:22 *is* significant: the latter verse conveys the status of believers, who are sealed with the deposit of the Spirit. It is likely that 1:21 is also best regarded as indicating status—the confirmation and anointing of believers *into Christ*—rather than the quality of their discipleship. If, therefore, βεβαιόω is regarded as expressing *confirmation* rather than *strengthening*, an instrumental reading of εἰς Χριστόν appears less convincing. If believers are *confirmed through Christ*, with respect to what are they so confirmed? The verb seems to require adverbial qualification, such that the confirmation of its objects is offered with reference to something.

As such, the most likely understanding of εἰς Χριστόν in this instance is that it conveys *a specific point of reference*, which is one of the functions of εἰς according to BDAG. Consequently, the phrase is best rendered, *Now the One who confirms us with you with respect to Christ....* The verse then expresses the status of believers, who are confirmed as being in some

---

20. BDAG, 173.

way defined by, or belonging to, Christ. This reading provides the best fit in the context, in which believers are also anointed and sealed with the Spirit—further markers that define and demarcate them.[21]

Phlm 6 ὅπως ἡ κοινωνία τῆς πίστεώς σου ἐνεργὴς γένηται ἐν ἐπιγνώσει παντὸς ἀγαθοῦ τοῦ ἐν ἡμῖν **εἰς Χριστόν**

*I pray that your participation in the faith may become effective through knowing every good thing that is in us **for the glory of Christ**.*

There are at least two possible options for understanding this use of the phrase εἰς Χριστόν. Before exploring these, it is worth noting that the translation above adds the phrase *the glory of,* which reflects the translator's understanding of the verse but does not reflect the Greek words. First, εἰς Χριστόν could express reference or respect, such that Paul refers to *every good thing that is in us with respect to Christ.* While this reading is certainly possible, it does seem to imply that Paul would be allowing room for good things in us that *do not* pertain to Christ, since the expression of reference or respect functions to delimit *every good thing.* Again, this is possible, but it seems unlikely.

Second, εἰς Χριστόν could express instrumentality, such that Paul is speaking of *every good thing that is in us through Christ.* The instrumentality of Christ in producing *every good thing that is in us* seems to accord more easily with Paul's thinking in general. Since every blessing that believers enjoy is found in and through Christ, such a notion fits well here. While not an impermeable account of the instrumental reading, it is the most likely alternative given its ease of accommodation within Paul's thinking in general.[22]

There are only two instances of εἰς Χριστόν in this subcategory, with 2 Cor 1:21 indicating a specific point of reference and Phlm 6 expressing instrumentality.

---

21. The conclusion of Hughes seems highly precarious: 'It is *God*, firstly, who *establishes* him, together with the Corinthian believers, into Christ—the present tense showing that this is a *constant* experience, and the graphic "into" (εἰς) that it is a *progressive* experience: in the purpose of God the stability is not only continuous, but is ever being intensified'; Hughes, *2 Corinthians*, 39. It is not clear what makes εἰς 'graphic' here, nor why it depicts a progressive experience that is intensified.

22. The ambiguity of this example is evidenced by Harris's approach that lists several options for understanding εἰς Χριστόν without arguing for any one of them; Harris, *Colossians and Philemon*, 252–53.

4.4 FAITH *INTO* CHRIST

Gal 2:16 εἰδότες [δὲ] ὅτι οὐ δικαιοῦται ἄνθρωπος ἐξ ἔργων νόμου
ἐὰν μὴ διὰ πίστεως Ἰησοῦ Χριστοῦ, καὶ ἡμεῖς **εἰς Χριστὸν** Ἰησοῦν
ἐπιστεύσαμεν, ἵνα δικαιωθῶμεν ἐκ πίστεως Χριστοῦ καὶ οὐκ ἐξ
ἔργων νόμου, ὅτι ἐξ ἔργων νόμου οὐ δικαιωθήσεται πᾶσα σάρξ

*[We] know that no one is justified by the works of the law but by
faith in Jesus Christ. And we have believed **in Christ** Jesus, so that we
might be justified by faith in Christ and not by the works of the law,
because by the works of the law no human being will be justified.*

This example of εἰς Χριστόν is probably best understood as the use
listed by BDAG as a *marker of goals involving affective/abstract/suitability
aspects*, and in particular its subcategory *of actions or feelings directed in
someone's direction in hostile or friendly sense*. Of the ten main categories of
the usage of εἰς listed in BDAG, this is the only serious contender. While
believing in Christ is not really an action nor a feeling—it is better understood as *trust*—nevertheless εἰς seems to function here as marking the
goal of such believing. Christ is the personal object toward whom trust is
extended.[23]

Col 2:5 εἰ γὰρ καὶ τῇ σαρκὶ ἄπειμι, ἀλλὰ τῷ πνεύματι σὺν ὑμῖν
εἰμι, χαίρων καὶ βλέπων ὑμῶν τὴν τάξιν καὶ τὸ στερέωμα τῆς **εἰς
Χριστὸν** πίστεως ὑμῶν

*For I may be absent in body, but I am with you in spirit, rejoicing to
see how well ordered you are and the strength of your faith **in Christ**.*

This instance of εἰς Χριστόν no doubt conveys the same sense as the
previous example: Christ is the goal toward whom trust is extended. He is
the object of the Colossians' faith.[24]

Both Gal 2:16 and Col 2:5 indicate Christ as the object of faith
through the function of εἰς Χριστόν to indicate the goal toward whom
trust is extended.

---

23. Longenecker, *Galatians*, 88.
24. Harris, *Colossians and Philemon*, 88.

4.5 NEW STATUS *INTO CHRIST*

Rom 6:3 ἢ ἀγνοεῖτε ὅτι, ὅσοι ἐβαπτίσθημεν **εἰς Χριστὸν** Ἰησοῦν, εἰς τὸν θάνατον αὐτοῦ ἐβαπτίσθημεν;

*Or are you unaware that all of us who were baptized **into Christ** Jesus were baptized into His death?*

To be baptized *into Christ* is best understood as reflecting Paul's conception of identification with Christ;[25] this is confirmed by the reference to being baptized into his death. Christ's death was, of course, a unique event, and the most plausible way in which believers might be understood as being 'baptized' into that death is through identification with Christ. BDAG's analysis handles this via the category *Other uses of εἰς* and a redirection to the entry for βαπτίζω, under which it is claimed that 'to be baptized εἰς Χρ. is for Paul an involvement in Christ's death and its implications for the believer'.[26] Such a description approximates the notion of identification with Christ, though not exactly. An 'involvement in Christ's death' implies participation — it is dynamic rather than stative, like Paul's 'with Christ' phrases (to be explored in ch. 5). While 'baptized' is dynamic, its destination εἰς Χριστόν implies a stative concept. To be baptized into Christ refers to a dynamic action that results in a new state — identification with Christ.

Gal 3:27 ὅσοι γὰρ **εἰς Χριστὸν** ἐβαπτίσθητε, Χριστὸν ἐνεδύσασθε

*For as many of you as have been baptized **into Christ** have put on Christ like a garment.*

This example of εἰς Χριστόν also involves being baptized into Christ; here it is related to the notion of putting on Christ rather than being baptized into his death (as in the previous example), though it is possible that 'baptized into Christ' is a truncation of 'baptized into Christ's death'. The metaphor of putting on Christ depicts him as a garment to be worn, which likely denotes incorporation into Christ.[27] This image will be explored

---

25. Dunn, *Romans 1–8*, 328.
26. BDAG, 164.
27. Bruce, *Galatians*, 186.

further in a subsequent chapter, but here we recognize that's Paul concern is to indicate the new status that believers enjoy. Those who have been baptized into Christ share the status of having put on Christ.

Thus, of the two instances of εἰς Χριστόν in this subcategory, Rom 6:3 expresses identification, while Gal 3:27 conveys incorporation.

4.6 *INTO CHRIST* AS A PERIPHRASIS FOR BELIEVERS

Rom 16:5 καὶ τὴν κατ' οἶκον αὐτῶν ἐκκλησίαν. ἀσπάσασθε Ἐπαίνετον τὸν ἀγαπητόν μου, ὅς ἐστιν ἀπαρχὴ τῆς Ἀσίας εἰς Χριστόν

Greet also the church that meets in their home. Greet my dear friend Epaenetus, who is the first **convert to Christ** *from Asia.*

This occurrence of εἰς Χριστόν is complicated by two difficult questions. The first is whether an additional verbal idea is to be supplied in this clause, which literally reads *who is the first fruit of Asia into Christ*. And if a verbal idea is to be supplied, it is not clear whether this should be *to convert* or some other possibility, such as *to believe*. If the latter, the sense of the clause would be that Epaenetus is the first fruit of Asia to believe in Christ. Since we have already witnessed two occurrences of *faith* or *believing* εἰς Χριστόν (Gal 2:16; Col 2:5, above), it is plausible that *to believe* might be supplied here.

The second difficult question, however, asks whether εἰς Χριστόν might be understood as a synonym for ἐν Χριστῷ, which is a possibility according to Harris (see §4.2) — at least as far as the prepositions εἰς and ἐν are concerned.[28] That is, Harris regards occasional synonymy between these two prepositions as possible. However, whether the *phrases* εἰς Χριστόν and ἐν Χριστῷ may occasionally be synonymous is not as simple as recognizing that the *prepositions* might be so. This is because of the strong likelihood that these phrases — certainly the latter — have an idiomatic function for Paul. While we have observed that such idioms do not restrict the meaning and function of the phrases, it nevertheless appears

---

28. Harris, 'Prepositions and Theology', 1185.

that Paul uses such phrases deliberately and with intent. Thus, synonymy between the two phrases may be less likely than otherwise might be the case. Consequently, it is probably best to err away from synonymy here.

A third option is possible. If emphasis in the clause is put on ἀπαρχή, *first fruit*, rather than on whether a verbal idea is to be supplied or whether εἰς Χριστόν and ἐν Χριστῷ are synonymous, it might be best to regard εἰς Χριστόν as expressing reference or respect. In this way, the clause would read *who is the first fruit of Asia with respect to Christ*. Given that this alternative respects the wording employed, does not require supplying an extra verbal idea, and does not require synonymy between εἰς Χριστόν and ἐν Χριστῷ, it is the preferred option.

4.7 TRINITY *INTO CHRIST*

2 Cor 1:21 ὁ δὲ βεβαιῶν ἡμᾶς σὺν ὑμῖν **εἰς Χριστὸν** καὶ χρίσας ἡμᾶς θεός

Now it is God who strengthens us, with you, in Christ and has anointed us.

This instance of εἰς Χριστόν is listed above as expressing reference or respect but is also included here for its trinitarian implications. The agency of God is in view, believers are the object of his agency, and his confirmation of believers is with respect to Christ.

4.8 OTHER USES OF *INTO CHRIST*

1 Cor 8:12 οὕτως δὲ ἁμαρτάνοντες εἰς τοὺς ἀδελφοὺς καὶ τύπτοντες αὐτῶν τὴν συνείδησιν ἀσθενοῦσαν **εἰς Χριστὸν** ἁμαρτάνετε

*Now when you sin like this against the brothers and wound their weak conscience, you are sinning **against Christ**.*

There are two main options for understanding this use of εἰς Χριστόν. The first is to regard the phrase as expressing reference or respect. The sense then would be *you are sinning with respect to Christ*. This reading is only convincing, however, if it can be shown that the parallel ἁμαρτάνοντες εἰς τοὺς ἀδελφούς, *sinning against the brothers*, also indicates reference and respect.[29] It is less likely, however, that Paul refers to sin *with respect to the brothers* rather than to sin *against the brothers*.

The second option is to understand this use as a marker of goal, under the subcategory of *actions or feelings directed in someone's direction in hostile or friendly sense*.[30] Under the 'hostile' uses of this subcategory, *to sin against someone* is noted by BDAG. Since this is the category under which BDAG would list this example, and because of the ease with which the category accommodates not only the concept of sinning against Christ but also that of sinning against the brothers, it offers a stronger reading than that of reference or respect.

> Gal 3:24 ὥστε ὁ νόμος παιδαγωγὸς ἡμῶν γέγονεν εἰς Χριστόν,
> ἵνα ἐκ πίστεως δικαιωθῶμεν
>
> *The law, then, was our guardian **until Christ**, so that we could be justified by faith.*

Since, in the context, Paul contrasts the age of law — 'before this faith came' (3:23) — with the age of faith in Christ (3:25), it is clear that his intent in v. 24 is to specify the law as guardian *until Christ*. This use of the phrase εἰς Χριστόν accords with the category that BDAG lists as expressing *extension in time*.[31] The relevant subcategory within the expression of extension in time is that which indicates the point up to which something continues. In other words, the law was guardian up to the point at which Christ came.[32]

> Eph 5:32 τὸ μυστήριον τοῦτο μέγα ἐστίν· ἐγὼ δὲ λέγω εἰς
> Χριστὸν καὶ εἰς τὴν ἐκκλησίαν

---

29. This parallel has implications for the wider discussion of union with Christ, since it raises the question of how sin against brothers equates sin against Christ. As Thiselton discusses, 'Since through participation in the death of Christ crucified the believer becomes *identified* with Christ, Christ *identifies* himself with those whom he has consecrated (1:2), enriched (1:5), and purchased as his own (6:20)'; Thiselton, *1 Corinthians*, 656.

30. BDAG, 290.

31. Ibid., 288–89.

32. Longenecker, *Galatians*, 148–49.

*This mystery is profound, but I am talking **about Christ** and the church.*

This instance of εἰς Χριστόν denotes the topic of reference; Paul is speaking *about Christ* (and the church).

Given the uses of εἰς Χριστόν in this subcategory, it appears that these occurrences do not relate to our topic of union with Christ (1 Cor 8:12; Gal 3:24; Eph 5:32). Thus, while some instances of εἰς Χριστόν provide evidence for our investigation, this is not universally the case.

4.9 INTO HIM

As the phrase ἐν αὐτῷ stands in for ἐν Χριστῷ, so εἰς αὐτόν may stand in for εἰς Χριστόν.[33] All the instances of this substitute phrase are categorized below.

4.9.1 FAITH INTO HIM

Phil 1:29 ὅτι ὑμῖν ἐχαρίσθη τὸ ὑπὲρ Χριστοῦ, οὐ μόνον τὸ **εἰς αὐτὸν** πιστεύειν ἀλλὰ καὶ τὸ ὑπὲρ αὐτοῦ πάσχειν

*For it has been given to you on Christ's behalf not only to believe **in Him**, but also to suffer for Him.*

This example of εἰς αὐτόν is clearly in keeping with those examples of εἰς Χριστόν that indicate the goal of faith and trust (Gal 2:16; Col 2:5, above).

4.9.2 INCORPORATION INTO HIM

Eph 4:15 ἀληθεύοντες δὲ ἐν ἀγάπῃ αὐξήσωμεν **εἰς αὐτὸν** τὰ πάντα, ὅς ἐστιν ἡ κεφαλή, Χριστός

*But speaking the truth in love, let us grow in every way **into Him** who is the head—Christ.*

There are two main options for understanding this instance of εἰς αὐτόν. First, the phrase might function as a marker of goal, though falling under a different BDAG subcategory to those cases above that are also

---

33. There are no instances of the phrase εἰς κύριον in the Pauline canon.

regarded as marking a goal. In this case, the relevant subcategory is most likely that *of change from one state to another with verbs of changing.*[34] The verb αὐξήσωμεν, *let us grow*, qualifies as a *verb of changing*, and, indeed, change is in part what is in view here. Paul is referring to growth to a deeper level of maturity as the body of Christ. One weakness of this reading, however, is that the change of state in view does not really involve a switch from one state to an altogether different state, but an alteration *within* the state of being *in him*. Consequently, this example does not tightly fit this subcategory.

Second, the phrase could reflect the subcategory that BDAG labels *the result of an action or condition indicated.* Understood this way, the phrase would indicate that believers are to be further *into him* by way of growing. A strength of this reading is that Ephesians 2:21 is included therein: αὐξάνειν εἰς ναόν, *grow into a temple.* Not only is this expression found within the same book, but it uses the same verbal lexeme together with εἰς. In the context of Ephesians 2, Paul addresses the growing-together of the corporate people of God—as he does here in Ephesians 4. Thus it seems likely that a similar intention runs through 4:15 and 2:21.

The condition that is reached through growing *into him* reflects incorporation into Christ.[35] This is clear from the context in which Paul is unfolding the metaphor of believers belonging to the *body* of Christ, which is explicitly referenced through the description of Christ as *Head*. The corporate metaphor of *body* is key for Paul's communication of the incorporation in which believers partake with Christ.

Col 1:20 καὶ δι' αὐτοῦ ἀποκαταλλάξαι τὰ πάντα **εἰς αὐτόν**,
εἰρηνοποιήσας διὰ τοῦ αἵματος τοῦ σταυροῦ αὐτοῦ,
[δι' αὐτοῦ] εἴτε τὰ ἐπὶ τῆς γῆς
εἴτε τὰ ἐν τοῖς οὐρανοῖς

And through Him to reconcile
*everything **to Himself***
by making peace
through the blood of His cross—
whether things on earth or things in heaven

---

34. BDAG, 290.
35. O'Brien, *Ephesians*, 312.

Note here is that εἰς αὐτόν possibly refers to God rather than Christ. Though God is not explicitly mentioned after 1:15 in the Christ hymn of 1:15–20, he is apparently the subject of the verb εὐδόκησεν in v. 19 and is implicitly the agent of δι' αὐτοῦ in 1:20. Consequently, reconciliation is most likely *to God* through Christ.[36] If this is the case, this example falls outside our scope of inquiry. Considering, however, that εἰς αὐτόν *could* refer to Christ rather than God, the example is worth pondering further.

This use of εἰς αὐτόν appears to indicate a sense of destination or goal, in that all things are reconciled to a particular end, which is Christ (if indeed he is the referent of αὐτόν). Within the BDAG category for εἰς that recognizes its function as a marker of a goal, this use of the phrase is best represented by the subcategory that denotes *actions or feelings directed in someone's direction in hostile or friendly sense.*[37] In this sense, the verse conveys the idea that all things are reconciled *toward* Christ through the peace-making of his cross.

As such, this use of εἰς αὐτόν is similar to that of Ephesians 4:15; just as believers may grow *into him*, so may all things be reconciled *into him*. It follows, then, that in both instances the notion of incorporation with Christ is at issue. While this may be so, the type of incorporation expressed in each instance is not quite the same. The incorporation in view in Ephesians 4:15 clearly pertains to believers, who are incorporated into the body of Christ. Such incorporation is unique to those who belong to Christ. Here in Colossians 1:20, however, the reconciliation of *all things* to Christ (or God) does not refer to same kind of incorporation.

For one thing, *all things* are not described as sharing in the body of Christ. Additionally, the reconciliation of all things does not necessarily refer to willing and 'friendly' reconciliation. While those who are of Christ are reconciled to him in a 'friendly' manner, the enemies of Christ are not reconciled willingly. In other words, the reconciliation of all things must, in part, refer to the *submission* of the hostile elements of the cosmos. If such is the case, any resulting sense of incorporation is not likely the intimate, organic, and spiritual union that believers share with Christ. The overthrown powers do not share in the death and resurrection of Christ; they are not seated with him in the heavens, nor do they share the

---

36. Harris, *Colossians and Philemon*, 50–51.
37. BDAG, 290.

blessings of Christ. Nevertheless, it is appropriate to regard the reconciliation of all things to Christ as conveying some kind of incorporation for the reason that all things are united around him—Christ is the centre of the cosmos, and holds all things together.[38]

4.9.3 OTHER USES OF INTO HIM

Rom 11:36 ὅτι ἐξ αὐτοῦ καὶ δι᾽ αὐτοῦ καὶ **εἰς αὐτὸν** τὰ πάντα· αὐτῷ ἡ δόξα εἰς τοὺς αἰῶνας, ἀμήν

*For from Him and through Him and **to Him** are all things. To Him be the glory forever. Amen.*

The antecedent of the pronoun *Him* in this instance is God rather than Christ. This example therefore falls outside the scope of our inquiry.[39]

1 Cor 8:6 ἀλλ᾽ ἡμῖν εἷς θεὸς ὁ πατὴρ ἐξ οὗ τὰ πάντα καὶ ἡμεῖς **εἰς αὐτόν**, καὶ εἷς κύριος Ἰησοῦς Χριστὸς δι᾽ οὗ τὰ πάντα καὶ ἡμεῖς δι᾽ αὐτοῦ

*Yet for us there is one God, the Father. All things are from him, and we exist **for Him**. And there is one Lord, Jesus Christ. All things are through Him, and we exist through Him.*

Again, it is clear that the pronoun αὐτόν has *the Father* as its antecedent, not Christ, and therefore is not relevant to our investigation.

2 Cor 2:8 διὸ παρακαλῶ ὑμᾶς κυρῶσαι **εἰς αὐτὸν** ἀγάπην

*Therefore I urge you to reaffirm your love **to him**.*

As with the two previous examples, this instance of the phrase εἰς αὐτόν does not have Christ as its antecedent; rather, it refers to the person about whom Paul instructed the Corinthian church regarding their disciplining of him.

Eph 1:5 προορίσας ἡμᾶς εἰς υἱοθεσίαν διὰ Ἰησοῦ Χριστοῦ **εἰς αὐτόν**, κατὰ τὴν εὐδοκίαν τοῦ θελήματος αὐτοῦ

---

38. See O'Brien's helpful discussion of these issues; O'Brien, *Colossians, Philemon*, 53–57.
39. Dunn, *Romans 9–16*, 701–2.

*He predestined us to be adopted through Jesus Christ **for Himself**, according to His favor and will.*

While it is possible that the antecedent of εἰς αὐτόν is Christ in this example, it is more likely to be the Father, who has predestined people for adoption through Christ, *for Himself*.[40]

Col 1:16–17 ὅτι ἐν αὐτῷ ἐκτίσθη τὰ πάντα
ἐν τοῖς οὐρανοῖς καὶ ἐπὶ τῆς γῆς,
τὰ ὁρατὰ καὶ τὰ ἀόρατα,
εἴτε θρόνοι εἴτε κυριότητες
εἴτε ἀρχαὶ εἴτε ἐξουσίαι·
τὰ πάντα δι᾽ αὐτοῦ καὶ **εἰς αὐτὸν** ἔκτισται.

For everything was created by Him,
in heaven and on earth,
the visible and the invisible,
whether thrones or dominions
or rulers or authorities—
*all things have been created through Him and **for Him**.*

Here again we see that εἰς αὐτόν indicates a sense of goal or destination: all things were created *for him*. The subcategory that seems most appropriate for this usage of the phrase is that *of actions or feelings directed in someone's direction in hostile or friendly sense*.[41] The action involved is the creation of all things, and we see here that this has not only occurred *through* Christ but is directed *toward* him and *for* him.[42]

Of the five instances of εἰς αὐτόν in this subcategory, Christ is not the antecedent in four cases (Rom 11:36; 1 Cor 8:6; 2 Cor 2:8; Eph 1:5), which renders these irrelevant to this study; the one remaining occurrence indicates action directed toward Christ (Col 1:16).

4.10 SUMMARY

Both εἰς Χριστόν and εἰς αὐτόν demonstrate some overlap with the thematic functions of ἐν Χριστῷ. The broad conceptual categories of *things*

---

40. Lincoln, *Ephesians*, 25.
41. BDAG, 290.
42. Harris, *Colossians and Philemon*, 46.

achieved for/given to people into Christ, faith into Christ, into Christ as a periphrasis for Christians, and *Trinity into Christ* represent the areas of overlap.

But εἰς Χριστόν and εἰς αὐτόν also evince a number of instances that are not related to the thematic uses of ἐν Χριστῷ. This is more the case with εἰς αὐτόν than with εἰς Χριστόν since the pronoun αὐτόν does not always refer to Christ as its antecedent. Consequently, we are able to conclude that these two phrases are used in relation to the concept of union with Christ. Our appreciation of the uses of these phrases, however, must be nuanced enough to recognise that not all instances may be regarded as relevant to our inquiry.

Beyond the broad thematic categories mentioned above, there is little overlap between the functions of εἰς and ἐν themselves when it comes to their contribution to the meaning of the phrases εἰς Χριστόν and ἐν Χριστῷ. The two most common uses of εἰς are the expression of goal, and reference or respect. These two functions are not carried at all by ἐν. Indeed, the only overlap of consequence between the two prepositions is the expression of instrumentality. This is a common function of ἐν and occasionally occurs with εἰς.

CHAPTER 5

Σὺν Χριστῷ

5.1 INTRODUCTION

To this point in our investigation the phrases under observation have involved either the preposition ἐν or εἰς, which of course share some lexical overlap. The next step, however, takes us outside the lexical range of these two prepositions. The preposition σύν has a distinct lexical capacity when compared to ἐν or εἰς, and yet the phrase σὺν Χριστῷ does apparently relate to ἐν Χριστῷ and εἰς Χριστόν. Their point of connection of σὺν Χριστῷ is the concept of participation with Christ, as is demonstrated below.

5.2 Σύν

The preposition σύν presents fewer difficulties than ἐν or εἰς. Robertson's definition is apposite: 'This is in little dispute. It is "together with."'[1] Of some interest is the history of usage of the word, especially in relation to μετά.[2] Outside of poetry, the occurrences of σύν within Attic writing are few compared to those of μετά. Demosthenes, for instance, has 346 occurrences of μετά, but only 15 of σύν. Aristotle has 300 and 8 respectively.[3]

---

1. Robertson, *Grammar*, 626.
2. According to Luraghi, 'The etymology of *sún* is obscure: a variant *xún* is also attested, mainly in Attic, which, according to some scholars, preserves the most ancient form. According to Chantraine (1968), *xún* could be connected with *metaxú*, "in the middle"'; Luraghi, *Prepositions and Cases*, 146.
3. Robertson, *Grammar*, 627. BDF (118, §221) claim that σύν 'is limited in classical Attic to the meanings "including" and "with the aid of", while μετά means "with". At the same time Ionic and accordingly Hellenistic ... retain σύν in the sense of "with" alongside μετά, and so it appears in the NT also'.

This pattern is somewhat reflected in the New Testament, though the statistics are less stark: μετά attests 469 occurrences while σύν occurs 128 times. Within the Pauline canon the figures are 73 to 39 respectively, and thus the pattern is even less pronounced. Nevertheless, one question that arises in light of these statistics is why Paul is prepared to coin the phrase σὺν Χριστῷ, but not once uses μετά for the same purpose. By contrast, Paul regularly ends his letters with the prayer that grace be *with* his readers, which is always μετά and never σύν.[4]

Porter suggests that the following distinction may be posited: 'σύν seems to imply at least in its fundamental sense the idea of like things being "with" each other.... This does not mean that they are exactly the same thing, but that the way they are being characterized by the author implies points of similarity.'[5] Additionally, Grundmann states that σύν has a personal character: 'It denotes the totality of persons who are together, or who come together, or who accompany one another, or who work together, sharing a common task or a common destiny, aiding and supporting one another.'[6] Σύν is more suited to express 'intimate personal union', while μετά denotes 'close association or attendant circumstances or simple accompaniment'.[7]

The main uses of σύν are listed by BDAG:[8]

1. marker of accompaniment and association
2. marker of assistance
3. marker of linkage

Immediately obvious is how simple this preposition appears in comparison to the previous two. While there are various nuances and subcategories within each of these main uses, it is nevertheless a significantly different state of affairs to attest only three main categories of usage.[9] BDAG appears

---

4. Harris, 'Prepositions and Theology', 1206.
5. Porter, *Idioms*, 174.
6. Walter Grundmann, 'σύν-μετά', *TDNT*, 7:770.
7. Harris, *Prepositions and Theology*, 200.
8. BDAG, 961–62.
9. While it may, in some instances, appear that σύν expresses instrument or means, this is probably not a legitimate function, as Harrison describes: 'Σύν with the dative case is used seemingly to express the instrument or means with which an action is performed: e.g. Soph. Phil. 1334–5, (πρὶν) τὰ πέργαμα | ... ξὺν τοῖσδε τόξοις ... πέρσας φανῇς, "before you shall be seen to have destroyed the citadel with these arrows." Here, however, σύν does no more, in fact, than introduce the concomitant circumstances or conditions of an action, or the accom-

to group σὺν Χριστῷ and related phrases under the first main category— accompaniment and association. Within this main category, σὺν Χριστῷ has a focus on association in activity, namely, co-experience and co-suffering.[10] In this light, it is interesting to note that σύν may denote 'in fellowship with', as a technical term in magic ritual, as demonstrated by Moulton and Milligan.[11]

Paul's use of the phrase σὺν Χριστῷ is apparently comparable with the phrases σὺν θεῷ and σὺν θεοῖς, which recur within Greek literature.[12] There is, however, no compelling evidence that Paul received the idiom from another source; it was most likely coined by him.[13] As Grundmann observes, Paul uses it to depict participation in Christ's life, glory, and victory (1 Thess 4:17), and salvation is fulfilled in fellowship with him (1 Thess 5:10).[14] The idiom can refer to the relationship of the community to Christ, but it may also denote the personal fellowship between Christ and the apostle (Phil 1:23).[15] The Christian's existence is his life with Christ, which is hidden in God (Col 3:3); the phrase here 'denotes the present, hidden, eschatological being of Christians'.[16]

One issue raised by the preposition σύν that is not of concern here for ἐν or εἰς is that of composition or compound words. According to Robertson, the use of σύν in composition 'illustrates the associative idea mainly as in συν-άγω (Mt. 2:4), συν-έρχομαι (Mk. 3:20), though the notion of help is present also, as in συν-αντι-λαμβάνομαι (Lu. 10:40), συν-εργέω (1 Cor. 16:16)'.[17] It would appear, then, that σύν in composition does not behave differently to σύν when it stands alone.

As for our theme of union with Christ, Dunn states that the σύν-compounds are even more significant in Paul's usage than the phrase σὺν Χριστῷ:

---

panying means, and not the simple instrument: the arrows of Philoctetus are not represented simply and directly as the instrument to be employed for the destruction of the Trojan citadel, but as that with which as a concomitant means the deed is to be accomplished'; Gessner Harrison, *A Treaty on the Greek Prepositions, and on the Cases of Nouns with Which These Are Used* (Philadelphia: Lippincott, 1858), 455.

10. BDAG, 962.

11. Moulton and Milligan, *Vocabulary of the Greek Testament*, 600, §4862.

12. Grundmann, 'σύν-μετά', 7:773, 781.

13. Ibid., 7:782, n. 79.

14. Ibid., 7:783.

15. Ibid., 7:784.

16. Ibid., 7:785–86.

17. Robertson, *Grammar*, 627.

For the real force of the 'with Christ' motif is carried by the remarkable sequence of about forty 'with' compounds which constitute yet another distinctive feature of Paul's writing. He uses them both to describe the common privilege, experience, and task of believers and to describe a sharing in Christ's death and life.[18]

Indeed, McGrath goes so far as to say that 'the quintessence of Saint Paul's doctrine of the solidarity of the body of Christians with Christ is contained in the concepts embodied in the words which we have been considering'.[19] Believers suffer with him (Rom 8:17), are crucified with him (Rom 6:6), are nailed to the cross with Christ (Gal 2:19), are united with him in his death (Rom 6:5), are fellow members of the same body (Eph 3:6), are built together in him (Eph 2:22), die with Christ (2 Tim 2:11), and are buried with him (Rom 6:4; Col 2:12). God brings believers to life with Christ (Eph 2:5; Col 2:13), who are raised up with him (Eph 2:6; Col 2:12; 3:1) and live together with him (Rom 6:8; 2 Tim 2:11). They become like Christ (Phil 3:10), are conformed to him (Rom 8:29; Phil 3:21), are joint-heirs with him (Rom 8:17; Eph 3:6), are joint-partakers of the promise (Eph 3:6), and are seated together with Christ (Eph 2:6) so that they may reign with him (2 Tim 2:12) and be glorified with him (Rom 8:17).[20] Before examining these compound expressions, however, we turn first to consider uses of the phrase σὺν Χριστῷ.

5.3 WITH CHRIST

Rom 6:8 εἰ δὲ ἀπεθάνομεν **σὺν Χριστῷ**, πιστεύομεν ὅτι καὶ συζήσομεν αὐτῷ

*Now if we died **with Christ**, we believe that we will also live with Him.*

This instance of σὺν Χριστῷ is best understood as conveying accompaniment and association; believers 'accompany' Christ in his death. The notion of dying with Christ most likely conveys 'participation in the salvation-history effects of Christ's death as marking and effecting the end

---

18. Dunn, *Paul the Apostle*, 402; see n. 62 for a list of these compound words.
19. Brendan McGrath, '"Syn" Words in Saint Paul', *CBQ* 14 (1952): 225.
20. Ibid., 226.

of the rule of sin and death'.[21] This will need to be explored further, but it is worth observing at this point that the concept is obviously not physical or concrete. Whether it is intended to be metaphorical must yet be ascertained, but it may be regarded as *spiritual*, either in a metaphorical sense or otherwise.

Col 2:20 εἰ ἀπεθάνετε **σὺν Χριστῷ** ἀπὸ τῶν στοιχείων τοῦ κόσμου, τί ὡς ζῶντες ἐν κόσμῳ δογματίζεσθε;

*If you died **with the Messiah** to the elemental forces of this world, why do you live as if you still belonged to the world? Why do you submit to regulations?*

In this example, the phrase σὺν Χριστῷ is again employed in order to convey an association of some kind to Christ. The believer is described as having died *with Christ*, which is best apprehended as participation with Christ. In this context, dying with Christ 'severs the bond that bound the Colossians to the slavery of the principalities and powers'.[22]

Col 3:3 ἀπεθάνετε γὰρ καὶ ἡ ζωὴ ὑμῶν κέκρυπται **σὺν τῷ Χριστῷ** ἐν τῷ θεῷ

*For you have died, and your life is hidden **with the Messiah** in God.*

Rather than conveying the notion of dying with Christ, this instance of σὺν τῷ Χριστῷ is used with reference to life being hidden with Christ. The preposition is nevertheless to be regarded as expressing accompaniment or association as it does in the previous examples, though it is better understood as conveying union with Christ[23] rather than participation. The two references to dying with Christ, above, envisage a sharing with Christ in the event of his death; participation in that event is in view. Here, however, the nature of believers' association with Christ does not refer to participation or sharing in an *activity* or *event*.

---

21. Dunn, *Romans 1–8*, 322.

22. O'Brien, *Colossians, Philemon*, 149.

23. O'Brien regards the phrase as expressing 'the intimate personal union of the believer with Christ'; O'Brien, *Colossians, Philemon*, 169–71. It is unlikely that the presence of the article in this instance has any bearing on the differing nuance of the phrase.

There are two possible ways in which to understand the nature of union here. First, being hidden with Christ in God might be regarded as sharing the *position* or *status* of Christ. As he is hidden in God, so believers are with him and share in his hiddenness. Second, being hidden with Christ might not imply that he is himself hidden in God. The verse may intend that believers are hidden in Christ, who is in God, but that does not mean that such hiddenness also describes Christ. In this case, union with Christ refers to a state of believers with reference to Christ, but it does not involve sharing in this position or status of Christ.

While the latter option is possible so far as this verse is concerned, it is weakened by the following verse: *When the Messiah, who is your life, is revealed, then you also will be revealed with Him in glory* (3:4). Since Christ will be *revealed*—and believers with him—it follows that the hiddenness of 3:3 *does* describe Christ after all. He who is hidden in God will later be revealed. Consequently, it is best to regard the nature of believers' union with Christ as sharing in his position and status as hidden in God. As he is hidden in God and later will be revealed, so believers are hidden with him in God and later will be revealed with him.[24]

Phil 1:23 συνέχομαι δὲ ἐκ τῶν δύο, τὴν ἐπιθυμίαν ἔχων εἰς τὸ ἀναλῦσαι καὶ **σὺν Χριστῷ** εἶναι, πολλῷ [γὰρ] μᾶλλον κρεῖσσον

*I am pressured by both. I have the desire to depart and be **with Christ**—which is far better.*

This example differs a little from the first three in that it does not indicate a *present* participation or union with Christ. Instead, it looks ahead to a *future* with Christ, which implies a hint of remoteness in Paul's current experience. While this remoteness should not be interpreted as contradicting the other uses of σὺν Χριστῷ, which convey participation with Christ, it is best to understand this usage as referring to a (quasi-?) physical proximity to Christ, which will only ensue in the case of Paul's death (or Christ's return, though the context has Paul's death in view).[25] The

---

24. Bruce, *Colossians, Philemon, Ephesians*, 135.
25. While it is possible to interpret Paul's words as indicating 'an even closer intimacy and deeper fullness beyond death than he has previously known', as Martin suggests, Paul does not here seem to be discussing *degrees* of intimacy. He does not say something akin to *I have the desire to depart and be* closer *to Christ*, but *to depart and be* with *Christ*. It is better, therefore, to regard *with Christ* here as indicating something different from other uses of the

former three examples apparently refer to a spiritual, or at least conceptual, identity with Christ and do not imply any sense of physical proximity to him. Consequently, this example expresses accompaniment with Christ but does not entail participation with him in a Christ-event or status.

Each of the four instances of σὺν Χριστῷ conveys accompaniment or association, with three of these expressing participation (Rom 6:8; Col 2:20; Phil 1:23) and one indicating union (Col 3:3).

5.4 WITH THE LORD

As with our investigation in previous chapters, a natural next step is to consider phrases that contain the title *Lord* or a pronoun — rather than the title *Christ* — that are otherwise identical to σὺν Χριστῷ. There is only one example of the phrase with *Lord*, but several that employ a pronoun.

1 Thess 4:17 ἔπειτα ἡμεῖς οἱ ζῶντες οἱ περιλειπόμενοι ἅμα σὺν αὐτοῖς ἁρπαγησόμεθα ἐν νεφέλαις εἰς ἀπάντησιν τοῦ κυρίου εἰς ἀέρα· καὶ οὕτως πάντοτε **σὺν κυρίῳ** ἐσόμεθα

*Then we who are still alive will be caught up together with them in the clouds to meet the Lord in the air and so we will always be **with the Lord**.*

This instance is similar to the use of σὺν Χριστῷ in Colossians 3:3 (see above, §5.3), which denotes a quasi-physical accompaniment with Christ rather than a conceptual or spiritual participation with him. As above, this statement points to a future reality of being with Christ[26] rather than a present identification with him.

5.5 WITH HIM

Rom 8:32 ὅς γε τοῦ ἰδίου υἱοῦ οὐκ ἐφείσατο ἀλλὰ ὑπὲρ ἡμῶν πάντων παρέδωκεν αὐτόν, πῶς οὐχὶ καὶ **σὺν αὐτῷ** τὰ πάντα ἡμῖν χαρίσεται;

---

phrase, rather than indicating a greater *degree* of what the phrase normally means. While the phrase normally refers to spiritual participation in Christ-events, here it refers to a quasi-physical proximity to Christ himself. See Martin, *Philippians*, 81.

26. Charles A. Wanamaker, *The Epistles to the Thessalonians* (NIGTC; Grand Rapids: Eerdmans, 1990), 175–76.

He did not even spare His own Son
but offered Him up for us all;
*how will He not also **with Him** grant us everything?*

This example of σὺν αὐτῷ can be understood in one of two ways, depending on who is regarded as associated with Christ. On the one hand, it is probably most natural to regard *with him* as associating believers with Christ. In this way, Paul's rhetorical question means that God will grant everything to Christ—and to us with him. On the other hand, σὺν αὐτῷ might associate God, rather than believers, with Christ. In this way, Paul means to say that God *with Christ* will grant us everything. In other words, God and Christ perform the action in partnership. Thus, the first reading regards Christ as the recipient of *everything*, while the second reading views Christ as the giver of *everything*.

While either option is grammatically and thematically possible, the former reading is probably the stronger of the two. One reason for this is that God is the sole agent of the two preceding clauses: *He did not even spare His own Son but offered Him up for us all*, and Christ is the object of both. Thus, it is natural to read Christ as the recipient of God's agency in the final clause.[27]

The BDAG category for σύν that best suits this use is one that describes it as a *marker of linkage, with focus on addition of a pers. or thing.*[28] Believers are added to Christ as the recipients of God's grant. Thus, while Paul may envision such an addition as an outworking of believers' participation with Christ, participation itself may not necessarily be in view.

2 Cor 13:4 καὶ γὰρ ἐσταυρώθη ἐξ ἀσθενείας, ἀλλὰ ζῇ ἐκ δυνάμεως θεοῦ. καὶ γὰρ ἡμεῖς ἀσθενοῦμεν ἐν αὐτῷ, ἀλλὰ ζήσομεν **σὺν αὐτῷ** ἐκ δυνάμεως θεοῦ εἰς ὑμᾶς

---

27. A third option is to include Christ in what is given to believers, as Moo paraphrases, 'along with Christ, God's Son whom God has already "handed over" for us, God will surely give us "all things"'; Moo, *Romans*, 541. This, however, is the most unnatural option for reading σὺν αὐτῷ, since its context appears to imply the reversal of Christ's fortunes in response to his self-giving death (cf. Phil 2:6–11). In other words, Paul is referring to what is given to Christ subsequent to his death; it is in this that believers partake.

28. BDAG, 962.

*In fact, He was crucified in weakness, but He lives by God's power. For we also are weak in Him, yet toward you we will live **with Him** by God's power.*

This example of σὺν αὐτῷ conveys participation with Christ in a conceptual or spiritual capacity. The first part of the verse states that Christ lives by God's power; to follow this with the phrase *we will live with him by God's power* indicates a sharing in Christ's living. Σὺν here expresses accompaniment and association, in that believers accompany Christ in his resurrected life by the power of God. It is worth noting that this expression of participation with Christ reflects a future (and presumably present) reality,[29] rather than participation in a past event, such as Christ's death, which has been more usual in the examples observed thus far.

Col 2:13 καὶ ὑμᾶς νεκροὺς ὄντας [ἐν] τοῖς παραπτώμασιν καὶ τῇ ἀκροβυστίᾳ τῆς σαρκὸς ὑμῶν, συνεζωοποίησεν ὑμᾶς σὺν αὐτῷ, χαρισάμενος ἡμῖν πάντα τὰ παραπτώματα

*And when you were dead in trespasses and in the uncircumcision of your flesh, He made you alive **with Him** and forgave us all our trespasses.*

While this instance of σὺν αὐτῷ also relates to life with Christ, it is used here with reference to the past event of Christ's resurrection. This is confirmed by the previous verse: *Having been buried with Him in baptism, you were also raised with Him through faith in the working of God, who raised Him from the dead* (2:12). Not only does that verse explicitly refer to Christ's resurrection, but it also indicates that believers were raised with him in that event. The notion of sharing in the resurrection of Christ—being made alive with him—expresses participation with him in that event.[30]

Col 3:4 ὅταν ὁ Χριστὸς φανερωθῇ, ἡ ζωὴ ὑμῶν, τότε καὶ ὑμεῖς σὺν αὐτῷ φανερωθήσεσθε ἐν δόξῃ

---

29. Some argue that the eschatological future is not in view at all here but only the present. See Kruse, *2 Corinthians*, 219, n. 1; Hughes, *2 Corinthians*, 479–80.

30. 'The Colossians have come to life with Christ, who was dead and rose again; their new life, then, is a sharing in the new life which he received when he rose from the dead'; O'Brien, *Colossians, Philemon*, 123.

*When the Messiah, who is your life, is revealed, then you also will be revealed **with Him** in glory.*

Here σὺν αὐτῷ could be functioning as a *marker of linkage*, as is the case in Romans 8:32 above,[31] or it may express accompaniment and association, as with most other instances. If it is a marker of linkage here, then σὺν αὐτῷ does not necessarily convey participation with Christ, though it may be an outworking of such participation. As a marker of linkage, the phrase would simply focus on the addition of believers with Christ when he is revealed.

The context, however, suggests that participation with Christ *is* in view here. First, the first half of the verse makes an overture to participation with the words *When the Messiah, who is your life, is revealed.* The mention of Christ's being *your life* connotes participation since we know that believers are made alive by participation with Christ. Furthermore, the previous verse conveys union with Christ, as observed above: *For you have died, and your life is hidden with the Messiah in God* (3:3). Since the revelation of Christ is mentioned in connection with his being *the life* of believers, it follows that our being revealed with him expresses participation with him.[32]

1 Thess 4:14 εἰ γὰρ πιστεύομεν ὅτι Ἰησοῦς ἀπέθανεν καὶ ἀνέστη, οὕτως καὶ ὁ θεὸς τοὺς κοιμηθέντας διὰ τοῦ Ἰησοῦ ἄξει **σὺν αὐτῷ**

*Since we believe that Jesus died and rose again, in the same way God will bring **with Him** those who have fallen asleep through Jesus.*

Σὺν αὐτῷ here could express linkage, that believers are regarded as additional to Christ when God brings him.[33] This would not necessarily convey participation with Christ (though may result from it), since it could be argued that being included as the object of God's agency is not the same as sharing in, say, the death of Christ.

---

31. So Harris, 'Σὺν αὐτῷ means "along with him" at his appearance (cf. Rom. 8:17), or "in his train" since he lives in heaven in a "body of glory" (Phil. 3:20–21) as the paradigm for believers' resurrection transformation (1 Cor. 15:20, 23, 49)'; Harris, *Colossians and Philemon*, 141.

32. 'The inward revelation of his saving glory which has come home to them already is the earnest of a fuller revelation yet to come, the grand consummation of the union between Christ and his people'; Bruce, *Colossians, Philemon, Ephesians*, 136.

33. Morris demonstrates that Paul most likely refers to the Parousia here rather than to the notion that Jesus will take such people with him into glory. 'It is their share in the events of that great day that is in view'; Morris, *Thessalonians* (NICNT), 140.

Nevertheless, as with Colossians 3:4 above, it is more likely that participation with Christ *is* in view here — σὺν αὐτῷ indicating accompaniment and association. While believers and Christ are indeed objects of God's action, this is not different from some other instances of participation in which Christ and believers are the objects of the Father's activity; being made alive with Christ (Eph 2:5) is one such example. Furthermore, union with Christ is arguably in view in the context, with believers described as having *fallen asleep through Jesus* (διὰ τοῦ Ἰησοῦ). Consequently, the idea is that believers who died before Christ's coming will participate in that great event by virtue of their union with him.

1 Thess 5:10 τοῦ ἀποθανόντος ὑπὲρ ἡμῶν, ἵνα εἴτε γρηγορῶμεν εἴτε καθεύδωμεν ἅμα **σὺν αὐτῷ** ζήσωμεν

*Who died for us, so that whether we are awake or asleep, we will live together **with Him**.*

This is an interesting example of σὺν αὐτῷ in that the force of the preposition is possibly strengthened by the adverb ἅμα, *together*. Under BDAG's listing for the adverb, the subcategory that recognizes its function as a *marker of association* seems most appropriate here; indeed, BDAG regards this instance as an example of such, claiming that ἅμα might be used as a preposition with the dative case and that this occurrence is apparently pleonastic in conjunction with σύν.[34]

It is best not to regard ἅμα as entirely pleonastic here, however, since it *does* contribute to our understanding of the function of σύν. Without the adverb, σύν might be construed as indicating either accompaniment and association or linkage. Since the adverb can itself function as a marker of association, it strengthens the likelihood of such a reading for σύν. In other words, ἅμα serves to indicate which way we should read σύν. Consequently, σὺν αὐτῷ is best regarded as expressing accompaniment and association with Christ and thus conveys participation with him.[35] Believers will live together with him who died for us.

Thus, of the six occurences of σὺν αὐτῷ in this subcategory, five

---

34. BDAG, 49.

35. Morris sees this as indicating believers' union with Christ; Morris, *Thessalonians* (NICNT), 162.

express participation with Christ through accompaniment or association (2 Cor 13:4; Col 2:13; 3:4; 1 Thess 4:14; 5:10), with one instance conveying linkage (Rom 8:32).

5.6 Σύν COMPOUNDS

There are eleven instances of σὺν (τῷ) Χριστῷ, σὺν κυρίῳ, and σὺν αὐτῷ in the Pauline canon, as observed above. There are as many instances of expressions that convey concepts related to these phrases. These are primarily encountered as σύν-compound words. We must ascertain the extent to which such compounds are comparable to the noncompound phrases.

> Rom 6:4 **συνετάφημεν** οὖν **αὐτῷ** διὰ τοῦ βαπτίσματος εἰς τὸν θάνατον, ἵνα ὥσπερ ἠγέρθη Χριστὸς ἐκ νεκρῶν διὰ τῆς δόξης τοῦ πατρός, οὕτως καὶ ἡμεῖς ἐν καινότητι ζωῆς περιπατήσωμεν
>
> *Therefore we were **buried with Him** by baptism into death, in order that, just as Christ was raised from the dead by the glory of the Father, so we too may walk in a new way of life.*

To be buried with Christ conveys participation with him in his death.[36] The function of the preposition is to express accompaniment and association, and the result is that believers share or participate in this Christ-event in a conceptual or spiritual manner.[37] The participatory nature of this concept is confirmed by the abundant presence of participation and identification motifs in the context. Romans 6:3 speaks of being baptized into Christ Jesus and in his death;[38] believers have been joined with him in the likeness of his death in 6:5, crucified with him in 6:6, and died and live with him in 6:8 (see below).

> Rom 6:5 εἰ γὰρ **σύμφυτοι** γεγόναμεν τῷ ὁμοιώματι τοῦ θανάτου αὐτοῦ, ἀλλὰ καὶ τῆς ἀναστάσεως ἐσόμεθα

---

36. Cranfield regards burial as the most emphatic way to indicate the fact of death; 'it is when a man's relatives and friends leave his body in a grave and return home without him that the fact that he no longer shares their life is exposed with inescapable conclusiveness'; Cranfield, *Romans*, 1:304.

37. Moo, *Romans*, 363–67.

38. See on this verse in chapter 4 (see §4.5).

*For if we have been **joined with Him** in the likeness of His death,*
we will certainly also be in the likeness of His resurrection.

The compound σύμφυτος pertains to *being associated in a related experience* and conveys identification with someone or something.[39] As such,
being *joined with him* most likely denotes participation with Christ. While
participation in Christ's death is a concept that has been observed on
several occasions, it is here complicated by the phrase τῷ ὁμοιώματι τοῦ
θανάτου αὐτοῦ, *in the likeness of His death*. What does it mean to be joined
to Christ in the *likeness* of his death? According to BDAG, this occurrence
of ὁμοίωμα is accommodated under the function that conveys a *state of
having common experiences*.[40] In this way, the phrase *the likeness of his death*
does not necessarily convey anything unusual with respect to sharing in
Christ's death.[41] In fact, BDAG paraphrases *if we have been united in the
likeness of his death (= in the same death that he died)*.[42]

One issue remains, however: participation language has thus far been
preserved for sharing in *events* rather than sharing in a *state*, and the phrase
σύμφυτοι γεγόναμεν indicates a state of being rather than an event. Nevertheless, ὁμοίωμα refers to a state of having common experiences, which
means that it reflects the reality of co-experience of an event. As such,
participation language remains apt since the verse refers to the state of
being associated in common experience — the death of Christ. Thus, the
phrase underscores the participation in which believers partake; they are
joined with Christ in the co-experience of his death.

Rom 6:6 τοῦτο γινώσκοντες ὅτι ὁ παλαιὸς ἡμῶν ἄνθρωπος
συνεσταυρώθη, ἵνα καταργηθῇ τὸ σῶμα τῆς ἁμαρτίας, τοῦ μηκέτι
δουλεύειν ἡμᾶς τῇ ἁμαρτίᾳ

---

39. BDAG, 960.
40. Ibid., 707.
41. So Moo, though he regards Paul's use of ὁμοίωμα as portraying Christ's death in a particular light. He concludes that this nuance brings out the conformity to Christ's death into
which believers enter, having participated in the event of his death; Moo, *Romans*, 369–70.
Dunn, who thinks that the 'very likeness of his death' implies some distinction from the
historical event (contra Moo), nevertheless comes to a similar conclusion in that the phrase
may refer to 'the actual equivalent of Christ's death as it comes to expression in conversion
and commitment'; Dunn, *Romans 1–8*, 330–31.
42. BDAG, 707.

*For we know that our old self was **crucified with Him** in order that sin's dominion over the body may be abolished, so that we may no longer be enslaved to sin.*

In this first of only two explicit references in the Pauline canon of crucifixion with Christ (see Gal 2:19 below),[43] it is clear that participation in the event of Christ's death is again in view.[44] The use of crucifixion language is striking in a context in which death language is normative, and thus it underscores the historical particularity of the death of Christ; it is his actual crucifixion outside Jerusalem in about AD 33 that focuses our thoughts. Consequently, the language of co-crucifixion highlights the extraordinariness of participation in Christ's death—for Paul's first readers an event that occurred decades before their coming to Christ.

Rom 6:8 εἰ δὲ ἀπεθάνομεν σὺν Χριστῷ, πιστεύομεν ὅτι καὶ συζήσομεν αὐτῷ

*Now if we died with Christ, we believe that we will also **live with Him**.*

This compound verb conveys participation with Christ in that believers will share in his life.[45] While the expression *live with Him* might communicate accompaniment without participation—in the sense of partaking in the life of Christ—this is unlikely. The first clause of this verse refers to having died with Christ, which is now a frequently observed concept that pertains to participation with Christ. Thus, the second clause likely expresses participation in the same manner. This is confirmed by 6:9, which indicates that Christ's ongoing life proceeds from his resurrection from the dead. Since believers participate in Christ's resurrection (6:5), it follows that they also participate in the life of Christ that proceeds from it. In fact, 6:11 seems to confirm this conclusion: believers are alive to God in Christ Jesus.[46]

---

43. There are, however, two implicit references to co-crucifixion in Gal 5:24 and 6:14.

44. Moo, *Romans*, 372.

45. Jewett takes this broadly, to refer to 'solidarity with Christ in the entirety of human life'; Robert Jewett, *Romans* (Hermeneia; Minneapolis: Fortress, 2007), 406. Given the symmetrical relationship of *live with him* to *died with Christ*, however, it is more likely resurrection life that is in view.

46. Thus Moo is correct to regard the phrase συζήσομεν αὐτῷ (6:8) as indicating a present

A second point of interest here is the fact that the first clause employs the noncompound phrase σὺν Χριστῷ, while the second clause uses the compound συζάω. Because of the obvious parallel between the two clauses, this constitutes evidence of no discernable difference between expressions that employ a σύν-compound and those that contain a noncompounded σύν.

Rom 8:17 εἰ δὲ τέκνα, καὶ κληρονόμοι· κληρονόμοι μὲν θεοῦ, **συγκληρονόμοι** δὲ **Χριστοῦ**, εἴπερ **συμπάσχομεν** ἵνα καὶ **συνδοξασθῶμεν**

*And if children, also heirs—heirs of God and **coheirs with Christ**—seeing that **we suffer with Him** so that **we may** also **be glorified with Him**.*

This is a particularly rich verse for participation with Christ. Believers are described as coheirs with Christ, as suffering with Christ, and as being glorified with Christ. However, while it is clear that the last two σύν-compound words ought to be classed as participatory, since they refer to sharing in activities, it is less clear that συγκληρονόμοι should also be classed as such. Believers are heirs of God (κληρονόμοι μὲν θεοῦ), which must be understood as indicating a positional state.[47] Since this is a state shared with Christ rather than an activity, it is better to label συγκληρονόμοι as indicating union with Christ.

It may be objected that it is inconsistent to identify one σύν-compound as expressing union while the following two in the immediate context indicate participation, but this is an unnecessary concern. Naturally, the two notions are closely connected—in fact, they may be understood as referring to the same ultimate spiritual reality, even though one term is reserved for a stative union with Christ while the other is a dynamic participation in the events of Christ's experience. The relatedness of the two terms will be explored at a later point in this book.

---

sharing in Christ's resurrection rather than a future anticipation of such; Moo, *Romans*, 377. Contra Dunn, *Romans 1–8*, 322.

47. Moo takes θεοῦ as a source or subjective genitive, indicating that believers will inherit what God has promised, which is shared only through, and in, Christ; Moo, *Romans*, 505.

Rom 8:29 ὅτι οὓς προέγνω, καὶ προώρισεν **συμμόρφους** τῆς εἰκόνος τοῦ υἱοῦ αὐτοῦ, εἰς τὸ εἶναι αὐτὸν πρωτότοκον ἐν πολλοῖς ἀδελφοῖς

*For those He foreknew He also predestined **to be conformed** to the image of his Son, so that He would be the firstborn among many brothers.*

This σύν-compound is included here for the sake of completeness, but it probably falls outside our scope of inquiry, since believers are portrayed as predestined to be conformed to the *image* of Christ. Whatever εἰκόνος means here,[48] it does not appear to refer directly to Christ himself, no matter to what extent his *image* conforms to his actual person. Cranfield regards it as probable that the growing conformity to Christ in suffering and obedience is in view here,[49] which thus effectively makes this an ethical image of sorts. Consequently, being conformed to the image of Christ cannot refer to quite the same reality as union with Christ himself; it refers rather to conformity of believers to the pattern and narrative of Christ.[50]

Gal 2:19 ἐγὼ γὰρ διὰ νόμου νόμῳ ἀπέθανον, ἵνα θεῷ ζήσω. **Χριστῷ συνεσταύρωμαι**

*For through the law I have died to the law, so that I might live for God. **I have been crucified with Christ.***

As with Romans 6:6 above, crucifixion with Christ evokes a striking image of participation in Christ's death. The dramatic nature of this participation is underscored by the fact that συσταυρόω is used in the Gospels to depict literally the simultaneous crucifixion of others with Jesus (Matt 27:44; Mark 15:32; John 19:32).[51]

Eph 2:5–6 καὶ ὄντας ἡμᾶς νεκροὺς τοῖς παραπτώμασιν **συνεζωοποίησεν τῷ Χριστῷ**—χάριτί ἐστε σεσῳσμένοι—καὶ

---

48. Cranfield regards the thought of man's creation according to the image of God (Gen 1:27) in the background here, as well as Christ's being the very image of God (2 Cor 4:4; Col 1:15); Cranfield, *Roman*, 1:432.

49. Ibid., 1:432.

50. See chapter 11 for further discussion of conformity, or cruciformity, to Christ.

51. Martyn, *Galatians*, 278.

συνήγειρεν καὶ **συνεκάθισεν** ἐν τοῖς ἐπουρανίοις ἐν Χριστῷ Ἰησοῦ

Even when we were dead in our trespasses, **made us alive together with Christ**—*by grace you have been saved*—*and* **raised us up with him** *and* **seated us with him** *in the heavenly places in Christ Jesus.* (ESV)

The three σύν-compounds in these two verses express accompaniment and association, indicating participation with Christ in his being made alive, his ascension, and his being seated in the heavens.[52] While Barth argues that the σύν-prefix contains a reference to Jews and Gentiles sharing in a common resurrection,[53] Lincoln demonstrates this to be false.[54] Believers partake in these central Christ-events, so what is true of Christ in his resurrection and ascension is true also of those who believe in him. 'A relationship with Christ is in view which affects believers' future destinies because it involves sharing in Christ's destiny.'[55]

Phil 3:10 τοῦ γνῶναι αὐτὸν καὶ τὴν δύναμιν τῆς ἀναστάσεως αὐτοῦ καὶ [τὴν] κοινωνίαν [τῶν] παθημάτων αὐτοῦ, **συμμορφιζόμενος** τῷ θανάτῳ αὐτοῦ

My goal is to know Him and the power of His resurrection and the fellowship of His sufferings, **being conformed** *to His death.*

This is an interesting verse since participation with Christ appears to be partly in view, but the notion is mixed with the *implications* of participation. The previous two verses speak of *gaining Christ* (3:8), *being found in him* (3:9), and *fellowship in his sufferings* (3:10), which may be viewed as conveying either union or participation in Christ. However, in v. 10 we also witness the concepts of *knowing him, knowing the power of his resurrection,* and *being conformed to his death.* These notions do not precisely specify participation in Christ, for they refer to Christ and his

---

52. Mitton describes these verses as reflecting participation, association, and identification with Christ; Mitton, *Ephesians*, 88–89.

53. See M. Barth, *Ephesians 1–3*, 220.

54. 'This is not in view in vv 5, 6, where the parallels with 1:20 show that the relationship between the believer and Christ is the writer's intended focus'; Lincoln, *Ephesians*, 101.

55. Ibid.

resurrection as the objects of Paul's knowledge. To know Christ is not the same as being found in him, since the former concept holds Christ as object, while the latter notion partakes in him. Knowing the power of his resurrection also differs from partaking in his resurrection for the same reason: one concept retains the resurrection as a known object, while the other shares in it. Likewise, being conformed to Christ's death is distinct to sharing in Christ's death; the former views his death as a pattern to which one may conform, while the latter involves participation in it.

Together with these observations, we note that the σύν-compound in question is defined by BDAG as *take on the same form.*[56] The reference to *form* suggests that the verb has to do with conduct. Paul has in mind, therefore, his conduct as a believer; he is to be conformed to the pattern of Christ's death in his life and ministry. The fact that his conduct is in view is confirmed in the following verses, in which Paul regards himself as not yet fully mature (3:12) and reaching toward what is ahead (3:13).

While we know that Paul regards himself as partaking in the death of Christ in participation with the Christ-event, the σύν-compound does not here convey that concept specifically. While the two things are no doubt related, Paul rather has in mind the shaping of his life and ministry to the pattern of Christ.[57] Such a manner of things is best not regarded as participation with Christ per se, though such participation leads to conformity of life and ministry to the death of Christ.[58] 'Now Paul — and by implication the Philippians should as well — sees his and their sufferings in Christ's behalf as God's way of "conforming" them into the likeness of Christ.'[59]

Phil 3:21 ὃς μετασχηματίσει τὸ σῶμα τῆς ταπεινώσεως ἡμῶν **σύμμορφον** τῷ σώματι τῆς δόξης αὐτοῦ κατὰ τὴν ἐνέργειαν τοῦ δύνασθαι αὐτὸν καὶ ὑποτάξαι αὐτῷ τὰ πάντα

*He will transform the body of our humble condition into the **likeness** of His glorious body, by the power that enables Him to subject everything to Himself.*

---

56. BDAG, 958.

57. Fee correctly rejects readings that see Paul's death and martyrdom in view here; 'Paul is not talking about dying, but about suffering — of a kind that is in keeping with Christ's death'; Fee, *Philippians*, 334, n. 66.

58. See chapter 11 for further discussion of cruciformity; that is, conformity to the death of Christ.

59. Fee, *Philippians*, 333–34.

While this σύν-compound adjective refers to a future reality, it is similar to the previous example—and in fact is a cognate of that verb—in that it refers to being conformed to the *likeness*, or *form*, of Christ. As with the previous example, this σύν-compound is best not regarded as expressing participation with Christ per se. It conveys the idea that believers' bodies will be *like* Christ's, but this is distinct to sharing in his own body.

While the previous example dealt with Paul's life and ministry being conformed to the pattern of Christ's death, here we see that believers' bodies will be transformed to the likeness or form of Jesus' resurrection body. In keeping with Gorman's concept of cruciformity, being conformed to Christ's death leads to sharing in his resurrection; the Christ-narrative of humiliation and suffering followed by exaltation and glory is manifested in the experience of the believer.[60]

Col 2:12 **συνταφέντες αὐτῷ** ἐν τῷ βαπτισμῷ, ἐν ᾧ καὶ **συνηγέρθητε** διὰ τῆς πίστεως τῆς ἐνεργείας τοῦ θεοῦ τοῦ ἐγείραντος αὐτὸν ἐκ νεκρῶν

Having been buried with Him *in baptism, you were also* ***raised with Him*** *through faith in the working of God, who raised Him from the dead.*

Both of these σύν-compounds convey accompaniment and association and express participation with Christ in the events of his burial and resurrection. Believers partake in these Christ-events in a spiritual manner. 'As the burial of Christ (1 Cor 15:4) set the seal upon his death, so the Colossians' burial with him in baptism shows that they were truly involved in his death and laid in his grave.'[61]

Col 3:1 εἰ οὖν **συνηγέρθητε** τῷ Χριστῷ, τὰ ἄνω ζητεῖτε, οὗ ὁ Χριστός ἐστιν ἐν δεξιᾷ τοῦ θεοῦ καθήμενος

---

60. In his words, '*the narrative of the crucified and exalted Christ is the normative life-narrative within which the community's own life-narrative takes place and by which it is shaped*'; Gorman, *Cruciformity*, 44 [italics are original]. He argues that because death and resurrection was the experience of Christ, so believers are to be conformed to the same narrative.

61. 'It is not as though they simply died like Jesus died, or were buried *as* he was laid in the tomb.... Rather, they died with him on the cross and were laid in his grave'; O'Brien, *Colossians, Philemon*, 118.

*So if **you have been raised with the Messiah**, seek what is above, where the Messiah is, seated at the right hand of God.*

Identical to the previous example, this σύν-compound refers to the participation of believers in Christ's resurrection. In this example, however, we witness the way in which Paul draws on believers' participation with Christ in order to issue instruction. Since believers have been raised with Christ, they are to think in light of this reality, seeking the things above, where Christ is. As Wright puts it, 'they have entered the new age, and, belonging there by right, do not have to struggle to attain the status of membership in God's people: they already have it. They must now simply allow its life to be worked out in them.'[62]

Of the seventeen occurrences of σύν-compounds in this subcategory, fourteen express accompaniment or association, with thirteen of these pointing to participation (Rom 6:4, 5, 6, 8; 8:17 [x2]; Gal 2:19; Eph 2:5, 6 [x2]; Col 2:12 [x2]; 3:1) and one indicating union (Rom 8:17). Three instances are not directly related to union with Christ (Rom 8:29; Phil 3:10, 21).

5.7 SUMMARY

Most occurrences of the σύν-compounds convey participation with Christ, though not all. In this respect, they match the usage of the noncompound phrases σὺν Χριστῷ and its variations, which also express participation in most instances. While they are capable of other functions, both σύν-compound and noncompound expressions share the fundamental tenor of participation: believers partake *with Christ* in his death, burial, resurrection, ascension, glorification, and session in heaven. Since these realities are each portrayed as highly significant for the believer's situation, the concept of participation that underpins them must constitute a crucial element of the apostle's theological framework.

---

62. Wright, *Colossians and Philemon*, 131.

CHAPTER 6

Διὰ Χριστοῦ

6.1 INTRODUCTION

Part of the usage of the phrase ἐν Χριστῷ denotes the instrumentality of Christ in various capacities. For instance, many things are done for believers *in Christ*, which often indicates that they are performed *through* Christ in some manner (see ch. 3). Consequently, it is reasonable to assume that other expressions denoting the instrumentality of Christ ought to be considered under the broad theme of union with Christ. To this end, the phrase διὰ Χριστοῦ and its variations will now be explored, since the preposition διά is a key way in which to express instrumentality in Greek.

6.2 Διά

According to Robertson, the etymology of διά begins with the word δύο ('two') and developed into the concept of 'by-twain, be-tween, in two, in twain'.[1] Thus the notion of '*interval* (be-tween) is frequent in the N.T. both in composition and apart from composition'.[2] Furthermore, the idea of 'interval between' leads to the notion of passing between two objects.[3]

---

1. Robertson, *Grammar*, 580. See also Harrison, *Greek Prepositions*, 187; Dutton, *Prepositional Phrases*, 14.

2. Robertson, *Grammar*, 580.

3. Ibid., 581.

As such, according to Robertson, "'through" is thus not the original meaning of διά, but is a very common one.[4]

The main uses of διά are listed by BDAG as following:[5]

With genitive case:

1. marker of extension through an area or object, *via, through*
2. marker of extension in time
3. marker of instrumentality or circumstance whereby someth. is accomplished or effected, *by, via, through*
4. marker of pers. agency, *through, by*

With accusative case:

1. marker of extension through an area, *through*
2. marker of someth. constituting cause

The two genitival categories of instrumentality (3) and personal agency (4) are the most pertinent uses of διά with respect to the phrase διὰ Χριστοῦ. While BDAG separates the categories, these are sometimes grouped together as instrumentality (personal or otherwise).[6] Indeed, the term *agency* may be used in at least two ways, either of which appears in the literature, often without definition. One way for *agency* to be employed is to regard it as synonymous with *instrumentality*. It thus refers to the person or thing through which deeds are accomplished. The other way *agency* may be understood is to denote the originator of an action rather than the instrument through which/whom it occurs.

For the sake of clarity, therefore, it is worth defining these categories as they will be employed here. *Instrumentality* is used in the standard manner, to refer to one through whom actions are accomplished, allowing for personal and impersonal instrumentality. *Agency*, on the other hand, will

---

4. Ibid. BDAG regard the fundamental idea that is expressed by this preposition to be that of separation; BDAG, 223.

5. BDAG, 223–26. Dutton, *Prepositional Phrases*, outlines several other uses of the preposition within Ancient Greek that are not commonly recognised: within idiomatic phrases (18–19); within proverbial phrases (20); with technical terms pertaining to the military, legal proceedings, the field of rhetoric, and the field of games (20–21); with verbs of motion, creating a periphrasis for the action or state described by the verb indicated by the noun in the phrase (29–30); in a distributive use (31); in pregnant expressions (32); and as plastic and picturesque expressions (32).

6. See, e.g., Albrecht Oepke, 'διά', *TDNT*, 2:66–67.

be restricted in its reference to the *originator* of an action and thus will not overlap with *instrumentality*. Finally, note that it is not the preposition itself that expresses instrumentality or agency, but these functions may be effected by its combination with suitable nouns, within appropriate contexts.[7] We turn now to consider the usage of διὰ Χριστοῦ and διὰ ... Χριστοῦ in the Pauline canon.

6.3 THINGS ACHIEVED FOR/GIVEN TO PEOPLE *THROUGH CHRIST*

Rom 5:1 δικαιωθέντες οὖν ἐκ πίστεως εἰρήνην ἔχομεν πρὸς τὸν θεὸν **διὰ** τοῦ κυρίου ἡμῶν Ἰησοῦ **Χριστοῦ**

*Therefore, since we have been declared righteous by faith, we have peace with God **through** our Lord Jesus **Christ**.*

This example of διὰ ... Χριστοῦ could be understood as conveying either instrumentality or agency. On the one hand, the phrase could express the agency of Christ, such that he is the originator of believers' peace with God. This reading seems possible since the agency of God does not, at first glance, appear to be evident in the verse. While possible, however, it does not seem to represent the stronger of the two options.

On the other hand, the phrase could indicate that Christ is the personal instrument through whom believers have obtained peace with God. God would be the agent of this instrumentality, initiating the peace granted to believers. Yet while this reading is congruent with Pauline thought, the clause in question does not explicitly refer to God as agent. We might suppose that believers' peace with God implies his agency, but it is not explicitly mentioned.

Nevertheless, the wider context *does* indicate the agency of God. From Romans 4:17–25 we observe that God is the one who justifies Abraham and all believers. When we thus read 5:1, the summary clause *Therefore, since we have been declared righteous by faith* assumes God's agency. He is the one who has declared believers righteous by faith. Such an understanding does not simply imply God's agency, but recognizes that it has been

---

7. Harrison, *Greek Prepositions*, 190.

in view leading up to this verse in relation to justification. In addition, the first half of v. 5 is a dependent participial phrase that expresses cause, which leads to the independent clause *we have peace with God through our Lord Jesus Christ*; because believers have been declared righteous, we have peace with God.

Consequently, the agency that pertains to the first half of the sentence must also inform the second. God is the agent of believers' righteousness, and this righteousness leads to peace with him; God is the agent of our peace with him. As such, the phrase *through our Lord Jesus Christ* expresses instrumentality, not agency. Christ is the personal instrument through whom God reckons peace.[8]

Rom 5:17 εἰ γὰρ τῷ τοῦ ἑνὸς παραπτώματι ὁ θάνατος ἐβασίλευσεν διὰ τοῦ ἑνός, πολλῷ μᾶλλον οἱ τὴν περισσείαν τῆς χάριτος καὶ τῆς δωρεᾶς τῆς δικαιοσύνης λαμβάνοντες ἐν ζωῇ βασιλεύσουσιν **διὰ** τοῦ ἑνὸς Ἰησοῦ **Χριστοῦ**

*Since by the one man's trespass, death reigned through that one man, how much more will those who receive the overflow of grace and the gift of righteousness reign in life **through** the one man, Jesus **Christ**.*

As with the previous example, the phrase διὰ … Χριστοῦ could here express agency or instrumentality. If the instrumentality of Christ is in view, the most obvious candidate for agency in the immediate context is believers: they will reign in life through Christ, and they would be the instigators of this reality. This option, however, it totally contrary to Paul's view of things. The agency of God in the reign of believers would be appropriate, but again is not explicitly present. Nevertheless, it might be argued that God's agency is implied through the phrases *the overflow of grace and the gift of righteousness*, especially since such grace is described as the grace *of God* in 5:15.[9]

Perhaps the strongest argument toward an instrumental reading, however, is the parallel between Christ and Adam in this verse. The phrases ἐβασίλευσεν διὰ τοῦ ἑνός and βασιλεύσουσιν διὰ τοῦ ἑνὸς Ἰησοῦ

---

8. Moo describes this as 'God's justifying act in Christ'; Moo, *Romans*, 299.

9. So Cranfield; 'After ἡ χάρις τοῦ θεοῦ καί it is natural to understand the gift to be the gift of God rather than of Christ'; Cranfield, *Romans*, 1:285–86.

Χριστοῦ are parallel in structure, both employing the same verbal lexeme (βασιλεύω) and the same prepositional phrase διὰ τοῦ ἑνός. With respect to Adam, we are told that *Since by the one man's trespass, death reigned through that one man* (διὰ τοῦ ἑνός), in which it seems clear that the agency of *death* is in view, enacted through the instrument of *that one man*. If the one man, Adam, is understood to be the instrument of the agency of death—as the text surely indicates—it is difficult to make any conclusion other than to regard Christ as instrumental also, mutatis mutandis. As death reigned through Adam, so believers will reign in life through Christ.

The apparent difficulty of this understanding, however, is that the parallel between the instrumentality of Adam and the instrumentality of Christ implies a parallel between the agency of death and the agency of believers. After all, it is death that reigns through Adam, and it is believers who reign through Christ. If, however, it is illegitimate to regard believers as possessing agency in this context—as has already been suggested—how then is the structural parallel between death and believers to be accounted? The key to answering this question is the description of believers as *those who receive the overflow of grace and the gift of righteousness*.

This description is not merely incidental; it provides the grounds on which Paul is able to claim that believers will reign in life. Believers have received God's grace and his gift of righteousness; because of this, they are compared favourably to the reign of death. If, then, believers are the agents of reigning in life, they are only able to be so through the prior agency of God. There are, in a manner of speaking, two layers of agency, in which God enables believers to reign in life through Christ. Or, perhaps it is better to regard God as the sole agent—since agency has to do with the origin, instigation, or source of an action—while believers can be regarded as those who are enabled to reign in life through the gifts of grace and righteousness.

> Rom 5:21 ἵνα ὥσπερ ἐβασίλευσεν ἡ ἁμαρτία ἐν τῷ θανάτῳ, οὕτως καὶ ἡ χάρις βασιλεύσῃ διὰ δικαιοσύνης εἰς ζωὴν αἰώνιον **διὰ** Ἰησοῦ **Χριστοῦ** τοῦ κυρίου ἡμῶν

> *So that, just as sin reigned in death, so also grace will reign through righteousness, resulting in eternal life **through** Jesus **Christ** our Lord.*

This example of διὰ ... Χριστοῦ could, once again, convey instrumentality or agency. If instrumentality, the sense would be that God, as agent, has brought about eternal life through Christ. Such a notion is possible — even likely — notwithstanding the fact that there is no explicit reference to the agency of God in the immediate or wider context. Since, however, such God-agency and Christ-instrumentality roles have been observed thus far, especially in relation to issues of salvation, it follows that such is the case here.[10]

Nevertheless, for situations in which there really is no God-agency expressed — either implicitly or explicitly — it is best not to second-guess Paul. It may well be that διὰ ... Χριστοῦ in this case does convey agency rather than instrumentality, specifying that Christ is the source of eternal life. Christ-agency has been observed in previous chapters and does not contradict Paul's thinking as we understand it. Thus, this instance may best be understood accordingly: Christ is the agent and source of eternal life.

> Rom 7:4 ὥστε, ἀδελφοί μου, καὶ ὑμεῖς ἐθανατώθητε τῷ νόμῳ **διὰ τοῦ σώματος τοῦ Χριστοῦ**, εἰς τὸ γενέσθαι ὑμᾶς ἑτέρῳ, τῷ ἐκ νεκρῶν ἐγερθέντι, ἵνα καρποφορήσωμεν τῷ θεῷ
>
> *Therefore, my brothers, you also were put to death in relation to the law **through** the crucified body of the **Messiah**, so that you may belong to another — to Him who was raised from the dead — that we may bear fruit for God.*

This example of διὰ ... Χριστοῦ specifies Christ's body as the vessel through which believers were put to death. The reference to Christ's *body* should not exclude the example from the *through Christ* category, since the idea clearly refers to something done through Christ; the only difference here is that this is made more specific and concrete through reference to his *body*.

The question remains, however, as to whether this example is to be understood as expressing instrumentality or agency. Once again here, there does not appear to be any explicit reference to the agency of God, so

---

10. So Dunn, *Romans 1–8*, 288.

that the agency of Christ (or Christ's crucified body) presents as a possible reading.

More likely, however, is the expression of the instrumentality of Christ's crucified body. The second half of the verse suggests this: *so that you may belong to another — to Him who was raised from the dead — that we may bear fruit for God.* Christ described as *him who was raised from the dead* implies the agency of God; Christ did not raise himself but was raised by his Father. With God's agency implied in relation to the resurrection of Christ, his agency may be implied with respect to his death. And if such is the case for Christ's death, so it is for the death of believers through Christ. Thus we may conclude that the agent of the death of believers is God, who puts them to death through the instrument of the crucified body of Christ.

Having established the instrumentality of the crucified body of Christ in this verse, it is worth reflecting on the manner in which believers are put to death through it. While there is nothing explicitly said about it, there seems to be an extra step to Paul's reasoning that has been left unsaid. For believers to be put to death through Christ's body, some association with that body is required. It could be speculative to suggest that the missing step here is the concept of participation with Christ. Yet the notion of participation makes sense, creating an association between believers and the body of Christ.[11] With such an association in place, God's putting believers to death through Christ's crucified body is achieved by believers' partaking in his death.

1 Cor 15:57 τῷ δὲ θεῷ χάρις τῷ διδόντι ἡμῖν τὸ νῖκος **διὰ** τοῦ κυρίου ἡμῶν Ἰησοῦ **Χριστοῦ**

*But thanks be to God, who gives us the victory **through** our Lord Jesus Christ!*

This example of διὰ ... Χριστοῦ expresses the instrumentality of Christ in a straightforward manner. The agency of God is explicit in the

---

11. So ibid., 362; contra Cranfield, who states: 'Paul is not saying that they have a share in Christ's death because they now are united to Him (in His body), but that Christ died for them (and this means that they also died in God's sight) in order that they might be united to Him'; Cranfield, *Romans*, 1:336.

two clauses *But thanks be to God, who gives us the victory.* The instrumentality of Christ in effecting this victory is the plain meaning of *through our Lord Jesus Christ!*[12]

2 Cor 1:5 ὅτι καθὼς περισσεύει τὰ παθήματα τοῦ Χριστοῦ εἰς ἡμᾶς, οὕτως **διὰ** τοῦ **Χριστοῦ** περισσεύει καὶ ἡ παράκλησις ἡμῶν

*For as the sufferings of Christ overflow to us, so **through Christ** our comfort also overflows.*

In this instance, διὰ τοῦ Χριστοῦ conveys the instrumentality of Christ in extending the comfort of God to believers. This is confirmed by the fact that the agency of God is plainly stated in 1:4: *He comforts us in all our affliction, so that we may be able to comfort those who are in any kind of affliction, through the comfort we ourselves receive from God.* Believers are comforted by God, whose comfort overflows through the person of Christ.[13]

2 Cor 5:18 τὰ δὲ πάντα ἐκ τοῦ θεοῦ τοῦ καταλλάξαντος ἡμᾶς ἑαυτῷ **διὰ Χριστοῦ** καὶ δόντος ἡμῖν τὴν διακονίαν τῆς καταλλαγῆς

*Everything is from God, who reconciled us to Himself **through Christ** and gave us the ministry of reconciliation.*

Once again, διὰ Χριστοῦ expresses the instrumentality of Christ in effecting the agency of God. God has reconciled believers to himself, and this has taken place through the person and work of Christ.

Gal 1:1 Παῦλος ἀπόστολος οὐκ ἀπ᾽ ἀνθρώπων οὐδὲ δι᾽ ἀνθρώπου ἀλλὰ **διὰ** Ἰησοῦ **Χριστοῦ** καὶ θεοῦ πατρὸς τοῦ ἐγείραντος αὐτὸν ἐκ νεκρῶν

*Paul, an apostle — not from men or by man, but **by** Jesus **Christ** and God the Father who raised Him from the dead.*

---

12. Ciampa and Rosner, *1 Corinthians*, 837.

13. 'In vv. 3–4 Paul blessed God for comfort in affliction, and here he goes on to explain that the honour of sharing in Christ's sufferings is always accompanied by the joy of sharing God's comfort'; Kruse, *2 Corinthians*, 61.

Literally, Paul describes his apostleship as having been designated *through Jesus Christ*. We see here that Christ performed this designation in concert with his Father. What remains to be ascertained, however, is whether this instance of διὰ … Χριστοῦ is to be regarded as expressing instrumentality or agency. On the one hand, an instrumental reading suffers from the fact that *through Jesus Christ* is connected to *and God the Father*, muting any discernable difference between the roles of Christ and his Father in this context. For an instrumental reading to be compelling, the agency of God should be evident, but the tight connection here between Christ and God does not give expression to such distinction.

It might be argued, however, that the phrase that qualifies God — *who raised Him from the dead* — indicates the agency of God: since he is the one who raised Christ, he stands behind Christ's work in appointing Paul as an apostle. This option seems unlikely, however. First, God's work in raising Christ does not appear to bear a direct causal relationship to Christ's appointment of Paul — and the agent-instrument correlation normally exhibits a direct relationship. Second, this description of God does not mitigate the fact that Christ and God are both the objects of the preposition διά. While the preposition may convey either instrumentality or agency, it is not likely able to convey both at the same time — one for its first object (instrumentality through Christ) and the other for its second (agency through God)!

Nevertheless, διὰ … Χριστοῦ here might express the agency of both Christ and God, such that a double agency is in view. Both figures are to be regarded as the originators and instigators of Paul's apostolic appointment.[14] This reading offers the best syntactical fit and may even serve a subtle role in the wider context. As Paul will go on to describe the revelation of Christ to him on the Damascus Road, at which point his apostleship was established (1:15 – 16), so this verse preempts the fact that Christ was not alone in effecting this apostolic appointment; the agency of Christ *and* his Father were complicit in Paul's calling. Indeed, that connection may also explain the description of God as the one who raised Christ from

---

14. This is in accordance with Martyn's comment, 'Both instances of *dia* in Gal 1:1 are best rendered with the word "by." In the whole of this verse Paul is concerned not with misunderstandings as to who may have mediated his sending, but rather with misconceptions as to who sent him'; Martyn, *Galatians*, 83.

the dead, since the revelation of Christ to Paul involved his encounter with the *risen* Lord.

Gal 1:12 οὐδὲ γὰρ ἐγὼ παρὰ ἀνθρώπου παρέλαβον αὐτὸ οὔτε ἐδιδάχθην ἀλλὰ **δι᾽** ἀποκαλύψεως Ἰησοῦ **Χριστοῦ**

*For I did not receive it from a human source and I was not taught it, but it came by a revelation **from** Jesus **Christ**.*

The phrase δι᾽ ἀποκαλύψεως Ἰησοῦ Χριστοῦ can be rendered one of three ways. The revelation could be *from* Jesus Christ (genitive of source) or *about* Jesus Christ (epexegetical genitive), or even *of* Jesus Christ (genitive of content). While it is standard to regard this expression as indicating *source*, such that the revelation comes *from* Jesus Christ, it may be more likely to indicate *content*: the gospel was received by Paul through a revelation *of* Jesus Christ. The main reason for this is that in 1:15–16 Paul says that God was pleased *to reveal His Son in me* (ἀποκαλύψαι τὸν υἱὸν αὐτοῦ ἐν ἐμοί). *His Son* is the direct object of the verb *to reveal*; thus, Paul is not saying that the message *about* Christ was revealed to him, but Christ himself.[15]

This is confirmed in the second half of 1:16: *so that I could preach Him among the Gentiles.* Again, Paul does not say *so that I could preach about Him*, but *so that I could preach* Him. Since, therefore, Jesus Christ is himself the revelation of God to Paul, it follows that here in 1:12 the genitive Ἰησοῦ Χριστοῦ should be taken to express content: Paul received the gospel through the revealing of Christ to him.

If such is the case, this example of δι᾽ ... Χριστοῦ does not refer to the instrumentality or agency of Christ himself, but to the instrumentality or agency of the *revelation of Christ*. As such, the notion is not personal since Paul does not speak of the activity of the person of Christ. This probably rules out the possibility of agency here; at least, according to BDAG, the category refers to *personal* agency.[16] It is more likely, then, that the phrase conveys the instrumentality of the revelation of Christ. While the agency of God in this revelation is not explicitly present in the verse, it may be

---

15. So Martyn, 'If v 12 is explicated in v 16, as seems likely, then in both of these verses Paul refers to God's act of invasively revealing Christ to him'; Martyn, *Galatians*, 144.

16. BDAG, 225.

observed a little further into the chapter: *But when God … was pleased to reveal His Son in me* (1:15–16). In these verses God is clearly regarded as the originator and instigator of the revelation of Christ to Paul, and so his agency may be understood in 1:12. Therefore, Paul did not receive the gospel through human means, but God revealed it to him through the instrumentality of the revelation of Christ.[17]

Eph 1:5 προορίσας ἡμᾶς εἰς υἱοθεσίαν **διὰ Ἰησοῦ Χριστοῦ** εἰς αὐτόν, κατὰ τὴν εὐδοκίαν τοῦ θελήματος αὐτοῦ

*He predestined us to be adopted **through** Jesus **Christ** for Himself, according to His favor and will.*

This occurrence of διὰ … Χριστοῦ conveys the instrumentality of Christ in the adoption of believers. God is clearly the agent of adoption, as the one who has predestined believers to be adopted, and he has acted according to his favour and will.

Phil 1:11 πεπληρωμένοι καρπὸν δικαιοσύνης τὸν **διὰ Ἰησοῦ Χριστοῦ** εἰς δόξαν καὶ ἔπαινον θεοῦ

*Filled with the fruit of righteousness that comes **through** Jesus **Christ** to the glory and praise of God.*

While this example of διὰ … Χριστοῦ might be understood as instrumental, it is probably better understood as expressing agency, since there is no indication of the agency of God in the immediate nor surrounding context. While it might be suggested that the phrase *to the glory and praise of God* implies the agency of God, this is not the case. The function of εἰς here is to indicate purpose;[18] it is for the glory and praise of God that Paul prays that believers might be filled with the fruit of righteousness, but this does not require God to be the agent of the action. As such, it is best to regard διὰ … Χριστοῦ as conveying agency: Jesus Christ is the one who fills believers with the fruit of righteousness in order to bring about the glory and praise of God.

---

17. Martyn, *Galatians*, 144.
18. Fee, *Philippians*, 105.

1 Thess 5:9 ὅτι οὐκ ἔθετο ἡμᾶς ὁ θεὸς εἰς ὀργὴν ἀλλὰ εἰς περιποίησιν σωτηρίας **διὰ** τοῦ κυρίου ἡμῶν Ἰησοῦ **Χριστοῦ**

*For God did not appoint us to wrath, but to obtain salvation **through** our Lord Jesus **Christ**.*

This instance of διὰ ... Χριστοῦ conveys the instrumentality of Christ in the salvation of believers. The agency of God in this is explicit: *For God did not appoint us to wrath, but to obtain salvation*, and Christ is the one through whom God's appointment of salvation to believers is achieved.

Titus 3:6 οὗ ἐξέχεεν ἐφ᾽ ἡμᾶς πλουσίως **διὰ** Ἰησοῦ **Χριστοῦ** τοῦ σωτῆρος ἡμῶν

*He poured out this Spirit on us abundantly **through** Jesus **Christ** our Savior.*

Once again the instrumentality of Christ is in view through this use of διὰ ... Χριστοῦ. The agency of God is expressed with God as the subject of the verb *He poured out*. He has poured out his Spirit on believers through the instrumentality of Jesus Christ our Saviour.

Of the thirteen instances of διὰ ... Χριστοῦ in this subcategory, ten are instrumental (Rom 5:1, 17; 7:4; 1 Cor 15:57; 2 Cor 1:5; 5:18; Gal 1:12; Eph 1:5; 1 Thess 5:9; Titus 3:6), and three express agency (Rom 5:21; Gal 1:1; Phil 1:11).

6.4 BELIEVERS' ACTIONS *THROUGH CHRIST*

Rom 1:8 πρῶτον μὲν εὐχαριστῶ τῷ θεῷ μου **διὰ** Ἰησοῦ **Χριστοῦ** περὶ πάντων ὑμῶν ὅτι ἡ πίστις ὑμῶν καταγγέλλεται ἐν ὅλῳ τῷ κόσμῳ

*First, I thank my God **through** Jesus **Christ** for all of you because the news of your faith is being reported in all the world.*

Here διὰ ... Χριστοῦ does not involve the agency of God or Christ; rather, we witness the phrase in relation to the agency of Paul. He is the instigator of thanksgiving to God, and this is somehow effected through Christ. According to the definitions adopted here, such a use of διὰ ...

Χριστοῦ is to be categorized as instrumental in function. BDAG, however, classes this occurrence as an example of agency, describing it as portraying Christ as an intermediary.[19] While we must regard the use as conveying instrumentality rather than agency, the notion of mediation does provide a good fit in this context. The idea is not that Paul uses Christ to perform an action—in the manner to which we are now accustomed vis-à-vis the agency of God; rather, Paul offers his thanks to God through the mediation of Christ.[20] As mediator, Christ is the means through which this occurs; thus, an instrumental reading is most appropriate.

Rom 5:11 οὐ μόνον δέ, ἀλλὰ καὶ καυχώμενοι ἐν τῷ θεῷ **διὰ** τοῦ κυρίου ἡμῶν Ἰησοῦ **Χριστοῦ** δι' οὗ νῦν τὴν καταλλαγὴν ἐλάβομεν

*And not only that, but we also rejoice in God **through** our Lord Jesus **Christ**. We have now received reconciliation through Him.*

As with the previous example, this occurrence of διὰ … Χριστοῦ expresses the instrumentality of Christ by way of mediation, with respect to the agency of believers.[21] Believers rejoice (or boast) in God through a relationship with him that is mediated by Christ.

Rom 7:25 χάρις δὲ τῷ θεῷ **διὰ** Ἰησοῦ **Χριστοῦ** τοῦ κυρίου ἡμῶν. Ἄρα οὖν αὐτὸς ἐγὼ τῷ μὲν νοῒ δουλεύω νόμῳ θεοῦ τῇ δὲ σαρκὶ νόμῳ ἁμαρτίας

*I thank God **through** Jesus **Christ** our Lord! So then, with my mind I myself am a slave to the law of God, but with my flesh, to the law of sin.*

Literally, the first sentence in this verse says *thanks [be] to God through Jesus Christ our Lord*. As such, it does not report an action performed by a believer. Rather, it *is* an action performed by a believer, in that Paul here gives thanks to God through Jesus Christ by this utterance.[22]

---

19. BDAG, 225.

20. Dunn, *Romans 1–8*, 28.

21. Ibid., 261.

22. Regardless of whether it is assumed that Paul is speaking as himself or as an unregenerate person in Rom 7:13–25, the first clause of this verse is to be regarded as Paul; 'On the unregenerate view, it must be assumed that Paul, the Christian, has at this point interjected his own thanksgiving'; Moo, *Romans*, 467.

Consequently, the reference may be included in this subcategory, even though it *performs*, rather than *reports*, an action *through Christ*. The phrase διὰ ... Χριστοῦ once again indicates the mediatorial instrumentality of Christ. It is through him that the agency of Paul in offering thanksgiving is enabled.

> Rom 15:30 παρακαλῶ δὲ ὑμᾶς, ἀδελφοί, **διὰ** τοῦ κυρίου ἡμῶν Ἰησοῦ **Χριστοῦ** καὶ διὰ τῆς ἀγάπης τοῦ πνεύματος συναγωνίσασθαί μοι ἐν ταῖς προσευχαῖς ὑπὲρ ἐμοῦ πρὸς τὸν θεόν

> *Now I appeal to you, brothers, **through** the Lord Jesus **Christ** and through the love of the Spirit, to join with me in fervent prayers to God on my behalf.*

The first question to address here is whether the clauses *through the Lord Jesus Christ* and *through the love of the Spirit* modify Paul's own action or the action that he wishes the Romans to adopt. That is, Paul might be saying that he personally implores the brothers through Christ, or he might be saying that they are to join in fervent prayer through Christ. While the latter option is grammatically possible, the former is more likely. First, it is more usual for such phrases to modify preceding material rather than subsequent content. Second, while Paul's imploring and the Romans' joining in prayer could both be understood as occurring through Christ, it is more difficult to conceive of their joining in fervent prayer as occurring through the love of the Spirit. Modifying Paul, however, 'the love of the Spirit' is Paul's way of indicating that his exhortation derives from love. Thus, it is best to regard these two clauses as modifying Paul's action rather than an action he desires the Romans to undertake.

Thus, διὰ ... Χριστοῦ is employed in connection to the agency of Paul, but in this case does not refer to mediation between Paul and God, as Paul's action is directed toward his readers. Indeed, it would seem that mediation is not in view at all. How then is the instrumentality of Christ to be understood here? The types of instrumentality observed thus far do not fit the context here, since mediation is not in view, and it also seems strained to suggest that Christ somehow effects Paul's action of imploring the Romans. Even less likely is the thought that the action is achieved by the love of the Spirit.

Rather, the type of instrumentality in view here may be that which is described by the BDAG subcategory *of manner, esp. w. verbs of saying*.[23] This function of διά describes the manner or mode in which an action takes place. One example that illustrates this is found in Acts 15:32: *Both Judas and Silas ... encouraged the brothers and strengthened them with a long message*. In this instance, διὰ λόγου πολλοῦ is translated *with a long message* and indicates the manner in which Judas and Silas encouraged the brothers. In a similar fashion, διὰ ... Χριστοῦ may be regarded as expressing the manner in which Paul implores his readers. He appeals to them *with Christ*, which means that he 'appeals to Christ's authority in order to drive home his entreaty'.[24]

Rom 16:27 μόνῳ σοφῷ θεῷ, **διὰ Ἰησοῦ Χριστοῦ**, ᾧ ἡ δόξα εἰς τοὺς αἰῶνας, ἀμήν

*To the only wise God, **through** Jesus **Christ**—to Him be the glory forever! Amen.*

This instance is similar to Romans 7:25 above, in that it *performs* an action of a believer *through Christ*. Here we see Paul offering praise to God through the mediatorial instrumentality of Christ.[25]

2 Cor 10:1 αὐτὸς δὲ ἐγὼ Παῦλος παρακαλῶ ὑμᾶς **διὰ** τῆς πραΰτητος καὶ ἐπιεικείας τοῦ **Χριστοῦ**, ὃς κατὰ πρόσωπον μὲν ταπεινὸς ἐν ὑμῖν, ἀπὼν δὲ θαρρῶ εἰς ὑμᾶς

*Now I, Paul, make a personal appeal to you **by** the gentleness and graciousness of **Christ**—I who am humble among you in person, but bold toward you when absent.*

The phrase here translated *by the gentleness and graciousness of Christ* can be literally translated *through ... Christ*. In effect, Paul's appeal to the Corinthians is conducted *through Christ*. In this case, however, a more specific facet of Christ's instrumentality is explicated, namely, his gentleness

---

23. BDAG, 224.
24. Cranfield, *Romans*, 2:776.
25. The relative pronoun ᾧ most likely refers to the 'only wise God' as antecedent; Moo, *Romans*, 941, n. 34.

and graciousness. The reference to these qualities makes it likely that the type of instrumentality in view is that *of manner*. Found especially with 'verbs of saying', this function of διά describes the manner or mode in which an action takes place.[26] As with Romans 15:30 (above), διά … Χριστοῦ expresses the manner in which Paul implores his readers.[27] He appeals to them *with the gentleness and graciousness of Christ*, which means that his action is informed and shaped by Christ's character.

Of the six instances of διά … Χριστοῦ in this subcategory, four adhere to the expected type of instrumentality (Rom 1:8; 5:11; 7:25; 16:27), while two express the instrumentality of manner (Rom 15:30; 2 Cor 10:1).

6.5 JUSTIFICATION *THROUGH* CHRIST

Rom 3:22 δικαιοσύνη δὲ θεοῦ **διὰ** πίστεως Ἰησοῦ **Χριστοῦ** εἰς πάντας τοὺς πιστεύοντας. οὐ γάρ ἐστιν διαστολή

That is, God's righteousness through **faith** *in Jesus* **Christ***, to all who believe, since there is no distinction.*

This, the first of Paul's three διὰ πίστεως [Ἰησοῦ] Χριστοῦ phrases, is widely debated concerning the nature of the genitive phrase. While traditional analyses regard πίστεως Ἰησοῦ Χριστοῦ as an objective genitive—*faith in Christ*—there is a growing wave of scholarship that regards it as a subjective genitive—*the faithfulness of Christ*.

It is impossible to engage this issue in sufficient depth, though a few observations are in order. Against an objective genitive reading is the apparent tautology: *God's righteousness through faith in Jesus Christ, to all who believe.* The first clause indicates that God's righteousness is received through faith in Christ, while the second clause approximates the same thing. A subjective genitive reading removes that apparent tautology, affirming that God's righteousness comes to all who believe through the faithfulness of Christ. In defense of an objective genitive reading, how-

---

26. BDAG, 224.

27. Contra Kruse, who seems to suggest that *the gentleness and graciousness of Christ* modifies the Corinthians' response to Paul's appeal rather than his appeal itself; 'he is intending that they receive and act upon the content of the appeal which follows in light of that by which he appeals'; Kruse, *2 Corinthians*, 172.

ever, is the possibility that the phrase *to all who believe* is not tautological but rather emphasizes that God's righteousness comes to *all* believers; πάντας is the additional element provided by the second clause. This is further supported by the final clause, *since there is no distinction*; all believers receive the righteousness of God through faith in Christ, without discrimination. While we could introduce several more arguments for either side,[28] an objective genitive reading seems mildly stronger than the subjective genitive.[29]

Nevertheless, regardless of whether πίστεως Ἰησοῦ Χριστοῦ is to be regarded as subjective or objective, either way it points to the instrumentality of Christ in believers' acquisition of righteousness. If *faith in Jesus Christ*, then trust in Christ brings about God's righteousness; if *faithfulness of Jesus Christ*, then the achievement of Christ enables participation in his righteousness. For our purposes, this observation is all that is required here.

Gal 2:16 εἰδότες ὅτι οὐ δικαιοῦται ἄνθρωπος ἐξ ἔργων νόμου
ἐὰν μὴ **διὰ** πίστεως Ἰησοῦ **Χριστοῦ**, καὶ ἡμεῖς εἰς Χριστὸν Ἰησοῦν
ἐπιστεύσαμεν, ἵνα δικαιωθῶμεν ἐκ πίστεως Χριστοῦ καὶ οὐκ ἐξ
ἔργων νόμου, ὅτι ἐξ ἔργων νόμου οὐ δικαιωθήσεται πᾶσα σάρξ

28. For a recent subjective genitive reading of this verse, see Douglas A. Campbell, 'The Faithfulness of Jesus Christ in Romans 3:22', in *The Faith of Jesus Christ: Exegetical, Biblical, and Theological Studies* (ed. Michael F. Bird and Preston M. Sprinkle; Milton Keynes: Paternoster/Peabody, MA: Hendrickson, 2009), 57–71; for an objective genitive reading, see R. Barry Matlock, 'Saving Faith: The Rhetoric and Semantics of πίστις in Paul', in *The Faith of Jesus Christ: Exegetical, Biblical, and Theological Studies*, 73–89. Watson also argues for an objective genitive reading by arguing that 'Paul's prepositional faith-formulations all derive from the ἐκ πίστεως of Habakkuk 2:4', which counts against the subjective genitive view; Francis Watson, 'By Faith (of Christ): An Exegetical Dilemma and its Scriptural Solution', in *The Faith of Jesus Christ: Exegetical, Biblical, and Theological Studies*, 162; see also idem, *Paul, Judaism, and the Gentiles: Beyond the New Perspective* (rev. ed.; Grand Rapids: Eerdmans, 2007), 243–44. From a linguistic point of view, Porter and Pitts argue that the objective genitive reading is mildly stronger than the subjective; Stanley E. Porter and Andrew W. Pitts, 'Πίστις with a Preposition and Genitive Modifier: Lexical, Semantic, and Syntactic Considerations in the πίστις Χριστοῦ Discussion', in *The Faith of Jesus Christ: Exegetical, Biblical, and Theological Studies*, 33–53.

29. Others propose a 'third view' that rejects the subjective-objective dichotomy, preferring to see πίστεως Χριστοῦ as a theological term (filled with whatever theological idea the interpreter prefers); see Preston M. Sprinkle, 'Πιστίς Χριστοῦ as an Eschatological Event', in *The Faith of Jesus Christ: Exegetical, Biblical, and Theological Studies*, 165–84.

[We] know that no one is justified by the works of the law but by faith in Jesus **Christ**. *And we have believed in Christ Jesus so that we might be justified by faith in Christ and not by the works of the law, because by the works of the law no human being will be justified.*

While the phrase διὰ πίστεως Ἰησοῦ Χριστοῦ can be rendered as an objective genitive—meaning *through faith in Jesus Christ* (cf. HCSB, above)—it could well be a subjective genitive—*through the faithfulness of Jesus Christ*.[30] The principal reason for this is the phrase that follows: *And we have believed in Christ Jesus*. To take διὰ πίστεως Ἰησοῦ Χριστοῦ as indicating *faith in Christ* makes the following clause tautological, effectively saying the same thing twice. The subjective genitive reading of πίστεως Ἰησοῦ Χριστοῦ allows two complementary ideas to be expressed: first, people are justified by *the faithfulness of Jesus Christ*; and second, we have been justified by believing in Christ.[31]

In this respect, Paul implies that Christ's faithfulness and consequent righteousness are shared with believers. While it is not directly stated, except perhaps by the διὰ ... Χριστοῦ language, the sharing of Christ's righteousness is presumably understood through participation with Christ. Certainly participation with Christ is in view in the following context, when Paul says that he has *been crucified with Christ* (2:19). Reconstructing Paul's thought, then, it can be discerned that by his participation in Christ's crucifixion (2:19) and consequently his life (2:20), he also participates in the declaration of Christ's righteousness, which has been achieved by Christ's faithfulness.

As with Romans 3:22 above, regardless of whether πίστεως Ἰησοῦ Χριστοῦ is to be regarded as subjective or objective, either way it points

---

30. For extensive argumentation for this position, see Martyn, *Galatians*, 263–75. See also Richard B. Hays, *The Faith of Jesus Christ: The Narrative Substructure of Galatians 3:1–4:11* (1983; repr. Grand Rapids: Eerdmans, 2002), 123–24, 162; D. W. B. Robinson, '"Faith of Jesus Christ"—A New Testament Debate', *RTR* 29 (1970): 79–80; Ardel B. Caneday, 'The Faithfulness of Jesus Christ as a Theme in Paul's Theology in Galatians', in *The Faith of Jesus Christ: Exegetical, Biblical, and Theological Studies*, 185–205. For the case against a subjective genitive reading, see James D. G. Dunn, 'Once More, ΠΙΣΤΙΣ ΧΡΙΣΤΟΥ', in *The Faith of Jesus Christ: The Narrative Substructure of Galatians 3:1–4:11*, 256–59, 261–62.

31. We cannot discuss here the full complexities of the debate concerning this issue; suffice to say, 'Recent decades have seen extensive discussion of the matter, sometimes even heated debate'; Martyn, *Galatians*, 251.

to the instrumentality of Christ in believers' acquisition of righteousness, contrasted with the (false) instrumentality of the works of the law.

Phil 3:9 καὶ εὑρεθῶ ἐν αὐτῷ, μὴ ἔχων ἐμὴν δικαιοσύνην τὴν ἐκ νόμου ἀλλὰ τὴν **διὰ πίστεως Χριστοῦ**, τὴν ἐκ θεοῦ δικαιοσύνην ἐπὶ τῇ πίστει

*And be found in Him, not having a righteousness of my own from the law, but one that is **through** faith in **Christ**—the righteousness from God based on faith.*

As with Galatians 2:16, there is debate about the meaning of the phrase διὰ πίστεως Χριστοῦ. A subjective genitive reading is also preferred here, that Paul's righteousness is based on the faithfulness of Christ.[32] Once again, regardless of whether the genitive is subjective or objective, this example of διὰ ... Χριστοῦ indicates the instrumentality of Christ in bringing about Paul's righteous status. As the phrase *the righteousness from God* expresses, this righteousness ultimately derives from the agency of God, who assigns it to believers on the basis of Christ's faithfulness (or faith in Christ).

All three instances of διὰ ... Χριστοῦ in this subcategory are instrumental (Rom 3:22; Gal 2:16; Phil 3:9).

6.6 CHARACTERISTICS OF BELIEVERS THROUGH CHRIST

2 Cor 3:4 πεποίθησιν δὲ τοιαύτην ἔχομεν **διὰ τοῦ Χριστοῦ** πρὸς τὸν θεόν

*We have this kind of confidence toward God **through Christ**.*

The characteristic in view is confidence. Such a characteristic is neither natural nor derived from inherent merit; rather, it comes through Christ. The kind of instrumentality that Christ enacts here is best described as mediatorial since it enables Paul to have confidence *toward God*—he is

---

32. See O'Brien for a detailed discussion that concludes in favour of this reading; O'Brien, *Philippians*, 391–400. Against this view, see Fee, *Philippians*, 325, n. 44.

assured with respect to God on the basis of Christ's mediation.[33] This is confirmed by the following verses, which indicate that 'our competence is from God' (3:5–6), demonstrating the agency of God and therefore the instrumentality of Christ in 3:4.[34]

6.7 TRINITY *THROUGH* CHRIST

Rom 2:16 ἐν ἡμέρᾳ ὅτε κρίνει ὁ θεὸς τὰ κρυπτὰ τῶν ἀνθρώπων κατὰ τὸ εὐαγγέλιόν μου **διὰ Χριστοῦ** Ἰησοῦ

*On the day when God judges what people have kept secret, according to my gospel **through Christ** Jesus.*

While the phrase διὰ Χριστοῦ could modify κατὰ τὸ εὐαγγέλιόν μου—in which case Paul is describing his gospel as *through Christ*—the phrase probably modifies ἐν ἡμέρᾳ ὅτε κρίνει ὁ θεός. The former alternative would envisage that Paul's gospel is *through Christ*, that is, that Paul's gospel is revealed through Christ. Even understood so, this option seems awkward at best. The latter alternative sees διὰ Χριστοῦ as continuing the thought of the previous clause, though preceded by κατὰ τὸ εὐαγγέλιόν μου, which may be regarded as parenthetic. If this is correct, the sentence might be paraphrased as *on the day when God judges **through Christ** Jesus what people have kept secret, according to my gospel.* This verse then indicates the instrumentality of Christ in God's judging activity[35] and thus constitutes a reference to the trinitarian nature of the work of God in Christ.

2 Cor 5:18 τὰ δὲ πάντα ἐκ τοῦ θεοῦ τοῦ καταλλάξαντος ἡμᾶς ἑαυτῷ **διὰ Χριστοῦ** καὶ δόντος ἡμῖν τὴν διακονίαν τῆς καταλλαγῆς

*Everything is from God, who reconciled us to Himself **through Christ** and gave us the ministry of reconciliation.*

---

33. Whether Bouttier is correct to regard this as indicative of Paul's role as one through whom Christ has worked, either way such confidence must derive from the mediation of Christ. See Bouttier, *En Christ*, 33 ff.

34. Kruse, *Corinthians*, 91–92.

35. Dunn, *Romans 1–8*, 103–4; Moo, *Romans*, 155; against Cranfield, *Romans*, 1:163.

The agency of God is in view in this verse in at least three ways. First, we are told that *everything is from God*; second, he *reconciled us to himself*; third, he *gave us the ministry of reconciliation*. Within these declarations of God's agency, we see that his reconciling us to himself is conducted *through Christ*.[36] Paul's implicit trinitarianism views Christ as the instrument of God's reconciliation.

Gal 1:1 Παῦλος ἀπόστολος οὐκ ἀπ᾽ ἀνθρώπων οὐδὲ δι᾽ ἀνθρώπου ἀλλὰ **διὰ** Ἰησοῦ **Χριστοῦ** καὶ θεοῦ πατρὸς τοῦ ἐγείραντος αὐτὸν ἐκ νεκρῶν

*Paul, an apostle — not from men or by man, but **by** Jesus **Christ** and God the Father who raised Him from the dead.*

Here Paul indicates that his apostleship is not derived *from* people (ἀπ᾽ ἀνθρώπων), nor assigned to him *through* people (δι᾽ ἀνθρώπου), but is through Christ and God (διὰ Ἰησοῦ Χριστοῦ καὶ θεοῦ). Rather than the instrumentality of Christ working in partnership with the agency of God, we see here that both Christ and God are modified by the one preposition, διά. Therefore are both regarded as the agents of this event (on this verse, see §6.3 above). Paul's apostleship is bestowed by Christ and God together in trinitarian unison.

Eph 1:5 προορίσας ἡμᾶς εἰς υἱοθεσίαν **διὰ** Ἰησοῦ **Χριστοῦ** εἰς αὐτόν, κατὰ τὴν εὐδοκίαν τοῦ θελήματος αὐτοῦ

*He predestined us to be adopted **through** Jesus **Christ** for Himself, according to His favor and will.*

The agency of God is once again clearly in view in this verse: he has predestined believers; their adoption is *for Himself*; and this is performed *according to His favour and will*. The work of God in adopting believers is accomplished through the instrumentality of Christ (on this verse, see §6.3 above), again reflecting Paul's implicit trinitarianism.

1 Thess 5:9 ὅτι οὐκ ἔθετο ἡμᾶς ὁ θεὸς εἰς ὀργὴν ἀλλὰ εἰς περιποίησιν σωτηρίας **διὰ** τοῦ κυρίου ἡμῶν Ἰησοῦ **Χριστοῦ**

---

36. Bouttier, *En Christ*, 31–35.

For God did not appoint us to wrath, but to obtain salvation **through** *our Lord Jesus* **Christ**.

In this verse, the agency of God is explicit in that he is the one who has appointed believers to obtain salvation. The obtaining of such salvation is executed through the instrumentality of Christ, and thus the work of Father and Son is inextricably linked in God's plan for salvation (on this verse, see §6.3 above).

Titus 3:6 οὗ ἐξέχεεν ἐφ ἡμᾶς πλουσίως **διὰ** Ἰησοῦ **Χριστοῦ** τοῦ σωτῆρος ἡμῶν

He poured out this Spirit on us abundantly **through** *Jesus* **Christ** *our Savior.*

The relative pronoun οὗ refers to the Holy Spirit mentioned in 3:5, who is poured out by God (the subject of the verb ἐξέχεεν). The Spirit is poured out on believers by God *through Jesus Christ*. Christ is the instrument for the agency of God in the giving of the Holy Spirit; thus we see all three persons of the Trinity involved here (on this verse, see §6.3 above).

Of the six occurrences of διὰ ... Χριστοῦ in this subcategory, five are instrumental (Rom 2:16; 2 Cor 5:18; Eph 1:5; 1 Thess 5:9; Titus 3:6), and one indicates agency (Gal 1:1). These instances of διὰ ... Χριστοῦ reflect the trinitarian nature of Paul's thought insofar as they point to the mutual cooperation of God and Christ.

6.8 VARIATIONS OF *THROUGH CHRIST*

As with other phrases investigated so far, there are variations to διὰ Χριστοῦ that are relevant to our investigation. These will primarily involve relative and personal pronouns that stand in place of Χριστοῦ.

6.8.1 *THINGS ACHIEVED FOR/GIVEN TO PEOPLE THROUGH CHRIST*

Rom 1:3 – 5 περὶ τοῦ υἱοῦ αὐτοῦ τοῦ γενομένου ἐκ σπέρματος Δαυὶδ κατὰ σάρκα, τοῦ ὁρισθέντος υἱοῦ θεοῦ ἐν δυνάμει κατὰ

πνεῦμα ἁγιωσύνης ἐξ ἀναστάσεως νεκρῶν, Ἰησοῦ Χριστοῦ τοῦ
κυρίου ἡμῶν, **δι᾽ οὗ** ἐλάβομεν χάριν καὶ ἀποστολὴν εἰς ὑπακοὴν
πίστεως ἐν πᾶσιν τοῖς ἔθνεσιν ὑπὲρ τοῦ ὀνόματος αὐτοῦ

*Concerning His Son, Jesus Christ our Lord, who was a descendant
of David according to the flesh and who has been declared to be the
powerful Son of God by the resurrection from the dead according to
the Spirit of holiness. We have received grace and apostleship **through
Him** to bring about the obedience of faith among all the nations, on
behalf of His name*

In v. 5, δι᾽ οὗ has 'Jesus Christ our Lord' as its antecedent (v. 3). Paul
asserts that the grace and apostleship that he has received is *through Him*.
While the agency of God in appointing grace and apostleship is not
explicit in v. 5, it is likely best understood so since God's agency *is* in view
through vv. 2–4. Thus Paul's reception of God's grace and his appointment as an apostle is effected through the mediatorial instrumentality of
Christ.[37]

Rom 5:1–2 δικαιωθέντες οὖν ἐκ πίστεως εἰρήνην ἔχομεν πρὸς
τὸν θεὸν διὰ τοῦ κυρίου ἡμῶν Ἰησοῦ Χριστοῦ **δι᾽ οὗ** καὶ τὴν
προσαγωγὴν ἐσχήκαμεν τῇ πίστει εἰς τὴν χάριν ταύτην ἐν ᾗ
ἑστήκαμεν καὶ καυχώμεθα ἐπ᾽ ἐλπίδι τῆς δόξης τοῦ θεοῦ.

*Therefore, since we have been declared righteous by faith, we have
peace with God through our Lord Jesus Christ. We have also obtained
access **through Him** by faith into this grace in which we stand, and
we rejoice in the hope of the glory of God.*

Again we observe that the antecedent of δι᾽ οὗ is 'our Lord Jesus Christ'
(v. 1),[38] and Paul says that *through Him* believers have obtained access into
the grace in which they stand. The agency of God is not explicitly in view
here, though believers are described as having peace with him through
Christ. Thus, the type of instrumentality in view is mediatorial; Christ
brings about the peace with God that believers enjoy.

---

37. Moo, *Romans*, 51.
38. See above (§6.3) on the mediatorial instrumentality of διὰ τοῦ κυρίου ἡμῶν Ἰησοῦ
Χριστοῦ in 5:1.

Rom 5:8–9 συνίστησιν δὲ τὴν ἑαυτοῦ ἀγάπην εἰς ἡμᾶς ὁ θεός, ὅτι ἔτι ἁμαρτωλῶν ὄντων ἡμῶν Χριστὸς ὑπὲρ ἡμῶν ἀπέθανεν. πολλῷ οὖν μᾶλλον δικαιωθέντες νῦν ἐν τῷ αἵματι αὐτοῦ σωθησόμεθα **δι' αὐτοῦ** ἀπὸ τῆς ὀργῆς.

*But God proves His own love for us in that while we were still sinners, Christ died for us! Much more then, since we have now been declared righteous by His blood, we will be saved **through Him** from wrath.*

Obviously, the antecedent of δι' αὐτοῦ is Christ (v. 8), and believers will be saved from wrath *through Him*. The agency of God in this action is introduced in v. 8: *But God proves His own love for us in that while we were still sinners, Christ died for us!* This verse implies that Christ's death was enacted because of God's love; thus, God's agency is ultimately behind that sacrifice, the declaration of righteousness through Christ's blood, and the salvation from wrath through Christ. The instrumentality of Christ, therefore, enables and enacts the agency of God in these things.[39]

Rom 5:11 οὐ μόνον δέ, ἀλλὰ καὶ καυχώμενοι ἐν τῷ θεῷ διὰ τοῦ κυρίου ἡμῶν Ἰησοῦ Χριστοῦ **δι' οὗ** νῦν τὴν καταλλαγὴν ἐλάβομεν

*And not only that, but we also rejoice in God through our Lord Jesus Christ. We have now received this reconciliation **through Him**.*

While the first half of this verse indicates the action of believers — that of rejoicing — through Christ (see §6.4, above), the second half indicates that reconciliation has been received *through Him*. Christ is the instrument for reconciliation, with the agency of God implied — after all, he is the one in whom believers rejoice.[40]

Gal 6:14 ἐμοὶ δὲ μὴ γένοιτο καυχᾶσθαι εἰ μὴ ἐν τῷ σταυρῷ τοῦ κυρίου ἡμῶν Ἰησοῦ Χριστοῦ, **δι' οὗ** ἐμοὶ κόσμος ἐσταύρωται κἀγὼ κόσμῳ

---

39. Murray, *Romans*, 1:169–71.

40. 'Paul again breaks forth into praise at the wonderful *reconciliation* which is ours by God's action in *our Lord Jesus*'; Ernest Best, *The Letter of Paul to the Romans* (CBC; Cambridge; Cambridge Univ. Press, 1967), 58.

*But as for me, I will never boast about anything except the cross of our Lord Jesus Christ, **through whom** the world has been crucified to me, and I to the world.* (pers. trans.)

This is an interesting example in that there is no explicit agency, and it is somewhat cryptic as to what Paul means by being crucified to the world (and vice versa). It is also not obvious in what sense the world is crucified to Paul *through* Christ. If δι᾽ οὗ is understood as expressing the instrumentality of Christ,[41] it is not immediately clear what action he has performed in order to achieve the world's being crucified to Paul and vice versa. It is best to regard this as metaphorical in some sense: Paul is speaking of the way in which the cares and desires of this world are 'dead' to him through Christ, and the way in which Paul himself is 'dead' to the world. He does not live to please the world, and the world is not pleasing to him. In this way, Paul most likely refers to the reality of his new spiritual life in Christ, in which the world, the flesh, and the devil do not rule him.[42]

If such is the case, it is significant that Paul describes this new spiritual life as occurring through the crucifixion of the world to him and his crucifixion to it. The use of such language obviously connotes Christ's crucifixion, which must be key to his instrumentality here. For Paul to refer to his own crucifixion, he evidently views himself as participating in the cross of Christ, which sheds light on the nature of Christ's instrumentality. It is through participation with Christ that he brings about the crucifixion of the world to Paul, and Paul's crucifixion to the world. In this way, this verse finds a parallel in Romans 7:4 (above), in which Paul indicates that believers have been *put to death in relation to the law through the crucified body of the Messiah.* In that verse, death to the law occurs through co-crucifixion with Christ; here death to the world occurs likewise.

---

41. The relative pronoun could refer to σταυρός as antecedent rather than Christ, but either way much the same point is made; 'Whether δι᾽ οὗ refers to the cross of Christ, or to the person of Christ, is of no consequence, since for Paul "Christ" is always the crucified redeemer Christ'; H. D. Betz, *Galatians: A Commentary on Paul's Letter to the Churches in Galatia* (Hermeneia; Philadelphia: Fortress, 1979), 318.

42. 'What identification with the crucified Christ does entail ... is no longer having "wordly" or "fleshly" advantages dominate one's thinking or living'; Longenecker, *Galatians*, 295.

Eph 2:17–18 καὶ ἐλθὼν εὐηγγελίσατο εἰρήνην ὑμῖν τοῖς μακρὰν καὶ εἰρήνην τοῖς ἐγγύς· ὅτι **δι᾽ αὐτοῦ** ἔχομεν τὴν προσαγωγὴν οἱ ἀμφότεροι ἐν ἑνὶ πνεύματι πρὸς τὸν πατέρα

*When the Messiah came, He proclaimed the good news of peace to you who were far away and peace to those who were near. For **through Him** we both have access by one Spirit to the Father.*

In this instance, it may not be best to regard δι᾽ αὐτοῦ as expressing instrumentality, since that function may belong to the Spirit, as the phrase ἐν ἑνὶ πνεύματι suggests. If so, it is probably best to regard δι᾽ αὐτοῦ as expressing *agency*: Christ instigates believers' access to the Father,[43] which is conducted by the instrumentality of the Spirit.

Of the six instances of δι᾽ οὗ/αὐτοῦ in this subcategory, five are instrumental (Rom 1:5; 5:2, 9, 11; Gal 6:14), and one expresses agency (Eph 2:18).

6.8.2 BELIEVERS' ACTIONS THROUGH CHRIST

Col 3:17 καὶ πᾶν ὅ τι ἐὰν ποιῆτε ἐν λόγῳ ἢ ἐν ἔργῳ, πάντα ἐν ὀνόματι κυρίου Ἰησοῦ, εὐχαριστοῦντες τῷ θεῷ πατρὶ **δι᾽ αὐτοῦ**

*And whatever you do, in word or in deed, do everything in the name of the Lord Jesus, giving thanks to God the Father **through Him**.*

In this instance, agency belongs to Paul's readers, who are to give thanks to God through Christ. While instrumentality is probably the best way in which to understand Christ's role in the thanksgiving of believers, it is unlikely that believers need Christ to *enable* each instance of this activity. It is more likely that a mediatorial instrumentality is in view, such that believers are able to address God because Christ has granted the necessary access to the Father.[44]

---

43. Larkin refers to δι᾽ αὐτοῦ as expressing 'intermediate agent'; Larkin, *Ephesians*, 43. This is a useful term in that it recognizes the agency of Christ while also pointing to the purpose of such agency here: to facilitate access to the Father.

44. Ernst Lohmeyer, *Die Briefe an die Philipper, an die Kolosser und an Philemon* (Göttingen: Vandenhoeck & Ruprecht, 1964), 152.

6.8.3 TRINITY THROUGH CHRIST

1 Cor 8:6 ἀλλ' ἡμῖν εἷς θεὸς ὁ πατὴρ ἐξ οὗ τὰ πάντα καὶ ἡμεῖς εἰς αὐτόν, καὶ εἷς κύριος Ἰησοῦς Χριστὸς **δι' οὗ** τὰ πάντα καὶ ἡμεῖς **δι' αὐτοῦ**

Yet for us there is one God, the Father. All things are from Him, and we exist for Him. And there is one Lord, Jesus Christ. All things are **through Him**, *and we exist* **through Him**.

There is symmetry between the agency of the Father in creation and the instrumentality of Christ in creation. All things are from the Father; all things are *through Christ*. The curious elements of this verse are the phrases καὶ ἡμεῖς εἰς αὐτόν and ἡμεῖς δι' αὐτοῦ.[45] At least the latter phrase appears to be coordinated with the fact that all things are *through Christ*; Paul may simply be indicating that the 'all things' includes humanity (or believers as a subset of humanity). The problem with this interpretation is that the same is not true of the former phrase; 'and we for Him' does not match 'from whom are all things' in the same way. Regardless, most likely Paul means that all things are created through Christ, and believers have participation in new creation through him.[46] 'Christ is understood to be the means of accomplishing all of the Father's intentions for his creation';[47] as such, this verse provides a clear representation of the trinitarian nuance of which *through Christ* language is capable.

2 Cor 1:20 ὅσαι γὰρ ἐπαγγελίαι θεοῦ, ἐν αὐτῷ τὸ ναί· διὸ καὶ δι' αὐτοῦ τὸ ἀμὴν τῷ θεῷ πρὸς δόξαν δι' ἡμῶν

For every one of God's promises is "Yes" in Him. Therefore, the "Amen" is also spoken **through Him** *by us for God's glory.*

There is an interesting parallel here between the phrases *every one of God's promises is "Yes" in Him* and *the "Amen" is also . . . through Him*; the

---

45. See Thiselton for a detailed discussion of these phrases; Thiselton, *1 Corinthians*, 635–38.

46. Ciampa and Rosner paraphrase, 'all creation has come into being through him and our experience of new creation was through him as well'; Ciampa and Rosner, *1 Corinthians*, 384.

47. Ibid.

prepositional phrases ἐν αὐτῷ and δι' αὐτοῦ appear to mean the same thing. In the first phrase, the *Yes* in Christ refers to his fulfilling the promises of God, which is best regarded as an instrumental use of ἐν αὐτῷ.[48] Likewise, δι' αὐτοῦ seems to express instrumentality as Christ is the one through whom the *amen* is achieved, which probably refers to the completion of God's promises also. The *amen* is offered through Christ for the purpose of God's glory, which in turn evidently occurs *through us*. Thus, it might be said that Christ's instrumentality in his *amen* facilitates the instrumentality of believers as glory to God is rendered through them.[49]

Eph 2:17–18 καὶ ἐλθὼν εὐηγγελίσατο εἰρήνην ὑμῖν τοῖς μακρὰν καὶ εἰρήνην τοῖς ἐγγύς· ὅτι **δι' αὐτοῦ** ἔχομεν τὴν προσαγωγὴν οἱ ἀμφότεροι ἐν ἑνὶ πνεύματι πρὸς τὸν πατέρα

*When the Messiah came, He proclaimed the good news of peace to you who were far away and peace to those who were near. For **through Him** we both have access by one Spirit to the Father.*

As noted above in §6.8.1, this example of δι' αὐτοῦ is best understood as indicating the agency of Christ rather than instrumentality, and it is included here for its evident trinitarian character: the agency of Christ, the instrumentality of the Spirit, and mediation toward the Father are in view.

Col 1:16–17 ὅτι ἐν αὐτῷ ἐκτίσθη τὰ πάντα
ἐν τοῖς οὐρανοῖς καὶ ἐπὶ τῆς γῆς,
τὰ ὁρατὰ καὶ τὰ ἀόρατα,
εἴτε θρόνοι εἴτε κυριότητες
εἴτε ἀρχαὶ εἴτε ἐξουσίαι·
τὰ πάντα **δι' αὐτοῦ** καὶ εἰς αὐτὸν ἔκτισται.

*For everything was created by Him,
in heaven and on earth,
the visible and the invisible,*

---

48. On the function of ἐν αὐτῷ in this verse, see ch. 3, §3.11.3.1.

49. So Kruse summarizes, 'it is only as we add our "Amen" to the promises of God which find their Yes in Christ that those promises become effective in our case, and we may on that account then truly glorify God for his grace to us'; Kruse, *2 Corinthians*, 76.

whether thrones or dominions
or rulers or authorities—
*all things have been created **through Him** and for Him.*

The antecedent of δι' αὐτοῦ is Christ the Son (1:13), who is here described as the instrument in God's work of creation. While the agency of God is not explicit, the passage infers it, since it addresses readers who share a biblical worldview in which God is creator.[50] Christ's activity in the work of creation is understood in light of that fact.[51] Thus, with the implicit agency of God in mind, together with the instrumentality of Christ, we see the trinitarian nature of the work of creation.

Col 1:19–20 ὅτι ἐν αὐτῷ εὐδόκησεν πᾶν τὸ πλήρωμα
 κατοικῆσαι
[20]καὶ **δι' αὐτοῦ** ἀποκαταλλάξαι τὰ πάντα εἰς αὐτόν,
εἰρηνοποιήσας διὰ τοῦ αἵματος τοῦ σταυροῦ αὐτοῦ,
[δι' αὐτοῦ] εἴτε τὰ ἐπὶ τῆς γῆς
εἴτε τὰ ἐν τοῖς οὐρανοῖς

[19] For God was pleased to have
all His fullness dwell in Him,
*[20]and **through Him** to reconcile*
everything to Himself
by making peace
through the blood of His cross—
whether things on earth or things in heaven.

In this passage the agency of God is clearly in view (*God was pleased*),[52] and Christ's instrumentality in God's work of reconciliation is the plain

---

50. 'Christ is … not the creator but the mediator in creation'; Eduard Schweizer, *The Letter to the Colossians: A Commentary* (trans. Andrew Chester; Minneapolis: Augsburg, 1982), 70, n. 39.

51. While we have elsewhere been reluctant to assign instrumentality to contexts in which the agency of God is not explicitly in view, creation is a special case since no one with a biblical worldview would doubt God's agency.

52. While ὁ θεός is not stated in the Greek text, there can be little doubt that God is the subject of the verb εὐδόκησεν in v. 19; Lightfoot, *Saint Paul's Epistles to the Colossians and to Philemon*, 158.

meaning of δι' αὐτοῦ here. God reconciles everything to himself through the blood of Christ's cross.

Col 3:17 καὶ πᾶν ὅ τι ἐὰν ποιῆτε ἐν λόγῳ ἢ ἐν ἔργῳ, πάντα ἐν ὀνόματι κυρίου Ἰησοῦ, εὐχαριστοῦντες τῷ θεῷ πατρὶ **δι' αὐτοῦ**

*And whatever you do, in word or in deed, do everything in the name of the Lord Jesus, giving thanks to God the Father **through Him**.*

This verse has already been discussed above (see §6.8.2) and is included here for its trinitarian import. Christ mediates our thanksgiving to the Father.

Of the seven instances of δι' οὗ/αὐτοῦ in this subcategory, six are instrumental (1 Cor 8:6 [x2]; 2 Cor 1:20; Col 1:16, 20; 3:17) and one indicates agency (Eph 2:18).

6.9 SUMMARY

The phrase διὰ Χριστοῦ in Pauline usage should be regarded as denoting instrumentality (and occasionally agency) and is sometimes best described as mediatorial: 'Christ mediates the action of another'.[53] Examples of such instrumentality and mediation relate to the action of God in creation (1 Cor 8:6; Col 1:16), the revelation of salvation and reconciliation (2 Cor 5:18; Col 1:20), and the impartation of the Spirit (Titus 3:6).[54]

Dunn regards the idiom διὰ Χριστοῦ to be closely parallel to ἐν Χριστῷ and σὺν Χριστῷ.[55] Paul uses the phrase to convey 'the saving or commissioning or final action of God as happening or coming to effect "through Christ"'.[56] However, Dunn helpfully acknowledges that Paul can use the phrase to speak of believers in their relationship with God; believers give thanks to God 'through Christ'. Paul also uses the phrase with respect to other believers; he 'appeals to his Roman audiences "through our Lord Jesus Christ"'.[57]

---

53. Oepke, 'διά', 2:67.
54. Ibid., 67.
55. Dunn, *Paul the Apostle*, 406.
56. Ibid.
57. Ibid.

CHAPTER 7

METAPHORS

7.1 INTRODUCTION

The previous four chapters have explored the language relating to union with Christ by way of the prepositions inherent to the theme. While it has been important to work through these prepositional phrases with care — especially since so much previous scholarship has focused on them — they do not exhaust the data that must be investigated. It would be a mistake to assume that because all the prepositional language has been canvassed, all of Paul's thinking relating to union with Christ has also been dealt with. On the contrary, one of the most important ways in which Paul expresses his thinking about union with Christ is through metaphor.[1] In this chapter we will explore the metaphors Paul uses to convey his thinking about union with Christ. They include Paul's portrayal of the church as the body of Christ, as the temple or building of God, and as the bride of Christ, and we will examine the language relating to the new clothing that believers are to 'put on'.

As with previous chapters, this chapter will seek to provide a thorough analysis of the apposite language, each passage in turn. One key difference here is that this chapter will offer a sustained engagement with Sang-Won Son's monograph, *Corporate Elements in Pauline Anthopology*.[2] Published

---

1. See Hans Burger, *Being in Christ: A Biblical and Systematic Investigation in a Reformed Perspective* (Eugene, OR: Wipf & Stock, 2009), 162–63.

2. Sang-Won (Aaron) Son, *Corporate Elements in Pauline Anthropology: A Study of Selected Terms, Idioms, and Concepts in the Light of Paul's Usage and Background* (AnBib 148; Rome: Editrice Pontificio Istituto Biblico, 2001).

in 2001, this fine study provides much of the work required by this chapter, and where possible its findings will be discussed and, as appropriate, adopted. Son's specific interest is the corporate elements of Paul's anthropology, and he investigates the ἐν Χριστῷ language and its related phrases, Paul's Adam–Christ typology, and the images of the church as the body of Christ, the temple or building of God, and the bride of Christ. For our purposes, we will engage Son's analysis of these images of the church, for now setting aside his treatment of ἐν Χριστῷ (and related language) and the Adam–Christ typology. Since his main interest is in Pauline anthropology rather than union with Christ per se, we are interested in slightly different questions here and will thus deviate from his approach at various points.

7.2 BODY OF CHRIST

The *body of Christ* is one of Paul's most important metaphors for describing the nature of the church.[3] Each passage that includes the metaphor is explored below. The full phrase *body of Christ* is not necessarily extant in each passage examined, since the term *body* is sometimes used alone as (so it seems) shorthand for the concept.

Furthermore, these passages do not exhaust the entire usage of the word *body* (σῶμα); only the occurrences that refer to the church are included. The reason for this is that we are interested in how the metaphor of the *body of Christ* may inform our understanding of union with Christ. If the church is Christ's body, of which he is head, the metaphor must convey connotations of union. The very nature of the idea of the *body of Christ* denotes incorporation, union, and identification of Christ and his people. 'Generally speaking, the qualification of the church as the body

---

3. The background to Paul's usage of 'body' language is not our concern here, though Ziesler's observations about the LXX are noteworthy: 'Paul clearly cannot be tied to Septuagintal meanings. There were other influences on his vocabulary, and at least in principle we must allow that sometimes he may have been an innovator. All we can safely conclude is that the biblical Greek he knew did normally employ σῶμα for the physical body, alive or dead, but that it sometimes employed it to indicate the person, seen through the medium of the physical.' John A. Ziesler, 'ΣΩΜΑ in the Septuagint', *NovT* 25 (1983): 144. Wedderburn likewise argues against finding the roots of Paul's usage in Gnostic thought: 'To turn first to the "Body of Christ" idea itself: any attempt to see in it a Gnostic doctrine runs into the very considerable problem of the absence of any good evidence of its use in non-Christian Gnostic sources before Mani; nor is it particularly prominent even in Christian ones'; A. J. M. Wedderburn, 'The Body of Christ and Related Concepts in 1 Corinthians', *SJT* 24 (1971): 85.

of Christ is a denotation of the special, close relationship and communion that exist between Christ and his church.[4] While we must explore to some extent the meaning of the metaphor *body of Christ*, our main priority is to unearth what it reveals about union with Christ, rather than to unpack its full dimensions.

Rom 12:4–5 καθάπερ γὰρ ἐν ἑνὶ **σώματι** πολλὰ μέλη ἔχομεν, τὰ δὲ μέλη πάντα οὐ τὴν αὐτὴν ἔχει πρᾶξιν, οὕτως οἱ πολλοὶ ἓν **σῶμά** ἐσμεν ἐν Χριστῷ, τὸ δὲ καθ᾽ εἷς ἀλλήλων μέλη

*Now as we have many parts in one **body**, and all the parts do not have the same function, in the same way we who are many are one **body** in Christ and individually members of one another.*

Here Paul compares the human body (12:4) to the body of believers in Christ (12:5). Just as a human body has different parts with different functions, so too the body of believers consists of many members and is yet *one body in Christ*. Furthermore, Paul explores the various functions of the members of the body in 12:6–8. Part of the value of the body metaphor is that it allows a strong conception of unity while also preserving the distinctiveness of individuals: the parts are united in one body, yet they perform different functions. Indeed, while the *many* are described as one body in Christ, individuals are regarded as *members of one another*. Finally, the *body* is here described as one body *in Christ*,[5] which provides an explicit connection between the metaphor and union language. As Best enunciates, 'those who are *united with Christ* are also *united* with one another and require therefore to behave in such a way that their mutual unity is furthered.'[6]

1 Cor 6:15–16 οὐκ οἴδατε ὅτι τὰ **σώματα** ὑμῶν μέλη Χριστοῦ ἐστιν; ἄρας οὖν τὰ μέλη τοῦ Χριστοῦ ποιήσω πόρνης μέλη; μὴ γένοιτο. [ἢ] οὐκ οἴδατε ὅτι ὁ κολλώμενος τῇ πόρνῃ ἓν **σῶμά** ἐστιν; ἔσονται γάρ, φησίν, *οἱ δύο εἰς σάρκα μίαν*

---

4. Herman Ridderbos, *Paul: An Outline of his Theology* (trans. John Richard de Witt; Grand Rapids: Eerdmans, 1975), 362.

5. 'The church is from one standpoint the "body of Christ" and from another, "one body in Christ"'; Son, *Corporate Elements*, 93.

6. Best, *Romans*, 141.

*Don't you know that your **bodies** are a part of Christ's body? So*
should I take a part of Christ's body and make it part of a prostitute?
Absolutely not! Don't you know that anyone joined to a prostitute
*is one **body** with her? For Scripture says, The two will become one*
flesh.

These verses do not explicitly mention the body of Christ, but the
concept is nonetheless implied. Believers' bodies are described as *a part
of Christ*; Paul uses the word μέλη (lit., 'members'), which he also used in
Romans 12:4–5 for the body parts of believers, paralleled to the body of
Christ.[7] To describe believers' bodies as 'members' of Christ is to envisage
them as his 'body parts'; thus the image evokes the concept of the body of
Christ, even if the phrase itself is absent.[8]

Second, the idea of believers as Christ's 'body parts' is not merely metaphorical; there appears to be a spiritual reality to which the metaphor
refers. This is evident through Paul's admonition *So should I take a part of
Christ's body and make it a part of a prostitute? Absolutely not!* It seems that
sexual union with a prostitute creates a concrete 'membership' with her
that is somehow (negatively) analogous with membership in Christ. It is
possible that the nature of this negative analogy is rooted in the indivis-
ibility of spiritual and physical realities. Being a member of Christ's body
must be a spiritual reality (rather than physical), but this spiritual reality
cannot be divorced from physical realities. It is inappropriate, then, for a
spiritual member of Christ's body to become physically united with a prostitute. That Paul regards such a union to be grossly inappropriate reveals
that his metaphorical language of membership in Christ's body refers to an
actual spiritual reality.[9] While it may be difficult to disentangle metaphor
from reality when it comes to spiritual realities, it is at least evident there
is a spiritual reality in view; Paul's *body* language is not merely illustrative.

A third issue here is the way in which sexual intercourse is regarded as
consummating bodily union. While this is no surprise with respect to two

---

7. Ciampa and Rosner, *1 Corinthians*, 257.

8. Son regards the phrase your bodies are members of Christ as being 'almost the same as'
you are members of Christ or you are members of the body of Christ; Son, *Corporate Elements*, 88.

9. As Ciampa and Rosner claim, '*union with Christ* is shown to be utterly incompatible
with union with a prostitute'; Ciampa and Rosner, *1 Corinthians*, 257 [italics are original].

people—so a biblical theology of marriage instructs—it is another matter with respect to Christ and his body.[10] This issue is probably best explored within the section of this chapter that deals with the metaphor of the marriage between Christ and his church, but it is worth noting here that the metaphors of body and marriage apparently intersect.

1 Cor 10:16–17 τὸ ποτήριον τῆς εὐλογίας ὃ εὐλογοῦμεν, οὐχὶ κοινωνία ἐστὶν τοῦ αἵματος τοῦ Χριστοῦ; τὸν ἄρτον ὃν κλῶμεν, οὐχὶ κοινωνία τοῦ **σώματος** τοῦ Χριστοῦ ἐστιν; ὅτι εἷς ἄρτος, ἓν **σῶμα** οἱ πολλοί ἐσμεν, οἱ γὰρ πάντες ἐκ τοῦ ἑνὸς ἄρτου μετέχομεν

The cup of blessing that we give thanks for, is it not a sharing in the blood of Christ? The bread that we break, is it not a sharing in the **body** *of Christ? Because there is one bread, we who are many are one* **body***, for all of us share that one bread.*

In this interesting example, the bread of the Lord's Supper is described as the *body of Christ*, just as the *cup of blessing* is the *blood of Christ*. Since there is only one bread—and therefore one body of Christ—the many are regarded as *one body* because all believers share in that one bread/body of Christ. Paul here uses one metaphor to explain another: the *one bread* refers, of course, to Christ's body rather than to the actual meal shared by believers, but that meal serves as an illustration of the other. As believers gather to share in one loaf of bread and are thus united in that sharing, so they share in the one body of Christ and are thus united in that sharing.[11]

The significance of this analogy for union with Christ is twofold. First, as already noted, the *body* metaphor facilitates the notion of the one and the many. Unity and diversity coexist in the body of Christ. Second, it seems that partaking in the 'bread' that is Christ's body actually *produces* the body. That is, believers constitute the *one body* by sharing in that *one bread*; stated otherwise, by partaking in the body of Christ, believers become part of the body. By being united to Christ, believers become part of his body.

---

10. See Ciampa and Rosner's discussion of the 'notion of the believer's nuptial union with Christ' in this passage (ibid., 259–60).

11. See Thiselton's extended discussion of these verses; Thiselton, *1 Corinthians*, 755–71.

1 Cor 11:29 ὁ γὰρ ἐσθίων καὶ πίνων κρίμα ἑαυτῷ ἐσθίει καὶ πίνει μὴ διακρίνων τὸ **σῶμα**

*For whoever eats and drinks without recognizing the **body**, eats and drinks judgment on himself.*

Occurring within a passage about the Lord's Supper and the Corinthians' abuse of it (11:17–34), this reference to the body is ambiguous. On the one hand, a natural reading suggests that *the body* refers to Christ's physical body offered on the cross, since the Lord's Supper proclaims his death (11:25–26). Whoever, therefore, partakes in the Lord's meal without recognizing the body of Christ given in death will bring judgment upon himself. On the other hand, the passage is ultimately about how the Corinthian congregation handles itself with respect to this supper and how they have shown lack of care for others, since they are divided through factions (11:18–22).

With this wider context in mind, *recognizing the body* may have to do with taking care of one another within the community of Christ. Whoever, therefore, partakes in the Lord's meal without recognizing the body of believers in Christ will bring judgment on himself. Indeed, Son acknowledges that 'it is difficult, if not impossible, to determine whether the body denotes the individual body of Christ or the church'.[12] His solution is to avoid a 'sharp distinction' between Christ's physical body and the body of the church.[13] It is probably correct, with Moule, to regard this instance as a *double entendre*, referring both to the crucified body of Christ and body of believers who share in Christ's body through the Lord's Supper.[14]

In terms of union with Christ, there is not much new to be gleaned from this verse. We have already seen that partaking in Christ results in believers partaking in one another. This reference reveals that not acting appropriately according to the body is worthy of judgment.

1 Cor 12:12–27 καθάπερ γὰρ τὸ **σῶμα** ἕν ἐστιν καὶ μέλη πολλὰ ἔχει, πάντα δὲ τὰ μέλη τοῦ **σώματος** πολλὰ ὄντα ἕν ἐστιν **σῶμα**,

---

12. Son, *Corporate Elements*, 91.
13. Ibid., 92.
14. C. F. D. Moule, *The Origin of Christianity* (Cambridge: Cambridge Univ. Press, 1977), 73.

οὕτως καὶ ὁ Χριστός· [13]καὶ γὰρ ἐν ἑνὶ πνεύματι ἡμεῖς πάντες εἰς ἓν **σῶμα** ἐβαπτίσθημεν, εἴτε Ἰουδαῖοι εἴτε Ἕλληνες εἴτε δοῦλοι εἴτε ἐλεύθεροι, καὶ πάντες ἓν πνεῦμα ἐποτίσθημεν. [14]καὶ γὰρ τὸ **σῶμα** οὐκ ἔστιν ἓν μέλος ἀλλὰ πολλά. [15]ἐὰν εἴπῃ ὁ πούς· ὅτι οὐκ εἰμὶ χείρ, οὐκ εἰμὶ ἐκ τοῦ **σώματος**, οὐ παρὰ τοῦτο οὐκ ἔστιν ἐκ τοῦ **σώματος**· [16]καὶ ἐὰν εἴπῃ τὸ οὖς· ὅτι οὐκ εἰμὶ ὀφθαλμός, οὐκ εἰμὶ ἐκ τοῦ **σώματος**, οὐ παρὰ τοῦτο οὐκ ἔστιν ἐκ τοῦ **σώματος**· [17]εἰ ὅλον τὸ **σῶμα** ὀφθαλμός, ποῦ ἡ ἀκοή; εἰ ὅλον ἀκοή, ποῦ ἡ ὄσφρησις; [18]νυνὶ δὲ ὁ θεὸς ἔθετο τὰ μέλη, ἓν ἕκαστον αὐτῶν ἐν τῷ **σώματι** καθὼς ἠθέλησεν. [19]εἰ δὲ ἦν τὰ πάντα ἓν μέλος, ποῦ τὸ **σῶμα**; [20]νῦν δὲ πολλὰ μὲν μέλη, ἓν δὲ **σῶμα**. [21]οὐ δύναται δὲ ὁ ὀφθαλμὸς εἰπεῖν τῇ χειρί· χρείαν σου οὐκ ἔχω, ἢ πάλιν ἡ κεφαλὴ τοῖς ποσίν· χρείαν ὑμῶν οὐκ ἔχω· [22]ἀλλὰ πολλῷ μᾶλλον τὰ δοκοῦντα μέλη τοῦ **σώματος** ἀσθενέστερα ὑπάρχειν ἀναγκαῖά ἐστιν, [23]καὶ ἃ δοκοῦμεν ἀτιμότερα εἶναι τοῦ **σώματος** τούτοις τιμὴν περισσοτέραν περιτίθεμεν, καὶ τὰ ἀσχήμονα ἡμῶν εὐσχημοσύνην περισσοτέραν ἔχει, [24]τὰ δὲ εὐσχήμονα ἡμῶν οὐ χρείαν ἔχει. ἀλλὰ ὁ θεὸς συνεκέρασεν τὸ **σῶμα** τῷ ὑστερουμένῳ περισσοτέραν δοὺς τιμήν, [25]ἵνα μὴ ᾖ σχίσμα ἐν τῷ **σώματι** ἀλλὰ τὸ αὐτὸ ὑπὲρ ἀλλήλων μεριμνῶσιν τὰ μέλη. [26]καὶ εἴτε πάσχει ἓν μέλος, συμπάσχει πάντα τὰ μέλη· εἴτε δοξάζεται [ἓν] μέλος, συγχαίρει πάντα τὰ μέλη. [27]ὑμεῖς δέ ἐστε **σῶμα** Χριστοῦ καὶ μέλη ἐκ μέρους.

*For as the **body** is one and has many parts, and all the parts of that **body**, though many, are one **body**—so also is Christ. [13]For we were all baptized by one Spirit into one **body**—whether Jews or Greeks, whether slaves or free—and we were all made to drink of one Spirit. [14]So the **body** is not one part but many. [15]If the foot should say, "Because I'm not a hand, I don't belong to the **body**," in spite of this it still belongs to the **body**. [16]And if the ear should say, "Because I'm not an eye, I don't belong to the **body**," in spite of this it still belongs to the **body**. [17]If the whole **body** were an eye, where would the hearing be? If the whole body were an ear, where would the sense of smell be? [18]But now God has placed each one of the parts in the **body** just as He wanted. [19]And if they were all the same part, where would the **body** be? [20]Now there are many parts, yet one **body**.*

*21So the eye cannot say to the hand, "I don't need you!" Or again, the head can't say to the feet, "I don't need you!" 22But even more, those parts of the **body** that seem to be weaker are necessary. 23And those parts of the **body** that we think to be less honorable, we clothe these with greater honor, and our unpresentable parts have a better presentation. 24But our presentable parts have no need of clothing. Instead, God has put the **body** together, giving greater honor to the less honorable, 25so that there would be no division in the **body**, but that the members would have the same concern for each other. 26So if one member suffers, all the members suffer with it; if one member is honored, all the members rejoice with it.*

*27Now you are the **body** of Christ, and individual members of it.*

In this salient discussion of the body of Christ, the unity and diversity of the body is given extended treatment. Paul labours the point that each part does its work within the body, and the diversity of its parts is essential to its proper functioning; it does the body no good if each part were an eye (12:16).

The key elements with respect to union with Christ pertain to vv. 12 and 27. Verse 12 makes the point that just as the body has many parts and is yet one body, so too is Christ.[15] The body of Christ is one body with many parts and is analogous to a human body; this idea will provide the impetus for the rest of the section that draws out the significance of diversity within the body.

Verse 27 underscores this reality with respect to the believers themselves by stating they *are the body of Christ, and individual members of it.* They form one body *and* they are parts of that body. Consequently, we see that the union that believers have with Christ has a totalizing effect on the one hand, and a distinguishing effect on the other. Believers are the body of Christ; they are all made into one, forming a single corporate identity. But believers are also individual parts of the body; their unity together does not quash their distinct and diverse otherness.

---

15. Son sees great significance in the fact that 'the analogy is made here to Christ rather than to the church.... This is significant because it indicates not only that σῶμα is more than a mere metaphor but also that there exists a special relationship between Christ and the church'; Son, *Corporate Elements*, 85.

Eph 1:22–23 καὶ πάντα ὑπέταξεν ὑπὸ τοὺς πόδας αὐτοῦ καὶ αὐτὸν ἔδωκεν κεφαλὴν ὑπὲρ πάντα τῇ ἐκκλησίᾳ, ἥτις ἐστὶν τὸ **σῶμα** αὐτοῦ, τὸ πλήρωμα τοῦ τὰ πάντα ἐν πᾶσιν πληρουμένου

*And He put everything under His feet and appointed Him as head over everything for the church, which is His **body**, the fullness of the One who fills all things in every way.*

With this reference to the *body* of Christ, we observe that the church is his body and that Christ is the *head over everything for the church*. This is the first reference that implies that Christ is the *head* of the body, and it introduces a couple of issues of potential confusion. First, until now, there has been no reason to question whether the church as the body of Christ has been conceived as a 'complete' body. While there has been some discussion relating to the diversity of its members, we have had no cause to doubt the comprehensiveness of this body.

Here, however, Paul writes that he regards Christ himself to be the head of his body.[16] This begs the question that has not, until now, been raised: if Christ is its head, does the church simply supply the remaining parts of the body? Second, the concept of Christ being the head of the body seems to imply that he himself does not constitute the rest of his body. Before the notion of *head* was introduced to the *body* metaphor, it followed that the body of believers were *part* of Christ; they were incorporated into Christ, becoming his members, with no explicit distinction between the part of the body that pertains to him and the parts that pertain to the church. But with the introduction of the *head* component

---

16. Ridderbos warns against this correlation, however, arguing that 'we must not form physiological conceptions derived from the relationships within the human body, but that the concept rather must be understood from the structures and connections of the human community'; Ridderbos, *Paul*, 382. While his point that headship ought be understood relationally rather than physiologically is to be affirmed, this does not necessarily contradict the correlation between the metaphors of head and body. When both are brought together in the same context, it strains credulity to suggest that their connectedness is unintended. So Williams acknowledges, 'when the two metaphors are found side by side, the association of "body" with "head" does give to "head" a particular meaning'; David J. Williams, *Paul's Metaphors: The Context and Character* (Peabody, MA: Hendrickson, 1999), 90. Likewise Bedale, 'Of course it seems hardly possible that St. Paul could use κεφαλή in the immediate context of σῶμα without any conscious reference at all to the anatomical image thereby evoked'; Stephen Bedale, 'The Meaning of κεφαλή in the Pauline Epistles', *JTS* 5 (1954): 214.

in relation to the *body* metaphor, the conceptual relationship between Christ and the church appears somewhat altered. There now seems to be a distinction between the head, which pertains to Christ, and the rest of the body.

While it may not be possible to address the first difficulty in its own right, it might be resolved through dealing with the second. This second difficulty can be assuaged by considering the final clause of the verse: *the fullness of the One who fills all things in every way* (1:23). This phrase stands in apposition to *his body* and apparently defines it in some manner. Christ's body is described as the *fullness* of the One who fills all things, and the principal point is that Christ permeates and fills all creation, with special reference to the church. Whatever the metaphysical reality to which this language refers, it suggests that any dichotomy between Christ and his body that might be posited is ultimately a false one.[17] Christ fills all things, and his body is his fullness; there can be no sense in which the headship of Christ over his body means that he does not also partake in the whole.

As for the implications for union with Christ that this passage offers, we note two new distinctions. First, it is clear that while believers are united to Christ and share in his body, Christ retains his own distinct person. The whole body shares in Christ and is his fullness, yet he alone may be described as its head. This kind of unity and distinction is similar to that observed above with reference to the unity of the body and the diversity of its parts. While believers are one body, they are each individually its members (1 Cor 12:27). In the same way, the whole body pertains to Christ, but it is his unique privilege to be the head.

Second, and related to the first point, our union with Christ through partaking in his body does not mitigate his authority over believers. Part of the distinction that remains between Christ and those united to him is his authoritative position over them. Consequently, no matter how pervasive and inclusive the reality of spiritual union with Christ may be, it does not erase every distinction.

---

17. Thus, Son is ultimately correct in claiming that Paul here 'represents the church not merely as the remaining parts of the body belonging to the head but as the whole body'; Son, *Corporate Elements*, 95.

Eph 2:14–16 αὐτὸς γάρ ἐστιν ἡ εἰρήνη ἡμῶν, ὁ ποιήσας τὰ ἀμφότερα ἓν καὶ τὸ μεσότοιχον τοῦ φραγμοῦ λύσας, τὴν ἔχθραν ἐν τῇ σαρκὶ αὐτοῦ, τὸν νόμον τῶν ἐντολῶν ἐν δόγμασιν καταργήσας, ἵνα τοὺς δύο κτίσῃ ἐν αὐτῷ εἰς ἕνα καινὸν ἄνθρωπον ποιῶν εἰρήνην καὶ ἀποκαταλλάξῃ τοὺς ἀμφοτέρους ἐν ἑνὶ σώματι τῷ θεῷ διὰ τοῦ σταυροῦ, ἀποκτείνας τὴν ἔχθραν ἐν αὐτῷ

*For He is our peace, who made both groups one and tore down the dividing wall of hostility. In His flesh, He made of no effect the law consisting of commands and expressed in regulations, so that He might create in Himself one new man from the two, resulting in peace. He did this so that He might reconcile both to God in one **body** through the cross and put the hostility to death by it.*

Son points out that 'scholars differ as to whether "one body" in 2:16 refers only to the individual body of Christ sacrificed on the cross or to the church'.[18] He argues for the latter; hence he includes this passage in his discussion of the *body* metaphor. I will argue that the passage refers to the former and hence does not directly contribute to our understanding of the metaphor.[19] The passage is included here, however, because of its place within scholarly discussion. We will proceed by engaging the three key points in Son's argument.

First, Son argues that 'if Paul was referring to the individual body of Christ, he would have spoken of "his body" rather than "one body"'.[20] It is a rather weak argument to proscribe what Paul might or might not say. The phrase *one body* can be explained simply by Paul's concern within the context to stress the reconciliation of two hostile parties. The expression *one body* simply underscores the fact that the two have become one.

Second, Son claims that 'the "one body" is clearly parallel to "one" (2:14) and "one new man" (2:15) and that all three expressions must, therefore, be interpreted as referring to the same entity'.[21] While this is

---

18. Ibid.
19. Admittedly, however, the majority of commentators advocate Son's position; see Best, *Ephesians*, 265. A notable exception is Barth, who regards 'one body' as designating 'the physical body of the Messiah, and more specifically, his crucified body'; M. Barth, *Ephesians 1–3*, 298.
20. Son, *Corporate Elements*, 95.
21. Ibid., 96.

a stronger argument than the first, it is not necessarily the case that *one body* must parallel *one* and *one new man*. Certainly, the common use of the word *one* is striking, but Son's analysis does not take into account another striking commonality through vv. 14–16, namely, the threefold use of the preposition *in* (ἐν). Paul says *in one body* in 2:16, which could be regarded as parallel to *in his flesh* (2:14) and *in himself* (2:15).

In fact, these apparent parallels are stronger than those suggested by Son. Each ἐν phrase refers to the sphere in which an activity takes place: **In His flesh**, *He made of no effect the law consisting of commands and expressed in regulations* (vv. 14–15); *so that He might create **in Himself** one new man from the two* (v. 15); *so that He might reconcile both to God **in one body*** (v. 16). The doing away of commandments is conducted in the sphere of his flesh; the creation of one new man is conducted in the sphere of himself; the reconciliation of the two is conducted in the sphere of one body. Since all three ἐν phrases refer to the spheres in which these key activities take place, it is more likely that *in one body* parallels the other two *in* phrases rather than *one* and *one new man*.

Third, Son points out that 'the phrase "in one body" occurs also in Colossians 3:15, and there it clearly refers to the church'.[22] This argument is similar to the first, in which Son proscribes what language Paul might or might not use. While he is correct that the same phrase refers to the church in 3:15, this does not mean it must refer to the church here. Given the strong connection between Christ's physical, crucified, body and his body the church, it does not seem beyond reason that Paul might employ the same phrase to refer to either body. After all, he uses the word *body* to refer to both without any compunction.

Consequently, *in one body* refers to Christ's crucified body, which makes best sense of the following phrases that make reference to the cross and the putting to death of hostility. Paul is therefore referring to the reconciling function of Christ's crucifixion, and his crucified body thereof.

Eph 4:4 ἓν **σῶμα** καὶ ἓν πνεῦμα, καθὼς καὶ ἐκλήθητε ἐν μιᾷ ἐλπίδι τῆς κλήσεως ὑμῶν

*There is one **body** and one Spirit—just as you were called to one hope at your calling.*

---

22. Ibid.

This reference to *body* no doubt refers to the church, since the immediate context is concerned with the unity among believers (4:1 – 3).[23] Verses 4 – 6 emphasize this unity by outlining the defining features of the church's existence: there is one body, one Spirit, one hope, one Lord, one faith, one baptism, and one God and Father. This section of the chapter — along with this reference to the oneness of the body — must be held in tension with 4:11 – 13, which details some of the facets of diversity within the body (see next discussion).

Eph 4:11 – 13 καὶ αὐτὸς ἔδωκεν τοὺς μὲν ἀποστόλους, τοὺς δὲ προφήτας, τοὺς δὲ εὐαγγελιστάς, τοὺς δὲ ποιμένας καὶ διδασκάλους, πρὸς τὸν καταρτισμὸν τῶν ἁγίων εἰς ἔργον διακονίας, εἰς οἰκοδομὴν τοῦ **σώματος** τοῦ Χριστοῦ, μέχρι καταντήσωμεν οἱ πάντες εἰς τὴν ἑνότητα τῆς πίστεως καὶ τῆς ἐπιγνώσεως τοῦ υἱοῦ τοῦ θεοῦ, εἰς ἄνδρα τέλειον, εἰς μέτρον ἡλικίας τοῦ πληρώματος τοῦ Χριστοῦ

*And He personally gave some to be apostles, some prophets, some evangelists, some pastors and teachers, for the training of the saints in the work of ministry, to build up the **body** of Christ, until we all reach unity in the faith and in the knowledge of God's Son, growing into a mature man with a stature measured by Christ's fullness.*

Following the reference to the body in the section that stresses the oneness of the church (4:1 – 6), Paul now specifies some of the distinct roles of which the church consists — hence accentuating the diversity of the body. There are several new elements that this passage contributes to our understanding of the metaphor.

First, part of the importance of the diversity of the body is that it facilitates the training of the saints in the work of ministry. The roles of apostle, prophet, evangelist, and pastor-teacher do not define all members of the body; they are for *some*, not *all*,[24] and the services they render toward the church issue directly from its diversity.

---

23. John Muddiman, *The Epistle to the Ephesians* (BNTC; New York: Continuum, 2001), 182 – 84.

24. Note the extended μέν ... δέ ... δέ ... δέ construction in the wording τοὺς μὲν ἀποστόλους, τοὺς δὲ προφήτας, τοὺς δὲ εὐαγγελιστάς, τοὺς δὲ ποιμένας καὶ διδασκάλους.

Second, it is clear that the body of Christ must be *built up*. This process of bodybuilding does not refer simply to the addition of new believers to the body but to its maturity and strength, as 4:13 evinces. It may be implied, therefore, that the body is not a static entity that simply shares in Christ; it changes and develops through the work of its members.

Third, not only does the body grow and mature in a dynamic way, but part of its development involves its increasing *unity*, as is expressed by the phrase *until we all reach unity in the faith*. The striking contribution here is its indication that the unity of the body is a work in progress, in spite of the consistent references to the oneness of the body in several instances, as noted above. This apparent juxtaposition between the consolidated oneness of the body on the one hand and the progress toward unity on the other can be explained in one of two ways. First, it might be an outworking of Paul's eschatological framework, in which the eschaton has been inaugurated in the present age. Such a framework is evident throughout Paul's writings and creates an expectation of a *now–not yet* tension. Thus, it could be suggested that the notion of the oneness of the body is an eschatological reality that belongs to the future but is referred to as a present reality because of the inaugurated eschatological thinking underpinning so much of Paul's theology. The need for the body to grow in unity is an expression, therefore, of the current reality of things, and this reality coexists in tension with the eschatological reality of completed unity.[25]

Second, a simpler solution may be preferable. Rather than viewing the apparent juxtaposition between mature oneness and unity as a work in progress from the outworking of Paul's inaugurated eschatology, it might be better explained through the coexistence of *spiritual* and *fleshly* realities.[26] In other words, the completed oneness of the body is a current spiritual fact: those who belong to Christ are now one body—indivisible and uncorrupted—since the believers' spiritual union with Christ cannot be compromised, and therefore their spiritual union with each other

---

25. So Lincoln; it is 'a version of the Pauline eschatological tension between the "already" and the "not yet" applied to the life of the Church'; Lincoln, *Ephesians*, 256.

26. O'Brien appears to combine both possibilities; 'The body metaphor reflects the "already–not yet" tension of the two ages.... It is a heavenly entity and yet it is an earthly reality'; O'Brien, *Ephesians*, 317.

is complete. Nevertheless, our fleshly existence in this world means that the spiritual oneness of the body is expressed through a corrupted and imperfect experience of the church.

Eph 4:15–16 ἀληθεύοντες δὲ ἐν ἀγάπῃ αὐξήσωμεν εἰς αὐτὸν τὰ πάντα, ὅς ἐστιν ἡ κεφαλή, Χριστός, ἐξ οὗ πᾶν τὸ **σῶμα** συναρμολογούμενον καὶ συμβιβαζόμενον διὰ πάσης ἁφῆς τῆς ἐπιχορηγίας κατ᾽ ἐνέργειαν ἐν μέτρῳ ἑνὸς ἑκάστου μέρους τὴν αὔξησιν τοῦ **σώματος** ποιεῖται εἰς οἰκοδομὴν ἑαυτοῦ ἐν ἀγάπῃ

*But speaking the truth in love, let us grow in every way into Him who is the head—Christ. From Him the whole **body**, fitted and knit together by every supporting ligament, promotes the growth of the **body** for building up itself in love by the proper working of each individual part.*

This passage refers to Christ as the *head* of the body, as well as the one who *promotes* its growing maturity. It also depicts the diversity of the parts of the body (*every supporting ligament*) and their service to the church (*by the proper working of each individual part*). Each of these ideas has been seen in previous passages, but two new points of interest surface here.

First, the body is described as growing *into Him who is the head* but also as growing *from Him*. Both expressions are odd when applied to the *body* metaphor, since the images of a body growing *into* its head or growing *out from* its head are equally strange. Paul seems to be stretching the metaphor beyond its anatomical limits and is content to do so for the sake of conveying the concepts he has in mind. Growing *into* the head likely refers to being conformed to Christ, becoming more like him, and 'growing into' the unity between believers and Christ. Growing *from* him depicts Christ as the source of the body; he is its origin and provides the stimulus for growth. Thus, while the notions of growing into and out from the head might be odd expansions of the body metaphor, they nevertheless enhance the organic nature of the body of Christ. The head is dynamically and organically infused with his body.

Second, while Christ is the source of the body and therefore promotes its growth, we observe that the body also builds up *itself.* Each individual part is involved in this growth, even while Christ is the one who grows the body. There is, therefore, a mutual cooperation and sharing in the work of growing the body of Christ. While the body may not shoulder responsibility for its own development apart from Christ, neither is the body free from burden.

In terms of union with Christ, these two developments of the body metaphor suggest that the union that believers share with Christ is organic, involving growth that flows from Christ but also into Christ. He is the source of our union and the goal of our union; we come from him and are to become like him.[27] Moreover, the dynamic growth of the body is promoted by Christ *and* involves the contribution of all its members.

Eph 5:23 ὅτι ἀνήρ ἐστιν κεφαλὴ τῆς γυναικὸς ὡς καὶ ὁ Χριστὸς κεφαλὴ τῆς ἐκκλησίας, αὐτὸς σωτὴρ τοῦ **σώματος**

*For the husband is head of the wife as Christ is head of the church. He is the Savior of the **body**.*

This reference (along with the next one) belongs to an extended analogy in which Christ is depicted as husband of the church. Since the metaphor of marriage will be explored later in this chapter, we will not deal with it in full here but rather limit our examination to the role of *body* language. Christ is again described as the *head of the church*, which is to be correlated with the reference to the body in the final phrase. Christ's headship of the church is likened to a husband's headship of his wife, an analogy to be explored later.

In addition to this, for the first time we encounter a description of Christ as *the Savior of the body*. Again, Paul is pushing the boundaries of the body metaphor with this description, since the *body* did not exist when Christ 'saved it'. The body was created through his death and resurrection; before those events there was no body to save. What Paul means, of course, is that Christ is the Saviour of all who would become members of his body.[28] In that sense, he is the Saviour of the body because he saved the believers who constitute that body.

---

27. So Best; 'the picture [is] not of a static church, but of one which is growing and maturing.... It is moving towards its goal (v. 13) and is enabled to do so through the love and power of its savior and head, Christ'; Best, *Ephesians*, 413.

28. O'Brien, *Ephesians*, 415.

Eph 5:29–30 οὐδεὶς γάρ ποτε τὴν ἑαυτοῦ σάρκα ἐμίσησεν ἀλλὰ
ἐκτρέφει καὶ θάλπει αὐτήν, καθὼς καὶ ὁ Χριστὸς τὴν ἐκκλησίαν,
ὅτι μέλη ἐσμὲν τοῦ **σώματος** αὐτοῦ

*For no one ever hates his own flesh but provides and cares for it, just
as Christ does for the church, since we are members of His **body**.*

Here Paul intensifies the body metaphor by likening the church to his
own flesh. While the presenting issue has to do with husbands caring for
their wives, nevertheless it is clear that Christ does likewise for the church
as a natural consequence of the body/flesh relationship.[29] With respect to
union with Christ, then, we may note that Christ provides and cares for
those united to him as members of his body; we are as his flesh.

Col 1:18 καὶ αὐτός ἐστιν ἡ κεφαλὴ τοῦ **σώματος** τῆς ἐκκλησίας·
ὅς ἐστιν ἀρχή,
πρωτότοκος ἐκ τῶν νεκρῶν,
ἵνα γένηται ἐν πᾶσιν αὐτὸς πρωτεύων

*He is also the head of the **body**, the church;
He is the beginning,
the firstborn from the dead,
so that He might come to have
first place in everything.*

Once again Christ is described as *the head of the body*, which stands in
apposition to *the church*. It is difficult to know whether or not the following phrase—*He is the beginning, the firstborn from the dead*—should be
understood with reference to the church or to the whole cosmos, which
is in view in the previous verses (1:15–17). Most likely the former option
is best, since the phrase *the firstborn from the dead* parallels the phrase *the
firstborn over all creation* in v. 15. Since vv. 15–17 refer to Christ's position over the entire cosmos and includes the aforementioned phrase, it is
plausible that all of v. 18 (at least) refers to the church, complete with its
firstborn parallel phrase.[30] Furthermore, the nature of the parallel between
the firstborn from the dead and *the firstborn over all creation* suggests as

---

29. Schnackenburg, *Ephesians*, 253.
30. Moule, *Colossians and Philemon*, 69.

much, since the former refers to resurrection, which pertains to the church and not the entire cosmos.

Thus, there is an implicit connection between the body of Christ and resurrection, since Christ is the firstborn from the dead. Without making too much of this nexus, it is plausible to suggest that the body is established through Christ's resurrection; he is the beginning of the church, and this is ultimately so that *He might come to have first place in everything.*

Col 1:24 νῦν χαίρω ἐν τοῖς παθήμασιν ὑπὲρ ὑμῶν καὶ ἀνταναπληρῶ τὰ ὑστερήματα τῶν θλίψεων τοῦ Χριστοῦ ἐν τῇ σαρκί μου ὑπὲρ τοῦ **σώματος** αὐτοῦ, ὅ ἐστιν ἡ ἐκκλησία

*Now I rejoice in my sufferings for you, and I am completing in my flesh what is lacking in Christ's afflictions for His **body**, that is, the church.*

In this notoriously difficult verse,[31] the church is again explicitly designated Christ's body. The difficulties are at least threefold. First, what are *Christ's afflictions for His body?* Second, in what sense are Christ's afflictions *lacking?* Third, what does Paul mean by his claim to complete in his flesh *what is lacking in Christ's afflictions?* We will attempt to answer each of these difficulties briefly.

First, most likely *Christ's afflictions* refer to his sin-bearing death.[32] While the church did not yet exist when Christ died (see Eph 5:23, above), his death and resurrection brought his body—the church—into being. It is not necessarily the case, however, that this is what Paul has in view here. To begin with, the phrase *for His body* may not actually modify *Christ's afflictions*, in spite of the natural reading of most English translations. The Greek word order has the phrase *in my flesh* (ἐν τῇ σαρκί μου) situated between the phrases *Christ's afflictions* (τῶν θλίψεων τοῦ Χριστοῦ) and *for His body* (τοῦ σώματος αὐτοῦ), such that the literal word order is *I am completing what is lacking in Christ's afflictions in my flesh for His body.* This raises at least two more questions.

It may mean, on the one hand, that Paul is completing what is lacking in his flesh for the sake of Christ's body; in other words, it is Paul's

---

31. See O'Brien, *Colossians, Philemon,* 75–81, for a detailed analysis.
32. Against this, see Schweizer, *Colossians,* 101.

action that is *for His body*, not Christ's afflictions. On the other hand, the prepositional phrase *in my flesh* may be situated where it is (after *Christ's afflictions*) to bracket *Christ's afflictions* between *I am completing* and *in my flesh*, so that all three elements are bound together as one thought. If this is the case, *in my flesh* need not be translated as following *Christ's afflictions*, such that it reads *I am completing in my flesh what is lacking in Christ's afflictions for his body*. This would mean that *Christ's afflictions* are *for His body*, rather than Paul's activity being for the body.

The second question raised by the word order is whether Christ's afflictions are lacking in general, or if they are lacking in Paul's flesh. This question is of great significance. If the former option is correct, Paul could be understood as suggesting that Christ's afflictions were not sufficient for the growth of the church. The latter option, however, implies that Paul is not commenting on the sufficiency of Christ's sufferings but the degree to which he himself has emulated those sufferings. The way in which we answer this question, and that of the previous paragraph, will shape how we understand the entire verse and will therefore answer the second and third questions raised in the first paragraph.

The best way to approach these issues is to refer to the context. Paul is speaking of his suffering for the church (1:24), his becoming its servant (1:25), his commission to preach to the Gentiles (1:27), and his methods and purpose (1:28). Paul does all this *striving with His strength that works powerfully in me* (1:29). This last verse is of particular interest, for we see that Paul regards his labour as powered by Christ's strength, which is at work in him. This notion reveals Paul's sense of union with Christ—Christ's strength works powerfully within him—and provides a clue for understanding 1:24. Since his sense of union with Christ in strength is revealed in 1:29, it is entirely plausible that 1:24 reveals Paul's sense of union with Christ in suffering. He regards Christ's afflictions as being 'in him' in the same way that Christ's strength is 'in him'.[33] Consequently, it is most likely that Christ's afflictions are lacking with respect to Paul's flesh—they are not lacking in general. Paul's point is that he is completing what is lacking in Christ's afflictions in his flesh. He is not yet fully conformed to the suffering servant, Christ, but is striving toward this.

---

33. So Wright, who regards this as an expression of Paul's incorporation into Christ's life; Wright, *Colossians and Philemon*, 88–89.

This in turn answers the prior question. If Paul is speaking of his own lack with respect to Christ's afflictions—and his addressing that lack—then the phrase *for His body* refers to Paul's activity, not to Christ's afflictions. Paul is addressing this lack of conformity to Christ's sufferings for the purpose of serving the church, which is what the entire passage is about.

We may put all these pieces together in the following way. Paul is discussing his own suffering and his desire to conform fully to Christ's afflictions.[34] He is completing in himself what is lacking with respect to Christ's afflictions, identifying himself with the suffering of Christ, just as he also identifies with Christ's strength (1:29). All of this is for the sake of the body of Christ, the church, of which he has become a servant.

Paul's identification and conformity to the afflictions of Christ inform our understanding of union with Christ. Not only does participation with Christ bestow blessings on believers as they share in the riches and privileges that belong to Christ, but it also involves sharing in Christ's suffering. For Paul, this sharing in affliction is expressed through his service to the church and his suffering for the gospel.

Col 2:19 καὶ οὐ κρατῶν τὴν κεφαλήν, ἐξ οὗ πᾶν τὸ **σῶμα** διὰ τῶν ἁφῶν καὶ συνδέσμων ἐπιχορηγούμενον καὶ συμβιβαζόμενον αὔξει τὴν αὔξησιν τοῦ θεοῦ

*He doesn't hold on to the head, from whom the whole **body**, nourished and held together by its ligaments and tendons, develops with growth from God.*

Found in the context of a warning against people who might be promoting the so-called Colossian heresy, this verse offers a telling description of the growth of the body. We note that the body develops *from* the head, as is the case in Ephesians 4:16 (discussed above). While the growth of the body stems from the head, this occurs in conjunction with the work of its *ligaments and tendons* (also seen in Eph 4:16), which most likely refers to the diverse roles and services provided by the members of the body.[35]

Furthermore, this growth of the body is described as being *from God.*

---

34. Bruce's position approximates this; Bruce, *Colossians, Philemon, Ephesians,* 83.
35. Though it does not refer to those who hold office in particular; Schweizer, *Colossians,* 164.

Thus, this verse provides a rich account of the forces involved in the body's growth and development: it grows from Christ the head, is nourished by the various gifts of the church, and develops with growth from God. As far as union with Christ is concerned, we see a vibrant, organic, and dynamic body that partakes of Christ, its head. The union that believers share together with Christ is not static, but develops through the work of God and the contribution of believers.

Col 3:15 καὶ ἡ εἰρήνη τοῦ Χριστοῦ βραβευέτω ἐν ταῖς καρδίαις ὑμῶν, εἰς ἣν καὶ ἐκλήθητε ἐν ἑνὶ **σώματι**· καὶ εὐχάριστοι γίνεσθε

*And let the peace of the Messiah, to which you were also called in one **body**, control your hearts. Be thankful.*

In this verse, believers are being called to the peace of Christ *in one body*. There is an interesting interplay between the singular *one body* and plural *your hearts*. Evidently, each member of the body is to allow the peace of Christ reign for the sake of the one body; after all, peace among the many facilitates the unity that is in view in the wider context of this passage, as the previous verse expresses: *Above all, put on love—the perfect bond of unity* (3:14). As love forms a bond of unity, so too peace shapes the body.

7.2.1 PUTTING THE BODY TOGETHER

From the numerous references above, we see that the *body* or *body of Christ* metaphor is rich and capable of several applications. The body is an organic being that is one in Christ and is also growing and maturing.[36] The body has many different parts, and is yet one. This oneness means that believers not only partake in Christ, but they are also joined to each other.[37] The diversity of gifts and roles shared among its members serve to enhance the unity of the body as the body grows and is built up. Christ is the head of the body, *from* whom and *into* whom the body grows. While the body grows by the work of God, it also builds itself through its supporting ligaments and tendons. The body is 'in Christ', partaking in him, while Christ nevertheless remains

---

36. See Burger's synthesis of Bavinck's ideas concerning the organic nature of the body; Burger, *Being in Christ*, 134.

37. 'It is a sense of belonging to Christ indeed, but of belonging together with others, with the obvious implication that one without the other would make the whole unbalanced and unhealthy'; Dunn, *Paul the Apostle*, 406. See also Davies, *Paul*, 55.

distinct—he alone is the head of the body. Finally, while the *body* language is metaphorical, it is not merely so.[38] There is a concrete reality to which it refers;[39] 'while Paul's reference to the "body" is certainly metaphorical, the unity which he expresses with this metaphor rests upon an ontological reality,[40] which has implications for the ways in which believers treat their own physical bodies.

It is plausible to suggest that union with Christ is a key element underpinning the metaphorical power of the *body* language.[41] 'Incorporated into Christ, believers form a corporate unity with him and Paul's designation of the church as the body of Christ basically denotes this unity.'[42] Indeed, Schweitzer goes so far as to suggest that *being-in-Christ* is the same thing as partaking in his body.[43] As suggested at the beginning of this section, the very concept of a body that is organically connected to its head implies union and participation. So Calvin states: 'Therefore, that joining together of Head and members, that indwelling of Christ in our hearts— in short, that mystical union—are accorded by us the highest degree of importance, so that Christ, having been made ours, makes us sharers with him in the first with which he has been endowed.'[44]

This is no decapitated body! It belongs to its head, who shares with it, shapes it, promotes its growth, and cares for it. The body is 'in Christ' (Rom 12:5), and it also grows into Christ, its head (Eph 4:15). While the prepositional language that is associated with union with Christ is fre-

---

38. See Son's survey of the two main views concerning the *body* language—'(1) Some understand it in a metaphorical sense and (2) others in a realistic sense'; Son, *Corporate Elements*, 102–8.

39. 'The Mystical Body of Christ is for Paul not a pictorial expression, nor a conception which has arisen out of symbolical and ethical reflections, but an actual entity'; Schweitzer, *Mysticism*, 127. See also Ridderbos, *Paul*, 376; Son, *Corporate Elements*, 108; J. Christiaan Beker, *Paul the Apostle: The Triumph of God in Life and Thought* (Edinburgh: T&T Clark, 1980), 307–8.

40. Daniel G. Powers, *Salvation through Participation: An Examination of the Notion of the Believers' Corporate Unity with Christ in Early Christian Soteriology* (Leuven: Peeters, 2001), 71.

41. So Ridderbos, 'As believers, by virtue of their being-of-Christ ... so are they also, if of Christ, his members and together his one body'; Ridderbos, *Paul*, 372. See also Ernst Käsemann, *Perspectives on Paul* (trans. Margaret Kohl; London: SCM, 1971), 106.

42. Son, *Corporate Elements*, 110.

43. 'The expression "being-in-Christ" is merely a brachyology [*sic*] for being partakers in the Mystical Body of Christ'; Schweitzer, *Mysticism*, 122.

44. John Calvin, *Institutes of the Christian Religion* (ed. John T. McNeill; trans. Ford Lewis Battles; Philadelphia: Westminster, 1960), 3.11.10 (p. 737).

quently absent with respect to the body metaphor, the concept of union is never far away and, in fact, is always implied by the metaphor itself.

7.3 TEMPLE AND BUILDING

The metaphor of temple or of a building is of significance for Paul's portrayal of the church. While *temple* and *building* might be treated separately as two different metaphors, they appear to be so closely related that we will discuss them together here. There are three lexical items that are of relevance: ναός, ἱερόν, and οἰκοδομή, which will be addressed in order. Each occurrence in Paul's usage of ναός is included below, since each one speaks metaphorically of the church—with one exception (see below). The second word, ἱερόν, only occurs once and is evidently not used metaphorically. It is included here, however, for the sake of completeness.

The third lexeme, οἰκοδομή, is more complex. There are two main ways in which Paul uses this word. The first, of interest here, is that which depicts a building or edifice that stands as the result of a construction process.[45] The idea of a constructed building is often used metaphorically to describe the church, and these instances are included below. The second way in which Paul uses οἰκοδομή is to refer to the *process* of building rather than the physical construction that stands as a result of building activity.[46] This usage also finds metaphorical employment, as Paul depicts the strengthening of believers and of the church as occurring through *building* or *edification*. Since this function of the word, however, does not refer to the church qua the church but rather a process that *affects* the church, it is not included here.[47] We are interested at this juncture in Paul's depiction of God's people as a building, not the edification of his people per se.

> 1 Cor 3:16–17 οὐκ οἴδατε ὅτι **ναὸς** θεοῦ ἐστε καὶ τὸ πνεῦμα τοῦ θεοῦ οἰκεῖ ἐν ὑμῖν; εἴ τις τὸν **ναὸν** τοῦ θεοῦ φθείρει, φθερεῖ τοῦτον ὁ θεός· ὁ γὰρ **ναὸς** τοῦ θεοῦ ἅγιός ἐστιν, οἵτινές ἐστε ὑμεῖς
>
> *Don't you yourselves know that you are God's **sanctuary** and that the Spirit of God lives in you? If anyone destroys God's **sanctuary**, God will destroy him; for God's **sanctuary** is holy, and that is what you are.*

---

45. BDAG, 697.

46. Ibid., 696–97.

47. This usage of οἰκοδομή is found in the following passages: Rom 14:19; 15:2; 1 Cor 14:3, 5, 12, 26; 2 Cor 10:8; 12:19; 13:10; Eph 4:12, 16, 29.

The Corinthians are here described as God's temple,[48] the corollary of which is that God's Spirit dwells within them.[49] 'If the presence of God is the feature that most essentially defines the temple, the indwelling of the Spirit so defines this congregation.'[50] Furthermore, as God's temple is holy, so too are the Corinthians since they are his temple.

Paul clearly applies the Old Testament image of God's holy temple to the people of God, thus using that (once) concrete (so to speak) reality as a metaphor to convey something about the new covenant congregation. Rather than being built of stone, this temple consists of people; and rather than God's Spirit dwelling within a physical structure, which could be accessed by people to varying degrees, he dwells within a people.[51]

While there is no reference here to the relationship of Christ to this temple, the metaphor is still useful for understanding the corporate identification of God with his people since his Spirit dwells among them. The people of God constitute the 'location' in which God dwells, and in that sense they have replaced the function of the temple of old. In so doing, they are apparently attributed with the sanctions once enjoyed by the original temple: God's punishment of those who would ruin it and his holiness.

1 Cor 6:19–20 ἢ οὐκ οἴδατε ὅτι τὸ σῶμα ὑμῶν **ναὸς** τοῦ ἐν ὑμῖν ἁγίου πνεύματός ἐστιν οὗ ἔχετε ἀπὸ θεοῦ, καὶ οὐκ ἐστὲ ἑαυτῶν; ἠγοράσθητε γὰρ τιμῆς· δοξάσατε δὴ τὸν θεὸν ἐν τῷ σώματι ὑμῶν

---

48. As with all instances of the word, the HCSB translates ναός as *sanctuary* rather than *temple*. Since, however, *temple* is a fitting translation for ναός and is probably better in the context of Paul's writing, we will refer to the entity described by ναός as *temple*, while retaining the translation provided by the HCSB.

49. Paul also refers to the church as God's building (οἰκοδομή) a few verses earlier (3:9; see below for discussion).

50. Constantine R. Campbell, 'From Earthly Symbol to Heavenly Reality: The Tabernacle in the New Testament', in *Exploring Exodus: Literary, Theological and Contemporary Approaches* (ed. Brian S. Rosner and Paul R. Williamson; Nottingham, UK: Apollos, 2008), 184.

51. Bonnington argues that Paul's agenda in 1 Corinthians is not to articulate a 'temple-replacement' theology; rather, the language relating to the temple is employed for the purpose of underscoring the holiness and purity of God's people. While Bonnington correctly observes that the context of these passages addresses holiness and purity issues, it is difficult to disavow any sense of a temple-replacement motif, even if it is not Paul's primary concern; see Mark Bonnington, 'New Temples in Corinth: Paul's Use of Temple Imagery in the Ethics of the Corinthian Correspondence', in *Heaven on Earth* (ed. T. Desmond Alexander and Simon Gathercole; Carlisle, UK: Paternoster, 2004), 152–58.

*Do you not know that your body is a **sanctuary** of the Holy Spirit*
who is in you, whom you have from God? You are not your own,
for you were bought at a price. Therefore glorify God in your body.

Here is the second reference in 1 Corinthians in which Paul describes believers as a temple. The differences in this case, when compared to 3:16–17 above, is that the *body* is specified as a temple, which is not the case in 3:16–17. Moreover, Paul appears to be commenting on the bodies of *individuals* in contrast to the corporate picture of 3:16–17, as I have argued elsewhere:

> Both references to the body are singular, though the possessive pronouns are plural. Syntactically, this could indicate that 'body' here is functioning collectively, referring to the one body that belongs to all concerned (the corporate temple). On the other hand, everything in the context seems to indicate that Paul indeed has the individual in mind, since he has been addressing the issue of prostitution and how any individual joined to a prostitute is one with her (6:16), and the 'sexually immoral [person] sins against his own body' (6:18). As such, the plural pronouns most naturally indicate the multiplicity of individual bodies that make up the Corinthian congregation.[52]

Again, it is the presence of the Holy Spirit within believers (as individuals, in this case) that demarcates each one's body as a temple; the temple is where God chooses to dwell. While addressed to individuals, the plural possessive pronouns indicate that Paul speaks to each in a corporate manner—they are a group of individuals.[53] As with the previous reference, there is no explicit mention of Christ's identification with believers here.

---

52. Campbell, 'Tabernacle', 185. See also Son, *Corporate Elements*, 123–24; R. J. McKelvey, *The New Temple: The Church in the New Testament* (London: Oxford Univ. Press, 1969), 52; Fee, *1 Corinthians*, 264; F. F. Bruce, *1 and 2 Corinthians* (NCB; London: Oliphants, 1971), 65; C. K. Barrett, *A Commentary on the First Epistle to the Corinthians* (HNTC; New York: Harper & Row, 1968), 151.

53. Son, *Corporate Elements*, 124. See also Spatafora: 'Paul's perspective is not, however, that of the Stoics who believed that the individual was, in himself, the temple of God. For the Apostle, it is a consequence of the believer's belonging to the Church which is first of all the temple. Nevertheless, members share in the nature of the whole'; Andrea Spatafora, *From the "Temple of God" to God as the Temple: A Biblical Theological Study of the Temple in the Book of Revelation* (Rome: Gregorian Univ. Press, 1997), 117, n. 101.

There is, however, identification of God with his people, since his Spirit dwells within them.

2 Cor 6:16 τίς δὲ συγκατάθεσις **ναῷ** θεοῦ μετὰ εἰδώλων; ἡμεῖς
γὰρ **ναὸς** θεοῦ ἐσμεν ζῶντος, καθὼς εἶπεν ὁ θεὸς ὅτι
ἐνοικήσω ἐν αὐτοῖς καὶ ἐμπεριπατήσω
καὶ ἔσομαι αὐτῶν θεὸς καὶ αὐτοὶ ἔσονταί μου λαός.

*And what agreement does God's **sanctuary** have with idols? For we
are the **sanctuary** of the living God, as God said:
I will dwell among them
and walk among them,
and I will be their God,
and they will be My people.*

Once again, God's people are equated with the temple of God. Paul says that *we are the sanctuary of the living God,* and he takes this further with a catena of Leviticus 26:12; Jeremiah 32:38; and Ezekiel 37:27, which states God's intention to dwell one day among his people. In this way, the *dwelling* of God with his people appears to be the key factor in designating the people as the temple.

Eph 2:21 – 22 ἐν ᾧ πᾶσα οἰκοδομὴ συναρμολογουμένη αὔξει
εἰς **ναὸν** ἅγιον ἐν κυρίῳ, ἐν ᾧ καὶ ὑμεῖς συνοικοδομεῖσθε εἰς
κατοικητήριον τοῦ θεοῦ ἐν πνεύματι

*The whole building, being put together by Him, grows into a holy
sanctuary in the Lord. You also are being built together for God's
dwelling in the Spirit.*

Speaking of the members of God's household (οἰκεῖοι τοῦ θεοῦ; 2:19), which is *built on the foundation of the apostles and prophets, with Christ Jesus Himself as the cornerstone* (2:20), Paul depicts God's people as a building, growing into a holy temple. Unlike the previous references to God's people as temple, these two verses specify incorporation into Christ—and this explicitly, three times. Christ is the antecedent of the two relative pronouns in 2:21 and 2:22 (ἐν ᾧ), such that the building is fitted together *in him* and is being built together for God's dwelling in the Spirit *in him.*

Furthermore, the building is growing into a holy temple *in the Lord*. As Peterson acknowledges, 'Paul affirms in Ephesians that *Christians in union with Christ* fulfil the Temple ideal.'[54]

These verses are full of interest for various reasons. First, we observe once again that the key component to God's people being described as his temple is his dwelling within them by his Spirit.

Second, the explicit incorporation into Christ in association with temple imagery develops the metaphor into a fully orbed trinitarian concept. The temple is *in the Lord* and is built for *God's dwelling in the Spirit*.

Third, the temple metaphor is dynamic, since God's people are *being built* together for his dwelling.[55] While the present indicative verb συνοικοδομεῖσθε could be translated *is built together* (2:22), the progressive *Aktionsart* rendering, *is being built*, is an equally valid understanding of the verb's imperfective aspect and is supported by the context.[56] Since the participle συναρμολογουμένη, *being fitted together*, and the present indicative αὔξει, *is growing* (2:21), both imply progression, so συνοικοδομεῖσθε should be understood.

Fourth, the metaphor is organic, in that God's people *grow* into a holy temple in the Lord (2:21). This organic nature creates a strange mixing of metaphors, in which a building can be described as *growing* as well as *being built* (2:22).

Fifth, it is somewhat ironic that the temple is described as a *building*, since the metaphor has been used by Paul to make the point that the

---

54. David Peterson, 'The New Temple: Christology and Ecclesiology in Ephesians and 1 Peter', in *Heaven on Earth* (ed. T. Desmond Alexander and Simon Gathercole; Carlisle, UK: Paternoster, 2004), 165 [italics are original].

55. 'One should not conceive of God (or Christ) merely as a static foundation of the house; he is actively building the house now.' Thomas R. Schreiner, *Paul: Apostle of God's Glory in Christ* (Downers Grove, IL: InterVarsity Press, 2001), 21. Regarding the ongoing growth of the temple, Beale notes that 'the borders of Eden and all subsequent temples were to be expanded until they circumscribed the globe with God's all-pervasive presence. Yet this purpose was never successfully pursued until it began to be accomplished in Christ. Here, as we have also seen in 1 Corinthians 3, the temple's expansion is beginning to be executed, in that its boundaries are expanding to include Gentiles from around the world. The temple will continue to expand to include more and more people until God's presence will pervade the entire earth at the end of the age (cf. Eph. 4:13)'; G. K. Beale, *The Temple and the Church's Mission: A Biblical Theology of the Dwelling Place of God* (NSBT 17; Downers Grove, IL: InterVarsity Press, 2004), 263.

56. Constantine R. Campbell, *Basics of Verbal Aspect in Biblical Greek* (Grand Rapids: Zondervan, 2008), 63.

temple is no longer a building but a people. The temple is a people, not a building, and yet the people are described as a building—in a metaphorical sense, of course.

2 Thess 2:4 ὁ ἀντικείμενος καὶ ὑπεραιρόμενος ἐπὶ πάντα λεγόμενον θεὸν ἢ σέβασμα, ὥστε αὐτὸν εἰς τὸν **ναὸν** τοῦ θεοῦ καθίσαι ἀποδεικνύντα ἑαυτὸν ὅτι ἔστιν θεός.

*He opposes and exalts himself above every so-called god or object of worship, so that he sits in God's **sanctuary**, publicizing that he himself is God.*

This verse refers to the *man of lawlessness*, described in the preceding verse. As such, it is not relevant to our current discussion.

1 Cor 9:13 Οὐκ οἴδατε ὅτι οἱ τὰ **ἱερὰ** ἐργαζόμενοι [τὰ] ἐκ τοῦ **ἱεροῦ** ἐσθίουσιν, οἱ τῷ θυσιαστηρίῳ παρεδρεύοντες τῷ θυσιαστηρίῳ συμμερίζονται;

*Don't you know that those who perform the **temple** services eat the food from the **temple**, and those who serve at the altar share in the offerings of the altar?*

This verse is found in the context of Paul's defending his right to be supported by the believers whom he serves. In such a context, Paul refers to the priests whose food was provided by the temple in which they served. While it might be supposed that Paul intends a *double entendre* here, so that the temple to which he refers also points to the Christian community (since he has already designated it God's new temple), this seems unlikely. As there is no hint in the context that Paul has the temple metaphor in mind, it is mostly likely that he is simply referring to the temple of old in order to illustrate and support his point.[57]

1 Cor 3:9 θεοῦ γάρ ἐσμεν συνεργοί, θεοῦ γεώργιον, θεοῦ **οἰκοδομή** ἐστε

*For we are God's coworkers. You are God's field, God's **building**.*

---

57. Ciampa and Rosner, *1 Corinthians*, 412.

This use of the building metaphor for God's people is mixed with that of being God's field. In the context, the previous three verses describe church growth using farming imagery (3:6–8), and here the metaphor abruptly switches to that of a building, which Paul explores in the following verses (3:10–15).[58] For our purposes, the significant facet of this use of the building metaphor is that God's building is founded on Christ: *for no one can lay any other foundation than what has been laid down. That foundation is Jesus Christ* (3:11). Here we glimpse the concept of incorporation into Christ: God's people are 'built' on Christ, and he must—by the very nature of the metaphor—be integrated with God's people, as the foundation of a building is essentially integrated with the structure of which it is a part.

2 Cor 5:1 οἴδαμεν γὰρ ὅτι ἐὰν ἡ ἐπίγειος ἡμῶν οἰκία τοῦ σκήνους καταλυθῇ, **οἰκοδομὴν** ἐκ θεοῦ ἔχομεν, οἰκίαν ἀχειροποίητον αἰώνιον ἐν τοῖς οὐρανοῖς

*For we know that if our temporary, earthly dwelling is destroyed, we have a **building** from God, an eternal dwelling in the heavens, not made with hands.*

This use of the building metaphor appears to refer to an individual's heavenly body, though this is not immediately clear. It might be argued, for instance, that the building refers to the people of God[59]—and this especially because of the mention of the *tent* (τοῦ σκήνους), a word that normally, in the New Testament, refers to God's dwelling among his people.[60]

However, the wider context does not prefer this reading. Paul says in 4:16: *Therefore we do not give up. Even though our outer person is being destroyed, our inner person is being renewed day by day.* The *outer person* here clearly refers to the physical, earthly body, which is given to decay

---

58. 'The transition from the image of the building to that of the temple seems rather sudden, but it is logical shift because the temple is a building and in the Old Testament (e.g., Ezra 5:3–4) it is indeed referred to as a building'; Son, *Corporate Elements*, 122.

59. See, e.g., E. Earle Ellis, 'The Structure of Pauline Eschatology (II Corinthians v. 1–10)', in *Paul and His Recent Interpreters* (Grand Rapids: Eerdmans, 1979), 35–48. Ellis argues that the concept of the heavenly house refers to the temple, used as a metaphor for the solidarity of believers with Christ.

60. See Campbell, 'Tabernacle', 177–95.

and frailty. This, then, correlates with the *earthly house, a tent*, which may be destroyed (5:1). In this vein, Paul continues in 5:6, 8: *So, we are always confident and know that while we are at home in the body we are away from the Lord ... and we are confident and satisfied to be out of the body and at home with the Lord.* Here the body is explicitly mentioned (τοῦ σώματος), and the burden of Paul's point is to demarcate the distinction between living in the earthly body, given to decay, and being *at home with the Lord*, which is eternal. Consequently, this use of the building metaphor is concerned with the resurrection bodies of individuals and does not directly contribute to the concept of incorporation into Christ. Having said that, however, it is worth noting Son's caveat:

> Hence, although 'our heavenly house' in 2 Cor. 5:1 has strong implications for the resurrection bodies of individual believers, it must be understood in the framework of the corporate solidarity in Christ in whom the new aeon is already fully actualized, just as both σῶμα ψυχικόν and σῶμα πνευματικόν described in 1 Cor. 15:44–49 are to be understood in the framework of the Adam–Christ typology introduced in the preceding passage (15:21–22).[61]

> Eph 2:21–22 ἐν ᾧ πᾶσα **οἰκοδομὴ** συναρμολογουμένη αὔξει εἰς ναὸν ἅγιον ἐν κυρίῳ, ἐν ᾧ καὶ ὑμεῖς συνοικοδομεῖσθε εἰς κατοικητήριον τοῦ θεοῦ ἐν πνεύματι

> *The whole **building**, being put together by Him, grows into a holy sanctuary in the Lord. You also are being built together for God's dwelling in the Spirit.*

As noted above, this use of the building metaphor is explicitly related to incorporation into Christ as well as the temple metaphor. This is a dynamic, organic, and trinitarian depiction of the people of God, in whom God dwells by his Spirit.

Before concluding this section, it is worth noting that Son also includes 1 Timothy 3:15 among the passages relating to the temple and building metaphors.[62]

---

61. Son, *Corporate Elements*, 130.
62. Indeed, Son's chapter on these metaphors includes that of *house* (οἶκος). We have not

1 Tim 3:15 ἐὰν δὲ βραδύνω, ἵνα εἰδῇς πῶς δεῖ ἐν **οἴκῳ** θεοῦ ἀναστρέφεσθαι, ἥτις ἐστὶν ἐκκλησία θεοῦ ζῶντος, στῦλος καὶ ἑδραίωμα τῆς ἀληθείας

*But if I should be delayed, I have written so that you will know how people ought to act in God's **household**, which is the church of the living God, the pillar and foundation of the truth.*

Son argues that 'the close connection of οἶκος θεοῦ with the architectural terms "pillar" (στῦλος) and "bulwark" (ἑδραίωμα) signifies that it more likely refers to the temple of God'.[63] This connection, however, is not sufficiently compelling, and we do not therefore accept that this passage employs the temple metaphor.[64]

7.3.1 THE SHAPE OF THE TEMPLE BUILDING

Paul uses the metaphors of temple and building with great effect. At their core, these metaphors convey the corporate nature of the church, and even in the few occasions in which they refer to individuals, they are nevertheless conditioned by the corporality of the church. As Son summarizes, 'The basic underlying concept is the corporate solidarity that believers form together in Christ. As the various parts of the body make up the single whole body and as the various parts of the building create the single whole building, so believers form a corporate solidarity. They are organically and structurally connected to one another.'[65]

The people of God are regarded as the new temple, since it is among them that God chooses to dwell by his Spirit; 'Both the individual believer and the church are spoken of as the temple of God because of the presence of the Holy Spirit.'[66] At one time this privilege was, by and large, reserved

---

included *house* in this section since 1 Tim 3:15 is the only passage that is added to the discussion through this metaphor, and it is questionable as to whether it really belongs here.

63. Son, *Corporate Elements*, 134.

64. Marshall recognizes the potential for temple reference here but rejects it; 'Thus the imagery employed is probably capable of expressing such 'new temple' ideas, but the shape of ethical thought in 1 Tim speaks against it as the dominant thought.' Furthermore, in the Pastoral Epistles 'there is no identification of the actual people of God with the οἶκος θεοῦ; it is an existing entity in which they live'; Marshall, *Pastoral Epistles*, 508.

65. Son, *Corporate Elements*, 136.

66. Edmund P. Clowney, 'The Biblical Theology of the Church', in *The Church in the Bible and the World* (ed. D. A. Carson; Exeter, UK: Paternoster, 1987), 26–27.

for the physical construction of the temple; now, in Christ, a congregation has superseded the construction. With the exception of Ephesians 2:21 – 22, the temple metaphor does not explicitly connect to incorporation into Christ, though it does clearly involve identification with God, as he dwells in his holy temple by his Spirit.

The people of God are also described metaphorically as a building, which has Christ as its foundation and is built by Paul as a master builder. Again, Ephesians 2:21 – 22 indicates that incorporation into Christ is conveyed by this metaphor through his being the foundation of the building.[67] That foundation is inextricably wedded to the building of which it is a part.[68] Furthermore, the building metaphor is here explicitly linked with the temple metaphor. As such, this passage provides the most direct account of both metaphors, offering a fully orbed trinitarian image of God's purposes for his people.

7.4 MARRIAGE

On a few occasions, Paul draws on marriage as a metaphor for the relationship between Christ and the church. While this metaphor is not as frequent as the others, it still constitutes a significant element in Paul's thinking. Note especially how the apostle grounds certain theological and ethical matters on the foundation of the nuptial union between Christ and the church. While the question must be raised at a later point as to whether Paul's theological thinking is shaped by this metaphor even when it is not explicitly in view, there is nonetheless much to be considered in connection with the explicit references explored below.

In addition to the paucity of examples, another difference between this metaphor and the ones addressed above is that there is no specific vocabulary associated with it. The metaphor is, rather, detected through a range of vocabulary and concepts that are inherently associated with marriage. Consequently, some passages are obviously concerned with the marriage metaphor, while others are subtler. This requires sensitivity to the nuances of

---

67. Thomas G. Allen, 'Exaltation and Solidarity with Christ: Ephesians 1:20 and 2:6', *JSNT* 28 (1986): 112.

68. Burger, *Being in Christ*, 239.

Paul's discussion in order to unearth the underlying logic that regards Christ as sharing in a one-flesh union with his people.

Rom 7:1 – 4 ἢ ἀγνοεῖτε, ἀδελφοί, γινώσκουσιν γὰρ νόμον λαλῶ, ὅτι ὁ νόμος κυριεύει τοῦ ἀνθρώπου ἐφ᾽ ὅσον χρόνον ζῇ; ἡ γὰρ ὕπανδρος γυνὴ τῷ ζῶντι ἀνδρὶ δέδεται νόμῳ· ἐὰν δὲ ἀποθάνῃ ὁ ἀνήρ, κατήργηται ἀπὸ τοῦ νόμου τοῦ ἀνδρός. ἄρα οὖν ζῶντος τοῦ ἀνδρὸς μοιχαλὶς χρηματίσει ἐὰν γένηται ἀνδρὶ ἑτέρῳ· ἐὰν δὲ ἀποθάνῃ ὁ ἀνήρ, ἐλευθέρα ἐστὶν ἀπὸ τοῦ νόμου, τοῦ μὴ εἶναι αὐτὴν μοιχαλίδα γενομένην ἀνδρὶ ἑτέρῳ. ὥστε, ἀδελφοί μου, καὶ ὑμεῖς ἐθανατώθητε τῷ νόμῳ διὰ τοῦ σώματος τοῦ Χριστοῦ, εἰς τὸ γενέσθαι ὑμᾶς ἑτέρῳ, τῷ ἐκ νεκρῶν ἐγερθέντι, ἵνα καρποφορήσωμεν τῷ θεῷ.

Since I am speaking to those who understand law, brothers, are you unaware that the law has authority over someone as long as he lives? For example, a married woman is legally bound to her husband while he lives. But if her husband dies, she is released from the law regarding the husband. So then, if she gives herself to another man while her husband is living, she will be called an adulteress. But if her husband dies, she is free from that law. Then, if she gives herself to another man, she is not an adulteress.

Therefore, my brothers, you also were put to death in relation to the law through the crucified body of the Messiah, so that you may belong to another—to Him who was raised from the dead—that we may bear fruit for God.

Paul does not explicitly apply the metaphor of marriage to the union between Christ and believers here, though it is arguably implied. He uses the legal norms of marriage to illustrate the relationship that believers have with the law of Moses. A married woman is bound to her husband until death, after which she is free from her bond (7:2). Paul argues that, in similar fashion, believers have been put to death with respect to the law and now belong to Christ (7:4).

Interestingly, Paul parallels the woman with the believer, yet the woman is freed through the death of her husband, while the believer is described as having been put to death (7:4). In this sense, the illustration does not appear to be congruent with the reality it illustrates, since it is the woman's husband who dies, but the believer *himself* (who is meant to parallel the woman) is the one who has died.[69] This apparent discrepancy between illustration and reality, however, is not as simple as it first appears. The believer is described as having been put to death to the law *through the crucified body of the Messiah.* Christ died under the burden of the law such that his death fulfills the requirement of the law. Consequently, *Christ-under-law* may be understood to parallel the dead husband of the illustration, in that the obligation to the husband is fulfilled upon his death. Since the requirement of the law has been fulfilled in Christ's death, those who share in his death might be described as having been *put to death in relation to the law*—its requirement of death has been met for each believer.

The consequence of the fulfillment of the law's requirement through the death of Christ is that believers are freed from the law (as the woman is free from her marriage bond when her husband dies) and now may belong to another (as the woman is free to remarry). While *Christ-under-law* parallels the first, and dead, husband, the resurrected Christ parallels the new husband to whom the woman will be married. As such, believers are freed from the law in order to belong to Christ.

Paul stops short of describing this 'belonging to another' as a marriage union between Christ and his believers, though it is possible that the passage hints as much. The parallel between the woman of the marriage illustration and believers suggests that, just as she is freed to remarry, believers are freed to belong to Christ through a similar bond. So Earnshaw concludes:

> Against this background, we can state the thesis that Paul's marriage analogy is properly understood only when *the wife's first marriage is viewed as illustrating the believer's union with Christ in his death and her second marriage is viewed as illustrating the believer's union with Christ in his resurrection.*[70]

---

69. Dodd apparently finds this frustrating; 'To make confusion worse compounded, it is not Law, the first husband, who dies: the Christian, on the other hand, is dead to the Law. The illustration, therefore, has gone hopelessly astray'; C. H. Dodd, *The Epistle to the Romans* (1932; repr. London: Fontana, 1959), 120. Most likely Dodd has not fully comprehended Paul at this point.

70. J. D. Earnshaw, 'Reconsidering Paul's Marriage Analogy in Romans 7.1–4', *NTS* 40 (1994): 72 [italics are original].

It might be objected, however, that an illegitimate transfer from illustration to reality is needed in order to describe this belonging to Christ as marriage. The legalities of marriage are simply illustrative of the believer's relationship to the law and Christ; to say that the believer is therefore 'married' to Christ misses the point. Indeed, if it is correct to adduce from the illustration that the believer is married to Christ, surely this would also require the believer to have been 'married' to the law, which is an unlikely inference.

These objections have some merit. Nevertheless, the text contains clues that suggest that there are similarities between marriage and the relationship between believers and Christ. The first is the participation evoked through the phrase *you also were put to death in relation to the law through the crucified body of the Messiah* (7:4). Believers share in the crucified body of Christ, which is an idea not altogether foreign to the concept of the one-flesh union of marriage. The second is the phrase *so that you may belong to another* (εἰς τὸ γενέσθαι ὑμᾶς ἑτέρῳ; 7:4). While this expression is rather vague in that it does not denote the nature of the 'belonging', nevertheless it is fair to assume that the bond it bespeaks has some affinity with the bond of marriage, given the context.[71]

Thus, it is appropriate to suggest that this passage evokes something akin to the bond of marriage with respect to the relationship between Christ and believers.[72] Participation with Christ is explicit and believers belong to Christ in a manner that characterizes the pledge of marriage.[73]

1 Cor 6:15 – 17 οὐκ οἴδατε ὅτι τὰ σώματα ὑμῶν μέλη Χριστοῦ ἐστιν; ἄρας οὖν τὰ μέλη τοῦ Χριστοῦ ποιήσω πόρνης μέλη; μὴ γένοιτο. οὐκ οἴδατε ὅτι ὁ κολλώμενος τῇ πόρνῃ ἓν σῶμά ἐστιν;

---

71. Best has no doubt that marriage between Christ and believers is in view; Ernest Best, *The Letter of Paul to the Romans* (CBC; Cambridge: Cambridge Univ. Press, 1967), 77 – 78.

72. Earnshaw restates the passage as follows: 'You, my readers, are free from the Mosaic law through sharing with Christ in his death, and have embarked on a new life in union with Christ in his resurrection. You are thus in many respects like a widow who has remarried, for such a woman is free from the law governing her first marriage through sharing in the legal consequences of her first husband's death and has embarked on a new life with a second husband'; Earnshaw, 'Marriage Analogy', 73.

73. Earnshaw (ibid., 88) regards Paul's 'participationist soteriology' as 'the interpretative key that can alone bring order out of the confusion'.

ἔσονται γάρ, φησίν, οἱ δύο εἰς σάρκα μίαν. ὁ δὲ κολλώμενος τῷ κυρίῳ ἓν πνεῦμά ἐστιν

Don't you know that your bodies are a part of Christ? So should I take a part of Christ and make it part of a prostitute? Absolutely not! Don't you know that anyone joined to a prostitute is one body with her? For Scripture says, The two will become one flesh. But anyone joined to the Lord is one spirit with Him.

The metaphor of marriage is more transparently in view in this passage and is expressed in two ways, both of which are related to the one-flesh element of marriage. First, Paul describes the bodies of believers as *members of Christ* (μέλη Χριστοῦ; 6:15). The word μέλος literally refers to a body 'part', with a figurative usage referring to a 'member' of a group.[74] Paul's frequent use of the body metaphor to refer to the people of God suggests that this use of μέλος metaphorically depicts believers as the *body parts* of Christ. Being *body parts* of Christ means that to become *[members] of a prostitute* (πόρνης μέλη) constitutes a grievous offense to the body of Christ.

If it is not already clear that Paul is addressing sexual relations here, he offers further clarification in the following verse: *Don't you know that anyone joined to a prostitute is one body with her?* (6:16). Clearly, sexual union with a prostitute is inappropriate because believers are body parts of Christ.[75] The point here, for our purposes, is that the sexual union—which is only appropriately expressed in marriage, according to the Bible—has some parallel to the relationship of Christ to his believers, since the same word (μέλος) is used for both relationships. There are significant differences, of course, between the two relationships—one is metaphorical, the other concrete; one is asexual, the other sexual; one is spiritual, the other physical—so that the parallel cannot be pressed too

---

74. BDAG, 628.

75. Son correctly notes that 'it is, however, not the sexual relationship itself but an immoral kind of sexual relationship that breaks one's union with Christ'; Son, *Corporate Elements*, 149. He develops this further in the following statement: 'The "one body" union created by sexual intercourse can either correspond to or contrast with the "one body (spirit)" union with Christ. Within the context of marriage, it provides a positive and compatible supplement to the "one body" union between believers and Christ, but in an immoral context ... it contradicts the corporate union with Christ' (p. 165).

far (see below). Nevertheless, a parallel does exist, and it is central to marriage: the sharing of one body. Believers share in Christ's body, so they are not to share in a prostitute's body. As Powers points out, 'The entire force of Paul's arguments against sexual abuses in Corinth is founded completely upon Paul's understanding of the believers' corporate unity with Christ. The Christians' unity with Christ forms the basis of Paul's entire argument.'[76]

Second, Paul quotes from Genesis 2:24 (LXX) — *For Scripture says, The two will become one flesh* — to support his statement that *anyone joined to a prostitute is one body with her* (6:16). Since Genesis 2:21–25 describes the first, and prototypical, marriage, Paul's use of the quote demonstrates that he regards sex with a prostitute as (inappropriately) creating the one-flesh relationship that is reserved for marriage. We noted above that it is this concept of sharing a body that Paul sees as the parallel between sex with a prostitute and Christ's body parts. Since the former has been linked to marriage through the quote of Genesis 2:24, it follows that Paul also regards the union between Christ and his body parts as an expression of the one-flesh relationship of marriage. In other words, if sex with a prostitute creates the one-flesh relationship of marriage, so too does the relationship between Christ and his body parts, since the sharing of a body is the parallel between these two images. The element that Genesis 2:24 brings to the table is that Paul depicts this as a *nuptial* union.[77]

Verse 17 sharpens Paul's point: *But anyone joined to the Lord is one spirit with Him*. First, the parallel between sex and the relationship of believers to Christ is reaffirmed with the phrase *anyone joined to the Lord*, which exactly parallels *anyone joined to a prostitute* (6:16) through the shared expression ὁ κολλώμενος, *anyone joined*. Second, Paul distinguishes the elements that are not paralleled between the two images: being joined to the Lord constitutes a *spiritual* union (*is one spirit with Him*), and thus the language of *body parts* is metaphorical. A spiritual union, with the concept of one flesh being therefore metaphorical, it is also best regarded as asexual (these distinctions are anticipated above).[78]

---

76. Powers, *Salvation through Participation*, 150.
77. So Ciampa and Rosner, *1 Corinthians*, 259–60.
78. 'This unity is no bodily union as sexual union is, but a unity ... in the Spirit.... Consequently, this image shows the presence of a moment of union, and further clarifies a little

Paul does not in this passage explicitly name the church as the bride of Christ or Christ as her husband, nor does he call their relationship *marriage*. Nevertheless, the evidence adduced above sufficiently supports the proposition that Paul regards the relationship between Christ and his people as a spiritual marriage. Believers are spiritually joined to the Lord, metaphorically expressing a one-flesh union. They share in one body, as do husband and wife.

2 Cor 11:2–3 ζηλῶ γὰρ ὑμᾶς θεοῦ ζήλῳ, ἡρμοσάμην γὰρ ὑμᾶς ἑνὶ ἀνδρὶ παρθένον ἁγνὴν παραστῆσαι τῷ Χριστῷ· φοβοῦμαι δὲ μή πως, ὡς ὁ ὄφις ἐξηπάτησεν Εὕαν ἐν τῇ πανουργίᾳ αὐτοῦ, φθαρῇ τὰ νοήματα ὑμῶν ἀπὸ τῆς ἁπλότητος [καὶ τῆς ἁγνότητος] τῆς εἰς τὸν Χριστόν

For I am jealous over you with a godly jealousy, because I have promised you in marriage to one husband—to present a pure virgin to Christ. But I fear that, as the serpent deceived Eve by his cunning, your minds may be seduced from a complete and pure devotion to Christ.

Here Paul explicitly refers to the marriage relationship between Christ and his people. Paul has betrothed (ἡρμοσάμην) the Corinthians to *one husband*, to whom he presents them as *a pure virgin* (παρθένον ἁγνὴν). While the verb ἁρμόζω does not necessarily imply a marriage betrothal,[79] and while ἑνὶ ἀνδρὶ can mean *to one man* rather than *to one husband*, the presentation of a *virgin* seals the matter: Paul is referring to marriage. The Corinthians—as God's people—are pictured metaphorically as the bride of Christ.

Two interesting issues arise from this text. First, the marriage between Christ and the Corinthians appears to be future-oriented, since Paul regards his work as that of *betrothing* the Corinthians to Christ. The idea of betrothal, by its nature, means that the marriage has not yet been consummated.

But this matter may not be as simple as it seems. If the aorist indicative

---

bit the nature of this union: real, and comparable with a sexual union in marriage, but more complex, for Christ and the Holy Spirit both play a role in it'; Burger, *Being in Christ*, 240.

79. BDAG, 132.

ἡρμοσάμην is translated *I have promised you in marriage*, the word *have* implies that the state of betrothal is current at the time of speaking, so that the promise has been made but not yet fulfilled. This translation, however, is not necessarily best. The aorist can just as easily be translated *I promised you in marriage*, eliminating the word *have* and thus removing the implication that the betrothal is current at the time of speaking (so NIV, ESV). If translated in this way, Paul may well refer to a past betrothal that has *already* been consummated.[80] The sense is that Paul had prepared the Corinthians to be joined to Christ in marital union, and having become believers they were henceforth united to him.[81] This understanding allows harmonization of this passage with others that employ the marriage metaphor as a present reality.

The second point of interest is what 11:3 contributes to our understanding of union with Christ. Paul fears that the Corinthians might be deceived—like the archetypal wife, Eve—becoming corrupted in their minds and turning away from pure devotion to Christ. It would seem, then, that turning away from devotion to Christ is an act of marital unfaithfulness. This fact underscores the spiritual reality of union with Christ: to be unfaithful in marriage is to swerve in spiritual devotion, perhaps being tempted by idols or led astray by false teachers. Such a notion should not surprise us given the common Old Testament theme of God's people—regarded as God's bride—repeatedly committing adultery with other gods.[82]

It might be argued, however, that 11:3 undermines our reading of 11:2, preferring the understanding of a current betrothal and future marriage. This argument would relate Paul's fear of the Corinthians' lack of devotion as spoiling their virginity before marriage. Certainly, this reading is coherent and seems, on one level, quite natural. It is equally natural, however, to regard their lack of devotion as affecting their marriage relationship—not necessarily their virginity—and the reference to Eve offers

---

80. It is standard among commentators to posit that consummation occurs at the parousia, but there is no evidence in the context that hints at this, let alone demands it. See, for example, Hughes, *2 Corinthians*, 374; Martin, *2 Corinthians*, 333.

81. Contra Burger: 'In conclusion, Christ and the church are portrayed here as a betrothed couple not married yet, awaiting their marriage when Christ comes again. Consequently, the moment of union receives an eschatological flavour'; Burger, *Being in Christ*, 241.

82. The marriage metaphor in the Old Testament will be explored in ch. 12.

some support to this reading. Being the prototypical wife, Eve was already united to her husband (Gen. 2:18–25) by the time she was deceived by the serpent (Gen. 3). As 3:12–16 indicates, this deception led to a strained relationship between Eve and her husband. Consequently, Paul may be drawing on these wider narratival matters in Genesis to demonstrate that deception and corruption lead to difficulties in marriage. The Corinthians are to avoid such things in order to remain devoted to Christ, their husband.

Eph 5:22–32 αἱ γυναῖκες τοῖς ἰδίοις ἀνδράσιν ὡς τῷ κυρίῳ, ²³ὅτι ἀνήρ ἐστιν κεφαλὴ τῆς γυναικὸς ὡς καὶ ὁ Χριστὸς κεφαλὴ τῆς ἐκκλησίας, αὐτὸς σωτὴρ τοῦ σώματος· ²⁴ἀλλὰ ὡς ἡ ἐκκλησία ὑποτάσσεται τῷ Χριστῷ, οὕτως καὶ αἱ γυναῖκες τοῖς ἀνδράσιν ἐν παντί. ²⁵Οἱ ἄνδρες, ἀγαπᾶτε τὰς γυναῖκας, καθὼς καὶ ὁ Χριστὸς ἠγάπησεν τὴν ἐκκλησίαν καὶ ἑαυτὸν παρέδωκεν ὑπὲρ αὐτῆς, ²⁶ἵνα αὐτὴν ἁγιάσῃ καθαρίσας τῷ λουτρῷ τοῦ ὕδατος ἐν ῥήματι, ²⁷ἵνα παραστήσῃ αὐτὸς ἑαυτῷ ἔνδοξον τὴν ἐκκλησίαν, μὴ ἔχουσαν σπίλον ἢ ῥυτίδα ἤ τι τῶν τοιούτων, ἀλλ᾽ ἵνα ᾖ ἁγία καὶ ἄμωμος. ²⁸οὕτως ὀφείλουσιν [καὶ] οἱ ἄνδρες ἀγαπᾶν τὰς ἑαυτῶν γυναῖκας ὡς τὰ ἑαυτῶν σώματα. ὁ ἀγαπῶν τὴν ἑαυτοῦ γυναῖκα ἑαυτὸν ἀγαπᾷ. ²⁹Οὐδεὶς γάρ ποτε τὴν ἑαυτοῦ σάρκα ἐμίσησεν ἀλλὰ ἐκτρέφει καὶ θάλπει αὐτήν, καθὼς καὶ ὁ Χριστὸς τὴν ἐκκλησίαν, ³⁰ὅτι μέλη ἐσμὲν τοῦ σώματος αὐτοῦ. ³¹ἀντὶ τούτου καταλείψει ἄνθρωπος [τὸν] πατέρα καὶ [τὴν] μητέρα καὶ προσκολληθήσεται πρὸς τὴν γυναῖκα αὐτοῦ, καὶ ἔσονται οἱ δύο εἰς σάρκα μίαν. ³²τὸ μυστήριον τοῦτο μέγα ἐστίν· ἐγὼ δὲ λέγω εἰς Χριστὸν καὶ εἰς τὴν ἐκκλησίαν.

²²Wives, submit to your own husbands as to the Lord, ²³for the husband is head of the wife as also Christ is head of the church. He is the Savior of the body. ²⁴Now as the church submits to Christ, so wives are to submit to their husbands in everything. ²⁵Husbands, love your wives, just as Christ loved the church and gave Himself for her, ²⁶to make her holy, cleansing her with the washing of water by the word. ²⁷He did this to present the church to Himself in splendor, without spot or wrinkle or anything like that, but holy and blameless. ²⁸In the same way, husbands are to love their wives as their own bodies. He

who loves his wife loves himself. [29] For no one ever hates his own flesh but provides and cares for it, just as Christ does for the church, [30] since we are members of His body.

[31] For this reason a man will leave
his father and mother
and be joined to his wife,
and the two will become one flesh.

[32] This mystery is profound, but I am talking about Christ and the church.

In this extended discussion about husbands and wives, Paul offers the most explicit application of the metaphor of marriage to the relationship of Christ to his church. Indeed, the application of the metaphor is so strong that Paul uses it to model proper relations between a husband and wife rather than the other way around. The husband is the head of the wife as Christ is the head of the church (5:23); the church submits to Christ, and wives are to do likewise toward their husbands (5:24); husbands are to love their wives in the same way that Christ loved the church (5:25); husbands are to love their wives as their own bodies, as Christ does the church (5:29); a man will leave his father and mother, be joined to his wife, and become one flesh with her — and this mystery refers to Christ and his church (5:32).

There is much here of interest, but we will restrict our investigation to the ways in which the marriage metaphor informs our understanding of union with Christ. There can be no doubt that Paul metaphorically designates the relationship between Christ and the church as marriage. Lest it be argued that 5:22–30 merely depicts the relationship between Christ and the church as an illustration for husband–wife relations without explicitly denoting the church as the wife of Christ or Christ as her husband, 5:30–31 leave no room for doubt. Quoting Genesis 2:24 in 5:30, Paul clarifies in 5:32 he is talking about Christ and the church.[83] It is to this relationship that Genesis 2:24 is applied, indicating that Christ

---

83. 'With a quotation of Gen 2:24 Paul situates marital unity within God's scriptural plan of creation as part of the great mystery regarding Christ and the church'; John Paul Heil, *Ephesians: Empowerment to Walk in Love for the Unity of All in Christ* (Studies in Biblical Literature 13; Atlanta: Society of Biblical Literature, 2007), 251.

is joined to his church as his wife, and the two are 'one flesh'.[84] Son summarizes the network of connections as follows:

> A certain typological comparison exists between the two relationships and Gen. 2:24, that is, the marriage relationship between Adam and Eve. As mathematical ratios it may be expressed as follows: Husband/wife (human marriage) = Christ/church (divine marriage) = Adam/Eve (original marriage). The human marriage relationship between husband and wife is explained in the framework of the divine union between Christ and the church, and both are grounded in the 'one flesh' marriage union between Adam and Eve constituted in Gen. 2:24.[85]

Consequently, 5:22–30 may be explored with this in mind, knowing that Paul truly regards Christ as husband and the church as wife. Before doing so, however, we must recognize the contribution of 5:30–31 toward our understanding of union with Christ. The metaphorical joining of husband and wife and their becoming one flesh indicate a profound union between Christ and the church. The metaphor is personal and implies a bond of intimacy that goes well beyond the other metaphors that Paul uses in portraying union with Christ. Indeed, the metaphor has a range of implications, most of which will not be explored here. As for the immediate implications of this one-flesh union, Paul draws out several points in 5:22–30.

First, the intimate bond of the marriage union does not erase the distinctions between Christ and his bride. Rather than some vague mysticism, in which the identity of believers is dissipated through union with the divine, we see here that husband and wife are clearly distinguished—though united—and each has particular roles within the relationship.

Second, the church appropriately submits to Christ, her head (5:22–24). Thus, their one-flesh union does not undermine the lordship of Christ, nor does it allow the church to indulge in disobedience. Submission is the church's only activity mentioned in the passage, which highlights both the significance of submission for the life of the church and

---

84. So Köstenberger, 'Thus, in one sense, Paul envisions Christ and his church as one person, inextricably united in this world, just like husband and wife (cf. Gen 2:24).' Andreas J. Köstenberger, 'The Mystery of Christ and the Church: Head and Body, "One Flesh"', *TJ* 12 (1991): 91.

85. Son, *Corporate Elements*, 155–56.

her passivity in relation to the other aspects of the marriage relationship, as Christ takes responsibility for her.

Third, the marriage is prepared, instigated, and sustained by Christ, with the wife identified as the recipient of his care. Christ is the Saviour of the body (5:23), having loved her and given himself for her (5:25). He makes her holy in order to present her to himself without blemish (5:26–27). He sustains her through provision and care (5:29). All of this underscores the reality that the one-flesh union with Christ is instigated by grace; it is not a union that believers 'achieve' or approach through mystical disciplines or spiritual advancement. The church is entirely the beneficiary of Christ's advances toward her.

These details demonstrate the importance of the marriage metaphor for understanding Paul's conception of the church's union with Christ. With the possible exception of the body metaphor, no other metaphor of union is exploited to this level of detail. Paul presses the marriage metaphor in such a way that several aspects of union with Christ are brought to light or at least sharpened. The metaphor confirms that union with Christ does not dissolve identity or distinction between Christ and the church, nor does it undermine Christ's lordship over the church. The metaphor explicates the assertive and proactive role of Christ in establishing this union and thus unveils it as a work of grace.

7.4.1 MARRIAGE MATTERS

There are only (at most) four occasions in which Paul explicitly draws on the metaphor of marriage to depict the relationship between Christ and his people. The paucity of occurrences should not, however, diminish the importance of the metaphor. Indeed, Paul's use of the metaphor is one of the most profound and informative ways in which he depicts union with Christ. He presses the metaphor for details in a way that is rarely seen with other metaphors, and it provides a significant theological foundation for Paul's ethical thinking.

The metaphor is personal because of the intimate nature of the one-flesh union of marriage. This means that union with Christ is not simply a general spiritual reality that designates believers as part of Christ's domain. While living under his domain is no doubt part of what it means to be united to Christ, the metaphor of marriage provides further nuance: the church is intimately and essentially wedded to Christ, to the exclusion of all others.

The metaphor preserves the identity of Christ as well as that of the church, since clearly within the marriage union, each occupies specific roles pertaining to husband and wife respectively.[86] In this way, the metaphor guards against some incorrect theories about union with Christ, particularly those related to mysticism that view believers as absorbed into the divine essence. The church does not dissipate in a spiritual sea of divinity, indistinguishable from her Lord and without proper identity. On the contrary, the church is identified as the bride of Christ, submitting to him and engaging in holy devotion. Furthermore, believers do not undergo 'the eradication of the individual's racial, social, and gender distinctives'.[87]

The metaphor has profound significance for the life of the church. It underpins ethical constraints related to sexual immorality, prohibits spiritual unfaithfulness, and requires the submission of the church to her husband. The marriage relationship also underscores the grace with which union with Christ is established, as Christ performs his husbandly duties in saving, preparing, and caring for his bride.

7.5 NEW CLOTHING

The final metaphor to be explored in this chapter has to do with *putting on Christ*. The concept metaphorically depicts Christ as clothing that adorns believers and that believers are exhorted to wear. The key lexical item for this metaphor is ἐνδύω, *put on*, the standard verb used for clothing oneself or another. It also has a metaphorical use, commonly referring to 'the taking on of characteristics, virtues, intentions, etc.'[88]

---

86. 'Husband and wife remain distinct individuals while they are, at the same time, one corporate body in marriage. The "one body" union does not eliminate their individual distinctions.... In the same manner, believers maintain their individuality when they form a corporate body with others and with Christ' (ibid., 168).

87. Ibid. 'Those who hold this view often appeal to Gal. 3:27–28.... Paul, however, does not teach in this passage that incorporation into Christ abrogates one's racial, social, and gender distinctives. He is primarily concerned here with the corporate unity of all believers in Christ which in some respects transcends and transforms but does not eradicate their racial, social, and gender distinctions.'

88. BDAG, 333–34.

At first glance, this metaphor stands apart from the others explored above in that it tends to imply that believers must make a choice *to put on Christ.* This is not the 'choice' of conversion to Christ but refers to the experience of the Christian life: those who are already regarded as being in union with Christ are exhorted *to put on Christ.* The other metaphors, by contrast, refer simply to a spiritual reality that is not dependent on believers' choices or actions. Believers are members of Christ's body; they are part of the temple or building of Christ; they are married to Christ in a one-flesh relationship. These are all nonnegotiable facets of Christian existence — they simply *are.* One question to be addressed, therefore, is whether the clothing metaphor really points to union with Christ or some other thing.

A second distinguishing feature, related to the first, concerns the way in which clothing differs from body, temple, building, and marriage. These latter metaphors imply permanence, while the clothing metaphor (unless understood counterintuitively) does not inherently imply as much — clothes can be changed after all. Furthermore, the other metaphors convey at their core the concept of being joined together with Christ in some manner. To be part of Christ's body means that a believer is connected to him as a member. To form part of the building of which Christ is the cornerstone means that the believer cannot be separated from the foundation of Christ without destroying the edifice. To be married to Christ entails a one-flesh union that will last forever. The metaphor of clothing, however, does not necessarily imply the notion of joining together with Christ since clothing is merely external apparel and is not 'joined' to its wearer. With these issues in mind, we turn now to the relevant passages.

Rom 13:12–14 ἡ νὺξ προέκοψεν, ἡ δὲ ἡμέρα ἤγγικεν. ἀποθώμεθα οὖν τὰ ἔργα τοῦ σκότους, **ἐνδυσώμεθα** [δὲ] τὰ ὅπλα τοῦ φωτός. ὡς ἐν ἡμέρᾳ εὐσχημόνως περιπατήσωμεν, μὴ κώμοις καὶ μέθαις, μὴ κοίταις καὶ ἀσελγείαις, μὴ ἔριδι καὶ ζήλῳ, ἀλλὰ **ἐνδύσασθε** τὸν κύριον Ἰησοῦν Χριστὸν καὶ τῆς σαρκὸς πρόνοιαν μὴ ποιεῖσθε εἰς ἐπιθυμίας

The night is nearly over, and the daylight is near, so let us discard the deeds of darkness and **put on** *the armor of light. Let us walk with decency, as in the daylight: not in carousing and drunkenness; not in sexual impurity and promiscuity; not in quarreling and jealousy. But* **put on** *the Lord Jesus Christ, and make no plans to satisfy the fleshly desires.*

This ethical passage uses ἐνδύω twice, first with reference to *the armor of light* and then with reference to *the Lord Jesus Christ*. If there is an intended parallel between 13:12 and 13:14, it would seem that *the deeds of darkness* parallels *the fleshly desires*, while *put on the armor of light* parallels *put on the Lord Jesus Christ*.[89] Whether or not the apparent parallel between these two verses is intentional, it appears that the exhortation *to put on Christ* is an ethical injunction. This is derived not only from the ethical nature of the context but from the fact that the exhortation is contrasted with the phrase *make no plans to satisfy the fleshly desires*; this suggests that putting on Christ offers an alternative lifestyle.

As such, it is not clear that this reference contributes to the theme of union with Christ since it does not seem to address spiritual union with him. Having said this, however, it is possible that there are two steps to Paul's logic, only one of which is ethical in nature. If there is a kind of shorthand at work, Paul may intend to convey the idea of union with Christ through the phrase *put on the Lord Jesus Christ* and assume the ethical corollaries that flow from such union. In other words, the ethical implications of union with Christ are of direct importance in this ethical context, even though the phrase itself denotes spiritual union. This is Kim's conclusion, who suggests that 'Paul probably means that as clothes, when put on, become a dominant part of ourselves, so Christ, when put on, becomes an essential part of the believer's nature, from which godly conduct is to spring'.[90]

1 Cor 15:51–54 ἰδοὺ μυστήριον ὑμῖν λέγω· πάντες οὐ κοιμηθησόμεθα, πάντες δὲ ἀλλαγησόμεθα, [52] ἐν ἀτόμῳ, ἐν ῥιπῇ ὀφθαλμοῦ, ἐν τῇ ἐσχάτῃ σάλπιγγι· σαλπίσει γὰρ καὶ οἱ νεκροὶ ἐγερθήσονται ἄφθαρτοι καὶ ἡμεῖς ἀλλαγησόμεθα. [53] Δεῖ γὰρ τὸ φθαρτὸν τοῦτο **ἐνδύσασθαι** ἀφθαρσίαν καὶ τὸ θνητὸν τοῦτο **ἐνδύσασθαι** ἀθανασίαν. [54] ὅταν δὲ τὸ φθαρτὸν τοῦτο **ἐνδύσηται** ἀφθαρσίαν καὶ τὸ θνητὸν τοῦτο **ἐνδύσηται** ἀθανασίαν, τότε γενήσεται ὁ λόγος ὁ γεγραμμένος· *κατεπόθη ὁ θάνατος εἰς νῖκος*

---

89. The latter phrase interprets the former, according to Cranfield; Cranfield, *Romans*, 2:688.

90. Jung Hoon Kim, *The Significance of Clothing Imagery in the Pauline Corpus* (JSNTSup 268; London: T&T Clark, 2004), 139.

Listen! I am telling you a mystery:
We will not all fall asleep,
but we will all be changed,
[52]in a moment, in the blink of an eye,
at the last trumpet.
For the trumpet will sound,
and the dead will be raised incorruptible,
and we will be changed.

*[53]For this corruptible must **be clothed***
with incorruptibility,
*and this mortal must **be clothed***
with immortality.

*[54]When this corruptible **is clothed***
with incorruptibility,
*and this mortal **is clothed***
with immortality,
then the saying that is written will take place:
Death has been swallowed up in victory.

In this remarkable passage about the resurrection of believers on the last day, the clothing metaphor refers to the transformation that believers will undergo: what is corruptible will be clothed with incorruptibility; what is mortal will be clothed with immortality. The clothing metaphor, therefore, refers to a future condition rather than the present, and to a state of affairs rather than an ethical injunction.

It is clear that the item of clothing here is not Christ, but *incorruptibility* and *immortality*, which raises the question as to whether union with Christ is in view or whether the metaphor is simply employed to convey a changed anatomical reality. While the metaphor here does not seem to connect to union with Christ directly, the wider context suggests that the notion of union is at least in the background. In 15:49 we read, *And just as we have borne the image of the man made of dust, we will also bear the image of the heavenly man.*[91] The heavenly man refers to Christ, in

---

91. Interestingly, Fee regards the verb ἐφορέσαμεν (*we have borne*) in 15:49 as 'a metaphor for putting on clothing'; Fee, *1 Corinthians*, 794.

contrast to Adam, the man made of dust. The notion of bearing *the image of the heavenly man* is at least suggestive of union with Christ, though it is unusual language for the concept.

Insofar as *incorruptibility* and *immortality* pertain to the image of the heavenly man, so we may conclude that being clothed with these qualities is a result of bearing the image of the heavenly man, Christ.[92] If bearing Christ's image can be shown to refer to (or imply?) union with Christ, then it follows that being clothed with incorruptibility and immortality is an outworking of this union with him.

2 Cor 5:1–4 οἴδαμεν γὰρ ὅτι ἐὰν ἡ ἐπίγειος ἡμῶν οἰκία τοῦ σκήνους καταλυθῇ, οἰκοδομὴν ἐκ θεοῦ ἔχομεν, οἰκίαν ἀχειροποίητον αἰώνιον ἐν τοῖς οὐρανοῖς. ²καὶ γὰρ ἐν τούτῳ στενάζομεν τὸ οἰκητήριον ἡμῶν τὸ ἐξ οὐρανοῦ ἐπενδύσασθαι ἐπιποθοῦντες, ³εἴ γε καὶ **ἐκδυσάμενοι** οὐ γυμνοὶ εὑρεθησόμεθα. ⁴καὶ γὰρ οἱ ὄντες ἐν τῷ σκήνει στενάζομεν βαρούμενοι, ἐφ᾽ ᾧ οὐ θέλομεν **ἐκδύσασθαι** ἀλλ᾽ **ἐπενδύσασθαι**, ἵνα καταποθῇ τὸ θνητὸν ὑπὸ τῆς ζωῆς

*For we know that if our temporary, earthly dwelling is destroyed, we have a building from God, an eternal dwelling in the heavens, not made with hands. ²Indeed, we groan in this body, desiring to put on our dwelling from heaven, ³since, when we are **clothed**, we will not be found naked. ⁴Indeed, we groan while we are in this tent, burdened as we are, because we do not want **to be unclothed** but **clothed**, so that mortality may be swallowed up by life.*

As with the previous passage, here the clothing metaphor refers to the future transformation to an immortal body.[93] That the resurrection body is in view here is less transparent than in 1 Corinthians 15:51–54, but it is evident by the progressively clearer set of contrasts between *our temporary, earthly dwelling* and *an eternal dwelling in the heavens*; *this body* and *our*

---

92. Kim approximates this; 'First of all, the imagery connotes that the present body, which is dominated by the fallen Adamic physicality, will be replaced by the resurrection body, which is pervaded by the second Adamic (that is, the risen Christ's) spirituality (v. 49)'; Kim, *Clothing Imagery*, 208–9.

93. Kim, *Clothing Imagery*, 221.

dwelling from heaven; *mortality* and *life*. The final contrast confirms that Paul has in mind the same transformation that is so elegantly described in 15:54—the mortal becomes immortal.

The phrase *when we are clothed* (5:3) parallels *our dwelling from heaven* (5:2) and *clothed* parallels *life* (5:4). This indicates that the metaphor of clothing again refers to the resurrection body; being *naked* is to be *in this body* (5:3).[94] It is unclear, however, whether union with Christ is to be implied by, or is in the background to, these images; the wider context does not suggest as much, unlike 1 Corinthians 15 above. While we might suppose from a wider understanding of Paul that resurrection and resurrection bodies are products of participation with Christ, the clothing metaphor here does not explicitly inform this understanding.

Gal 3:26–27 πάντες γὰρ υἱοὶ θεοῦ ἐστε διὰ τῆς πίστεως ἐν Χριστῷ Ἰησοῦ· ὅσοι γὰρ εἰς Χριστὸν ἐβαπτίσθητε, Χριστὸν **ἐνεδύσασθε**

*For you are all sons of God through faith in Christ Jesus. For as many of you as have been baptized into Christ have **put on** Christ like a garment.*

The context here has to do with the status of believers as children of God, as people baptized into Christ. These things refer to spiritual realities that pertain to all believers after their conversion; in fact, being *baptized into Christ* arguably refers to conversion.[95] Consequently, putting on Christ is not here an exhortation but a statement of fact: all who have been baptized into Christ have put on Christ. This is reflected in the language, which employs an aorist indicative (ἐνεδύσασθε), whereas Romans 13:14 has an imperative (ἐνδύσασθε).[96]

This example overrides some of the assumptions about the clothing metaphor that were raised in the introduction to this section. Here, to

---

94. Martin takes the image of being naked (v.3) to refer to an intermediate state between death and the parousia, but this is unconvincing. There is an inverse parallelism in vv.2–3: A B B′ A′, in which A *this body* parallels A′ *naked*, while B *our dwelling from heaven* parallels B′ *clothed*. See Martin, *2 Corinthians*, 105–6.

95. See ch. 10 (§10.17).

96. The forms are almost identical, but the augment in ἐνεδύσασθε reveals its indicative mood.

put on Christ does not imply impermanence; since it is linked to being baptized into Christ, which is a once-for-all event, the metaphor refers to a permanent spiritual reality. In addition, there is no 'choice' implied by the use of the metaphor here. Believers are not at liberty to make a decision about whether or not they will put on Christ. Rather, the metaphor is a statement of fact — a nonnegotiable corollary of being baptized into Christ.

In other words, this use of the clothing metaphor quite possibly refers to union with Christ.[97] In fact, with reference to this example, Burger declares that 'the image of clothing makes clear the union between Christ and the believer who is in Christ'.[98] The permanence of its meaning here, its connectedness to baptism, and its place within a context concerned with the spiritual status of believers are features consistent with union.[99]

> Col 3:9–10 μὴ ψεύδεσθε εἰς ἀλλήλους, ἀπεκδυσάμενοι τὸν παλαιὸν ἄνθρωπον σὺν ταῖς πράξεσιν αὐτοῦ καὶ **ἐνδυσάμενοι** τὸν νέον τὸν ἀνακαινούμενον εἰς ἐπίγνωσιν κατ' εἰκόνα τοῦ κτίσαντος αὐτόν
>
> *Do not lie to one another, since you have put off the old self with its practices and have **put on** the new self. You are being renewed in knowledge according to the image of your Creator.*

This example of the clothing metaphor is different again. While found in an ethical context similar to Romans 13:12–14, the phrase does not issue an exhortation as it does there, nor does it refer to the putting on of Christ, but *the new self*. This occurrence is similar to Galatians 3:26 (above) in the way that it expresses a permanent reality rather than an exhortation that implies 'choice'. Yet it differs from Galatians 3:26 in that the permanent spiritual reality referred to involves putting on *the new self*, not Christ.

---

97. 'Paul's "clothed yourselves with Christ" conveys the sense of sharing Christ's nature as a result of being united to Christ, since the image of outer clothing in Scripture most frequently refers to inner transformation.' William J. Dumbrell, *Galatians: A New Covenant Commentary* (Blackwood, South Australia: New Creation Publications, 2006), 64.

98. Burger, *Being in Christ*, 243.

99. So Kim, 'All of these observations support our opinion that the putting-on-Christ imagery in Gal. 3.27 symbolizes a believer's baptismal union with Christ'; Kim, *Clothing Imagery*, 116.

The first question to be resolved is who *the new self* is. The contrast with *the old self* does not settle the matter, since *the old self* might be contrasted to Christ himself or to a believer who has been reconstituted in Christ. However, the phrase that indicates that this new self is being *renewed in knowledge according to the image of your Creator* counts against reading the new self as Christ.[100] Though Christ is elsewhere described as the image of God (Col 1:15), the language of *being renewed* (ἀνακαινούμενον) favours the reading that regards *the new self* as the believer, who has a new life in Christ.

In context, this new self is best understood in relation to 3:3: *For you have died, and your life is hidden with the Messiah in God.* The *old self* has spiritually died, and the *new self* lives with Christ. This new life with Christ forms the basis for Paul's following ethical appeal (3:5–10), beginning with *Therefore, put to death what belongs to your worldly nature* (3:5). Thus, the ethical context in which 3:9–10 occurs is grounded on the believers' union with Christ.[101]

Putting these elements together, we may conclude that the phrase *put on the new self* in Colossians 3:10 does not speak directly of believers' union with Christ, but it refers to the new life that exists in union with him. In this way, the ethical injunctions that are appropriate for the new life arise from the spiritual reality of being hid with Christ.

Col 3:12 ἐνδύσασθε οὖν, ὡς ἐκλεκτοὶ τοῦ θεοῦ ἅγιοι καὶ ἠγαπημένοι, σπλάγχνα οἰκτιρμοῦ χρηστότητα ταπεινοφροσύνην πραΰτητα μακροθυμίαν

*Therefore, God's chosen ones, holy and loved, **put on** heartfelt compassion, kindness, humility, gentleness, and patience.*

Following the previous section on *putting on the new self,* this occurrence of the metaphor demonstrates its flexibility, even within the space of a few verses. As demonstrated above, *put on the new self* (3:10) refers to

---

100. So Kim, "'The new man", however, cannot be directly equated with Christ himself. If such were the case, we would have to say that Christ (= the new man) has been renewed after his own model, which does not make sense': Kim, *Clothing Imagery*, 163.

101. 'The new humanity is the solidarity of those who are incorporated into, and hence patterned on, the Messiah who is himself the true Man.... At last, in Christ, human beings can be what God intended them to be.' Wright, *Colossians and Philemon*, 138.

the new life of the believer, and it is with respect to this new reality that
ethical injunctions follow. The exhortation evident in 3:12 is one such
example of the ethical outworking of the new life in Christ. As God's chosen ones—as his people—believers are to *put on* compassion, kindness,
humility, gentleness, and patience.

As with Romans 13:12, the exhortation *to put on* such characteristics
implies a 'choice' that believers must make with respect to the Christian life.
While such an action is required of believers (and therefore is not really subject
to 'choice' in one sense), nevertheless the nature of ethical injunctions is such
that believers must decide to act appropriately rather than in ways contrary to
their status as the people of God.

It is difficult to discern how such an injunction might relate to the
concept of union with Christ, except through the two-step logic suggested
above, in which ethical injunctions are the corollaries of a preexisting
union with Christ. Indeed, there is some hint of this in the verse that
completes the sentence begun in 3:12: *accepting one another and forgiving
one another if anyone has a complaint against another. Just as the Lord has
forgiven you, so you must also forgive* (3:13). Here we see that the forgiveness
that believers are to extend to one another is inspired by the forgiveness
that the Lord has extended to believers. Since the Lord has forgiven them,
they are to be characterized by forgiveness.

Admittedly, this inspiration to forgiveness comes through *modeling*
rather than union with Christ per se. Nevertheless, 3:13 provides an example in which ethical behaviour is based on believers' relationship with the
Lord.[102] Furthermore, it might be argued that the characteristics listed
in 3:12—compassion, kindness, humility, gentleness, and patience—are
likewise derived from the Lord as a model for behaviour.

Eph 4:20–24 ὑμεῖς δὲ οὐχ οὕτως ἐμάθετε τὸν Χριστόν, [21]εἴ γε
αὐτὸν ἠκούσατε καὶ ἐν αὐτῷ ἐδιδάχθητε, καθώς ἐστιν ἀλήθεια
ἐν τῷ Ἰησοῦ, [22]ἀποθέσθαι ὑμᾶς κατὰ τὴν προτέραν ἀναστροφὴν
τὸν παλαιὸν ἄνθρωπον τὸν φθειρόμενον κατὰ τὰς ἐπιθυμίας
τῆς ἀπάτης, [23]ἀνανεοῦσθαι δὲ τῷ πνεύματι τοῦ νοὸς ὑμῶν [24]καὶ

---

102. 'The one who is in Christ will demonstrate what it means to be renewed in Christ
when problems and complaints arise in the body; then graciousness toward the other appears';
Thompson, *Colossians and Philemon*, 84.

ἐνδύσασθαι τὸν καινὸν ἄνθρωπον τὸν κατὰ θεὸν κτισθέντα ἐν δικαιοσύνῃ καὶ ὁσιότητι τῆς ἀληθείας

*But that is not how you learned about the Messiah, [21]assuming you heard about Him and were taught by Him, because the truth is in Jesus, [22]you took off your former way of life, the old self that is corrupted by deceitful desires; [23]you are being renewed in the spirit of your minds; [24]you **put on** the new self, the one created according to God's likeness in righteousness and purity of the truth.*

At first glance, this example appears identical to Colossians 3:9, in which the phrase *put on the new self* refers to an existing spiritual reality of the new life in Christ. The reality, however, is more complex. While the translation offered above—*you put on the new self*—implies a prior fact of existence, this is probably not the best translation. The infinitive ἐνδύσασθαι occurs within a series of infinitives following the indicative ἐδιδάχθητε (*you were taught*) in 4:21. The structure is as follows: *you were to taught* (ἐδιδάχθητε) *by him* (4:21) *to put off* (ἀποθέσθαι) *your old self* (4:22), *to be renewed* (ἀνανεοῦσθαι) *in the spirit of your minds* (4:23), and *to put on* (ἐνδύσασθαι) *the new self* (4:24). This structure consequently demonstrates that *to put on the new self* constitutes part of the teaching of Christ to believers. They are taught to put off the old, to be renewed, and to put on the new.

Since, then, 4:24 deals with content that is taught by Christ for the right behaviour of believers, it does not refer to a preexisting state in which believers have already decisively put on the new self. In this way, 4:24 differs from Colossians 3:9, which employs the phrase *put on the new self* to refer to the spiritual reality of the new life that believers enjoy in Christ. This spiritual reality, however, is not far from view in 4:24, since its final clause refers to this new self as *the one created according to God's likeness in righteousness and purity of the truth* (4:24). As such, we see that the new self itself is a created preexisting reality, and the first part of 4:24 instructs believers to put on this new man. In other words, the ethical injunction requires believers to *be* what they already *are*.[103] They are to put on the new self, who already exists through the work of God.

---

103. Schnackenburg, *Ephesians*, 201.

This example, therefore, expresses an ethical injunction — unlike Colossians 3:9 — but it is an injunction that involves the application of a preexisting created reality. Believers are to be what they already are; they are to behave in a way that is consistent with who they are in Christ.

Eph 6:10 τοῦ λοιποῦ, ἐνδυναμοῦσθε ἐν κυρίῳ καὶ ἐν τῷ κράτει τῆς ἰσχύος αὐτοῦ. ἐνδύσασθε τὴν πανοπλίαν τοῦ θεοῦ πρὸς τὸ δύνασθαι ὑμᾶς στῆναι πρὸς τὰς μεθοδείας τοῦ διαβόλου

Finally, be strengthened by the Lord and by His vast strength. **Put on the full armor of God so that you can stand against the tactics of the Devil.**

Once again, this use of the clothing metaphor is found in connection with an ethical injunction. While the notion of putting on the full armour of God is more ambiguous than previous examples, it is clear from the context that the injunction has to do with Christian living; by putting on the armour of God, believers are enabled to *stand against the tactics of the Devil*. Being an injunction, this occurrence implies the kind of 'choice' that has been observed in other examples above and does not refer to a preexisting state of any kind.

In terms of union with Christ, this use of the metaphor hints at a close association with the Lord, since believers are to be *strengthened by the Lord* (6:10) and are to *put on the full armor of God* (6:11). It is God's armour that believers put on,[104] which is presumably how they will be strengthened by the Lord. The sharing of his armour implies a sense of participation or union between believers and the Lord, though the nature of this cannot be pressed.

7.5.1 PUTTING ON LANGUAGE

It is evident from the analysis above that the clothing metaphor is capable of three main uses. The first is its use in ethical contexts, in which the language of *putting on* refers to the adoption of certain behavioural characteristics. Believers are to 'choose' to put on humility, gentleness, patience, as well as the *new self* and Jesus Christ. Such ethical usage does not directly

---

104. T. Y. Neufeld, *Put on the Armour of God: The Divine Warrior from Isaiah to Ephesians* (Sheffield: Sheffield Academic, 1997), 118.

address the concept of union with Christ, though it arguably arises from such union.

The second main use of the clothing metaphor is to refer to the transformation of mortal bodies into immortal at the parousia. This is a future, rather than current, reality, and it arises from bearing the image of Christ. As Kim states, 'Paul's clothing imagery in 1 Cor. 15.49, 50, 51–54 and 2 Cor. 5.1–4 is associated with his strong assurance that believers will experience a great change in their existence at the parousia.'[105]

The third main use of the clothing metaphor has to do with the permanent (and current) spiritual state of believers. Believers have put on Christ, and this is apparently coincident with their baptism with Christ; it refers to the reality of their conversion. For Tannehill, 'the ideas of dying and rising with Christ and of stripping off the old man and putting on the new man have, in fact, the same significance for the author'.[106] As such, the metaphor in this usage does not imply a 'choice' or decision regarding their conduct but conveys a permanent reality. It is also evident that, at least in some cases, this use of the metaphor conveys union with Christ.

It is difficult to press the clothing metaphor as it applies to Christ. In what sense do believers 'wear' Christ? Paul does not elaborate with specifics, which is part of the power, but also the difficulty, of metaphor. Wikenhauser, however, offers a reasonable elucidation of the metaphor as follows:

> The expression 'to put on Christ' is a metaphor in which Christ is compared to a heavenly robe which is ready for all men; by putting on this robe men enter a new world and are enveloped in this new world. The new relationship to Christ is not merely ethical, it is ontological. It is not simply a fresh rule of conduct. The man who 'puts on Christ' gains a share in Christ's being, and this participation produces 'Christ in us', the 'new man'.[107]

While Wikenhauser's elucidations generally fit the evidence adduced above, at no point does Paul explicitly refer to Christ as 'a heavenly robe' or the entering of a new world through 'putting on this robe'. Furthermore,

---

105. Kim, *Clothing Imagery*, 222.
106. Tannehill, *Dying and Rising*, 52.
107. Wikenhauser, *Mysticism*, 32.

while he is correct to affirm that the metaphor is not merely ethical in nature, it is not clear how 'ontological' it is. May we really conclude at this point that the 'man who "puts on Christ" gains a share in Christ's being'? There is no evidence from the textual usage of the metaphor to support such claims.

Wedderburn suggests a different tack. 'Priests, priestesses and worshippers seem often in the ancient world to have been seen and depicted wearing the clothes and insignia of their deities.'[108] He points out that such phenomena did not symbolize deification, but dedication and 'belonging to the one whose garb is worn'.[109] By applying these insights to Paul's language, Wedderburn concludes that 'the Christian who puts on Christ does not thereby become Christ, but does share the character and consecration to God of Christ ... and does belong to Christ ... and is part of that new humanity created by God in Christ.'[110] A problem with this reconstruction, however, is that Paul does not restrict his using of *putting on* language to Christ; he can use it for behavioural characteristics and for the *new self.* Of course it may be argued that such things are the outworking of putting on Christ (as I have suggested at various points), but this nevertheless weakens the likelihood that Paul is drawing on established religious traditions.[111]

We can say with confidence that a believer *has* put on Christ and *is to* put on Christ. In this, two of the three main uses (the resurrection use being excluded) of the clothing metaphor become connected in that it denotes both the permanent spiritual reality of union with Christ[112] and the ongoing ethical requirement to apply this reality to daily existence. The metaphor therefore evokes permanence in some contexts and impermanence in others. It also evokes 'choice', or at least instruction, in some

---

108. A. J. M. Wedderburn, *Baptism and Resurrection: Studies in Pauline Theology against Its Graeco-Roman Background* (WUNT 44; Tübingen: Mohr, 1987), 337.

109. Ibid.

110. Ibid., 338–39.

111. In fact, 'the possession in one's life of the divine qualities and powers characteristic of that deity' is included by the religious traditions cited by Wedderburn, ibid., 337. The difference, however, is that while such divine qualities and powers derive from the deity named upon believers' garments, in Paul's language such qualities and behavioural characteristics are themselves named. It is not simply the case that believers put on Christ and patience is thereby imputed; rather, patience itself is 'put on'.

112. 'There is little doubt that the putting on of Christ basically indicates baptismal union with Christ'; Kim, *Clothing Imagery*, 227.

contexts, and pure statement of fact in others. Finally, as Burger summarizes, the metaphor 'can be used to refer to the resurrection (Corinthians), to the old and new self (Colossians and Ephesians), to virtues (Col 3:12), but also to Christ himself (Gal 3:27; Rom 13:14)'.[113] In conclusion, Kim appears to be correct in interpreting the clothing metaphor as a symbol for union with Christ that entails ethical conformity to Christ; 'he who has entered this state of wearing Christ as if he were a garment (that is, the state of union with Christ) should manifest an ethical change in his practical life.'[114]

7.6 SUMMARY

Paul's metaphorical language is one of his most potent tools for elucidating the spiritual reality of union with Christ. The metaphor of the body of Christ depicts the church as an organic being as each member partakes in Christ and is joined one to another. The metaphor implies union by its very nature. The metaphors of temple and building convey the corporate nature of the church, with the temple depicting the dwelling of God by his Spirit among his people, and the building denoting a structure incorporated into Christ, its foundation. The metaphor of marriage profoundly depicts the church's spiritual union with Christ as a personal and exclusive bond as he saves, prepares, and cares for her, while she submits to his headship. The metaphor of clothing depicts the reality of conversion to Christ as well as its attendant ethical expectations; the believer *has* put on Christ and *is to* put on Christ. It is a symbol for union with Christ that entails conformity to Christ.

CONCLUSION TO PART 2

Part 2 has collated and examined the evidence within Paul's writings that relates to the theme of union with Christ. The starting point for this task was the phrase ἐν Χριστῷ and variations thereupon, including ἐν κυρίῳ and ἐν αὐτῷ. These phrases are interchangeable and are capable of a wide range of meanings, with a preference for instrumental and locative functions.

---

113. Burger, *Being in Christ*, 244.
114. Kim, *Clothing Imagery*, 225.

From there, it was natural to proceed to the phrase εἰς Χριστόν and variations thereupon. While the movement from the preposition ἐν to εἰς does not represent a significant leap from a lexical perspective, nevertheless the latter preposition yields different, though overlapping, results compared to the former preposition. The phrase εἰς Χριστόν most commonly expresses movement toward a goal, and reference and respect. It occasionally generates translations such as *against Christ, until Christ, about Christ,* and *for Christ,* which do not relate to the theme of union with Christ as established by the phrase ἐν Χριστῷ.

After ἐν Χριστῷ and εἰς Χριστόν, we explored the phrase σὺν Χριστῷ, together with its variations. While σύν does not share the lexical range of ἐν or εἰς, nevertheless σὺν Χριστῷ relates to the theme of union with Christ as already established by the other phrases, conveying a sense of participation with Christ.

Then we examined the phrase διὰ Χριστοῦ since the concept of the instrumentality of Christ had already been established through the previous phrases. Since διὰ Χριστοῦ expresses the same notion of instrumentality, this phrase was included among the expressions that denote union with Christ.

Finally, we investigated a range of metaphors for their expression of union with Christ. The metaphors of body, temple and building, marriage, and clothing each contribute to the theme. The body, temple and building metaphors convey the incorporation of God's people, as each member is united to Christ. The metaphor of marriage communicates a spiritual union between Christ and his bride. The clothing metaphor indicates that believers are to be characterized by their union with Christ.

The explorations of part 2 have led to many insights into Paul's thinking, and there is an enormous amount of data — with much detail and nuance — to be processed. The processing of this information is, in part, the burden of part 3. We will draw on the observations of part 2 in order to explore the meaning and significance of Paul's conception of union with Christ and its relationships to the major spheres of Pauline thought.

THEOLOGICAL STUDY

CHAPTER 8

UNION WITH CHRIST AND THE WORK OF CHRIST

8.1 INTRODUCTION

While a plethora of approaches to the theme of union with Christ abound — with its multivariate descriptions, its relative significance debated, and its implications variously conceived — one fact remains constant: in the mind of Paul, union with Christ is inextricably linked to the work of Christ. Part of the burden of this chapter, therefore, is to state the obvious. This will be done, however, in an explicit fashion with reference to the particularities of Paul's language that have been analyzed in earlier parts of this book, while also seeking to uncover the nature of the relationship between the work of Christ and union with Christ.

To begin, Dunn correctly notes that the phrase ἐν Χριστῷ and its related forms take on a relatively objective usage in relation to the work of Christ, 'referring particularly to the redemptive act which has happened "in Christ" or depends on what Christ is yet to do'.[1] Gaffin labels this usage 'the *redemptive-historical* "in Christ"'.[2] This may be distinguished from a more subjective usage that refers to believers as *being* in Christ,[3] which has traditionally been regarded as the mystical element of Paul's

---

1. Dunn, *Paul the Apostle*, 397.
2. Richard B. Gaffin, 'Union with Christ: Some Biblical and Theological Reflections', in *Always Reforming: Explorations in Systematic Theology* (ed. A. T. B. McGowan; Leicester, UK: Apollos, 2006), 275.
3. Dunn, *Paul the Apostle*, 398.

thought. As Wikenhauser states, 'there are texts containing the phrase "in Christ" where he is speaking of Christ as the vehicle of 'God's work'[4] and in which there is no mystical meaning.

Furthermore, Wikenhauser acknowledges the problem that all English-speaking interpreters of Paul encounter, namely, that he 'often wrote "in Christ" in places where we would have expected to read "by Christ"'.[5] On the one hand, this might be dismissed on a linguistic level such that we simply acknowledge that Greek is capable of expressing instrumentality through multiple means, of which the preposition ἐν happens to be favoured by Paul. To ask, then, why Paul says 'in Christ' (woodenly translated) rather than 'by Christ' — when clearly that is meant in some instances — becomes a meaningless question since ἐν Χριστῷ is merely another way to say 'by Christ'.

On the other hand, the apparent instrumentality of ἐν Χριστῷ in several texts could connote a subtle distinction compared to 'by Christ'. It will likely never be known with certainty if that is the case or what that distinction may be. Nevertheless, Wikenhauser suggests that by the instrumental uses of ἐν Χριστῷ Paul evidently 'wished to bring out the point that to some extent Christ was the abode of God's gracious presence, the place where God willed and worked the salvation of men'.[6] In other words, the phrase points not only to the instrumental work of Christ, but also to Christ as the 'location' of God's enacted will. This notion will be explored further in the subsequent chapter on the Trinity, but for now we note its implications for the work of Christ. It means that even 'objective' uses of ἐν Χριστῷ and related language — pertaining to Christ as the vehicle of God's will — are not disconnected from the overarching theme of union. God the Father operates in union with Christ so that the instrumental work of Christ is an expression of their divine communion.

Requiring further consideration with respect to the work of Christ is the way in which believers may partake in his accomplishments. This moves beyond the strictly objective nature of the redemptive-historical

---

4. Wikenhauser, *Mysticism*, 24.

5. Ibid., 25. See also Wedderburn: 'there will seemingly be relatively little difference between these uses of 'in Christ' and those passages where something is done to us 'through Christ', using διά with the genitive'; A. J. M. Wedderburn, 'Some Observations on Paul's Use of the Phrases "In Christ" and "With Christ"', *JSNT* 25 (1985): 90.

6. Wikenhauser, *Mysticism*, 25.

work of Christ to what Gaffin describes as 'the *existential*, or perhaps better, *applicatory* "in Christ"', which refers to 'union in the actual possession or application of salvation'.[7] Calvin understood this applicatory 'in Christ' to be essential for salvation: 'First, we must understand that as long as Christ remains outside of us, and we are separated from him, all that he has suffered and done for the salvation of the human race remains useless and of no value for us.'[8] While the redemptive-historical (objective) 'in Christ' language apparently reveals something of the Father's union with Christ, this existential or applicatory 'in Christ' language speaks to the union that believers share with him.

In order to address these and other matters, it is necessary first to turn to the results of the analytical work conducted in part 2. It will be of no surprise that through a multitudinous array of references the work of Christ is explicitly related to union with Christ.[9] A selective survey of the various chapters of part 2 will bear this out.

8.2 Ἐν Χριστῷ

In chapter 3, on the prepositional phrase ἐν Χριστῷ, we note the results of §3.3, 'Things Achieved for/Given to People *in Christ*', that the phrase is directly connected to Christ's work in relation to the following themes: redemption (Rom 3:24), the gift of eternal life (Rom 6:23; 2 Tim 1:1), sanctification (1 Cor 1:2), the gift of God's grace (1 Cor 1:4; 2 Tim 1:9), reconciliation (2 Cor 5:19), the gift of freedom (Gal 2:4), the gift of the blessing of Abraham to the Gentiles (Gal 3:14), the gift of every spiritual blessing (Eph 1:3), being raised with Christ and seated with him in the heavens (Eph 2:6), the creation of believers for good works (Eph 2:10), forgiveness (Eph 4:32), the provision of God (Phil 4:19), and salvation (2 Tim 2:10). As the concluding summary of §3.3 indicates, there is a clear tendency toward the instrumental function of ἐν Χριστῷ in connection to these themes. God's acts toward his people are performed through Christ, or are conditioned by or associated with him. God's gifts toward his people are extended toward believers through Christ.

---

7. Gaffin, 'Union with Christ', 275.
8. Calvin, *Institutes*, 3.1.1 (p. 725).
9. The theme of justification will be dealt with independently in ch. 11.

8.3 Ἐν αὐτῷ

Also in chapter 3, this time dealing with the prepositional phrase ἐν αὐτῷ, we note the results of §3.11.3.1, 'Things achieved for/given to people *in Him*', that the phrase is directly connected to Christ's work in relation to the following themes: the gift of spiritual riches (1 Cor 1:5), the fulfilment of God's promises (2 Cor 1:19–20), election (Eph 1:4), creation (Col 1:16), union with Christ (Col 2:10), and the glorification of believers (2 Thess 1:12). Unsurprisingly, several of these instances indicate the instrumentality or agency of Christ.

8.4 Σὺν Χριστῷ

In chapter 5, on the prepositional phrase σὺν Χριστῷ, we note the results of §5.3, '*With Christ*', that the phrase is directly connected to Christ's work in relation to dying with Christ (Rom 6:8; Col 2:20). Both of these references indicate participation with Christ in his death.

8.5 Σὺν αὐτῷ

Also in chapter 5, this time dealing with the prepositional phrase σὺν αὐτῷ, we note the results of §5.5, '*With him*', that the phrase is directly connected to Christ's work in relation to his resurrection (2 Cor 13:4; Col 2:13; 1 Thess 5:10). Each of these references indicates participation with Christ in his resurrected life.

8.6 Σύν COMPOUNDS

Again in chapter 5, this time dealing with σύν-compound words, we note the results of §5.6, 'Σύν Compounds', that such compound words are directly connected to Christ's work in relation to his death (Rom 6:4–5; Phil 3:10; Col 2:12), his resurrected life (Rom 6:8; Eph 2:5; Phil 3:21; Col 2:12; 3:1), his suffering and glorification (Rom 8:17), and his ascension (Eph 2:6). Believers participate with Christ in these aspects of his work.

8.7 Διὰ Χριστοῦ

In chapter 6, on the prepositional phrase διὰ Χριστοῦ, we note the results of §§6.3 and 6.8.1, 'Things Achieved for/Given to People *through*

Christ', that the phrase is directly connected to Christ's work in relation to the following themes: the gift of grace (Rom 1:5), the gift of peace with God (Rom 5:1), eternal life (Rom 5:21), death to the law (Rom 7:4), victory over death (1 Cor 15:57), reconciliation (Rom 5:11; 2 Cor 5:18), predestination and adoption (Eph 1:5), access to the Father (Eph 2:18), salvation (Rom 5:9; 1 Thess 5:9), and the gift of the Spirit (Tit 3:6). With the exception of Romans 5:21 and Ephesians 2:18, in which διὰ Χριστοῦ expresses agency, these references indicate the instrumentality of Christ.

8.8 BODY OF CHRIST

In chapter 7, which deals with the various metaphors that Paul uses in connection to union with Christ, we note that §7.2 on the body of Christ indicates the connection of this metaphor to Christ's work in relation to his headship of the church (Eph 1:22–23; 4:15–16; Col 1:18; 2:19), reconciliation of Jew and Gentile to God (Eph 2:14), and salvation (Eph 5:23).

8.9 TEMPLE AND BUILDING

Also in chapter 7, we note that §7.3 on the temple and building metaphors indicates the connection of these metaphors to Christ's work in relation to the establishment and growth of God's people (Eph 2:21–22).

8.10 MARRIAGE

Again in chapter 7, we note that §7.4 on the metaphor of marriage indicates the connection of this metaphor to Christ's work in relation to his love and self-giving for the church (Eph 5:25), his sanctification and cleansing of the church (5:26), his presentation of the church as holy and blameless (5:27), and his provision for the church (5:29).

8.11 SYNTHESIS

This brief and selective survey reveals that virtually every element of Christ's work that is of interest to Paul is connected in some way to union with Christ. Salvation, redemption, reconciliation, creation, election, predestination, adoption, sanctification, headship, provision, his death, resurrection, ascension, glorification, self-giving, the gifts of grace, peace, eternal life, the Spirit, spiritual riches and blessings, freedom, and the fulfillment of God's promises are all related to union with Christ.

The ways in which the various elements of Christ's work relate to union with Christ differ according to the nature of the work and the language employed. Instances that use the prepositional phrases ἐν Χριστῷ and διὰ Χριστοῦ tend to refer to the instrumentality of Christ in association with the agency of God, or, more rarely, the agency of Christ. As such it is fitting to understand this kind of 'union' in mediatorial terms, as Christ performs the will of God toward his people. This mediatorial instrumentality is most often found in a humanward direction, proceeding from the Father, through the Son, to his people.

Instances that employ the preposition σύν, whether independently or as part of a compound word, indicate participation with Christ in various elements of his work. The scope of Christ's work that is found in connection to σύν-expressions is more defined than that found in connection to ἐν Χριστῷ and διὰ Χριστοῦ, being limited, largely, to Christ's suffering, death, resurrection, ascension, and glorification. Participation with Christ in his work envisages a type of union that is not mediatorial so much as representative. As Christ performs his works, he represents believers while in some spiritual sense they partake in the events that he undergoes. It is also personally encompassing in that a believer's whole person is defined by their participation in Christ's death, resurrection, ascension, and so forth.

The uses of the metaphors of body, building, temple, and marriage convey yet another type of union with respect to the work of Christ. The metaphors envisage an almost 'static' union in which the relationship between Christ and believers is pictured in a stative manner. Believers are not depicted as participants in the work of Christ in the manner in which the σύν-expressions envisage, though they are beneficiaries. Rather, God's people are portrayed as members of the body of which Christ is head; they are part of the building he constructs; they constitute the marriage partner for whom he cares and loves. The metaphors convey incorporation and unity, and they depict realities that have been created by Christ and continue to be nurtured by him.

8.12 DYING AND RISING WITH CHRIST

Clearly one of the most significant elements in the relationship between union with Christ and the work of Christ is that of dying and rising with him. Christ's death for sin and his resurrection to new life are appropriated to the believer through participation in these events. We turn now to consider this theme.

8.12.1 CRANFIELD ON ROMANS 6

Writing of Romans 6:1–14, Cranfield argues that there are four different senses in which we may speak of our dying with Christ and (corresponding to them) four senses in which we may speak of our being raised with him.[10] According to Cranfield, these senses of dying and rising with Christ must be carefully distinguished while also held in close relation to one another.[11] They are (1) the juridical sense; (2) the baptismal sense; (3) the moral sense; (4) the eschatological sense.[12]

With respect to (1) the juridical sense, Cranfield observes 'God's decision to take our sin upon himself in the person of his own dear Son', with believers regarded as having died with him.[13] God has chosen to relegate the sinful life of the believer to the past, which Cranfield sees in view in Romans 6:2 and 8 in particular, thus affecting their status with him.[14] 'God willed to see them as having died in Christ's death and having been raised in his resurrection.'[15]

With respect to (2) the baptismal sense, Cranfield observes in Romans 6:3–4a the close relationship between believers' baptism and Christ's death; 'they were baptized into his death; through their baptism they were buried with him into death.'[16] He points out, however, that new life does not come through baptism, since 'it is based on the gospel events themselves'; 'it is clear that [Paul] did not think of baptism as actually effecting this death with Christ. Baptism does not establish the relationship. It

---

10. C. E. B. Cranfield, 'Romans 6:1–14 Revisited', *ExpTim* 106 (1994): 40–41.
11. Cranfield, 'Romans 6 Revisited', 40.
12. Ibid., 40–41.
13. Ibid., 41.
14. Ibid.
15. Ibid.
16. Ibid.

attests a relationship already established.'[17] Moreover, Cranfield correctly remarks that the motif of baptism is not explicitly connected to being raised with Christ, though he argues that such is surely implied: 'if baptism were only the seal of their interest in his death and not also the seal of their interest in his resurrection, it would be of but little value, for Christ's death has no saving efficacy apart from its sequel in his resurrection.'[18]

With respect to (3) the moral sense, Cranfield regards Romans 6:2 as key: '"We who died to sin, how shall we any longer live therein?" in v. 2 is recognition that, instead of continuing to live in sin, we must try to die to it.'[19] The objective nature of believers' death with Christ entails the subjective obligation to live out death to sin, as it were. Likewise, Cranfield regards 6:4 as indication that believers are to live according to Christ's resurrection: 'the moral conduct denoted by "walk in newness of life" is being regarded as a resurrection.'[20]

With respect to (4) the eschatological sense, Cranfield finds less direct evidence in Romans 6:1–14, though he regards it as understood nonetheless. Physical death will bring about final death to sin, and 'this is the one item in our eightfold scheme which is unquestionably obvious without being stated'.[21] He does, however, regard 6:8b as secondarily referring to believers being raised in the final resurrection.[22]

Cranfield's eightfold scheme of dying and rising with Christ provides a helpful guide in delineating the complex thought of Romans 6:1–14, while also shedding light on the nuances involved in the notion of dying and rising with Christ. The third and fourth quarters of his scheme, which respectively refer to the moral and eschatological aspects of dying and rising with Christ, relate to the chapters in this book on Christian living (ch. 10) and the definition of union with Christ (ch. 12, in which eschatology is discussed), so they will not be discussed further here. The first two quarters, however, require further examination. The second quarter— regarding the baptismal sense of dying and rising with Christ—will be addressed first with discussion of the juridical sense to follow.

---

17. Ibid.
18. Ibid., 42.
19. Ibid.
20. Ibid.
21. Ibid., 43.
22. Ibid.

The notion of being baptized into Christ's death is by no means a straightforward one, and while Cranfield's solution appears sensible, it is not without its detractors.[23] Cranfield claims that baptism in Romans 6:3 does not imply that the believer's union with Christ, or new life, or conversion, comes about through the baptismal rite. He seems to think this is obvious ('it is clear that [Paul] did not think of baptism as actually effecting this death with Christ'), but it is worth testing this claim. For Cranfield to be correct, Paul must refer to baptism in a metaphorical sense, for if he does not, it would be difficult to deny that believers are united with Christ through the baptismal rite in a literal sense.[24] In support of a metaphorical reading of baptism in Romans 6:3 is the phrase 'we were buried with him by baptism', found in 6:4, which must refer to burial metaphorically since a literal reading would be nonsensical.[25]

It is difficult to say more without a broader appreciation of Paul's

---

23. Bousset, for example, pushes strongly in the other direction: 'It is quite clear that here (Romans 6) Paul connects one of the most characteristic presentations of his Christ mysticism to cultic events and representations which were bound up with the sacrament of baptism. One cannot escape the impression that here Paul proceeds from a conviction, already present in the communities, of the cultically sacramental intimacy of the Christians with Christ which is accomplished in baptism'; Bousset, *Kyrios Christos*, 157. Dunn offers a more balanced view: 'In itself the phrase leaves open the question of whether the divine act happens in and through the ritual act ... is rather imaged by the ritual act.... I am more persuaded in favour of the latter'; Dunn, *Romans 1–8*, 311 (see also 327–29).

24. Bousset takes Paul's reference to baptism literally and so concludes: 'For him baptism serves as an act of initiation in which the mystic is merged with the deity, or is clothed with the deity.... Thus in baptism the Christians have become one with the Son, and hence themselves have become sons'; Bousset, *Kyrios Christos*, 158. This accords well with Bousset's claim that 'there remains a certain affinity between the Pauline Christ mysticism' and the mystery piety of Hellenism; Bousset, *Kyrios Christos*, 170. While he discerns many significant differences between Paul and the Hellenistic mystery cults, nevertheless Bousset sees some parallels too, and the preponderance of initiation rites in such cults makes for a convenient parallel with baptism. It may be the case, therefore, that Bousset has too quickly assumed in Romans 6 a parallel with various initiation rites of mystery cults, and in so doing has misrepresented Paul's wider thinking on the matter of baptism.

25. This point appears to be missed by Dunn, who regards baptism in 6:4 as 'almost certainly' the ritual act (despite opting for metaphorical baptism in the previous verse); Dunn, *Romans 1–8*, 313. If 'metaphor' is not the most appropriate description of Paul's phrase in 6:4, perhaps 'spiritual' is better, as long as it is clear that burial with Christ is not a literal description. Beasley-Murray aptly summarizes: '"We were buried with Him" indicates that the action of baptism primarily means, not that the baptistery becomes our grave, but that we are laid in the grave of Christ. To be buried along with Christ in a Jerusalem grave *c.* A.D. 30 means unequivocally that the death we died is the death *He* died on Golgotha'; G. R. Beasley-Murray, *Baptism in the New Testament* (London: Macmillan, 1962), 133.

thinking about baptism in general. While a thorough analysis of this question is beyond our scope here, a few points are pertinent.[26] First, Paul mentions baptism a number of times, which might be construed as indicative of its importance to him as a theme.[27] Second, however, Paul appears to downplay the significance of physical baptism in 1 Corinthians 1:14–17, not quite remembering whom he baptized among the Corinthians (v.16) and famously declaring that 'Christ did not send me to baptize, but to evangelize' (v.17). Third, this latter point means that in all likelihood, when Paul does refer to baptism, he does so in a metaphorical sense (except for when it is obvious from the context that this is not the case, such as in 1 Cor 1:16). In this way, we can harmonize his apparent downplaying of physical baptism with the apparent seriousness with which he speaks of baptism elsewhere. These things are not contradictory if the latter is metaphorical—that is, if baptism depicts a spiritual rather than a physical reality. Paul is serious about spiritual baptism; physical baptism is a secondary issue.

This means we can confirm Cranfield's statement that baptism into Christ's death does not depict the physical rite of baptism as the means through which the believer is united to Christ in his death. Baptism into Christ's death is a metaphorical description of the spiritual reality of dying with Christ. This leads us to consider the first quarter of his schema: the juridical sense of dying and rising with Christ.

Paul says that believers have died to sin (Rom 6:2) and will live with Christ (6:8). It is highly significant that these statements closely follow the juridical material of 5:12–21. This section acknowledges the link between sin and death (5:12), sin and law (5:13), sin and judgment (5:16), and sin and condemnation (5:16). In response to these things, the remainder of Romans 5 reflects on the gift of God in Jesus Christ, through whom righteousness reigns resulting in eternal life (5:17–21). Given this context, a juridical interpretation of dying and rising with Christ is certainly feasible.

The next pericope of Romans 6:1–14 is primarily concerned with the moral implications of the new life in Christ, but the juridical backdrop of 5:12–21 is never far from the surface. By speaking of dying and rising

---

26. See Beasley-Murray, *Baptism*, for an extended treatment of the subject.

27. Cognates of the βαπτιζ- word group occur thirteen times in the Pauline canon: Rom 6:3–4; 1 Cor 1:13–17; 10:2; 12:13; 15:29; Gal 3:27; Eph 4:5; Col 2:12.

with Christ, Paul appears to be delving into the mechanics of how the gift of God in Jesus Christ has overturned the juridical implications of sin and death. The logic appears to be as follows. The consequence of sin is death, judgment, and condemnation. By dying a representative death for sinful humanity, Christ fulfilled the legal requirement for sin. Once this legal requirement had been satisfied by death, the new life of Christ is no longer bound by sin or the juridical consequences it entails. The way in which the benefits of Christ's representative death are apprehended is by identification with him in his death. This is where participation and representation come together: believers spiritually partake in the death and resurrection of Christ, who has represented them in these acts.[28] Thus, Paul can boldly proclaim that those who have died with Christ were crucified with him (6:6), entailing both the end of enslavement to sin (6:6–7) and resurrection that is free from death (6:8–9).

Cranfield is correct, therefore, to identify a juridical sense in dying and rising with Christ in Romans 6:1–14. In fact, it is probably not possible to situate the passage in its proper context without an appreciation of the juridical nature of this motif. The reason that believers have been set free from the condemnation of the law and death is that the righteous requirements of the law have been met through their dying and rising with Christ.

8.12.2 TANNEHILL ON ROMANS 6

Tannehill provides another important contribution concerning the motif of dying and rising with Christ. His basic thesis is as follows: 'If the believer dies and rises with Christ, as Paul claims, Christ's death and resurrection are not merely events which produce benefits for the believer, but also are events in which the believer himself partakes. The believer's new life is based upon his personal participation in these saving events.'[29]

With reference to Romans 6, Tannehill observes one central idea emanating from the motif of dying and rising with Christ: '[Paul] is interested in the idea of dying and rising with Christ because it implies death to the

---

28. 'Paul teaches that it is not only within the facticity of Christ's crucifixion that the individual died, but it is also the case that in his personal history it is the old sin-dominated self that has been crucified with Christ'; Michael Parsons, 'In Christ in Paul', *VE* 18 (1988): 31.

29. Tannehill, *Dying and Rising*, 1.

old dominion of sin and new life to God.'[30] This claim suggests that Tannehill views eschatology—the fourth quarter of Cranfield's schema for Romans 6—as the dominant concern in the passage, since the distinction between the dominion of sin and new life is ultimately eschatological in character.

This takes an interesting turn for our understanding of Romans 6, if indeed Tannehill is correct, for the element that Cranfield found little direct evidence to support is now to be regarded as the central idea of the passage. In this respect, it is first important to acknowledge that Cranfield's use of the term 'eschatology' is apparently limited to its literal application: the study of 'the end things', which is why he uses it with reference to the 'final death to sin' and the 'final resurrection'. Tannehill, however, is primarily concerned with the relationship between the dominion of sin and death and the dominion of life, and this distinction of realms is regarded as eschatological in nature. In other words, Tannehill's understanding of eschatology is not limited to what happens at 'the end of time', but includes the present significance of these opposing dominions. He writes:

> It is not a great step for Paul to move from a reference to present participation in newness of life to a reference to the future resurrection, as he does in vss.4–5. For Paul these are two aspects of the Christians' participation in eschatological life, and he can easily move from the one to the other.[31]

Thus, we observe a subtle difference between Tannehill and Cranfield with respect to what the term 'eschatology' refers. This is not problematic, but it simply requires acknowledgment since this terminological difference explains why Cranfield finds little direct evidence for the eschatological nature of dying and rising with Christ in Romans 6 while Tannehill finds it everywhere.

Indeed, for Tannehill the whole of Romans 6 is eschatological in nature: 'From the beginning to the end of the chapter Paul is concerned

---

30. Ibid., 9. So Wisnefske, 'Christianity announces a cataclysmic breach in the ages: our former lives are moribund and passing away; but new life, the very life of God, is united with us and recreating us'; Ned Wisnefske, 'Living and Dying with Christ: Do We Mean What We Say?', *WW* 10 (1990): 254.

31. Tannehill, *Dying and Rising*, 11.

with the Christian's relation to the dominion of sin.'[32] Furthermore, the concept of two opposing dominions (sin/death vs. new life in Christ) is of central significance to Tannehill's understanding of dying and rising with Christ:

> In order to understand what Paul means by dying and rising with Christ, we must investigate the related idea of the two dominions. The contrast between two dominions and their lords is not only basic to the whole of Rom. 6, but is also a feature of all of the passages which speak of dying with Christ as a past event. It is only by bringing out the full significance of this fact that we can understand the meaning of the motif of dying and rising with Christ for Paul.[33]

According to Tannehill's understanding, the connection between the two dominions and the motif of dying and rising with Christ has to do with a change of lordship: 'It means dying to an old master and living to a new one.'[34] By dying with Christ, the believer dies to the powers of the old aeon and enters into a new life under a new power.[35]

There is much to commend Tannehill's approach to the motif of dying and rising with Christ, and its role in portraying the transfer of dominions is powerful indeed. While this rests on his assertion that Romans 6 portrays 'sin' as a domain, realm, or aeon, such is not necessarily immediately obvious and it is important to test this claim further.

In support of Tannehill's view, Romans 6:6 refers to no longer being 'enslaved to sin' (τοῦ μηκέτι δουλεύειν ἡμᾶς τῇ ἁμαρτίᾳ). In 6:7, it is through death that a person is 'freed from sin's claims' (δεδικαίωται ἀπὸ τῆς ἁμαρτίας), as though sin is a force of captive power. In 6:9, death is described as no longer ruling over Christ (θάνατος αὐτοῦ οὐκέτι κυριεύει). Believers are instructed in 6:12 not to let 'sin reign' (μὴ οὖν βασιλευέτω ἡ ἁμαρτία), and in 6:13 not to offer any parts of the body to sin (as weapons for unrighteouesness; παριστάνετε τὰ μέλη ὑμῶν ὅπλα ἀδικίας τῇ

---

32. Ibid., 10.
33. Ibid., 14–15.
34. Ibid., 18.
35. Ibid., 21. So also Hooker: 'To be "in Christ", therefore, to be joined to him in baptism, and so to die with him and rise with him, means to share in his death to sin and in his release from the power of sin'; Morna D. Hooker, *From Adam to Christ: Essays on Paul* (Cambridge: Univ. of Cambridge Press, 1990; repr. Eugene, OR: Wipf & Stock, 2008), 34.

ἁμαρτίᾳ). In 6:14, we are told that 'sin will not rule over you' (ἁμαρτία γὰρ ὑμῶν οὐ κυριεύσει). In 6:16, Paul states that believers will be slaves either to sin or to obedience (δοῦλοί ἐστε ᾧ ὑπακούετε, ἤτοι ἁμαρτίας εἰς θάνατον ἢ ὑπακοῆς εἰς δικαιοσύνην). In 6:17, Paul says that his readers 'used to be slaves of sin' (ἦτε δοῦλοι τῆς ἁμαρτίας). Again, in 6:20, believers are described as previously being 'slaves of sin' (δοῦλοι ἦτε τῆς ἁμαρτίας), and in 6:22 as having been liberated from sin (νυνὶ δὲ ἐλευθερωθέντες ἀπὸ τῆς ἁμαρτίας).

To be sure, some of these references could be interpreted in a more existential manner, such that Paul is referring to sin as a subjective experience through which people are enslaved to their own sinful desires. It is a better reading of the context, however, to regard these references as depicting sin as a domain, or realm, under which people are enslaved by its captive power. This reality does not deny the potency of the subjective experience of sin—in fact, the two go together—but it simply clarifies what is in view in Romans 6. Paul is concerned to depict the transition that believers undertake in Christ from being under the rule of the realm of sin and death to that of new life and righteousness. As such, Tannehill is undoubtedly correct to recognize the importance of the 'two domains' in this chapter, and therefore the connection of dying and rising with Christ to this eschatological concern.

Tannehill develops the connection between dying and rising with Christ and the eschatology of the two domains through the concept of Christ as an inclusive figure. When Paul speaks of being baptized into Christ's death, Tannehill regards 'baptism as entry into Christ, who is an inclusive or corporate person'.[36] Christ as an inclusive person is closely related to the concept of the new dominion in Paul's thought: 'Christ, as inclusive person, represents and embodies the new dominion in himself.'[37] For Tannehill, Paul can say that the believer participates in Christ's death because he is included in Christ. 'It is through this connection with inclusive patterns of thought that we must understand dying and rising with Christ.'[38]

For Tannehill, this concept of Christ as an inclusive figure is not dependent on the notion of 'corporate personality', which may or may not

---

36. Tannehill, *Dying and Rising*, 24.
37. Ibid.
38. Ibid.

be derived from the thought of the Old Testament.[39] Rather, the inclusivity of Christ is dependent on the eschatological nature of his death and resurrection. His logic is as follows: Paul associates dying and rising with Christ with the end of the old dominion and the foundation of the new,

---

39. Ibid., 29. This is a subject of much debate (for an overview of the history of the discussion, see David Timms, 'The Pauline Use of *en Christo*: Re-examining Meaning and Origins—A Linguistic Analysis' [PhD thesis, Macquarie University, 2000], 40–47); a sample of representative views is appropriate here. Two issues are pertinent: first, whether or not a concept of 'corporate personality' exists in the Old Testament, and if so in what capacity; second, whether or not such a concept (however defined) lies in the background of Paul's thought. In favour of the term's Old Testament credibility and Pauline significance, Ridderbos claims that the single representative of a whole people stands in relationship with said people such that they are identified with their representative; 'It is this corporate connection of the all-in-One that Paul applies to Christ and his people'; Ridderbos, *Paul*, 62. Likewise, Beker regards Paul's 'incorporation motif' as originating in the Jewish notion of corporate personality, with several of its components to be found in Paul: '(1) the one for all; (2) the one in all; (3) the once for all'; Beker, *Paul the Apostle*, 310. Son is also in favour of the concept and regards it as better than other explanations of 'being in Christ' because '(1) it recognizes the locative use of the formula and (2) it conceives of Christ as a person'; Son, *Corporate Elements*, 27, 119. Ahern frequently finds the concept in the Old Testament and regards it as important for understanding Paul; Barnabas M. Ahern, 'The Christian's Union with the Body of Christ in Cor, Gal, and Rom', *CBQ* 23 (1961): 201. Against the concept of corporate personality, Porter claims that this 'sacred cow' is already dead 'and is now more than ready to be buried'. He argues that the corporate life of Israel is better conveyed by the term 'corporate representation'; Stanley E. Porter, 'Two Myths: Corporate Personality and Language/ Mentality Determinism', *SJT* 43 (1990): 289–307. Timms regards the evidence for corporate personality in Old Testament as scant and debatable; Timms, 'Pauline Use of *en Christo*', 47. Rogerson suggests that adherence to the concept of corporate personality adds nothing but confusion; John W. Rogerson, 'The Hebrew Conception of Corporate Personality: A Re-Examination', *JTS* 21 (1970): 15. Wedderburn holds a mediating position that acknowledges the difficulties of the term 'corporate personality', while remaining 'thoroughly appreciative of the idea expressed by it as long as exaggerated claims are not made for it'; Wedderburn, *Baptism and Resurrection*, 352. Schreiner agrees that some have taken the concept of corporate personality too far, while he acknowledges the representative character of Paul's Christology; Schreiner, *Paul*, 158. If 'corporate personality' is understood to refer to the solidarity of the tribe or nation with one person as representative of the whole, Tannehill suggests that 'this has something to contribute to our understanding of Paul but is not a sufficient explanation of Paul's corporate or inclusive patterns of thought'; Tannehill, *Dying and Rising*, 29. Bassler likewise acknowledges the representational elements of corporate personality but sees this as 'a far cry from the notions of union and incorporation that Paul's language suggests'; Jouette M. Bassler, *Navigating Paul: An Introduction to Key Theological Concepts* (Louisville: Westminster John Knox, 2007), 41. The best evaluation of the evidence appears to favour Porter's notion of 'corporate representation', which retains the legitimacy of Israelite solidarity without the problematic complexities of a shared *personality*. Nevertheless, as Tannehill and Bassler suggest, corporate representation does not account for Paul's thought in full and can only be a constituent factor therein.

and because of this they are eschatological events.[40] And, 'because they are eschatological events, affecting the old dominion as a whole, they are also inclusive events'.[41] All people are included in one of these two dominions; the dominions themselves entail inclusion for good or for ill. Since Christ's death and resurrection *affect* the old dominion and *effect* the new, these events are not only eschatological but inclusive as well. Insofar as believers pertain to the new domain, they participate in the eschatological death and resurrection of Christ; it is part and parcel of their membership in the new realm. 'Because the existence of all within an aeon is based upon and determined by the founding events, the whole of the aeon shares in these events. The inclusive terminology which appears in connection with dying and rising with Christ has a similar sense.'[42]

This schema removes the difficulty of temporal remoteness with respect to believers participating in events that predate them: 'the fact of temporal distance creates no major problem for Paul in connection with dying and rising with Christ'.[43] Individuals are not isolated from the power sphere in which they exist, and 'the new dominion is not an epoch of world history, which could be superseded in the course of historical development, but something which is hidden within history'.[44]

Ultimately, Tannehill's reconstruction of Paul's thought in Romans 6 provides a brilliant account of how dying and rising with Christ relates to the two dominions, is eschatological in nature, and transcends time and space. Furthermore, this reconstruction does not contradict Cranfield's observations cited above but complements them. As Cranfield points out, the chapter's references to dying and rising with Christ include juridical, baptismal, moral, and eschatological elements. Tannehill's explication, however, searches the 'deep structure' of Paul's thought and provides a lucid account of how these things cohere. In addition, this 'deep structure' has value beyond Romans 6 as Tannehill demonstrates its coherence in Galatians, Ephesians, Colossians, and 2 Corinthians, about which he summarizes: 'The passages discussed above make clear that Paul's use of dying and rising with Christ must be understood in the context of his eschatology. This motif is used to

---

40. Tannehill, *Dying and Rising*, 30.
41. Ibid.
42. Ibid., 39–40.
43. Ibid., 40.
44. Ibid.

indicate the decisive transfer of believers from the old to the new aeon which has taken place in the death of Christ as an inclusive event.[45]

8.13 THE NEW ADAM

No discussion of the work of Christ would be complete without some attempt to wrestle with Paul's thought concerning Christ as the new Adam. While it may seem counterintuitive that this section should follow the discussion of Romans 6—since the primary text for the Adam Christology is the preceding pericope, Romans 5:12–21—there is method in this madness. Tannehill has provided a credible account of the 'deep structure' of Paul's thought in Romans 6 and it has potential to aid our understanding of 5:12–21 since it is likely that it is built on the same foundations, as Tannehill suggests: 'the connection between the two sections becomes clear if we note the importance of the contrast between the two dominions in both.'[46]

8.13.1 ROMANS 5

While it is commonplace to interpret Romans 5:12–21 through some notion of 'corporate personality', this seems misguided.[47] A typical reading that uses such a notion regards Adam and Christ as two corporate identities into whom all of humanity is absorbed: those enslaved to sin are incorporated into Adam while those with new life are incorporated into Christ.[48] Kreitzer provides an example of this in the following statement: 'Adam and Christ are complemented in that both are representative

---

45. Ibid., 70.

46. Ibid., 26.

47. Drawing on Best's distinction between solidarity and corporate personality, Beasley-Murray claims on the one hand that 'Adam is seen to be in unique solidarity with the race as the head who affects all but who is not affected by them; yet we cannot go so far as to say that all in the race express the personality of Adam; each individual may sin and die because of Adam but the whole race is not made into a personality which sins and dies'; Beasley-Murray, *Baptism*, 137. On the other hand, however, Beasley-Murray retains corporate personality with respect to Christ; 'In the case of the Second Adam, however, we see One who may be viewed as an inclusive personality; when He died those who are included in Him died with Him; when He rose, they rose with Him'; Beasley-Murray, *Baptism*, 137.

48. Schreiner offers a balanced view of the matter: 'Doubtless some have gone too far when they speak of corporate personality. But the contrast between Adam and Christ supports the representative character of Paul's christology, and it is clear that they are the heads of humanity'; Schreiner, *Paul*, 158.

figures for their followers. Both encompass humanity within themselves. Both stand as the typological figures of an aeon. Both, by their respective acts, set the pattern for the people who follow them.[49]

There is much to affirm here, but a problem lies with the statement that 'both encompass humanity within themselves'. One of the difficulties for this kind of reading of Romans 5:12–21 is that it is not clear from a theological point of view why Adam should be given such a privilege. Why is all humanity outside Christ encompassed by Adam? Why is humanity incorporated into him? Why should Adam's actions be 'imputed' to all? While there are no doubt some compelling examples of this kind of reading that might give us pause, they are nevertheless built on the wrong foundation. It is not 'corporate personality' that is the controlling notion in the comparison between Adam and Christ, but rather the contrasting domains they represent. If Tannehill is correct about Romans 6—and we have argued above that he is—then it is more likely that the underpinning framework of Paul's thought in 5:12–21 is concerned with the 'two domains' of sin and life rather than corporate personality.

Kreitzer's statement reflects this notion also with the sentence: 'Both stand as the typological figures of an aeon.' Thus, Kreitzer's view is not wholly at odds with Tannehill's position, since both acknowledge the significance of the domains or aeons represented by Adam and Christ. The strength of Tannehill's position, however, is that it does not also require that all humanity is incorporated into Adam; humanity participates in the domain *represented* by Adam, but Adam is not in himself a corporate *personality* standing over humanity.

The way in which Romans 5:12–21 connects to the underpinning framework—or 'deep structure'—of Paul's thought is that Adam and Christ are the entry points into the two domains.[50] The first domain of

---

49. L. Joseph Kreitzer, 'Christ and Second Adam in Paul', *CV* 32 (1989): 87. So also Dodd, *Romans*, 100–101. In similar a vein, the following statement from Barcley is not so much incorrect as not quite precise enough: 'To be "in Adam" or "in Christ," then, carries the notion of solidarity, participation, belonging, corporate inclusion. Believers who are "in Christ" have a solidarity with Christ; they belong to him who is their corporate representative'; William B. Barcley, *"Christ in You": A Study in Paul's Theology and Ethics* (Lanham, MD: Univ. Press of America, 1999),113. Solidarity with Adam or Christ pertains to their domains in particular rather than simply their corporate persons.

50. So Dunn: 'Paul indicates that he wants this figure [Adam] to be seen not so much as an individual in his own right, but as a more than individual figure, what we might call an

sin and death was established when 'sin entered the world through one man, and death through sin' (5:12). To read this first statement through the lens of corporate personality, we are left wondering why Paul continues with the rest of the sentence: 'in this way death spread to all men, because all sinned'. If, as the corporate personality view suggests, Adam's sin is imputed to all he represents, there is little point adding 'because all sinned', since Adam's sin is their sin too. The second half of the sentence would need to be understood as meaning that 'all sinned' in a metaphorical sense — that is, in Adam's sin 'all sinned'. However, this twist is an unnecessary complication if corporate personality is not in view. Paul is not suggesting that Adam's sin is imputed to all humanity, but that he opened the door to a dark domain through which all people subsequently walked, because 'all sinned' in a concrete rather than figurative way.[51] Consequently, Adam's role is that he marks the beginning of this dark domain; he held the door open as all humanity walked through.

It is in this respect that Paul can say 'by the one man's trespass the many died' (5:15). He is not claiming that Adam's one sin is imputed to all humanity, but that the domain of sin and death claims 'the many'. Likewise, the statement 'by the one man's trespass, death reigned though that one man' (5:17) does not mean that Adam is death's vice-regent, operating as 'lord' of its domain; rather, it means that as the 'entry point' to the domain of sin and death, Adam allows death to rule over all those who follow in his footsteps. Again, the statements 'through one trespass there is condemnation for everyone' (5:18) and 'through one man's disobedience the many were made sinners' (5:19) refer to the pervading rule of sin and death, which is initiated through Adam. Adam stands as the gateway to its dominion, since death spread to all men, because all sinned (5:12).[52]

By the same token, then, the presentation of Christ as the new Adam in Romans 5:12–21 is not concerned with corporate personality but with entrance into the new domain of life and righteousness. This means that

---

"epochal figure" — that is, as the one who initiated the first major phase of human history and thereby determined the character of that phase for those belonging to it'; Dunn, *Romans 1–8*, 289. Likewise, Moo comments that 'Paul's focus is not at this point on the corporate significance of Adam's act but on his role as the instrument through whom sin and death were unleashed in the world'; Moo, *Romans*, 321.

51. Dunn, *Romans 1–8*, 290.

52. Moo, *Romans*, 339.

'the overflow of grace and the gift of righteousness' (5:17) reigns through
Jesus Christ by virtue of his providing access to this new domain. When
Paul says that 'through one righteous act there is life-giving justification for everyone' (5:18), this then refers to everyone who enters the new
domain of life; 'the many will be made righteous' (5:19) likewise refers to
members of the new realm of Christ. Chapter 6 then goes on to emphasize the contrast between the two domains and the means through which
believers access the new realm: through sharing in Christ's death and
resurrection.

This approach to Romans 5:12–21 has many of the same implications
as those approaches that rely on the notion of corporate personality. It
is still appropriate to describe Adam and Christ as the two representatives of humanity; Adam represents enslaved humanity under condemnation, while Christ represents liberated humanity under righteousness. The
nature of this representation, however, is not dependent on imputation
of sin (with respect to Adam) or righteousness (with respect to Christ).
It is, rather, both a mechanical and symbolic representation at the same
time. It is mechanical in the sense that Adam and Christ open the door to
their respective domains, providing the means through which others may
enter in. Adam is the mechanism through which all humanity accesses the
domain of death, just as Christ is the mechanism through which redeemed
humanity accesses the domain of new life. Both figures are also symbolic
representatives of their respective domains since both are the 'first man'
of each. This is captured well by Ridderbos:

> Adam is the one through whom sin entered the world and death through
> sin, so Christ is the one who gives righteousness and life. Christ and
> Adam stand over against one another as the great representatives of the
> two aeons, that of life and that of death. In that sense, as representing a
> whole dispensation, a whole humanity, Adam can be called the type of
> "him who was to come" (v. 14), i.e., of the second man and of the coming
> aeon represented by him. For as the proto-father brought sin and death
> into the world, so Christ by his obedience (that is, by his death) and his
> resurrection has made life to dawn for the new humanity.[53]

---

53. Ridderbos, *Paul*, 57. He views the same thinking at work in 1 Cor 15:45: 'The intention
of the apostle is here again not merely to point to the resurrection of Christ as the token or
as the possibility of the future resurrection of all believers. Rather, Christ as second man and

Morna Hooker likewise detects the importance of the transfer of dominion from Adam to Christ in the deep structure of Paul's thought: 'Yet it is arguable that for Paul the idea of human solidarity is a vitally important factor in the substructure of his thought, more fundamental than all the images he uses; and that for him, man's redemption is seen primarily in terms of moving from the sphere of Adam to the sphere of Christ.'[54]

With this we return to our primary concern, which is union with Christ, or 'human solidarity', as Hooker puts it. Dying and rising with Christ is an expression of such solidarity with Christ and participation in these key events. This participation enables the transition out of the old domain of sin and death represented by Adam and facilitates entrance into the new domain of life and righteousness represented by Christ.

8.13.2 1 CORINTHIANS 15

It is important also to consider Paul's two references to Adam in 1 Corinthians 15. Commenting on 15:22, 'For as in Adam all die, so also in Christ shall all be made alive', Beker says: 'The phrase has essentially a participatory-instrumental meaning and signifies the transfer to the new age that has been inaugurated with the death and resurrection of Christ.'[55] Such an interpretation provides a compelling parallel with our reading of Romans 5:12–21.

This is not, however, how some interpreters read the verse. Son understands 1 Corinthians 15:22 as indicating 'that the whole of humanity now exists corporately either in Adam or in Christ'.[56] Tellingly, Son acknowledges the difficulty in explaining why Paul should come to this conclusion: 'Unfortunately, Paul does not explain how Adam and Christ determined

---

last Adam is the one in whose resurrection this new life of the recreation has already come to light and become reality in this dispensation'; Ridderbos, *Paul*, 57.

54. Hooker, *From Adam to Christ*, 41.

55. Beker, *Paul the Apostle*, 272.

56. Son, *Corporate Elements*, 63. Son acknowledges the criticisms that have been leveled at the notion of 'corporate personality' (p. 79). He nevertheless regards the concept as legitimate: 'As [Paul] applies the Adam-Christ typology to his teaching about redemption and resurrection, he clearly assumes some sort of solidarity of humanity. This assumption can probably be best explained in terms of the Old Testament conception of "corporate personality"'; Son, *Corporate Elements*, 82.

the destiny and the mode of existence of the whole of humanity.'[57] Nevertheless, Son argues that the preposition ἐν in the phrase 'in Adam' and 'in Christ' of 15:22 'indicates Adam and Christ as spheres of human existence. This means that in 1 Cor 15:22 Adam and Christ are more than representational figures. They are corporate persons who include in themselves their respective followers'.[58]

This seems a bold claim considering it is based solely on Paul's choice of preposition. Rather than interpreting the phrases 'in Adam' and 'in Christ' in 15:22 as indicating the corporate nature of these persons, it seems just as likely (if not more so) that the phrases are shorthand for 'in the realm of Adam' and 'in the realm of Christ'.[59] Indeed, the immediate context supports the view that Paul has the contrast between the two dominions in view, as is the case in Romans 5 and 6. He refers to Christ's handing over 'the kingdom' to the Father (15:24), the abolishment of 'all rule and authority and power' (15:24), Christ's reign over his enemies (15:25), and the abolishment of death (15:26). These references speak to the underlying thought structure that views two dominions in conflict with one another. It is this underlying thought structure that provides the best interpretative guide to the phrases 'in Adam' and 'in Christ' in 15:22: Paul means to point to the respective dominions represented by each figure.

The second reference to Adam in 1 Corinthians 15 is found in vv. 45–49. Again these verses contrast Adam with Christ: Adam 'became a living being', while 'the last Adam became a life-giving Spirit' (15:45); the first man 'was from the earth and made of dust, the second man is from heaven' (15:47). All of humanity is then associated with one or the other of these two 'Adams': 'Like the man made of dust, so are those who are made of dust; like the heavenly man, so are those who are heavenly' (15:48), and 'just as we have borne the image of the man made of dust, we will also bear the image of the heavenly man' (15:49).

The question here, however, is whether Paul means to present Adam and Christ as corporate persons (as Son claims) or simply as representatives of their respective realms. In this passage, there is no expression parallel

---

57. Ibid., 64.
58. Ibid.
59. So Thiselton, 'Paul uses the shorthand *those in Adam* and *those in Christ* to express this nexus of thoughts'; Thiselton, *1 Corinthians*, 1282.

to the phrases 'in Adam' and 'in Christ' as found in 15:22, which Son
interprets as indicating corporate personalities. Instead, we find the curious expressions 'like the man made of dust' (οἷος ὁ χοϊκός) and 'like the
heavenly man' (οἷος ὁ ἐπουράνιος; 15:48). While these expressions might
be interpreted through the lens of corporate personality, they might be
read just as well without it. With Adam and Christ as representatives who
have led the way into their respective domains, those who belong to their
domains are depicted as following in their footsteps. They are 'like' Adam
or 'like' Christ because they belong either to Adam's realm or to Christ's
realm; Paul is not necessarily stating that the former are incorporated into
Adam himself and the latter into Christ himself. It is most likely that once
again the deep structure of Paul's thought is concerned with the contrast
between two domains, which finds expression on the 'surface' level of his
language through the two representatives of these domains.[60]

8.14 PARTICIPATION AND SALVATION

The redemptive-historical elements of salvation form an important component of the work of Christ, and we turn now to consider an area of
debate related to this of which union with Christ—and participation in
particular—has become the centrepiece. It has been argued that theological approaches to salvation that understand the work of Christ to be substitutionary are mistaken by way of disregard for the participatory nature
of salvation. While there are several possible interlocutors with whom we
might engage on this issue, the 2001 work of Daniel Powers holds especial
interest.[61] Powers has approached this question by careful examination of
the relevant Pauline passages, arguing that Paul does not regard salvation to

---

60. These conclusions accord well with some of Timm's summary statements concerning the relationship between Adam and Christ in Paul's thought: 'There is no clear Adam-
theology in the Jewish sources nearest the first century which would see Adam as a corporate
figure.... In light of the preceding discussion we might legitimately conclude that the phrase
ἐν τῷ Ἀδάμ does not connote union—and even less a mystical union. It is true that there
are some texts which might lead us to conclude that Adam is the "universal man" and the
progenitor of humankind but this does not justify a locative understanding of ἐν τῷ Ἀδάμ.
In fact, to the contrary, the contextual evidence would suggest that ἐν takes a predominantly
instrumental nuance, with Adam being the cause or the instigator of the fate which belongs
to all of his progeny. This latter point is the one emphasised by those who exegete the rabbinic
writings.' Timms, 'Pauline Use of en Christo', 60.

61. Powers, Salvation through Participation.

be accomplished by the substitution of Christ but rather through participation with Christ. An example of this is Powers' treatment of Galatians 2:20:

> When Paul asserts that Christ 'loved me and gave himself for (ὑπὲρ) me,' he means that Christ represented the believers in his death. Paul did not intend to say that Christ died instead of, or in the place of, the believers, because he sees the believers as also being involved in Christ's death. Rather, Paul sees Christ as being so bound up in the fate of the believer that he represents the believer in his death; he gave himself *on behalf of* the believer.[62]

Powers emphasizes the significance of participation with Christ in salvation. He stresses that Christ and the believer are 'so bound up' together that representation is facilitated. Elsewhere he writes, 'Paul's notion of salvation is inherently entwined with his presupposition that believers are united with Christ. For Paul, salvation is possible inasmuch as the believers participate in the death and resurrection of Christ.'[63] From the evidence observed thus far in this book, we must concur with Powers concerning the importance of participation in Paul's conception of salvation. Galatians 2:20 is but one example in support of this fact, and Powers convincingly argues the same point through several other passages.

While Powers is correct in what he affirms, it is not apparent that he is correct in what he denies. Is it really the case that substitution is absent from Paul's discussions of salvation because participation is so pervasive? By pitting participation against substitution in such sharp relief, one wonders if Powers has endorsed a false dichotomy. The essence of this dichotomy for Powers appears to be that one cannot describe as substitutionary an action in which both parties participate. Commenting on 2 Corinthians 5:21, to which we will return in a subsequent chapter, and outlining the position against which he argues, Powers states: 'Through substitution, the substitute takes the place of another so that the other does not personally participate in the condition which is rightfully his.'[64]

Given this understanding of substitution, we observe why Powers regards it as mutually exclusive of participation: if one acts as a substitute,

---

62. Ibid., 124 [italics are original].
63. Ibid., 169.
64. Ibid., 79–80.

'the other does not personally participate' with him — by definition. The coherence of this conclusion appeals to common sense; after all, it is a truism that one who is replaced by a substitute does not at the same time retain her position with the substitute. In common parlance this would be oxymoronic. And yet, while observations from common sense and parlance are important, the ultimate guide must be the inner logic of the apostle as evidenced by his own words. In view of this, we ask: Does Paul regard the notion of participation as contrary to substitution?

This is not easy to answer, but a few points deserve consideration. To begin, Paul never speaks of his own contribution to salvation. While he can refer to sharing in the sufferings of Christ (e.g., 2 Cor 1:5), this most likely refers to the role of suffering in Paul's apostolic ministry. Nowhere does he even hint that somehow by participating in Christ's work he has himself died for his own sins, paid his own price for sin, and by his work conquered evil. Christ has done all these things, and Paul glorifies God for it because it is by grace — precisely *because* Paul cannot contribute to these things. This is not to suggest that Powers regards Paul as semi-Pelagian. Rather, it provokes us to ponder the nature of Paul's participation in Christ's death and resurrection. If Paul regards himself a participant in the work of Christ and yet attributes no credit to himself for the salvation achieved and victory won — but attributes all to Christ — then his participation is of such nature that benefits from Christ's activity, yet does not contribute to it. This is not participation according to common parlance or practice. It is, rather, the gracious inclusion in the achievements of another. Paul's understanding of his participation with Christ does not, therefore, compromise the uniqueness of Christ in the work of Christ; Christ is the Son of God, the Saviour, the resurrected Lord — and Paul is none of these things. Since there is this sense of the uniqueness of Christ in Paul's understanding of participation with Christ, there is therefore space for the notion of substitution, properly understood.

The conceptual link between these things is representation. Powers freely uses this term, regarding it as more accurate than substitution for describing Paul's thought. However, it is here that the latter concept is permitted space, since representation envelops substitution within its lexical denotation. According to normal English usage,[65] representation denotes acting on behalf of another. It is difficult to imagine this concept without

---

65. We are, after all, dealing with English terms to analyze these theological distinctions.

evoking something of what we normally mean by substitution.[66] By its very nature, the phrase 'on behalf of another' speaks of standing in someone else's stead—acting for them so that they need not act for themselves. Thus, to speak of representation is to recognize substitution—at least to some degree.[67] In this way, representation—with its attendant substitutionary overtones—protects Paul's understanding of participation from semi-Pelagianism (anachronism notwithstanding). While Paul is a participant with, and beneficiary from, Christ and his work, Christ remains Paul's representative in bearing sin and death—and in overturning them too.

Thus we conclude that Powers is correct in what he affirms—the centrality of participation and representation in Paul's understanding of salvation—but not in what he denies, since substitution is folded within representation and does not contradict participation. As Wright affirms, 'The Messiah is able to be the substitute *because* he is the representative.'[68]

8.15 CONCLUSION

This chapter draws together the exegetical results of part 2 that relate to the work of Christ, and it is observed that virtually every element of his work is connected to union with him. Dying and rising with Christ means that believers identify with his representative death and resurrection, and it facilitates a change of lordship as the believer dies to the dominion of sin and death and enters new life in the realm of Christ. Paul's theme of the new Adam relates to these two dominions, with Adam and Christ as the entry points into their respective domains. Thus, participation in the representative and substitutionary acts of Christ brings forth resurrection life.

---

66. According to Stewart, Paul's thought of Christ as substitute always went hand-in-hand with the thought of Christ as representative; James S. Stewart, *A Man in Christ: The Vital Elements of St. Paul's Religion* (London: Hodder & Stoughton, 1935; repr. Vancouver: Regent College, 2002), 242.

67. As Dahms puts it, our representative Christ actualized 'the full surrender to God that we could will but could not actualize'; John V. Dahms, 'Dying with Christ', *JETS* 36 (1993): 23.

68. N. T. Wright, *Justification: God's Plan and Paul's Vision* (London: SPCK, 2009), 84–85.

CHAPTER 9

Union with Christ and the Trinity

9.1 Introduction

A significant theological theme in Paul's writings involves the interactions between Father, Son, and Spirit, and we turn now to observe the ways in which union with Christ relates to Paul's implicit trinitarianism. A selective survey of the chapters of part 2 will bear this out. It is to be expected that there will be some overlap here with the previous chapter concerning the work of Christ; the two discussions are not mutually exclusive, but they are kept distinct for the sake of clarity. Following the insights gained from the exegetical material, the discussion turns to consider some pertinent issues within modern trinitarian thought that directly bear on union with Christ.

9.2 Ἐν Χριστῷ

In chapter 3, on the prepositional phrase ἐν Χριστῷ, we note the results of §3.10, 'Trinity *in Christ*', which indicate that the phrase is directly connected to the Father and/or the Spirit in relation to the following themes: the Spirit of life (Rom 8:2), the love of God (8:39), the grace of God (1 Cor 1:4; Eph 2:7), God's work of reconciliation (2 Cor 5:19), the promise of the Spirit (Gal 3:14), the fatherhood of God toward his people (3:26), the blessing of God (Eph 1:3), creation (2:10), the glory of God (3:21; Phil 4:19), God's forgiveness (Eph 4:32), God's calling (Phil 3:14), the peace of God (4:7), and the will of God (1 Thess 5:18). Unsurprisingly, most of these references depict a working relationship between Father and Son in which God is the agent and Christ the instrument of his will. This further highlights the mediatorial element of union with Christ as expressed by the phrase ἐν Χριστῷ. While humanity's interest in such a union is as the beneficiary of the work and gifts of God, it is clear that the other side of that mediation involves the expression of God's will toward humanity through Christ.

9.3 Ἐν αὐτῷ

Also in chapter 3, this time dealing with the prepositional phrase ἐν αὐτῷ, we note the results of §3.11.3.4, 'Trinity *in Him*', which indicate that the phrase is directly connected to the Father and/or the Spirit in relation to the following themes: the fulfillment of God's promises (2 Cor 1:20), the righteousness of God (5:21), election (Eph 1:4), the revelation of God's will (1:9), the fullness of God's nature (Col 2:9), and God's triumph over the rulers and authorities (2:15). As with ἐν Χριστῷ, most of these express the instrumentality of Christ in relation to the agency of God.

9.4 Σὺν Χριστῷ

Chapter 5 does not include distinct sections on the Trinity because (nearly) all the σύν-related language is analyzed in terms of believers' participation with Christ in his work. Nevertheless, there are some passages in which such language is directly connected to the Father and/or the Spirit, and in §5.3 on the phrase σὺν Χριστῷ we note its connection to life with God (Col 3:3).

9.5 Σὺν αὐτῷ

Also in chapter 5, this time dealing with the prepositional phrase σὺν αὐτῷ, we note the results of §5.5 that indicate that the phrase is directly connected to the Father and/or the Spirit in relation to the following themes: God's provision of all things (Rom 8:32), God's power (2 Cor 13:4), and resurrection (1 Thess 4:14; 5:10).

9.6 Σύν COMPOUNDS

Again in chapter 5, this time dealing with σύν-compound words, we note the results of §5.6, which indicate that such compound words are directly connected to the Father and/or the Spirit in relation to the following themes: the inheritance of God (Rom 8:17), resurrection (Eph 2:5; Col 2:12), and ascension (Eph 2:6).

The σύν-related language indicates participation with Christ, and yet we have noted that, even with such focused attention on believers' identification with him, there are further connections to the Father and the Spirit. It is thus clear that participation with Christ is not simply a one-to-one relationship between believers and Christ; it also conveys trinitarian overtones as the persons of the Father and the Spirit are never far from view.

9.7 Διὰ Χριστοῦ

In chapter 6, on the prepositional phrase διὰ Χριστοῦ, we note the results of §6.7 that indicate the phrase is directly connected to the Father and/or the Spirit in relation to the following themes: judgment (Rom 2:16), reconciliation (2 Cor 5:18), predestination and adoption (Eph 1:5), salvation (1 Thess 5:9), and God's pouring out of the Spirit (Tit 3:6).

9.8 VARIATIONS OF Διὰ Χριστοῦ

Again in chapter 6, this time on phrases related to διὰ Χριστοῦ, we note the results of §6.8.3 that indicate that such phrases are directly connected to the Father and/or the Spirit in relation to the following themes: creation (1 Cor 8:6; Col 1:16), the fulfillment of God's promises (2 Cor 1:20), access to the Father by the Spirit (Eph 2:18), reconciliation (Col 1:20), and thanksgiving (3:17). The usage of διὰ Χριστοῦ and its variations normally envisage an instrumental relationship of Christ with respect to the agency of God, parallel to such uses of the ἐν Χριστῷ language.

9.9 BODY OF CHRIST

In chapter 7, which deals with the various metaphors that Paul uses in connection with union with Christ, we note that §7.2 on the body of Christ indicates the connection of this metaphor to the Father and/or the Spirit in relation to baptism in the Spirit (1 Cor 12:13), God's ordering of the body (12:18, 24), reconciliation of Jew and Gentile to God (Eph 2:16), and the uniqueness of the Spirit (4:4).

9.10 TEMPLE AND BUILDING

Also in chapter 7, we note that §7.3 on the temple and building meta-phors indicates the connection of these metaphors to the Father and/or the Spirit in relation to the following themes: believers as God's temple (1 Cor 3:16–17; 2 Cor 6:16) in whom the Spirit lives (1 Cor 3:16), indi-vidual believers as a sanctuary of the Holy Spirit (6:19), the temple as God's dwelling in the Spirit (Eph 2:22), and believers as God's building (1 Cor 3:9).

9.11 SYNTHESIS

This brief and selective survey demonstrates that there are several instances in which language and metaphors that relate to union with Christ also relate in some way to Paul's implicit trinitarianism. With respect to God the Father, we have observed that the following concepts are all con-nected to union with Christ: the love of God, his grace, his fatherhood, his blessings, his glory, his forgiveness, his calling, his peace, his will, his inheritance, his promises, the fullness of his nature, his triumph over his enemies, his power, his temple, his building, God's work of creation, rec-onciliation, resurrection, ascension, predestination, adoption, judgment, salvation, and access to the Father. With respect to the Spirit, the themes of his being promised, his being poured out, baptism in the Spirit, and the temple of the Spirit are also connected to union with Christ.

The ways in which Paul's implicit trinitarianism relates to union with Christ differ according to the theme addressed and the language employed. The strong tenor of instrumentality that has been observed in the usage of ἐν Χριστῷ and διὰ Χριστοῦ (and their respective variations) points to the mediatorial nature of Christ's work. This observation does not, however, only shed light on Christ's work as it relates to union with Christ; it also demonstrates that union with Christ has a robust God-ward concern. Christ's mediatorial work is related to humanity on one side and God on the other. It is apparently necessary, therefore, to acknowledge that union with Christ does not merely address believers' union with him; it also addresses Christ's union with his Father and with the Spirit.

The participation with Christ that is captured by Paul's various σύν-expressions is not mediatorial, and yet we have observed significant con-nections with God here too. This demonstrates that relationship between union with Christ and the two other members of the Trinity is not simply derived from the nature of mediation, which requires more than two parties. In other words, the trinitarian aspect of union with Christ is not limited to its function in the mediation of Christ between God and humanity.

Moreover, the metaphors of incorporation are also intertwined with trinitarian elements. We have observed that God has a direct interest in the body of Christ as the one who orders it, and through it he brings about his reconciliation between Jew and Gentile. Baptism in the Spirit is also directly related to the body of Christ. Alongside the body of Christ, the corporation of believers is also referred to as God's temple, in whom he dwells and the Spirit lives, and as God's building. Consequently, such metaphorical language not only speaks to the issue of union with Christ both directly and indirectly, but it also has a place in understanding God's relationship to the corporate nature of his people.

Before continuing the discussion on the trinitarian aspects of union with Christ, it is worth reflecting on the significance of the observations that have been summarized in the preceding material. In exploring the God-ward elements of union with Christ, we move against the trend in New Testament scholarship to consider union with Christ simply from humanity's standpoint. Most discussions of the subject regard the theme solely as involving our relationship to Christ, exploring what it means for believers to be united to him and to participate in his works. Yet we have observed that the same language used to depict the unity, participation, and identification of believers with Christ is also used with respect to the relationships between Father, Son, and Spirit. Such unity, participation, and identification exists within the members of the Godhead and describes their interaction as the Father's will is enacted through Christ and by the Spirit. As Karl Barth acknowledges:

> This historical being in Christ is decisively determined, of course, by the fact that first and supremely God was 'in Christ' reconciling the world to Himself (1 Cor. 5[19]).... As they [believers] are in Christ, they acquire and have a direct share in what God first and supremely is in Him, what was done by God for the world and therefore for them in Him, and what is assigned and given to them by God in Him.[1]

---

1. K. Barth, *Dogmatics*, IV/3.2, 546.

Consequently, it is appropriate to regard union with Christ as dealing with more than just humanity and Christ; indeed, it may well be a significant mistake to do so. The Pauline theme of union with Christ is as much about the Father and the Spirit's union with him as it is about ours.

We turn now to consider particular theological issues raised by the topic of the Trinity in connection to union with Christ. First, our attention turns to God the Father and union with Christ. A key question here is whether or not union with Christ entails union with the Father. Second, our attention turns to the Spirit and union with Christ. Third, we will explore the nature of union with Christ with reference to the nature of the Trinity and assess the extent to which these are related.

9.12 GOD THE FATHER AND UNION WITH CHRIST

Schweitzer points out that Paul never speaks of being one with God or being in God. While he does assert the divine sonship of believers, Paul 'does not conceive of sonship to God as an immediate mystical relation to God but as mediated and effected by means of the mystical union with Christ'.[2] Consequently, 'in Paul there is no God-mysticism; only a Christ-mysticism by means of which man comes into relation to God'.[3]

Indeed, Paul rarely refers to God the Father as indwelling believers. Wikenhauser states, 'It is significant that there are only two texts where Paul says that God—as distinct from the Spirit of God—dwells in men: both texts are Old Testament citations [2 Cor 6:16 (Lev 26:12); 1 Cor 14:25 (Isa 45:15)].'[4] While several commentators regard believers' union with Christ as implying, or leading to, union with the Father as a theological necessity,[5]

---

2. Schweitzer, *Mysticism*, 3.

3. Ibid. In fact, Schweitzer does acknowledge a 'God-mysticism' in Paul's thought, but it is not contemporaneous with Christ mysticism; 'They are chronologically successive, Christ-mysticism holding the field until God-mysticism becomes possible.' This, then, is part of the eschatological significance of Christ mysticism in Schweitzer's understanding; it is a penultimate reality that will eventually give way to God-mysticism (ibid., 12–13).

4. Wikenhauser, *Mysticism*, 67.

5. See, e.g., Stewart: 'Union with Christ, as Paul conceives it, *is* union with God. He knows nothing of a mysticism which stops short of faith's final goal. Behind every expression his intense intimacy with Jesus stands the great ultimate fact of God Himself.' Stewart, *A Man in Christ*, 170.

this is not directly reflected by Paul's language. Paul restricts himself to references to believers being in Christ or in the Spirit. In the first instance, then, the relationship between union with Christ and union with the Father is a nonstarter; Paul does not address it, nor does it appear to feature in his thinking. One can argue that Paul's implicit trinitarianism is not only suggestive of the believer's union with the Father through Christ, but it is entailed by such and is therefore an unstated facet of Paul's thinking. Paul the theologian is not restricted by what he did or did not say in his extant occasional letters, and his theological thinking is no doubt deeper and broader than we might be able to reconstruct from the evidence left behind.

There is, nevertheless, a middle ground here that ought to be considered. This involves respecting the insights of both positions and seeking to bring them together. First, it is significant that Paul does not use language of the Father that parallels the phrase 'in Christ' or its related language. This fact ought not be too quickly dismissed, for it raises the question as to why Paul would refrain from this possibility, especially since 'in Christ' is so frequently employed. Let us refrain, then, from using the term 'union with God' or 'in the Father' as though those phrases reflect something that Paul would have said. It is likely that Paul's emphasis on 'in Christ' language—and 'in the Spirit', to a lesser extent—reflects a particular function of his Christology and pneumatology. It is Christ who indwells believers through his Spirit, and it is *to* Christ that believers are joined through the Spirit. The same is not said of the Father because such would undermine the unique role of the Son and the ancillary role of the Spirit.

Second, the power of Paul's implicit trinitarianism ought not be underestimated. There can be little question that Paul regards union with Christ as having significant implications for the believer's relationship to the Father. This is not simply because Christ mediates people to the Father, facilitating access to the Holy One who is otherwise unapproachable to sinful humanity. It is also because Paul knows that Christ is the divine Son who is united to his Father in a profound manner. The union between Father and Son means that a believer in union with the Son is brought into relationship with the Father.

Putting these two things together, it is best to acknowledge the trinitarian implications of union with Christ in terms of relationship with the Father, in the Son, through the Spirit. Union with Christ brings about real and meaningful relationship with the Father, but it is best not to describe this as 'union' with him, since that language is reserved for Christ. After all, the church is the bride of *Christ* and therefore becomes one flesh with him; nowhere does Paul use that metaphor with reference to the Father. Through the notion of relationship with the Father, we are able to preserve the integrity of Paul's language while also acknowledging one of the theological implications of union with Christ, namely, that through Christ we are brought into fellowship with the Father.

While it may be appropriate to caution against referring to 'union with God', there is another significant way in which 'in Christ' language is related to the Father. As observed above, it is clear that 'union with Christ' is as much about the Father's union with the Son as it is about believers' union with Christ.[6] God the Father is 'in Christ' and works in and through him. Christ is the instrument of the Father's will, and all his acts toward humanity are mediated through the Son. In this respect, we must appreciate that according to Paul's language, union with Christ is not simply about our unity with him and the resulting relationship with the Father. It is also about the Father's relationship to the Son and his 'reaching' toward humanity through Christ. Only by acknowledging 'both sides' of union with Christ will we do justice to the cut and thrust of Paul's language and, indeed, his theology.

9.13 THE SPIRIT AND UNION WITH CHRIST

The role of the Spirit in understanding Paul's thinking about union with Christ has many facets.[7] One important element of this role is to effect

---

6. In this way, Stewart's concern that 'God retreats to the background' if union with Christ does not entail union with God is alleviated, and it is still possible to affirm with him that 'it is not true that God is thrust into the background. God is everywhere. He is in every thought of Paul's heart, and in every Christward motion of Paul's will' (ibid., 172).

7. Of note is Horton's observation that Calvin begins his treatment of the Spirit's work (the application of redemption) by returning to the theme of union with Christ; 'Christ's work for us must be distinguished but never separated from his union with us and work within us, both of which are accomplished by the Spirit'; Horton, *Covenant and Salvation*, 146. Reaching further back, Kelly notes that the ancient theologian Epiphanius (ca. AD 310–403) taught that 'not only was the Holy Spirit the bond of the Holy Trinity, he was also the bond of the believer's union with Christ'; Douglas F. Kelly, 'Prayer and Union with Christ', *SBET* 8 (1990): 121.

the presence of Christ in believers.[8] While Paul states that Christ is seated at the right hand of the Father, it is also the case that Christ is present in believers. And yet, as Wikenhauser correctly identifies, these statements are not incompatible since 'the Spirit provides the link between the two'.[9] The Spirit mediates the presence of Christ among believers in such a way that he may be regarded as 'with the Father' and also at the same time 'among his people'.[10] As Smedes puts it, 'the Spirit is the living contact between the victorious Jesus and all who are united with Him.... Between Him and us there is no gulf in time or space.'[11] This is due to the fact 'the Spirit represents Jesus Christ, wholly and completely'.[12] As Barth summarizes, 'the gift and work of the Holy Spirit in us is that Jesus Christ should live in us by faith, that He should be in solidarity and unity with us and we with Him.'[13]

Paul is capable of using the language 'in the Spirit' alongside 'in Christ'. Wikenhauser observes: '"In the Spirit" is a phrase which Paul uses nineteen times, and he often makes exactly the same statement about the Spirit as he makes about Christ.'[14] Smedes claims that Paul does not make a distinction between our life in the Spirit and our life in Christ.[15] Nevertheless, it also

---

8. Son demonstrates the organic connection between the reception of the Spirit and Paul's metaphor of 'putting on Christ'; 'Receiving the Spirit is the essential part of the "putting on Christ". When Christ is put on, the Spirit of Christ enters into the believer and occupies his whole being, resulting in the completion of his unification with Christ (cf. Gal. 4.19).' Son, *Clothing Imagery*, 120. For more on the language of 'putting on Christ' and the clothing imagery it reflects, see ch. 7.

9. Wikenhauser, *Mysticism*, 89.

10. This fact should, however, be qualified by the acknowledgment that Christ's sitting at the right hand of the Father is an expression that denotes his rule and authority more than his 'physical location'; Wikenhauser, *Mysticism*, 89.

11. Lewis B. Smedes, *Union with Christ: A Biblical View of the New Life in Jesus Christ* (rev. ed.; Grand Rapids: Eerdmans, 1983), 26.

12. Ibid., 48.

13. K. Barth, *Church Dogmatics* II/2, 780.

14. Wikenhauser, *Mysticism*, 53.

15. Smedes, *Union with Christ*, 45. So Bousset: 'The two formulas coincide so completely that they can be interchanged at will. The Christian is ἐν Χριστῷ as he is ἐν πνεύματι. As the Spirit dwells in the believers, so also Christ dwells in them.' Bousset, *Kyrios Christos*, 160. Tannehill, likewise: 'The changing terms "Spirit of God," "Spirit of Christ," and "Christ" indicate the one power which is active in the new aeon, dwelling in the believers and at work in them. The movement from one phrase to another shows that there is no sharp distinction between being "in the Spirit," having the Spirit of God dwell "in you," having the "Spirit of Christ," and Christ being "in you."' Tannehill, *Dying and Rising*, 60.

appears to be the case that 'in the Spirit' language displays a special connection to the life of the believer. Wikenhauser elaborates:

> Close examination of the cases where Paul uses these two phrases with the same ideas reveals an interesting fact: Paul always uses the phrase 'in Christ' when he is speaking of salvation as such, while he reserves the phrase 'in the Spirit' for the conduct of the faithful as contrasted with the life of the natural man, and especially for the new sphere of life as contrasted with the life of the 'the flesh' (σάρξ), or when he is dealing with the effects of the Spirit on the interior life of the believer.[16]

Schweitzer correctly points to the role of the Spirit in confirming the reality of sharing the death and resurrection of Jesus: 'In regarding the possession of the Spirit as a sign of the resurrection which is already in process of being realised in the believer, Paul is asserting something which, from the point of view of an eschatology which has Christ's death and resurrection behind it, is self-evident.'[17] The Spirit thereby provides assurance to believers that they share in the resurrection of Christ, but also 'that they are Children of God and are justified in His sight'.[18] In this regard, Ridderbos points out that 'being-in-the-Spirit is therefore not in the first place a personal, but an ecclesiological category'.[19] The believer who is incorporated into Christ is also baptized into the Spirit; 'to belong to the one body of Christ signifies also to share in the one Spirit.'[20]

In the life of the believer, the Spirit becomes the means through whom union with Christ is lived out. 'Thus, for the mystical doctrine of the being-in-Christ, ethics is nothing else than the Spirit's working.'[21] Indeed, for Paul 'the Spirit is primarily a divine power which operates in man', from whom a person derives strength.[22] In part, the implications of the Spirit's work are

---

16. Wikenhauser, *Mysticism*, 54.

17. Schweitzer, *Mysticism*, 160.

18. Ibid., 166–67.

19. Ridderbos, *Paul*, 221.

20. Ibid. This association between the Spirit and Christ finds its roots in prophetic eschatology, in which it is established that 'the Messiah of David's line is endowed with the Spirit of God, and thereby becomes capable of the bringing in the Kingdom of Peace'; Schweitzer, *Mysticism*, 160. In such a manner, the Spirit is 'the form of manifestation of the powers of the resurrection' (ibid., 166).

21. Ibid., 294.

22. Wikenhauser, *Mysticism*, 57.

related to the corporate nature of the Christian life, as Dunn recognizes: 'Paul's language indicates rather a quite profound sense of participation with others in a great and cosmic movement of God centred on Christ and effected through his Spirit.'[23] Furthermore, the Spirit is of fundamental importance to the prayer life of those in Christ, with 'the influence of the union upon the very prayers themselves as they rise out of the deep places of the lives of Christians, who are indwelt by the eternal Spirit'.[24]

9.14 THE TRINITARIAN CHARACTER OF UNION WITH CHRIST

A key question related to the trinitarian nature of union with Christ is the manner in which the union that believers share with Christ reflects the union between Christ and God the Father. To what extent are these two things related, and how meaningful is such a comparison? Douty offers the interesting observation that the mutual indwelling of Christ and the Father is stressed in the gospels, while the mutual indwelling of Christians and Christ is stressed in the New Testament letters.[25] This is no doubt due, in part, to the teaching of Jesus about himself and his ministry found in the gospels (and John in particular), while Paul demonstrates—through the occasional nature of his letters—a strong concern to explore the implications of Christ's person and work for the life of believing communities. Thus, it is not surprising that the mutual indwelling of Christ and the Father is more prominent in the gospels, since Jesus' teaching is about himself, while the mutual indwelling of Christians and Christ is more prominent in the letters, since Paul's concern is for the churches.

An important theme in recent trinitarian theology draws on the concept of *perichoresis* (περιχώρησις) to attempt to describe the nature of the inner life of Trinity. An ancient term, used in this connection since Gregory of Nazianzus (c. AD 329–389) and explored further by John of Damascus (c. AD 676–749), it focuses on the mutual indwelling of Father, Son, and Spirit as each person partakes in the being of the other. Such thinking resonates with Jesus' prayer of John 17: *May they all be one, as you, Father,*

---

23. Dunn, *Paul the Apostle*, 404.
24. Kelly, 'Prayer and Union', 135.
25. Norman F. Douty, *Union with Christ* (Swengel, PA: Reiner, 1973), 147.

are in me and I am in you. May they also be one in us.... I am in them and you are in me (John 17:21, 23). Also apparently in keeping with Jesus' words is the extension of the concept of *perichoresis* beyond the inner life of the Trinity to envelop humanity. As Speidell summarizes, this has to do with 'God in us, we in God, and we in one another. The tripersonal God shares his divine life of communion with humans so that humans may live as a union of persons in communion with God and one another'.[26]

Nevertheless, Douty wisely cautions against too closely associating the mutual indwelling of believers and Christ with that of his Father: 'But the mutual indwelling of Christ and believers is only similar to that existing between the Father and Himself as Man, and not equivalent to it.'[27] While it may be true that believers' union with Christ is patterned after the Father's, it 'cannot possibly be said to be equal to it'.[28] Similarly, Seifrid cautions that while the term περιχώρησις is 'beautiful and useful in its simplicity', it is inadequate to describe 'the distinction between God and the sinner who interpenetrate one another in union'.[29]

Related to this is the question of the deification of believers, or *theosis*. While there is a long tradition of reflection on this subject, especially in Orthodox theology, we will restrict this discussion to a few recent contributors. Explicating the Orthodox doctrine of *theosis*, Meyendorff and Tobias declare that 'deification does not mean that human beings "become God" in a pantheistic sense'.[30] What is in view, rather, is personal relationship with God and participation 'in God's life through the sacraments in the church, the body of Christ, [and] the community of the people of God'.[31]

---

26. Todd H. Speidell, 'A Trinitarian Ontology of Persons in Society', *SJT* 47 (1994): 284.

27. Douty, *Union with Christ*, 147.

28. Ibid., 148.

29. Mark A. Seifrid, 'Paul, Luther, and Justification in Gal 2:15–21', *WTJ* 65 (2003): 228–29.

30. John Meyendorff and Robert Tobias, eds., *Salvation in Christ: A Lutheran–Orthodox Dialogue* (Minneapolis: Augsburg, 1992), 20.

31. Ibid. While deification is normally associated with Orthodox theology, recent appraisals of Luther and Calvin identify a type of deification in their writings too. Billings argues that Calvin teaches deification of a particular sort: 'Drawing upon the language of participation, ingrafting, and adoption in select Pauline and Johannine passages, Calvin teaches the participation of humanity in the Triune God, affirming the differentiated union of humanity with God in creation and redemption'; J. Todd Billings, 'United to God through Christ: Assessing Calvin on the Question of Deification', *HTR* 98 (2005): 316–17. According to Billings, Calvin believed that 'believers participate not just in the divine nature of Christ,

Similarly, Metzger regards union with Christ as 'a dynamic of inclusion and personal participation in the life of the Trinity through the personal mediation of the Spirit who unites our hearts in faith to Christ'.[32]

Yet Breck describes the Orthodox view as holding that 'divinization' or 'deification' means 'a literal "ontological" participation in the being of God', while avoiding any hint of absorption into the divinity with a consequent loss of individual personality.[33] In spite of the strong language of 'ontological participation in the being of God', deification does not suggest that believers become God, but that 'humans as creatures are introduced into personal relationships of participation in the uncreated, divine energies or grace'.[34] Helminiak argues that it is union with Christ—together with his incarnation—that makes human divinization possible. 'In Jesus Christ, for the first time, divinization became a real human possibility; what has happened is certainly possible';[35] 'the solidarity that constitutes the divine-human possibility is collective union in Christ.'[36]

Such a theory of divinization ought not be caricatured as a pathway to uncreatedness or lack of distinction between Creator and created being. According to Helminiak, 'divinized humans remain distinct not only from one another but also from the divine substance and so from the divine persons, as well'.[37] By this understanding of divinization, it is clear that humans may only be described as 'divine' in a strictly qualified sense; they do not become God, nor are they mingled with his divine being. Thus, while Helminiak can draw a comparison 'between collective union in Christ and the unity of the divine Persons in the Trinity',[38] he also affirms that 'human collective union in Christ differs from the union of the three divine persons'.[39]

---

but in the whole person of Christ. Through this participation in Christ, believers participate in the Trinity' (ibid., 327).

32. Paul Louis Metzger, 'Luther and the Finnish School—Mystical Union with Christ: An Alternative to Blood Transfusions and Legal Fictions', *WTJ* 65 (2003): 208–9.

33. John Breck, 'Divine Initiative: Salvation in Orthodox Theology', in *Salvation in Christ: A Lutheran–Orthodox Dialogue* (ed. John Meyendorff and Robert Tobias; Minneapolis: Augsburg, 1992), 117.

34. Ibid., 117–18.

35. Daniel A. Helminiak, 'Human Solidarity and Collective Union in Christ', *AThR* 70 (1988): 53.

36. Ibid., 54.

37. Ibid. 58.

38. Ibid., 57.

39. Ibid., 58.

On this point, Helminiak is surely correct; union with Christ may be seen as a type of relationship in parallel to that between the persons of the Godhead, but it does not constitute the same thing nor does it divinize humans in the way we would think of the Trinity as divine.[40] Consequently, the question is raised as to whether the term 'divinization' is actually helpful or if it dies the death of a thousand qualifications. Perhaps it is analogous to the term 'mysticism' with reference to Paul's theology of union with Christ. It had to be qualified to such an extent that it ultimately failed to be useful.[41]

Murray identifies the nub of the issue when he points to the distinction between analogy and identity:

> Union with Christ does not mean that we are incorporated into the Godhead. That is one of the distortions to which this great truth has been subjected. But the process of thought by which such a view has been adopted neglects one of the simplest principles which must always guide our thinking, namely, that analogy does not mean identity. When we make a comparison we do not make an equation.[42]

While it is true that the nature of the Trinity informs our understanding of union with Christ, it cannot be taken too far. The persons of the Trinity relate to one another through mutual indwelling, and such mutual indwelling characterizes the nature of the relationship between believers and Christ. Murray's point, however, is that this comparison provides an analogy only and does not entail the divinization of believers or even the sense that our relationship with Christ is the same as those within the Godhead. There is no question, however, that it is appropriate to acknowledge that union with Christ entails relationship for believers with the

---

40. Similarly, Wesche describes *theosis* as 'the mystery of human nature's perfection, not its alteration or destruction, because *theosis* is the mystery of eternal life in communion with God in the divine Logos and communion with God in the divine Logos is the very essence of human being as "created in the image and likeness of God"'; Kenneth Paul Wesche, 'Eastern Orthodox Spirituality: Union with God in Theosis', *ThTo* 56 (1999): 31. The distinction between humanity and God that Wesche affirms here, however, does not prevent his use of the strong language 'that humanity might become God' (ibid., 33).

41. Perhaps this highlights a fundamental difference between Eastern and Western approaches to theology. While the former resists systematic formulation, the latter drives toward an organized system replete with nuance and qualification.

42. Murray, *Redemption*, 208–9.

members of the Trinity. Believers' fellowship with God the Father and the Holy Spirit is a spiritual reality 'that union with Christ draws along with it'.[43]

Gorman has developed a slightly different approach to *theosis* via his understanding of cruciformity, which refers to conformity to the crucified Christ. His argument is that cruciformity is really theoformity, or *theosis*, since 'to be one with Christ is to be one with God; to be like Christ is to be like God; to be in Christ is to be in God'.[44] Gorman also suggests that Paul's language of being 'in Christ' is his 'shorthand for "in God/ in Christ/in the Spirit"'.[45] While we cannot affirm the full extent of this claim,[46] Gorman is probably correct to point out that Paul's christocentricity is really an implicit trinitarianism.[47] Gorman helpfully identifies that the Eastern tradition does not mean that people become little gods, but that 'theosis means humans become *like* God'.[48] 'Theosis is about divine intention and action, human transformation, and the *telos* of human existence—union with God.'[49]

9.15 CONCLUSION

This chapter draws together the exegetical results of part 2 that relate to Paul's implicit trinitarianism. Christ is the instrumental mediator of the Father's will toward humanity, and incorporation into Christ spells membership in God's temple in which the Spirit dwells. Moroever, Christ's mediatorial work is related to humanity on one side and God on the other; thus union with Christ addresses believers' union with him *and* Christ's union with his Father and the Spirit. Union with Christ brings believers into fellowship with the Father, being indwelt by the Spirit, though Paul

---

43. Ibid., 212.

44. Gorman, *Inhabiting the Cruciform God*, 4.

45. Ibid. In another book, Gorman adds: 'To say that believers live in the Spirit of Christ is to say that they inhabit the three-in-one cruciform God'; Michael J. Gorman, *Reading Paul* (Eugene, OR: Cascade, 2008), 127.

46. It has been demonstrated that 'in Christ' is not a formula that indicates the *one* concept in every instance of usage. It has a broad spectrum of meanings according to context (see ch. 3).

47. Gorman, *Inhabiting the Cruciform God*, 4.

48. Ibid.

49. Ibid., 4–5.

reserves union language for being 'in Christ' and 'in the Spirit', not 'in the Father'. The Spirit effects the presence of Christ in believers and confirms in them the reality of participation in his death and resurrection. He also enables believers to live out the implications of their union with Christ. While believers' union with Christ is patterned after the Father's union with him, it is not equal to it; our union does not entail that believers become members of the Godhead. Rather, a carefully qualified sense of *theosis* points to human transformation that we might become like God.

CHAPTER 10

UNION WITH CHRIST AND CHRISTIAN LIVING

10.1 INTRODUCTION

Paul's concern for the way in which believers live, identify themselves, and conduct themselves in relation to God, other believers, and the world is obviously intense and widespread. Such concern occupies significant portions of each of his letters, often as the practical outworking of his exposition of profound theological themes. We turn now to consider the ways in which the issue of Christian living—the term used here encompasses a wide range of issues, including identity and activity—is explicitly related to union with Christ. This will include specific activities of individuals, such as Paul himself, as well as matters that pertain to his readers and general issues that relate to all believers.[1] As has been the practice thus far,

---

1. Indeed, it has been argued that Pauline anthropology in general rests on Paul's understanding of humanity's relation to Christ. Nelson claims that, according to Paul, 'man only becomes truly man in relation to Christ', and as such Pauline anthropology is essentially Christocentric; William R. Nelson, 'Pauline Anthropology: Its Relation to Christ and His Church', *Int* 14 (1960): 27. Son explores this notion also, but with respect to the corporeality of humanity: 'Paul understands man as a being whose existence is not limited to his individual person. Although an individual man is separated from others by the limits of his physical body, his existence is by no means limited to himself. In certain respects his existence extends beyond his individual boundaries to form a corporate unity (body) with others and with Christ but without losing his individuality'; Sang-Won (Aaron) Son, 'Implications of Paul's "One Flesh" Concept for His Understanding of the Nature of Man', *BBR* 11 (2001): 121–22. For a trinitarian approach to the same issue, Speidell says that 'because God is a preeminently tripersonal being, humans created in God's image must, and may, live as persons in relation to God, other persons, and the world'; Speidell, 'Trinitarian Ontology', 283.

a selective survey of the chapters of part 2 will facilitate the consideration of this relationship.

10.2 Ἐν Χριστῷ

In chapter 3, on the prepositional phrase ἐν Χριστῷ, we note the results of §3.4, 'Believers' Actions *in Christ*', which indicate that the phrase is directly connected to the sphere of Christian living in relation to the following themes: speaking (Rom 9:1; 2 Cor 2:17; 12:19), boasting in Christ rather than in oneself (Rom 15:17; Phil 3:3), and Paul's conduct (1 Cor 4:17).

Continuing with ἐν Χριστῷ, we note the results of §§3.5 and 3.6, 'Characteristics of Those *in Christ*' and 'Faith *in Christ*', which indicate that the phrase is directly connected to the sphere of Christian living in relation to the following themes: boasting in Christ Jesus (1 Cor 15:31), confidence in Christ Jesus (Phil 1:26), encouragement in Christ (Phil 2:1), an attitude of Christ Jesus (Phil 2:5), maturity in Christ (Col 1:28), faith and love in Christ Jesus (2 Tim 1:13), being strong in grace (2:1), living a godly life (3:12), boldness in Christ (Phlm 8), and faith in Christ (1 Cor 15:19; Gal 3:26; Eph 1:1; Col 1:4; 1 Tim 3:13; 2 Tim 3:15).

Again with respect to ἐν Χριστῷ, we note the results of §3.8, 'New Status *in Christ*'. The status of believers in Christ is an essential element of Christian living, since Paul is concerned to teach believers how properly to identify and understand themselves in light of Christ. Ἐν Χριστῷ is directly connected to the sphere of Christian living in relation to the following themes: being alive to God (Rom 6:11), being free from condemnation (8:1), being part of one body (12:5), being a new creation (2 Cor 5:17), being children of God (Gal 3:26), being one in Christ Jesus (3:28), and Gentiles being partners with Jews in the promise of God (Eph 3:6).

Another subtopic involving ἐν Χριστῷ is explored in §3.9, '*In Christ* as a Periphrasis for Believers'. This section deals with the instances of the phrase in which it functions as a label for people who are Christian. This use of ἐν Χριστῷ is included because the identification of believers falls under the sphere of Christian living. The results of §3.9 indicate that the phrase functions this way in describing various individuals or groups as coworkers in Christ (Rom 16:3, 9), converted (Rom 16:7; 1 Cor 16:24; 2 Cor 12:2), babies in Christ (1 Cor 3:1), an instructor in Christ (4:15), churches in Christ (Gal 1:22; 1 Thess 2:14), saints in Christ (Phil 1:1; 4:21), brothers in Christ (Col 1:2), and a prisoner in Christ (Phil 1:13; Phlm 23).

10.3 Ἐν κυρίῳ

In chapter 3, this time on the prepositional phrase ἐν κυρίῳ, we note the results of §3.11.2.2, 'Believers' actions *in the Lord*', which indicate that the phrase is directly connected to the sphere of Christian living in relation to the following themes: welcoming and greeting other believers (Rom 16:2; 1 Cor 16:19), working in the Lord (Rom 16:12; 1 Cor 15:58), boasting in the Lord (1 Cor 1:31; 2 Cor 10:17), testifying in the Lord (Eph 4:17), obeying parents (6:1; Col 3:20), rejoicing (Phil 3:1; 4:4, 10), standing firm (4:1; 1 Thess 3:8), agreeing in the Lord (Phil 4:2), wives submitting to their husbands (Col 3:18), encouraging other believers (1 Thess 4:1; 2 Thess 3:12), and leading others (1 Thess 5:12).

Also on the phrase ἐν κυρίῳ, the results of §§3.11.2.3 and 3.11.2.4, 'Characteristics of those *in the Lord*' and 'Faith *in the Lord*', indicate that the phrase is directly connected to the sphere of Christian living in relation to the following themes: confidence (Gal 5:10), being a prisoner (Eph 4:1; 2 Thess 3:4), being light (Eph 5:8), joy (Phlm 20), and faith (Eph 1:15; Phil 2:19).

Again with reference to ἐν κυρίῳ, the results of §3.11.2.5, '*In the Lord* as a periphrasis for believers', indicate that the phrase functions to describe various individuals or groups as friends in the Lord (Rom 16:8), converted (Rom 16:11; 1 Cor 7:39), a child in the Lord (1 Cor 4:17), an apostle (9:2), a servant (Eph 6:21), brothers (Phil 1:14; Phlm 16), and a slave (Col 4:7).

Clearly ἐν Χριστῷ and ἐν κυρίῳ language is strongly intertwined with the sphere of Christian living, with the full variety of believers' actions, characteristics, and status defined by these phrases. Furthermore, this language is Paul's shorthand for describing people as believers in Christ. Evidently, the phrases are so comprehensive that they connote a person's spiritual state and allegiance to Christ with sufficient clarity.

10.4 Σὺν Χριστῷ

Chapter 5 does not include distinct sections on Christian living because all the σύν-related language is analyzed in terms of solidarity with Christ in his work. Nevertheless, there are some passages in which such language is directly connected to the actions, characteristics, and status of believers; in §5.3 on σὺν Χριστῷ, we note its connection to the following themes: having died with Christ (Rom 6:8; Col 2:20) and life hidden with Christ (Col 3:3).

10.5 Σὺν αὐτῷ

On the prepositional phrase σὺν αὐτῷ, we note the results of §5.5, 'With Him', which indicate that the phrase is directly connected to living with Christ (2 Cor 13:4; 1 Thess 5:10) and being made alive with him (Col 2:13).

10.6 Σύν COMPOUNDS

On the σύν-compound words, we note the results of §5.6, which indicate that such compound words are directly connected to Christian living through the following themes: having died with Christ (Rom 6:4–5), living with Christ (6:8), being coheirs with Christ (8:17), suffering with Christ (8:17), being glorified with Christ (8:17), being made alive with Christ (Eph 2:5), ascending with Christ (2:6), having been buried with Christ (Col 2:12), and having been raised with Christ (2:12; 3:1).

The σύν-related language indicates participation with Christ, which has clear implications for Christian living. They are regarded as suffering with Christ, having died with Christ, being raised with him, living with Christ, ascending with him to the heavens, and being glorified with Christ, among other things. Paul understands these profound realities to have essential significance for the ways in which believers are to live and identify themselves.

10.7 Διὰ Χριστοῦ

In chapter 6, on the prepositional phrase διὰ Χριστοῦ, we note the results of §6.4, 'Believers' Actions *through Christ*', that indicate the phrase is directly connected to the sphere of Christian living in the following activities: thanksgiving (Rom 1:8; 7:25), rejoicing (5:11), encouragement (15:30; 2 Cor 10:1), and praise (Rom 16:27). Evidently, these behaviours are conducted through the instrumentality of Christ; he enables believers to offer thanks and praise God, to rejoice, and to encourage others.

10.8 BODY OF CHRIST

In chapter 7, which deals with the various metaphors that Paul uses regarding union with Christ, in §7.2 the metaphor of the body of Christ is connected to the sphere of Christian living in relation to the unity and diversity of believers in the body (Rom 12:4–5; 1 Cor 12:12–27), sexual purity (1 Cor 6:15–16), sharing in the one body (10:16–17; 11:29; Eph 4:4; Col 3:15), building the body (Eph 4:12, 15–16), and being members of Christ's body (5:30).

10.9 TEMPLE AND BUILDING

In §7.3 the metaphors of temple and building are connected to Christian living in relation to the status of believers as the temple of God (1 Cor 3:16; 6:19; 2 Cor 6:16; Eph 2:21), in whom the Spirit lives (1 Cor 3:16; Eph 2:21–22), and as God's building (1 Cor 3:9; Eph 2:21).

10.10 MARRIAGE

In §7.4 the metaphor of marriage is connected to Christian living in relation to the status of believers as one with Christ (1 Cor 6:16–17), promised in marriage to Christ (2 Cor 11:2–3), one flesh with him (Eph 5:31–32), with the practical implications of sexual purity (1 Cor 6:15–17), and submission to Christ (Eph 5:24).

10.11 NEW CLOTHING

The final metaphor explored in chapter 7 is that of new clothing (§7.5), which refers to *putting on* Christ or things pertaining to him. This metaphor is directly related to Christian living, with strong behavioural implications, as seen in relation to resisting fleshly desires (Rom 13:14), putting on compassion, kindness, humility, gentleness, and patience (Col 3:12), and putting on the armour of God (Eph 6:11).[2] The metaphor can also denote the status of believers: those who have been baptized have put on Christ (Gal 3:27) or the new self (Col 3:9; Eph 4:24).

10.12 SYNTHESIS

This brief and selective survey demonstrates that there are several instances in which the language and metaphors that relate to union with Christ inform the sphere of Christian living. The *identity and status* of believers are effected through their union with Christ and are described in terms of being alive to God, free from condemnation, one body, a new creation, children of God, coheirs, one in Christ Jesus, members of his body, married to Christ, one flesh with him, having died with Christ, being buried with him, having been raised with him, being glorified with him, having put on Christ, living with Christ, and being God's temple and building.

The *activities* of believers are conditioned by their union with Christ; these include speaking, boasting, welcoming others, working, testifying, obeying, rejoicing, standing firm, agreeing with one another, submitting to Christ, encouraging each other, leading, suffering, praising God, maintaining sexual purity, sharing, building God's people, and putting on his armour.

The *characteristics* of believers are also conditioned by their union with Christ; these include faith, confidence, maturity, love, grace, godliness, boldness, joy, compassion, kindness, humility, gentleness, and patience.

Finally, the very *terminology* Paul uses to call someone a Christian is taken directly from the vocabulary of union with Christ since the reality of their connection to Christ is of such significance that it summarizes their entire Christian existence. Various individuals and groups are so described as friends in the Lord, converted, a child, an apostle, a servant, brothers, a slave, a coworker, a prisoner, an instructor, churches in Christ, and saints.

---

2. Kim points out the several ways in which clothing imagery communicates ethical content. He sees it relating 'to the entirety of the Christian's life' and to an 'ethical change in his practical life'; Kim, *Clothing Imagery*, 2. The metaphor's ethical power draws on the assumption that as a garment reveals its wearer's character, 'so Christ reveals a Christian's character' (ibid., 117–18).

In sum, virtually every aspect of the Christian life is informed in some way by a believer's union with Christ. The status and identity that believers enjoy, which is so programmatic for Paul's ethical framework and instruction, are inextricably bound up with union with Christ. From there flow the activities and characteristics of believers, which again are entwined with union with Christ. The Christian life is so weaved of the fabric of union with Christ that the most appropriate moniker for believers is 'in Christ'. As Campbell claims, it cannot be denied that Paul 'is laying out a distinctive ethical system informed by participation in Christ through the Spirit'.[3]

We turn now to consider in greater depth some of the important strands of discussion in relation to the Christian living in union with Christ.

10.13 LIVING OUT THE DEATH AND RESURRECTION OF CHRIST

As we have seen, Paul freely speaks of believers participating with Christ in the events of his death and resurrection. He also draws on this reality to construct the framework through which believers are to understand their present state of being and consequent moral obligations.[4] Tannehill remarks, 'These events continue to give their stamp to the life of the believer, for he continues to participate in Christ's death and resurrection in his daily life.'[5] The following discussion addresses the ways in which dying and rising with Christ affect Paul's convictions about the Christian life.

For Cranfield, the Christian life correlates to the 'moral' sense of dying and rising with Christ that he finds in Romans 6. The implicit answer, he

---

3. Douglas A. Campbell, *The Deliverance of God: An Apocalyptic Rereading of Justification in Paul* (Grand Rapids: Eerdmans, 2009), 607. According to Stewart, union with Christ is not merely 'the mainstay of Paul's religion', but *'the sheet-anchor of his ethics'*; Stewart, *A Man in Christ*, 194 [italics are original]. Thuruthumaly notes that 'Christ is the sphere of Paul's spiritual life'; J. Thuruthumaly, 'Mysticism in Pauline Writings', *Bible Bhashyam* 18 (1992): 147. See also Morna D. Hooker, 'Interchange in Christ and Ethics', *JSNT* 25 (1985): 5–7.

4. Wisnefske laments how little the reality of dying and rising with Christ animates the thoughts of believers in the current state of the church; 'we are listening to cosmic news but only hear more pedestrian religious views'; Wisnefske, 'Living and Dying', 254.

5. Tannehill, *Dying and Rising*, 1.

argues, to Paul's question in v. 2 — 'We who died to sin, how shall we any longer live therein?' — is that believers must try to die to sin in their day-to-day experience.[6] In other words, dying with Christ involves not only participation in the historical event of his death, but also in the daily battle against sin, for which Christ died in the first place. Furthermore, the responsibility that believers face of walking in newness of life is, Cranfield suggests, an expression of sharing in the resurrection of Christ. Resurrection brings about new life, and being conformed to Christ's resurrection is expressed 'in our concrete daily living' of that new life.[7]

There is an apparent eschatological tension in the framework of Paul's thinking when it comes to sharing in the death and resurrection of Christ. On the one hand, believers have already died and risen with Christ, participating with him in the particular events of history. On the other hand, believers live out the death and resurrection of Jesus in their lives, as the significance of their sharing in his historical death and resurrection takes hold for everyday living.[8] Tannehill prefers to describe this tension by saying that the believer continually dies with Christ in that there takes place in his life 'a continual manifestation and affirmation of his past death with Christ'.[9] The reality of this eschatological tension means that believers who become united to Christ in his death and resurrection may not appear any different in the first instance; rather, their conformity to Christ must unfold with increasing significance. Schweitzer acknowledges the implications of this tension:

> But whereas this dying and rising again has been openly manifested in Jesus, in the Elect it goes forward secretly but none the less really. Since in the nature of their corporeity they are now assimilated to Jesus Christ, they become, through His death and resurrection, beings in whom dying

---

6. Cranfield, 'Romans 6 Revisited', 42.

7. Ibid.

8. So Ejenobo: 'In more than one sense, the Christian has already died and has been raised with Christ; but in another sense, his dying and being raised with Christ is a matter of present obligation, something which ought now to be in the process of being fulfilled, and in yet another sense, it lies ahead of him as an eschatological promise.' David T. Ejenobo, 'Union with Christ: A Critique of Romans 6:1–11', *AJT* 22 (2008): 312.

9. Tannehill, *Dying and Rising*, 81. So too Gorman: 'For Paul, this intimate identification with Christ symbolized in baptism is not merely a one-time event but an experience of *ongoing* death, of *ongoing* crucifixion. Paul paradigmatically envisions his entire faith experience with Christ as "co-crucifixion"'; Gorman, *Cruciformity*, 32.

and rising again have already begun, although the outward seeming of their natural existence remains unchanged.[10]

Something very real has changed for the person who participates with Christ in his death and resurrection, and yet outwardly the profound significance of this change may not be immediately obvious.

The ethical implications of participating with Christ in his death and resurrection derive from the purpose of these events. Wikenhauser offers an interesting approach to this when he describes Christ's death as 'a supreme ethical act',[11] performed in obedience to the Father, 'for the thoroughly ethical-religious purpose of liberating mankind from sin'. Since the purpose of Christ's death was 'ethical-religious', the implications therefore of participating with Christ in his death follow suit: 'That is why the mystical fellowship with Christ is not complete until it becomes an ethical-religious relationship.'[12] While we may not retain Wikenhauser's language here, the connection between the purpose of Christ's death and the purpose of living in light of it is worthy of further consideration. If the purpose of Christ's death — in part at least — is to bring rebellious humanity into relationship with the holy God, it follows that, once reconciled, believers will live in a manner that befits such a relationship with such a God.

Such reasoning will avoid a common problem afflicting modern believers who may struggle to see a clear rationale for holy living when they understand that reconciliation with God is through the work of Christ, not according to works. Since salvation is by grace, the importance of righteous living can be muted in the name of avoiding moralism or legalism. While such -isms ought to be avoided in the Christian life, it does not follow that holiness and righteous conduct are not the proper calling for believers. Indeed, as suggested above, if the purpose of Christ's death and resurrection is to restore human beings to the holy God, then the purpose of the Christian life is live according to that restored relationship. Barth eloquently expresses this reality for the believer:

He believes, obeys and confesses as, now that Christ has united Himself with him, he unites himself with Christ, giving himself to the One who

---

10. Schweitzer, *Mysticism*, 110.
11. Wikenhauser, *Mysticism*, 146.
12. Ibid., 146–47.

first gave Himself to him, and thus choosing Him as the starting-point and therefore the goal of His thinking, speech, volition and action, quite simply and non-paradoxically because this is what He is, because there is no other starting-point or goal apart from Him, because in truth he is not outside Him but within Him.[13]

Gorman approaches the issue by drawing on the 'life-narrative' of Christ to which believers are conformed: *the narrative of the crucified and exalted Christ is the normative life-narrative within which the community's own life-narrative takes place and by which it is shaped.*'[14] In other words, Gorman argues that because death and resurrection were what Christ experienced—indeed, the necessary 'path'—so believers are to be conformed to the same narrative. This pattern is not merely imitation of Christ; in fact, for Gorman that word does not sufficiently capture Paul's meaning. He argues instead for the usefulness of the word 'cruciformity' in this connection:

> Cruciformity, I therefore suggest, is a term more appropriate for what has often been referred to as the 'imitation' of Christ. Cruciformity is an ongoing pattern of living in Christ and of dying with him that produces a Christlike (cruciform) person. Cruciform is what being Christ's servant, indwelling and being indwelt by him, living with and for and 'according to' him, is all about, for both individuals and communities.[15]

Cruciformity, according to Gorman, evokes Paul's 'narrative spirituality', such that the life of a believer is shaped by the narrative events of Christ's death and resurrection. More than that, the necessary link between his death, resurrection, and exaltation provides the logic underpinning Paul's understanding of life in union with Christ. To be united to Christ is '*to be a living exegesis of this narrative of Christ*', in which humiliation is a voluntary renunciation of rights in order to serve and obey, and in which exaltation follows humiliation.[16] Gorman, summarizes this in

---

13. K. Barth, *Dogmatics*, IV/3.2, 544–45.

14. Gorman, *Cruciformity*, 44 [italics are original].

15. Ibid., 48–49. Hooker also champions the word 'conformity' to capture Paul's thought: 'Of course this is not imitation, it is conformity, and it is a central theme in Paul'; Hooker, *From Adam to Christ*, 92.

16. Gorman, *Cruciformity*, 92.

the following statement: 'Paul's spirituality of cruciformity is a narrative spirituality, and the master narrative that shapes his spirituality is Philippians 2:6–11.'[17]

Gorman's approach is interesting and seems a more powerful appropriation of Paul's thought than the simple 'imitation of Christ' approach. While it may be argued that Gorman has improperly emphasized conformity to the *death* of Christ at the expense of the resurrection (seen especially in the term *cruciformity*), Gorman resists this problem. According to Paul's narrative spirituality, which rests on Philippians 2:6–11, humiliation and death lead to resurrection and exaltation. Such was the case for Christ, and such is the case for the believer who is conformed to the death of Christ. In other words, cruciformity entails conformity with the resurrection and exaltation of Christ as well as conformity to his death.[18]

As long as this link is taken into account, one need not assume that the term *cruciformity* neglects the end of the story, as it were. Conformity to Christ in his death and resurrection recognizes the role of union with Christ in Paul's ethical thinking in a way that mere imitation does not. The believer is not simply 'retracing the steps' of Christ, but participating in his work in a manner that is expressed in the believer's life. In this respect, Gorman's thesis may also provide a helpful way of thinking about the eschatological tension discussed above; by becoming conformed to Christ's death and resurrection, the believer is both partaking in the historical events of salvation while also living them out in his or her own time and experience.

---

17. Ibid. Hooker makes much the same point regarding this passage: 'Phil. 2 is equally practical: the pattern of Christ's self-humiliation is the basis of the Christian's life and of his dealings with his fellow men. This is not simply a question of following a good example: he *must* think and behave like this, because the behaviour of Christ is the ground of his redemption; if he denies the relevance of Christ's actions to his own, then he is denying his very existence in Christ. He must behave like this because he is *in* Christ, and this is the mind of Christ'; Hooker, *From Adam to Christ*, 25. And Hooker again (ibid., 90–91): 'Paul has a very profound understanding of the relationship between the saving events of the gospel and the conduct appropriate to those who are in Christ; of course he did not consider Christian ethics to be simply a matter of imitating the example of Christ; rather it is a conformity to the true existence which belongs to those who are in Christ.'

18. Again, Hooker makes a similar point: 'Just as Christ's resurrection brings resurrection and glory (to those who are prepared to suffer with him), so Paul's experience of comfort brings comfort to the Corinthians (provided they share in his sufferings)'; Hooker, *From Adam to Christ*, 49.

10.14 UNION WITH CHRIST AND SUFFERING

Suffering, in Paul's thought, is related to Christ in at least two ways. First, suffering ensues in the believer's life as he or she follows Christ. Since Christ suffered, believers will inevitably follow him in his suffering. Second, suffering also occurs through participation with Christ in his suffering. In fact, Schweitzer goes as far as saying that 'the thought of following Christ in the path of suffering hardly occurs apart from that of fellowship with Christ in suffering'.[19] In other words, Schweitzer regards the first and second points as being tied together: believers follow Christ in suffering by participating with him in it.

Paul's own experience of suffering provides a valuable model by which we might appreciate how suffering derives from participation with Christ. On this issue, Tannehill observes that Paul often refers to his own suffering as 'death' or 'dying', which may suggest that he understands his suffering as participation in Christ's death.[20] If such is the case, it is little wonder that Paul regards suffering as a normal part of the Christian experience. Proudfoot states that suffering is not optional for the person in Christ, since every believer 'is brought into fellowship with Christ's suffering at baptism'.[21] This is how Paul can describe his own sufferings as sharing in the sufferings of Christ, because 'the nature of the believer's spiritual union with Christ is such that he recapitulates in his own life the two-fold soteriological experience of his Lord — death and resurrection'.[22]

Proudfoot's recognition of 'the two-fold soteriological experience' of Christ is significant, as Paul seems to relate suffering to resurrection as well as to death. With respect to the role of suffering in the new life of the believer, Tannehill suggests that 'the pattern of saving events' stands behind Paul's conviction that suffering leads to life. 'By God's power Jesus' death led to his resurrection. So also God brings life from death in the existence of the believer.'[23] Gorman expresses a similar notion while emphasizing the significance of the co-prefix for understanding Paul's

---

19. Schweitzer, *Mysticism*, 144.
20. Tannehill, *Dying and Rising*, 86.
21. C. Merrill Proudfoot, 'Imitation or Realistic Participation? A Study of Paul's Concept of "Suffering with Christ"', *Int* 17 (1963): 151. See §10.17 for further discussion of baptism.
22. Ibid., 152.
23. Tannehill, *Dying and Rising*, 89.

thought: 'if we co-suffer with Christ we are co-heirs with him and will be co-glorified with him.'[24]

All of this points to the fact that sharing in Christ's death and resurrection is not simply about the status of the believer with respect to salvation. As Proudfoot summarizes, 'Now we see that just as the "resurrection-power" is not simply a *status,* neither is the "death-power": it is working itself out in Paul's daily experience. He is continually *being conformed* ... to it as his fellowship with Christ extends to suffering.'[25] The conclusion, then, to the issue of suffering and the Christian life is that suffering is to be viewed as a *participatio Christi* and not as an *imitatio Christi* only.[26] Believers share in the ongoing force of Christ's death and the power of his resurrection, and one consequence of this is that believers will undergo suffering.[27]

10.15 BEING THE BODY OF CHRIST

One of the most powerful metaphors for union with Christ is that of believers being his body, or part thereof.[28] The metaphor is also of crucial importance for understanding Paul's theology of the church and, indeed, the responsibilities that believers bear with respect to one another. As Dunn observes, 'It is a sense of belonging to Christ indeed, but of belonging together with others, with the obvious implication that one without the other would make the whole unbalanced and unhealthy.'[29] The body metaphor also provides a brilliant means through which Paul teaches of the importance of unity and diversity within the people of God. As Käsemann puts it, 'for Paul, unity in the body of Christ does not mean the sameness of all the members; it means the solidarity which can endure the

---

24. Gorman, *Cruciformity,* 46.

25. Proudfoot, 'Suffering with Christ', 152 [italics are original].

26. Ibid., 160.

27. Ibid.

28. Pelser surveys the nonmetaphorical interpretations of Paul's *body* language, arguing both that it must be taken metaphorically and, following Perriman, that such metaphoric language is able to refer to something *real.* 'The fact that Paul referred to the church by means of the body metaphor is therefore in itself no indication that it should be interpreted figuratively'; Gert M. M. Pelser, 'Once More the Body of Christ in Paul', *Neot* 32 (1998): 525–39. Field agrees and discusses the educational force of metaphors; Barbara Field, 'The Discourses behind the Metaphor "The Church is The Body of Christ" as Used by St Paul and the "Post-Paulines"', *AJT* 6 (1992): 88–107.

29. Dunn, *Paul the Apostle,* 406.

strain of the differences—the different gifts and different weaknesses of the different members.'[30]

Powers' study of 1 Corinthians demonstrates the ethical power of the body metaphor, with particular reference to sexual conduct. He argues that the entire force of Paul's arguments against sexual abuses in Corinth 'is founded completely upon Paul's understanding of the believers' corporate unity with Christ'.[31] Reflecting more broadly on the significance of the body metaphor in 1 Corinthians, Powers summarizes, 'Paul asserts that the believers are united with Christ who "died for" them. And by virtue of their solidarity with Christ, the believers are also united with each other.'[32] Similarly, Bowe states that believers 'live out their Christian existence in the organic unity of the one body of Christ. All else flows from this claim.'[33]

The power of the metaphor is dependent on its entailment of union with Christ. It is possible, however, that the metaphor merely refers to the corporate nature of believers rather than the organic picture of a body growing out of and into Christ. Ridderbos regards such a possibility as 'highly superficial', rejecting the idea that the metaphor is restricted to the unity and diversity of believers, 'and that the addition "of Christ" is then to be taken only as a qualifying genitive'.[34]

Rather than pointing simply to the unity and diversity of believers, the body metaphor originates in the notion of being members of Christ.[35] When believers first partake in Christ, they are engrafted into his body as its members,[36] and so 'as each person is joined to Christ by the incoming of the Holy Spirit, it necessarily follows that all those who are thus

30. Käsemann, *Perspectives on Paul*, 3. Indeed, it is Paul's concern for diversity within the body that makes his use of this metaphor distinct from most of the other ancient writers who employed it. In Stoic usage, for example, diversity was not regarded as politically expedient; Field, 'Body of Christ', 96.

31. Powers, *Salvation through Participation*, 150. So also Ellis, who says that the body metaphor 'underlies the whole of [Paul's] theology and is decisive for understanding his sexual ethics and his teachings on the Lord's Supper, on ministry, and on the Christian hope'; E. Earle Ellis, 'Sōma in First Corinthians', *Int* 44 (1990): 144.

32. Powers, *Salvation through Participation*, 55.

33. Barbara Bowe, '"You Are the Body of Christ": Paul's Understanding of the Human Person', *TBT* 29 (1991): 144.

34. Ridderbos, *Paul*, 370.

35. 'Paul uses the image "the body of Christ" to give the sense of *corporate unity* in Christ'; Parsons, 'In Christ in Paul', 37 [italics are original].

36. Brian Daines, 'Paul's Use of the Analogy of the Body of Christ: With Special Reference to 1 Corinthians 12', *EvQ* 50 (1978): 78.

united to Him, are also united to one another'.[37] To be sure, the unity and diversity of believers are in view through the metaphor, but not to the exclusion of the logically prior reality of union with Christ. Indeed, Ridderbos explains wherein the unity of the church is founded and why it can be called Christ's body: 'because already in his suffering and death he represented it in all its parts and united it in himself into a new unity.'[38]

Consequently, one of Paul's most powerful metaphors for his understanding of the nature of the church, its unity and diversity, its ethical standards, and its corporate membership one to another is grounded in union with Christ. As believers are included in him, so they are incorporated into his body and become its members.

10.16 BEING THE BRIDE OF CHRIST

Another powerful metaphor through which Paul depicts union with Christ is that of marriage, or the church being the bride of Christ. Paul is not alone among biblical writers in using this metaphor, for the Hebrew Scriptures provide 'a rich mine for exploring metaphors of marriage as an expression of a divine-human relationship'.[39] God's covenantal relationship with Israel is often depicted as that of a husband and wife, and it becomes a familiar theme in the Old Testament. Indeed, the metaphor is also found elsewhere in the New Testament.[40] The use of the metaphor of marriage, then, is not as peculiar to Paul as some other metaphors.

---

37. Douty, *Union with Christ*, 238.

38. Ridderbos, *Paul*, 377.

39. Richard D. Patterson, 'Metaphors of Marriage as Expressions of Divine-Human Relations', *JETS* 51/4 (2008): 691. Patterson points out that while literature of the ancient Near East depicted divine-human relations, the Scriptures are unique in employing the metaphor of marriage for divine-human relationships (ibid., 690–91). While it may be the case that marriage as a metaphor is unique to the Bible, Batey demonstrates that the concept of 'one flesh' certainly was not. This concept in the first century was a symbol of unity, used to express religious and philosophical ideas, and was intelligible to both Jew and Greek; Richard Batey, 'The MIA ΣAPΞ Union of Christ and the Church', *NTS* 13 (1967): 271. Batey does, however, regard Paul's application of the 'one flesh' concept as unique in that it expressed a personal and permanent union between Christ and the church (ibid., 279–80).

40. See Patterson for a discussion of the relevant passages, which include John the Baptist's self-identification as assisting Jesus the bridegroom (John 3:27–30), Christ's likening his mission to that of a bridegroom (Matt 9:15–16; Mark 2:19–20), and the depiction in Revelation of Christ's return through the metaphor of a wedding; Patterson, 'Metaphors of Marriage', 698–700.

While there are only four instances (at most) in which Paul explicitly employs the metaphor of marriage, it is still a significant means through which union with Christ is to be understood. As demonstrated in chapter 7, this metaphor is uniquely pressed in its details, with Ephesians 5:22–32, for example, extrapolating at length on the husbandly duties of Christ with respect to his bride. The intimacy of the 'one-flesh' union of Christ and his church underscores the personal nature of union with Christ.[41] The church is not simply saved by Christ and put under his rule in his domain, but shares in a profound spiritual bond with her groom.

The metaphor of marriage entails a number of implications for Christian living. As demonstrated in chapter 7, Paul uses this metaphor to prohibit sexual immorality and spiritual unfaithfulness and to promote the submission of the church to her head. Through all this, the metaphor calls attention to God's grace in Christ, since the husband saves, washes, and cares for his bride.

10.17 Union with Christ and the Sacraments

The issue of the sacraments—baptism and the Lord's Supper—and their relationship to union with Christ is not straightforward. This is partly due to the fact that on one end of the spectrum it is possible to see no relation at all between the sacraments and union with Christ, and on the other end one can see a close and important connection.

The former view might be summarized along the following lines. When Paul speaks of being baptized into Christ's death, he does not refer to the sacrament (or act) of baptism but is speaking purely metaphorically. Baptism in Christ's death is parallel to burial with Christ and is simply another way of referring to union with Christ in his death; it says nothing about the practice of baptism. As for the Lord's Supper, Paul does not even mention it with reference to union with Christ, so it is a nonissue.

The latter view takes the opposite approach. When Paul speaks of being baptized into Christ's death, he is interpreting the act of baptism.[42]

---

41. Son captures this well: 'The sexual union between husband and wife and the spirit union between Christ and the church are related typologically to the sexual union between Adam and Eve (Gen 2:24)'; Son, 'One Flesh', 114.

42. Wedderburn notes that for some scholars baptismal traditions are in the background

Baptism is the means through which believers participate with Christ in his death. Far from being metaphorical, Paul uses such language in a concrete and particular way that is instructive and meaningful with respect to the sacrament of baptism: it is the initiation into union with Christ. As for the Lord's Supper, Paul quotes Jesus' statements about the bread being his body and the cup being his blood in 1 Corinthians 11. To partake in the Lord's Supper then — to eat his body and drink his blood — is communion with Christ; it is an act of participatory devotion.[43]

It is best to find a position between these two poles, for there are commendable elements to both, but there are also points at which either might be critiqued. A strength of the first position is that when Paul speaks of being baptized into Christ's death, the context suggests that he is indeed referring to baptism metaphorically. The use of this phrase in Romans 6 was explored in chapter 9, where we noted that the parallel phrase 'buried with Christ' must be metaphorical, which strongly supports a metaphorical reading of baptism. In support of the second position is that the Lord's Supper in particular is genuinely suggestive of union with Christ, given the symbolism that Christ himself assigned to the bread and the cup.

A weakness of the first position is that it is difficult to disassociate completely Paul's language of baptism into Christ's death from the specific act of baptism. Even while he may use the term metaphorically in Romans 6, the reason the metaphor is coherent is that it draws on a shared understanding of baptism. Paul may not be addressing the physical act of baptism in such contexts, but that does not negate any relationship between the metaphor and the practice.[44] A weakness of the second position is that it is unlikely that Paul means to say that it is through the act of baptism that believers are actually united to Christ in his death. This goes against the metaphorical context in Romans 6, but it also stands in tension with Paul's clear conviction that believers are united to Christ by *faith*, not by

---

wherever dying and rising with Christ is mention in connection with baptism; A. J. M. Wedderburn, 'Hellenistic Christian Traditions in Romans 6', *NTS* 29 (1983): 341.

43. Storz provides an example of such a view: 'Through the Lord's Supper Christ dwells in us — we bear Christ's wounded body in our own. Through Baptism we dwell in Christ — we are borne in Christ's wounded body'; Martha Ellen Stortz, 'Indwelling Christ, Indwelling Christians: Living as Marked', *CurTM* 34 (2007): 178.

44. 'Paul is here reflecting, not upon the meaning of baptism, but upon the meaning of having been baptized, that is, upon the nature of Christian existence'; Wedderburn, 'Romans 6', 341.

an external *rite*. Furthermore, it does not do justice to Paul's apparently indifferent attitude toward the act of baptism; after all, if union with Christ was understood to be effected by the act of baptism, one would expect it to register more highly among Paul's priorities.

A mediating position affirms the strengths of both positions while avoiding their weaknesses. This means that when Paul speaks of being baptized into Christ's death, he refers to baptism metaphorically. He does not imply that union with Christ is effected through the act of baptism, as though it is some sort of initiation rite. Union with Christ is effected by faith.[45] However, Paul's expression does provide symbolic content to the act of baptism; it is a physical sign that points to our union with Christ in his death and resurrection. In this way, we observe a connection between the sacrament of baptism and union with Christ, without making the errors of reading the sacrament into Romans 6 or viewing baptism as an initiation rite.

Concerning the Lord's Supper, it is difficult to deny that its symbolic content is at least suggestive of union with Christ. To eat Christ's 'body' and drink his 'blood' is a powerful symbol that gives expression to one's partaking in Christ; indeed, there could hardly be a more apt visual expression of such communion.[46] However, it probably goes too far to regard the Lord's Supper—in Paul's mind at least—as an actual act of sharing in Christ's death rather than simply symbolic of such.[47]

While Paul certainly takes this sacrament seriously (1 Cor 11:27–32),

---

45. Contra Letham: 'Baptism comes first, the Holy Spirit efficaciously uniting us to Christ in and through it'; Robert Letham, *Union with Christ: In Scripture, History, and Theology* (Phillipsburg, PA: Presbyterian and Reformed, 2011), 138–39.

46. This is made all the more likely by 'Paul's concern for the communal participation in the body and blood of Christ as an essential component for the unity and proper worship practice within the Corinthian church body'; Lace Marie Williams-Tinajero, 'Christian Unity: The Communal Participation in Christ's Body and Blood', *One in Christ* 40 (2005), 51. The point is that participation in Jesus' body and blood not only signals a sharing in his death, but 'a new reality of worshippers united with the personal incarnate living God that connected them with each other' (ibid., 51). Since union with Christ entails the incorporated union of his people, the Lord's Supper is also a communal reality. As Wedderburn notes, the Eucharist gives tangible expression to the idea that all believers share in the one person of Christ; Wedderburn, 'Body of Christ', 79.

47. The difficulty, however, of proving this point is elucidated by Williams-Tinajero, who claims there is no biblical basis 'for determining "how" Christ's body and blood relate to the bread and cup. It is difficult to deduce the meaning of the elements from vague texts'; Williams-Tinajero, 'Christian Unity', 57. This is why mystical, physical, real presence, and symbolic interpretations are each represented by various quarters of the church.

he does not give it the widespread emphasis one might expect if he regarded it as a profoundly significant act of participation with Christ in and of itself. He clearly does regard *suffering* this way, and so it is unsurprising that his references to sharing in Christ's sufferings are frequent. Such is not the case with respect to the Lord's Supper. It simply is not something with which Paul is particularly occupied. In conclusion, then, Paul seems to regard the sacraments as symbolic acts that give expression to union with Christ. He does not, however, regard the sacraments as effecting or actualizing union with Christ; they are important symbols, but symbols nonetheless.

10.18 CONCLUSION

This chapter draws together the exegetical results of part 2 that relate to Christian living. It is clear that union with Christ relates to the full variety of believers' actions, characteristics, and status. This is such that 'in Christ' language serves as shorthand for indicating that a person is a believer. Participation with Christ means that believers will suffer with Christ, having died to the world, and ought to live according to their new identity in him. As members of the body of Christ, believers are to respect the body in matters of unity and diversity as well as sexual purity. Having put on Christ, believers are to be conformed to him.

Thus, 'Christian discipleship means identification with the crucified Lord'.[48] Indeed, the widespread implications of union with Christ for Christian living means that it is impossible to understand Paul's expectations of believers without appreciating the derivational significance of this union. Wikenhauser summarizes the state of affairs: 'In spite of their diversity these texts all agree that Christ is the vital principle of Christians. Their new life depends on this mystical union with him.'[49] Truly, we may say that 'the Christian lives in Christ, draws all vital power from him, and indeed is a Christian only as long as he lives in this union with Christ'.[50] Barcley sum it up: 'To be "in Christ" means to belong to, to serve, to be ruled by Christ.'[51]

---

48. Hooker, *From Adam to Christ*, 55.
49. Wikenhauser, *Mysticism*, 31.
50. Ibid.
51. Barcley, *"Christ in You"*, 111.

CHAPTER 11

UNION WITH CHRIST AND JUSTIFICATION

11.1 INTRODUCTION

There has been much controversy within recent New Testament scholarship surrounding the Pauline theme of justification, and part of this controversy has involved its relationship to union with Christ.[1] Two issues in particular have generated discussion. The first, having been raised famously by Schweitzer in 1930, is concerned with the relative importance of union with Christ in Paul's thinking vis-à-vis justification. Is union with Christ more important to Paul than justification? Is the latter merely a subsidiary crater within the former?

---

1. Douglas Campbell's recent massive tome challenges the entire legitimacy of 'Justification Theory', which he describes as individualistic, modernistic, rationalistic, and introspective. He argues in effect that the entire Protestant tradition has been misguided in its reading of Paul—a bold claim that attacks New and Old Perspectives alike. Instead, Campbell proposes an apocalyptic rereading of Paul in which God's deliverance occurs through Christ's assumption of Adamic ontology, which is executed in his death. Believers respond by dying with Christ, who then receive a new 'in Christ' ontology, which is communal and participatory. Campbell pits this apocalyptic–participatory gospel against justification, arguing that 'Paul's account of sanctification *is* the gospel. His description of deliverance and cleansing "in Christ," through the work of the Spirit, at the behest of the Father, the entire process being symbolized by baptism, *is* the good news'; Campbell, *Deliverance of God*, 934. While Campbell's startling contribution cannot be engaged here, it has not adequately demonstrated that an apocalyptic–participatory schema is unable to be reconciled to justification theory; indeed, Campbell has overplayed this tension (if it is a tension at all). Ultimately, Campbell's rereading strains credulity in arguing for the complete absence of justification theory in Paul.

The second issue deals with the relationship between union with Christ and the concept of imputed righteousness. While some quarters regard imputation as the mechanism through which righteousness is credited to believers, others deem union with Christ as the means through which this occurs. Both of these issues require consideration. We will begin by surveying elements in part 2 in order to facilitate the discussion of these matters.

11.2 Ἐν Χριστῷ

In chapter 3, on the prepositional phrase ἐν Χριστῷ, the results of §3.7, 'Justification *in Christ*', indicate that this phrase is explicitly connected to justification in Romans 3:24 and Galatians 2:17. In the first reference, justification occurs by God's grace through redemption, which is described as ἐν Χριστῷ. We argued that grace is the agent bringing about justification, while *in-Christ-redemption* is its instrument. In the second reference, justification is linked directly to ἐν Χριστῷ, with the prepositional phrase most likely expressing the agency of Christ in producing justification.

11.3 Ἐν αὐτῷ

Also in chapter 3, on the prepositional phrase ἐν αὐτῷ, the results of §3.11.3.4, 'Justification *in Him*', indicate that the phrase is directly connected to justification in 2 Corinthians 5:21 and Philippians 3:9. In the former reference, ἐν αὐτῷ expresses instrumentality, so that Christ is the instrument through whom believers 'might become the righteousness of God'. In the latter reference, ἐν αὐτῷ expresses Paul's union with Christ: he has gained Christ and shares in his righteousness.

11.4 Διὰ Χριστοῦ

In chapter 6, on the prepositional phrase διὰ Χριστοῦ, the results of §6.5, 'Justification *through Christ*', indicate the phrase is directly connected to justification in Galatians 2:16 and Philippians 3:9. In the first reference, the phrase 'though the faith of Jesus Christ' indicates the instrumentality of Christ in the work of justification in contrast to the (false) instrumentality of works of the law. In the second reference, the phrase 'through faith in Christ' expresses the instrumentality of Christ in bringing about Paul's righteous status.

11.5 SYNTHESIS

Given the significance of the debates concerning the relationship between justification and union with Christ, it is surprising that there are few references in which the two concepts are explicitly linked. Compared to the degree to which union with Christ is directly connected to the Pauline themes of Christian living, trinitarianism, and the work of Christ, its connection to justification seems insignificant.

This assessment, however, is not completely accurate for three reasons. First, justification has been somewhat artificially separated out in this analysis, when it in fact belongs to the sphere of the work of Christ, and it has some connection to Paul's trinitarian thinking and the area of Christian living as well. This separation has been undertaken in order to treat justification independently, given its significance in scholarly discussion. Second, as with other themes, the concept of justification is not limited to specific vocabulary, and it should be considered from all angles. Third, while there are few references with explicit connection between the language of union with Christ and that of justification, nevertheless, these connections are strong and evince the instrumentality of Christ in justification.

11.6 JUSTIFICATION: WHAT IS IT?

Before proceeding to the issues raised above, an essential element of any discussion about justification must include its definition. No longer may the meaning of 'justification' be assumed, and with particular reference to the contributions of various scholars associated with the New Perspective on Paul, we turn now to explore what justification is for Paul. The caveat here is that justification is an enormous topic in its own right in New Testament studies, and the following discussion will be necessarily brief.

Part of the process by which we seek to understand Paul's thinking about justification involves its place in Paul's theological framework. As is the case with union with Christ, the relationship between justification and other key elements in Paul's thinking bears significance for uncovering its meaning and function. Also in parallel to union with Christ, the relation between justification and eschatology is of especial interest.

Schweitzer's analysis of justification begins with eschatology: 'Our starting-point must be the observation that the righteousness belongs, strictly speaking, to the future.'[2] That is, righteousness, or the status of having been justified, has to do with the pronouncement of righteousness at the coming judgment.[3] Since union with Christ, according to Schweitzer, is the means through which Paul understands the future to be connected to the present, it bears an eschatological relationship to justification. Justification belongs to the future, but through union with Christ believers may partake in it ahead of time. Righteousness 'can only be considered as already attained as a consequence of the being-in-Christ, by means of which believers possess in advance the state of existence proper to the Messianic Kingdom.'[4]

Given this logic, it is obvious that Schweitzer must also conclude that union with Christ is the more basic category for Paul, since it produces justification; 'this righteousness is really the first effect of the being-in-Christ. From it comes all the rest.'[5] Consequently, when Paul speaks of righteousness through faith, Schweitzer views it as a shorthand expression that assumes union with Christ as the middle step. All the blessings of redemption flow from being-in-Christ, so that faith only becomes operative through union with Christ.[6] Thus, Schweitzer can say, 'In consequence of believing in Christ we possess righteousness through being-in-Christ'.[7]

For Wright, righteousness is not simply a future reality: 'Justification is *both* future … *and* present.'[8] There are four key elements to Paul's

---

2. Schweitzer, *Mysticism*, 205.

3. Ibid.

4. Ibid.

5. Ibid.

6. Ibid., 206.

7. Ibid. Deissmann expresses a similar notion when he says that 'justification "out of" faith or "through" faith is really justification "in" faith, justification "in Christ," justification "in the name of Jesus Christ," justification "in the blood of Christ." Faith is not the pre-condition of justification, it is the experience of justification'; Deissmann, *Paul*, 169–70. So too Gaffin: 'Not justification by faith but union with the resurrected Christ by faith (of which union, to be sure, the justifying aspect stands out perhaps most prominently) is the central motif of Paul's applied soteriology'; Gaffin, *Resurrection*, 132.

8. N. T. Wright, *The New Testament and the People of God* (Christian Origins and the Question of God 1; Minneapolis: Fortress, 1992), 336 [italics are original]. Käsemann expresses this in the following manner: 'What Christ once did has continuing efficacy and gives us a part in him, so that 'in Christ' means belonging to the historical extension of the saving event which once took place in the past and the sphere which is indicated by that event'; Käsemann, *Perspectives on Paul*, 99–100.

doctrine of justification, according to Wright. First, righteousness is about the work of Jesus the Messiah of Israel. Second, justification is about the covenant God made with Abraham, whose purpose was the salvation of the world. Third, justification is focused on the divine lawcourt. Fourth, justification is bound up with eschatology.[9] Of these four elements, three are hardly controversial, since most would agree that justification is about the work of Christ, focused on the lawcourt, and is eschatological. The element that proves somewhat contentious is Wright's emphasis on the covenantal nature of justification.

Wright contends that righteousness properly refers to 'conformity with a norm', and when it is applied to God, 'the strong probability is that this refers to God's fidelity to the norm he himself has set up, in other words, the covenant'.[10] Thus Wright's understanding of the covenantal nature of righteousness is reconstructed from the idea of God conforming to his own 'norm' in Jesus Christ. All four elements of righteousness are established by what God has done in Christ. First, righteousness is about the work of the Messiah. Second, God's covenant promises to Abraham are fulfilled in Christ. Third, Jesus was vindicated, and so all those who belong to him are vindicated also. Fourth, the new world had begun.[11] These elements fulfill the messianic, covenantal, juridical, and eschatological facets of righteousness.

Wright acknowledges that for Paul, justification was something that happened 'in the Messiah'; the believer's righteous status is possessed through incorporation into Christ.[12] Such incorporation is the basis on which the other elements of justification are established — 'the lawcourt verdict, the covenantal declaration, and the inaugurated-eschatological pronouncement'.[13] This last element — the inaugurated-eschatological pronouncement — gives expression to Paul's resurrection eschatology, since those who are in Christ share his vindicated status *in advance* of the final vindication of the last day.[14]

Unfortunately, some critics have caricatured Wright's position as *purely* covenantal or sociological, which it clearly is not; it retains juridical

---

9. Wright, *Justification*, ix–x.
10. Ibid., 46.
11. Ibid., 80.
12. Ibid., 119.
13. Ibid., 128.
14. Ibid., 134.

and eschatological elements alongside covenantal and sociological.[15] In Wright's own words, '"Righteousness", within the lawcourt setting—and this is something that no good Lutheran or Reformed theologian ought ever to object to—denotes *the status that someone has when the court has found in their favour*.'[16]

Gorman, influenced by Wright, sees three elements in the meaning of justification. These are, first, right relations with God; second, right relations with others; third, acquittal on the day of judgment.[17] 'In other words, justification, righteousness, and their related terms in English refer to *covenant faithfulness with respect to God and neighbor*, and *ultimate divine approval*.'[18] Covenantal approaches to righteousness emphasize right relations to other covenant members, with God in the role of covenant partner who establishes believers in right relationship to himself.[19] Thus justification refers to the establishment of right covenant relations, 'both "vertical" or theological (toward God) and also, inseparably, "horizontal" or social (toward each other)'.[20] It ought to be clear that such covenantal approaches to justification, therefore, do not negate its juridical aspects, since the verdict of the law court is in view. Such juridical elements, however, are regarded as only part of what justification means for Paul. 'The judicial image must be understood within a wider covenantal, relational, participatory, and transformative framework.'[21]

Schreiner, however, has critiqued such 'covenantal' approaches to justification. While he affirms that God's righteousness *expresses* his faithfulness to his covenant, this is not the same thing as saying that God's righteousness *is* his faithfulness to the covenant.[22] 'God's righteousness surely fulfils his covenantal promises, but it does not follow from this that

---

15. As Bird notes, 'Dunn and Wright do not deny that justification has a bearing upon a person's standing before God and so establishes their status before God in view of the eschatological judgment'; Michael F. Bird, *The Saving Righteousness of God: Studies on Paul, Justification and the New Perspective* (Milton Keynes, UK: Paternoster, 2006), 29. Nevertheless, Bird also acknowledges that Dunn and Wright 'often give the impression' of reducing justification to sociological and ecclesiological conceptions (ibid., 100).

16. Wright, *Justification*, 69 [italics are original].

17. Gorman, *Cruciformity*, 136.

18. Ibid. [italics are original].

19. Bassler, *Navigating Paul*, 68.

20. Gorman, *Inhabiting the Cruciform God*, 52–53.

21. Ibid., 54–55.

22. Schreiner, *Paul*, 199.

we should define righteousness as covenantal faithfulness.'[23] Schreiner has a point. There appears to be linguistic confusion at the core of covenantal definitions of righteousness. While, as Schreiner acknowledges, there is a connectivity between God's righteousness and his covenant faithfulness, such an association is not one of denotation; they are related, but they are not therefore the same thing.[24] It is preferable, therefore, to conclude with Bird that justification is 'a vertical category dealing with a person's status' before God, which has covenantal *implications* as Paul argues for 'the inclusion of the Gentiles *as Gentiles* into Christian fellowship'.[25]

Moving beyond Wright, Gorman binds the juridical aspects of justification with ethical elements. Justification makes the unjust into the just; 'that is, justification is the divine act of transforming people into the righteousness/justice of God.'[26] Thus, believers become capable of practicing the justice of God displayed on the cross.[27] This is the corollary of God's declaration of righteousness, so that 'a real, existential process of transformation' takes place;[28] 'God's declaration of "justified!" now is a "performative utterance," an effective word that does not return void but effects transformation.'[29] This does not, according to Gorman, undermine a sacrificial understanding of Christ's death. Rather, his death is polyvalent in character, such that the justified are 'able to fulfill the law and do the works of love because they are forgiven *and* liberated *and* restored *and* filled with the Spirit'.[30]

While few would deny that, according to Paul, justification leads to transformation, Gorman seems to argue that transformation is part of what justification *means*. That is, transformation is not simply an application, or outworking, of justification, but is partly what justification is. On this point, Gorman has gone too far. Justification in Paul's thought is

---

23. Ibid., 199.
24. Likewise Bird, 'Righteousness appears elsewhere not as God's action, but as the basis and rationale for his saving actions. As such it can connote God's faithfulness to his covenantal promise to Israel.... The righteousness of God then is the character of God embodied and enacted in his saving actions which means vindication (for Israel and the righteous) and condemnation (for the pagan world and the wicked)'; Bird, *Saving Righteousness*, 15.
25. Ibid., 113.
26. Gorman, *Inhabiting the Cruciform God*, 99.
27. Ibid., 99.
28. Ibid., 101.
29. Ibid.
30. Ibid., 102.

based on the work of Christ, is juridical and eschatological in nature, and possibly with covenantal overtones. But to claim that the term denoting God's declaration of acquittal also denotes the unfolding righteousness in the life of the believer is too broad. His suggestion that justification is polyvalent, including both declaration of righteousness and the ethical achievement of righteousness, is not ultimately persuasive.

Part of the problem here is parallel to the one described above with reference to covenantal definitions of justification. The connectivity between the declaration of righteousness and the expected ethical conduct flowing from it does not indicate that these two things are the same. Again, Schreiner points to this problem, arguing that the collocation of ethical and righteousness terms does not demonstrate that the words used all bear the same definition.[31]

Another part of the problem with Gorman's argument is based on Paul's broader ethical structure. It has widely been acknowledged that Paul's ethic can be summarized as 'be what you are'; if you have been declared righteous, then be righteous in your conduct. This ethical structure means that ethical conduct arises out of grace-effected status. God decrees to sinners the status of being right with him, and so they are to live accordingly. Gorman's reconstruction of justification, however, collapses these two parts into one: there is no status leading to right action, since status and right action are both parts of the same thing. While we may agree with Gorman in the final outcome—that God's grace in assigning righteous status to believers entails the expectation of righteous living—we must disagree in defining this whole picture as what Paul means by 'justification'. Justification leads to right living, to be sure, but right living is not part of what Paul means by justification; it is the eschatological-juridical declaration of God based on the work of Christ, in fulfillment of his covenant promises.

11.7 UNION WITH CHRIST AND JUSTIFICATION: LEVELS OF IMPORTANCE?

Schweitzer's proclamation that righteousness by faith is but a subsidiary crater formed within the rim of the main crater—being-in-Christ—

---

31. Schreiner, *Paul*, 206–7.

remains influential.[32] While Schweitzer's statement has drawn many detractors,[33] the observations leading to Schweitzer's conclusions are nevertheless potent. If it is to be measured by sheer numerical frequency, there is no question that union with Christ far exceeds justification as a topic of concern. Paul uses union language at virtually every opportunity, connecting it to a rich variety of concepts and themes, as we have already observed. However, raw frequency is not necessarily a sound criterion by which to judge the level of significance. Wright suggests that one need not choose between justification and being in Christ as the 'centre' of Paul's thought; 'the two must not be played off against one another, and indeed they can only be understood in relation to one another'.[34]

Nevertheless, the findings of this study thus far seem to accord with the suggestion that justification occurs as an outworking of union with Christ. This can be claimed by virtue of the fact that union with Christ language is employed in an instrumental fashion with respect to justification, as observed above; justification occurs through and in Christ. Moreover, broader consideration suggests that because such a multiplicity of Christ's works are related to union with Christ, often with an instrumental relationship in view, it follows that union is an originating theme through which others derive. On that score, justification is likewise derived through union with Christ and coheres with Christ's other works by virtue of their common source in Christ. As Ridderbos acknowledges, 'the foundation for the doctrine of justification ... lies in the corporate unity of Christ and his own'.[35]

This suggestion is supported by an understanding of the way in which justification relates to themes such as Christ's death, resurrection, and vindication. At each step along the path to the righteousness of believers, we

---

32. Schweitzer, *Mysticism*, 224–25.

33. See, for example, Beker: 'The contextual nature of Paul's argument does not imply a language split, as if a "central crater" of ontological participation in Christ is "the real core" of Paul's gospel and justification by faith is purely secondary and a survival'; Beker, *Paul the Apostle*, 286. See also Schreiner, *Paul*, 194.

34. Wright, *Justification*, 201–2. In fact, in Wright's analysis, justification and being in Christ are held together by the overarching category of covenant; Wright, *Justification*, 203. See also Burger, *Being in Christ*, 259; Beker, *Paul the Apostle*, 259–60; Schreiner, *Paul*, 156–57; Bird, *Saving Righteousness*, 86.

35. Ridderbos, *Paul*, 169. 'The justification of the ungodly is a justification "in Christ," that is to say, not only on the ground of his atoning death and resurrection, but also by virtue of the corporate inclusion in him of his own' (ibid., 175).

see that they share in the crucial elements of Christ's own righteousness; they participate in Christ's death for sin and likewise in his vindicating resurrection. Consequently, it follows that sharing with Christ gives rise to justification—it is an outworking of union with Christ. Thus, Gorman is correct to reject the view that Paul has two 'soteriological models',[36] one being juridical and the other participationist. Rather, Paul's one soteriological model is justification by co-crucifixion.[37]

11.8 RESURRECTION AS VINDICATION

Several scholars have drawn a connection between justification and resurrection in Paul's thought.[38] Jewish eschatology anticipated resurrection for the righteous on the last day, and Paul likely drew on this expectation for his understanding of the theological significance of Christ's resurrection.[39] Christ's resurrection signals his vindication in God's sight; he has been declared righteous through his resurrection from the dead.[40] As Letham states, 'In his resurrection, Christ himself was justified, or vindicated, as the second Adam.'[41]

If the justification of Christ occurs through his resurrection, it can be argued that the justification of believers occurs by their participation with him.[42] So Burger describes: 'Just as Christ participated in our unrighteousness, we now participate in his vindication and become justified. Our

---

36. He cites Bart Ehrman and Douglas Campbell as proponents of such a view; Gorman, *Inhabiting the Cruciform God*, 42.

37. Gorman, *Inhabiting the Cruciform God*, 45.

38. For instance, Burger, *Being in Christ*, 250; Bird, *Saving Righteousness*, 40–59; Michael F. Bird, 'Progressive Reformed View', in *Justification: Five Views* (ed. James K. Beilby and Paul Rhodes Eddy; Downers Grove, IL: InterVarsity Press, 2011), 150. This is by no means taken for granted, however. Wright laments that 'there seems to be something about the joining together of resurrection and justification which some of our Western traditions have failed to grasp'; Wright, *Justification*, 219.

39. Powers says that while Paul probably developed most of his understanding of believers' eschatological resurrection as a participation in Jesus' resurrection, 'one should not too readily dismiss the possibility that Paul borrowed the principal elements of this conception from Jewish tradition. Indeed, in the *Assumption of Moses*, there are certain eschatological motifs which seem to parallel, and perhaps even underlie, Paul's understanding of the believers' eschatological resurrection as a participation in Jesus' resurrection'; Powers, *Salvation through Participation*, 215.

40. Ibid., 82–83; Hooker, *From Adam to Christ*, 40.

41. Letham, *Union with Christ*, 137.

42. So Hooker, 'Christ's death and resurrection lead to "justification" for many precisely

justification is a gracious participation of the ungodly in the vindication of Christ.[43] Believers share in the vindication of Christ's resurrection by dying and rising with him; they are declared righteous by virtue of their participation in these events.[44] Gaffin endorses such logic: 'In view of the solidarity involved, being raised with Christ has the same significance for believers that his resurrection has for Christ.'[45] In fact, Gaffin goes much further; he argues that whenever Paul speaks of the believer's justification, adoption, sanctification, glorification, or any other benefit connected to them, in such instances the underlying consideration is resurrection with Christ.[46]

After his death for sin, the righteousness of Christ is declared by his resurrection, which is the sign of his vindication. Believers are regarded as having died with Christ, having been raised with him, and likewise therefore as being righteous with him. The justification of believers is the result of their death and resurrection with Christ, just as the righteousness of Christ results from his own death and resurrection.[47] Thus, Gorman correctly states that 'for Paul justification is an experience of participating in Christ's resurrection life that is effected by co-crucifixion with him'.[48]

---

because he himself is "justified" by God and acknowledged as righteousness'; Hooker, *From Adam to Christ*, 31.

43. Burger, *Being in Christ*, 248. Also Bird, 'Jesus' resurrection is his justification and believers are justified in so far as they have union with the justified Messiah'; Bird, *Saving Righteousness*, 2; and 'Consequently, union with Christ is union with the justified Messiah and the now Righteous One. Jesus by fact of his resurrection is the locus of righteousness and redemption and believers are justified only because they have been united with the justified Messiah' (ibid., 56).

44. So Hooker, again: 'To be in Christ is to be identified with what he is. It is not surprising, then, if his resurrection and vindication as the righteous one lead both to the acknowledgement of believers as righteous, and to their resurrection'; Hooker, *From Adam to Christ*, 37.

45. Gaffin, *Resurrection*, 129; 'To be more exact, the notion that the believer has been raised with Christ brings into view all that now characterizes him as a result that he has been justified, adopted, sanctified, and glorified with Christ, better, that he has been united with the Christ, who is justified, adopted, sanctified, and glorified, and so by virtue of this (existential) union shares these benefits' (ibid.).

46. Ibid. So Powers: 'Paul views reconciliation, justification, and the non-reckoning of sins to the believer as being the result of the mutual participation and identification of Christ with the believer and the believer with Christ'; Powers, *Salvation through Participation*, 83–84.

47. So Gaffin: 'For Christians, then, Christ's justification, given with his resurrection, becomes theirs, when united, by faith, to the resurrected Christ, that is, the justified Christ, his righteousness is reckoned as theirs or imputed to them'; Richard B. Gaffin, 'Justification and Eschatology', in *Justified in Christ: God's Plan for Us in Justification* (ed. K. Scott Oliphant; Fearn, Scotland: Mentor, 2007), 6.

48. Gorman, *Inhabiting the Cruciform God*, 40.

11.9 IMPUTATION

The second key issue addressed in recent scholarship is the relationship between union with Christ and imputed righteousness. How is it that believers are declared righteous? Is it through imputation or through union with Christ?[49] It remains difficult for defenders of imputation to mount a persuasive exegetical case in its favour. Romans 4 has become the key text in discussions about imputation,[50] which, Vickers says, 'has the best claim as an "imputation text"'.[51] But even here, he admits, the text 'does not contain every detail associated with the doctrine'.[52] In fact, according to Bird, 'there simply is no text in the New Testament which categorically states that Christ's righteousness is imputed to believers'.[53]

However, theological approaches have merit; so Carson asks, 'Even if we agree that there is no Pauline passage that *explicitly* says, in so many words, that the righteousness of Christ is imputed to his people, is there biblical evidence to substantiate the view that the substance of this thought is conveyed?'[54] Is imputation the implicit mechanism by which Christ's righteousness is conferred on believers? On the other side of the debate it is claimed that there is no need for imputation to be derived from Paul's theological framework since Christ's righteousness is conferred on

---

49. For Gundry, the issue goes much further than *how* believers receive Christ's righteousness; he argues that they do not receive or participate in it at all, since the relevant Pauline texts speak of *God's* righteousness rather than Christ's. Our sins are imputed to Christ, but his righteousness is not imputed to us. Rather, God counts faith as righteousness. Robert H. Gundry, 'The Nonimputation of Christ's Righteousness', in *Justification: What's at Stake in the Current Debates* (ed. Mark Husbands and Daniel J. Treier; Downers Grove, IL: InterVarsity Press, 2004), 17–45.

50. See Visscher's helpful analysis of Romans 4 in light of New Perspective approaches and those who oppose them. Gerhard H. Visscher, *Romans 4 and the New Perspective on Paul: Faith Embraces the Promise* (Studies in Biblical Literature 122; New York: Peter Lang, 2009). On imputation in particular, see 167–77.

51. 'The reason for this is simple: the word λογίζομαι appears more often in Romans 4 than in any other single text in the Bible'; Brian J. Vickers, *Jesus' Blood and Righteousness: Paul's Theology of Imputation* (Wheaton, IL: Crossway, 2006), 71.

52. Ibid., 111.

53. Bird, *Saving Righteousness*, 2.

54. D. A. Carson, 'The Vindication of Imputation', in *Justification: What's at Stake in the Current Debates* (ed. Mark Husbands and Daniel J. Treier; Downers Grove, IL: InterVarsity Press, 2004), 50 [italics are original]. Vickers argues the same: 'While no single text contains or develops all the "ingredients" of imputation, the doctrine stands as a component of Paul's soteriology'; Vickers, *Imputation*, 18.

believers by virtue of their union with him.[55] That is, through union with Christ believers are made righteousness, not through imputation.

From an exegetical standpoint, the latter position is easier to maintain than the former. It has been demonstrated that the instrumentality and agency of Christ, along with union with Christ, produces justification in believers (Rom 3:24; 2 Cor 5:21; Gal 2:16–17; Phil 3:9). While there are only a few direct references connecting union with Christ to justification, these are nevertheless superior to the *absence* of explicit references to the imputation of righteousness. Such an approach also has theological validity alongside its exegetical soundness.

One is left wondering, however, whether this debate has been shaped around a false dichotomy. Is it necessary to pit union with Christ against imputation? Is it not possible that the two concepts might cohere and in fact belong together? It is my contention that imputation is a theological concept that might properly be understood as an outworking of union with Christ; through their union with Christ, his righteousness is imputed to believers. Indeed, in his robust defence of the doctrine of imputation, Vickers comes to the same conclusion: 'It is difficult to overemphasize that the imputation of Christ's righteousness takes place in union with Christ. Only as a person is identified with Christ is Christ's righteousness imputed to that person.'[56]

For such a synthesis to function properly, however, imputation must not be regarded as a mechanical 'removal' of Christ's righteousness from him, which is then impersonally applied to others, like the transfer of funds from one bank account to another. This would hardly do justice to the union between believers and Christ. Carson recognizes this:

---

55. Powers, for example, argues strongly against any notion of imputation in Paul's writings. Two key points he makes are that imputation is absent in all of the key texts regarding justification, and that righteousness is conferred on believers through their participation with Christ. For Powers, participation with Christ cancels the possibility of imputation or substitution: 'the principal notion behind the earliest believers' assertion that "Christ died for us" is that of representation and participation, and not substitution'; Powers, *Salvation through Participation*, 234. It is not clear, however, that the reality of participation with Christ—and indeed, representation by Christ—is mutually exclusive of substitution or imputation as theological concepts.

56. Vickers, *Imputation*, 237. See also Lane G. Tipton, 'Union with Christ and Justification', in *Justified in Christ: God's Plan for Us in Justification* (ed. K. Scott Oliphint; Fearn, Scotland: Mentor, 2007), 23–49.

On the one hand, justification is, in Paul, irrefragably tied to our incorporation into Christ, to our union with Christ.... If we speak of justification or of imputation ... *apart* from a grasp of this incorporation into Christ, we will constantly be in danger of contemplating some sort of transfer *apart* from being included in Christ, *apart* from union with Christ.[57]

Imputation ought to be understood as the unmerited reception of a righteousness that belongs wholly to another, and this reception of 'alien' righteousness is facilitated through the 'un-alienation' of two parties; once believers are joined to Christ, his righteousness is shared with them.[58] In this way, imputation and union with Christ coexist, with one flowing from the other.[59]

11.9.1 LUTHER

It should be noted that this understanding of imputation is not foreign to the Reformed Protestant tradition; in fact, it has been argued that such is the position held by Luther and Calvin. For Luther, the imputation of righteousness occurs through the one flesh union in which believers share with Christ. As Metzger observes:

We are not one flesh with Christ because we are declared righteous. Rather, we are declared righteous because we are one flesh with Christ. One should not take this to imply a denial of imputed righteousness, for

---

57. Carson, 'Vindication', 72.

58. The concept of 'alien righteousness' is helpfully defended by Gaffin. 'The righteousness that justifies is apart from us; it is not our own, of our own doing, but Christ's. At issue here is the concern, not only understandable but necessary, not to confuse Christ's righteousness, as the sole ground for justification, with anything, any change or transformation, that takes place within the sinner. The concern here, again, is not to obscure that justifying righteousness is perfect and complete, in what Christ has done, once for all, in his finished work, apart from anything the believer does or is done in the believer. In this sense, to speak of "alien righteousness" is surely defensible, even helpful'; Gaffin, 'Union with Christ', 285.

59. For Gaffin, understanding that righteousness for the believer comes through being raised with Christ avoids one problem that some versions of imputation might entail, namely, that the justification of the ungodly 'is not arbitrary but according to truth: it is synthetic with respect to Christ (as resurrected)'; Gaffin, *Resurrection*, 132. Justification by faith, then, is not a legal fiction as some critics have claimed, but is the justification of Christ shared with believers who participate in his resurrection. See also Bird, *Saving Righteousness*, 8–9; Vickers, *Imputation*, 216–22.

imputed or alien righteousness conveys the essential truth that we are not righteous on our own, that is, by nature. We are only righteous in relation to Christ.[60]

Luther apparently saw no contradiction between the imputation of righteousness and union with Christ;[61] the latter entails the former. From one point of view, Luther regarded righteousness as alien and passive, in that it is not produced by anything that believers do; yet the marriage between Christ and his people means that his righteousness really becomes their own.[62]

While the father of the Reformation held a view of imputation that depended on union with Christ, the trajectory of later Protestantism followed Melanchthon rather than Luther. Melanchthon thought primarily of the cross as a transaction and, according to Seifrid, 'the later Protestant formulaic description of justification as the "imputation of Christ's righteousness" was a development of the Melanchthon view'.[63] Imputation functioned differently in Luther and Melanchthon's thought. For the latter, '"imputation" was necessary in order to mediate Christ's cross-work to the believer', while for Luther, 'Christ's saving

---

60. Metzger, 'Luther and the Finnish School', 206–7. Jenson observes the same feature in Luther's thought, that 'in faith the soul is united with Christ as a bride with the groom, to be "one body" with him and so possess his righteousness'; Robert W. Jenson, 'Response to Tuomo Mannermaa, "Why Is Luther So Fascinating?"', in *Union with Christ: The New Finnish Interpretation of Luther* (ed. Carl E. Braaten and Robert W. Jenson; Grand Rapids: Eerdmans, 1998), 23. Likewise, Mannermaa, Peura, and Juntunen: 'Justifying faith means participation in God in Christ's person'; Tuomo Mannermaa, 'Justification and *Theosis* in Lutheran-Orthodox Perspective', in *Union with Christ: The New Finnish Interpretation of Luther*, 32; 'The Christian then hangs onto Christ and trusts him to be righteous in respect to him. This union with Christ is the basis of the Christian's salvation'; Simo Peura, 'Christ as Favor and Gift *(donum)*: The Challenge of Luther's Understanding of Justification', in *Union with Christ: The New Finnish Interpretation of Luther*, 55; 'According to Luther a Christian is "in Christ"; the Christian exists in him through participation in him. One is righteous because one is posited in Christ'; Sammeli Juntunen, 'Luther and Metaphysics: What Is the Structure of Being according to Luther?' in *Union with Christ: The New Finnish Interpretation of Luther*, 152.

61. Vickers, *Imputation*, 27.

62. Stephen Westerholm, *Perspectives Old and New on Paul: The "Lutheran" Paul and His Critics* (Grand Rapids: Eerdmans, 2004), 32–33.

63. Mark A. Seifrid, 'Luther, Melanchthon and Paul on the Question of Imputation', in *Justification: What's at Stake in the Current Debates* (ed. Mark Husbands and Daniel J. Treier; Downers Grove, IL: InterVarsity Press, 2004), 144. Also Seifrid, 'Justification in Galatians 2', 229–30.

benefits are already mediated in the union of faith'.[64] Seifrid therefore argues that any insistence to define justification in terms of imputation 'is to adopt a late-Reformational, Protestant understanding'.[65] Furthermore, 'it is impossible to force Luther into this paradigm. Melanchthon himself tried and failed. Shall we then declare Luther outside the Reformation?'[66]

11.9.2 CALVIN

Calvin was much more in line with Luther than Melanchthon on this issue. Gaffin aptly summarizes Calvin's position: 'In expressing himself on justification, including imputation, he always, explicitly or implicitly, relates it to union with Christ.'[67] So Calvin says:

> Therefore, that joining together of Head and members, that indwelling of Christ in our hearts — in short, that mystical union — are accorded by us the highest degree of importance, so that Christ, having been made ours, makes us sharers with him in the first with which he has been endowed. We do not, therefore, contemplate him outside ourselves from afar in order that his righteousness may be imputed to us but because we put on Christ and are engrafted into his body.... For this reason, we glory that we have fellowship of righteousness with him.[68]

This, and several other passages from Calvin's *Institutes*, give credence to McCormack's view that Calvin appears to make union with Christ 'logically, if not chronologically, prior to both justification and

---

64. Seifrid, 'Luther, Melanchthon and Paul', 144–45.
65. Ibid., 149.
66. Ibid.
67. Gaffin, 'Union with Christ', 285.
68. Calvin, *Institutes*, 3.1.10 (p. 737). There are several other similar statements to be found in Calvin. Other representative examples include: 'You see that our righteousness is not in us but in Christ, that we possess it only because we are partakers in Christ; indeed, with him we possess all its riches.... To declare that by him alone we are accounted righteous, what else is this but to lodge our righteousness in Christ's obedience, because the obedience of Christ is reckoned to us as if it were our own?' (3.1.23; p. 753); 'But we define justification as follows: the sinner, received into communion with Christ, is reconciled to God by his grace, while, cleansed by Christ's blood, he obtains forgiveness of sins, and clothed with Christ's righteousness as if it were his own, he stands confident before the heavenly judgment seat' (3.17.8; p. 811).

regeneration'.[69] According to Billings, 'Calvin's theology of justification fit within his theology of union with Christ'.[70] Horton discerns complementary emphases in Calvin's account of justification, such that the righteousness of Christ is 'outside' the believer, but by virtue of union with Christ it cannot remain outside us.[71] An alien righteousness belongs to Christ, not believers, but Christ himself does not remain alien, 'but joins himself to us and us to him'.[72] Thus Calvin 'avoids a strict realism on one side and an arbitrary nominalism on the other'.[73]

As we have seen, Luther and Calvin's understanding of imputation is useful for preserving the notion that the righteousness pertaining to believers is not their own; it has been granted to them and is a bestowal of God's grace. In their context, imputed righteousness had special significance with respect to the Reformers' concern to correct medieval Catholicism, which diluted the 'alien' nature of righteousness and thus the grace of God. In protecting the alien righteousness of Christ, however, imputation did not imply that it was an abstract substance that could be separated out from Christ's person. Quite clearly, this was not Luther or Calvin's understanding, since they both regarded the righteousness of Christ as being shared with believers through their spiritual union with him. The marriage of the church to Christ means that what belongs to the husband is shared with his bride; it is hers only because her husband has brought it to the marriage, as it were.

11.10 CONCLUSION

This chapter draws together the exegetical results of part 2 that relate to justification, which reveal that there are few instances in which it is explicitly linked to union with Christ. Nevertheless, these references clearly convey the instrumentality of Christ in justification. Matters of definition are

---

69. Bruce L. McCormack, 'What's at Stake in Current Debates over Justification? The Crisis of Protestantism in the West', in *Justification: What's at Stake in the Current Debates* (ed. Mark Husbands and Daniel J. Treier; Downers Grove, IL: InterVarsity Press, 2004), 101.

70. J. Todd Billings, *Union with Christ: Reframing Theology and Ministry for the Church* (Grand Rapids: Baker, 2011), 7.

71. So Vickers' reading of Calvin; 'Christ's righteousness is imputed to the believer in the context of the believer's union with Christ'; Vickers, *Imputation*, 36–37.

72. Horton, *Covenant and Salvation*, 145; Billings, *Union with Christ*, 27.

73. Horton, *Covenant and Salvation*, 146.

discussed, concluding that justification is juridical and eschatological but does not denote covenantal faithfulness or ethical transformation, though it has covenantal overtones *by implication* and *leads to* transformation. The instrumental facet of 'in Christ' language means that justification occurs as an outworking of union with Christ, and the two concepts ought not be set against each other, but rather, must be understood in their relatedness. The justification of believers stems from their participation in the death and resurrection of Christ; his vindicating resurrection becomes the vindication and righteousness of those united to him. Finally, the theological conception of imputation is understood as the unmerited reception of Christ's righteousness, which is received through union with him.

CHAPTER 12

DEFINING 'UNION WITH CHRIST'

12.1 INTRODUCTION

The previous chapters in part 3 have explored the ways in which union with Christ relates to the major spheres of Paul's theological thought—the work of Christ, Trinity, Christian living, and justification. Having completed these theological discussions, built on the exegetical analyses of part 2, we must now engage the matter of defining 'union with Christ'. While a definition was posited from the outset (see §1.7), we turn now to demonstrate that this is derived from the exegetical and theological study that comprises the bulk of this book. Once the definition of 'union with Christ' is established, it will be possible to discuss the issue of antecedents for Paul's conception of the theme.

12.2 UNION, PARTICIPATION, IDENTIFICATION, INCORPORATION

The discussion here turns to defining union with Christ and the validity of this term itself alongside related appellations. The conclusions of this section have already been stated in §1.7, yet a concerted discussion of the matter has been avoided thus far for two main reasons.

First, this study has been conducted with a commitment to an inductive approach, and as far as possible this commitment has shaped the methodology and structure of the book. Admittedly, such a study cannot be entirely inductive, and certain decisions about 'union with Christ' have had to be made along the way, not least of which has been the determination of Pauline language that is related to the concept. The difficulty of this particular matter was acknowledged at the beginning of part 2, since there is an inevitable circularity involved in deciding which material is related to a theme when we are not yet sure what that theme actually is. Only by positing some predetermined understanding of union with Christ were we able to deduce which prepositional phrases and metaphors belonged or related to the theme. Nevertheless, this has been done with the goal of building an inductive approach to the topic based on Paul's language. Consequently, it is proper to arrive at the final destination once all the data has been considered, and this destination involves a definition and description of union with Christ that do justice to the sweep and detail of our findings.

Second, a proper understanding of union with Christ cannot be developed without due attention to the many ways in which it relates to other Pauline themes. As we have seen, the language of union is inextricably tied to the major spheres of Paul's thought, informing and being informed by each. Because of this, union with Christ is not to be regarded as an isolated concept; in fact, to do so would be to distort it significantly. Thus, a definition and description of union with Christ is only possible through understanding its role in the entirety of Paul's theological framework. Just as linguistic items may only be understood as they relate to other linguistic items, so too union with Christ may only be understood as it relates to other themes. Having traced these relationships, we are only now in a position to reach conclusions.

12.2.1 DESCRIBING 'UNION WITH CHRIST'

Before *defining* union with Christ, it is appropriate to *describe* it. This is complex and therefore difficult because of the many ways in which Paul employs 'union' language and because of the intricate web of connections between union with Christ and other themes in Paul's theological framework.[1]

---

1. Billings makes much of the imagery of *adoption* in his understanding of union with Christ; Billings, *Union with Christ*, 15–21. While adoption is no doubt an important concept in Paul's thought (see Rom 8:15, 23; 9:4; Gal 4:5; Eph 1:5) and must be *conceptually* related to union with Christ, there is only one instance in which it is *explicitly* connected to the language of union—Ephesians 1:5, which states that adoption occurs *through Christ* (διὰ Ἰησοῦ Χριστοῦ). This would suggest that adoption—like blessings, redemption, and forgiveness—is received *through* our union with Christ, but it is not what union with Christ *is*.

While it is fitting at this stage to offer a summary of our observations, this will inevitably flatten much of the nuance of Paul's thinking, since we cannot rehearse everything all over again. As such, the reader is invited to revisit previous parts of this book for relevant details.

In no particular order, the following observations must inform our definition of union with Christ.

12.2.1.1 Location

First, union with Christ involves our location within the realm of Christ. Believers are situated under his rule, and our lives are conducted within the spiritual sphere of his dominion. This reality informs the nature of the Christian life as the lordship of Christ defines appropriate behaviour within his realm and characterizes our being, especially in contradistinction to existence within the realm of sin and death.

12.2.1.2 Identification

Related to location, union with Christ involves the identification of believers with Christ. Situated within the realm of his rule,[2] believers' identity is shaped by their belonging to Christ, the Second Adam.[3] We are marked off as his rather than belonging to Adam, and this is to shape believers' sense of who they are and to whom they owe allegiance.[4]

12.2.1.3 Participation

Third, union with Christ involves the participation of believers in the events of Christ's narrative, including his death and burial, resurrection, ascension, and glorification.[5] Believers are described as having died with Christ, having been raised with him, and so forth, such that the significance of these events pertain to us as it pertains to him.

---

2. Gorman, *Cruciformity*, 36; Walter Bartling, 'The New Creation in Christ: A Study of the Pauline ἐν Χριστῷ Formula,' *CTM* 21 (1950): 403.

3. Kreitzer, 'Second Adam', 75–78.

4. Indeed, 'Christians' entire existence is outlined by their identification with Christ'; Powers, *Salvation through Participation*, 166.

5. Tannehill, *Dying and Rising*, 119; John D. Harvey, 'The "With Christ" Motif in Paul's Thought', *JETS* 35 (1992): 340; Gert M. M. Pelser, 'Could the "Formulas" *Dying* and *Rising with Christ* be Expressions of Pauline Mysticism?', *Neot* 32 (1998): 132.

12.2.1.4 Incorporation

Fourth, union with Christ also involves the incorporation of believers into his body, temple, church, and building. Believers are grafted into a community that is founded, shaped, and directed by Christ.[6] Their belonging to this Christ-community affects how they are to live in a way that honours the body. Thus, belonging to Christ means that we belong to one another.

It is, however, an overstatement to claim that incorporation into the body of Christ exhausts the meaning of 'union with Christ', as Schweitzer claims: 'The expression "being-in-Christ" is merely a shorthand reference for being partakers in the Mystical Body of Christ.'[7] While partaking in the body of Christ is a significant element of union with Christ, as we have observed, there are several other notions that are not satisfied by Schweitzer's claim.

12.2.1.5 Instrumentality

Fifth, union with Christ involves the way in which he effects the will of God toward us. Christ is the instrument of God's agency for the benefit of humanity, and this role is largely mediatorial. Thus one aspect of our union with Christ is that it enables us to partake in the blessings of God. Apart from Christ, we are without God and without his acts toward us.

12.2.1.6 Trinity

Sixth, union with Christ involves the inner life of the Trinity. It refers to the Father's relationship to the Son, and their union in the Spirit; it does not merely pertain to the relationship of believers to Christ. The Father's will is enacted through the Son, by the Spirit, for the glory of Christ and the benefit of humanity. This represents the other side of the mediatorial function of union with Christ; God the Father act towards humanity through the Son and by virtue of his union with him.

---

6. Ian A. McFarland, 'The Body of Christ: Rethinking a Classic Ecclesiological Model', *IJST* 7 (2005): 239–45.

7. Schweitzer, *Mysticism*, 122. Bultmann also regarded the phrase 'in Christ' as 'primarily an *ecclesiological* formula', referring to 'the state of having been articulated into the "body of Christ" by baptism'. He does, however, recognize other uses of the phrase, such as expressing the state of 'being determined by Christ whereby it supplies the lack of the not yet coined adjective "Christian" or a corresponding adverb', and eschatological meaning; Bultmann, *New Testament*, 311.

12.2.1.7 Union

Seventh, union with Christ involves an actual spiritual union with him.[8] Believers are described as being 'in' Christ and he being in them such that there is a mutual indwelling by the Spirit.[9] Likened to a nuptial union,[10] this mutual indwelling appears to be derivative of the nature of relationships within the inner life of the Godhead, in which Father, Son, and Spirit co-inhere one another. As the Father indwells the Son, so the Son indwells his people. Consequently, there is some sense in which believers participate in the 'divine-nature-of-relating', while not themselves becoming divine. Such union with Christ does not compromise the personhood of Christ or the believer, since 'each retains his own personality and they are not fused by one person absorbing the other'.[11]

12.2.1.8 Eschatology

Eighth, union with Christ has eschatological dimensions.[12] This is implicit through Paul's references to the realm of Christ and participation in Christ's resurrection in particular. The realm of Christ is an eschatological entity in which the future age of righteousness has broken into the present world, set in opposition to the realm of sin and death. Moreover,

---

8. 'Mystical union is what it is because it is spiritual. This is so not in an immaterial, idealistic sense, but because of the activity and indwelling of the Holy Spirit. This circumscribes the mystery and protects against confusing it with other kinds of union. As spiritual, that is, effected by the Holy Spirit, it is neither ontological, like that between the persons of the Trinity, nor hypostatic or unipersonal, like that between Christ's two natures, nor psychosomatic, like that between body and soul in human personality, nor somatic, like that between husband and wife; nor is it merely intellectual and moral, a unity in understanding, affections, purpose'; Gaffin, 'Union with Christ', 273–74. Murray likewise; 'This brings us to note, in the second place, that union with Christ is *Spiritual* because it is a spiritual relationship that is in view. It is not the kind of union that we have in the Godhead — three persons in one God. It is not the kind of union we have in the person of Christ — two natures in one person. It is not the kind union we have in man — body and soul constituting a human being. It is not simply the union of feeling, affection, understanding, mind, heart, will, and purpose. Here we have union which we are unable to define specifically. But it is union of an intensely spiritual character consonant with the nature and work of the Holy Spirit so that in a real way surpassing our power of analysis Christ dwells in his people and his people dwell in him'; Murray, *Redemption*, 206 [italics are original].

9. Gorman, *Cruciformity*, 38.

10. Son, 'One Flesh', 120–22.

11. Wikenhauser, *Mysticism*, 75; see also p. 102; K. Barth, *Dogmatics*, IV/3.2, 540.

12. Dunn, *Paul the Apostle*, 411–12.

Christ's resurrection 'in the middle of time', as it were, is an eschatological inbreaking of the future resurrection of the dead.[13] To participate, then, in Christ's resurrection is to partake in an eschatological event. Further-more, the synthesis between union with Christ and justification involves eschatological overtones, since justification — in connection to resurrec-tion — is the eschatological declaration of righteousness brought into the present time.

Schweitzer, however, overplays this element of union with Christ. He regards Christ mysticism's *sole* function as eschatological, developed in order to solve Paul's eschatological problems.[14] If Christ's resurrection was the beginning of the resurrection of the dead in general, Paul's eschatologi-cal problem was how believers are to partake in the future — while they themselves are in the present. For Schweitzer, Christ mysticism solved this problem (see §2.4): 'Thus the direction of his thought was forced from all sides by the problems of eschatology itself to the paradoxical assertion that the powers manifested in the dying and rising of Jesus were already at work in those who are elect to the Messianic Kingdom.'[15] While the escha-tological nature of union with Christ is to be affirmed, it is reductionist to view it entirely in terms of a solution to an eschatological problem.[16] There are several other 'non-eschatological' elements to union with Christ that are not mere solutions to problems.

12.2.1.9 Spiritual Reality

Finally, union with Christ is a spiritual *reality*.[17] It is not merely meta-phorical, being understood as a poignant way in which to depict 'rela-tionship with Christ' or some other such notion. While Paul employs various corporate metaphors — which we have explored at length — in his discussions of church and union with Christ, these have always pointed

---

13. Paul 'cannot regard the resurrection of Jesus as an isolated event, but must regard it as the initial event of the rising of the dead in general'; Schweitzer, *Mysticism*, 98.

14. See, for example, Schweitzer, *Mysticism*, 100–105.

15. Ibid., 100.

16. 'Schweitzer wrongly suggested that Paul's view of the believer's incorporation into Christ grew out of the dilemma of the temporal separation between Christ's resurrection and His second advent'; D. N. Howell, 'The Center of Pauline Theology', *BSac* 151 (1994): 60–61.

17. 'The participatory union is not a figure of speech for something else; it is, as many scholars have insisted, real'; Sanders, *Palestinian Judaism*, 455.

to a concrete referent.[18] This referent is *spiritual*, but nonetheless *real*. As Schweitzer acknowledges, 'One thing which surprises us in the Pauline Christ-mysticism is its extraordinarily realistic character'; it is 'a real co-experiencing of His dying and rising again.'[19]

12.2.2 DEFINING 'UNION WITH CHRIST'

Going hand in hand with defining union with Christ is the terminology used to invoke the concepts involved. From the observation of these concepts above, it seems unlikely that a single term could possibly capture the full breadth of ideas that cohere in this theme. This problem has beset the scholarly community since Deissmann's launch of the modern discussion of Pauline mysticism.

First, the term *mysticism* failed on several levels. It was an unhelpfully vague term that, at its best, seemed only to refer to some kind of relatedness to the divine.[20] It did not give expression to the defined ideas expressed by Paul's language. Furthermore, *mysticism* created confusion since the term was taken from the history of religions movement and was normally associated with pagan mystery and mystic spiritualities. By the time the likes of Deissmann (see §2.2) and Schweitzer (§2.4) had stressed the differences between Paul's mysticism and those of mystical spiritualities,[21] the term had died the death of a thousand qualifications.

Second, the term *union* has its own problems. It is still perhaps the most universal of terms (indeed, it is the working terminology employed here), and the primary strength of the term is that it captures the faith union between believers and Christ; in addition, it can also be used with respect to the mutual indwelling of Father, Son, Spirit and the parallel

---

18. So, e.g., Powers: 'While Paul's reference to the "body" is certainly metaphorical, the unity which he expresses with this metaphor rests upon an ontological reality. The believer is truly "in" Christ'; Powers, *Salvation through Participation*, 71. See also Ellis, 'Sōma in First Corinthians', 138; Field, 'Body of Christ', 88–94; Andrew C. Perriman, '"His Body, Which Is the Church...": Coming to Terms with Metaphor', *EvQ* 62 (1990): 140–41.

19. Schweitzer, *Mysticism*, 13. However, Schweitzer overstates this insofar as he regards Christ mysticism as a quasi-*physical* reality—'But in reality the dying and rising again with Christ is not a metaphorical but a quasi-physical conception' (ibid., 295). Union with Christ is *real*, but spiritual; it is not physical.

20. '"Mysticism" is a vague term, and discussions around this subject are apt to be lost in the bog of terminology'; Davies, *Paul*, 13–14.

21. See Deissmann, *Paul*, 149–53; Schweitzer, *Mysticism*, 15–16, 22–23.

mutual indwelling of Christ and his people. The nuptial union between Christ and the church is another concept that union with Christ is able to convey. The chief problem for the term *union*, however, is that it is *static*, referring to a state of affairs or mode of existence; it reflects a spiritual reality but is not able to convey more dynamic notions. In particular, the term does not adequately capture participatory elements—the dynamic, active partaking in the *events* of Christ's narrative. To *participate* is a 'doing' word, while *union* is a 'being' word. Arguably, union with Christ does better with the concepts of identification and incorporation (by implication), but these require explication—they are not automatically implied by the term.

Third, the term *participation* has the opposite problem. It obviously suits participatory elements, conveying participation in the events of Christ's narrative, but it insufficiently conveys union elements, such as the faith union or mutual indwelling of Christ and his people. Nor does it point to identification or incorporation, except perhaps by implication. Thus, the term fails to elucidate any key concept apart from participation itself. While participation is currently the in-vogue term within New Testament studies (since Sanders, §2.12), it is not a stronger alternative to 'union' with Christ and ultimately ought to be superseded.

These single-idea terms are not sufficiently broad to encapsulate all that Paul envisions by our relatedness to Christ, and most likely no single term will do justice to the theme. Instead, I propose that this theme is best conveyed through four terms: union, participation, identification, and incorporation. *Union* gathers up faith union with Christ, mutual indwelling, trinitarian, and nuptial notions. *Participation* conveys partaking in the events of Christ's narrative. *Identification* refers to believers' location in the realm of Christ and their allegiance to his lordship. *Incorporation* encapsulates the corporate dimensions of membership in Christ's body. Together these four terms function as 'umbrella' concepts, covering the full spectrum of Pauline language, ideas, and themes that are bound up in the metatheme of 'union with Christ'. Furthermore, all four terms entail ethical expectations, as Paul draws on the implications of union, participation, identification, and incorporation to inform the Christian life.

The ordering of these four terms is not reflective of their relative importance, nor does it reflect the share of data to which each term relates.

It could be argued, however, that the ordering of terms reflects a kind of 'logical' or 'theological' priority—not a priority of importance but of sequence. Whether Paul conceived of a 'logic' underpinning these concepts is not clear, nor can such be demonstrated from his extant corpus. Nevertheless, an attempted reconstruction of the logical sequence of these concepts follows.

It should first be noted that such a *logical* sequence does not imply *temporal* sequence; it is not as though union occurs, *then* participation, *then* identification, and *then* incorporation. Rather, in a kind of 'union-with-Christ *ordo salutis*', this ordering is (theo)logical only, and most likely 'occurs' all at the 'same time'. A believer is united to Christ at the moment of coming to faith; their union is established by the indwelling of the Spirit. The person united to Christ therefore enters into participation with Christ in his death, resurrection, ascension, and glorification. As a participant in Christ's death and resurrection, the believer dies to the world and is identified with the realm of Christ. As a member of the realm of Christ, the believer is incorporated into his body, since union with Christ entails union with his members.

Since, however, the expression *union, participation, identification, incorporation* is a bit unwieldy as a label, the term *union with Christ* will continue to be used for the sake of convenience. But from this point on, it must be understood as shorthand for 'union, participation, identification, incorporation'.

12.3 ANTECEDENTS OF UNION, PARTICIPATION, IDENTIFICATION, INCORPORATION

One of the most important questions that has engaged scholarship with respect to union with Christ has been whether antecedents to Paul's thought can be found in Greco-Roman or Jewish thought. Especially of interest in the first half of the twentieth century, this question has all but been abandoned in recent discussions, and it is no accident that it has not been directly addressed here until now.

One of the problems facing past explorations was methodological. Commonly an interpretative priority was given to reconstructions of supposed antecedents, which were then utilized to uncover Paul's understanding of union with Christ. But the difficulty here is that it is pointless searching for 'antecedents' to union with Christ if it is not first understood what 'union with Christ' actually is. Once an antecedent is established, it inalterably affects how the theme is handled. Union with Christ is either interpreted *in accord with* its antecedents, or it is defined *against* its antecedents — in demonstration of how Paul's conception differs from others. The latter approach is not ultimately conclusive because union with Christ can only be understood negatively (what it is *not*), and the former approach is methodologically corrupt for assuming what union with Christ is before establishing its meaning from Paul's own mind.

The approach taken here has been to sidestep the whole issue of antecedents until an understanding of union with Christ could be developed from the Pauline canon. In what could be regarded by some as a backward step, we are now in a position to evaluate potential antecedents to union with Christ because we have arrived at a useful appreciation of what Paul means by this theme.

First, we consider Greco-Roman antecedents to union with Christ. Moves by Bultmann and others to anchor Paul's conception in Greco-Roman thought were never persuasive[22] and have ultimately been rejected.[23] Greco-Roman parallels could only be used negatively, as it became increasingly clear that Paul did *not* follow such antecedents.[24] The various species of pagan mysticism have little in common with Paul. Even the apparently parallel practice of baptism has been shown to convey a significantly different meaning for Paul when compared to Greco-Roman practice.

Second, Jewish theology of the Second Temple period informs Paul's categories of thought, forming the conceptual backdrop to his theological thinking,[25] but ultimately it does not account for the full-orbed nature of

---

22. See Bultmann, *New Testament*, 298–300.

23. Generally speaking, Davies notes that those scholars 'who have emphasized the Hellenistic aspects of Paul's thought, generally find it necessary to reject much New Testament evidence'; Davies, *Paul*, 2. More specifically, 'Paul's "mysticism" cannot be Hellenistic. Paul never speaks of being deified as the Hellenistic mystics do. The distinction between Creator and creature always remains for Paul, a fact which shows his affinities to Jewish not Hellenistic "mysticism"' (ibid., 15; cf. also 88–93).

24. Bousset, *Kyrios Christos*, 164–66.

25. Davies, *Paul*, 15–16, 323.

Pauline union with Christ.[26] Schweitzer depended on late-Jewish apocalyptic eschatology for his reading of Paul (see §2.4),[27] and while his insistence on the eschatological aspect of Pauline mysticism became influential, the rigidity with which Schweitzer appropriated Paul in light of apocalyptic has largely been rejected.[28] Beyond apocalyptic eschatology,[29] Davies has pointed out various affinities between Paul and rabbinic Judaism, such as his distinction between the σάρξ and πνεῦμα[30] and the Adamic representation of humanity (see §2.11).[31] While such affinities are illuminating and no doubt resonate with Pauline theology, again they do not fully explicate Paul's conception of union with Christ, which remains startlingly original against his Jewish background.

Third, the Old Testament has received comparatively little treatment on the question of antecedents to union with Christ. There are no parallels for Paul's entire conception of union with Christ to be found in the Old Testament, nor is his union with Christ vocabulary and prepositional usage to be found there. Some strands of Paul's thought, however, can find antecedents in the Old Testament, and these strands primarily relate to Pauline metaphors for union. The metaphors of marriage,[32] temple, and clothing all find antecedents in the Old Testament,[33] and this not particularly controversial. The contexts in which God refers to Israel as his bride are well known (e.g., Ezek 16). The symbolic nature of the temple as the locality in which God dwells with his people is even better known (e.g., 1 Kings 8:27–30). Related to the temple cult, priestly garments were symbols of representation and mediation.

Each of these strands resonates well with Paul's metaphorical descriptions of union with Christ. Paul has reappropriated the divine marriage

---

26. Wedderburn, *Baptism and Resurrection*, 356.

27. Schweitzer, *Mysticism*, 37.

28. See Davies, *Paul*, xii–xv, 10.

29. Schweitzer regards the general features of mainstream Judaism as 'opposed to mysticism'; Schweitzer, *Mysticism*, 36. Davies, however, contends that Schweitzer oversimplified the distinction between 'normative Pharisaic Judaism standing over against apocalyptic'. Rather, Judaism is much more varied and complicated than Schweitzer could have appreciated, a fact that further confirmed by the Dead Sea Scrolls; Davies, *Paul*, xii.

30. Ibid., 17–20.

31. Ibid., 52–57.

32. Patterson, 'Metaphors of Marriage', 692–99.

33. Kim, *Clothing Imagery*, 102.

of the Old Testament so that Christ is the husband and the church his bride. Temple imagery now refers to the people of God among whom God dwells. Believers clothe themselves with Christ himself, the one true mediator. While Paul's christological configuration of marriage, temple, and clothing is boldly innovative, the Old Testament antecedents to such themes ought to be obvious.

Nevertheless, the Old Testament does not appear to anticipate such notions as mutual indwelling, the instrumentality of Christ, the *other-worldly* realm of Christ,[34] and the body of Christ. Thus, while we may affirm that certain important strands of Paul's thought find antecedents in the Old Testament, other major strands do not.

Fourth, it could be argued that these strands just mentioned — mutual indwelling, the instrumentality of Christ, the otherworldly realm of Christ, and the body of Christ — are all to be found in the gospel of John.[35] Before exploring these connections, we must consider whether it is even *possible* for John to provide theological antecedents for Paul. In all likelihood, the gospel of John was not written before Paul's death — even if an early date is adopted for the gospel.[36] It is historically plausible that Paul was aware of some of the Jesus traditions that found their way into the composition of John.[37] Moreover, *John* may have been familiar with *Paul's* writings, so that the situation might be reversed; that is, Paul may be the antecedent. Thus it is theoretically possible that there are genuine parallels between Paul and John. However, it might be wise to avoid the term 'antecedent' for John.

---

34. While an *earthly* reign of the Messiah is envisaged in Old Testament prophecy, the *otherworldly* nature of the realm of Christ remains a unique feature of New Testament expectation (though it could be argued that Dan 7 presents a step on the trajectory toward the New Testament understanding).

35. So Taylor: 'In substance the Johannine mysticism closely resembles the Pauline mysticism, the principal differences being that the former also discloses a God-mysticism and does not make use of the dying and rising with Christ'; Vincent Taylor, *Forgiveness and Reconciliation: A Study in New Testament Theology* (2nd ed.; London: Macmillan, 1956), 145.

36. An early date (before AD 70) would at least open the possibility of Paul's familiarity with the final form of the gospel, though such dating is not widely accepted. See Leon Morris, *The Gospel According to John* (NICNT; rev. ed.; Grand Rapids: Eerdmans, 1995), 25–30.

37. Brown regards the historical tradition underlying John's gospel as reaching back as far as AD 40–60; Raymond E. Brown, *The Gospel According to John (i–xii)* (AB; Garden City, NY: Doubleday, 1966), lxxxvi. See also Richard Bauckham, *Jesus and the Eyewitnesses: The Gospels as Eyewitness Testimony* (Grand Rapids: Eerdmans, 2006), esp. 264–89.

What are these parallels? First, the notion of mutual indwelling is prevalent in John. Note these sayings of Jesus:

- *The one who eats My flesh and drinks My blood lives in Me, and I in him* (John 6:56).
- *Remain in Me, and I in you. Just as a branch is unable to produce fruit by itself unless it remains on the vine, so neither can you unless you remain in Me* (John 15:4; see also 15:5–7).
- *May they all be one, as You, Father, are in Me and I am in You. May they also be one in Us, so the world may believe You sent Me* (John 17:21).
- *I am in them and You are in Me. May they be made completely one, so the world may know You have sent Me and have loved them as You have loved Me* (John 17:23; also 17:26).

It is remarkable how well these statements of Jesus cohere with Paul's references to the mutual indwelling of Christ and believers.

Second, the instrumentality of the Son performing the Father's will occurs at several places:

- *The Father, in fact, judges no one but has given all judgment to the Son* (John 5:22).
- *But I have a greater testimony than John's because of the works that the Father has given Me to accomplish* (John 5:36).
- *For I have come down from heaven, not to do My will, but the will of Him who sent Me* (John 6:38).
- *The works that I do in My Father's name testify about Me* (John 10:25b).
- *So the things that I speak, I speak just as the Father has told Me* (John 12:50).

It is clear that Christ views his own activities as dependent on, and enacting, the will of the Father.

Third, the idea of the otherworldly realm of Christ is also to be found in John:

- *If you were of the world, the world would love you as its own. However, because you are not of the world, but I have chosen you out of it, the world hates you* (John 15:19).

- *My kingdom is not of this world.... If My kingdom were of this world, My servants would fight, so that I wouldn't be handed over to the Jews. As it is, My kingdom does not have its origin here* (John 18:36).

These references refer to the otherworldly domain over which Christ rules, with which believers are identified.

Fourth, John conveys a notion very similar to Paul's body of Christ:

- *I am the true vine, and My Father is the vineyard keeper. Every branch in Me that does not produce fruit He removes, and He prunes every branch that produces fruit so that it will produce more fruit. You are already clean because of the word I have spoken to you. Remain in Me, and I in you. Just as a branch is unable to produce fruit by itself unless it remains on the vine, so neither can you unless you remain in Me. I am the vine; you are the branches. The one who remains in Me and I in him produces much fruit, because you can do nothing without Me* (John 15:1–5).

The image of the vine and the branches parallels the body and its members — both metaphors are organic, envisaging a profound connection to Christ. Unless a believer is a branch of the vine, or a member of the body, he or she does not belong to Christ.

Thus, at least four central concepts associated with Paul's theology of union with Christ can be found resonating throughout John's gospel. Does union with Christ find antecedents in John? Possibly, though perhaps it is more accurate to say that union with Christ finds antecedents *in the words of Jesus*.[38] Putting the Johannine words of Jesus together with Jewish eschatology and Old Testament strands of thought about divine-human marriage, temple, and priestly clothing, we find connections to most elements of thinking about Paul's union with Christ. While such connections do not fully account for its development, for Paul's conception is boldly original in its language, scope, and pervasiveness, there do appear to be threads of influence from Jesus, Judaism, and the Old Testament. In this way, it is obvious that Paul has not simply plucked union with Christ out of thin air, so to speak.

---

38. While he takes a different route to get there, Schweitzer also acknowledges the influence of Jesus on Paul's understanding of union with Christ; 'for the preaching of Jesus itself contains Christ-mysticism'; Schweitzer, *Mysticism*, 105; 'Paul's mystical doctrine of redemption has its roots in the Gospel of Jesus' (ibid., 396).

In fact, the original catalyst for the development of Paul's theology of union with Christ may be seen as Jesus' words *to Paul* on the Damascus Road. Deissmann regards Paul's encounter with the risen Christ on the road to Damascus as his 'basal mystical experience', and 'all that can be called Paul's Christ-mysticism is the reaction to this initial experience' (see §2.2).[39] In particular, Jesus' words "Saul, Saul, why are you persecuting Me?" and "I am Jesus, the One you are persecuting" (Acts 9:4, 5) speak directly to the theme of union with Christ. Paul's *persecution of Christians* is regarded as *persecution of Christ*, which reveals a strong sense of identification between Jesus and his followers. While Paul does not explicitly acknowledge that these words sparked his thinking about union with Christ, they are certainly suggestive of such a possibility.

12.4 CONCLUSION

This chapter presents the major conclusions of the book, offering a definition and descriptions of union with Christ, along with an exploration of the possible antecedents to Paul's thought. Union with Christ is defined as *union, participation, identification, incorporation* — terms that together do justice to the widespread variety and nuance of Paul's language, theology, and ethical thought about our relatedness to Christ. *Union* conveys faith union with Christ, mutual indwelling, trinitarian, and nuptial notions. *Participation* refers to the partaking in the events of Christ's narrative. *Identification* encapsulates believers' location in the realm of Christ and their allegiance to his lordship. *Incorporation* gathers up the corporate dimensions of membership in Christ's body. These terms provide sufficient breadth through which the various characteristics of union with Christ are to be understood — the notions of locality, identification, participation, incorporation, instrumentality, Trinity, union, eschatology, and spiritual reality are all ably represented.

The conceptual antecedents for Paul's thought are to be found in Jewish theology, the Old Testament, and the words of Jesus, beginning with his encounter with Christ on the Damascus Road. The revelation that Saul, the persecutor of Christians, was in fact persecuting the risen Christ himself forever transformed Paul's life and understanding of the universe.

---

39. Deissmann, *Paul*, 130–31.

CHAPTER 13

IMPLICATIONS AND FUTURE DIRECTIONS

13.1 INTRODUCTION

This final chapter explores two issues arising from the conclusions of the study and sets an agenda for future directions of research. The two issues discussed here are, first, the *importance* of union with Christ within Paul's theological framework and, second, the theological *structure* of his thought. In Paul's mind, how important is union with Christ? What place does union with Christ occupy in the structure of his theology? Is it central or does it play some other role? These are not simple questions, nor are they independent of each other. Nevertheless, we must attempt to answer them. Following this, we turn to consider future directions of research that might profitably grow out of the exegetical and theological study of Paul and union with Christ.

13.2 IMPORTANCE

The question of how important the concept of union with Christ is in Paul's mind is not as simple as it first appears. If the matter is addressed purely from a statistical standpoint, the sheer number of instances in which Paul uses language related to union with Christ is overwhelming. With scores of prepositional phrases that express union, such as the multiple uses of ἐν Χριστῷ, εἰς Χριστόν, σὺν Χριστῷ, and διὰ Χριστοῦ, and a variety of metaphors such as marriage, temple, building, body, and clothing, a statistical approach leads us to conclude that union with Christ is one of the most important themes in Paul's thought—if not *the* most important. Certainly it is more common than, for example, justification language; this realization would *seem* to support Schweitzer's claim that the latter is but a subsidiary crater within the main crater of being-in-Christ.

It is unlikely, however, that statistics alone can answer this question. Is the importance of a theme to be determined simply by how many times it is evoked?[1] Such an approach could conceivably lead to a distortion of reality in a variety of matters. For example, are television advertisements more important than news programs? They are many times more frequent, but it is doubtful that any thinking adult would therefore conclude that they matter more (to the viewer, at least) than news. On the contrary, frequency and repetition are crude measures by which to estimate importance. They are not irrelevant, however, and it ought to be acknowledged that repeated reference to certain themes is one way in which an author may attribute prominence to various topics. But prominence involves more than pure frequency, since there are other ways an author may draw attention to matters of significance.

One such indicator of prominence, or importance, is the degree to which an author *directly addresses* the matter in question. If, for example, an author expounds a theme at some length and with attention to detail, it should be evident that he wants us to regard that with some consequence. The prominence that direct address achieves is not necessarily undermined by a lack of frequency. In other words, a particular theme may be addressed only once in a discourse, but by its allocation of significant space within the discourse and the directness with which it is expounded, its importance is assured.

By the same token, a theme that is raised *indirectly* or is not addressed with a similar level of directness as another theme will naturally be perceived as less prominent. This is the case even if the theme enjoys relatively high frequency; if it is not addressed directly but only occurs in connection to other themes, its frequent mention will not elevate its prominence.

These realities inevitably affect the theme of union with Christ and the question of its importance to Paul's theological framework. As indicated above, it is a frequent theme—a fact in favour of its significance. Less immediately ascertained, however, is the extent to which union with

---

1. Not according to Howell: 'pervasiveness does not equal centrality'; Howell, 'Center', 62.

Christ is addressed *directly* by Paul. On the one hand, many of the references to union with Christ either appear to be incidental or are evoked in passing. This is especially the case with many occurrences of the prepositional phrases ἐν Χριστῷ, εἰς Χριστόν, σὺν Χριστῷ, and διὰ Χριστοῦ. On a good number of occasions we find these phrases used in connection with other themes. Some instances are idiomatic, forming part of Paul's standard vocabulary and offering little direct contribution to the discussion at hand. It would be a mistake, therefore, to assume that union with Christ is of great importance to Paul merely on the basis that he uses the phrase ἐν Χριστῷ with high frequency.

On the other hand, some occurrences of the prepositional phrases ἐν Χριστῷ, εἰς Χριστόν, σὺν Χριστῷ, and διὰ Χριστοῦ appear to be employed as part of a direct exposition of union with Christ. How often this occurs and which passages may be included under such auspices will be addressed below.

The metaphors that convey union with Christ are likewise complex when it comes to assessing the importance of the theme. As with the prepositional phrases, some uses of the metaphors of body, church, building, marriage, and clothing are not employed *in order to* address union with Christ directly. Such uses may be incidental or idiomatic, and are not the focus of Paul's direct attention. In other cases, these metaphors may indeed be the focus of Paul's attention, but they are not necessarily for the purpose of expounding the theme of union with Christ. Indeed, these metaphors often *imply* union with Christ without it being the *main* purpose of the metaphor. Then again, there will be some occasions in which metaphors receive Paul's direct attention and in which union with Christ is squarely in view. Again, the question of how often this occurs, and in which passages, will be dealt with below.

All of this is to say that the matter of how important union with Christ is to Paul's theological framework is not straightforward and requires careful consideration of the various elements that contribute to prominence in discourse. We turn first to identifying those passages that *directly address* the theme of union with Christ. There is no foolproof methodology for this, but we will proceed by paying close attention to each passage in its context, identifying key themes, and assessing whether union with Christ receives direct exposition. Each relevant passage will be cited again here for the sake of convenience, though the exegesis offered in part 2 will not repeated (references to the previous analyses will be included). Rather, each passage will be discussed with a view to the present purpose.

13.2.1 IMPORTANT PASSAGES

Rom 6:3 ἢ ἀγνοεῖτε ὅτι, ὅσοι ἐβαπτίσθημεν εἰς Χριστὸν Ἰησοῦν, εἰς τὸν θάνατον αὐτοῦ ἐβαπτίσθημεν;

Or are you unaware that all of us who were baptized into Christ Jesus were baptized into His death?

This verse speaks of being baptized into Christ, as Paul indicates that all who were so baptized were therefore baptized into his death. Through these notions of being baptized into Christ and into his death, it is clear that participation with Christ is in view. Furthermore, since Paul's primary concern in this verse is to indicate such participation with Christ in his death, it is apparent that participation is directly addressed here. See §4.5.

Rom 6:4 συνετάφημεν οὖν αὐτῷ διὰ τοῦ βαπτίσματος εἰς τὸν θάνατον, ἵνα ὥσπερ ἠγέρθη Χριστὸς ἐκ νεκρῶν διὰ τῆς δόξης τοῦ πατρός, οὕτως καὶ ἡμεῖς ἐν καινότητι ζωῆς περιπατήσωμεν

Therefore we were buried with Him by baptism into death, in order that, just as Christ was raised from the dead by the glory of the Father, so we too may walk in a new way of life.

Continuing the thought of v. 3, Paul here expresses participation with Christ in his burial by baptism into death, with the result that Christ's resurrection issues in a new way of life for believers. The last clause of the verse points to Paul's wider ethical concern, and it is evident that participation with Christ is directly addressed for this purpose. See §5.6.

Rom 6:5 εἰ γὰρ σύμφυτοι γεγόναμεν τῷ ὁμοιώματι τοῦ θανάτου αὐτοῦ, ἀλλὰ καὶ τῆς ἀναστάσεως ἐσόμεθα

For if we have been joined with Him in the likeness of His death, we will certainly also be in the likeness of His resurrection.

This verse clearly addresses the matter of participation with Christ in a direct fashion. It refers to participation in the likeness of Christ's death and the certainty therefore of participation with him in the likeness of his resurrection. See §5.6.

Rom 6:8 εἰ δὲ ἀπεθάνομεν σὺν Χριστῷ, πιστεύομεν ὅτι καὶ συζήσομεν αὐτῷ

Now if we died with Christ, we believe that we will also live with Him.

Again, participation with Christ is of direct concern here, as Paul reiterates that participation in his death results in participation with him in life. See §5.6.

Rom 7:4 ὥστε, ἀδελφοί μου, καὶ ὑμεῖς ἐθανατώθητε τῷ νόμῳ διὰ τοῦ σώματος τοῦ Χριστοῦ, εἰς τὸ γενέσθαι ὑμᾶς ἑτέρῳ, τῷ ἐκ νεκρῶν ἐγερθέντι, ἵνα καρποφορήσωμεν τῷ θεῷ

Therefore, my brothers, you also were put to death in relation to the law through the crucified body of the Messiah, so that you may belong to another—to Him who was raised from the dead—that we may bear fruit for God.

Paul here addresses the issue of believers no longer being under law since they participate in Christ's crucifixion, which results in their belonging to Christ. Participation in Christ's crucifixion and belonging to Christ both refer to union with Christ in a direct manner. See §6.3.

Rom 8:17 εἰ δὲ τέκνα, καὶ κληρονόμοι· κληρονόμοι μὲν θεοῦ, συγκληρονόμοι δὲ Χριστοῦ, εἴπερ συμπάσχομεν ἵνα καὶ συνδοξασθῶμεν

And if children, also heirs—heirs of God and coheirs with Christ—seeing that we suffer with Him so that we may also be glorified with Him.

Paul's primary point here is that believers are heirs of God and coheirs with Christ; this point is founded on believers' participation with Christ in his suffering and consequently his glorification. While participation with Christ may not be the primary issue here, it is nevertheless addressed directly as a necessary supporting argument. See §5.6.

> Rom 12:5 οὕτως οἱ πολλοὶ ἓν σῶμά ἐσμεν ἐν Χριστῷ, τὸ δὲ καθ' εἷς ἀλλήλων μέλη
>
> *In the same way we who are many are one body in Christ and individually members of one another.*

Paul's concern here has to do with unity and diversity within the church, and key to this argument is the fact that believers are incorporated into Christ. Thus, incorporation into Christ is directly addressed here. See §3.8.

> 1 Cor 1:30 ἐξ αὐτοῦ δὲ ὑμεῖς ἐστε ἐν Χριστῷ Ἰησοῦ, ὃς ἐγενήθη σοφία ἡμῖν ἀπὸ θεοῦ, δικαιοσύνη τε καὶ ἁγιασμὸς καὶ ἀπολύτρωσις
>
> *But it is from Him that you are in Christ Jesus, who became God-given wisdom for us—our righteousness, sanctification, and redemption.*

This whole verse addresses union with Christ as it expresses some of the corollaries of being in Christ: he has become for us wisdom, righteousness, sanctification, and redemption. Christ is these things *for us*, and they flow from the union with Christ that is expressed by the phrase *in Christ Jesus*. Plainly, then, union with Christ is of direct importance here. See §3.10.

> 1 Cor 6:15–16 οὐκ οἴδατε ὅτι τὰ σώματα ὑμῶν μέλη Χριστοῦ ἐστιν; ἄρας οὖν τὰ μέλη τοῦ Χριστοῦ ποιήσω πόρνης μέλη; μὴ γένοιτο. οὐκ οἴδατε ὅτι ὁ κολλώμενος τῇ πόρνῃ ἓν σῶμά ἐστιν; ἔσονται γάρ, φησίν, οἱ δύο εἰς σάρκα μίαν
>
> *Don't you know that your bodies are a part of Christ's body? So should I take a part of Christ's body and make it a part of a prostitute? Absolutely not! Don't you know that anyone joined to a prostitute is one body with her? For Scripture says, The two will become one flesh.*

Essential to Paul's ethical concern here is the reality of union with Christ: believers' bodies are members of Christ, which is why a believer is not to become one with a prostitute. While the primary concern has to do with the conduct of believers, union with Christ is directly addressed as the rationale underpinning Paul's injunction. See §§7.2, 4.

1 Cor 8:6 ἀλλ᾽ ἡμῖν εἷς θεὸς ὁ πατὴρ ἐξ οὗ τὰ πάντα καὶ ἡμεῖς εἰς αὐτόν, καὶ εἷς κύριος Ἰησοῦς Χριστὸς δι᾽ οὗ τὰ πάντα καὶ ἡμεῖς δι᾽ αὐτοῦ

Yet for us there is one God, the Father. All things are from him, and we exist for Him. And there is one Lord, Jesus Christ. All things are through Him, and we exist through Him.

Paul's central concern here is to affirm the uniqueness of the one God and the one Lord, Jesus Christ. As part of the uniqueness of Christ, Paul views all things having their being through him, and believers in particular. While this verse is unlike the others investigated thus far, the notion of participation with Christ is expressed by the claim that believers have their being through Christ. And while such participation is not the primary concern, it is directly addressed as a key factor in establishing the uniqueness of Christ. See §6.8.3.

1 Cor 10:16–17 τὸ ποτήριον τῆς εὐλογίας ὃ εὐλογοῦμεν, οὐχὶ κοινωνία ἐστὶν τοῦ αἵματος τοῦ Χριστοῦ; τὸν ἄρτον ὃν κλῶμεν, οὐχὶ κοινωνία τοῦ σώματος τοῦ Χριστοῦ ἐστιν; ὅτι εἷς ἄρτος, ἓν σῶμα οἱ πολλοί ἐσμεν, οἱ γὰρ πάντες ἐκ τοῦ ἑνὸς ἄρτου μετέχομεν

The cup of blessing that we give thanks for, is it not a sharing in the blood of Christ? The bread that we break, is it not a sharing in the body of Christ? Because there is one bread, we who are many are one body, for all of us share that one bread.

Sharing in the blood and body of Christ, as expressed by sharing the cup and the bread of the Lord's Supper, is indicative of union with Christ. The direct implication of this union in the body of Christ is that the many are one. These verses plainly address union with Christ in a direct manner. See §7.2.

1 Cor 15:22 ὥσπερ γὰρ ἐν τῷ Ἀδὰμ πάντες ἀποθνῄσκουσιν, οὕτως καὶ ἐν τῷ Χριστῷ πάντες ζῳοποιηθήσονται

For as in Adam all die, so also in Christ all will be made alive.

Participation with Christ is directly in view here, as believers will be made alive in him. See §3.11.1.1.

2 Cor 5:17 ὥστε εἴ τις ἐν Χριστῷ, καινὴ κτίσις· τὰ ἀρχαῖα παρῆλθεν, ἰδοὺ γέγονεν καινά

Therefore, if anyone is in Christ, he is a new creation; old things have passed away, and look, new things have come.

The description of believers as a new creation is grounded in their being in Christ. Union with Christ, therefore, is a direct concern of this verse. See §3.8.

2 Cor 5:21 τὸν μὴ γνόντα ἁμαρτίαν ὑπὲρ ἡμῶν ἁμαρτίαν ἐποίησεν, ἵνα ἡμεῖς γενώμεθα δικαιοσύνη θεοῦ ἐν αὐτῷ

He made the One who did not know sin to be sin for us, so that we might become the righteousness of God in Him.

The notion that Christ would become *sin for us* expresses the union that believers have with him in his sin-bearing death. Similarly, believers become the righteousness of God through their union with Christ. It is evident that this verse, therefore, offers a direct account of union with Christ. See §§3.11.3.4, 5.

2 Cor 11:2 ζηλῶ γὰρ ὑμᾶς θεοῦ ζήλῳ, ἡρμοσάμην γὰρ ὑμᾶς ἑνὶ ἀνδρὶ παρθένον ἁγνὴν παραστῆσαι τῷ Χριστῷ

For I am jealous over you with a godly jealousy, because I have promised you in marriage to one husband—to present a pure virgin to Christ.

The metaphor of marriage to Christ conveys a profound sense of union with him; this is therefore directly in view. See §7.4.

2 Cor 13:4 καὶ γὰρ ἐσταυρώθη ἐξ ἀσθενείας, ἀλλὰ ζῇ ἐκ δυνάμεως θεοῦ. καὶ γὰρ ἡμεῖς ἀσθενοῦμεν ἐν αὐτῷ, ἀλλὰ ζήσομεν σὺν αὐτῷ ἐκ δυνάμεως θεοῦ εἰς ὑμᾶς

In fact, He was crucified in weakness, but He lives by God's power. For we also are weak in Him, yet toward you we will live with Him by God's power.

Paul describes his apostolic band as weak in union with Christ, while also affirming that they will live in union with him. While his main concern in the context is to affirm his own apostolic authority, the union he has with Christ is a key element in his claim, and thus it is a direct concern of this verse. See §§3.11.3.3; 5.5.

Gal 3:27 ὅσοι γὰρ εἰς Χριστὸν ἐβαπτίσθητε, Χριστὸν ἐνεδύσασθε

For as many of you as have been baptized into Christ have put on Christ like a garment.

The notions of baptism into Christ and putting on Christ are both concerned with union, which is, thus, the direct concern of this verse. See §4.5.

Gal 3:28 οὐκ ἔνι Ἰουδαῖος οὐδὲ Ἕλλην, οὐκ ἔνι δοῦλος οὐδὲ ἐλεύθερος, οὐκ ἔνι ἄρσεν καὶ θῆλυ· πάντες γὰρ ὑμεῖς εἷς ἐστε ἐν Χριστῷ Ἰησοῦ

There is no Jew or Greek, slave or free, male or female; for you are all one in Christ Jesus.

The primary concern here is to indicate the unity of believers in the realm of Christ and the fact that the distinctions that exist among believers do not undermine or compromise such unity. This unity is founded on the common identification with the realm of Christ; because believers are in the sphere of Christ, they are all one in him. Thus, identification with Christ is directly addressed as the theological underpinning of the unity of believers. See §3.8.

Eph 1:22–23 καὶ *πάντα ὑπέταξεν ὑπὸ τοὺς πόδας αὐτοῦ καὶ αὐτὸν ἔδωκεν κεφαλὴν ὑπὲρ πάντα τῇ ἐκκλησίᾳ, ἥτις ἐστὶν τὸ σῶμα αὐτοῦ, τὸ πλήρωμα τοῦ τὰ πάντα ἐν πᾶσιν πληρουμένου*

And He put everything under His feet and appointed Him as head over everything for the church, which is His body, the fullness of the One who fills all things in every way.

Paul's primary concern here is to address the nature of Christ's relationship to the church: he is its head, and it is his body; the church is the *fullness* of Christ, who fills all things. The metaphors of head and body convey a profound sense of incorporation of believers into Christ; this is therefore another example in which incorporation into Christ is directly addressed. See §7.2.

> Eph 2:5–6 καὶ ὄντας ἡμᾶς νεκροὺς τοῖς παραπτώμασιν συνεζωοποίησεν τῷ Χριστῷ,—χάριτί ἐστε σεσῳσμένοι—καὶ συνήγειρεν καὶ συνεκάθισεν ἐν τοῖς ἐπουρανίοις ἐν Χριστῷ Ἰησοῦ
>
> *[He] made us alive with the Messiah even though we were dead in trespasses. You are saved by grace! Together with Christ Jesus He also raised us up and seated us in the heavens.*

Participation with Christ is directly in view in these two verses, as seen in the notions of being made alive with Christ, being raised with him, and being seated with him in the heavens. See §5.6.

> Eph 2:15 τὸν νόμον τῶν ἐντολῶν ἐν δόγμασιν καταργήσας, ἵνα τοὺς δύο κτίσῃ ἐν αὐτῷ εἰς ἕνα καινὸν ἄνθρωπον ποιῶν εἰρήνην
>
> *He made of no effect the law consisting of commands and expressed in regulations, so that He might create in Himself one new man from the two, resulting in peace.*

The creation of *one new man from the two* refers to the unity of Jewish and Gentile believers, and Paul indicates that this unity is created in Christ. To describe the *one new man* as being created *in* Christ conveys the sense that the two alienated parties are reconciled through their common incorporation into Christ. This unity between Jew and Gentile is the primary concern here, and the foundation for this unity is incorporation into Christ. Consequently, clearly incorporation into Christ is directly addressed, if not the principal issue. See §3.11.3.1.

> Eph 2:21 ἐν ᾧ πᾶσα οἰκοδομὴ συναρμολογουμένη αὔξει εἰς ναὸν ἅγιον ἐν κυρίῳ
>
> *The whole building, being put together by Him, grows into a holy sanctuary in the Lord.*

The idea of a building being put together and growing in Christ conveys incorporation into Christ. Such incorporation is obviously of direct concern here. See §§3.11.4.1; 7.3.

Eph 4:15–16 ἀληθεύοντες δὲ ἐν ἀγάπῃ αὐξήσωμεν εἰς αὐτὸν τὰ πάντα, ὅς ἐστιν ἡ κεφαλή, Χριστός, ἐξ οὗ πᾶν τὸ σῶμα συναρμολογούμενον καὶ συμβιβαζόμενον διὰ πάσης ἁφῆς τῆς ἐπιχορηγίας κατ᾽ ἐνέργειαν ἐν μέτρῳ ἑνὸς ἑκάστου μέρους τὴν αὔξησιν τοῦ σώματος ποιεῖται εἰς οἰκοδομὴν ἑαυτοῦ ἐν ἀγάπῃ

But speaking the truth in love, let us grow in every way into Him who is the head—Christ. From Him the whole body, fitted and knit together by every supporting ligament, promotes the growth of the body for building up itself in love by the proper working of each individual part.

Believers are to grow into Christ, from whom the whole body promotes its own growth. This body is organically connected to its head, and in this way the concept of union with Christ is firmly established. While addressing the growth of the body through the work of its various parts, it is evident that union with Christ is of direct concern in these verses. See §§4.9.2; 7.2.

Eph 5:29–32 οὐδεὶς γάρ ποτε τὴν ἑαυτοῦ σάρκα ἐμίσησεν ἀλλὰ ἐκτρέφει καὶ θάλπει αὐτήν, καθὼς καὶ ὁ Χριστὸς τὴν ἐκκλησίαν, ³⁰ ὅτι μέλη ἐσμὲν τοῦ σώματος αὐτοῦ. ³¹*ἀντὶ τούτου καταλείψει ἄνθρωπος [τὸν] πατέρα καὶ [τὴν] μητέρα καὶ προσκολληθήσεται πρὸς τὴν γυναῖκα αὐτοῦ, καὶ ἔσονται οἱ δύο εἰς σάρκα μίαν.* ³²τὸ μυστήριον τοῦτο μέγα ἐστίν· ἐγὼ δὲ λέγω εἰς Χριστὸν καὶ εἰς τὴν ἐκκλησίαν.

For no one ever hates his own flesh but provides and cares for it, just as Christ does for the church, ³⁰since we are members of His body.

³¹*For this reason a man will leave*
his father and mother
and be joined to his wife,
and the two will become one flesh.
³²*This mystery is profound, but I am talking about Christ and the church.*

Paul indicates in Ephesians 5:32 that his reason for citing Genesis 2:24 is to explicate the nature of the relationship between Christ and the church. In doing this, Paul describes the church as Christ's own flesh, members of his body, and his wife. The metaphor of marriage offers profound insight into the union between Christ and his people, addressed directly here. See §§4.8; 7.2.

Phil 3:8–9 ἀλλὰ μενοῦνγε καὶ ἡγοῦμαι πάντα ζημίαν εἶναι διὰ τὸ ὑπερέχον τῆς γνώσεως Χριστοῦ Ἰησοῦ τοῦ κυρίου μου, δι' ὃν τὰ πάντα ἐζημιώθην, καὶ ἡγοῦμαι σκύβαλα, ἵνα Χριστὸν κερδήσω καὶ εὑρεθῶ ἐν αὐτῷ, μὴ ἔχων ἐμὴν δικαιοσύνην τὴν ἐκ νόμου ἀλλὰ τὴν διὰ πίστεως Χριστοῦ, τὴν ἐκ θεοῦ δικαιοσύνην ἐπὶ τῇ πίστει

More than that, I also consider everything to be a loss in view of the surpassing value of knowing Christ Jesus my Lord. Because of Him I have suffered the loss of all things and consider them filth, so that I may gain Christ and be found in Him, not having a righteousness of my own from the law, but one that is through faith in Christ—the righteousness from God based on faith.

Paul refers here to gaining Christ, being found in him, and having righteousness through Christ. Each of these indicates union with Christ in some sense and is set against those things he now considers *loss* and *filth*. Union with Christ is directly in view. See §§3.11.3.3; 6.5.

Col 2:9–10 ὅτι ἐν αὐτῷ κατοικεῖ πᾶν τὸ πλήρωμα τῆς θεότητος σωματικῶς, καὶ ἐστὲ ἐν αὐτῷ πεπληρωμένοι, ὅς ἐστιν ἡ κεφαλὴ πάσης ἀρχῆς καὶ ἐξουσίας

For the entire fullness of God's nature dwells bodily in Christ, and you have been filled by Him, who is the head over every ruler and authority.

Two types of union with Christ are evoked in these verses. The first is the union between God and Christ, as we are told that the fullness of God's nature dwells in Christ. The second is the union between believers and Christ, as we are told that they have been filled with him. These two types of union are the focus of these verses. See §§3.11.3.1, 4.

Col 2:12–13 συνταφέντες αὐτῷ ἐν τῷ βαπτισμῷ, ἐν ᾧ καὶ
συνηγέρθητε διὰ τῆς πίστεως τῆς ἐνεργείας τοῦ θεοῦ τοῦ ἐγείραντος
αὐτὸν ἐκ νεκρῶν· καὶ ὑμᾶς νεκροὺς ὄντας [ἐν] τοῖς παραπτώμασιν
καὶ τῇ ἀκροβυστίᾳ τῆς σαρκὸς ὑμῶν, συνεζωοποίησεν ὑμᾶς σὺν
αὐτῷ, χαρισάμενος ἡμῖν πάντα τὰ παραπτώματα

*Having been buried with Him in baptism, you were also raised with
Him through faith in the working of God, who raised Him from the
dead. And when you were dead in trespasses and in the uncircumcision of
your flesh, He made you alive with Him and forgave us all our trespasses.*

Participation with Christ is squarely in view in these verses, with references to believers being buried with him, raised, and made alive with him.
See §§3.11.4.1; 5.5, 6.

Col 2:20 εἰ ἀπεθάνετε σὺν Χριστῷ ἀπὸ τῶν στοιχείων τοῦ
κόσμου, τί ὡς ζῶντες ἐν κόσμῳ δογματίζεσθε;

*If you died with the Messiah to the elemental forces of this world, why
do you live as if you still belonged to the world?*

Again, participation with Christ is featured here, through reference to
believers having died with Christ. See §5.3.

Col 3:1 εἰ οὖν συνηγέρθητε τῷ Χριστῷ, τὰ ἄνω ζητεῖτε, οὗ ὁ
Χριστός ἐστιν ἐν δεξιᾷ τοῦ θεοῦ καθήμενος

*So if you have been raised with the Messiah, seek what is above,
where the Messiah is, seated at the right hand of God.*

Participation with Christ is once again featured here, through reference to believers having been raised with Christ. See §5.6.

Col 3:3–4 ἀπεθάνετε γὰρ καὶ ἡ ζωὴ ὑμῶν κέκρυπται σὺν τῷ
Χριστῷ ἐν τῷ θεῷ· ὅταν ὁ Χριστὸς φανερωθῇ, ἡ ζωὴ ὑμῶν, τότε
καὶ ὑμεῖς σὺν αὐτῷ φανερωθήσεσθε ἐν δόξῃ

*For you have died, and your life is hidden with the Messiah in God.
When the Messiah, who is your life, is revealed, then you also will be
revealed with Him in glory.*

Paul says that believers' lives are hidden with Christ in God, and that when Christ is revealed they will be revealed with him. Both of these notions are strong indicators of union with Christ, which is therefore of central concern here. See §§5.3, 5.

1 Thess 4:14 εἰ γὰρ πιστεύομεν ὅτι Ἰησοῦς ἀπέθανεν καὶ ἀνέστη, οὕτως καὶ ὁ θεὸς τοὺς κοιμηθέντας διὰ τοῦ Ἰησοῦ ἄξει σὺν αὐτῷ

Since we believe that Jesus died and rose again, in the same way God will bring with Him those who have fallen asleep through Jesus.

Paul indicates here that believers who have died before the coming of Christ will be brought with him at his coming (see 4:15). Since believers will accompany Christ, the notion of participation with Christ is again in view in a direct manner. See §5.5.

1 Thess 5:10 τοῦ ἀποθανόντος ὑπὲρ ἡμῶν, ἵνα εἴτε γρηγορῶμεν εἴτε καθεύδωμεν ἅμα σὺν αὐτῷ ζήσωμεν

Who died for us, so that whether we are awake or asleep, we will live together with Him.

Living together with Christ expresses participation with him and is a direct concern of this verse. See §5.5.

The list above has been generated by attempting to identify those passages that treat union, participation, identification, and incorporation in a direct manner. However, such a compilation cannot be constructed with absolute objectivity, and I acknowledge that the list is best regarded as a rough guide rather than a definitive one. It could be argued that two or three other passages should be included in this list, and conversely others might argue that some of those listed should not be included. With this caveat in place, it appears from the compilation above that union with Christ is directly in view in approximately thirty-two instances. A further complicating factor is that some of these texts refer to union with Christ more than once, which thus adds to the direct occurrences.

We return now to consider the importance of union with Christ in Paul's thinking. While many more passages allude to union with Christ, we have narrowed these down to approximately thirty-two instances where it is addressed as a *direct concern*. The question before us, then, is this: How significant is a theme that receives direct attention in thirty-two instances? I suggest that it is significant indeed. To be sure, its significance could be exaggerated if one were to regard all nondirect references on the same level as direct references, and yet we see that even avoiding this error it must be acknowledged that union with Christ is of great significance in the apostle's thought.[2]

Beyond the number of direct references to union with Christ, another measure of the importance of the theme is its role in the structure of Paul's thought. We turn now to consider this complex matter.

13.3 The Structure of Paul's Thought

The structure of Paul's thought involves many interconnected themes, which are obviously not presented to us in a systematic fashion. Scholars have spent considerable energy over the years trying to delineate the logic of the relationships between themes—a fact that reveals the complexity of the task. In particular, some strands of scholarship have sought to identify the 'key' to Paul's theological framework. Scholars have believed that by correctly identifying this key, they would then be able to 'unlock' Paul's mind and thus both understand what he really means and delineate the matters of most importance to him. The purported consequences of such investigations could be as dramatic as redefining Paul's understanding of what the gospel is, how salvation occurs, what justification means, and so forth. It is possible that this quest for the 'key' to understanding Paul's mind dates back to Martin Luther's discovery that the righteousness of God is credited to believers through faith in Christ. In Luther's own estimation, that discovery unlocked Paul's writings and changed his entire conception of what it means to be a Christian.

A closely related matter is the quest for the 'centre' of Paul's theology.

---

2. This is not a thoroughgoing statistical result, since that would require the comparison of the figure of thirty-two occurrences with the number of instances in which other Pauline themes are directly addressed. Such analysis is beyond the scope of this book and is not necessarily helpful. There is no reason to suggest that the level of importance of one theme as compared to another can meaningfully be determined by comparing their respective number of direct references. In fact, such an approach could easily lead to misjudgment. On the contrary, the statistic of thirty-two direct references to union with Christ is useful for the purpose of speaking about the theme in broad terms and to demonstrate that there are more than just a handful of direct references to it, but also far fewer than the number of indirect references.

While a 'key' unlocks the whole or provides the missing piece of the puzzle, a 'centre' of Paul's thought refers to one theme that is central to all others. It is the foundation of the framework and its lifeblood. It is the most essential element, deserving recognition above all others.

Whether the search for the 'centre' of Paul's theology is a beneficial endeavour—or even a legitimate one—it has potential for far-reaching consequences. Whatever idea or theme is posited as the 'centre' of the apostle's thinking, it requires a thorough rereading of Paul as the effects of said theme are understood vis-à-vis the other ideas and themes throughout the interconnected network of thought. In other words, one interpreter will read Paul in a certain way based on what he or she considers to be Paul's 'great concern', while another interpreter will read him differently by virtue of an alternate understanding of that 'great concern'.

While this fact is a mere truism, it also has potential to be abused as a form of manipulation. A desire to understand Paul in a way that makes him more palatable to the reader will be, for some, strong indeed. One way to do this, while basically maintaining the integrity of the structure of Paul's thinking, is to read him with an underlying presupposition that predetermines what Paul is 'really' concerned about. In this way, Paul's 'great concern' becomes a controlling idea to be found everywhere—one that flattens out the diversity, nuance, and detail of his thought. This 'great concern' functions as a hermeneutical principle that can distort the entire warp and weft of the apostle's theology.

Thus, while this search for the 'centre' of Paul's theology may or may not be beneficial or legitimate, there can be no question that it is of dramatic importance. In fact, I venture to say that much of the scholarly debate about Paul in the latter half of the twentieth century effectively reduces to this concern. Indeed, even a passing acquaintance with the scholarly discussion regarding Paul's conception of union with Christ will reveal that it has largely focused on the place of this theme in the apostle's thinking. Following Schweitzer, there is a long line of proponents who view that union with Christ is Paul's central concern, to which all others themes in Paul's letters are subordinate, or at least derivative.[3] Given this trend and the evident importance of the question, it is worth reflecting on the issue with care.

---

3. See, e.g., Terrance Callan, *Dying and Rising with Christ: The Theology of Paul the Apostle*

13.3.1 THE 'CENTRE' OF PAUL'S THEOLOGY?

Is the search for a 'key' or 'centre' of Paul's theology a legitimate exercise? Since the notions of 'key' and 'centre' are subtly different, we will deal with them separately. Underlying the search for the 'centre' of the apostle's thought is an assumption about its shape. A metaphor that might capture this is that of a wheel whose spokes emanate from a centre. Each element of Paul's thought — it is assumed — emanates from the 'centre' of his theology, and it is this centre that provides coherence to the whole as apparently unrelated 'spokes' of the wheel are in fact related by their common centre.[4] This assumption regarding the shape of Paul's thinking, however, is normally unsubstantiated and, by definition, merely supposed. Presumably this is due to the difficulty of demonstrating such a thing.

If we reject such a presupposition about the shape of Paul's thinking, the existence of a 'centre', as a consequence, becomes less tenable.[5] It might be posited, for example, that Paul's thought is more like a web of interconnected ideas than a wheel with spokes emanating from its centre. Such a web may or may not have a centre; a spider's web, for instance, has a centre, even though the rest of the web does not emanate from it — rather, it is the first in a set of concentric circles connected to each other. Another kind of web, such as a fishing net, has no discernable centre. To assume that the shape of Paul's theology is like a web of interconnected ideas is nevertheless also an assumption, and on that level it is not necessarily any more authoritative than the assumption of a wheel shape.[6]

(New York: Paulist, 2006); Sanders, *Palestinian Judaism*, 502; Gorman, *Inhabiting the Cruciform God*, 171.

4. 'The notion of a center suggests one or two images. One is that of a wheel consisting of a hub and spokes, in which the spokes proceed from and are all independently related to the hub. The other image is that of a solar system, in which the planets all revolve around the center at various distances, some close and some more peripheral to the center of the system. In each of these two images, the center does not function to relate the parts to one another and therefore does not truly integrate the system'; Gorman, *Cruciformity*, 370.

5. Gorman (ibid.) points out that recent narrative approaches to Paul's theology call into question the legitimacy of the language of a theological center; 'Stories have plots and patterns and even midpoints, but not centers.' Elsewhere, however, Gorman is prepared to operate within scholarly discussion as it has been framed and proposes *theosis* as the center of Paul's theology; Gorman, *Inhabiting the Cruciform God*, 171.

6. Another proposal is the image of a house, in which God is the foundation on whom other themes are laid; Schreiner, *Paul*, 19–22.

We must, therefore, proceed with caution, since we are attempting to discern between two (or more) competing presuppositions. Nevertheless, there are good reasons for preferring one over another. Against the wheel-shaped model is the fact that its centre is not easily derived, as evidenced by the ongoing debates about what it is. Surely the degree to which scholarship has fluctuated concerning this matter lends some weight to the possibility that there is, in fact, no centre.[7] After all, it is not unreasonable to expect that something that is so crucially significant to all other ideas — as the centre of the wheel must be — would present itself with some degree of clarity. Insofar as protracted debate has failed to reach any consensus hitherto, this is simply not the case.[8]

As a corollary of this point, the dangers inherent in assuming a wheel-shaped model are increased by virtue of the apparent arbitrariness with which a centre of the wheel is derived.[9] Since a wheel-shaped model necessarily prioritizes certain data that is perceived to belong to its centre, uncertainty about what that centre is gives licence to distortion of potentially great magnitude.[10] Finally, against a wheel-shaped model is that fact that Paul does not present his mind this way; his thought is far too complex, with myriad connections between ideas, to allow it to be reduced to a common denominator.

Conversely, a web-shaped model of the apostle's thought seems to have a natural attractiveness in that it does not require a reconstruction over and against the way in which his thinking is presented. His letters develop thematically and pastorally, with ideas leading to other thoughts, sometimes circling back again, and other times stretching out to new concepts. The occasional and nonsystematic manner in which he writes does not preclude the strong likelihood that his thought is ordered, but it does seem to fit with a web-shaped order more naturally than a wheel-shaped one. A further element in support of a web-shaped order is its neutrality vis-à-vis

---

7. 'To speak of a "center" or "core" would imply that there could be only one such result, which might be the first mistake to correct'; Jonathan Bishop, 'The Gospel(s) According to Paul', *AThR* 76 (1994): 296.

8. Howell, 'Center', 90.

9. 'Again it is hazardous to speculate on the direction of Paul's inner logic and then construct a theory around the results' (ibid., 65).

10. Schreiner helpfully reflects on these dangers, which include the possibility of domesticating Paul, creating a 'canon within a canon', giving one theme hegemony over others, and sweeping aside material than conflicts with the central theme; Schreiner, *Paul*, 16–17.

the prioritization of some data over others; without a centre, this kind of order encourages analysis of how ideas interconnect rather than how they might be reduced to a core. It consequently allows for the preservation of complexity and diversity.

Consideration of these factors leads to the conclusion that a web-shaped model for Paul's thought is best, and so it is assumed here. This assumption cannot be proved, nor can it be defended by exegetical data; it is, rather, the positing of a theory that does better justice to the nature of Paul's writings than the alternatives. As such, it seems therefore inappropriate to seek the centre of Paul's thought, since a web-shaped model does not allow for one. Even if the model is assumed to be analogous to a spider's web, with a series of concentric circles, its centre is not one out of which other ideas emanate, like spokes from a wheel. Indeed, no circles beyond the second one are directly connected to the centre.

13.3.2 THE 'KEY' TO PAUL'S THEOLOGY?

A distinction ought to be understood between a *centre* and a *key* to Paul's thought. While a *centre* implies that there is one element that controls the others and creates coherence between all, a *key* provides something that is missing in order to make sense of the whole. In other words, a key to Paul's thought is about access rather than control. It is still important, as a centre would be if one existed, but its importance lies in unlocking the door, as it were, rather than reducing all else to itself. Once the door has been unlocked, the key has no further inherent significance apart from its own place within the structure of thought.

If this understanding of a key is adopted, it means that such a key is occasional rather than fixed. It refers to an element that has been misplaced, forgotten, or misunderstood, like a missing piece in a jigsaw puzzle. What that element is may differ according to time and place, in that differing theological traditions can have their own lacunae. If a particular theological tradition has neglected an element of Paul's thought—whatever it might be—that tradition may have difficulties appreciating the coherence of his thinking until the missing element is (re)discovered and appropriated.

In Luther's case, for example, the key to Paul's theology was justification by faith, since that element had not been properly appreciated. Once

Luther was able to appropriate it, the rest of Paul fell into place for him. In current Pauline scholarship, it might be argued that some other element is to be understood as a key to his thought, such as his Jewish theological heritage or the resurrection of Christ.

In this case, it seems entirely appropriate to speak of a key to Paul's theology if such a key is needed. If it can be demonstrated that an element of Paul's thought has been neglected, misunderstood, or misplaced in current thinking about him, then rectifying the situation may well provide access to a new appreciation of the apostle. By describing this as a 'new appreciation', it should be understood that it is 'new' with respect to the theological community in question rather than 'new' in the history of Pauline interpretation, since it may well signal a return to a (perhaps forgotten) state of affairs.

While the discovery of such a key is no doubt of great significance, this does not mean that the key will necessarily enjoy the same kind of importance as a centre would. As noted above, its significance lies in opening the door and not necessarily in ordering everything else. Unfortunately, it is human nature to overemphasize a new discovery. As a result, it often happens that a key to Paul's thought is treated as though it is the centre of his thinking, and this can lead to distortion. By all means, the key must be appreciated for its function in opening the door, and it must be properly appropriated (back) into our understanding of Paul's thinking, but it would likely be a mistake to subordinate all other elements to it.

It is possible, then, that union with Christ might properly be regarded as a key to Paul's theology. Certainly prior to Deissmann and Schweitzer, this theme had been neglected at least in some spheres of Protestant Pauline scholarship. It arguably remained so until their work—particularly Schweitzer's—had been absorbed. Indeed, the more recent fascination with the theme belongs to the period of Pauline scholarship beginning with Sanders, and in that respect it is still relatively new in the slow-moving world of scholarship, whose trends take even longer to filter through to more popular levels of theology.

Part of the evidence that union with Christ is a modern key to Paul's theology is the fact that it features so prominently in Luther and Calvin, but not consistently in the Reformed tradition that has followed them. It is possible to view it as a theme that has been 'discovered' by Reformed Protestant circles only to find it a prominent feature of their theological forebears. Consequently, it may function as a route back to an understanding of Paul (or certain elements of him, at least) that has remained elusive for a time.

To regard union with Christ as a key to Pauline thought, however, does not ultimately answer what place it occupies in his theological framework, since our understanding of the function of the key is to provide access rather than to occupy the centre. Instead, we must draw on the exegetical results of this book in order to ascertain the ways in which union with Christ interacts with other themes within Paul's theological framework, and it is to this we now turn.

13.3.3 THE ROLE OF UNION WITH CHRIST IN PAUL'S THOUGHT

We observed above that the theme of union with Christ is directly addressed in approximately thirty-two instances in Paul's letters. The prominence of the theme, therefore, both in frequency of reference and theological significance, is substantial. However, there are many more instances—by far the majority—in which union with Christ is referenced in passing and in connection to other themes. Indeed, virtually every topic that Paul addresses is in some measure connected to union with Christ.

What are we to make of this? If, as suggested above, Paul's thought is metaphorically shaped like a web (rather than a wheel), it is my contention that union with Christ is the 'webbing' that holds it all together. Union with Christ is connected to everything else, perhaps, as Bouttier expresses, as 'the light that illuminates the others'.[11] Every Pauline theme and pastoral concern ultimately coheres with the whole through their common bond—union with Christ.[12] The metaphor of webbing does justice to the fact that union with Christ is mentioned so often: it is enormously widespread. It also does justice to the fact that, while widespread, it is only addressed *directly* roughly thirty-two times; it is therefore not the main issue *most* of the time, but is also never out of sight. It is essential, without

---

11. Bouttier, *Christianity*, 118.

12. This may be similar to Gorman's description of cruciformity—by which he means participation in the death and resurrection of Christ—as the 'integrative narrative experience' of Paul's life. It is integrative in the sense that conformity to Christ defines Paul's entire experience and permeated every dimension of it; Gorman, *Cruciformity*, 371.

suppressing other themes. In this way, we can affirm what Schweitzer (see §2.4) and Sanders (§2.12) observed, that mysticism or participation significantly characterizes Paul's theology, but we can deny that union with Christ is his central concern.

As such, I believe that the metaphor of a web helpfully accounts for the structure of Paul's thought, and union with Christ is the webbing that holds it all together. It is not the centre of his thought, though possibly should be regarded as a key to rediscover the richness and vitality of Paul's theology. Thus, union with Christ is indispensable but not the 'great concern'. Ultimately, it is most likely that Paul's great concern is the glory of God in Christ. As Howell concludes:

> Christ's Person and work has as its reference point the Person and redemptive purposes of God the Father. The Son of God came to fulfill the redemptive mission of the Father (Rom. 8:3; Gal. 4:4). Even His acclamation as King and Lord is ultimately intended for the Father's glory (1 Cor. 15:28; Phil. 2:11). God alone is the Source of all things (Rom. 11:36; 1 Cor. 8:6a). It is God from whom mankind is alienated and by whom he must finally be judged. God the Father plans (foreknowledge and election), superintends (salvation history), and both inaugurates and consummates the redemption of His created universe (Rom. 8:18–25).[13]

Thus, I argue that union with Christ is not Paul's 'great concern', nor is it the centre of his theological framework. It is, rather, the essential ingredient that binds all other elements together; it is the webbing that connects the ideas of Paul's web-shaped theological framework. It is for this reason that we can say that every blessing we receive from God is through our union with Christ. It is by being united to him in faith by the Spirit, dying, suffering, rising, and glorying with him, having been predestined and redeemed in him, being identified with his realm, and being incorporated into his people that believers enjoy the manifold grace of God.

13.4 FUTURE DIRECTIONS

The first and most obvious future direction to arise from the results of this study is the careful consideration of the study itself. I hope that its conclu-

---

13. Howell, 'Center', 70.

sions will shape subsequent discussions of Paul in general and union with Christ in particular. First, the definition of union with Christ as *union, participation, identification, incorporation* does justice to Paul's varied and nuanced language and thought. These terms envelop the characteristics of locality, identification, participation, incorporation, instrumentality, Trinity, union, eschatology, and spiritual reality.

Second, Pauline scholarship will benefit from the blend of thorough exegetical analysis and theological reflection offered here. No previous study of union with Christ has been so ambitious in the scope of its detailed analysis, and few have attempted such a deliberate integration of exegesis with theology.

Third, if union with Christ has been neglected, it ought to be recovered, since a faithful understanding of Paul is impossible without it.

Fourth, if the significance of union with Christ has been overplayed, it ought to be understood as essential while not central. Its function as the connecting fabric of Paul's theology has great power of explanation that accounts for both its prevalence and its relatively infrequent direct exposition.

Fifth, the web-shaped conception of Paul's theological framework suits the occasional nature of his writings and the fact that there is no obvious 'centre' of his theology, and it will help to resolve some of the problems within Pauline scholarship.

Sixth, the acknowledgment that antecedents to Paul's thought may be found in the words of Jesus, Jewish theology, and the Old Testament is sensible without claiming too much, and it allows for Paul's boldly original language and approach.

Another future direction arising from this work ought to be the investigation of union with Christ outside the Pauline canon. An exegetical and theological approach to the topic outside Paul, in conjunction with this study, would facilitate the articulation of the theme for biblical theology in general. One such investigation could, for instance, further explore the proposed relationship between the Pauline canon and the gospel of John. Another avenue would be to examine further the proposed Old Testament antecedents of the theme. Non-Pauline New Testament expressions of union with Christ could be compared and contrasted to the Pauline conception of the theme. This direction for research needs to be undertaken since the topic outside Paul has hardly been addressed in New Testament scholarship.

Finally, a future direction stemming from this study could be the exploration of the pastoral and devotional implications of union with Christ. This could take place on a more popular—rather than academic—level, for the sake of distilling important theological observations to be of widespread benefit to the life of the church. It ought to be clear that union with Christ offers a wealth of pastoral and devotional potential and should be extolled from every pulpit and basic to every believer.

13.5 CONCLUSION

Following the major conclusions of this book presented in the previous chapter, this final chapter discusses the importance of union with Christ within Paul's theological framework and the theological structure of his thought. Union with Christ is seen to be an essential theme that serves to connect the various elements of Paul's theology. If the shape of Paul's theological framework is regarded as a web of interconnected ideas, union with Christ is the webbing that holds it all together. Its role in the greater theological schema accounts for the widespread prevalence of the theme while also allowing for its not being the centre of Paul's thought.

It is fitting to conclude with a call for the results of this study to be considered and discussed within Pauline scholarship, for research into the non-Pauline expressions of union with Christ, and for pastoral and devotional reflection on the theme for the benefit of the church.

BIBLIOGRAPHY

Aageson, J.W. 'Paul and Judaism: The Apostle in the Context of Recent Interpretation'. *Word and World* 20 (2000): 249–56.

Adams, Edward. *Constructing the World: A Study in Paul's Cosmological Language*. Studies of the New Testament and its World. Edinburgh: T&T Clark, 2000.

Ahern, Barnabas M. 'The Christian's Union with the Body of Christ in Cor, Gal, and Rom'. *Catholic Biblical Quarterly* 23 (1961): 199–209.

Allan, John A. 'The "In Christ" Formula In Ephesians'. *New Testament Studies* 5 (1958): 54–62.

———. 'The "In Christ" Formula in the Pastoral Epistles'. *New Testament Studies* 10 (1963): 115–21.

Allen, Thomas G. 'Exaltation and Solidarity with Christ: Ephesians 1:20 and 2:6'. *Journal for the Study of the New Testament* 28 (1986): 103–20.

Arens, Edmund. 'Participation and Testimony: The Meaning of Death and Life in Jesus Christ Today'. *Concilium* 1 (1997): 112–19.

Barcley, William B. *"Christ in You": A Study in Paul's Theology and Ethics*. Lanham, MD: University Press of America, 1999.

Barnard, Jody A. 'Unity in Christ: The Purpose of Ephesians'. *The Expository Times* 120 (2009): 167–71.

Barnett, Paul. *The Message of 2 Corinthians: Power in Weakness*. The Bible Speaks Today. Leicester, UK: Inter-Varsity Press, 1988.

Barrett, C.K. *A Commentary on the First Epistle to the Corinthians*. Harper's New Testament Commentaries. New York: Harper & Row, 1968.

Barth, Karl. *Church Dogmatics* II/2: *The Doctrine of God*. Ed. G. W. Bromiley and T. F. Torrance. Trans. G. W. Bromiley et al. Edinburgh: T&T Clark, 1957.

———. *Church Dogmatics* IV/3.2: *The Doctrine of Reconcilation*. Ed. G. W. Bromiley and T. F. Torrance. Trans. G. W. Bromiley. Edinburgh: T&T Clark, 1962.

Barth, Markus. *Ephesians: Introduction, Translation, and Commentary on Chapters 1–3*. Anchor Bible. Garden City, NY: Doubleday, 1974.

———. *Ephesians: Introduction, Translation, and Commentary on Chapters 4–6*. Anchor Bible. Garden City, NY: Doubleday, 1974.

Bartling, Walter. 'The New Creation in Christ: A Study of the Pauline ἐν Χριστῷ Formula'. *Concordia Theological Monthly* 21 (1950): 401–18.

Bassler, Jouette M. *Navigating Paul: An Introduction to Key Theological Concepts.* Louisville: Westminster John Knox, 2007.

Batey, Richard. 'Jewish Gnosticism and the "Hieros Gamos" of Eph V: 21–33'. *New Testament Studies* 10 (1963): 121–27.

———. 'The MIA ΣΑΡΞ Union of Christ and the Church'. *New Testament Studies* 13 (1967): 270–81.

Bauckham, Richard. *Jesus and the Eyewitnesses: The Gospels as Eyewitness Testimony.* Grand Rapids: Eerdmans, 2006.

Beale, G.K. *The Temple and the Church's Mission: A Biblical Theology of the Dwelling Place of God.* New Studies in Biblical Theology 17. Downers Grove, IL: InterVarsity Press, 2004.

Beasley-Murray, G.R. *Baptism in the New Testament.* London: Macmillan, 1962.

Bedale, Stephen. 'The Meaning of κεφαλή in the Pauline Epistles'. *Journal of Theological Studies* 5 (1954): 211–16.

Beker, J. Christiaan. *Paul the Apostle: The Triumph of God in Life and Thought.* Edinburgh: T&T Clark, 1980.

Berkhof, Hendrik. *Christ and the Powers.* Trans. John H. Yoder. Scottdale, PA: Herald, 1977.

Best, Ernest. *The Letter of Paul to the Romans.* The Cambridge Bible Commentary. Cambridge: Cambridge University Press, 1967.

———. *Ephesians.* International Critical Commentary. London: T&T Clark, 1998.

Betz, H.D. *Galatians: A Commentary on Paul's Letter to the Churches in Galatia.* Hermeneia. Philadelphia: Fortress, 1979.

Billings, J. Todd. 'United to God through Christ: Assessing Calvin on the Question of Deification'. *Harvard Theological Review* 98 (2005): 315–34.

———. *Union with Christ: Reframing Theology and Ministry for the Church.* Grand Rapids: Baker, 2011.

———. 'John Calvin's Soteriology: On the Multifaceted "Sum" of the Gospel'. *International Journal of Systematic Theology* 11 (2009): 428–47.

Bird, Michael F. 'Incorporated Righteousness: A Response to Recent Evangelical Discussion Concerning the Imputation of Christ's Righteousness in Justification'. *Journal of the Evangelical Theological Society* 47 (2004): 253–75.

———. *The Saving Righteousness of God: Studies on Paul, Justification and the New Perspective*. Milton Keynes, UK: Paternoster, 2006.

———. *Introducing Paul: The Man, His Mission and His Message*. Downers Grove, IL: InterVarsity Press, 2008.

———. 'Progressive Reformed View'. Pages 131–57 in *Justification: Five Views*. Ed. James K. Beilby and Paul Rhodes Eddy. Downers Grove, IL: InterVarsity Press, 2011.

Bishop, Jonathan. 'The Gospel(s) According to Paul'. *Anglican Theological Review* 76 (1994): 296–312.

Black, C. Clifton, II. 'Pauline Perspectives on Death in Romans 5–8'. *Journal of Biblical Literature* 103 (1984): 413–33.

Black, Matthew. 'The Pauline Doctrine of the Second Adam'. *Scottish Journal of Theology* 7 (1954): 170–79.

Bonnington, Mark. 'New Temples in Corinth: Paul's Use of Temple Imagery in the Ethics of the Corinthian Correspondence'. Pages 151–59 in *Heaven on Earth*. Ed. T. Desmond Alexander and Simon Gathercole. Carlisle, UK: Paternoster, 2004.

Bortone, Pietro. *Greek Prepositions: From Antiquity to the Present*. Oxford: Oxford University Press, 2010.

Bousset, Wilhelm. *Kyrios Christos: A History of Belief in Christ from the Beginnings of Christianity to Irenaeus*. Trans. John E. Steely. Nashville: Abingdon, 1970.

Bouttier, Michel. *En Christ: Étude d'exégèse et de théologie Pauliniennes*. Études d'histoire et de philosophie religieuses 54. Paris: Presses Universitaires de France, 1962.

———. *Christianity According to Paul*. Trans. Frank Clarke. Studies in Biblical Theology 49. London: SCM, 1966.

Bowe, Barbara. '"You Are the Body of Christ": Paul's Understanding of the Human Person'. *Bible Today* 29 (1991): 139–44.

Braaten, Carl E., and Robert W. Jenson, eds. *Union with Christ: The New Finnish Interpretation of Luther*. Grand Rapids: Eerdmans, 1998.

Breck, John. 'Divine Initiative: Salvation in Orthodox Theology'. Pages

105–20 in *Salvation in Christ: A Lutheran–Orthodox Dialogue*. Ed. John Meyendorff and Robert Tobias. Minneapolis: Augsburg, 1992.

Brown, Raymond E. *The Gospel According to John (i–xii)*. Anchor Bible. Garden City, NY: Doubleday, 1966.

Bruce, F.F. *1 and 2 Corinthians*. New Century Bible. London: Oliphants, 1971.

———. *The Epistle to the Galatians*. New International Greek Testament Commentary. Exeter, UK: Paternoster, 1982.

———. *The Epistle to the Colossians, to Philemon, and to the Ephesians*. New International Commentary on the New Testament. Grand Rapids: Eerdmans, 1984.

———. *Philippians*. New International Biblical Commentary. Peabody, MA: Hendrickson, 1989.

Bryan, C. 'Law and Grace in Paul: Thoughts on E. P. Sanders'. *St Luke's Journal of Theology* 34 (1991): 33–52.

Büchsel, Friedrich. '"In Christus" bei Paulus'. *Zeitschrift fur die neutestamentliche Wissenschaft und die Kunde* 42 (1949): 141–58.

Bultmann, Rudolf. *Theology of the New Testament*. Trans. Kendrick Grobel. London: SCM, 1952.

———. *Der zweite Brief an die Korinther*. Göttingen: Vandenhoeck & Ruprecht, 1976.

Burdon, Christopher J. 'Paul and the Crucified Church'. *Expository Times* 95 (1984): 137–41.

Burger, Hans. *Being in Christ: A Biblical and Systematic Investigation in a Reformed Perspective*. Eugene, OR: Wipf & Stock, 2009.

Burrell, David B. 'Indwelling: Presence and Dialogue'. *Theological Studies* 22 (1961): 1–17.

Byrne, Brendan. 'Living out the Righteousness of God: The Contribution of Rom 6:1–8:13 to an Understanding of Paul's Ethical Presuppositions'. *Catholic Biblical Quarterly* 43 (1981): 557–81.

Callan, Terrance. *Dying and Rising with Christ: The Theology of Paul the Apostle*. New York: Paulist, 2006.

Calvin, John. *Institutes of the Christian Religion*. Ed. by John T. McNeill. Trans. Ford Lewis Battles. Philadelphia: Westminster, 1960.

Campbell, Constantine R. *Verbal Aspect, the Indicative Mood, and Narrative: Soundings in the Greek of the New Testament*. Studies in Biblical Greek 13. New York: Peter Lang, 2007.

———. *Verbal Aspect and Non-Indicative Verbs: Further Soundings in the Greek of the New Testament*. Studies in Biblical Greek 15. New York: Peter Lang, 2008.

———. *Basics of Verbal Aspect in Biblical Greek*. Grand Rapids: Zondervan, 2008.

———. 'From Earthly Symbol to Heavenly Reality: The Tabernacle in the New Testament'. Pages 177–95 in *Exploring Exodus: Literary, Theological and Contemporary Approaches*. Ed. Brian S. Rosner and Paul R. Williamson. Nottingham:, UK Apollos, 2008.

Campbell, Douglas A. *The Deliverance of God: An Apocalyptic Rereading of Justification in Paul*. Grand Rapids: Eerdmans, 2009.

———. 'The Faithfulness of Jesus Christ in Romans 3:22'. Pages 57–71 in *The Faith of Jesus Christ: Exegetical, Biblical, and Theological Studies*. Ed. Michael F. Bird and Preston M. Sprinkle. Milton Keynes, UK: Paternoster; Peabody, MA: Hendrickson, 2009.

Campbell, James M. *Paul the Mystic: A Study in Apostolic Experience*. London: Andrew Melrose, 1907.

Caneday, Ardel B. 'The Faithfulness of Jesus Christ as a Theme in Paul's Theology in Galatians'. Pages 185–205 in *The Faith of Jesus Christ: Exegetical, Biblical, and Theological Studies*. Ed. Michael F. Bird and Preston M. Sprinkle. Milton Keynes, UK: Paternoster; Peabody, MA: Hendrickson, 2009.

Canlis, Julie. 'Calvin, Osiander, and Participation in God'. *International Journal of Systematic Theology* 6 (2004): 169–84.

Carpenter, Craig B. 'A Question of Union with Christ? Calvin and Trent on Justification'. *Westminster Theological Journal* 64 (2002): 363–86.

Carson, D.A. 'The Vindication of Imputation'. Pages 46–78 in *Justification: What's at Stake in the Current Debates*. Ed. Mark Husbands and Daniel J. Treier. Downers Grove, IL: InterVarsity Press, 2004.

Childs, Brevard S. *The Church's Guide for Reading Paul: The Canonical Shaping of the Pauline Corpus*. Grand Rapids: Eerdmans, 2008.

Ciampa, Roy E., and Brian S. Rosner. *The First Letter to the Corinthians*. Pillar New Testament Commentary. Grand Rapids: Eerdmans, 2010.

Clowney, Edmund P. 'The Biblical Theology of the Church'. Pages 13–87 in *The Church in the Bible and the World*. Ed. D.A. Carson. Exeter, UK: Paternoster, 1987.

Cranfield, C.E.B. *The Epistle to the Romans*. 2 vols. International Critical Commentary. London: T&T Clark, 1975.

———. 'Romans 6:1–14 Revisited'. *Expository Times* 106 (1994): 40–43.

Dahms, John V. 'Dying with Christ'. *Journal of the Evangelical Theological Society* 36 (1993): 15–23.

Daines, Brian. 'Paul's Use of the Analogy of the Body of Christ: With Special Reference to 1 Corinthians 12'. *Evangelical Quarterly* 50 (1978): 71–78.

Davies, W.D. *Paul and Rabbinic Judaism*. 3rd ed. London: S.P.C.K., 1970.

Deissmann, Adolf. *Die Neutestamentliche Formel "In Christo Jesu"*. Marburg, Germany: N.G. Elwert, 1892.

———. *Paul: A Study in Social and Religious History*. 2nd ed. Trans. William E. Wilson. London: Hodder and Stoughton, 1926.

Dillistone, F.W. 'How Is the Church Christ's Body?: A New Testament Study'. *Theology Today* 2 (1945): 56–68.

Dodd, C.H. *The Epistle to the Romans*. London: Hodder & Stoughton, 1932; repr. London: Fontana, 1959.

Douty, Norman F. *Union with Christ*. Swengel, PA: Reiner, 1973.

Dumbrell, William J. *Galatians: A New Covenant Commentary*. Blackwood, South Australia: New Creation, 2006.

Dunn, James D.G. 'Salvation Proclaimed: VI. Romans 6:1–11: Dead and Alive.' *Expository Times* 93 (1982): 259–64.

———. 'Once More, ΠΙΣΤΙΣ ΧΡΙΣΤΟΥ'. Pages 249–71 in *The Faith of Jesus Christ: The Narrative Substructure of Galatians 3:1–4:11*. Grand Rapids: Eerdmans, 2002 [originally published in *Pauline Theology*, Vol. 4: *Looking Back, Pressing On*. Society of Biblical Literature, 1997].

———. *Romans 1–8*. Word Biblical Commentary. Dallas: Word, 1988.

———. *Romans 9–16*. Word Biblical Commentary. Dallas: Word, 1988.

———. *The Theology of Paul the Apostle*. Grand Rapids: Eerdmans, 1998.

Dutton, Emily Helen. *Studies in Greek Prepositional Phrases: διά, απó, έκ, εἰς, ἐν*. Chicago: University of Chicago, 1916.

Earnshaw, J.D. 'Reconsidering Paul's Marriage Analogy in Romans 7.1–4'. *New Testament Studies* 40 (1994): 68–88.

Ejenobo, David T. 'Union with Christ: A Critique of Romans 6:1–11'. *Asia Journal of Theology* 22 (2008): 309–23.

Ellis, E. Earle, 'The Structure of Pauline Eschatology (II Corinthians

v. 1–10)'. Pages 35–48 in *Paul and His Recent Interpreters*. Grand Rapids: Eerdmans, 1979.

———. 'Sōma in First Corinthians'. *Interpretation* 44 (1990): 132–44.

Fee, Gordon D. *The First Epistle to the Corinthians*. New International Commentary on the New Testament. Grand Rapids: Eerdmans, 1987.

———. *Paul's Letter to the Philippians*. New International Commentary on the New Testament. Grand Rapids: Eerdmans, 1995.

Field, Barbara. 'The Discourses Behind the Metaphor "The Church is The Body of Christ" as Used by St Paul and the "Post-Paulines"'. *Asia Journal of Theology* 6 (1992): 88–107.

Fitzmyer, Joseph A. *Romans*. Anchor Bible. New York: Doubleday, 1993.

Furnish, Victor Paul. *2 Corinthians*. Anchor Bible. Garden City, NY: Doubleday, 1984.

Gaffin, Richard B. *The Centrality of the Resurrection: A Study in Paul's Soteriology*. Grand Rapids: Baker, 1978.

———. 'Justification and Eschatology'. Pages 1–21 in *Justified in Christ: God's Plan for Us in Justification*. Ed. K. Scott Oliphant. Fearn, Scotland: Mentor, 2007.

———. 'Union with Christ: Some Biblical and Theological Reflections'. Pages 271–88 in *Always Reforming: Explorations in Systematic Theology*. Ed. A.T.B. McGowan. Leicester, UK: Apollos, 2006.

Gager, John G. *Reinventing Paul*. Oxford: Oxford University Press, 2000.

Garcia, Mark A. 'Imputation and the Christology of Union with Christ: Calvin, Osiander and the Contemporary Quest for a Reformed Model'. *Westminster Theological Journal* 68 (2006): 219–51.

———. 'Imputation as Attribution: Union with Christ, Reification and Justification as Declarative Word'. *International Journal of Systematic Theology* 11 (2009): 415–27.

Garlington, Don B. 'Imputation or Union with Christ? A Response to John Piper'. *Reformation & Revival* 12 (2003): 45–113.

Gorman, Michael J. *Cruciformity: Paul's Narrative Spirituality of the Cross*. Grand Rapids: Eerdmans, 2001.

———. *Reading Paul*. Eugene, OR: Cascade, 2008.

———. *Inhabiting the Cruciform God: Kenosis, Justification, and Theosis in Paul's Narrative Soteriology*. Grand Rapids: Eerdmans, 2009.

Green, Gene L. *The Letters to the Thessalonian*. Pillar New Testament Commentary. Grand Rapids: Eerdmans, 2002.

Gundry, Robert H. 'The Nonimputation of Christ's Righteousness'. Pages 17–45 in *Justification: What's at Stake in the Current Debates*. Ed. Mark Husbands and Daniel J. Treier. Downers Grove, IL: Inter-Varsity Press, 2004.

Guthrie, Donald. *The Pastoral Epistles*. Tyndale New Testament Commentaries. 2nd ed. Leicester, UK: Inter-Varsity Press, 1990.

Harink, Douglas. *Paul among the Postliberals: Pauline Theology beyond Christendom and Modernity*. Grand Rapids: Brazos, 2003.

Harris, Murray J. 'Appendix: Prepositions and Theology in the Greek New Testament'. Pages 1171–1215 in *New Interational Dictionary of New Testament Theology*, vol. 3. Ed. Colin Brown. Carlisle: Paternoster, 1976.

———. *Colossians and Philemon*. Exegetical Guide to the Greek New Testament. Grand Rapids: Eerdmans, 1991.

———. *The Second Epistle to the Corinthians*. New International Greek Testament Commentary. Grand Rapids: Eerdmans, 2005.

———. *Prepositions and Theology in the Greek New Testament*. Grand Rapids: Zondervan, 2012.

Harrison, Gessner. *A Treaty on the Greek Prepositions, and on the Cases of Nouns with Which These Are Used*. Philadelphia: Lippincott, 1858.

Hart, Trevor A. 'Humankind in Christ and Christ in Humankind: Salvation as Participation in our Substitute in the Theology of John Calvin'. *Scottish Journal of Theology* 42 (1989): 67–84.

Harvey, John D. 'The "With Christ" Motif in Paul's Thought'. *Journal of the Evangelical Theological Society* 35 (1992): 329–40.

Hays, Richard B. *The Faith of Jesus Christ: The Narrative Substructure of Galatians 3:1–4:11*. Grand Rapids: Eerdmans, 2002 [originally published by the Society of Biblical Literature, 1983].

Heil, John Paul. *Ephesians: Empowerment to Walk in Love for the Unity of All in Christ*. Studies in Biblical Literature 13. Atlanta: Society of Biblical Literature, 2007.

Heinfetter, Herman. *An Examination into the Significations and Senses of the Greek Prepositions*. London: Cradock, 1850.

Helminiak, Daniel A. 'Human Solidarity and Collective Union in Christ'. *Anglican Theological Review* 70 (1988): 34–59.

Hoch, Carl B. 'The Significance of the Syn–Compounds for Jew–Gentile

Relationships in the Body of Christ'. *Journal of the Evangelical Theological Society* 25 (1982): 175–83.

Hodge, Charles. *A Commentary on the Epistle to the Ephesians*. Geneva Series Commentary. London: Banner of Truth, 1964 [previously published in New York, 1856].

Hooker, Morna D. 'Were there False Teachers in Colossae?' Pages 315–31 in *Christ and Spirit in the New Testament*. Ed. Barnabas Lindars and Stephen S. Smalley in honor of C.F.D. Moule. Cambridge: Cambridge University Press, 1973.

———. 'Interchange in Christ and Ethics'. *Journal for the Study of the New Testament* 25 (1985): 3–17.

———. *From Adam to Christ: Essays on Paul*. Eugene, OR: Wipf & Stock, 2008 [previously published by Cambridge University Press, 1990].

Horton, Michael S. *Covenant and Salvation: Union with Christ*. Louisville: Westminster John Knox, 2007.

Howard, George. 'The Head/Body Metaphors of Ephesians'. *New Testament Studies* 20 (1974): 350–56.

Howell, D. N. 'The Center of Pauline Theology'. *Bibliotheca Sacra* 151 (1994): 50–70.

Hughes, Philip Edgcumbe. *Paul's Second Epistle to the Corinthians*. New International Commentary on the New Testament. Grand Rapids: Eerdmans, 1962.

Hunn, Debbie. 'Debating the Faithfulness of Jesus Christ in Twentieth-Century Scholarship'. Pages 15–31 in *The Faith of Jesus Christ: Exegetical, Biblical, and Theological Studies*. Ed. Michael F. Bird and Preston M. Sprinkle. Milton Keynes, UK: Paternoster; Peabody, MA: Hendrickson, 2009.

Jeal, Roy R. 'A Strange Style of Expression: Ephesians 1:23'. *Filología Neotestamentaria* 10 (1997): 129–38.

Jenson, Robert W. 'Response to Tuomo Mannermaa, "Why Is Luther So Fascinating?"'. Pages 21–24 in *Union with Christ: The New Finnish Interpretation of Luther*. Ed. Carl E. Braaten and Robert W. Jenson. Grand Rapids: Eerdmans, 1998.

———. 'Response to Mark Seifrid, Paul Metzger, and Carl Trueman on Finnish Luther Research'. *Westminster Theological Journal* 65 (2003): 245–50.

Jewett, Robert. *Romans*. Hermeneia. Minneapolis: Fortress Press, 2007.

Johnson, Marcus P. 'Luther and Calvin on Union with Christ'. *Fides et Historia* 39 (2007): 59–77.

Jones, R. Tudur. 'Union with Christ: The Existential Nerve of Puritan Piety'. *Tyndale Bulletin* 41 (1990): 186–208.

Juntunen, Sammeli. 'Luther and Metaphysics: What Is the Structure of Being according to Luther?' Pages 129–60 in *Union with Christ: The New Finnish Interpretation of Luther*. Ed. Carl E. Braaten and Robert W. Jenson. Grand Rapids: Eerdmans, 1998.

Käsemann, Ernst. *Essays on New Testament Themes*. Translated by W. J. Montague. London: SCM, 1964.

———. *New Testament Questions of Today*. Trans. W. J. Montague and Wilfred F. Bunge. London: SCM, 1969.

———. *Perspectives on Paul*. Trans. Margaret Kohl. London: SCM, 1971.

Kelly, Douglas F. 'Prayer and Union with Christ'. *Scottish Bulletin of Evangelical Theology* 8 (1990): 109–27.

Kennedy, H.A.A. 'Two Exegetical Notes on St. Paul'. *Expository Times* 28 (1916–1917): 322–23.

Kilpatrick, George Dunbar. 'Parallel to the New Testament use of SŌMA'. *Journal of Theological Studies* 13 (1962): 117.

Kim, Jung Hoon. *The Significance of Clothing Imagery in the Pauline Corpus*. Journal for the Study of the New Testament Supplement Series 268. London: T&T Clark, 2004.

Konstan, David, and Ilaria Ramelli. 'The Syntax of ἐν Χριστῷ in 1 Thessalonians 4:16'. *Journal of Biblical Literature* 126 (2007): 579–93.

Köstenberger, Andreas J. 'The Mystery of Christ and the Church: Head and Body, "One Flesh"'. *Trinity Journal* 12 (1991): 79–94.

Kreitzer, L. Joseph. 'Christ and Second Adam in Paul'. *Communio Viatorum* 32 (1989): 55–101.

Kruse, Colin G. *The Second Epistle of Paul to the Corinthians*. Tyndale New Testament Commentaries. Leicester, UK: Inter-Varsity Press, 1987.

Larkin, William J. *Ephesians: A Handbook on the Greek Text*. Baylor Handbook on the Greek New Testament. Waco, TX: Baylor University Press, 2009.

Lee, John A.L. *A History of New Testament Lexicography*. Studies in Biblical Greek 8. New York: Peter Lang, 2003.

———. 'The Present State of Lexicography of Ancient Greek'. Pages 66–74 in *Biblical Greek Language and Lexicography: Essays in Honor of Frederick W. Danker*. Ed. Bernard A. Taylor et al. Grand Rapids: Eerdmans, 2004.

Lee, Kye Won. *Living in Union with Christ: The Practical Theology of Thomas F. Torrance*. Issues in Systematic Theology 11. New York: Peter Lang, 2003.

Letham, Robert. *Union with Christ: In Scripture, History, and Theology*. Phillipsburg: Presbyterian & Reformed, 2011.

Lightfoot, J.B. *Saint Paul's Epistles to the Colossians and to Philemon*. Grand Rapids: Zondervan, 1963 [originally published by MacMillan, 1879].

Lincoln, Andrew T. *Ephesians*. Word Biblical Commentary. Dallas: Word, 1990.

Lohmeyer, Ernst. *Die Briefe an die Philipper, an die Kolosser und an Philemon*. Göttingen: Vandenhoeck & Ruprecht, 1964.

Longenecker, Richard N. *Galatians*. Word Biblical Commentary. Dallas: Word, 1990.

Luraghi, Silvia. *On the Meaning of Prepositions and Cases: The Expression of Semantic Roles in Ancient Greek*. Amsterdam: John Benjamins, 2003.

McCormack, Bruce L. 'What's at Stake in Current Debates over Justification? The Crisis of Protestantism in the West'. Pages 81–117 in *Justification: What's at Stake in the Current Debates*. Ed. Mark Husbands and Daniel J. Treier. Downers Grove, IL: InterVarsity Press, 2004.

MacGregor, G.H.C. 'Principalities and Powers: The Cosmic Background of Paul's Thought'. *New Testament Studies* 1 (1954–55): 17–28.

Maloney, Elliot C. 'God's Power in Christ Jesus'. *The Bible Today* 36 (1998): 349–53.

Mannermaa, Tuomo. 'Justification and *Theosis* in Lutheran-Orthodox Perspective'. Pages 25–41 in *Union with Christ: The New Finnish Interpretation of Luther*. Ed. Carl E. Braaten and Robert W. Jenson. Grand Rapids: Eerdmans, 1998.

———. 'Why is Luther so Fascinating? Modern Finnish Luther Research'. Pages 1–20 in *Union with Christ: The New Finnish Interpretation of Luther*. Ed. Carl E. Braaten and Robert W. Jenson. Grand Rapids: Eerdmans, 1998.

Marshall, Bruce D. 'Justification as Declaration and Deification'. *International Journal of Systematic Theology* 4 (2002): 3–28.

Marshall, I. Howard. *The Pastoral Epistles*. International Critical Commentary. London: T&T Clark, 1999.

Martin, Ralph P. *2 Corinthians*. Word Biblical Commentary. Waco, TX: Word, 1986.

———. *The Epistle of Paul to the Philippians*. Tyndale New Testament Commentaries. Rev. ed. Leicester, UK: Inter-Varsity Press, 1987.

Martin, T. 'But Let Everyone Discern the Body of Christ (Colossians 2:17)'. *Journal of Biblical Literature* 114 (1995): 249–55.

Martyn, J. Louis. *Galatians*. The Anchor Bible. New York: Doubleday, 1997.

Matlock, R. Barry. 'Saving Faith: The Rhetoric and Semantics of πίστις in Paul'. Pages 73–89 in *The Faith of Jesus Christ: Exegetical, Biblical, and Theological Studies*. Ed. Michael F. Bird and Preston M. Sprinkle. Milton Keynes, UK: Paternoster; Peabody, MA: Hendrickson, 2009.

McFarland, Ian A. 'The Body of Christ: Rethinking a Classic Ecclesiological Model'. *International Journal of Systematic Theology* 7 (2005): 225–45.

McGrath, Brendan. '"Syn" Words in Saint Paul'. *Catholic Biblical Quarterly* 14 (1952): 219–26.

McKelvey, R.J. *The New Temple: The Church in the New Testament*. London, Oxford University Press, 1969.

Mead, James K. '"All of Our Griefs to Bear": A Biblical and Theological Reflection'. *Reformed Review* 56 (2002): 5–18.

Merz, Annette. 'Why Did the Pure Bride of Christ (2 Cor. 11.2) Become a Wedded Wife (Eph. 5:22–33)? Theses about the Intertextual Transformation of an Ecclesiological Metaphor'. *Journal for the Study of the New Testament* 79 (2000): 131–47.

Metzger, Paul Louis. 'Luther and the Finnish School—Mystical Union with Christ: An Alternative to Blood Transfusions and Legal Fictions'. *Westminster Theological Journal* 65 (2003): 201–13.

Meyendorff, John, and Robert Tobias, eds. *Salvation in Christ: A Lutheran–Orthodox Dialogue*. Minneapolis: Augsburg, 1992.

Mitton, C. Leslie. *Ephesians*. New Century Bible. London: Oliphants, 1976.

Moo, Douglas J. *The Epistle to the Romans*. New International Commentary on the New Testament. Grand Rapids: Eerdmans, 1996.

Morris, Leon. *The Epistles of Paul to the Thessalonians*. Tyndale New Testament Commentaries. Rev. ed. Leicester: Inter-Varsity Press, 1984.

———. *The First Epistle of Paul to the Corinthians*. Tyndale New Testament Commentary. Rev. ed. Leicester, UK: Inter-Varsity Press, 1985.

———. *The First and Second Epistles to the Thessalonians*. New International Commentary on the New Testament. Grand Rapids: Eerdmans, 1991.

———. *The Gospel According to John*. New International Commentary on the New Testament. Rev. ed. Grand Rapids: Eerdmans, 1995.

Moule, C.F.D. *The Epistles to the Colossians and to Philemon*. Cambridge Greek Testament Commentary. Cambridge: Cambridge University Press, 1958.

———. *An Idiom Book of New Testament Greek*. 2nd ed. Cambridge: Cambridge University Press, 1959.

———. *The Origin of Christianity*. Cambridge: Cambridge University Press, 1977.

Moulton, James Hope. *A Grammar of New Testament Greek*. Vol. 1: *Prolegomena*. 3rd ed. Edinburgh: T&T Clark, 1908.

Moulton, James Hope, and George Milligan. *Vocabulary of the Greek Testament*. Peabody, MA: Hendrickson, 2004.

Mounce, William D. *Pastoral Epistles*. Word Biblical Commentary. Nashville: Nelson, 2000.

Muddiman, John. 'Adam, the Type of the One to Come'. *Theology* 87 (1984): 101–10.

———. *The Epistle to the Ephesians*. Black's New Testament Commentary. Peabody, MA: Hendrickson, 2001 [originally published by Continuum, 2001].

Murray, John. *Redemption—Accomplished and Applied*. Grand Rapids: Eerdmans, 1955.

———. *The Epistle to the Romans*. 2 vols. New International Commentary on the New Testament. Grand Rapids: Eerdmans, 1959.

Nardoni, Enrique. 'Partakers in Christ (Hebrews 3.14)'. *New Testament Studies* 37 (1991): 456–72.

Neder, Adam. *Participation in Christ: An Entry into Karl Barth's* Church Dogmatics. Columbia Series in Reformed Theology. Louisville: Westminster John Knox, 2009.

Nelson, J. Robert. 'The Hard Reality of Dying and Living with Christ'. *Theology Today* 18 (1961): 133–41.

Nelson, William R. 'Pauline Anthropology: Its Relation to Christ and His Church'. *Interpretation* 14 (1960): 14–27.

Nestle, E. and E., K. Aland, J. Karavidopoulos, C. Martini, and B. M. Metzger. *Novum Testamentum Graece*. 27th ed. Stuttgart: Deutsche Bibelgesellschaft, 1993.

Neufeld, T.Y. *Put on the Armour of God: The Divine Warrior from Isaiah to Ephesians*. Sheffield: Sheffield Academic, 1997.

Neugebauer, Fritz. 'Das paulinische "in Christo"'. *New Testament Studies* 4 (1957–58): 124–38.

———. *In Christus: Eine Untersuchung zum paulinischen Glaubensverständnis*. Göttingen: Vandenhoeck & Ruprecht, 1961.

O'Brien, Peter T. *Colossians, Philemon*. Word Biblical Commentary. Waco, TX: Word, 1982.

———. *The Epistle to the Philippians*. New International Greek Testament Commentary. Grand Rapids: Eerdmans, 1991.

———. *The Letter to the Ephesians*. Pillar New Testament Commentary. Grand Rapids: Eerdmans, 1999.

O'Neill, John. 'The Absence of the "In Christ" Theology in 2 Corinthians 5'. *Australian Biblical Review* 35 (1987): 99–106.

Parsons, Michael. 'In Christ in Paul'. *Vox Evangelica* 18 (1988): 25–44.

Patterson, Richard D. 'Metaphors of Marriage as Expressions of Divine-Human Relations'. *Journal of the Evangelical Theological Society* 51/4 (2008): 689–702.

Pelser, Gert M.M. 'Could the "Formulas" *Dying* and *Rising with Christ* be Expressions of Pauline Mysticism?' *Neotestamentica* 32 (1998): 115–34.

———. 'Once More the Body of Christ in Paul'. *Neotestamentica* 32 (1998): 525–45.

Perriman, Andrew C. '"His Body, Which Is the Church. . . .": Coming to Terms with Metaphor'. *Evangelical Quarterly* 62 (1990): 123–42.

Peters, Albert. 'Union with Christ—An Indissoluble Union'. *The Banner of Truth* 460 (2002): 17–21.

Peterson, David. 'The New Temple: Christology and Ecclesiology in Ephesians and 1 Peter'. Pages 161–76 in *Heaven on Earth*. Ed. T. Desmond Alexander and Simon Gathercole. Carlisle: Paternoster, 2004.

Peura, Simo. 'Christ as Favor and Gift *(donum)*: The Challenge of Luther's Understanding of Justification'. Pages 42–69 in *Union with Christ: The New Finnish Interpretation of Luther*. Ed. Carl E. Braaten and Robert W. Jenson. Grand Rapids: Eerdmans, 1998.

———. 'What God Gives Man Receives: Luther on Salvation'. Pages 76–95 in *Union with Christ: The New Finnish Interpretation of Luther*. Ed. Carl E. Braaten and Robert W. Jenson. Grand Rapids: Eerdmans, 1998.

Piper, John. 'A Response to Don Garlington on Imputation'. *Reformation & Revival* 12 (2003): 121–28.

Porter, Stanley E. *Verbal Aspect in the Greek of the New Testament with Reference to Tense and Mood*. SBG 1. New York: Peter Lang, 1989.

———. 'Two Myths: Corporate Personality and Language/Mentality Determinism'. *Scottish Journal of Theology* 43 (1990): 289–307.

———. *Idioms of the Greek New Testament*. 2nd ed. Biblical Languages: Greek 2. Sheffield: Sheffield Academic, 1994.

Porter, Stanley E., and Andrew W. Pitts. 'Πίστις with a Preposition and Genitive Modifier: Lexical, Semantic, and Syntactic Considerations in the πίστις Χριστοῦ Discussion'. Pages 33–53 in *The Faith of Jesus Christ: Exegetical, Biblical, and Theological Studies*. Ed. Michael F. Bird and Preston M. Sprinkle. Milton Keynes, UK: Paternoster; Peabody, MA: Hendrickson, 2009.

Powers, Daniel G. *Salvation through Participation: An Examination of the Notion of the Believers' Corporate Unity with Christ in Early Christian Soteriology*. Leuven: Peeters, 2001.

Proudfoot, C. Merrill. 'Imitation or Realistic Participation? A Study of Paul's Concept of "Suffering with Christ"'. *Interpretation* 17 (1963): 140–60.

Raunio, Antti. 'Natural Law and Faith: The Forgotten Foundations of Ethics in Luther's Theology'. Pages 96–124 in *Union with Christ: The New Finnish Interpretation of Luther*. Ed. Carl E. Braaten and Robert W. Jenson. Grand Rapids: Eerdmans, 1998.

Reinhard, Donna R. 'Ephesians 6:10–18: A Call to Personal Piety or Another Way of Describing Union with Christ?' *Journal of the Evangelical Theological Society* 48 (2005): 521–32.

Ridderbos, Herman. *Paul: An Outline of his Theology*. Trans. John Richard de Witt. Grand Rapids: Eerdmans, 1975.

Robertson, A.T. *A Grammar of the Greek New Testament in the Light of Historical Research.* 4th ed. Nashville: Broadman, 1934.

Robinson, D.W.B. "'Faith of Jesus Christ'—A New Testament Debate'. *Reformed Theological Review* 29 (1970): 71–81.

Rogerson, John W. 'The Hebrew Conception of Corporate Personality: A Re-Examination'. *Journal of Theological Studies* 21 (1970): 1–16.

Sabou, Sorin. 'A Note on Romans 6:5: The Representation (ΌΜΟΙΩΜΑ) of his Death'. *Tyndale Bulletin* 55 (2004): 219–29.

Sanders, E.P. *Paul and Palestinian Judaism: A Comparison of Patterns of Religion.* Minneapolis: Fortress, 1977.

Schnackenburg, Rudolf. *The Epistle to the Ephesians.* Trans. Helen Heron. Edinburgh: T&T Clark, 1991.

Schreiner, Thomas R. *Paul: Apostle of God's Glory in Christ.* Downers Grove, IL: InterVarsity Press, 2001.

Schweitzer, Albert. *The Mysticism of Paul the Apostle.* Trans. William Montgomery. Baltimore: John Hopkins University Press, 1998.

Schweizer, Eduard. 'Dying and Rising with Christ'. *New Testament Studies* 14 (1967): 1–14.

———. *The Letter to the Colossians: A Commentary.* Trans. Andrew Chester. Minneapolis: Augsburg, 1982.

Seifrid, Mark A. 'Paul, Luther, and Justification in Gal 2:15–21'. *Westminster Theological Journal* 65 (2003): 215–30.

———. 'Luther, Melanchthon and Paul on the Question of Imputation'. Pages 137–52 in *Justification: What's at Stake in the Current Debates.* Ed. Mark Husbands and Daniel J. Treier. Downers Grove, IL: InterVarsity Press, 2004.

Smedes, Lewis B. *Union with Christ: A Biblical View of the New Life in Jesus Christ.* Rev. ed. Grand Rapids: Eerdmans, 1983.

Smyth, Herbert Weir. *Greek Grammar.* Rev. Gordon M. Messing. Cambridge, MA: Harvard University Press, 1920.

Son, Sang-Won (Aaron). *Corporate Elements in Pauline Anthropology: A Study of Selected Terms, Idioms, and Concepts in the Light of Paul's Usage and Background.* Analecta Biblica 148. Rome: Editrice Pontificio Istituto Biblico, 2001.

———. 'Implications of Paul's "One Flesh" Concept for His Understanding of the Nature of Man'. *Bulletin for Biblical Research* 11 (2001): 107–22.

Spatafora, Andrea. *From the "Temple of God" to God as the Temple: A Biblical Theological Study of the Temple in the Book of Revelation*. Rome: Gregorian University Press, 1997.

Speidell, Todd H. 'A Trinitarian Ontology of Persons in Society'. *Scottish Journal of Theology* 47 (1994): 283–300.

Sprinkle, Preston M. 'Πιστίς Χριστοῦ as an Eschatological Event'. Pages 165–84 in *The Faith of Jesus Christ: Exegetical, Biblical, and Theological Studies*. Ed. Michael F. Bird and Preston M. Sprinkle. Milton Keynes: Paternoster, UK; Peabody, MA: Hendrickson, 2009.

Stendahl, Krister. 'The Apostle Paul and the Introspective Conscience of the West'. *Harvard Theological Review* 56 (1963): 199–215.

Stewart, James S. *A Man in Christ: The Vital Elements of St. Paul's Religion*. Vancouver, BC: Regent College, 2002 [originally published London: Hodder & Stoughton, 1935].

Stortz, Martha Ellen. 'Indwelling Christ, Indwelling Christians: Living as Marked'. *Currents in Theology and Mission* 34 (2007): 165–78.

Tamburello, Dennis E. *Union with Christ: John Calvin and the Mysticism of St. Bernard*. Columbia Series in Reformed Theology. Louisville: Westminster John Knox, 1994.

Tannehill, Robert C. *Dying and Rising with Christ: A Study in Pauline Theology*. Eugene, OR: Wipf & Stock, 2006 [previously published by Berlin: De Gruyter, 1967].

Taylor, Vincent. *Forgiveness and Reconciliation: A Study in New Testament Theology*. 2nd ed. London: Macmillan, 1956.

Thiselton, Anthony C. *The First Epistle to the Corinthians*. New International Greek Testament Commentary. Grand Rapids: Eerdmans, 2000.

Thompson, Marianne Meye. *Colossians and Philemon*. Two Horizons New Testament Commentary. Grand Rapids: Eerdmans, 2005.

Thuruthumaly, J. 'Mysticism in Pauline Writings'. *Bible Bhashyam* 18 (1992): 140–52.

Timms, David. 'The Pauline Use of *en Christo*: Re-examining Meaning and Origins — A Linguistic Analysis'. PhD dissertation. Macquarie University, 2000.

Tipton, Lane G. 'Union with Christ and Justification'. Pages 23–49 in *Justified in Christ: God's Plan for Us in Justification*. Ed. K. Scott Oliphint. Fearn, Scotland: Mentor, 2007.

Turner, Nigel. *Grammatical Insights into the New Testament*. Edinburgh: T&T Clark, 1965.

Van Kooten, George H. *Cosmic Christology in Paul and the Pauline School: Colossians and Ephesians in the Context of Graeco-Roman Cosmology, with a New Synopsis of the Greek Texts*. Wissenschaftliche Untersuchungen zum Neuen Testament 2.171. Tübingen: Mohr Siebeck, 2003.

Vickers, Brian J. *Jesus' Blood and Righteousness: Paul's Theology of Imputation*. Wheaton, IL: Crossway, 2006.

Visscher, Gerhard H. *Romans 4 and the New Perspective on Paul: Faith Embraces the Promise*. Studies in Biblical Literature 122. New York: Peter Lang, 2009.

Wallace, Daniel B. *Greek Grammar beyond the Basics: An Exegetical Syntax of the New Testament*. Grand Rapids: Zondervan, 1996.

Wanamaker, Charles A. *The Epistles to the Thessalonians*. New International Greek Testament Commentary. Grand Rapids: Eerdmans, 1990.

Watson, Francis. *Paul, Judaism, and the Gentiles: Beyond the New Perspective*. Rev. and exp. Grand Rapids: Eerdmans, 2007.

——. 'By Faith (of Christ): An Exegetical Dilemma and its Scriptural Solution'. Pages 147–63 in *The Faith of Jesus Christ: Exegetical, Biblical, and Theological Studies*. Ed. Michael F. Bird and Preston M. Sprinkle. Milton Keynes, UK: Paternoster; Peabody, MA: Hendrickson, 2009.

Wedderburn, A.J.M. 'The Body of Christ and Related Concepts in 1 Corinthians'. *Scottish Journal of Theology* 24 (1971): 74–96.

——. 'Hellenistic Christian Traditions in Romans 6'. *New Testament Studies* 29 (1983): 337–55.

——. 'Some Observations on Paul's Use of the Phrases "In Christ" and "With Christ"'. *Journal for the Study of the New Testament* 25 (1985): 83–97.

——. *Baptism and Resurrection: Studies in Pauline Theology against Its Graeco-Roman Background*. Wissenschaftliche Untersuchungen zum Neuen Testament 44. Tübingen: Mohr, 1987.

Wesche, Kenneth Paul. 'Eastern Orthodox Spirituality: Union with God in Theosis'. *Theology Today* 56 (1999): 29–43.

Westerholm, Stephen. *Perspectives Old and New on Paul: The "Lutheran" Paul and His Critics*. Grand Rapids: Eerdmans, 2004.

Williams, David J. *Paul's Metaphors: The Context and Character*. Peabody, MA: Hendrickson, 1999.

Williams-Tinajero, Lace Marie. 'Christian Unity: The Communal Participation in Christ's Body and Blood'. *One in Christ* 40 (2005): 45–61.

Wikenhauser, Alfred. *Pauline Mysticism: Christ in the Mystical Teaching of
St. Paul.* Trans. Joseph Cunnigham. New York: Herder and Herder,
1960.

Wisnefske, Ned. 'Living and Dying with Christ: Do We Mean What We
Say?'. *Word and World* 10 (1990): 254–59.

Woodhouse, John. *Colossians and Philemon: So Walk in Him.* Fearn, Scotland: Christian Focus, 2011.

Worgul, George S. 'People of God, Body of Christ: Pauline Ecclesiological
Contrasts'. *Biblical Theology Bulletin* 12 (1982): 24–28.

Wright, N.T. *Colossians and Philemon.* Tyndale New Testament Commentaries. Leicester, UK: Inter-Varsity Press, 1986.

———. *The New Testament and the People of God.* Christian Origins and
the Question of God 1. Minneapolis: Fortress, 1992.

———. *Justification: God's Plan and Paul's Vision.* London: SPCK, 2009.

Yates, Roy. 'A Note on Colossians 1:24'. *Evangelical Quarterly* 42 (1970):
88–92.

———. 'A Re-examination of Ephesians 1:23'. *Expository Times* 83 (1972):
146–51.

Zerwick, Maximilian. *Biblical Greek: Illustrated by Examples.* English edi-
tion adapted from 4th Latin ed. by Joseph Smith. Scripta Pontificii
Instituti Biblici 114. Rome: Pontificio Instituto Biblico, 1963.

Ziesler, John A. 'ΣΩΜΑ in the Septuagint'. *Novum Testamentum* 25
(1983): 133–45.

Scripture Index

Subject Index

Abraham: blessing of, 133; covenant with, 392

Adam: and Christ, 240–41, 268; contrast to, 313; and Eve, 384; the new, 343–48; representative nature of, 142; the second, 397

adoption: is for himself, 257; imagery of, 407

adverbial function, understanding, 165

afflictions, Christ's, 284–85

agency: the term, 238–48, 255–57; use of, 82, 94

agreement, Christian, 162

alive, to God, 116

Ampliatus, 171

Andronicus, and Junia, 121

antecedents, of union, 414–20

anthropology, Pauline, 369

Apelles, description of, 101

apocalyptic eschatology, 416

apostleship: in the Lord, 173; Paul's, 257, 259

Aquila, and Priscilla, 159

Archippus, ministry of, 153

armour, of God, 320, 374

association, with Christ, 233, 235

authority, of his testimony, 160

baptism, 316, 321, 384–86; as its antecedent, 197; buried with Christ in, 181; and Christ's death, 333–36, 424, 429; established by, 43; and mysticism, 34; relationship between, 62–63; suffering at, 380; through, 53. See also sacraments

believer(s): achieved for, 73; actions, 94–95, 101, 154, 182, 248–52, 262; body of, 269–70; characteristics of, 255, 374; as children of God, 315; are in Christ, 132; comfort to, 244; conduct as a, 234; exhorted to, 310; are filled, 181; justification of, 405;

as a new creation, 428; new life of, 318–19; participation of, 408; periphrasis for, 120, 171, 175, 208, 370; predestination of, 177; received by, 194; resurrection of, 313; saved from wrath, 260; are spiritually joined, 304; as a temple, 291; and union with Christ, 364; unity of, 429. See also Christian

betrothal, 305

blessing, comes by Christ, 82

boasting: that glorifies, 157; Paul's action of, 96, 99

body of Christ, 63; being the, 381–83; and Christ's work, 331; and Christian living, 373; as metaphor, 268–89; mystical, 38; sharing in the, 213; and the Trinity, 355

boldness, 198; in Christ, 110; speak with, 185

bread, described as, 271

brethren, means 'Christians,' 174. See also brother(s)

bride, 383–84, 416–17

brother(s), in the Lord, 126, 174

building, 151; and Christian living, 373; idea of a, 430; temple and, 289–98; and the Trinity, 356. See also temple

call, of God, 138, 148–49

Calvin, John, 288, 329, 360, 364, 401, 403–4, 440

canon, 23, 27–28

cause: expresses, 161; might indicate, 90, 95, 99, 105, 110, 111

chains, for Christ, 125

characteristics: of believers, 255; of those in Christ, 101–11, 167, 184; of those in whom, 198

Christ: Adam and, 142; and the church, 274, 298; death of, 230, 234–35; dying with, 221; and God, 245; is the

AUTHOR INDEX

Note: Bolded numbers reflect an extended discussion of this author